Living Law

Living Law

Jewish Political Theology from Hermann Cohen to Hannah Arendt

MIGUEL VATTER

OXFORD
UNIVERSITY PRESS

Oxford University Press is a department of the University of Oxford. It furthers the University's objective of excellence in research, scholarship, and education by publishing worldwide. Oxford is a registered trade mark of Oxford University Press in the UK and certain other countries.

Published in the United States of America by Oxford University Press
198 Madison Avenue, New York, NY 10016, United States of America.

First issued as an Oxford University Press paperback, 2026

Library of Congress Cataloging-in-Publication Data
Names: Vatter, Miguel E., author.
Title: Living law : Jewish political theology from
Hermann Cohen to Hannah Arendt / Miguel Vatter.
Description: New York, NY : Oxford University Press, 2021. |
Includes bibliographical references and index.
Identifiers: LCCN 2020027302 (print) | LCCN 2020027303 (ebook) |
ISBN 9780197546505 (hardback) | ISBN 9780197828045 (paperback) | ISBN 9780197546529 (epub)
Subjects: LCSH: Judaism and politics. | Political theology. | Jewish law—Philosophy. |
Judaism—Philosophy. | Jewish philosophy—19th century. | Jewish philosophy—20th century.
Classification: LCC BM645.P64 V38 2021 (print) | LCC BM645.P64 (ebook) |
DDC 296.3/820904—dc23 LC record available at https://lccn.loc.gov/2020027302
LC ebook record available at https://lccn.loc.gov/2020027303

DOI: 10.1093/oso/9780197546505.001.0001

Paperback Printed by Marquis Book Printing, Canada

The manufacturer's authorized representative in the EU for product safety is
Oxford University Press España S.A. of Parque Empresarial San Fernando de Henares,
Avenida de Castilla, 2 – 28830 Madrid (www.oup.es/en or product.safety@oup.com).
OUP España S.A. also acts as importer into Spain of products made by the manufacturer.

This book is dedicated to the memory of my grandmother Johanna Hirsch and her cousin Margarete Katzenstein, who, exiled at opposite ends of the American continents, kept the German Jewish experience alive for me and passed on the love of learning.

Contents

Acknowledgments ix

Introduction: What Is Jewish Political Theology? 1

1. Philo and the Origins of Political Theology 11
2. Hermann Cohen and Socialist Democracy 35
3. Franz Rosenzweig and Religious Constitutionalism 81
4. Gershom Scholem and the Mystical Foundations of Authority 133
5. Leo Strauss and the Concrete Order of Law 191
6. Hannah Arendt and Federalism 237

Conclusion: The Empty Throne: From Theocracy to Anarchy 285

References 295
Index 327

Acknowledgments

I did not have the opportunity of undertaking formal studies in religion, nor in Jewish thought. Therefore, I am particularly obligated to a number of people over the years who discussed with me some of these ideas, read, and commented on some of my texts, and guided me to further readings, either directly or through their own writings: William Altman, Jeffrey Bernstein, Wendy Brown, Judith Butler, Julie Cooper, Agnes Heller, Bruno Karsenti, Thomas Meyer, Fabián Ludueña Romandini, Bruno Quélennec, Vasileios Syros, Emmanuel Taub, Mark C. Taylor, and Shmuel Trigano. I owe an especially great debt of gratitude to Bruce Rosenstock for encouraging my explorations in this area, for our discussions on these topics, and for his careful, patient, and generous reading of several chapters in this volume. The ideas in this book were presented in conferences and seminars over the years, but I have especially fond memories of the workshop I organized with Robert Buch at the University of New South Wales in Sydney in November 2016, where we had the pleasure of hosting for an intense week of discussions James Martel, Agata Bielik-Robson, and Gil Anidjar. In this book they are sure to see the continuation of those discussions. I am particularly grateful for the friendship of Simona Forti and her encouragement and suggestions in relation to this project and especially about my interpretations of Arendt over the years. I thank my editor at Oxford, Angela Chnapko, for supporting the decision to publish my work on political theology. As always, my gratitude goes to Vanessa Lemm , who understands my obsession with German-Jewish thought, and to our children Lou, Esteban, Alizé and Sebastian for reminding me daily what natality entails.

The idea for this book came out of my now more than two decades long interest in and writing on Leo Strauss, and my concurrent engagement with Giorgio Agamben's oeuvre. While researching Strauss's intellectual context, back in 2006, I had the good sense to order and then study the dusty, hardly cracked volumes of the "Jewish Writings" of Hermann Cohen. This experience unlocked for me a new vista on the later development of German-Jewish philosophy in the 20th century. I first presented some of my ideas on Jewish political theology in a paper on "Political Philosophy as Rhetoric: The Case of Leo Strauss," read at the international conference "Possibility and Paradox: Rhetoric and Political Theory," Northwestern University, Chicago, April 2009. I thank Keith Topper and Dilip Gaonkar for their invitation. A version of this paper is finally forthcoming in their edited volume, *The Oxford Handbook on Rhetoric and Political Theory.*

Roberto Esposito's kind invitation to present a series of lectures in his graduate seminar at the Istituto Scienze Umane, Naples, Italy, in November 2009 was also instrumental in my early articulation of this project. I am also thankful for the opportunity to present some of these ideas at two talks I gave on Strauss and on Rosenzweig, respectively, at Princeton University, Department of Religion, May 2011, and at the international colloquium "Guerra y Paz. Desde la pregunta por la memoria hasta las aporías de la democracia," Universidad Diego Portales, Santiago, Chile, September 2011.

Chapters 1 and 2 on Cohen and Rosenzweig draw on some material previously published as Vatter, Miguel, 2016, "Cosmopolitan Political Theology in Cohen and Rosenzweig," *Philosophy Today* 60(2): pp. 295–324; and Vatter, Miguel, 2017, "Nationality, State, and Global Constitutionalism in Hermann Cohen's Wartime Writings," in *Crisis and Reconfigurations: 100 Years of European Thinking since 1914*, edited by Matthew Sharpe, Rory Jeffs, and Jack Reynolds, pp. 43–63 (New York: Springer). Chapter 6 on Arendt is a greatly expanded and revised version of Vatter, Miguel, 2018, "Roman Civil Religion and the Question of Jewish Politics in Arendt," *Philosophy Today* 62(2): pp. 573–606. I thank Peg Birmingham for hosting me at De Paul University and inviting me to present my work on Rosenzweig there, and then welcoming my submissions on this topic. I am grateful to the editors and publishers for permission to use this material.

Introduction

What Is Jewish Political Theology?

Methodological precautions and genealogical hypothesis

In his 1935 treatise on divine sovereignty, the Jewish philosopher Martin Buber introduced the idea of an "anarchic soul of theocracy."[1] A decade earlier, the German jurist Carl Schmitt had coined the term "political theology" in order to designate the Christian theological foundations of modern sovereignty and legal order.[2] In a specular and opposite gesture, Buber argued that the covenant at Sinai established YHWH as the King of the Israelites and simultaneously promulgated the principle that no human being could become sovereign over this people. In so doing, Buber offered an interpretation of Jewish theocracy that is both republican and anarchic: republican because, by pivoting on the idea that democracy is a function of a people's fidelity to a prophetic *higher law*, theocracy displaces the central role of the human sovereign;[3] anarchic because this divine law is saturated with the messianic aim to *put an end to relations of domination* between peoples.[4] In this book I show that this republican and anarchic articulation of the discourse of political theology characterizes the development of Jewish political theology in the 20th century from Hermann Cohen to Hannah Arendt.

Despite the recent currency of the term, it is not self-evident that a "Jewish" discourse on "political theology" exists.[5] A given discourse does not qualify as

[1] The phrase is "*dem anarchischen Seelengrund die Theokratie*" (Buber 1964, 686).

[2] For the term "political theology" see (Schmitt 1988, 2008). Schmitt's political theology is treated at length in (Vatter 2020).

[3] For the topos of Hebraic republicanism in early modern political thought, see (Nelson 2010); and for Spinoza's democratic reading of the covenant at Sinai, see (Cooper 2017).

[4] For this sense of *an-arche* as "no-rule," see Arendt's claim that "perhaps the greatest American innovation in politics as such was the consistent abolition of sovereignty within the body politic of the republic" (1990, 153) and the idea of "a political body in which rulers and ruled would be equal, that is, where actually the whole principle of rulership no longer applied" (1990, 172). For a discussion of no-rule in contemporary political theory, see (Vatter 2012).

[5] The term "Jewish political theology" appears to have a relatively recent origin. It is employed in (Elazer 1997; Novak 2005; and Melamed 2012). However, these authors do not comment on its connection with the Schmittian and post-Schmittian discourse on political theology. This connection becomes central in discussions of Jewish political theology inspired by (Taubes 2003). For some recent examples, see (Anidjar 2003; Rashkover 2005; Lilla 2007; Schmidt 2009; Kavka and Rashkover 2014; and Butler 2014).

Living Law. Miguel Vatter, Oxford University Press (2021). © Oxford University Press.
DOI: 10.1093/oso/9780197546505.003.0001

being an instance of Jewish political theology simply because it offers some discussion of biblical politics, or of the political assumptions of Rabbinic Judaism, or of the political theory of Zionism, and so on. In this book I adopt the methodological precaution that, for a given discourse to qualify as Jewish political theology, it should have an internal, not contingent connection with the central themes and the method of political theology as Schmitt understood them and as they were subsequently elaborated upon by other 20th-century authors from Eric Peterson and Ernst Kantorowicz to Jacob Taubes, Hans Blumenberg, and Giorgio Agamben. This internal connection, in part helped by the shared language and cultural context, is at its closest and most evident with the German Jewish thinkers I have chosen to focus on.[6]

For Schmitt, the basic themes of political theology as a discourse center on the concept of sovereignty and its reliance on the analogy between God and the human sovereign representative. In this book, I show that Jewish political theology offers an alternative conception of divine sovereignty and of its democratic political implications. Likewise, for Schmitt, the method of political theology is based on the hypothesis of structural analogies between the sciences of theology and of jurisprudence. In this book I argue that significant portions of the philosophical and mystical developments of the Jewish tradition are characterized by similar analogies, based on the assumption that the revealed Torah is the highest exemplar of the Greek philosophical term for law, *nomos*.[7]

This methodological precaution needs to be followed along two registers: one that treats of the genealogy of Jewish political theology in the philosophical and mystical developments of the Greek and Jewish streams of the Western tradition; the other that bridges the analytic-conceptual content of Jewish political theology to concepts employed in 20th-century democratic theory. The authors treated in this book work out their views on the divine law in relation to their interpretations of specific periods and texts of the Jewish tradition and the

[6] Admittedly, given this methodological precaution, some French Jewish thinkers who articulate a politico-theological discourse close to anarchism, like Simone Weil and Emmanuel Levinas, could also have been included. However, in the case of Weil one encounters the problem of her apparent rejection of most aspects of the Jewish tradition; and in the case of Levinas there is the explicit reliance and borrowings from the German Jewish thought that is central to this book. That said, Weil and Levinas are discussed in compressed fashion in the Conclusion.

[7] The idea of "the Jewish tradition" does not designate a univocal concept. The complexities of this idea of tradition are discussed throughout this volume. Stated in very general terms, the authors treated here draw more from the philosophical and the mystical traditions of Judaism than from the tradition of so-called normative or Rabbinic Judaism. A discussion of the latter remains entirely outside the scope of this book. Emil Fackenheim, although standing on the shoulders of the Jewish political theology I discuss here, ultimately rejects its discourse because he believes, much like Joseph Soloveitchik or David Hartman, that the tradition of Rabbinic Judaism is the most adequate form for the historico-political realization of the biblical teachings. Fackenheim believes that the Talmudic principle of the co-originality of Written and Oral Torah is the best expression of "the Grace that is in the 'law'" (1973, 118).

Western history of philosophy. And all of these authors develop the complex relation between divine sovereignty and democracy by placing special emphasis on one dimension of it. Hence, in each chapter I pair the discussion of the individual author with one significant concept of contemporary democracy: social democracy, global constitutionalism, charismatic authority, legality, and federalism.

For the genealogical approach to Jewish political theology, I adopt the hypothesis that the remote origins of Jewish political theology are found in the syncretistic discourse of the Hellenistic philosopher Philo Judaeus. Philo's thought combines a Platonic conception of politics with the contents of the Pentateuch into a novel doctrine of the Law of Nature. In the late 1920s, the historian of religions Erwin Goodenough proposed the hypothesis that Christian political theology originated in the reception of Philo's philosophy. On Goodenough's radical and contested interpretation, Philo modeled the Jewish conception of the kingship of YHWH on the Pythagorean-Platonic conceptions of philosophical kingship and *nomos phuseos* (law of nature). As is well known, one of Schmitt's axioms about political theology is that modern political and legal concepts are secularized versions of theological concepts. Goodenough's interpretation of Philo starts from the premise that in Hellenistic Judaism, the relation of derivation is the reverse, so that theological concepts can be said to translate more primordial politico-philosophical and juridical concepts.[8] The direct connection between Schmitt's political theology and the 20th-century debate on Philo initiated by Goodenough was sealed by the German theologian Erik Peterson, who used Goodenough's hypothesis in order to show that a *Christian* "political theology," in the sense of Schmitt, was strictly speaking impossible because the analogy between divine and human sovereignty was an invention of Hellenistic Judaism.[9]

Schmitt never cites Goodenough's work, so it is unclear whether he was aware of it. However, Schmitt rejected Peterson's claim that political theology was an invention of Jewish philosophy. Schmitt's well documented anti-Semitic beliefs would have made it problematic for him to acknowledge the role of the Jewish tradition in the discourse which he claimed to have discovered. Nor is the main problem that, if Goodenough and Blumenberg are correct, Jewish political theology undermines the very idea of secularization. I think the main reason for Schmitt's rejection is simply that he found it difficult to understand how the prophetic and messianic motifs of the Pentateuch, with their revolutionary and antinomian charge, could serve as foundation for a stable form of political sovereignty, which was the conservative function he wanted to assign to political

[8] See (Goodenough 1928). His interpretation anticipates the methodological critique raised by Hans Blumenberg against Schmitt's idea of secularization as a translation from theological to juridical concepts in (Blumenberg 1985), which is taken up again in (Agamben 2011).

[9] See the famous essay "Monotheism as a Political Problem" in (Peterson 2011).

theology. Hermann Cohen—the towering figure in German Jewish thought at the start of the 20th century—instead believed that the Jewish conception of divine sovereignty, when properly understood as a "religion of reason," in the tradition of Philo's philosophical interpretation of the Torah, was a laboratory of radical social democracy. Cohen's hypothesis was that the immanent, revolutionary, and egalitarian logics of the modern social world, in prefiguring a post-sovereign political organization of the world, were oriented toward the social realization of the prophetic and messianic figurations of the Kingdom of God. It is in this sense that in this book I take Cohen's Jewish writings to have inaugurated Jewish political theology at the turn of the 20th century, years before Schmitt coined the term.

Jewish political theology connects divine sovereignty to the philosophical idea of a "Law of Nature," or *nomos phuseos*. This connection expresses the belief that it is possible to bridge the idea of political salvation coming from fidelity to the law given to a people by a divine King with the Greek philosophical doctrine contained in the formula *nomos basileus*, a term that is usually rendered as the "sovereignty" of law.[10] Although Schmitt identified this idea of "law as king" as a formula for the legitimacy of the absolutist state, I show that the discourse of Jewish political theology addresses the problem of why and how a divine revelation takes the form of *nomos phuseos*, of principles of natural justice that offer the basis for a constitutional, democratic government. More precisely, this discourse investigates the idea that the rule of law, standing on the basis of the Law of Nature, is established and legitimated by an idea of "constituent power" that lies outside the powers of the state *and* of government.

From divine sovereignty to pastoral government and return

According to philosophers Michel Foucault and Giorgio Agamben, Christian political theology was not, pace Schmitt, the legitimate discourse of state sovereignty as much as the conduit for a pastoral idea of government that they associate with liberal democracy.[11] On this hypothesis, the distinction between sovereignty and government, or between political theology and economic theology, is helpful in order to account for the emergence of alternative forms of power and legitimacy disconnected from the state and linked to the economy

[10] Originally found in Pindar Fr. 169a, then taken up by Plato in *Gorgias* 484b1–c3, the formula is usually rendered as "the law, king of all." For a discussion of the formula, see, among others, (Stier 1928; Heinemann 1965 [1942]; Gigante 1956; Ostwald 1986; Stefou 2015; and Zartaloudis 2019). The formula plays a central role in (Agamben 1998). For a wide-ranging discussion of the history of the rule of law from the perspective of *nomos* see (Loughlin 2010).

[11] See (Foucault 2009; and Agamben 2011).

and to the law in their relative autonomy and self-referential operations.[12] My hypothesis in this book is that Jewish political theology is a discourse developed in the 20th century that draws from heterodox interpretations of the philosophical and mystical aspects of the Jewish tradition on divine government in order to articulate anew the ideal of the rule of law and its constituent power that brings human sovereignty to an end. The same discourse also offers some of the richest resources to critically respond to the shift from sovereignty to government and its significance for modern politics.

Neither Agamben nor Foucault discusses at any length the distinction between Christian and Jewish conceptions of divine government or providence. On the contrary, they tend to assume that Christian pastoral conceptions of government stand in continuity with the Jewish teachings on divine government. I believe that this is a misleading assumption. It prevents one from appreciating how some of the Jewish teachings on divine providence are subversive with respect to both Christian and modern conceptions of government. In other words, this assumption of continuity blocks from sight the possibility that Jewish political theology is democratic while not being governmental.

Prior to the recovery of the problem of government in Foucault and Agamben, the relation between divine providence and political power made its way into social and political theory through Max Weber's conception of charisma as ground of the legitimate exercise of power. Schmitt claimed that charisma was Weber's own, original contribution to the discourse of political theology.[13] Weber's thesis on charismatic authority states that sociopolitical reality receives its original form of legitimacy thanks to the providential category of charisma, the biblical idea of a historical dispensation of divine grace or gift (*hesed, charis*) of leadership.[14] Charismatic authority is the fundamental source of what Weber calls *Lebensführung*, that is, the self-reflexive capacity to guide or lead people's innerworldly conduct.[15]

Weber's idea of charismatic authority as the first and fundamental form of legitimacy is closely related to his interpretation of the prophetic tradition in Judaism. Weber's introduction of charisma into sociology confirmed Cohen's thesis that modern society is structurally oriented toward the realization of Jewish messianic expectations. Far from seeing in the concept of a divinely

[12] See now the different paths traced between Foucaultian and Agambenian approaches to governmental power and economic theology in (Leshem 2016; and Heron 2018). For an overview on the shifts from sovereignty to governmentality, see (Esposito 2008; Dean 2013; McLoughlin 2015; Vatter 2018; and Stimilli 2019), among others.

[13] (Schmitt 2008).

[14] See (Weber 1952, 1968).

[15] This element of religion as *Lebensführung* is capacious enough to encapsulate the typical opposition between a Protestant idea of "religion" as belief- or faith-based versus the post-secular idea of religion that understands it as internally connected with "ethics" in the sense of bodily practices and rituals that constitute a "way of life," as discussed in (Mahmood 2005, ch. 4).

guided political leader a remnant of the mythical past, without a place or function in modern liberal democracies, it is fair to say that democratic theory after Weber thoroughly embraced the idea of charismatic leadership.[16]

Jewish political theology in the 20th century develops the implications of divine sovereignty by a thoroughgoing reconceptualization of the Weberian category of charismatic leadership. The German-Jewish thinkers addressed in this book were all extremely conscious of the ominous rise of what Weber called *plebizitäre Führerdemokratie* (plebiscitarian leadership democracy), and, so my hypothesis, they sought to divert its course toward the shores of that other crucial development of 20th-century political thought, namely, the global constitutionalization of human rights. Whether they had in mind the unsuccessful Bavarian Soviet revolution of 1918, led by Jewish communists and anarchists,[17] or the diverse Zionist proposals and experiments in the first half of the 20th century, it is no exaggeration to say that all of the German Jewish thinkers treated in these pages, from Franz Rosenzweig to Gershom Scholem, from Leo Strauss to Hannah Arendt, intuitively grasped what Cohen was after. In their different, even opposed ways, these thinkers carried forward the impulse of his central idea: to articulate the social-revolutionary significance of Jewish theocracy.

Liberal approaches to religion believe that modern constitutions establish a "two-way protection" of religion where "the state protects freedom of religion and abstains from establishing, endorsing, or promoting any religion."[18] Those who believe that late modern democracy requires a liberal regulation of religion in the public sphere consequently adopt the view that every kind of theocracy threatens democracy. The treatments of theocracy developed by Jewish political theology in the 20th century suggest a different possibility. Contemporary democratic theorists are familiar with Claude Lefort's famous claim that modern democracies are characterized by the "empty place" of sovereign power.[19] I propose to consider the discourse of Jewish political theology in the 20th century as offering ways to analyze this absence of sovereignty in democracy through the analogy with the messianic idea according to which God seeks to realize His Kingdom on earth in an emancipatory, egalitarian, and cosmopolitical form. More specifically, the thinkers treated in this book work through Jewish prophetic and messianic motifs and teachings in order to develop both a *charismatic* understanding of democratic leadership in revolutionary practice and in order to innovate the

[16] For charisma as the root of radical democratic ideas, see (Badiou 2003; Kalyvas 2009; and Hardt and Negri 2019). For a discussion of charismatic leadership in the Schumpeterian idea of democracy and its new populist forms, see now (Urbinati 2019).

[17] See (Kets and Muldoon 2019).

[18] (Laborde 2017, 26).

[19] On the importance and influence of Lefort's theory of democracy for post-metaphysical conceptions of politics, see the discussions in (Rosanvallon 1998; Marchart 2007; and Esposito 2020).

constitutional idea of democratic legitimacy based on higher law or natural right. The exploration of this paradoxical coincidence of legalism with anarchism is the central aim of this book.

From Cohen to Arendt, Jewish political theology develops the motif of the higher law by drawing inspiration from the philosophical and mystical elaborations of the idea of God's law as a "living law" found in the Jewish tradition. The discourse of Jewish political theology recovers importance for contemporary political theorizing because of what it has to say about maintaining the freedom and power of a people in and through its *living relationship to legality*. For this reason, in the chapters that follow my discussion of these authors is focused on what they have to teach us about fundamental political concepts tied to the function of law and legality in modern politics and government. Whereas Christian political theology tends to unify legal authority with governmental power, I suggest that the discourse of Jewish political theology tends to separate these. Thereby, legality itself becomes the fundamental resource of a people's constituent power to undermine sovereignty and resist government. In sum, the strand of Jewish political theology discussed here is characterized by a basic messianic *and* republican insight according to which the life of the higher law has deep-rooted *anarchic* dimensions and consequences.[20]

The Weberian idea of charismatic leadership serves to suspend the validity of late modern theorems of secularization which rest on the belief in human progress, phylogenetic learning processes, and evolutionary transformations of human sociality characteristic of 19th-century philosophy of history.[21] If one adds to the sociology of religion the vistas opened by the history of religion, at least on Goodenough's hypotheses, then one can say that Jewish political theology is a discourse that calls into question the very idea of secularization, not only in its late modern variation as a theory of human progress leading to the salvation of humankind, but also in Schmitt's post-secular variant whereby modern and secular political and legal concepts are assumed to be secularized versions of medieval Christian theological formulas.

Divine providence and history can be combined in two fundamentally opposed ways. According to 19th-century political theology, *history itself* is a providential process. A supra-historical order develops in and through the historical

[20] Recent work on political theology has also emphasized its relation to anarchist theories. For (Diamantides and Schütz 2018), Byzantine political theology is the discourse that best articulates the anarchic dimension of theocracy. Diamantides and Schütz deconstruct the so-called Caesaro-Papism of Byzantine political theology to unmask it as a teaching of the necessary failure of all government, where government is understood as a practice that is tied to an ideal of crisis management. (Newman 2019) also highlights the anarchic reception of political theology in contemporary political theory but he does not connect it with a particular religious tradition.

[21] See the discussions of secularization and philosophy of history in (Taylor 2007; Brunkhorst 2014; and Hunter 2017). For the latest formulation of the modern faith in progress, see (Pinker 2019).

progression, and this order comes to its full realization at the "end" of this history. The providential meaning of history finds its most influential expression with Hegel's political theology, but its premises remain operative in modern historicist doctrines of progress.[22] By way of contrast, for 20th-century Jewish political theology, divine providence and historical process are at odds with each other because history is ultimately part of an order (that of eternal nature) which is *not itself historical*.

In his later thought, Schmitt linked political theology with philosophy of history through the Pauline conception of the *katechon* ("restrainer"), a historical force that holds back the advent of ultimate evil. Saint Paul formulated this obscure theological concept in 2 Thessalonians 2:6–7, where he opposes the "restrainer" to a "secret power of lawlessness" that is also at work throughout history.[23] Traditionally, the *katechon* refers to the belief that the Holy Spirit is active in history in order to stop the advent of the "man of sin" or "lawless one" or Anti-Christ that precedes the End (*eschaton*) of history. More generally, for Schmitt the *katechon* stands for any governmental power that "slows down" the progression toward the End. This action of restraining the advent of disorder, the action of managing and administering chaos, is the ultimate source of the legitimacy of governmental power.

In this book, I argue that the confrontation with the idea of the *katechon* is an important theme in the discourse of Jewish political theology. Whereas Christian political theology seeks to restrain the advent of disorder by slowing down progress, Jewish political theology considers the possibility of *reversing* the direction of progress and effecting a *return* to the eternal order of Creation that preceded history. On this view, divine government operates through what Cohen and Rosenzweig call "historical eternity," that is, the political or constitutional actualization of the divinely revealed order within the historical development of nations and peoples. This "return to beginnings" in which history is arrested, in which there is a (re)turn away from progress because divine law is placed above political sovereignty coincides, paradoxically, with the acceleration of revolutionary changes. The "end" of history is accelerated by returning to the "beginning" of history. This is the paradoxical formula of Jewish political theology in the 20th century, where the idea of divine government is internally connected with a messianic conception of politics that adopts charismatic leadership and direct democracy.

22 For a discussion of this claim, see (Löwith 1964; and Esposito 2015).

23 There is a lot of literature on Schmitt's interpretation of the *katechon* in his juridical and political thinking. For interpretations of the concept in Schmitt, see (Meuter 1994; Palélogue 2004; and Maraviglia 2006). For the clearest explanation of the theological concept and its history, see now (Cacciari 2017).

Outline of chapters

Chapter 1 discusses why Philo became an essential source for the development of political theology in the West through his conception of the prophet as *nomos empsychos*, or living law. The chapter addresses the controversial interpretation of Philo proposed by Goodenough which establishes a new paradigm on how to think about the relation between Athens and Jerusalem, pagan philosophy and Jewish revelation, in Hellenistic Judaism. The chapter argues that this interpretative approach to Philo sheds light on why he became a decisive source for the renaissance of Jewish political theology in the 20th century, starting with Cohen's foundational work.

Chapter 2 is dedicated to Cohen's renewal of Jewish theologico-political thought. Cohen is the first to establish an internal, systematic connection between the Jewish messianic idea and a universalistic conception of democracy. He articulates a political theology of socialist democracy, not based on the analogy between One God and One King, but on that between One God and One Humanity. Cohen rejected Zionism as a solution to the political problem caused by the condition of minority nationality in which the Jewish people lived in European states. But he did not believe in assimilation either. He maintained that its messianic religion assigned the Jewish people the task of pointing the way to an international order based not on state sovereignty but on the supremacy of international law founded on human rights that recognized the plurality and right to self-determination of nationalities.

Chapter 3 discusses Rosenzweig's political theology in light of the tension between nationalism and cosmopolitanism. Christian political theology is based on a message of universal love and brotherhood, but Rosenzweig points out how the reception of this message in the West took the form of nationalism and a sanctification of imperialism. Rosenzweig's political theology opens an alternative path to peoplehood based on the possibility of a cosmopolitan empire of law that is not territorially delimited and an access to citizenship that is not ethnoculturally predetermined.

Chapter 4 is dedicated to reconstructing Gershom Scholem's analysis of Jewish messianism in light of political theology. Scholem's political thought is often associated with a critique of any attempt to endow Zionism with messianic traits. In this chapter, I instead focus on his conception of legal authority. I argue that his historiographical work on the mystical tradition of Judaism shows that the authority of the law is a function of the abdication of divine sovereignty and of a mystical idea of God's Nothingness. Scholem articulates Jewish political theology around motifs found in Nietzsche's critique of Christianity and nihilism. His is a political theology of the law after the "death of God."

Chapter 5 is dedicated to Leo Strauss's attempt at giving a philosophical foundation to legality beyond legitimacy, based on a recovery of medieval Islamic and Jewish conceptions of the prophet as a political founder of the perfect legal order. Christian political theology has always pivoted around the polemical claim that Mosaic law was "tyrannical" in some way. Strauss's contribution to Jewish political theology consists in examining Jewish and Islamic prophetology by formulating it in terms of the so-called tyrannical teaching of Platonic political philosophy.

Chapter 6 discusses the relation between Arendt's conceptions of Judaism, its relation to the history of the Jewish people, and her theory of republicanism. I argue that Arendt reconstructs the tradition of republicanism as a fusion of Greco-Roman "direct" democracy and post-Weberian motifs like the federalist character of the Jewish covenant. In so doing, Arendt was following Buber's lead, who was the first 20th-century thinker to explicitly identify the anarchic core of Jewish political theology. Buber conceives God's Kingship as the inner meaning of the Jewish faith *and* articulates this Kingship in the post-Weberian terms of the idea of charismatic leadership. The charismatic leader on his interpretation is the leader who establishes the "promised Land" not in the form of a conquest or occupation of a specific territory through "holy war," but as the opening of a political space of no-rule established within any given society. In contrast with Heidegger's political theology in the 1930s, which attempts to determine peoplehood as a function of opening a space for the manifestation of the gods of the Earth, I argue that Arendt recovers Roman civil religion in order to unify republican federalism with an anarchic conception of political freedom.

The Conclusion discusses the symbol of the empty Throne, understood as an image for the connection between theocracy and anarchy. The chapter contrasts Agamben's hypothesis that anarchy is the secret engine of liberal government with the central hypothesis of this book, namely, that Jewish political theology thematizes the paradoxical unity of rule of law and anarchic democracy. The argument is carried out, first, in relation to the idea of a "principle of anarchy" proposed by Reiner Schürmann. The chapter ends by discussing Simone Weil's hypothesis on the unity between Pythagoreanism and the book of Job and proposing her meditation as an apt interpretation of the meaning of the empty Throne.

1

Philo and the Origins of Political Theology

On the genealogy of political theology

One of the most influential texts in the 20th-century discourse of political theology is Erwin Goodenough's 1928 article on Hellenistic kingship.[1] In his critique of Carl Schmitt's political theology, Erik Peterson relied heavily on Goodenough's findings in order to support his claim that Eusebius's pre-Trinitarian theological legitimation of the Roman emperor Constantine was rooted in a reception of Philo's interpretation of the biblical God as a divine monarch.[2] Peterson took up the controversial connection that Goodenough made between Hellenistic ideas of kingship and Philo's allegorical readings of the Bible in order to assert the claim that political theology has a pagan-Jewish, rather than a Christian, origin. Ernst Kantorowicz likewise relies on Goodenough's article in his famous treatise on medieval political theology, *The King's Two Bodies*, when he interprets Frederick II's project of establishing a secular polity separate from the Church as the rebirth of Hellenistic kingship in the Middle Ages.[3]

In the space of its few compressed pages, Goodenough's article on "The Political Philosophy of Hellenistic Kingship" claims to have found the origin of political theology in the Pythagorean-Platonic idea of divine kingship, and shows how Philo establishes a new relation between Judaism and Hellenism, or Jerusalem and Athens, in which the Hellenistic king receives the form of the Jewish, and later Christian, Messiah. Although often cited by authors who have contributed to the discourse of political theology, Goodenough's seminal article has to date, as far as I can tell, not received an interpretation of its own.

[1] (Goodenough 1928). To date, this article remains an unsurpassed source for every discussion of "sacred kingship" as evidenced by (Oakley 2006). For commentary on the work and reminiscences on the person of Goodenough, see (Neusner 1968).

[2] Peterson refers to Philo, *De decal.*, 155: "the first commandment contains the laws concerning monarchy." He interprets it to mean that the monotheistic God becomes here a cosmic God, and the Jewish people become a "cosmopolitan" people, in the specific sense of owing obedience only to God as monarch of the universe. In so doing, this people takes over the role of "priest and prophet" of humankind (Philo, *De spec. leg.* II:163) cited in (Peterson 2011, 73). Goodenough's work is also the main source for important and encyclopedic accounts of Hellenistic, Judeo-Hellenistic, and early Patristic political theologies in (Dvornik 1966; Oakley 2010).

[3] There seems to be no reference to Goodenough's oeuvre in Giorgio Agamben's works on political theology, which rely on Peterson. This absence is curious given that in *Homo sacer* Agamben argues that the political theology of sovereignty takes up the conception of the "animate law," or *nomos empsychos*, which features centrally in Philo's interpretation of the Patriarchs.

Living Law. Miguel Vatter, Oxford University Press (2021). © Oxford University Press.
DOI: 10.1093/oso/9780197546505.003.0002

In particular, scarce attention is given to the fact that Goodenough's ground-breaking interpretation of Philo also contains an account of the origins of Jewish political theology out of the reception of Platonic political philosophy in Hellenistic Judaism. Goodenough's hypothesis offers, in my opinion, the most convincing genealogical account for the connection between Jewish political theology, divine sovereignty, and charismatic authority that forms the backbone of the contemporary debate on governmentality in political theory. Additionally, Goodenough's interpretation of Philo offers the historical-religious background within which to understand both the critique of the universalistic pretenses of the Christian conception of empire and the claims made on behalf of the peculiar universalism of Jewish messianism. Both would play a crucial role in the development of Jewish political theology in the 20th century, from Hermann Cohen to Hannah Arendt.

The historiography of Philo in the 20th century is contested between the legacy of two intellectual giants: on one side, Goodenough himself, and on the other, Harry Austryn Wolfson. Goodenough led the way in 1935 with his magisterial study, *By Light, Light: The Mystic Gospel of Hellenistic Judaism*. There followed a companion study, *The Politics of Philo Judaeus*, in 1938, and *An Introduction to Philo Judaeus* in 1940.[4] Wolfson's masterpiece, the two volumes of *Philo: Foundations of Religious Philosophy in Judaism, Christianity and Islam*, came out in 1947 and contained a quick dismissal of Goodenough's hypothesis on Hellenistic Judaism.[5] Subsequent interpretations of Philo tended to distance themselves from the theologico-political issues that animated the debate between Goodenough and Wolfson.[6] However, more recently the earlier question of Philo's role in establishing the problem of political theology has been recovered by Carlos Fraenkel.[7] In this chapter my interest is not to intervene on the merits of these erudite debates on Philo's philosophy, but simply to situate Goodenough's interpretation in a way that explains its crucial role in the development of the discourse of political theology in the 20th century.

The central issue in the debate between Goodenough, Wolfson, and now Fraenkel has to do with how one understands the conjunction of "Athens and Jerusalem" or philosophy and revelation in Hellenistic Judaism and then in Western medieval philosophy. Wolfson proposed the thesis that Philo was the giant on whose shoulders stood all of Christian, Jewish, and Islamic medieval philosophy. He believes that Philo was responsible for turning the Greek

[4] (Goodenough 1969, 1938, 1962).

[5] (Wolfson 1947). To which Goodenough replied in his long and critical review of Wolfson's book (Goodenough 1948).

[6] See the monumental interpretation in (Runia 1990) and for the debate on the philosophical status of Philo's thought, see (Borgen 1996).

[7] (Fraenkel 2012).

philosophy of Plato and Aristotle into the handmaiden of revealed religions. As Goodenough puts it: "Philo is to him the dramatic point where revelation entered to dominate reason. And the revelation which came into Western thought through Philo seems for Wolfson to be specifically Jewish revelation. What Wolfson is really demonstrating is that medieval thought began with the confluence of Greek and Jewish points of view" (Goodenough 1948, 89). Wolfson essentially claimed that Philo poured the molten gold of ancient philosophy into the normative mold offered by the interpretation of Mosaic law given by Rabbinic Judaism (and later by Christianity and Islam) and in so doing inaugurated medieval philosophy as a "religious philosophy." Medieval philosophy was "religious" because it accepted without question the priority of prophetically revealed law as the expression of morality over the freedom of human intellect. Only with the advent of Spinoza was the very idea of giving a rational or allegorical account of the Bible discredited. Only after Spinoza, so Wolfson, did philosophy manage to "emancipate" itself from the authority of revelation.

Fraenkel's hypothesis, on the other hand, reverses Wolfson's order of priority. His claim is that Philo is the founder of medieval philosophy because he formulates the teaching of the Platonic idea of a "philosophical religion" under conditions of belief in divine revelation.[8] According to Fraenkel, some of the greatest minds in Western medieval philosophy turned revealed religion into the handmaiden of Platonic philosophy. On this view, normative interpretations of revealed religions serve to communicate, in allegorical form, the Greek teaching that the philosophical life is the highest form of life. "Religion is conceived [by Philo] as the means allowing non-philosophers to have a share in the perfection of philosophers."[9] By adopting religious beliefs and following religious practices, the multitude of individuals who are not philosophers can approximate the idea of the Good that is cognized only by philosophers. They can approximate it, however, only at the inferior, moral level of conduct, not at the superior level of rational thought.

Goodenough's hypothesis on Philo is in many respects more radical than both Wolfson's and Fraenkel's interpretations:

> There is revealed in Philo an elaborate transformation of Judaism into a mystic philosophy, *one that ultimately draws its sources largely upon Orpheus, Isis, and Iran, as these were interpreted by the mystic philosophers of Greek background.*

[8] "Philo, I contend, interpreted Judaism as what I propose to call a *philosophical religion*. In this way he could make a case for what he considered to be the excellence of both, Judaism and philosophy, addressing doubts about the value of Judaism expressed by Gentiles and assimilated Jews and doubts about the value of philosophy harboured by Jewish traditionalists" (Fraenkel 2011, 24).

[9] (Fraenkel 2011, 27). The point is rehearsed systematically in Fraenkel's book-length treatment of the hypothesis.

> This mystic philosophy with almost monotonous reiteration brings all the incidents of the Pentateuch into an account of the Mystic Royal Road to God through the Powers or through Sophia. . . . It seems that Philo must hereafter be treated as the great source from whom we learn of *a Judaism so thoroughly paganised* that its postulates and its objectives were those of Hellenistic Mysteries rather than of any Judaism we have hitherto known. For all of its passionate Jewish loyalty, it was not fundamentally a Judaism with Hellenistic veneer; it was a Hellenism in Jewish symbols and allegories, to be sure, but still a Hellenistic dream of the solution of the problem of life by ascent higher and higher in the Stream-Light of God. (Goodenough 1969, 263)

Goodenough argues that Philo's enormous significance lies in having modeled Judaism on the Greek philosophical conception of God as the Mystery of Being (*to on*). This Pythagorean-Platonic conception of God is equiprimordially a mystical conception of a Hidden God who reveals Himself in the form of a "Stream of Light" or *Logos* that has simultaneously a philosophical (scientific) and a messianic (redemptive) dimension. The Stream of Light reveals the existence of a universal Law of Nature which corresponds to no positive set of religious or political laws, and which promises human beings their emancipation from the factual or positive power and authority exercised over them by given political and religious institutions.

In contrast to Wolfson, Goodenough's interpretation places the Mystery of God higher than the legal interpretation offered by institutional religions of the revelations of prophets like Moses or Muhammad. The Jewish Torah, for instance, is not only "bundles of commands which were written by Moses" but also contains, in the figures of the Patriarchs, the teachings of the Unwritten Law of Nature, "the unwritten representation of God's revealed nature and will" (Goodenough 1969, 73). The Stream of Light or *Logos* is expressed by a conception of *Nomos* that is embodied by prophets as living law: "Moses, the ideal king, had as his essential quality the fact that he was *nomos empsychos*, an incarnation of the great Law of Nature. . . . Thus to be incarnation of *nomos* was to be the incarnation not only of the divine force which ruled the world but of the Platonic ideas" (Goodenough 1969, 189). This living law is directly political or charismatic; it is not institutional or organized around a church. For Goodenough, Philo's Judaism is not the "normative" form of Judaism associated with the Pharisaic and Rabbinic traditions.[10]

In contrast to Fraenkel, Goodenough emphasizes the messianic or redemptive dimension of the idea of a Stream of Light issuing from the Mystery of God. For Fraenkel, the Platonic conception of God is purely speculative or theoretical; its

[10] Goodenough refers to (Moore 1924) for the idea of a "normative" Judaism.

practical dimension is secondary and "pedagogical"; it is mediated by institutional religion as a check on the non-philosophical multitudes. For Goodenough, instead, the basis of the *Logos-Nomos* in the Mystery of God means that philosophy is equiprimordially mystical and political; it is an instrument of divine providence, but divine providence is carried forward by no specific church or religion; it offers a form of salvation that is radically universal precisely because it is accessible by everyone and because it is radically *extra ecclesiam*.

The key demonstration of Goodenough's hypothesis lies in his claim that Philo's reinterpretation of Judaism adopts the Pythagorean-Platonic Hellenistic doctrines of kingship according to which "what was said of God must somehow be said of the King—so the King is *nomos empsychos* [living law] because God's nature is *nomos tes phuseus* [law of nature]" (Goodenough 1969, 39). To indicate this parallelism he cites passages from Philo and from the pseudo-Aristotelian or neo-Pythagorean treatise *De mundo*.[11] According to the latter treatise, "the rule of God, Himself enthroned and inaccessible . . . [extends] His government through the world as he sends forth His *dunameis* [power] into all things. This conception of kingship . . . seems to be the background for Philo's doctrine of *dunameis*" (Goodenough 1969, 39). The crucial idea here is that the *nomos tes phuseus* is "the Law of God since Nature is God" (51). The divine *Nomos* is not a law that is immanent or inherent in things as it was for Stoicism, but it is the law of God's Nature. Thus, although the One God is distinct from the world and so is transcendent, "in a sense the world shares in God's nature as well as power, in God's being as well as in His activity" (37).

This doctrine of Hellenistic kingship is adopted by Philo in order to make sense of the core of the Jewish religion, the teaching of the Ark of the Covenant:

> The Presence, the One who Spoke, is the highest God, *to on*. From Him radiate all the lower manifestations. First is the *Logos tou ontos* [of Being] corresponding to the voice heard by Moses. From the Logos the Stream goes on out in two branches, the two Cherubim, who are called the Creative power (*dunamis poietike*) and the Royal or Ruling power (*dunamis basilike*). . . . The Creative power sends forth the Merciful power or Benevolence (*dunamis eleos*), the Mercy Seat, and the Royal power sends forth the legislative power (*dunamis nomothetike*), the law within the box, which is also the Punishing power. The seventh and last member of this pleroma, the one typified by the box of the ark is the Conceptual world (*kosmos noetos*) the Platonic world of forms. (Goodenough 1969, 23–5)

[11] *De mundo*, vi:398a ff; and Philo, *Agr.* 51, 78; *Opif.* 71; *Cher.* 29; *Post.* 101; *Gig.* 45, 64; *Mig.* 146; *Cong.* 116; *Spec.* iv:78; *Legat.* 3.

Philo's mystical-philosophical translation of Judaism therefore brings its monotheism in close relation to Hellenistic and Persian astral religions, where the Sun stands for the One God whose Logos radiates forth as the Light-Stream and divides into several powers, represented by astral gods, in and through which the One God exercises His providence or government of the world. In this way, Judaism opens itself to pantheism and even polytheism, and, conversely, Greek philosophy reveals itself as containing a mystical monotheism.

Politically speaking, the important point of this analogy between Hellenistic philosophical kingship and Judaism is the principle of equality before the law of nature. Justice is always a function of following God's law of nature.[12] For Philo, "God is also the father-ruler, good shepherd, helmsman and charioteer, with rulership always *kata nomon kai diken* [according to law and justice]. And the Law of the Universe is directly the product of God; it is His providence, but more importantly it is the imitation of his Nature" (Goodenough 1969, 52). The crucial thesis is that the essence of divine sovereignty is strictly constitutional. God exists as universal law of nature. In turn, "God is referred as creating *isotes* (equality) and in His rulership as always being guided by it" (Goodenough 1969, 62).[13] The model of divine kingship is therefore that of a divine constitutional democracy.

The significance of Goodenough's hypothesis can be garnered by comparing it with the genealogy of Western governmentality proposed by Michel Foucault. In his lectures on *Security, Territory, Population*, Foucault argued that the idea of government as a "conduct of conduct" was introduced into Western political through the "pastoral" conception of power developed by Christianity. According to him, this conception of pastoral power was "not a Greek idea" but had an "Eastern" origin coming from Egyptian, Assyrian, and especially Jewish teachings on God as Father and Shepherd.[14] For Foucault, governmentality is a politico-theological conception because of its roots in this pastoral conception of power. The difference with Goodenough's account, however, is that Foucault *opposes* the rule of law, which he considers to be a Greek conception, to the governmentality of pastoral power which is based on the personal relation of command and obedience that Foucault believes to be modeled on the biblical commandments. For Goodenough, to the contrary, Philo presents a conception of God's sovereignty that expresses itself *exclusively* in terms of a government of the law of nature and that does not require individuals to enter into relations of personal submission.

[12] "To Philo, as to all Greek tradition, the legal was always the just," citing Xenophon, *Mem.* IV, iv:12 in (Goodenough 1969, 59).

[13] Goodenough paraphrases from *Spec.* iv:232, 237: "in the universe *isotes* is represented by cosmic order, in cities by democracy, in bodies by health, and in souls by *kalokagatheia* [nobility, goodness]" (1969, 62).

[14] (Foucault 2009, 123–4).

Foucault admits that Plato's texts put into question his hypothesis that pastoral power has no place in Greek political thought: "to be a good shepherd is to be not only the good magistrate, but quite simply the true, ideal magistrate. You find this in *Critias* 109b–c; *The Republic* I:343a, 345e, III:416a–b, 440d; *The Laws* V:735b–e, and the *Statesman* 267c–277d" (2009, 138). Without mentioning Goodenough, Foucault gives a brief *compte rendu* of extant scholarship that identified Plato's use of the shepherd metaphor as a debt to Pythagorean political thought, in which the metaphor of pastoral power was central to the formulation of legitimate kingship. He mentions the hypothesis held by some scholars according to which these pastoral metaphors indicated a reception of Jewish motifs in Pythagoreanism, and thus also in Platonism.[15] He also refers to Armand Delatte's 1922 study *Essai sur la politique pythagoricienne*, which argued that the belief in Zeus as "the god-shepherd" (137) is autochthonous to Greek political thought and from Pythagoras found its way to Isagoras and Plato.[16]

Foucault explicitly refers to Delatte's claim that according to the Pythagorean etymology, *nomos* (law) derived "from *nomeus*, that is to say, the shepherd. The shepherd is the lawmaker insofar as he distributes food, directs the flock, indicates the right direction, and says how the sheep must mate so as to have good offspring. All this is the function of the shepherd who gives the law to his flock. Hence the title of Zeus as *Nomios*" (1922, 137). But he does not connect the theses of Delatte's study with Schmitt's discussion of the roots of *nomos* in the practice of land-grabbing, distribution, and production tied to shepherding.[17] Nor does he connect Delatte's hypothesis to the genealogy of political theology which traced it back to Hellenistic conceptions of kingship in the work of Goodenough and Peterson. Foucault's sole concern is to show that Plato, despite what the preceding evidence suggests, does not himself adopt the Pythagorean paradigm of shepherding and is not dependent on this doctrine of Hellenistic kingship.

By way of contrast, Goodenough claims that Philo receives this Pythagorean doctrine of kingship through Plato and employs it to model Judaism on the paradigm of a pagan mystery religion. Foucault wants to separate the political teaching of Platonism from Judaism in order to claim that governmentality is non-political because the "religious" idea of Hebrew provenance that is received by Christianity leads eventually to modern governmentality. Conversely, Goodenough's genealogy shows that Philo introduced a continuity between

[15] Foucault does not refer to the belief found in parts of Hellenistic culture according to which Plato was a "student" of Moses. The idea is central in Philo and from there came to the Latin Church Fathers. On this belief, see my discussion of Goodenough in the following, and (Fraenkel 2012).

[16] (Delatte 1922). Not to be confused with Louis Delatte's book on Hellenistic kingship (1941) that Goodenough reviewed critically in 1949 (Goodenough 1949).

[17] (Schmitt 2003) and for commentary (Ojakangas 2009). For a critique of Schmitt's interpretation of the archaic Greek idea of *nomos* see now (Zartaloudis 2019).

Platonism and Judaism in order to develop a theory of divine sovereignty through *Nomos-Logos* that lies equally distant both from Schmitt's attempts to ground human sovereignty in the archaic idea of Greek *nomos* as land-grabbing and from the Christian pastoral power of governmentality.

On this reading of Philo, the Mystery of the divine economy is not articulated in terms of a division between sovereign Being and governmental Action as proposed in Giorgio Agamben's interpretation of Trinitarianism.[18] Rather, Philo's Judeo-Hellenistic articulation of the Mystery remains unitarian: One Being, One Stream of Light, One Law under which all human beings are in principle equal. Consequently, the conception of divine democracy that is received by Jewish political theology is not reducible to the idea of democracy that follows from Foucault's and Agamben's hypotheses on governmentality and pastoral power. The teachings of the prophets, above all Moses's teachings, articulate this law of Nature into a redeemed form of life that is, in one, religious, philosophical, and democratic.

On the idea of living law

The Hellenistic political philosophy of kingship is characterized by undoing the normative distinction between lawful kingship and unlawful tyranny. In his dialogue on Philip II, king of Macedonia and father of Alexander the Great, Isocrates "is pleased with every tyrant or king who rules his subjects well" (Goodenough 1928, 56). With Isocrates, the classical Socratic distinction between king and tyrant begins to give way to the possibility of an "affirmative" idea of tyranny.[19] Isocrates brings together the Sophistic reading of *nomos basileus* understood as the supra-legal "right of the strong to enslave the weak" with "the theorizing of Socrates, Plato, and Xenophon about kings" (Goodenough 1928, 56). By applying Platonism to the Sophist idea of "might as right," Isocrates determines that the king who is a "model" of virtue and of self-rule "must so modify and improve the laws that they will be just, consistent and capable of direct and speedy application, while the king's own judgments are to be fixed and just as the best of laws" (Goodenough 1928, 57). Two apparently irreconcilable ideas of natural right—which according to Gorgias and Thrasymachus means "might is right," whereas for Socrates and Plato it means "wisdom is right"—are joined by Isocrates in the principle that the written laws of the city suffer from a fundamental problem of

[18] (Agamben 2011).

[19] Not entirely coincidentally, in a footnote illustrating the preceding statement, Goodenough points to Xenophon's *Hiero* as a crucial philosophical source for this development. He thereby seems to have anticipated Leo Strauss's thesis about the "tyrannical teaching" contained in Xenophon political thought. For further discussion of this question see (Vatter 2010).

application. Civil laws are just only to the extent that they are applied, or judged, by a wise or knowing king who, in so doing, becomes a lawmaker, and thus comes to stand over the given customary constitution.

A few years before Goodenough's article, Schmitt argued in *Political Theology* that the paradox of legal application—that is, the fact that no legal norm can be applied by another norm except through the decision of an authoritative person—is the basis on which a theory of absolute sovereignty rests.[20] Goodenough's article is, to my knowledge, the first attempt to employ this paradox of legal application in order to shed light on Platonic political philosophy as a whole.[21] In so doing, he discovered the origins of Western political theology in Hellenistic kingship, where Schmitt had never thought to look for it. For according to this paradox, if a king is to be "lawful"—that is, constitutional—and thus fall in with Plato's reading of natural right, then he must also be "above the law"—that is, tyrannical, and thus fall in with Gorgias's reading of natural right. Political theology begins by setting aside the distinction between king and tyrant in and through the guise of a discourse on natural right.

In *Homo sacer*, Agamben offers a reading of the idea of *nomos basileus* in both its Sophistical and Platonic readings.[22] This formula, he argues, contains the secret of sovereignty in the Western political tradition. This secret is that the rule of law is made possible by a conception of sovereignty that places a moment of *anomie* or violence at the heart of the law. Agamben then proceeds to show that sovereignty both makes possible the rule of law and at the same time undermines it through its logic of exception. Goodenough's genealogy of political theology lends partial support to Agamben's claim insofar as the *nomos* in question is imposed by a sovereign (*basileus*) who lies "above" the law, and in this sense undermines the traditional opposition between lawful king and unlawful tyrant. Agamben radicalizes this line of thought by prioritizing the Sophist connection between sovereignty and force or violence. He thus suggests that by recognizing sovereignty at the heart of the rule of law, the formula *nomos basileus* sacralizes the idea that "might is right" in the form of the state of exception.

However, Goodenough's genealogy can also be interpreted in the opposite manner than Agamben does. By emphasizing the Platonic, rather than Sophist, meaning of *nomos basileus* as "right is might," the sovereign moment of the rule of law does not designate an instance of violence as much as one of (divine) Justice, which gets formulated as law of Nature, and underlies the legitimacy of all positive legislation. In this view, the role of a political constitution is to allow principles of justice to stand "tyrannically" over the parts of the state and limit

[20] See the discussion of this point in (Vatter 2017d).

[21] He calls it "the problem of royalty or tyranny" (Goodenough 1928, 57).

[22] *Nomos basileus* is the decisive formula for sovereignty in (Agamben 1998, 30–39).

the struggle over power, thus reining in the temptation to make the mightier force also the legislative power. In this other, more Platonic sense, the subversion of the traditional distinction between lawful king and unlawful tyrant points ahead to the development of the idea of constituent power, which is a power to make constitutions, not a power to rule through force and violence.

Goodenough is clear that the reason why the legitimate king must stand above the positive laws of the city is because this legitimacy depends exclusively on the king's reception of the transcendent Stream of Light (*Logos-Nomos*) coming from the hidden God. This element of the Platonic teaching of *Nomos* is missing in Schmitt's reconstruction of sovereignty, and it is also not developed in Agamben's interpretation.[23] Indeed, the Platonic-Pythagorean conception of *Nomos* brings it within close proximity to the function of the Jewish Torah handed down to the Jewish people by Moses after receiving divine illumination on Mount Sinai. "The Jews had much of the best Greek thought with them in seeking salvation in Law" (Goodenough 1969, 72).

A secondary, but essential thesis of Goodenough's article is that the legitimacy of the new kind of king exemplified by Alexander the Great does not come from the adoption of Stoic motifs, with their notion of a world monarch who corresponds to Zeus's cosmic rulership of the world in accordance with the Stoic natural law of the cosmos, as had been previously generally assumed.[24] On the contrary, Goodenough argues that the Hellenistic philosophy of kingship must be reconstructed from "a lost Peripatetic tradition on kingship" (Goodenough 1928, 59). From this point of view, the Aristotelian corpus is not only the source of Christian, then humanist political ideals,[25] but also a source of a "lost" tradition of extra-constitutional kingship, or charismatic leadership.

This other tradition of Aristotelianism offers the basis for an alternative reading of the Pindaric formula of natural right, namely, *nomos basileus*: the law is king. Drawing upon the fragments of the neo-Pythagorean Archytas, Goodenough interprets this formula to mean that the king is legitimate insofar as he can be the "animate" or "living" law, *nomos empsychos*. On this view, the king's judgments are the living applications of one and the same natural or divine law (*nomos tes phuseus*) that stands higher than the written laws (*nomoi* and *psephismata*) of the cities (Goodenough 1928, 59). The distinction between rulers and ruled, typical for Greek political thought, receives a mediation by the

[23] Although, in all fairness, Agamben does suggest that the Platonic reading of *nomos basileus* may contain an emancipatory sense that places it at the polar opposite of Schmitt's elaboration of sovereignty. In this context, Agamben refers to the thought of Leo Strauss, but he does not develop this interpretation (Agamben 1998, 35).

[24] For the reception of this Stoic ideal of the king in the Roman and Renaissance theories of principality, see (Stacey 2007).

[25] For the discussion on Christian Aristotelianism, see (Nederman 1991). For the humanist reception, see (Baron 1988; Pocock 1975; Skinner 1978).

third term of *nomos*, where it refers to the "will of the gods" which must receive its "vivid representation to men" in the figure of the king (61). This Hellenistic king is "tyrant" because he administers justice from a position that stands above the customary laws of the cities, but he is also "legitimate" insofar as he stands under and incorporates the natural or divine Law. The king has ceased to be a representative of the will of the citizens of a city, and instead has become the representative of the trans-political will of the god(s): as such he represents to human beings the rational principle which stands above and separate from the body politic.[26]

Goodenough anticipates Agamben's connection of sovereignty with a doctrine of *living law* (*nomos empsychos*). However, the contraposition of both interpretations shows the vastly different paths that this notion took in Western political thought. Following suggestions found in Hannah Arendt's analysis of totalitarianism, where she argues that the totalitarian leader destroys all positive law because he is imbued with the belief that his commands are the incarnation of the true "laws of History," Agamben claims that Hitler represented the climax of the doctrine of *nomos empsychos* or *lex animata* found throughout the Western canon of political thought since Aristotle. In contrast, Goodenough's reading of this Aristotelian motif is determined by the history of its reception in Philo and then in the philosophical and mystical developments of the Jewish tradition, according to which Moses (as well as the other patriarchs) represents "the ideal king, [and] had as his essential quality the fact that he was *nomos empsychos*, and incarnation of the great Law of Nature."[27]

Although Plato and Aristotle agree that the king as living law is only a theoretical possibility for the Greeks, precisely because the Greek cities held on to a belief in *isegoria* and *isonomia* according to which everyone has a (justifiable) right to exercise rule, Aristotle considered that other, non-Hellenic peoples existed for whom this kind of divine kingship was a real possibility: "if a people is capable by nature of producing a race superior in virtue and political talent, it is fitted for kingly rule" (Goodenough 1928, 63).[28] Three distinct peoples, according to Goodenough, believed in the real possibility of such an "overman": Persians, Romans, and Jews.

If Goodenough's hypothesis is correct, it means that Persian and Egyptian motifs of cosmic kingship and sun worship enter Greek thought precisely thanks to the terrain prepared by Socrates and the Socratic school, not in tension with it. On this hypothesis, there is an underlying harmony between political

[26] "The king is personally a representation and revelation of divine-natural law in the kingdom" (Goodenough 1928, 64).

[27] (Goodenough 1969, 188). On Moses as ideal king, see (Meeks 1968).

[28] Goodenough refers to *Politics* III,17 1288a 15–20, where Aristotle raises the possibility of an individual "who is so superior that his virtue exceeds that of all others."

theology and Platonic political philosophy. Goodenough indicates that if Plato's thought may justifiably be opposed to a certain notion of political theology as "cosmic rulership"—much in the way that Foucault attempted to show—by the same token his thought can hardly be opposed to a higher notion of political theology as a doctrine of living (natural) law. Writing in 1928, Goodenough was likely aware that German and French right-wing intellectuals were recurring to "Aryan" mythologemes of being a "superior race" in order to oppose the Jewish people's self-understanding as God's chosen people.[29] As I discuss in the following chapters, German Jewish thinkers like Cohen, Rosenzweig, Buber, Strauss, and Arendt did not have to wait for Schmitt's racialization of political theology in the 1930s in order to recognize the racial or biopolitical stakes in the genealogy of political theology.

Goodenough's article develops the fundamental politico-theological theme of the king as living law in two ways. The first way employs the idea of a "living" rational law in order to secure directly the "common good" of the people without the mediation of positive or customary law. This first sense is directly related to the treatment of sovereignty in the discourse of political theology. Goodenough offers an interpretation of the fragment *On Kingship* collected by Stobaeus and attributed to Diotogenes, a "Pythagorean," whose exact dates are not known. The fragment is worth citing: "For justice is in the law, and the law is the source of justice. But the king is Animate Law [*nomos empsychos*] or is a legal ruler [*nomimos archon*]. So for this reason he is most just and most lawful" (Goodenough 1928, 65). Goodenough reads this passage to mean that the office of the king is to be occupied for the purpose of doing justice. He opposes this claim to the Cynic belief that all virtuous men are "kingly" because virtue makes them self-sufficient. In other words, the claim is that social justice is possible only because there is a kind of kingly office that communicates the will of the gods to the people: "The perfect king must be a good commander, judge, and priest. . . . For the task of a pilot is to save the ship . . . while the task of the king and captain is to save those who are in danger in war. For each of these is overseer and fashioner [*demiourgos*] of the organization of which he is the dictator" (66). This fragment from Diotogenes seems to anticipate Schmitt's category of the "constituent" dictator whose legislation in times of emergency ("in danger in war") is redemptive for his people, that is, for their common good. The image that gets sealed here,

[29] For Nazi versions of Platonism in German philosophy, see (Forti 2006). But see also the discourse on sovereignty developed in the interwar period by Georges Dumezil in works like *Mitra-Varuna. Essai sur deux représentations indo-européennes de la Souveraineté* (Dumézil 1988), published in 1940, where the "trifunctional" conception of sovereignty as conjunction of king, warrior, and priest was ascribed to "Aryan" civilizations and supposedly was inherited by Germanic and Roman peoples (in opposition to Jewish and Christian peoples).

and which Goodenough will talk about further in what follows, is that of a dictator or tyrant, the living law, as savior of the people.

A crucial element of the juridical conception of the living law is the idea that *Nous*, or the active divine intellect, governs the world by way of the legislation of this perfect king. The scheme is providential. As Diotogenes says, "it is right for the king to act as does God in his leadership and command of the universe" (Goodenough 1928, 67). The question is left open as to how exactly God governs the world. This question becomes of central importance not only for Jewish political theology but also for the theme of "economic" theology. In order to describe the idea of divine government expressed in the pseudo-Aristotelian *De mundo* 398a–398b, where God's government of the world is compared to that of Persian emperor Xerxes, Peterson anachronistically applies the 19th-century liberal formula "le roi règne mais il ne gouverne pas" (the king reigns but does not govern). This pseudo-Aristotelian, Hellenistic idea of kingship is meant to convey the belief that the king does not govern the particulars of individual's lives (the king is not a shepherd), but that his administration (*oikonomia*) takes charge of the worldly affairs. Agamben would see here the origin of an economic theology that fills the vacuum of Aristotelian monarchism by the Christian Trinitarian idea of divine government (Agamben 2011).

The analogy between One God and One King that for Peterson is definitive of political theology is captured in another fragment by Diotogenes: "the king bears the same relation to the state as God to the world. . . . For the state, made as it is by a harmonizing together of many different elements, is an imitation of the order and harmony of the world, while the king who has an absolute rulership, and is himself Animate Law, has been metamorphosed into a deity among men" (Goodenough 1928, 68). The crucial point here is that the king stands above the great nation or empire much like God stands above the world: they are no longer a part of this world, and it is this transcendence of the king with respect to the polity that necessitates his separation from mankind and his becoming divine. Order is imposed on a polity in the same way that God imposes order on the world: by a transcendent act of legislation whose stipulations account for the order in which everything happens in the world, up to and including the least particular.[30]

The image of a king who is separate from the body politic but nevertheless controls all of its parts and motions poses the "political problem of monotheism" (Peterson). According to Agamben, Christianity resolved this problem through the idea of divine *oikonomia* where the Father's monarchy is administered by the Son's government (Agamben 2011, 17–50). For Goodenough, however,

[30] (Goodenough 1969, 51) cites Philo: "The cosmos is matter put into order under a divine regimentation" (*Fuga* 9ff).

Hellenistic political philosophy offered another solution which passes through a theory of imitation or *mimesis*:

> He [the human king] must separate himself from the human passions and draw himself up close to the gods. . . . So will he succeed in putting in order those who look upon him, amazed at his majesty, at his self-control, and his fitness for distinction. . . . And equity and mercy share the throne of justice. . . . For the gods, and especially Zeus, the ruler of all things, have such attributes. . . . He inspires fear by the fact that he punishes evil doers, and control and rules all things. . . . In all these respects . . . royalty is an imitation of divinity. (Diotogenes, cited in Goodenough 1928, 72)

The ruler must become god-like in his virtues and attributes, so that order will flow into the society he rules by virtue of his subjects being desirous to imitate him. Here the crucial function is that of intellect, or *nous*, through which the king can become god-like, can achieve *homoiosis* with the divine, and through this act, shine out the light that guides his subjects, which light is his glory: "he who is both king and wise will be a lawful imitator and servant of God" (Goodenough 1928, 74). The Platonic philosopher-king, having become living law, reveals himself to be not only legislator but also priest insofar as his power to provide law comes from his capacity to "serve" God.

Goodenough thus anticipates the hypothesis of the political function of liturgy which is also of decisive importance in Agamben's development of economic theology.[31] For this Hellenistic doctrine of kingship, the king governs through prayer. The people's prayers enhance the glory of the king, whose prayers in turn enhance the glory of God. Goodenough believes this liturgical conception of kingship is not of Christian nor even of Jewish origin, but should be traced back to the Socratic-Platonic principle of *imitatio dei*. "Socrates and Plato agreed with Pythagoras that the end of life is to achieve a likeness to God" (Goodenough 1928, 74). For this *imitatio dei* to be the principal way in which God governs the world, God must be separate from the world, and not immanent in it: "for imitation of God could be imagined only by philosophers who considered God as a moral existence ruling a world objective to himself. If God is the all, as in Stoic pantheism, one may live in conformity with God's legal nature, but can hardly imitate him" (74–5). Thus the kind of political order achievable by the king as living law depends on a providential understanding of God's actions in the world, that is, it presupposes a God that is separate from the world and that seeks to be worshipped by this world. This doctrine entails that political order is established through a divine or natural law that is "religious," not in the sense of

[31] (Agamben 2011, 211, 222–30)

conforming a separate Church, but in the sense that it controls every aspect of the individual's life or conduct and has as its ultimate aim transforming a people who are subject to the living law into a "holy" people.

This point leads Goodenough to discuss the second way in which the discourse of Hellenistic kingship understands the motif of the living law, which concerns the problem of the "salvation" of a people through their faith in the king. This second, soteriological aspect of the living law is ultimately responsible for shifting the discourse of political theology from a monarchic to a democratic paradigm. The Platonic teaching that the authentic king is the individual of superior philosophical virtue and capacity for self-rule is formulated by Ecphantus, a "Pythagorean" contemporary of Archytas, as an "alien and foreign thing which has come down from heaven to man, so anyone would suppose that his virtues were the work of God, and have become the king's through God."[32] Ecphantus unifies these Platonic motifs with "an Egyptian sun symbolism" according to which "royalty is a stream of light which goes out of the deity lighting one high point in each order of existence. Among men it touches the king alone" (Goodenough 1928, 78). The Neoplatonic theory of emanation finds here its political correlate.

There are two principal sources of the sun symbolism for royalty adopted by Hellenism. The first one derives from the Egyptian pharaoh Akhenaton, whose monotheism of sun worship (the cult of Aton, "the singular solar deity of the world") is adopted in synthesis with Platonism: "the king's sharing in the Solar Power made him the Animate Law of his realm" (Goodenough 1928, 82). In connecting Philo's interpretation of the Mosaic religion with the Platonic reinterpretation of the sun worship derived from Akhenaton, Goodenough's 1928 article seems to anticipate Freud's hypothesis of Moses "the Egyptian," first published in 1939 as *Moses and Monotheism*. The other source of sun symbolism is of Persian origin. It is in this context that the image of light streaming from the sun corresponds to the idea of glory: "a divine kingly glory made by Mazda which shone upon true kings" (Goodenough 1928, 78). Xenophon (*Cyropaedia* VIII, 1, 40–2) is again indicated as the Greek thinker who receives the Persian sun symbolism and applies it to the Hellenistic motif of the superhuman king.

In 1938 Eric Voegelin, following suggestions derived from Peterson, published his book *Political Religions* in which he suggested that Fascism and Nazism were the latest incarnations of a "political religion" turning around the sun symbolism invented by Akhenaton and adopted by Moses "the Egyptian." Voegelin would then argue that this "political religion" needed to be opposed by returning to the

[32] On the "communion" of the king with God which transmits royalty, Goodenough cites Plato's *Laws* 716a, and *Minos* 319c.

values of Platonism and Christianity.[33] However, according to Goodenough's hypothesis, neither Persia nor Egypt originally had the idea of a living law, which is a purely Greek, Pythagorean-Platonic invention. Indeed, Goodenough's article shows that the cult of the sun-king is part of a theory of king by divine grace or glory that is entirely compatible with Platonism as well as with Christianity and Judaism. The messianic or redemptive component of the doctrine of Hellenistic kingship leads Goodenough to conclude that "Persia, then, seems to be the race of people referred to by Aristotle [in *Politics* 1288a] which claimed to be able to produce a kingly race of a different sort from the rest of the citizens." But there is little doubt that Goodenough was also thinking about another exalted "race of people" who identify Moses as their divine king and living law, from Philo onward.

The connection between Platonism and Judaism relies on the fact that the redemptive force of the idea of living law in Ecphantus works through the development of the intellect:

> Rather, self-sufficiency, being a primal entity [*arche*], leads all things, but is itself led by nothing, and precisely this is a property alike of God and the king himself to be the ruler (when he is called the "Self-ruling") but *to be ruled by no one*. Now that this could not occur apart from intelligence [*phronesis*] is clear, while it is obvious that God is the intelligence of the universe. For the universe is held together in arrangement and proper order, and this could not obtain without mind [*nous*]. Nor could the king without intelligence have these virtues: I mean justice, continence, communion, and their sisters. (Goodenough 1928, 86, emphasis mine)

The idea of *nous* as a providential overflow or emanation from the God to the kingly individual is therefore not so much a theory of the transmission of "ruling power" as of "no-rule": the philosophical conception of sovereignty means "to be ruled by no one" because one is self-ruling thanks to the power of the intellect.

Politically speaking, this means that if God in fact governs the world through *nous* then He does not rule through ministers or servants.[34] God "makes no use of anyone in giving His orders." Instead, this divine government depends on God "offering Himself as one worthy of imitation. God implants a desire to imitate Him in every man who has a nature like God's. God is Himself good, and to be

[33] See (Voegelin 1998) and (Assmann 1998) who picks up Voegelin's hypothesis about Moses in terms of a supposed "Mosaic distinction' between "true" (viz., monotheistic) and "false" (viz., polytheistic, pagan) religions. There is no mention of Goodenough in Assmann's study.

[34] Goodenough thus refutes Peterson's claim that political theology is essentially a theory about how divine government is carried through by angelic (or demonic) ministers. See (Peterson 1951). Agamben's focus on the angelic dimension of Christian economic theology follows Peterson. I discuss this theme at more length in Chapter 4.

so is His sole and easy function [*ergon*], while those who imitate Him do as a consequence all things better than other people. The resemblance which each man can achieve consists in self-sufficiency" (Goodenough 1928, 89). Here, the redemptive declension of Hellenistic political theology begins to turn away from a Persian, monarchic conception of empire to a Jewish, democratic conception of messianic rule.

Indeed, Goodenough's discussion of Ecphantus recalls Maimonides' understanding of the imitation of God: first, because God is only imitable in His actional attributes; second, because these attributes are perceived through intellect (*nous*) rather than through will; third, because a people who live according to God's *nous* will be self-sufficient and thus will be happy, having been cared for by God's providence. Providential rule has the grammar of *imitatio dei* or *homoiosis* (becoming the same as God). *Homoiosis* is political in a democratic and messianic sense because it promises that everyone can become kingly, that is, intellectually self-sufficient. But it is also democratic because such providential rule requires that no one be enslaved: the people ought to follow God's law *out of intelligence* and, vice versa, the education of *nous*, the education toward a philosophical life, becomes the privileged way to follow God's law.

Jewish political theology in the 20th century wrestles with the idea, voiced by Philo and Maimonides, that obedience to divine law and freedom of human intellect belong together. Spinoza's rather Machiavellian understanding of this idea was to say that Moses developed his "monotheistic religion" in order to enslave a people in such a way that they did not realize they were being enslaved but, on the contrary, thought of their "yoke" to the divine law as the source of their freedom. Spinoza opposed his doctrine of natural right based on natural reason to the "ideology" of Mosaic religion. But for Philo and Maimonides, Mosaic law is the basis of a "religion of reason," in the sense that it is a divine law or teaching for which philosophy and religion, freedom and bondage through divine law, go together. Goodenough reveals the Platonic background of this reading of Mosaic law, when he points out that the idea of a "spontaneous obedience based upon a sincere conviction on the part of subjects that the king is actually wiser than they" is found in Xenophon's *Cyropaedia* I,1,5, where the Persian subjects "desire" that they be "guided by his [Cyrus] will." Goodenough comments: "the idea remerges as a distinction in Plato and Aristotle between a king and a tyrant, that the king rules over willing, the tyrant over unwilling subjects" (Goodenough 1928, 90), except that now this "willingness" is obtained only because of the religious character of the kingly rule, because of the "piety" and the priestly qualities of the king.

As political theology, the doctrine of Hellenistic kingship develops on two divergent paths. On the one hand, it teaches that "the king is personally the constitution of his realm, that all the laws of localities under him must be ultimately moulded by and express his will." This is the idea of the king as living law which gives rise to extra-constitutional legislation, or, the law of sovereignty that Schmitt designates by the term "political theology." But for Goodenough the theory of Hellenistic kingship has also a redemptive component that is activated in messianic monotheisms: "But more, he is the saviour of his subjects from their sins by giving them . . . a dynamic and personal revelation of deity" (Goodenough 1928, 91). Clearly, only two possible figures can be meant here: Moses as the prefiguration of the Jewish Messiah, and Jesus as the Christ (Messiah). Goodenough's seminal article therefore has an esoteric agenda of its own, that is, to show that by way of Hellenistic political theology one inevitably ends up with messianism, whether it be based on Moses (as developed by Philo) or on a Pauline understanding of theocracy, where living in imitation of Jesus Christ permits the believers to be equal sons of the king, and no longer slaves to other human beings. Goodenough is the first to hypothesize that political theology can end up in Jewish or Christian ideals of (democratic) theocracy.

Philo and the origins of the "anti-Roman affect"

After his groundbreaking article, Goodenough dedicated a great deal of his work to Philo as a political thinker.[35] Philo represents the democratic trajectory of the idea of Hellenistic kingship, distinct and indeed opposed to the trajectory of the idea which leads from the Roman emperors to Eusebius and Constantine into the terrain later marked out by Peterson and pursued in the Middle Ages by those medieval political theorists who wanted to create the sovereignty of the state free from the influence of the Church and to that end called the "true secular prince" the *lex animata*. The alternative trajectory that Philo gives to the doctrine of Hellenistic kingship upholds the Hellenistic ideal in the context of Jewish messianism and is constituted around the opposition to the Roman Empire. One can say that the tradition of the living law splits up between Moses and Augustus, and these two possibilities, that of Jewish theocracy and Christian political theology, although they have a common root, inevitably oppose each other.

Many of Philo's works were composed in the genre of an "Apology for the Jews." The central message that these works intended to convey to gentiles was that "Moses is characterized basically in terms of the contemporary ideal of the king, who was to be a 'divine man' and so link the people with the spiritual order. This was a personality of whom the pagan world had been dreaming. He would be the ideal Sage of the Stoics, the 'divine man' of the Pythagoreans, the 'saviour' of the Mysteries" (Goodenough 1962, 33). Indeed, Goodenough's central

[35] See (Goodenough 1938; and 1962, first published in 1940).

thesis is precisely that Philo writes not merely defensively, to protect Jews from persecution, but also in view of making proselytes. This is shown by the text of *On Virtues* where, after discussing the virtues of the Jewish laws that show their "harmony with the best tradition of Greek ethics," Philo moves on to discuss two virtues that are particularly Jewish, those of repentance and nobility (Goodenough 1962, 44). Philo intends to show that gentiles, as long they enact *Teshuvah* (repentance) and turn toward the true God, can be "superior to those who are Jews only by birth, and not also by virtue and observance. For true nobility is not a matter of Jewish birth . . . but of the heart" (Goodenough 1962, 45). Greek philosophy is the path to Judaism for those not born Jews.[36] The motif is taken up again by Maimonides, and possibly in the same sense as in Philo, namely, that Judaism is the *telos* of Greek philosophy, just as God is the *telos* of nature.

The heart of Goodenough's reading of Philo consists in identifying the exact point at which Judaism adopts Hellenism in order to overcome it. This point is the true relation between God, law, and cosmos. In Philo's interpretation of Genesis, *On the Creation of the World*, he is not simply trying to show the Hellenistic world how much Greek cosmology is to be found in Moses's account of the Creation. He is also showing that the created world corresponds perfectly to the conception of the revealed divine law, so that "the fact that one obeys true Law is thereby living in accord with nature and nature's God" (Goodenough 1962, 36). It is not as if the revealed law is unmasked as cosmic law or astrology. Philo's Moses is not a Stoic: he is not saying that to be a faithful Jew means living in accordance with Nature and its fatal law. His point is exactly the opposite: to live in accordance with natural law—the Greek philosophical ideal—means to recognize the transcendence of God with respect to nature and thus to orient oneself to revealed law given by Moses as ideal man or divine king.

For in Philo the divine law has two manifestations: first as "the mind of God, the ideal world, and the material cosmos," that is, as Creation. But "the revelation of Law . . . takes its second form in the person of the ideal human being, the man who conquered his material nature (as poor Adam proved unable ultimately to do) and so whose life is a revelation of true Law in the human microcosm" (Goodenough 1962, 39). Such superior human beings are the Patriarchs, who are living law, *nomoi empsychai kai logikoi*. For Philo "the laws of the Code [of Moses] are nothing but memoirs of the life of the ancients, discussions of antiquities, namely the deeds and words of their active careers" (Goodenough 1962, 39). Philo's Abraham is the first representative of the charismatic structure

[36] Goodenough interprets *On the Special Laws* I as teaching "that only those who have the correct Platonic philosophy of life can truly share in Jewish ritual. He is obviously still writing for pagan enquirers" (Goodenough 1962, 40).

of rule in Jewish theocracy: "Abraham, by virtue of being the unwritten law of God, was a merciful benefaction (*charis*) from God with abiding power to benefit man" (40).

As living law, Moses "had the power of taking a Law which was spirit and divine purpose, and of applying it to human problems. Through him the Law, or Nature, of God could become statutory laws" (Goodenough 1962, 34). If Abraham as living law represents natural law to humankind, Moses does more: he applies natural law and, in that way, generates the "perfect" civil legislation, unlike any other set of national laws.

Spinoza and Rousseau surmised that Judaism was organized as one of many pagan civil religions; it was characterized by a positive legislation given by Moses as political founder, which ceased to have application once the Jewish temple-state was destroyed. Goodenough reads Philo as offering an *ante litteram* reply to these early modern interpretations: Moses's legislation is itself the application of divine or natural right. In other words, the Jewish people, living under the laws of Moses, are the representatives on earth of natural right. Their particularism has become the vehicle of universalism. It is this crucial shift that Cohen picks up in his own refutation of Spinoza, accusing the latter of having forgotten that Judaism, prior to being a civil religion, is a teaching of natural right.

While Peterson argued that Philo's political theology only led to the ideology of Roman emperors as human gods, and from there culminated in Constantine's Caesaropapism, in his later work on Philo, Goodenough shows that the Jewish philosopher is the initiator of a political theology that is compatible with the teaching of Christ as Logos (something which has long been recognized and plays a crucial role in Cohen) and yet is also profoundly anti-Roman. "The spirit of Roman rule corresponds most closely in modern times to fascism, for Augustus and his successors were fascist rulers in the sense that they had no constitutional warrant for their totalitarian authority" (Goodenough 1962, 53). By way of contrast, Philo's Moses is representative of an "anti-Roman affect" because his legislation has the "constitutional warrant" of being under God's law, and not above it.[37]

Philo's political thought holds that the human state should be modeled after God's state, not after the Roman state:

> His [God's] very existence has the result that a flow of power streams forth from him. The analogy for this was the sun with its rays. . . . It is not only the creative power, but also the governing. . . . From the point of view of God this rule is, like the rule of the father in the home [*oikonomia*], monarchy. . . . The *material world is then a monarchy* in that it gets its regulation from above, *but it*

[37] The expression comes from Schmitt's *Roman Catholicism and Political Form*.

is a democracy within itself in so far as all created things (except man, and even men among themselves) are equal before the higher reality of the Logos-Law. (Goodenough 1962, 65, emphasis mine).

This passage expresses the unique sense in which Jewish political theology is a teaching of "divine democracy" and not just of "divine sovereignty" or of "divine government."

It is instructive to compare Goodenough's interpretation of Philo's idea of divine *oikonomia* with Agamben's interpretation of Christian divine *oikonomia.* Both share the belief that the rule of the head or sovereign in a household works in and through the "nature" of the parts of the household.[38] The rule of the *oikos* is the model for how transcendent sovereignty unites with nature, and thus only an "economic" theology can resolve the "political problem of monotheism." However, Agamben argues that in Christianity this solution receives its definitive politico-theological form with Saint Thomas Aquinas's philosophy, where the "nature" of created things corresponds to the activity of divine government as *dispositio* [arrangement], whereas the Creation itself corresponds to God as transcendent sovereign of the world. On this model, "the good of order" emerges in and through the contingent unfolding of events by secondary causes rather than through the intervention *ex machina* of a divine sovereign (Agamben 2011, 132–4). For Philo, instead, God does not only "reign" above His Creation, but He also "governs" this Creation through His providence in the form of a Logos-Nomos, as opposed to the Second Person of the Trinity. The two forms of divine government are natural right, on the one hand, and living law (Abraham's knowledge) on the other. Abraham is living natural law that is applied by Moses in his positive laws of the state of Israel. Natural right establishes itself as the constitution of God's state.[39]

Since the law of nature is God's constitution or divine law for the world, Philo opposes the undivided rule of God, or theocracy, to the many legislations decreed by statesmen on the basis of their "covetousness, their want of good faith towards and confidence in one another. . . which have appeared to be for the common advantage of the agreeing and unanimous multitudes" and are to be considered "additions to the one great general constitution of nature."[40] That is why Philo considers that "the one true manifestation of divine law in the form of a social

[38] For the analogy of the head of the household with a monarch, see Aristotle *Oeconomicus* I, 1343[a] and the discussion in (Agamben 2011, 116–9).

[39] In this sense, Goodenough's interpretation of Philo has a remarkable overlap with Strauss's interpretation of Maimonides, in which natural right becomes the placeholder of theocracy, and with Buber's interpretation of theocracy as the other side of democracy in virtue of the equality of all created natures to the natural law. Both of these interpretations are discussed in more detail in Chapter 5 and Chapter 6, respectively.

[40] (Goodenough 1962, 66) citing *On Joseph*, 31 (Philo 2006, 438).

code, the Jewish law, had to be given to a people in the desert where they were isolated from the pressures and entanglements of ordinary life" (Goodenough 1962, 66). The only political or civil laws that are not "additions" to divine or natural law are those given by Moses to Israel; it is in order to distinguish the constitution of the Israelites from that of other cities, from the civil theologies of other cities, that Philo claims a priority of the "desert" over the city or civilization.

If all political states, with the exception of the Mosaic constitution, which is the only political state that corresponds to natural law, are artificial constructions made by dominant groups, the question arises how to reunite God's city with the human city. The answer is contained in the concept of a messianic king, "a ruler . . . who would be more than human." For Philo, Moses becomes "the king [who] could do no wrong, it was everywhere held, because while he codified in his decrees the law of Nature for men, told them what was 'right' and 'wrong,' he himself was essentially a citizen of the heavenly city: subject to its standards alone, men could not judge him by the laws which regulated the conduct of others. Still today the state has this superhuman prerogative" (Goodenough 1962, 69).[41] Philo sets up Moses as the first figure of sovereignty, that is, as the king who is at the same time priest (in that he worships God) and judge (in that he applies divine law) and legislator (in that his application of divine law is law-making for the city).

But, on Goodenough's reading the legitimate purpose of the divine king, of the sovereign who is "above the law," is none other than the institution of a primordial democracy. In Philo's conception of theocracy, the divinity of the king stands for a messianic politics. Despite his reservations with respect to Peterson's reading of Philo's political theology as the source of the doctrine of sovereignty, Schmitt was not capable of taking up the opposite suggestion—formulated by Goodenough—that Philo's political theology was that of a "divine democracy."[42] Goodenough's interpretation of Philo is strongly indicative of that connection between messianism and democracy "to come" that Jacques Derrida thematizes, but that in reality characterizes a great deal of Jewish political theology in the 20th century.

As Goodenough formulates this transition from divine kingship to messianism, "when the Jewish people shall have at last developed political leaders who, like the guardians of Plato's *Republic*, are able to guide the people according to the truth of immaterial reality; when the Jews as a whole shall have been

[41] For Paul, this role is taken over by Jesus Christ. For a discussion of how Paul takes up Philo's idea of the messianic king, see (Blumenfeld 2001).

[42] More exactly, Schmitt says that the Jewish analogy between One God and One People should have allowed Philo to speak of a "divine democracy" [*Göttlicher Demokratie*] but that instead he only uses the term "divine monarchy." Schmitt refers to Peterson's claim that Philo is "a friend of democratic ideals . . . but it is clear that the Jewish faith in God prohibited him from speaking of a divine democracy" (Schmitt 1996b, 47).

transformed into virtue; then a deliverer will come who will be more divine than human. . . . [He] will set up a kingdom in which *the true democracy of nature will at last appear*, the equality of every man in the heavenly city of which all are at last citizens" (Goodenough 1962, 70, emphasis mine). Philo's messianism, therefore, sets a democratic goal to the Platonic philosopher king, that is, a "return to nature" that is fundamentally democratic in nature. Put in more messianic language, the "true democracy of nature" is destructive of the division of humanity into political states at war with each other. In the chapters that follow I hope to show that Philo's attempt to turn Plato's philosopher-king back into a democratic discourse by way of messianism is a leitmotif of all Jewish political theology in the 20th century.

2

Hermann Cohen and Socialist Democracy

Monotheism as a political problem in Cohen's Jewish Writings

The development of political theology in the 20th century can be understood as a series of answers to what Erik Peterson calls the "political problem of monotheism."[1] When God is conceived as the Lord of the world, the political problem is to understand how God manifests His presence in and through history without thereby destroying the freedom of His subjects, that is, without becoming a tyrant. The answers to this politico-theological problem depend on how the distinction between God's "metaphysical" essence and His "historical" or "political" existence is conceptualized. My claim in this chapter is that Hermann Cohen offers the first answer to this problem in the form of a discourse that can be rightly called a "Jewish political theology."[2] By working out an original Platonic-Maimonidean approach to the Jewish messianic ideal, Cohen's Jewish political theology undoes the oppositions between reason and faith, nature and revelation, that Saint Paul articulated in messianic form.[3] These oppositions were foundational for medieval Christian political thought, which, according to Carl Schmitt's hypothesis, were also secularized in modern political and juridical thought. The consequence of Cohen's political articulation of Jewish messianic teaching is that the discourse of political theology in the 20th century was no longer exclusively tied to the legitimacy of the nation state and of sovereignty, but was imparted another trajectory, oriented toward a supranational, cosmopolitan ideal of the rule of law. The chapters that follow discuss this alternative trajectory of Jewish political theology, which has become fundamental to radical democratic political thought in our own times.

[1] See the treatise by the same name in (Peterson 2011).

[2] For the problem of "Jewish political theology," see (Kavka 2014a). On Judaism as it touches on the question of political theology in early modernity and in its reception in 20th-century political theory, see also (Hammill and Lupton 2012; and Kahn 2014). For a sober presentation of "Jewish political theology" coming from the perspective of Jewish political thought, see (Melamed 2012, 35–49). As Melamed admits, talk of "Jewish political theology" begins in earnest only with the reception of Leo Strauss's studies in the history of political thought and in his direct engagement with Carl Schmitt. For two opposed perspectives on this engagement, see (Meier 1995; and Vatter 2004b).

[3] For a representative example of post-Marxist, Pauline political theology, see (Žižek, Santner, and Reinhard 2013).

Living Law. Miguel Vatter, Oxford University Press (2021). © Oxford University Press.
DOI: 10.1093/oso/9780197546505.003.0003

Starting with Augustine, Christian political theology gave a Trinitarian answer to the political problem of monotheism.[4] On this view, God the Father guides human beings spiritually though God the Son, whose mystical body is the Church, and materially, through the government of the State. These "Two Cities" stand in a hierarchical relationship, where spirit informs matter. The concrete formations of power found in medieval Christian Europe, namely, Empire and Church, as well as the early modern *jus publicum Europaeum* (public law), composed by the concert of European sovereign nation-states that replaced the definitive breakup of the medieval world order, remained Trinitarian in their politico-theological structure. Generalizing and simplifying to an extreme, one can say that both the medieval (Gelasian) and the modern (Grotian) concrete normative orders depend on the vicarious representation of God through hierarchical organizations of legitimate domination, be these conceived as Empire or as Church, or as a fusion of both as happens in the early modern states.[5]

With Spinoza and the spread of Spinozist libertine thought, this Trinitarian answer came under attack, eventually leading to the formation of a "liberal" concrete political and juridical order.[6] Spinoza's answer to the political problem of monotheism, very roughly, was to say that God no longer has a political existence after the downfall of the Hebrew Republic founded by Moses. As he says in the "Preface" to his *Theologico-Political Treatise*, "the law revealed by God and Moses was simply the laws of the Hebrew state alone, and was therefore binding on none but the Hebrews, and not even on them except while their state still stood" (Spinoza 2002, 392). For Spinoza, Jesus founded no concrete political order but simply offered a universal ethical teaching of brotherly love (*Theologico-Political Treatise*, chapters 7 and 14). After Jesus, true religion is what the democratically established, human sovereign says it is (*Theologico-Political Treatise*, chapter 19). This religion is a "civil" religion that enjoins obedience and respect for laws given by the sovereign people to itself and as long as it protects natural individual rights.

Against this background, my hypothesis is that Cohen opens a new discourse on political theology that is anti-Trinitarian because it is based on a strict or pure conception of God's singularity [*Einzigkeit*]. Cohen identifies this conception of God as the core teaching of Judaism as a "religion of reason." The conception of God's singularity only offers itself as model for radically egalitarian, non-hierarchical, democratic associations based on the recognition of the singular humanity shared by all individuals. However, contra Spinoza, Cohen

[4] I refer to the treatment of Christian political theology in (Vatter 2020).

[5] For the medieval world order, see (Schmitt 2008). On the modern world order, see (Taylor 2004). On the presence of Trinitarianism in modern governmentality, see now (Agamben 2011).

[6] On Spinoza as initiating modern liberalism, see (Strauss 1997; James 2012; and Israel 2002) for three narratives.

maintains that Judaism, both as a nationality and as a teaching, is assigned a crucial transhistorical role as carrier of a messianic political ideal best understood as a teaching of natural right as human rights, which transcends the idea of individual rights protected by the sovereignty of the nation-state.

Two problems seem to stand in the way of clarifying the real contribution of Cohen to the development of political theology in the 20th century. The first is the widespread tendency to see in his philosophical system a creative reinterpretation of Kant's critical thought, without taking into due consideration his turn to Platonism and his interpretation of Maimonides and medieval Arabic philosophers, and this despite the best efforts of Leo Strauss's indications.[7] The second problem consists in the relative lack of scholarly studies of his posthumously published Jewish writings, the three volumes of the *Jüdische Schriften*, only a small fraction of which are translated into English and only in excerpted fashion (at the time of writing there exists no critical edition of these writings in German or Hebrew). Most of the studies on Cohen that address his political thought tend to rely on his posthumous book *Religion of Reason Out of the Sources of Judaism*, which is Cohen's late attempt to present in systematic fashion the body of work that he wrote over decades and which was posthumously collected in the *Jüdische Schriften*.[8] The later work, admirable as it is, cannot give an exact appreciation of Cohen as a theologico-political thinker. Apart from leaving out crucial texts, such as the monograph on Maimonides and the long treatments of Plato and Spinoza, *Religion of Reason* tends to emphasize the "theological" elements of Judaism over its politico-philosophical ones, and thus in a sense makes it harder to grasp the central tenets of Cohen's political theology.

Franz Rosenzweig's introduction to the 1924 edition of Cohen's *Jüdische Schriften* has the great merit of shining light on the political character of Cohen's religious writings as a function of a return to Platonic political philosophy. For Rosenzweig, Cohen's oeuvre is characterized by two distinct critiques of contemplative reason: the first is elaborated in his commentaries on Kant's critiques, and then in his own reconstruction of a neo-Kantian system of philosophy; the second work of critique is developed in his Jewish writings, where Cohen departs from his neo-Kantian orientation and takes up Plato's critique of reason as his normative horizon. Cohen's approach to monotheism is more Platonic than Kantian because God is understood from the Idea of the Good, which lies "beyond being" [*epekeina tes ousias*], and so can be approximated not scientifically but only ethico-politically. Rosenzweig's point is that one errs from the

[7] See here (Hollander 2014).

[8] See (Cohen 1924 and 1995) respectively. For the English edition of excerpts from the Jewish Writings, see (Cohen 1993). Translations from the *Jüdische Schriften* are mine.

beginning if one assumes that Cohen's "religion of reason" is an interpretation of Judaism along neo-Kantian or "liberal" lines.[9]

The connection between Platonism and Judaism, between God as Idea and the God of Israel, is worked out by Cohen through an original reading of Maimonides as a Platonist, discussed in the following. By returning to Platonism through a reconstruction of medieval Arabic and Jewish philosophy, Cohen is able to assign to religion a fundamental role within the development or evolution of human culture that he thought was denied to it within the liberal conception of culture, based on the self-assertion of the individual.[10] Thus, in a late text of 1914 entitled "The Religious Movements of the Present," he explains that the fundamental question posed by religion to human culture (by which Cohen means the development of human reason from out of its own power) is whether the concept of humanity requires or not the Idea of God. Referring to the so-called *Kulturkampf* (culture war) between Bismarck and Catholicism, which found parallels all over Europe in the 19th and early 20th centuries, Cohen asserts that "all culture wars turn on this question [*Alle Kämpfe der Kultur drehen sich um diese Frage*]" (1924, I:37). Cohen gives a radical answer to this question: to attain the standpoint of "humanity" it is necessary to establish the "cor-relation" [*Korrelation*][11] to God, for deprived of this ethico-political relation to God, human beings will not be able to overcome their natural political condition, rooted in wars between national and ethnical groupings. The correlation to God opens the horizon for a politics oriented by the singularity of humanity, which Cohen understands as a political life oriented by the Idea of the Good. Such a qualified political life receives the name of *Sittlichkeit*.[12] The political meaning of God as Idea is expressed in the task presented by what Cohen calls the "the social ideal," namely, the task of realizing the humanity of human beings in the form of a messianic or socialist democracy (1924, I:xxxii–xxxiv).[13] The internal relation between God as Idea of the Good and the ideal of a messianic community determines the sense in

[9] For a recent reading of Cohen as a neo-Kantian, German "liberal theologian," see now (Lilla 2007). There is no mention whatsoever of Cohen's interpretations of Maimonides or Plato in Lilla's account. Lilla also misses the deep continuities between Cohen and Rosenzweig discussed in the next chapter.

[10] For a discussion of the liberal conception of culture and culture wars as understood in the Weimar context, see (Vatter 2004b; and Kahn 2014).

[11] *Korrelation* is Cohen's technical term for the biblical idea of a covenantal, that is, political relation between God and a people. It plays a crucial role in Rosenzweig and is discussed further in the next chapter.

[12] *Sittlichkeit* is often translated as "ethics," but to do so is to miss the way in which Cohen employs and plays with the post-Hegelian connotations of the term, which are best captured if the term is understood as the equivalent of the Greek *politeia*, both an organization of citizens and a constitutional order. I shall translate it as "ethico-political reality." For discussions of *Sittlichkeit* in Cohen, see (Bienenstock 2009; Zank 2006; and Loick 2015).

[13] On Cohen's adherence to a socialist form of democracy, see (Schwarzschild 1956).

which Cohen's interpretation of Jewish monotheism is a form of Platonic political philosophy.

God and His Kingdom: Cohen and messianic political theology

Contemporary post-Marxist thinkers like Alain Badiou, Giorgio Agamben, and Slavoj Žižek have theorized their radical conceptions of emancipatory politics by appealing to Saint Paul's messianism, which turns on the truth-event that Jesus is the Messiah who both fulfills and brings to an end the rule of law. At stake in this discussion is the degree to which Saint Paul's interpretation of Jesus's teaching remains linked to a Jewish understanding of the Messiah, as Jacob Taubes and Eric Santner forcefully argue. Santner even claims that "Saint Paul was the first great German-Jewish thinker, equal in stature to Rosenzweig, Freud and Benjamin."[14] But Cohen's massive contribution to the renewal of messianic politics during the same period remains much less explored.[15] It is not commonly acknowledged by those theorists of the post-Marxist Left who today adopt theologemes from Jewish messianism, that prior to Rosenzweig, Benjamin, and Scholem, it was Cohen who insisted that the central importance of Judaism to politics is due to its single-minded adherence to the teaching of messianism.[16]

The messianic solution to monotheism as a political problem can be rendered, according to Cohen, in one pithy formula: "God and His Kingdom [*Gott und sein Reich*]" (1924 III,175). The Platonic approach to Jewish monotheism advocated by Cohen is charged with elucidating the two components of this formula. The first task is the demonstration of the singularity of God; the second consists in the messianic establishment of His Kingdom on earth. Cohen carries out the first task mainly through an interpretation of Maimonides as a Platonic political philosopher. Maimonides accounts for God's singularity both through a negative theology and through an ethical conception of God as Idea of the Good, as discussed next. However, the problem of realizing the messianic ideal in history calls for what I shall name the Philonic strategy in Cohen's Jewish writings. This strategy climaxes in Cohen's highly controversial wartime text, *Germanism*

[14] See (Santner 2003, 132). On Saint Paul's "Jewish" conception of messianism, see (Taubes 1993; and Agamben 2005b).

[15] A good pointer to this failed reception is the early study by Taubes on messianic thinking in the Western tradition, which does not mention Cohen at all, but starts from Bloch and Rosenzweig (Taubes 2009).

[16] The question of messianism is missing in the discussion of Benjamin's and Scholem's early reception of Cohen discussed in (Ng 2012). Evidence of Benjamin's extensive debts to Cohen are now documented in (Deuber-Mankowsky 2000, 2015), although without focusing on the question of political messianism.

and Judaism, discussed in the second half of the chapter, which sets out to explain the complicated and dialectical relation between Judaism, nationalism, and cosmopolitanism.

The Kingdom of God, or an ethico-political reality [*Sittlichkeit, politeia*] oriented by the Idea of the Good, is possible only if individuals direct their actions and beliefs toward the imitation or *mimesis* of God's singularity (Cohen 1924, I:20–1). For Cohen, the "Bible science" developed by German Jewish thinkers at the end of the 19th century needed to be oriented by the demonstration that the Torah is primarily the *Lehre* (teaching) of God's singularity and the messianic consequences that follow from it.[17] The study of Torah thus becomes equivalent to the knowledge of *Sittlichkeit*, that is, to "political philosophy": "The love of God is the love of *Sittlichkeit*. Spiritual love is only the care of *Sittlichkeit*. But *Sittlichkeit* requires knowledge . . . so the Thora must also be the teaching, the knowledge of *Sittlichkeit*."[18] According to Cohen, the Torah indicates that this knowledge of *Sittlichkeit* must be made accessible to all human beings. The knowledge or *scientia* of God (i.e., theology), which is now understood by Cohen as the science of the true ethico-political reality (*Erkenntnis der Sittlichkeit*), is not the exclusive possession of the priestly class.[19] In this sense, one can say that the Torah as a teaching of political science is not constitutive of a concrete normative order like that of a Church, an Empire, or a State.

Cohen's point is that if the Torah can be understood as political philosophy, then for Judaism there can be no ultimate distinction between faith and knowledge, just as there can be no ultimate distinction between a class of priests initiated into wisdom and a class of laypeople who lack this *scientia*. That is why Cohen refers to Judaism as "our philosophy [which is] at the same time our faith": a formula that renders the sense of his expression "religion of reason." The project of interpreting the Torah as political philosophy reverses the process of secularization as Schmitt conceived it, namely, as the translation of Christian theological categories into political-juridical ones. Since from Cohen's perspective there is no true politics that is not also messianic, political philosophy

[17] There is no space to discuss the complicated question of the different meanings and discourses taken by the ideas of a "Bible science," of a "Science of Judaism" [*Wissenschaft von Judentum*] in Germany in the 19th and early 20th centuries, up to the *Akademie für die Wissenschaft des Judentums* founded by Rosenzweig with Cohen's imprimatur. However, the stakes at issue in defining the conditions of possibility of such a science are addressed in all the following chapters. On the history of the *Akademie*, see (Myers 1992). For the classic version of its picture of Jewish philosophy, see (Guttmann 1973). For the critique of a "science of Judaism," especially in its 19th-century form in Germany, see (Scholem 1963, 1997).

[18] "Die Liebe zu Gott ist die Liebe zur Sittlichkeit. Das geistige Lieben ist einzig und allein die Pflege der Sittlichkeit. Die Sittlichkeit aber fordert Erkenntnis . . . so muss denn auch die Thora die Lehre, die Erkenntnis der Sittlichkeit sein" (Cohen 1924, I:23).

[19] Cohen puts the same point by saying that "the study of the Thora prevails over all commandments [*Das Studium der Lehre alle Gebote überwiegt*]" (1924, I:24).

becomes a question of translating Greco-Roman political categories into Jewish theological ones. The recent project of recovering a tradition of "Jewish political thought," associated mainly with the names of Daniel Elazar and Michael Walzer, is inconceivable outside of the horizon opened by Cohen's politico-theological approach to the project of a "Bible science."[20]

To interpret the Torah as "political philosophy," in other words, to see in messianic theology the translation and realization of pagan philosophical politics, is to erect Israel, in the words of Saadja (whom Cohen considers to be "the founder of Jewish philosophy"), as a counter-education with respect to Greek *paideia*: "our nation is a nation only through its teaching (Torah) [*Unsere Nation ist nur Nation durch ihre Lehre (Torah)*]." That is why (the rest of) Israel, who corresponds to all those who study the Torah as a (Platonic) political philosophy, is designated in the Bible as constituting a "kingdom of priests and a holy people" (Cohen 1924, I:23). Martin Buber, Gershom Scholem, and Leo Strauss will adopt from Cohen, and articulate in their distinct, even opposite ways, the belief that biblical theocracy requires that God ought to govern over the whole of life, *das ganze Leben*, and such a conception of divine government troubles and subverts any radical separation between "the priests and the Israelites," between Church and State, and between the sacred and the profane (Cohen 1924, I:26).

Whereas the Greco-Roman ideal of the education of humankind leads to the elevation of the arts and of the national state (an ideal that the Renaissance recovers in the belief that the state is humanity's greatest work of art, Hobbes's *machina machinarum*, the technical artifact that makes all technological innovations possible), the political content of this messianic teaching, of this counter-education of mankind, is "the subjugation of the nation under humanity [*die Unterwerfung der Nation unter die Menschheit*]" (Cohen 1924, III:173). For Cohen, an ethico-political action is world-historical only when it aims to transcend the "natural" horizon of separate nations living in a Hobbesian state of war. The truly political act is the one that expresses the perspective of humanity as the only relevant political subject, and this politics calls for nothing short of a "fundamental fight against war understood as historical idol worship" [*gründsatzliche Bekämpfung des Krieges als des geschichtlichen Götzendienstes*] (Cohen 1924, III:143). On this view, (the remnant of) Israel would be the one "nation" on earth that stands for the messianic ideal of a world without nations, and thus without wars, by carrying forth the political ideal of a life dedicated to study and scholarship. In short, as a "religion of reason," Judaism contains a political theology of anti-nationalism, or cosmopolitanism.[21]

[20] On "Jewish political thought," see the discussion in (Cooper 2016).

[21] For a reading of Cohen's political theology as counter to Julius Wellhausen's *Prolegomena to the History of Israel*, who famously argued that Judaism is first of all a national religion and only secondarily a universal "religion of Law," see (Weidner 2014).

Cohen's conception of *Sittlichkeit* in his Jewish writings is not simply intended to express the idea that the Torah contains the true principles of the *politeia*, but it is also intentionally meant to contrast with the Hegelian politico-theological conception of *Sittlichkeit*, a point picked up soon thereafter by Rosenzweig. Cohen's employment of the Hegelian term reflects his awareness that Christian political theology and philosophy of history, in a sense, climaxed with Hegel's theory of the national state as the *Da-sein* of God.[22] Cohen's response to Hegel's divinization of the nation-state (and his claim that it is best represented by a constitutional monarchy) is that only a messianic realization of God's Kingdom corresponds to world history: "the Kingdom of the Messiah is God's Reign . . . God's Reign as the Ideal of world history" (Cohen 1924, III:174). Unlike the Hegelian conception of *Sittlichkeit*, where God governs in history in and through the (national) state as highest expression of objective spirit, for Cohen the rule of God in history is entirely oriented by a messianic conception of theocracy that leads beyond the horizon of the nation-state. Where Eric Voegelin and Karl Löwith later argued that Jewish messianism was the true source of Hegelian philosophy of history and its secularization of *Heilsgeschichte* (history of salvation), Cohen's Jewish political theology places the messianic end of history beyond the state from the start.[23]

God's Kingdom is the name Jews give to that ideal form of society which has managed to abolish its main world-historical character, namely, the division between rich and poor. "That is why the Sabbath represents the ideal unity of humanity in terms of the equalization of the basic oppositions of human history" (Cohen 1924, I:173). On Cohen's account, the Sabbath stands for the belief that in the day dedicated to the study of God's ways there can be no difference between rich and poor, masters and slaves. Expressed otherwise, Cohen's conception of the actuality of freedom requires the end of (forced and wage) labor and the universal access to free ("liberal") education.[24]

For Cohen, God's Kingdom is not found in the "other world," in a heavenly City of God, but is to be established here on earth. Only polytheism, not a rigorous or strict monotheism, believes in a "beyond" and in the "resurrection" of the individual (Cohen 1924, I:26). Cohen calls into question the belief in the resurrection of the individual because, on his account of messianism, salvation cannot be an individual matter, but is essentially a political condition, dependent

[22] For a recent discussion of Hegel and modern political theology, see (Esposito 2015). For other classic treatments of the theme, see (Theunissen 1970; Shanks 1991; Kervégan 2005; and Böckenfoerde 2006). On the depiction of Judaism within German Idealism, see (Mack 2003; and Loick 2014).

[23] See (Löwith 1957; and Voegelin 1952). For an excellent defense of Cohen's conception of world history against the interpretation offered by Löwith, see (Bienenstock 2012).

[24] Both requirements reappear in Agamben's conception of "inoperativity" (Agamben 2000). See the discussions in (Whyte 2014; and Prozorov 2009).

on the correlation of a people to God. However, salvation is not political in the sense of Voegelin's "political religion," but in the sense that the subject of salvation or happiness is the entire human species or *Gattungswesen*, as Marx would have it. "The people does [*sic*] not die, but has [*sic*] a history which continues. . . . Immortality acquires the meaning of the historical living-on of the individual in the historical continuity of his people. . . . The individual soul acquires its immortality in the historical continuation of the human species" (Cohen 1995, 301). Since salvation is not personal, there is no personal savior, or, put more drastically, whoever promises individual salvation is thereby shown to be a false Messiah (Cohen 1924, I:31).

Reversing Schmitt's theological formula for sovereignty ("Jesus is the Christ"), for Cohen the Christ, the anointed ("Messiah"), cannot be Jesus as conceived by Saint Paul, as that divine man who, by sacrificing himself, took upon his person the sins of all individuals, and thus became their personal savior. That is why Cohen insists that the messianic must be separated from the personality of the Messiah. Nearly a century before Jacques Derrida's *Spectres of Marx*, Cohen anticipated the concept of the "messianic without Messiah" as corresponding to a "people of the future, as the humanity of the future [*Volk der Zukunft, als die Menschheit der Zukunft*]" (1924, I:32). It would not be incorrect to say that one possible designation for Cohen's conception of God's Kingdom is Derrida's concept of "a democracy to come," the final form of *Sittlichkeit* here on earth. Not the universal state, as Alexandre Kojève has it, but the ideal of a "democracy to come" contains the cipher of a true "world" or "global" history, that is, of a history which is truly worldly because it moves the human species beyond the political limits determined by the sphere of the "national."

When the Sabbath is understood world-historically, it denotes the messianic time in which the natural history of the human species comes to its end. Cohen helpfully distinguishes this social democratic messianism from the Pauline messianism, to the extent that the former is oriented toward a messianic "future time," whereas the latter is oriented toward a messianic "future world" (1924, III:146; 1995, 447, 461). The content or truth-event of Jesus as the Christ, according to Saint Paul's messianism, is the actuality of individual resurrection from the dead. Such resurrection only makes sense on the assumption of a "future world." Schmitt claimed that the Christian conception of world history depended on the Pauline concept of the *katechon*. In his view, world history was characterized by the struggle led by the Christian Church, in conjunction with an earthly Empire, to restrain the anomic or anarchic force of the Anti-Christ. For Schmitt, the Anti-Christ takes on Promethean qualities, falsely promising that humankind can reach "world peace" before the actual End of the world is attained by the Second Coming of Jesus Christ. The point being that, for Schmitt, the "future world" is not something that can happen historically, and that is why it is good and right that the possibility of political wars or wars between states not vanish from this world.

For Cohen, on the contrary, war is the result of a mythical conception of politics and of the state which needs to be fought against in order to redeem history and politics from their tendency toward self-destruction, in order for history to have a future at all. In his view, the fundamental political myth is the belief in the possibility of individual salvation which rests upon the dualism of Church and Empire. Thus, one can say that for Cohen it is faith in Jesus as the Christ that comes to play the Promethean role. In this sense, Jewish political theology also develops its own idea of the *katechon* or restrainer, as I discuss further in the next chapter dedicated to Rosenzweig. But such a Jewish *katechon* would have to be understood in terms of a messianic politics that restrains the Christian restrainer itself. The messianic political task is that of restraining the very earthly powers that proclaim civil peace can be secured only if one upholds the "one necessary belief" (Hobbes) that "Jesus is the Christ." Cohen believes that a proper Jewish "restraining" of Paulinian messianism can only be achieved through a return to Platonic political philosophy, as represented in the thought of Philo and Maimonides.

The underlying opposition between Philo and Saint Paul over the messianic reading that needs to be given to the Hellenistic tradition of divine kingship remains very much present, if not explicitly thematized, in Cohen's messianism. It is my contention that Cohen's democratic messianism echoes Philo's idea of a "democracy of nature." Tellingly, Cohen defines human freedom as "purity of heart" (1924, I:28): in human beings, purity corresponds to holiness (*Heiligkeit*) in God. This notion of purity is one of Philo's four cardinal virtues, related to the "nobility" of those who study Torah. It is not surprising—given his understanding of political monotheism—that Cohen establishes an opposition between this Philonic purity of heart and the Pauline conception of original sin. Whereas purity is only achievable in one's lifetime and on condition of acting ethico-politically, and does not require the intervention on the part of God's "representatives" or vicars, Cohen thinks that in Saint Paul the political freedom of human beings plays no part in their salvation: true freedom, the "freedom of God's children" in Romans 8:21, depends on the individual's participation in God's glory through the faith in a Beyond (1924, I:28).

Cohen's use of Philo in developing his Jewish political theology is overdetermined and ambivalent. For Cohen also charges Philo with the responsibility of attempting to join Athens and Jerusalem, "religion and Greek philosophy," in a way that led to Christianity and left Jews "perplexed": "The *Logos* of Philo Judaeus emerged in the direction of the question of an intermediary between God and man: the greatest deviation that is possible within the horizon of prophetism. A profanation of God's transcendence" (1924, III:131). Cohen believes that by positing the *Logos* as a divine-human intermediary between God and Man, Philo opened the door for the identification of the Christ or Messiah with such a *Logos*.[25] In contrast, the Jewish philosopher who saves Judaism from the "perplexity" produced by Christian faith in Jesus as the Messiah, and offers the correct way to conceptualize "Athens" and "Jerusalem," is Maimonides, not Philo. Cohen's "religion of reason" calls for another permutation of "Athens and Jerusalem," one which goes back from Philo to Plato and from Plato to Moses. This other return to Plato and from Plato to the Jewish prophetic tradition is the great achievement of Maimonides: it is what makes him, in Cohen's opinion, the "eternal teacher" of Israel. In particular, this return, or *Teschuvah*, is made possible, for Cohen, through Maimonides' negative theology, the idea of the unknowability of God's essential attributes, which keeps Judaism from the temptation of "profanating" God's transcendence, as occurred with Philo's doctrine of the *Logos*.

Maimonides: Platonist and radical democrat

Cohen's central insight is that Maimonides avoids the risk of profanating God's transcendence because he reduces metaphysics and theology to the level of practical or political philosophy. For Maimonides, "ethics constitutes the core and the effective center of his metaphysics" (Cohen 2004, 23). In this way, God's essence is left entirely untouched by human reason; it is radically other and remains transcendent. Only God's existence, that is, only His practical or actional attributes, are accessible to human knowledge. Cohen adduces as proof of this claim the concluding appendix to the *Guide of the Perplexed* (comprising chapters 51–54) that crowns the treatise with "the problem of the love of God, or ethics" (2004, 25). Cohen is referring to the passages in *Guide* 3:53–4 where Maimonides offers the interpretation of *hesed* (loving-kindness or *charis*), *mishpat* (judgment), and *sedaqah* (righteousness or justice) to clarify the fact that "it is My purpose that there should come from you *loving-kindness, righteousness, and judgment in the earth* [Jeremiah 9:23] in the way we have explained with regard to the *thirteen attributes*: namely, that the purpose should be assimilation to them and that this should be our way of life" (Maimonides 1963, III:54).

God's revelation occurs entirely in terms of the criteria or standards for human ethico-political life and actions, of which He becomes their Idea or Model: "God has His being [*sein Wesen*] exclusively in ethico-political reality.

[25] It is of course a highly contested question whether Philo's *Logos* corresponds to a second divinity, just as it is a contested question whether for Philo human beings can "divinize" themselves through their *nous*, or intellect, which is the "divine" part of the human being. For an excellent review of these questions, see (Runia 1988).

He is the model and archetype [*das Vorbild und das Urbild*] of ethico-political reality. But humanity is lord of this ethico-political reality: it is up to human beings to implement it and to be responsible for it" (Cohen 1924, III:133). As a reality, God becomes a possible object of knowledge for human beings only in an ethico-political sense: theology is transposed from metaphysics to political philosophy. In a striking phrase, Cohen says that for the prophets "God's innermost attribute is simply the Messiah" (1924, I:30). In other words, the "action" closest to God's hidden essence is the establishment in world history of the humanity of human beings. This ethico-political knowledge of God, finds its innermost meaning in the messianic attribute of God, that is, in the fact that God's actional attributes, which correspond to His Kingdom, are nothing other than the ideal human ethico-political reality. Platonic political philosophy becomes here the veritable meaning of Jewish political theology, once God's non-actional attributes are left entirely in ignorance.

Cohen's novel interpretation of Maimonides as a radical messianic thinker is based on his equally innovative interpretation of Plato's doctrine of Ideas. Cohen believes that metaphysics is crowned by ethics already in Plato, thanks to the possibility of attaining knowledge of the Idea of the Good. For Cohen, such an identification of the Idea with the Good represents Plato's appropriation and completion of the Socratic identification of virtue with knowledge: "Socrates plays the role of the herald Elijah and Plato that of the Messiah [Malachi 3:23]," he says, setting up the parallelism between Platonism and Jewish prophetic tradition that is the pillar of his reading of Maimonides (Cohen 2004, 2). The Socratic identity of virtue with knowledge entails the identity between ethics and metaphysics. Put in the terms of the Jewish tradition, the Socratic identity expresses the belief that the Torah, the guide of ethics, also contains philosophy, or is the climax of theoretical reason as well. The Torah therefore is a work of reason; it calls for a rational or allegorical interpretation: more than Philo, it is Maimonides who achieved such an interpretation. But if the Torah is to be understood as the highest point of philosophy, precisely due to the fact that it is an ethics or a political philosophy, then Aristotle's division and ranking of the contemplative and the practical lives must be rejected across the line: Maimonides could not have been the Aristotelian thinker he was universally thought to be.[26]

If virtue is knowledge, then it must be possible to give ethics a scientific form: this presupposes that the Good must be an Idea. According to Cohen, the notion of Idea in Plato has two meanings: that of giving an account (*logon didonai*, *Rechenschaft*) of a concept (*eidos*, *Begriff*); and that of a mathematical hypothesis,

[26] For other excellent readings of Cohen's Platonic reading of Maimonides, see (Rose 1993; Hollander 2014), who do not, however, thematize the politico-theological context of Cohen's Platonism.

an axiom (Cohen 2004, 4ff). The two aspects are related as follows: science means to give an account of, or a justification, of one's concepts, but there is only such a justification on the basis of axioms or hypotheses that provide the ground that justifies, that is, that provide the *explanans* (*Grundlegung*). The problem with this conception of scientific knowledge is that, if there is to be a science of the Good, then this would seem to require that the Good itself be only a hypothesis, an *explanans*. If so, then the Good can, in principle, be corrected in and through the progress of science. But this would make its normative validity merely relative (Cohen 2004, 8). Cohen believes that Plato resolved the dilemma of having to opt either for a rigorous concept of science or for a pure concept of ethics by giving the Idea of the Good a different status than all the other scientific ideas or hypotheses. Plato turned the Good into something *anhypotheton*.[27] In so doing, Plato saved science for ethics, de facto making possible a philosophical ethics. If the ideas are grounds or principles (*arche*), the Good as Idea is the groundless or non-hypothetical ground (*an-arche*) of all hypotheses. "The idea of the Good may be defined as that hypothesis which constitutes the *telos* or end of reason" (Cohen 2004, 11).

But it is not only that the ethical Idea of the Good stands at the origin of ideas as scientific hypotheses, and thus at the origin of science. Cohen believes that the progress of science is itself oriented toward an ethico-political goal. For Cohen, the Idea of the Good "is a prophecy of wisdom." This corresponds to a second sense of the Idea of the Good as *an-arche*, namely, the messianic finality of knowledge according to which everyone will be capable of attaining, in the messianic time, an authentic proximity to, or knowledge of God. On Cohen's account, the only reason that Nature favors the scientific discoveries of human beings is so that humanity may thereby attain its true, ethico-political nature, that is, its politically redeemed or messianic condition. In this way, progress in natural science and progress in democracy are intimately intertwined. In sum, Cohen's interpretation of Plato shows that the very possibility of natural science is preceded by an ethico-political relationship, corresponding to the correlation between God and His Creation, and it is finalized by another ethico-political relationship, corresponding to the ethico-political correlation of humanity with itself, the messianic condition.

This Platonic understanding of ethics as science is then employed by Cohen to explain the Maimonidean solution to the apparent antinomy between the

[27] As formulated in the famous passage from the *Republic*: "I mean that which reason itself grasps by the power of dialectic. It does not consider these hypotheses as first principles but truly as hypotheses—stepping stones to take off from, enabling it to reach the unhypothetical first principle of everything. Having grasped this principle, it reverses itself and, keeping hold of what follows from it, comes down to a conclusion without making use of anything visible at all, but only of forms themselves, moving on from forms to forms, and ending in forms" (Plato 1992, 511b).

autonomy of human reason, evidenced by the human pursuit of knowledge through scientific hypotheses, and the obedience to divine commandments that makes possible ethical action. This is the antinomy that Spinoza had brought to the fore in his critique of Maimonides and of the Bible. According to Cohen, Maimonides' solution is that all divine commandments are rational because in God, will and reason are the same. The establishment of Judaism as a religion of reason turns on the identity of divine wisdom with divine will. For human beings, the highest goal is the knowledge of God's wisdom, which, since it is identical to God's will, means that knowing God is not different from doing His will, that is, becoming like God in an ethico-political sense (Cohen 2004, 65). That is why to obey the divine commandments because these are willed by God is not contrary to human reason but is its highest purpose; it is equivalent to knowing God: "according to Maimonides, cognition is the task and *telos* of religion, and consequently of ethics" (Cohen 2004, 66).

It is not often pointed out that Cohen's Platonic interpretation of Maimonides culminates with the adoption of Abraham and Moses as exemplars of the sage who unites both faith and philosophy, ethics and cognition of God. In so doing, Cohen identifies the Maimonidean sage with Philo's conception of the Hebrew prophets as *nomos empsychos* or "living law," and opposes it to both Aristotle's and Spinoza's conception of the sage as someone who stands above "good and evil," above ethics, in his or her capacity to contemplate the whole of Being:

> How much Maimonides himself attributes his overcoming Aristotle to the Jewish tradition he himself attests by stating his aversion to *eudaimonia* more explicitly in his halakhic code than in the *Guide*: "The one who serves God out of love is engaged in the pursuit of Torah and its law, and follows the path of wisdom, not for the sake of some mundane or earthly interest, not for the sake of avoiding pain or suffering . . . but rather one is engaged in the pursuit of truth for truth's sake . . . and this level is a very high one, and not every wise person attains it." And he continues: "This is the level of our forefather Abraham . . . the level that God required of us through Moses" [*Hilchot Teshuvah* 10:2]. It seems beyond doubt that the phrase "not every sage" alludes to Aristotle and is derived from Maimonides' devotion to his own tradition rather than from the irony of any criticism in point. (Cohen 2004, 157)

Cohen's efforts to present a democratic, even revolutionary Maimonides rest on his claim that Maimonides adopts the biblical attitude that the reward for following the commandments are the commandments themselves, and that he rejects the Aristotelian claim that the end of ethics is merely happiness (but not wisdom). For if, unlike what Aristotle maintained, the contemplative life is *not* identical with the knowledge of God because the knowing of God is fundamentally achieved in and through living the true ethico-political life (*Sittlichkeit*) rather than in an exercise of intellectual self-perfection, then it follows that authentic self-perfection, or true knowledge of God, is in principle accessible to everyone and not just to the few philosophers. Conversely, the Aristotelian idea of human happiness is composed, on the one hand, by the self-sufficiency of the philosophers in their contemplative, supra-political life, and, on the other, by the happiness of the non-philosophers in their practical life oriented toward the "common material good" (Cohen 2004, 169). This Aristotelian ideal of happiness is shown to be a profoundly ideological construction that underpins a division of humanity into social classes and hierarchical institutions like Church and Empire. For Cohen, this Aristotelian distinction between contemplative and political forms of life is radically anti-messianic, and the "common good" with which it seduces the many to support the rule of the few who know better is a base lure to distract the multitudes from embarking on the philosophical enterprise of knowing God and achieving true justice on earth.

Maimonides, atheism, and nihilism

In his path-breaking interpretation of Maimonides, Cohen also offers a second demonstration of his claim that for Maimonides the crowning achievement of human reason as the true knowledge of God is ethico-political, rather than metaphysical or theological. This second demonstration turns on an innovative reading of Maimonides' so-called negative theology. Maimonides teaches that "there are no other divine attributes other than those posited by revelation. It is philosophy's impotence that is exposed here" (Cohen 2004, 66). Thus, Maimonides' theory of divine attributes assigns priority to divine revelation over human reason because what this reason can know about God is only what God reveals to human reason about Himself.[28] Ethics, or philosophy, is the cognition of God; but God can be cognized only through the attributes He reveals (Exodus 34:6–7), and "revelation posits those attributes that reveal God solely and exclusively as an ethical being . . . compassionate and gracious, abounding in kindness, and faithfulness. This is the focus of Maimonides' doctrine of attributes: he pinpoints and limits the concept of a divine attribute to an ethical attribute, thus identifying the concept of God with the ethical concept of God" (Cohen 2004, 69). Ethics is not separated from cognition because ethics is the cognition of God; and God, as object of cognition, is an ethical being. Therefore, the knowable

[28] I discuss in chapter 5 on Strauss how he takes up Cohen's claim in terms of the priority of the revealed (Mosaic) Law over philosophy.

divine attributes correspond to the thirteen ethical attributes manifest in the revealed Law understood as the terms of the covenant between God and Israel.

Cohen's point is that ethics is the cognition of God, and God can be known only according to His actions (Exodus 33:13), not His substance: "divine actions are only attributes insofar as they serve as paradigms for human conduct" (2004, 71). These paradigms of ethical conduct are the revealed laws. Thus, to know God means to follow His laws: "the cognition of God actually means the cognition of these paradigms, translated into rules, into legislation for human action, by virtue of which the action obtains the character of ethical conduct" (2004, 72). Since God's being is His existence or His actions, knowledge of God's being (which, for Aristotelianism, designates theology or metaphysics) is nothing other than knowledge of God's laws. As paradigms of action, divine laws refer to ethico-political action. Ultimately, knowledge of God is nothing other than political theology. The doctrine of divine attributes, in Cohen's interpretation of it, is the heart of Maimonides' Jewish thought as a Platonic political philosophy.[29]

Cohen himself admits that Maimonides' doctrine of negative attributes raises the suspicion of atheism (2004, 83).[30] In effect, everything here turns on the understanding the meaning of the alpha privative in "a-theism." The first thing that needs to be said in this context is that for Cohen, Maimonides' negative theology is not counter to rational faith but functions as its foundation, for all representation of God by way of positive attributes does nothing but anthropomorphize God and thus falls into idolatry. Cohen begins with a comparison between Maimonides and Spinoza: both prohibit the determination of God, for it entails a negation of God (Spinoza's *omnis negatio est determinatio*). The difference is that Spinoza's God is "the God of Nature" and not the "God of ethico-political action." If one assumes, following Spinoza, that God is Nature, then God loses all ethico-political meaning because He ceases to have any correlation to the Good (the "social ideal," in Cohen's language). It is to Cohen that one owes the discovery that Spinoza's attack against teleology in nature serves the purpose of obviating the question as to the (ethical) purpose of nature.

If to attribute something to God means to negate God, then it follows that to say anything about God must entail negating the negation. Cohen believes

[29] Cohen gives the source of Maimonides' doctrine of God's thirteen actional attributes as based on Exodus 34:6–7, "You shall become holy." It is the meaning of the concept of *imitatio Dei* or *mechake lamelekh* (to imitate the king), as well as Deuteronomy 11:22 with regard to the command to "keep close to Him." With respect to the discussion of actional attributes in the *Guide*, Cohen cites from I:54 to the effect that "the utmost virtue of man is to become like Him . . . we should make our actions like unto His." Here it becomes evident that for Maimonides, ethics, or more particularly, theocracy (following the guidance of God as *melekh*) is the core of his philosophy or metaphysics.

[30] For Maimonides, the doctrine of negative attributes "should not be divulged to the vulgar. For this kind of speculation is more suitable to the elite who consider that the magnification of God does not consist in their saying improper things but in their understanding properly" (*Guide* I:59). Strauss will say in his correspondence that he discovers the atheism of Maimonides.

that Maimonides' doctrine of negative attributes depends on a theory of negation that originates with Plato. For Plato's crucial innovation was to clarify two senses of negation: *ou* or negation ("not"), and *me* or privation ("un-" or "-less"). Maimonides applies this distinction in his negative theology: "it is not through negation [*ou*] but rather through a negation that is only apparent [*me*] that we attain a true and fast affirmation of God" (Cohen 2004, 88). The negative attributes of God are not to be understood as simple negations, but as negations of privations. Cohen cites Maimonides: "He exists, but not through an existence other than His essence; and similarly He lives, but not through life; He is powerful, but not through power; He knows, but not through knowledge" (*Guide* 1:57). The problem is how to understand God's existing by not-existing, God's living by not-being-alive.

In the discussion of *Guide* 1:58, Maimonides employs Alexander of Aphrodisias's discussion of negation, found in his commentary to Aristotle's *Metaphysics*. Alexander divides negation into two meanings. For instance, one can say that the "wall does not see" and that the "wall is not-seeing or blind." In the former sense, the wall does not have the potential to see at all; seeing is negated of the wall. In the latter sense, though, one is saying that the wall is deprived of sight, but that it could have the capacity of seeing. The privative at the level of being asserts something at the level of the ideal or ought. If one says, "that man is ignorant," one is depriving him of knowledge, but at the same time asserting that he could and ought to know. No privative can apply to God, because it would imply that He could be more perfect than what He already is, that He is expected to be something that He is not. Maimonides points out that the pious often praise God, saying that He is not envious, but this only reflects their expectation that He be generous. This is the incorrect idea of negative attributes for Maimonides. On Cohen's reading, the proper doctrine of negative attributes is to "admit only those negative attributes that imply the negation of a privative attribute" (2004, 98).[31] For example, one can say of God that He is "not unjust," where "un-just" is the privative and "not" is the negation. Only through such a notion of "double" or "determinate" negation, which is not an identification, does one "approach" God correctly, namely, accordingly to His revelation.

In conclusion, Cohen's interpretation of Maimonides' negative theology evacuates any reference to what Heidegger will shortly after start to call

[31] Cohen is referring to passages like: "the meaning of its perfection being . . . that all deficiencies are negated with respect to it" (*Guide* 1:58); "you come nearer to the apprehension of Him, may He be exalted, with every increase in the negations regarding Him; and you come nearer to that apprehension than he who does not negate with regard to Him that which, according to what has been demonstrated to you, must be negated" (*Guide* 1:59); "For on every occasion on which it becomes clear to you by means of a demonstration that a thing whose existence is thought to pertain to Him, may He be exalted, should rather be negated with reference to Him, you undoubtedly come nearer to Him by one degree" (*Guide* 1:60).

"onto-theo-logy." Instead, Cohen substitutes metaphysics and theology with a political theory of messianic *Sittlichkeit*. By following Plato, and placing God's essence *epekeina ousias*, "beyond being," while at the same time arguing that God's existence offers itself only as an ethico-political paradigm, Cohen's conception of messianism leads to a conception of world-historical politics that must adopt nihilism as its method. This insight is later developed and radicalized in different directions by Rosenzweig, Benjamin, Scholem, and Strauss, as shown in the following chapters. Each of these thinkers adopts Cohen's methodological nihilism and gives it a different content and orientation.[32] At the same time, by demonstrating that the progress of scientific knowledge receives both its beginning and its end from a conception of God as *an-arche*, Cohen shows that when God's singularity is taken as model of political relation between human beings, this relation must also be characterized by "an-archy," or by the absence of relations of domination. Thus, Cohen's messianism turns out to be also an an-archism. In this sense, his political theology anticipates the sense in which Hannah Arendt, Emmanuel Levinas and Reiner Schürmann, among others, will later articulate a politics of anarchy.[33]

Cohen's internal critique of Platonism

Cohen's late conception of religion is complex. If "religion" is understood as a strict or pure conception of God's singularity, then Cohen's later thesis is that human beings cannot establish a polity based on humanity without such religion: "religion constitutes the whole being of human beings [*die Religion das ganze Wesen der Menschen ausmache*]" (1924, III:102). At the same time, Cohen rejects the traditional, conservative belief that "without religion, no true *Sittlichkeit* exists" (1924, III:112). Here "religion" is understood to refer to a sphere of myth that is exclusively centered on the vertical relation between humans and the divine (the gods), considered as something standing independent of and above the horizontal condition of political relations between human beings.[34] Only a "mythical" (pre-Platonic) conception of politics can be based on this latter sense of religion, whereas the messianic conception of politics that follows from a teaching of the strict singularity of God is based on the Platonic critique of political and religious myths. For Cohen, Socratic

[32] For two discussions of methodological nihilism in Cohen and Rosenzweig, see (Fiorato 2004; Bertolino 2013), but their conceptions of nihilism in Cohen do not show its politico-theological presuppositions.

[33] Here I cannot follow (Kavka 2014a, 112–113), who claims that Cohen thinks of God as *arche* and it is only Benjamin's and Scholem's messianism that is truly *anarchic*.

[34] On the different senses of the term religion in Cohen, see (Borda 2005).

philosophy is the highest guise taken by human culture because it demands that the condition of the ethico-political relation between human beings be placed above, and stand higher than, considerations of "sacredness" which regulate the vertical relation between human beings and their gods. There is no true, that is, non-mythical, concept of religion without Platonic philosophy.[35] Bible science, as Cohen understands it, has as its sole objective to de-mythologize the biblical revelation and uncover its immanent rationality.

For Cohen, strict monotheism—the teaching of God's singularity—stands to mythical conceptions of the divine as "the natural right of religion [*das Naturrecht der Religion*]" (1924, III:102). The expression is highly paradoxical: it means that all mythical religions have something like an inalienable natural right to the revelation of God's singularity that remains valid no matter the stage of cultural development of humankind. Indeed, for Cohen the progress of human culture must be measured against the criterion offered by revelation as a rational doctrine of natural right. Between divine revelation(s) and human natural right there is no mutual exclusion. This means that Cohen rejects equally the belief that human salvation occurs only within a Church (*nulla salus sine ecclesia*) and by strength of faith alone, and the opposite belief, espoused by Spinoza, that a true doctrine of natural right can only lead to a civil religion that supports the sovereign's provision of physical security and "freedom to philosophize" to human beings and is entirely disconnected from the possibility of their eternal salvation. Cohen charges Spinoza of having placed the "natural right" of egoism over and above the "natural right" of revelation, which is figured, as discussed in the following, by the Noahidic divine natural laws that apply equally to believers and non-believers in divine revelation.

Ultimately, on my interpretation, the function of Platonic political philosophy in Cohen's thought is to account for the paradoxical thesis of a fundamental compatibility between natural right (what is right according to nature) and divine revelation (what is right according to God). For Cohen, the development of natural right by Socrates and Plato established the definitive standard for political life (*Sittlichkeit*) as a life lived in accordance with the Idea of the Good, and as the space of action where human beings realize their common humanity. Following Socrates and Plato, no ethico-political reality is possible unless it be grounded on (natural) reason or a scientific knowledge of ethics. By conceptualizing revealed religion out of the Idea of the Good, Cohen argues that an authentic messianic politics must be grounded on reason, or, that messianic politics must be a philosophical politics (1924, III:111).

[35] This is the source of Jan Assmann's account of the so-called Mosaic difference between true and untrue religion. Assmann understands this distinction as an exclusively Mosaic or Jewish invention (Assmann 2009). For Cohen it is equally a Socratic-Platonic one.

Cohen's brilliant intuition is that if a conception of politics is to break free from its dependency on religion or myth, then this will occur only if philosophy becomes political, as occurs with Socrates and Plato. Platonic political philosophy breaks into the mythical precincts of religion with two concepts: the philosophical conception of nature, and the philosophical conception of politics (*Sittlichkeit*) (Cohen 1924, III:121). Together they constitute the idea of natural right or law of nature. By attending to its political vocation, Platonic philosophy makes possible what Cohen calls "true religion" (i.e., the teaching of God's singularity and its messianic reality). For Cohen, a "true religion" can only be a "religion of reason" in the double sense that it is a religion which has been purified of its mythical aspects by passing through the sieve of Platonic critique, but also in the sense that it leads Platonic political philosophy toward its real end, namely, the messianic realization of the Idea of the Good. For Cohen, Platonism stands in need of the prophets as much as the prophets stand in need of Platonism.

Indeed, philosophy or science is unable to break with myth by itself unless it takes into itself the monotheism introduced by the prophetic tradition. Without the prophetic God, Platonism itself remains mythical: this is another source of the motif of the "dialectic of Enlightenment."[36] The prophetic God has as its sole task that of turning human beings toward their good, namely toward an authentic conception of politics (Cohen 1924, III:124). Platonism and the prophetic tradition coincide on the Idea of the Good. For the Socratic-Platonic tradition, the Idea of the Good is philosophical; for the prophetic religion, God is approximated only in and through the ethico-political relation between human beings (Cohen 1924, III:125). Thus "true religion" or pure monotheism is always already inscribed, as it were, within the field opened by Plato, that is, the directedness of the human being toward the Idea of the Good, even if Plato's philosophy on its own cannot attain its political realization: "The establishment of the Good is not the task of gods; for that he [Plato] needs a new kind of divinity . . . this new type refers to the unity of God [*die Einheit Gottes*]" (Cohen 1924, III:126). The singularity of God is that additional an-hypothetical principle needed to attain the Good as the oneness of humanity, that is, the ideal human ethico-political association. It is in this sense that without pure monotheism, without Judaism as "religion of reason," humanity falls short of realizing its political potential.

The fundamental difference between Plato's Idea of the Good and the Prophet's knowledge of God as He who is Good, according to Cohen, is symbolized by the

[36] A variant of this affirmative circle between philosophy and divine revelation is to be found in Walter Benjamin, whose notion of critique is not understandable unless its Platonism is joined with the prophetic tradition. That reason is caught up in its own myth, that there is a "dialectic" of Enlightenment, is not only a Hegelian discovery, but is also an idea that Cohen derives from completely anti-Hegelian premises—premises which are at play, though in a disguised way, in Max Horkheimer and Theodor Adorno.

fact that Plato has no conception of the Sabbath (1924, I:313). Throughout his *Jüdische Schriften*, Cohen always holds on to the necessary limitation of a philosophical or Socratic conception of ethics based on its ultimate incapacity to take into account the prophetic dimension of messianism. These limits of Platonism are highlighted in Cohen's last public lecture of 1916, "The social ideal in Plato and the Prophets" (*Das soziale Ideal bei Platon und den Propheten*). In this lecture, Cohen argues that the ideal politics cannot rest exclusively on the Platonic transcendence of the Idea of the Good because this Idea, although "beyond being," is not "beyond nature." An ideal or messianic politics requires the transcendence of the Good as understood by the prophets, namely, a Good that is characterized by the *absence* of the concept of nature (1924, I:310).[37] For Cohen, the absence of a concept of nature in the Bible indicates that the prophets do not have a philosophical knowledge of the Idea of Good, because for them God is not Idea, but is He who is the Good (1924, I:313). The correlate of this Good (but not of the Idea of the Good) is the concept of messianic humanity: "Plato still had no idea of humanity" (1924, I:314). This prophetic idea of humanity is connected by Cohen to the fact of suffering: the prophets identify suffering with a social evil, with poverty, and the pious with the poor, the "suffering servants" of God.

The tension between Plato's Idea of the Good and the Hebrew prophets' experience of God as He who is the Good has a political meaning: it is the tension between security (from war) and freedom (from necessity). Cohen believes that Plato ultimately thinks of the (political) Good in terms of security, whereas the Hebrew prophets do so in terms of freedom. Cohen never says that the prophetic tradition can do away with this fundamental tension or problem, which is nothing short of the problem of the political: "at the ame time it becomes clear that compassion alone cannot be the impulse behind sociability. Rather, in the last instance we must dig up and revive the source of knowledge if security and social development are to contribute to resolving social problems. That is why we need to turn our attention from the prophets to Plato" (Cohen 1924, I:316). The philosophical or scientific knowledge of politics, that is, Platonic political philosophy, is fundamental for the historical realization of God's Kingdom, and that is why "the divine Plato remains for all times the admonisher of truthfulness [*der Mahner zur Wahrhaftigkeit*], the guardian of scientific knowledge, as the sole unmistakeable heart of truth" (Cohen 1924, I:316).

However, Cohen believes that Plato's idealism is limited by its underlying political realism.[38] He identifies Plato's realism, the place where Plato's own discourse departs from its Idealism, precisely in the doctrine of the philosopher-king.

[37] The same point is often rehearsed by Strauss in his explanations of the difference between biblical teaching and Greek philosophy: see (Strauss 1953, 1986).

[38] "The caste of warriors does not originate from the land of Ideas but from political reality" (Cohen 1924, I:321).

This is the very doctrine that Erwin Goodenough had seen as the source for the Hellenistic conception of kingship, and which, in turn, via the reception of Philo and Saint Paul, reaches Christianity and then medieval Islam and Judaism.[39] Whereas it is generally thought that Plato's doctrine of the philosopher-king is the most "utopian" and unrealizable part of his political philosophy, Cohen sees in this figure the quintessence of Plato's "realism."[40]

Cohen rejects Plato's doctrine of the philosopher-king because it is based on the assumption that only a few human beings can ever attain a perfect ethico-political existence (or, what is the same, that not all human beings can reach the true knowledge of God). Since for Plato not everyone can be *sittlich*, since not everyone can live politically—in the highest sense of the term—the many non-philosophers must let the few philosophers, who know God, govern them (Cohen 1924, I:317). For Cohen, by way of contrast, Plato's philosopher-king stands opposed to the prophetic ideal of the abolition of the difference between rulers and ruled, the an-archic core of Jewish messianism: "In the relation of God and human beings no difference can be made between those who rule and those who are ruled [*In bezug auf Gott und den Menschen darf es keinen Unterschied geben zwischen Regierenden und Regierten*], nor between philosophers and non-philosophers. Moses says: 'may the whole people of God be prophets'" (1924, I:318). Cohen calls this Mosaic principle of an-archy the "principle of God" and opposes it to Plato's "principle of scientific knowledge," which is strictly oriented around the discovery of the *arche* (1924, I:318).[41]

To indicate the salient difference between Plato and the prophets, Cohen significantly refers to the other ideal Republic in the Western tradition, namely, the model of the Three Crowns characteristic of Moses's Hebrew Republic, according to which the king must make for himself a copy of the Torah and make sure to follow its statutes (Deuteronomy 17).[42] Cohen takes this to mean that the king in the Hebrew Republic, as opposed to the philosopher-king in Plato's *Republic*, is thereby "placed at the same level with each member of the people" (1924, I:318). This reference to the doctrine of the Three Crowns is crucial in a few respects.

[39] See (Melamed 2003) on the reception of the Platonic idea of the philosopher-king in medieval and Renaissance thought. For the career of this idea in late antiquity and early Middle Ages, see (O'Meara 2003). For the similarities between Platonic philosopher-king and conceptions of tyranny in the Greek tradition and in early Renaissance, see now (Gastaldi and Pradeau 2009).

[40] For an excellent discussion of the key debates in the reception of Platonic political philosophy in modernity, see (Vegetti 2009); for "postmodern" 20th-century reception debates, see (Zuckert 1996).

[41] On the phrase "principle of anarchy" in relation to Heidegger and Arendt, see (Schürmann 1990). See also the discussion of Scholem's debts to Cohen in (Lazier 2008, 182–90). But Lazier does not refer to Cohen's political theology, and its relation to Platonic political philosophy, and thus misses how Rosenzweig, Benjamin, Scholem, and Strauss further articulate politically the debate on nihilism and anarchy that Cohen unleashed. I discuss this in the next chapters and return to the contemporary debate on anarchism and political theology in the Conclusion.

[42] On the Three Crowns, see (Trigano 1991, Cohen 2007; and Nelson 2010). I discuss further this political model in the next chapters.

First, it demonstrates clearly that Cohen's critique of Platonism is internal to the development of a Jewish political theology which is both cosmopolitan and republican in character. Second, it exposes the mistake in Peterson's claim, later adopted by both Löwith and Voegelin, according to which Schmitt's political theology of sovereignty paradoxically finds its origins in Jewish monotheism rather than in Christian Trinitarianism. Cohen agrees that Judaism is compatible with a political theology, but it is an essentially republican and an-archic one.

The priority assigned to the philosopher-king in Plato's ideal city corresponds to the fact that, in this city, the caste of guardians is ultimately a caste of warriors. Plato's ideal or perfect republic is ideal only *within* the horizon according to which the state of nature between peoples and nations is still the primary reality. The Hobbesian horizon of permanent war is the "abyss" that separates Plato's ideal from the social ideal of the biblical prophets. "According to Josiah's characteristic expression, peoples should not learn war any longer. And learning means literally custom [*die Gewöhnung*]" (Cohen 1924, I:320). The Torah, that is, learning as custom [*Lernen als Gewöhnung*], is an education in peace, not in war; whereas the Platonic state educates to war because it is an ideal warrior state.[43] Cohen's point is that the Platonic ideal falls short of the messianic and cosmopolitical biblical ideal of peace because what is needed, aside and apart from security, is the abolition of poverty. The latter, in turn, requires an organization of society such that everyone can come to learn the truth because the truth is the capability of everyone's mind. Plato, the father of Idealism, nonetheless falls short of Idealism because he remains attached only to the idea of the Idea, and misses "the idea of the Good in every human mind [*die Idee des Gutes in jeden Menschengeiste*]" (Cohen 1924, I:318). In the next section, Cohen's own idealistic conception of the state is discussed in light of this democratic conception of intelligence.

Cohen believes that Plato's philosopher-kings belong to the caste of warriors because of two crucial Platonic principles: first, the belief that philosophical knowledge of the Good belongs to the few; it is aristocratic rather than democratic. The second Platonic principle is that social order requires the division between rulers and ruled. Plato holds these two principles as unconditionally valid because he lacks an idea of humanity as a singular universal. In support of these claims, Cohen refers to a famous passage in Book 7 of the *Laws*, where Plato states that "while God is the real goal of beneficent serious endeavour, man, as we said before, has been constructed as a toy for God, and this is, in fact, the finest thing about him" (Plato 1985, *Laws* 803c, translated by A.E. Taylor). Conceived as a plaything of God, the human being cannot live up to the idea of *Korrelation* between the God of Abraham and Israel.

[43] Again, this Cohenian interpretative insight is elevated to an axiom in Strauss's reading of Plato, where Socrates stands in secret agreement with Thrasymachus. See (Strauss 1964).

The universalism of the Torah, without which the messianic interpretation of Jewish monotheism falls apart, requires that philosophy not be reduced to a form of life that is exclusive of the many. According to Plato, "philosophy is not possible for the many. . . . The prophets are not philosophers. For them it is enough that human beings come to recognize God and through him recognize human beings. They are confident that all human beings are capable of this knowledge of God" (Cohen 1924, I:329).[44] For Cohen, any distinction between those who know and those who do not know inevitably applies to politics: the distinction between priests and laity, between the Crown and its subjects (the people as a minor, that requires a tutor to be represented before God), which sets up Church and Empire and denies the messianic, anti-nationalist core of theocracy whose formula is precisely the opposite, namely, the idea of a "people" (the supranational "remnant of Israel") entirely conformed by "priests" (the students of the teaching of the Torah as political philosophy).

Prophetic messianism also stands or falls on the possibility of transcending national barriers and differences: "The difference between Platonism and Prophetism is approximated sociologically in the difference between the resident foreigner [*Ger*] and the barbarian. The Hellene is autochtonous. The Torah commands unity between natives and foreigners" (Cohen 1924, I:327). The singularity of God calls forth a unified humanity in which national barriers will cease to have meaning, and with that, war will be abolished. This is the social ideal represented by the Hebrew prophets, and which Plato cannot ascribe to. Cohen gives two kinds of evidence that in Jewish monotheism there is no strict distinction between those who are born into a nation and resident foreigners. The first, is that the prophets see God's glory even in the destruction of their own state (1924, I:328). Cohen speaks here of the "domination" exercised by "ethics" [*Herrschaft der Sittlichkeit*] in Judaism, which stands over and above the goal of preserving Israel's own state. The defenders of political Zionism could not forgive Cohen for this claim, as detailed in the following. But his fundamental point is that the Torah must be understood as something radically other than the law of a particular nation: it should be understood as containing also a teaching of natural right that establishes peoplehood on the basis of abolishing the exception to humankind that is contained in the concept of barbarian.[45] If the Torah is not only a national law, then it must be understandable also as a form of natural law, and thus its teaching must be accessible by the natural reason of everyone. This

[44] For another contemporary defense of the equal intellectual capacity of everyone as a fundamental principle of democracy, see now (Rancière 2009). Rancière, though, does not see the connection of this belief to the messianic tradition.

[45] For a critique of the "civilizational discourse" that Cohen is rejecting, see now (Brown 2008, chs. 6–7). On the question of the foreigner and democratic cosmopolitanism, see (Honig 2003). For these themes in Cohen, see the excellent treatment in (Bouretz 2003).

will be the point of contention with Spinoza, who takes up exactly the opposite view, as discussed in the following sections.

The problem of nationality, or *Germanism and Judaism*

Cohen's infamous 1915 wartime manifesto, *Germanism and Judaism* [*Deutschtum und Judentum*], written in order to rally the support of Jews in the diaspora for the German cause in the war against France, England, and Russia, is greatly responsible for the general lack of favor that has met Cohen's rehabilitation of religion in his later work. In the moderate words of Judith Butler, *Germanism and Judaism* "has become increasingly painful to read over time, since he [Cohen] believed that Germany would protect Jews against anti-Semitism. His essay maintains a tenacious belief that Jewishness and Germanness are interlinked, and that it is not possible to think the one mode of belonging without the other. . . . Of course, it seems like Zionism wins the day, if we consider Cohen's tragic embrace of Germany as fatherland as the only alternative" (Butler 2014, 140–1). The text received immediate replies from Buber and Jacob Klatzkin in the pages of Buber's journal *Der Jude*, which also published Cohen. More recently, *Germanism and Judaism* has been interpreted either as a sign of Cohen having given up his Kantian commitments to "perpetual peace" and succumbing to the pressures of militarism and nationalism, or, conversely, as evidence that he held a hopelessly idealistic faith in human progress and in civilization. Thus, some scholars argue that the Great War forced Cohen to re-theologize his approach to Judaism, making his political thought vulnerable to *völkisch* (populist or ethnicist) positions that stand in tension with his previous commitments toward democratic socialism.[46] Conversely, his rejection of political Zionism has been condemned by some as if he had been a naïve pawn of the very German nationalism that would later bring Hitler to power.[47]

None of these interpretations situates *Germanism and Judaism* within the discourse on Jewish political theology that Cohen had developed over the previous

[46] See (Kartheininger 2006).

[47] See the superficial but quite typical interpretation of Cohen's political thought given in (Lilla 2007). The positive discussion of Cohen in (Gordon 2012a) does not quite redress this situation, mainly because it downplays Cohen's political and theological thought. The article on Cohen in *The Cambridge Companion to Modern Jewish Philosophy* by (Poma 2007) entirely bypasses a politico-theological reading of Cohen. Another interpretation suggests Cohen (and Rosenzweig) put forward a non-political conception of Judaism due to their critiques of sovereignty. For this kind of argument, see (Batnitzky 2012) and (Mittleman 2009, 202–20). For an excellent attempt to understand Cohen and Rosenzweig as bringing forth a form of Jewish political theology, see (Taub 2013), who does not articulate the relation between Philonic and Maimonidean elements in these authors. For a balanced reconstruction of Cohen's thought that attempts to consider the political and religious dimensions, see (Bouretz 2003).

decades. Critics and supporters agree on the fact that Cohen began to engage the "Jewish Question" already in 1880, when he published *Ein Bekenntnis in der Judenfrage*, in which he sought to counter the Prussian nationalist historian Heinrich Treitschke's anti-Semitic claim that Judaism was nothing other than the "political religion" of a "foreign," non-Germanic "people" (Cohen 1924, I:xxviii). What is usually missed is that already this early skirmish is indicative of Cohen's constant effort to conceptualize Judaism in opposition to the categories of "political religion" or "civil theology," while not giving up the insight that the pulsing heart of Jewish monotheism is political. Precisely because Cohen does not conceive of Jewish monotheism as an instrument for militaristic nation-building, that is, as the equivalent of a Roman civil theology, he reconstructs a Jewish political theology entirely out of a messianic horizon. Likewise, this understanding of Judaism as carrier of the most radical form of political messianism determines the sense of his later polemical writing against Spinoza, for Cohen takes aim at Spinoza as the originator of the idea that Judaism is mainly the civil theology of a now defunct Hebrew republic.[48]

In the same vein, Cohen's anti-nationalist messianic Judaism sets him on a collision course with the early Zionist movement, among whose youthful militants were Buber, Strauss, and Scholem.[49] Not surprisingly, these authors all perceived Cohen's messianism as anti-political, where "political" meant a more "realistic" perspective that assumes the impossibility of transcending the "natural" state of national wars, and that countenanced the more Machiavellian requirements of state-founding (in this case, in Palestine). At the same time, they also considered that Cohen's messianism was not "nihilistic" enough, that is, was not sufficiently oriented toward effecting a radical break not only with current sociopolitical conditions, but perhaps also with modernity as a whole. These early judgments, however, fail to take the measure of Cohen's politico-theological approach to the problem of nationalism, and they miss entirely Cohen's subversive employment of Philo's Jewish political thought which, on Goodenough's hypothesis discussed earlier, was designed precisely to contrast the hegemony of Roman imperial political religion.[50]

Perhaps it is most useful to begin the treatment of *Germanism and Judaism* with the critique coming from the most nationalist members of the Zionist camp

[48] This Spinozist motif, as well as the implicit or explicit critique of Spinoza's view of Judaism, is found in all the authors treated in this book, and therefore it is examined from different perspectives in all the chapters that follow. For an excellent recent discussion of the meaning of Spinoza for contemporary Jewish political thought, see (Cooper 2017).

[49] For this debate, see (Hollander 2006). Hollander, correctly in my opinion, brings Cohen closer to Buber and Rosenzweig than is usually done, for reasons that will become clear in my discussion of these two thinkers.

[50] The complex relation between Judaism and Roman civil religion will turn out to be decisive in Arendt as well, as I show in chapter 6.

in Germany, best expressed by Klatzkin's essay.[51] Klatzkin offers a three-pronged attack on Cohen's text: first, he denies root and branch any "creative alliance" between Judaism and Hellenism of the kind offered by Philo and Maimonides, and instead asserts "the deep gap between their world-views" (Klatzkin 1980, 67). Next, he claims that Cohen's argument for the rootedness of Germanism in Christianity and of Christianity in Philo's Judaism undoes the radical opposition between Judaism and Christianity asserted by Cohen himself (in his critique of Saint Paul's messianism), as well as belittles the fact that "competent representatives of Germanism proudly called themselves anti-Christian. They were fighting for the purity of Germanism, for the liberation of the Siegfried soul [*sic*]" (Klatzkin 1980, 76). Lastly, he charges Cohen with glorifying "the nationalism of others . . . while Jewish nationalism is condemned. Cohen lauds the state as the highest ethical form of life, he advocates an army, but he prohibits Jews from having a conception of statehood and praises the prophets of Israel for abandoning their Fatherland in their cosmopolitanism. . . . They, the prophets, are made to testify against Zionism. What nation would have tolerated such blasphemy?" (84).

Klatzkin's critique of *Germanism and Judaism* is blind to the politico-theological strategy behind Cohen's appropriation of Plato, Philo, and of Maimonides as a Platonist. While free from the widespread misreading of Cohen as a proponent of "liberal theology" such as found in Mark Lilla's recent interpretation—which simply ignores the import of Plato and Maimonides in Cohen's thought—Klatzkin's claim that "Athens" and "Jerusalem" are irreconcilable does not recognize Cohen's point that Judaism as a political theology is possible only on condition of its internalization of Platonic political philosophy. Unlike Rosenzweig and even Buber, Klatzkin misses entirely Cohen's point that such a turn to Platonism is absolutely essential in order to offer a political vision of Judaism that is of "world-historical" and not just of "national" significance. Klatzkin claims that Maimonides introduced the Greek sciences "into the vestibule of our Law 'as female cooks and makers of spiced sauce'" (1980, 67). As shown previously in relation to Cohen's interpretation of Maimonides, and as discussed in the next chapters in relation to the readings of Maimonides in Rosenzweig and Strauss, Klatzkin's claim is ludicrous.

With respect to Klatzkin's second charge, that Cohen disparages Germanism as nationalism, this too is superficial because it assumes that the limits of nationalism are also the limits of philosophy, whereas Cohen is involved in a complicated discourse on "philosophical nationalisms" that allows the self-definition of a nation to be determined by the "culture wars" that take place in the discourse of philosophy. The importance of this point will be noticed only decades later by

[51] See (Klatzkin 1980).

Derrida.[52] Lastly, Klatzkin's charge that Cohen denies the claims made on behalf of the Jewish nationality is untrue. To the contrary, his late Jewish writings traverse the dialectical or internal relation between Judaism and the phenomenon of nationality in order to develop it in a non-Zionist sense. Cohen is interested in showing one way in which Jewish nationality relates, on one side, to the idea of the legal state (or nation) and, on the other side, to the cosmopolitan and messianic ideal of humanity. Klatzkin, and Buber also to an extent, argues that Cohen's recognition of Jewish nationality "would have to lead Cohen to recognize Zionism" (Klatzkin 1980); or, as Buber puts it, and distinguishing Zion from the nation-state, "we believe that Zion restored will be the House of Prayer for all nations and the center of the new earth. . . . The new humanity needs us. Not scattered and striving with each other, but gathered and united . . . serving him faithfully forming a community of mankind according to his sense" (1980, 94). Cohen disagreed with Buber's claim that the realization of the messianic ideal required Zionism. For him this "solution" to the "Jewish Question" was perhaps not cosmopolitan, not world-historical enough. Whatever the case, in the pages and chapters that follow it will be shown that Cohen established the fundamental terrain on which the discussion on Jewish political theology, and its relation to both nationalism and cosmopolitanism, would take place after him, starting with Rosenzweig.

In the *Ethik des reinen Willens* of 1904,[53] Cohen considers that the idea of a people or nation (*Volk*) is an expression of "nature," whereas law and state are products of "spirit," or *Sittlichkeit*.[54] However, the later placement of a "religion over reason," drawn from Judaism, over individual morality is already anticipated in Cohen's *Ethics* insofar as its central hypothesis is that the organon of pure practical reason is found in jurisprudence rather than in morality.[55] Breaking with the liberal tradition of natural right, for Cohen the juridical person is not modeled on the isolated individual in the state of nature, but on a conception of the *Genossenschaft* (union or cooperative) which he draws from the German jurist Otto von Gierke.[56] The unity of the cooperative is constructed out of the

[52] This has been nicely captured by (Hollander 2008) who also discusses Derrida's interpretation of *Germanism and Judaism* and in general Derrida's studies on "the double exemplarity of the German and the Jewish" beyond "symbiosis, affinity, or harmony" (Hollander 2008, 128).

[53] (Cohen 1904). Henceforth referred to as *Ethics* and abbreviated as ErW. Translations from German are mine. In this and the following section, I draw extensively from the discussion in (Vatter 2017c).

[54] Schwarzschild reconstructs Cohen's political thought as a process of "idealisation" that maps onto a progressive conception of history leading from nature to culture: "Individual (natural man)—nationality—people (Volk, territory)—state (from power state to legal state = from community to society, i.e. socialism—federation of states—humanity" (Schwarzschild 1979, 149).

[55] For discussions of Cohen's ethics in relation to jurisprudence, see (Winter 1980; Gibbs 2005; Zank 2006; Holzhey 2006; Bienenstock 2009; Igor 2011; and Loick 2015).

[56] For a discussion of the contemporary relevance of Gierke's theory of legal personality, see now (Vatter 2016).

category of "totality" or "allness" (*Allheit*). The category of "allness" corresponds in the last instance to the idea of humanity. It is the category employed in Kant's second formulation of the categorical imperative, according to which individuals, in respect to their shared humanity, ought never to be treated as means, but as ends in themselves. Cohen argues that humanity or allness refers to that trans-individual unity found in every individual of the human species, the consciousness of which constitutes the "self-consciousness" of the state.

In order to appreciate the intention behind's Cohen's rather Hegelian-sounding conception of the state, it is useful to recall that in Christian political theology the bearer of humanity is ultimately the sovereign state, and sovereignty is structured on the model of the "King's Two Bodies," leading to a distinction in principle between the person of state and the person of the individual, which is fundamental for the jurisprudence of the modern system of nation-states, the *jus publicum Europaeum* developed from Hobbes to Schmitt.[57] The distinction between the person of the state and the person of its individual subjects is often pictured by making the state into the "head" of a "body" composed by citizens, following here the early Christian conception of Christ as the head of a "mystical body" composed of those who believe that "Jesus is the Christ."[58]

Cohen's conception of the state rejects any dualistic construction of the legal personality of the state. In so doing, Cohen's *Ethics* rephrases the Hegelian language of *Sittlichkeit* in Spinozist terms: "this constitution of the self-consciousness of the state is the analogon of the unity of nature, the object of the theoretical consciousness. Just like each single natural body is a case, a mode, a form of the movement internal to the preservation of the substance [this appears to be a clear reference to the theory of *conatus*], so too each willing subject is . . . called a mind [*Geist*]. . . . And in this way the state becomes the world of minds, the model of minds, the legal constitution of minds [*Und so wird der Staat zu der Welt der Geister; zu dem Inbegriff, zu der rechtlichen Verfassung der Geister*]" (ErW 232–3). The constitution of the state presupposes every citizen not as part of the "body" of the state, but as composing the "mind" of the state.[59]

If all individuals are considered to be political actors because they are valued for their "mind," then the constitution of the state is necessarily expressed by

57 For a recent discussion of this model and its permanence in liberal democracy, see (Santner 2011).

58 I refer to the discussion of these Pauline motifs in Schmitt, Kantorowicz, and Maritain found in (Vatter 2020).

59 My claim that Cohen's *Ethics* contains a strong Spinozist undercurrent, despite his well-known later critique of Spinoza, diverges from the received reading of Cohen's thought as motivated fundamentally by a moral rejection of pantheism, for which see (Simon 1935). I thank Thomas Meyer for this reference. A full discussion of Cohen's interpretation of Spinoza has to be left for another occasion. In the preceding citation, Cohen is probably harkening back to Bartolus's formula of the "council that represents the mind of the people [*concilium representat mentem populi*]" (Canning 1987, 198). Bartolus was discussed in von Gierke's history of medieval legal and political thought.

the public use of reason or by "the common mind," and politics comes to be internally connected to the expansion of what Cohen calls a "theoretical culture" (i.e., the liberal arts) (ErW 233). This explains why Cohen's two most important requirements for a legal state are, first, that the will of the state needs to be formulated democratically, in the sense that all individuals have the right to express their mind through public discussion leading to a binding legal resolution; and, second, that a legal state must have as its foundation the universal right to a free and public education.

Lastly, the correlation between self and law that defines Cohen's conception of autonomy climaxes in a conception of human rights which, in the constitution of the state, corresponds functionally to the role of natural right":

> Human rights in the state is the natural right of the law and of the state [*Das Menschenrecht im Staate ist das Naturrecht des Rechtes und des Staates*]. Without the [legal] state there are no human rights. But also without human rights there is no legal state as state of justice. Without human rights in the state what will rule in the state is the law of the powerful [*Machtrecht*] and class law [*Klassenrecht*]. . . . Only justice is the foundation of the state. . . . All virtues climax in justice. (ErW 583)

In this complex passage, Cohen is trying to counteract a typical republican understanding of the "Rights of Man" which makes these rights accessible only to those citizens whose interests find protection in their state, namely, those citizens that already belong to the ruling classes.[60] Cohen's argument is that a state cannot become a legal state, and thus do away with its class character, unless its constitution is turned inside out, by giving those who are excluded by its legal order the possibility to preserve and assert their human rights, the rights that they have "by nature" and in virtue of the "humanity" they bear. Thus, the conception of the legal state must confront the question of natural right, or the question of the "natural" basis of humanity. Formulated in abstract terms in 1904, by 1915 the task of reconstructing the complex genealogy of this idea of *Geist*, and its internal relation to human rights as "natural right" of the legal state, would become the central problem of *Germanism and Judaism*.

Perhaps the fundamental question of a politics of human rights in the 20th century concerns the link between the "natural" and the "religious" components of the concept of humanity. If human rights are distinct from political and civil rights, then human beings must bear them independently of their being members of a state. Human rights are legal rights that belong to humanity as a whole (which in the case of Cohen means they are tied to a conception of the

[60] See the critique of the Rights of Man in (Arendt 1973).

singularity of God), and yet they must also somehow exist in the state of nature where no positive law is given (that is, they must exist prior to the Mosaic revelation). How does Cohen's Jewish political theology make sense of this apparent paradox?

Cohen gives two related answers to this politico-theological quandary. The first turns on the idea that the state of nature contains a cosmopolitan legal condition: the technical name for this construction is the biblical belief in the Noachite laws that God gave to the human species after the Flood. This idea will be discussed in the final sections of this chapter. The second answer is given by the attempt Cohen makes in *Germanism and Judaism* to engage the "Jewish Question" in order to conceptualize the condition of the possibility of human rights, namely, in order to bridge the "natural" conception of a people or nation to the messianic and cosmopolitan idea of the whole of humanity through the "spiritual" or "idealist" conception of the legal state.

In his important treatment of *Germanism and Judaism*, Steven Schwarzschild rejects the superficial objections that are generally made against it: that Cohen was unaware of the depths of German anti-Semitism and that he was himself taken in by the tide of German nationalism.[61] Schwarzschild instead shows that Cohen was perfectly aware that the "actual, historical German culture" from 1880 to 1914 was one characterized by the rise of reactionary political thought and of anti-Semitism. Thus, in the second edition of the *Ethics*, Cohen explicitly manifests his opposition to "this modern style of Germanism . . . [and instead] harkening back to the original power of the essence of the German spirit" (Schwarzschild 1979, 139). As Schwarzschild says, *Deutschtum* "is then in these Jewish mouths a rational, ideal, normative construction, which, far from being identical with, in fact constantly opposes and challenges *Deutschland* to moralize, 'idealize' itself radically and infinitely" (1979, 141).

However, Schwarzschild's reading of *Germanism and Judaism* remains caught within the traditional "progressive" or "idealist" conception of Cohen's messianism that is tributary to a moralistic, Kantian interpretation and ignores the crucial problem of the internal connection between revealed religion and (Platonic) natural law. This Kantian interpretation somehow assumes that culture always already transcends nature, just like the legal state is self-evidently capable of mastering the nation. By the time World War I had broken out, Cohen no longer

[61] This includes the well-known critique of the Judeo-German "symbiosis" put forward by Scholem in various texts, among which are (Scholem 1970, 1984). Often cited, but perhaps not always carefully read, in these texts Scholem argues that German intellectuals and politicians never conceived of Jewish emancipation in terms of the recognition of Jewish nationality, but only in classical "liberal" terms by considering Jews as individual representatives of humankind (Scholem 1970, 25–6, 35, 40). None of these arguments affects at all Cohen's discourse on Jewish nationality. And, indeed, a careful reading of Scholem will not find him singling out Cohen as one of those German Jews who believed in the "myth" of the Judeo-German "symbiosis."

had any illusions on the wrong-headedness of these assumptions, if only because they tended to sublate the very idea that Jews form a nation. The linear progression through stages of idealization fails to capture the constitutive importance of the problem of nationality in Cohen: the "normative ideal" of a cosmopolitan and republican conception of statehood cannot be realized by recursive moments of universalization.[62] In the "Critical Epilogue" to the second edition of *Germanism and Judaism*, Cohen writes: "A Germanism that might demand of me that I surrender my religion and my religious inheritance, I would not acknowledge as an ideal peoplehood in which the power and dignity of statehood inhere" (Schwarzschild 1979, 143). Thus, for Cohen the idealization of the state into a true legal state, or *Rechtsstaat*, is not intended to sublate or transcend the question of nationality, but rather is inseparable from it.

The construction of Germanism as a "cosmopolitan nationality" can only become a reality if its idealist conception of the state can assume the kind of monotheism that Jews, and not just German Jews, are given to bear in and through their self-preservation and self-assertion. That is why Cohen's plea to North American Jews to help keep the United States out of the war is made in the name of supporting a country (Germany) that had legally and culturally recognized Jews in its war against another country (Russia) in which Jews were subject to pogroms. In this sense, there is much truth to Schwarzschild's claim that "it would not be very hard to show how Cohen, had he been, say, a Frenchman and immersed in French historical culture as he in fact was in German sources, would doubtless have written about 'Frankism and Judaism'" (Schwarzschild 1979, 145). In other words, for Cohen "a worldwide federation of social republics" will only come to pass when other nations traverse their own moment of "Germanism and Judaism."

Although Schwarzschild's reading of *Germanism and Judaism* is indispensable to understand the political intention of the manifesto, it leaves untouched the central issue of that text, namely, the character of that "spirit" capable of asserting and preserving the "ideal" of a German-Jewish symbiosis (for lack of a better term) over against the "real" Germany. For Cohen the "internal kinship" between Germanism and Judaism is made possible by the common reception of Hellenistic philosophy exemplified by Philo's "idealism," the Alexandrian Jewish Platonist.[63] *Germanism and Judaism* argues that the meaning of "Germanism" in philosophy lies in its commitment to idealism. Cohen's thesis is that "German" idealism is in effect a variant of Platonism which was bequeathed to it through the mediation of Philo, the first to offer a philosophical and cosmopolitan

[62] A strategy still employed by (Benhabib 2004), among others.

[63] (Cohen 1915, 5). Subsequent references are made in the text, preceded by DJ and page number. I follow the translation found in (Derrida 1991) whenever possible, otherwise translations are mine.

interpretation of Judaism and simultaneously the source of Saint Paul's foundation of Christianity on the idea of *logos* as "holy spirit" [*heilige Geist*] incarnated by Christ.[64] Cohen was aware, of course, that there were at least two other significant claims to determine the meaning of "Germanism" in philosophy: the first of them links Germanism to materialism in Marx but also in Friedrich Lange, Cohen's mentor at Marburg. The second of them links Germanism to nihilism in the figure of Nietzsche.[65] Cohen opts for the connection between Germanism and idealism because, on his Philonic hypothesis, Germanism could only receive a philosophical, or spiritual, expression on the grounds of the symbiosis with Judaism because it is through the Jewish community that Platonism is brought over from Al-Andalus to Christian Germany in the Middle Ages.[66]

For Cohen, the Jewish reception and transmission of Platonism gives the connection of Germanism to idealism a very particular form, namely, the form of modern empirical science. Here Cohen puts to use his interpretation of Platonic ideas as hypotheses, discussed earlier: "as a hypothesis, the idea is then by no means the solution of the problem, but only the exact definition of the problem itself" (DJ 7–8). It is this priority of the hypothesis over the observation that connects Plato to Kepler and Galileo: for these founders of modern science, the hypothesis is not a mere "fiction" (Galileo's *hypotheses non fingo*), but rather what "accounts for" or "saves" the phenomena (*sozein ta phainomena*), in accordance with the Platonic definition of philosophy.[67] Likewise, just as modern science is said to originate from a recovery of the Platonic conception of the idea as hypothesis, so too the Platonic demand to provide a justification for the way in which things appear (*logon didonai*) leads to the movement of the Protestant Reformation, understood as a movement to submit all authority to a critical examination (DJ 9). In this way Cohen brings religion (truthfulness of conscience that demands justification) on the side of ethics and science, not against it.

[64] Here Cohen is taking up themes found in the left-Hegelian Bruno Bauer, the object of Marx's critique in "On the Jewish Question," and who later in life was the author of a book on Philo, *Philo, Strauss und Renan und das Urchristentum* (1874). But Bauer's reading of Philo was anti-Semitic, whereas Cohen entirely subverts this usage of Philo.

[65] Of course, neither Marx nor Nietzsche thought of himself as a "German philosopher."

[66] Thus, Cohen's connection of Germanism to Idealism is not Hegelian, insofar as Hegel saw in absolute Idealism an overcoming of Judaism. Cohen's hypothesis is not all that different from the one recently proposed by (Flasch 2006). Kurt Flasch argues that there was a crucial reception of Arab and Latin Averroism in German mysticism, mainly by Meister Eckhart, which reception became the source of the sense of *Geist* in German idealism. In a later chapter I discuss Strauss's much more Nietzschean approach to the relation between Averroism, Platonism, and Jewish philosophy.

[67] (Duhem 2015). This definition of the idea as a problem will be taken up verbatim by Strauss. Notice that Derrida gives it a Husserlian-Levinasian interpretation by bringing into play the connection between idea and infinity (as opposed to totality): "What we have here, then, under the name of hypothesis is indeed a determination of the idea as an opening to the infinite, an infinite task for 'philosophy as a rigorous science'" (Derrida 1991, 58).

In his interpretation of *Germanism and Judaism*, Derrida argues that Cohen's connection of German idealism to Platonism through Judaism is another expression of the mythical "identification" of Germany with Greece, an identification that would also give rise to Fascist outgrowths.[68] Thus, in direct opposition to Schwarzschild's hypothesis, Derrida claims that for Cohen "the point is to prove that not only is the German moment of this syllogism essential and necessary, but that there is no other Judeo-X psyche (Spanish, Italian, French—still less Arab, that is, non-Christian) which measures up to this syllogism. . . . It is strictly Judeo-Protestant, that is to say, thanks to Luther, Judeo-German" (Derrida 1991, 54). On such a reading, Cohen would be arguing that for a religion to internalize the Platonic conception of the Idea is equivalent to becoming a Protestant religion: "the Jew himself being, as we shall verify, a Protestant and the Protestant a Platonic Jew" (Derrida 1991, 60). For Derrida, Cohen's reading of Philo as the inventor of the concept of "spirit" symbolizes "Judeo-Protestantism" and signals the advent of "world logocentrism," thereby making Cohen into the first philosopher of "globalization." Derrida even suggests that, in the end, Cohen's *Germanism and Judaism* did manage to "convert" the United States, insofar as North American society would come to reflect the hegemony of such "Judeo-Protestantism" and has managed to globalize its "logocentric psychosis" (1991, 60–1).[69]

Derrida's thesis downplays the significance of the Jewish transmission of Platonism, which is indissolubly bound up with the Jewish diaspora and its multiple symbioses in the Arab, Spanish, Italian, and French "psyches."[70] More importantly, Derrida's thesis limits the effects of the introduction of Platonism into the discursive space of monotheistic religions. As shown earlier, Cohen makes simultaneously two points: first, that the introjection of Platonism into monotheistic religions allows these to undergo a process of "reformation" and embark on their own trajectory of critique; second, that the contact with monotheism

[68] On this identification, see (Nancy 1990; and Schmidt 2001). See (Forti 2006) on Nazi biophilosophy and its appropriation of Platonic motifs. See also (Derrida 1991) on the problem of "spirit" and Nazism in Heidegger.

[69] This thesis is the opposite of Lilla's claim that "the noble experiment of [Cohen's] liberal theology [*sic*]" ended with the Nazi concentration camps (2007, 247). For another critique of Derrida's reading see (Altman 2011, 391).

[70] Additionally, as a brief glance at his *Ethics* and *Aesthetics* attests, there is in the early 20th century hardly a more cosmopolitan philosopher than Cohen, whose thought incorporates not only medieval Arabic and Jewish thinkers, but also the canonical authors of a "world literature" like Cervantes, Dante, and Shakespeare. It is no coincidence that José Ortega y Gasset, one of the major advocates of the importance of Spanish culture for European philosophy, spent two formative years in Marburg studying with Cohen, whom he considered to be his mentor, and with whom he had a reading group on Cervantes. Ortega y Gasset's first important book is *Meditaciones del Quijote*, which he wrote upon his return from Marburg. Ortega always claimed, with some reason, that this book anticipated the existential turn of philosophy found in Jaspers and Heidegger. For a study of Derrida's discourse on "the Jew, the Arab," see now (Anidjar 2003).

allows Platonism or philosophy to become self-critical.[71] The encounter with "Jerusalem" allows "Athens" to be something other than "logocentrism." Thus, for Cohen, Jewish messianism allows Plato's an-hypothetical Idea of the Good to be understood in terms of God as the only Being, expressed in the biblical formula of "I am who I shall be" (i.e., God as the only Being who is not hypothetical like all other beings). Because God is an-hypothetical, knowledge of God is not accessible by natural science (which always remains hypothetical knowledge), but only in and through a messianic realization of the "love of the stranger," which in Cohen takes the form of a struggle for equal human rights: "Only the Bible recognized the dignity of all human beings. 'Messianic humanity' Cohen proclaims, 'was foreshadowed in the stranger who has equal rights.'" (Schwarzschild 1990, 41). The sense in which Judaism is a priori open to the claims for equal treatment of non-believers will be addressed later in some detail.

In *Germanism and Judaism*, Cohen's treatment of German Idealism culminates with Fichte, the philosopher who discovered that "the social Self is a national Self" (DJ 41). Derrida argues that for Cohen the transition from Kant to Fichte means that "the subject is in its origin and through and through, substantially, subjectally national. It has a universal form, but this universality does not occur to its truth except as nationality" (1991, 80). Conversely, "the truth of nationality in general is German idealism." However, Cohen also considers Judaism to be a nationality, and he never says that the "truth" of Judaism as nationality lies with German Idealism, quite to the contrary. Forgetting that Judaism is also a nationality (of a peculiar kind) leads Derrida to claim erroneously that the "cosmopolitan proposition" in Cohen falls entirely within his Germanism because "the German spirit is the spirit of humanity." In fact, Cohen says that "the spirit of humanity is the originary spirit [*Urgeist*] of our ethics. In this ethical determinacy, the German spirit is the spirit of cosmopolitanism and of the humanity of our classical period" (DJ 44). What this means is that if Germanism is to remain faithful to its "spirit," then it must assert and preserve the spirit of cosmopolitanism and humanity, not that of nationality. Germanism will be able to do so only by harkening back to the *Urgeist* that underlies the *Geist* of the German "classical period," namely, the originary spirit of Philo's Platonic Judaism and the messianic idea of the prophets (DJ 48).

Although it is true that Cohen argues that the ideal of a perpetual peace preserved through a confederation of socialist republics can only be pursued

[71] This intuition was later appropriated by Derrida himself in (Derrida 2000), but he never acknowledged his debt to Cohen. Paradoxically, in this text Derrida gives the last word to Bergson, who was Cohen's "antagonist" in the international philosophical polemic that followed the publication of *Germanism and Judaism*. This context is missing in analyses of Derrida's late "turn" to religion, as found for instance in (Vries 2001), which mentions neither Philo nor Cohen in his discussion of the political theology of cosmopolitanism.

through the might of national states rather than in the name of a disembedded capitalism (DJ 47), this is only because the legal state makes it possible for military service to be universal and mandatory, such that all social classes, and not just the working classes, will feel equally the consequences and the burdens of war. Likewise, only the legal state makes the universal right to vote the condition for a legitimate exercise of power, such that all those who are supposed to fight in a war will have an equal voice in deciding whether to go to war in the first place. Lastly, only the legal state can assure the free and universal access of all nationalities to a public system of education that makes it in principle possible for all to participate in determining the common mind. It is clear that for Cohen the adequacy of German Idealism to the spirit of humanity does not follow from German statehood and this statehood from the German nation, as Derrida wrongly imputes, but, inversely, it follows from orienting the German nation in and through the public education and democratic system imposed by German statehood toward the spirit of cosmopolitanism and humanity that lies beyond the horizon of statehood itself: "It is all too certain that confederation is the end that the State must pursue so that the ideal of the State can be achieved elsewhere than in itself" (DJ 48).[72]

For Cohen, Judaism brings forward a messianic politics because it is a nationality that belongs within a state but does not form the state: "Judaism constitutes a nationality precisely because it does not seek statehood" (cited in Wiedebach 2012, 3). This way of presenting Judaism brings Cohen's manifesto close to what today is called the politics of multiculturalism. The primary reason why Cohen worked out this concept of nationality was to defend European Jews from the anti-Semitic charge of building "a state within the state" that spread all over Europe and Russia with the Dreyfus Affair. However, Judaism is a "pre-political" religion only insofar as it is also a "cosmo-political" religion: "The monotheistic idea of God has the purpose of organizing a religious state constitution as world organization, that is, as one of a federation of states of humankind developing according the idea of messianism" (cited in Wiedebach 2012, 30, fn. 81). How are these two seemingly opposed dimensions of Judaism to be reconciled? How can a nationality be both pre- and post-political in this sense?

Hartwig Wiedebach argues that Cohen's recovery of the idea of nationality has both an exoteric and an esoteric form. Exoterically, Cohen works out an idea of "nationality as 'plurality' under the unifying umbrella of a nation" (2012, 75). This is the idea of a federal nation-state which contains within it several nationalities. But for Cohen, this multicultural approach to Jewish nationality is ultimately "an anthropological means for the procreation of religion" (Wiedebach

[72] I address the problem of federalism and its connection with Jewish political theology in chapter 6 on Arendt.

2012, 77). Although Cohen sees no "political" reason to maintain a difference between German Jews and non-Jewish Germans in a truly legal state, he does see a crucial "pre-political" and "constitutional" reason to maintain the religious difference. Cohen's idea of nationality does not collapse onto the Zionist "ideology of peoplehood (*Volkstum*) which was derived from much the same sources (Hegel, Nietzsche, etc.) as and paralleled the theories of German ethnicism. Not infrequently they even expressed their Jewish approval of at least some of the planks in the anti-Jewish platform" (Schwarzschild 1979, 152). Nevertheless, by holding on to a pre- and post-political meaning of the Jewish nationality, Cohen exhibits what Wiedebach calls "an esoteric dualism of nationality" (2012, 83).[73]

This "esoteric" conception of Jewish nationality is related to its function as bearer of the messianic idea. Cohen's approach to the "Jewish Question" is not a liberal one: he does not advocate the reduction of Judaism to a religious denomination with "equal rights" to other religious denominations established by a secular constitution that prohibits the state from imposing any religion on its citizens. The reason Cohen does not take this approach is because he believes Judaism is a religion only in virtue of its "religious constitution" which entails that Jews must "hold fast to the essential core of the ancient God of the prophets" (Cohen 1924, II:77).

Wiedebach thinks that Cohen contradicts himself here: he cannot at one and the same time argue that Judaism is a pre-political religion, and that Judaism is a religion in virtue of its "political" constitution. But here Wiedebach conflates a sense of the political linked with sovereignty and statehood to a sense of the political linked with constitutionalism and cosmopolitanism. Cohen's key idea is that the Jewish "religious constitution" expresses a doctrine of natural right, that is, a natural and legal condition of humanity that precedes its division into nations and states. In the Torah this natural right is figured by the Noachite laws, which grounds the belief that strangers are not without rights in the Jewish religious constitution. Therefore, there is no contradiction in claiming that Judaism is not "political" insofar as it is a nationality that does not seek to establish another state within the nation-state, and, at the same time, that Judaism is "political" insofar as its teaching expresses a post-national idea of global constitutionalism.[74]

Wiedebach argues that Cohen's esoteric teaching on nationality advocates a "reversal" of the Noachite laws, such that instead of Judaism welcoming the

[73] Compare with Schwarzschild's idea of Cohen's esoteric practice: "'Germany is the spirit of Kant and Beethoven' is now seen also to imply that in fact Germany is at least a lot of other things . . . but we must make people believe, rightly or in part wrongly, that Germany 'is' ('being' having been understood as, in the Platonic/radically Kantian tradition, an ultimately ethical term) only the spirit of Kant and Beethoven and their likes, because then they are likely to act accordingly and thus in fact make it into what it is already (normatively and 'ideally') claimed to be" (Schwarzschild 1979, 153).

[74] Both my interpretation and the one offered by Wiedebach reject Lilla's reading of Cohen's Jewish messianism as a form of "universal nationalism" (Lilla 2007, 33).

plurality of nations through the legal equality between believer and unbeliever established in its religious constitution, in the future it will be up to the "united nations" of the world to welcome and protect the singularity of the Jewish nationality and, by extension, of all stateless peoples. In its symbiosis with Judaism, Germanism is supposed to be the exemplar for the other nations of the wisdom of this arrangement (2012, 231). But Wiedebach seems to forget that Cohen does not actually employ the resources of Germanism as a mediation between Judaism as nationality and the messianic notion of a cosmopolitan confederation of socialist republics. Rather, Cohen's other texts of this period show the inherent limits of German Idealism as a vehicle to return toward natural right. With Fichte and then Hegel, German Idealism leaves the doctrine of natural right in favor of historicism and philosophy of history: it thus becomes prey to nationalism and to the internal relation between state and war with which Hegel closes his *Philosophy of Right*, something that would exercise Rosenzweig in *Hegel and the State*.

Cohen's teaching on natural right and the problem of Noachite laws

Cohen argues that the Torah, that is, the "religious constitution" of the Jewish people, teaches that God revealed certain laws to Noah's sons while in the state of nature, and made them accessible by the natural reason of everyone, enjoining the preservation of believers and unbelievers alike. As Schwarzschild has brilliantly discussed, for Cohen "the Jewish concept of the Noachite as the ethical person pleasing to God purely on the basis of natural, rational moral law without religious commitment holds foremost place of pride and glory" (1990, 41). Cohen's hypothesis regarding the world historical significance of Judaism is contained in the claim that the religious constitution of this nationality points humanity beyond the state-form. "The religious human being is not born with Moses; he exists already since Noah. And this natural religion was established by the true God Himself" (Cohen 1924, III:346). Thus, for Cohen, the Mosaic laws are not the exemplary ethical laws: Judaism is a universalistic teaching of natural law before being a "positive" religion.

Cohen's famous critique of Spinoza belongs to the same period as *Germanism and Judaism*. In many ways these two texts are mirror opposites: whereas in the latter text Cohen takes up Judaism as a nationality, in the former text he criticizes Spinoza for turning Judaism into a national, particularistic religion, rather than as an exemplar of the universal and natural religion of humanity (Cohen 1924, III:329). In Chapter 5 of the *Theologico-Political Treatise* Spinoza argues that Moses is a political leader, but not an ethical teacher. Moses teaches no universal and rational ethics, but merely achieves the submission of the Jewish people to a tyrannical God who deprives that people of their status as *sui iuris* (Cohen 1924, III:342). For Cohen, Spinoza's portrayal of Judaism as a political religion is mistaken on two counts: first, it misses entirely the "social spirit" of Jewish prophetology, something which Cohen believes was first recovered by the English republican revolutionaries of the 17th century; second, Spinoza interprets the Jewish "religious constitution" as if it modeled a church with temporal powers, a state within the state, and which, in Hobbesian fashion, must be fought in the name of a sovereign, liberal state (Cohen 1924, III:344). According to Cohen, Spinoza's construal of Judaism intentionally ignores Noachite laws, just as much as it ignores the Sabbath laws, and instead chooses to interpret the "natural divine laws" as corresponding only to the teachings of Jesus, at the same time elevating Jesus to the status of a philosopher (1924, III:335). Spinoza makes Christianity, rather than Judaism, the fountainhead of human rights.[75]

Cohen's polemic against Spinoza turns on the latter's claim that Maimonides himself understood Judaism as Spinoza understands it, namely, as a form of national or political religion. Spinoza gives as evidence of this charge the interpretation of the Noachite laws that Maimonides provides in the *Mishneh Torah*, "Laws of the Kings," Chapter 11:

> Everyone who accepts the seven (Noachite) laws and is careful to fulfil them is one of the righteous of the nations of the world and has a share in the world to come. This is so if he accepts and practices them on the ground that God commanded them in the Torah and that He informed us through Moses our teacher that the sons of Noah had earlier been given these commandments. But if he practices them on the basis of his own rational considerations, then he is not a resident stranger-convert [*ger-toshav*] nor one of the righteous men of the nations of the world nor one of their sages.[76]

For Spinoza, this passage clearly shows Maimonides to be less of a rationalist than he seems to be because he states that those Gentiles who follow Noachite laws purely because they are rational (according to their natural light of reason), that is, on universalistic grounds, are *not* going to be saved (*Theologico-Political Treatise*, chapter 5). Spinoza suggests that Maimonides' teaching is that outside of Moses, there is no salvation. Likewise, Spinoza accuses Maimonides of

[75] On the problem of "Christian human rights" in the early 20th century, see (Moyn 2015). However, Moyn misses the importance of the German-Jewish debate on the theological roots of human rights.

[76] I refer to the translation and commentary on the problem of Noachite laws in Maimonides found in (Schwarzschild 1990, 31ff).

holding on to the belief in Creation (as something whose truth is indemonstrable by reason but nonetheless possible) because he thinks that Maimonides wants to secure for philosophers a political role akin to those of a king or pope.

Cohen's critique of Spinoza is made in full awareness that he and Spinoza are fighting for the same cause: against the tradition in the Christian West that received the Hellenistic idea of philosopher-kings and transformed it into the politico-theological conception of divine kingship, a doctrine that would found the ideologies of both Church and Empire (Cohen 1924, III:354).[77] Cohen also shares with Spinoza a rejection of any conception of religion based on the hatred of foreigners. The disagreement between them concerns the status of the religious constitution of the Jewish nation: for Spinoza this is the constitution of a state, and thus Judaism is another form of political religion where piety toward God is ultimately identified with love of the nation and hatred of its enemies (*Theologico-Political Treatise*, chapter 17). Spinoza argues that a legal and democratic state can only be built on the basis of a natural right that excludes reference to divine revelations of any kind. For Cohen, instead, the Torah is a religious constitution, but not of a state, rather of a supra- and cosmo-political legal order based on human rights. What is unique about the Torah for Cohen is that it connects a legal constitution to a messianic politics: that this occurs in the form of divine revelation only signifies that the destiny of natural rights is to become the rights of humanity.

Schwarzschild is correct when he says that, ultimately, the debate between Cohen and Spinoza is about the status of natural right. On the one hand, the dualism between natural and positive law is suspicious to Cohen, as it was later to Hans Kelsen: if positive legislation is to depend on some "natural" law, then it loses its "autonomy" as the expression of a democratic and legal procedure in which the "mind" of everyone is taken into consideration with equal respect.[78] On the other hand, without an appeal to something like natural right, one risks incurring into the typical objection addressed to legal positivism, namely, that it loses sight of the distinction between justice and law. Schwarzschild believes that this dilemma is precisely reflected in Maimonides' seemingly self-contradictory belief about Noachite laws: "this is exactly what Maimonides said to the Noachite: the fulfillment of the moral law insures you of God's approval: the law of nature provides you with an inkling of the moral law, but by itself it is neither enough nor reliable; to know the moral law you also have to submit to Revelation, and you have to know God" (1990, 59).

[77] On this fundamental role played by sacral kingship in the West, see now (Oakley 2006).

[78] Cohen and Kelsen share the aim of gaining an understanding of law that would dismantle or deconstruct what they considered the pernicious dualism of natural and positive laws, for in their mind this dualism justified non-democratic philosophies of law and of politics, both liberal and anti-liberal ones. On Kelsen's critique of dualism, see now (Brunkhorst 2011).

Unlike Schwarzschild, Cohen argues that Spinoza was mistaken about Maimonides' view, and there is no priority assigned to revelation over reason in his thought: one does not need to adopt Mosaic law in order to become part of the wise, that is, part of the rest of Israel. For Cohen, Maimonides is a "religious liberal" (Cohen 1924, III:350). But what Cohen means by this expression is not a point about denominationalism. Rather, in his defense of Maimonides, Cohen silently recovers a claim first established by Philo, namely, that those who follow Noachite laws as if they expressed a philosophical or Platonic conception of natural right or of the law of nature are Jews out of choice, and are even more "noble" than those who are Jews by birth but who might not understand the divine reason of the commandments (1924, III:346ff).[79] In other words, Cohen's point is that Maimonides means that there is a crucial distinction between following the Noachite laws merely "on the basis of his own rational considerations" and following them on the basis of "the righteous men of the nations of the world nor one of their sages": not any "rational" justification of the Noachite laws will do, but only a Platonic or political-philosophical justification of these laws will have redemptive force.[80]

Cohen's defense of Maimonides and critique of Spinoza thus shed light on the esoteric teaching of *Germanism and Judaism*. This teaching is captured neither by Derrida's hypothesis that Judaism overcomes its national limits by transposing itself into a Judeo-Protestantism that pursues a globalized techno-scientific rationalism, nor is it captured by Wiedebach's hypothesis that Germanism stands for the "reversal" of the Noachite laws by establishing an international law that protects national minorities from persecution. Instead, Cohen's esoteric teaching is that the same affinity that German philosophy feels toward Greek philosophy is what opens for Germans, as for other nations, the possibility of becoming Jews "by choice," and in this sense become part of the "rest of Israel." The messianic state is not accessible unless the nations of the world come to understand themselves as the "rest of Israel" and, conversely, unless Jews themselves shall "return" (*Teshuvah*) to their religion of birth, but as a rational choice since it has been purified of all its mythical aspects through its adoption of Platonism. This is the only way in which the question of nationality can be addressed in order that it may give rise to a cosmopolitan idea of the legal state whose constitution expresses the natural rights of humanity.

Notice that Cohen's proposal is a far cry from the liberal solution to the question of nationality. The liberal position is that human beings are by nature free to choose their own religion, and this natural freedom is not religiously

[79] For this interpretation of Philo, see the discussion of Goodenough in the previous chapter.

[80] In other words, according to Cohen, Maimonides is vindicating Noachite laws as part of what the ancients called their "ancient theology." On this idea, see now (Fraenkel 2012).

constituted. But for Cohen, human freedom, the freedom of humanity, consists in the freedom to choose to be Jewish when one was not born a Jew: this is the functional equivalent to the freedom to philosophize. And it entails the practical corollary that a truly human freedom is the choice to take the place of the foreigner, and in this way practically abolish the distinction between native and barbarian. Unlike the liberal natural freedom, this human freedom is constituted religiously: it is the natural religion of Noah's children. For Cohen, "Moses did not care only for the people of Israel, but before and after Noah for the peoples which, although they are not the children of Israel, nevertheless they are the sons of Noah. And as such they participate in the blessedness which is the expression of religious congeniality [*Ebenbürtigkeit*, which translates into 'equality' but also perhaps 'symbiosis,' a common life]" (Cohen 1924, III:351). The point of the "symbiosis" of *Germanism and Judaism* is that human freedom takes the form of a double birth or rebirth that occurs in a return to beginnings, in a return from national law to a divine natural law.

Cohen's critique of Spinoza was spurred by the latter's suggestion that only Jesus, and not also Moses, taught of divine natural law, that is, a pure love of the stranger. But it may well be that Cohen himself, in the end, leaves unanswered the real question: not whether the "peoples of the world" can become Jewish by choice, but why would a Jew like Spinoza "choose" to give up his religion and embrace the freedom to philosophize? Was Spinoza's choice not an expression of the spirit of liberalism? After all, if non-Jews can choose to become Jews, why cannot Jews choose to become non-Jews or even atheists? Spinoza chose Nature's God over God as Creator of Nature as the foundation of natural right. In so doing, he frayed open another path for the realization of the messianic ideal, one that entails understanding Moses himself as a tyrant insofar as he helped establish the fateful idea of a "true religion," and seeing in Jesus the representative of a natural religion of brotherly love who attempts to redress this problem by separating for good the pursuit of truthfulness from the pursuit of ethics.[81] This other Spinozist path, which itself breaks off in many different directions, will be taken by those Jewish thinkers who follow Cohen in the attempt to delineate a Jewish response to Christian political theology: from Rosenzweig and Buber, to Scholem, Strauss, and Arendt.

Messianism and the eternity of the world

Cohen's politico-theological thought and his messianic conception of world history have often been reduced to a Kantian approach to the indefinite progress of

[81] I discuss this modern, republican interpretation of Jesus in chapter 6, dedicated to Arendt.

the human species.[82] True enough, Cohen rejects the necessity of the aristocratic principles of Platonic political philosophy because he opposes the "present" of war, and thus of Plato's ideal state, to the messianic "future" of peace, and thus the prophets' "state of humanity." For Cohen, the contradictions between nations in political space can be overcome by transposing them into the "infinity" of time, the analogon of God's eternity (Cohen 1924, I:325). But one does not understand Cohen's conception of the "future time" of messianism if one collapses it onto a neo-Kantian conception of indefinite progress in empty time. This is to misunderstand Cohen's project, which consists in fighting Spinoza's battle for a universal and egalitarian conception of freedom of thought, for a return to natural right, even for the eternity of the world, but by transposing it on the terrain of Maimonides' and Philo's attempts to understand Judaism as a "religion of reason."

Cohen's cosmopolitan political theology ultimately rests on his interpretation of Maimonides' distinction between a future time (the messianic Kingdom) and a future world: "the right meaning of the Messianic Age is only fulfilled through its connection with the present, and Maimonides elucidated this meaning not only by making a distinction between the future time and the future world, but also through his entire connection of religion with ethics" (Cohen 1995, 386).[83] The key to this Maimonidean messianism is Cohen's insistence that the messianic time is this-worldly, and not to be projected into another world, an eschatology of the Hereafter. For Cohen, it is only a materialist conception of self-perfection that leads to positing a Hereafter (one sees this direction in Scholem and Benjamin, and in the early fusion of Nietzschean-Marxist themes with Sabbatian eschatology), whereas he proposes an idealistic reading of the messianic age, that is, an interpretation of the messianic age as an effort to change the present from within history, oriented by the future of humanity.

Here Cohen is, in the last instance, far more Marxist than other interpreters of Maimonides' messianism, whether the conservative reading by Hartman, or the apocalyptic reading of Scholem. For Cohen, following Marx's notion that communism is always already present in any given historical age as its dream, Maimonides' messianism depends on understanding that "the world-to-come is already present... for the individual, however, life in the world-to-come becomes accessible only after his life in this world has expired" (Cohen 2004, 175), citing *Hilchot Teshuvah* 8:8. In other words, just as Marx says that the fetishism of the commodity already presupposes the socialization of all productive forces, but

[82] For this widespread belief, see: "It is astonishing to see how easily they were lulled to sleep by their faith in the natural goodness of man and the benevolence of the historical process that had issued in their bourgeois world" (Lilla 2007, 249).

[83] Cohen sees in Maimonides a messianism that turns on the conception of a future-to-come (*atid lavo*) and of the "messianic time" (*yemoth hamaschiach*) (Cohen 2004, 169).

in an alienated form, separate from the workers (who work in anti-social ways), so Maimonides sees the messianic age in the social or political existence of each individual, which socialization seems, to the individual, to lie not in establishing a different ethico-political relation with human beings, but in seeking another world. For Cohen, the messianic age is the self-awakening of humanity to its proper social or ethico-political nature. This is what Cohen means when he writes that for Maimonides "eternal life constitutes a surplus of life of the human individual for the sake and in the cause of her developing toward an ethical being [*einem Zuwachs des menschlichen Individuums für seine Entwicklung . . . zum sittlichen Wesen*]. . . . Eternal life exists, insofar as it may come, because it obtains only for the ethical individual, for whom it must come [*es (das ewige Leben) besteht nur, sofern es kommt, weil es nur für das sittliche Individuum besteht, für das es kommen muss*]" (2004, 175) .[84] Eternal life appears as a surplus of earthly life, and thus as something to come, only to the extent that the individual has not yet appropriated its productive forces, that is, has not yet appropriated its social essence, its ethical being: once the individual reappropriates the surplus that it itself produces, once the individual lives with others in a truly social relationship, then earthly and eternal life coincide. Cohen's Maimonides therefore fits entirely coherently with Marx's notion of communism and Nietzsche's perfectionism as the self-overcoming of humankind toward a messianic condition: "the idea of perfection in the Hereafter as the paradigm for the amelioration of human nature . . . that a person aspires to perfect herself, that human nature be perfected, that nature should not obstruct the existence of the soul and its cognitive pursuit: this is the meaning of eternal life" (2004, 177).

Properly understood, the Cohenian idea of God's singularity or uniqueness does not mean the radical transcendence of God from Nature such that a supernatural or other-worldly dimension would open up. Cohen rejects Spinoza's apparent pantheism that identifies God with Nature because such an identity would deprive the messianic construction of ethics of any meaning. However, it is also the case that Cohen does not oppose the "creator of the world" to the idea of the eternity of the world.[85] Both the messianic ideal in Saint Paul and the idea of messianism in Judaism aim for an eternal life, but whereas the former rests on the belief that eternal life belongs in another world or "beyond," Cohen's Jewish messianism places eternal life in this world and articulates it in terms of the idea of a future time.

[84] My translation; the version given by Bruckstein is not acceptable.

[85] See Wiedebach's excellent discussion of the doctrine of Creation, which points out that in Cohen there is both a *creatio ex nihilo* and one that is *ab nihilo* so that "a Creation 'in the beginning' stands side by side with a continuous 'renewal of the world'" in (Wiedebach 2010, 120). However, this reading cannot be reconciled with Cohen's belief in eternal life and in the eternity of the world, which is stronger than a mere "renewal of the world."

For Cohen, the messianic end leads to a conception of eternal life and this life entails the eternity of this world, not the transition to "another" world: "Eternity . . . is the meaning, the goal, the end of the whole of human life. . . . It is significant for the Hebrew linguistic consciousness that the Hebrew word for world, *olam*, at the same time means eternity: "He hath set the world [*olam*] in their heart" (Ecclesiastes 3:11)" (Cohen 1995, 461). In other words, the messianic goal of peace is synonymous with the attainment of eternal life in an eternal world. For Cohen, redemption is not the apocalyptic transcendence of nature, but merely its redemption. Expressed otherwise, the redemption of nature is the proper task of a messianic politics. It is most significant, then, that he concludes *Religion of Reason* with the following, seemingly paradoxical thought:

> But for this [Hebrew] religious consciousness for which the world is God's creation and revelation, neither the world nor man could be simply perishable. The presentiment of the immortality of man and the eternity of the world manifests itself in this deep word, *olam*. . . . But this eternity is only the continuation of the earthly life—the same root of the word comprises both sides of existence; hence, peace, as it leads to eternity, is also the guide of earthly life, to the beginning of all historical survival, which lies in it. . . . In this historical eternity the mission of peace of messianic mankind is completed. (Cohen 1995, 462)

Cohen will never specify how the geopolitical opposition between Jerusalem and the world of nations can be overcome in historical time, by understanding the logic behind the "historical eternity" of the "remnant" of Israel and the universalization of the messianic ideal. This task was first attempted by Rosenzweig in the *Star of Redemption*.

3

Franz Rosenzweig and Religious Constitutionalism

Introduction

Liberal constitutionalism adheres to the principle of non-establishment of religion through the state. It thereby posits an antithesis between theocracy and constitutionalism. But does the idea of biblical theocracy—which "*does not recognize state sovereignty as such* . . . only God is sovereign and He entrusts the exercise of His sovereign powers mediated through His Torah-as-constitution to the people as a whole"[1]—harbor something affirmative for contemporary democratic constitutionalism? In this chapter I argue that Franz Rosenzweig recasts the idea of the Torah-as-constitution in terms of a theory of globalization and addresses the relation between state-denying divine sovereignty and the discourses on geopolitics and biopolitics.[2] In so doing, he contributes to conceptualizing constitutionalism beyond nationalism and the sovereignty of the state. Rosenzweig's Jewish political theology critically engages with Western nationalism and imperialism, precisely the two factors that cast a shadow on the universalist and egalitarian claims made on behalf of liberal constitutionalism.[3]

In recent times, the juridical and political significance of theocracy has made inroads into the discourse of comparative constitutionalism through the concepts of "constitutional theocracy" and "religious constitutionalism." The former intends to capture developments after the Iranian Islamic Revolution as well as the constitutional peculiarities of the State of Israel,[4] while the latter has been used to describe the inscription of religion in the ongoing efforts at constitutionalizing the European Union.[5] In in his much debated reporting on the

[1] (Elazer 1997, 6, emphasis mine). On this motif in the "Jewish political tradition," see (Walzer, Lorberbaum, and Zohar 2000; and Walzer 2006) and (Mittleman 1996, ch. 2).

[2] Herzfeld (2013) points out that Rudolf Kjellén, the Swedish political scientist who coined the terms "geopolitics" and "biopolitics," was studied carefully by Rosenzweig and his "Patmos Circle," which included Eugen Rosenstock-Huessy. Björk (2018) offers an interesting discussion of Kjellén together with Rosenzweig.

[3] On liberal imperialism, see (Losurdo 2004; Pitts 2006; and Bell 2019). On liberal nationalism, see (Tamir 1995; Miller 1997; and Gustavsson and Miller 2020).

[4] On theocratic constitutionalism, see, among others, (Hirschl 2010; and Ghobadzadeh 2015).

[5] On the early modern idea of a religious constitution, see (Hunter 2018). Samuel Moyn points out that several contemporary European constitutions, foremost among them the German one,

Living Law. Miguel Vatter, Oxford University Press (2021). © Oxford University Press.
DOI: 10.1093/oso/9780197546505.003.0004

early days of the Iranian Revolution, Michel Foucault noticed the resurgence of theocratic constitutionalism at the end of the 20th century. Foucault glimpsed a strange coincidence of opposites between civic republican aspirations and Shiʿa messianic impulses, a curious mutual attraction between what he described as an anarchic "resistance to the power of the state" and an idea of "government" based on divine law (Foucault 2001, 694).[6] My claim is that the recovery of this internal connection between theocracy and republicanism found one of its first formulations in the Jewish political theology developed by Rosenzweig.

Rosenzweig carried forward Hermann Cohen's project to show the significance of Jewish nationality for a democratic and cosmopolitan discourse on political theology. Yet, he shared Carl Schmitt's premise that every legal order depends on partitions of land that, from the start, inscribe constitutionalism within a logic of war and enmity whose ultimate projection on a global scale transcends the form of the nation-state. This chapter shows how Rosenzweig reconstructs Jewish messianism as the more radical form of cosmopolitanism because it is the most republican in spirit, that is, because it is founded on the twin priority of the rule of law over the rule of concrete orders, and of peoplehood over nationhood. When read along these lines, Rosenzweig's thought contains important insights for moving beyond "the standoff we seem to have between theocratic principles of the Jewish tradition and the democratic principles of the societies in the world where Jews have survived and flourished."[7]

This chapter begins by drawing a connection between the synthesis of Judaism and republicanism in Moses Hess—critic of the "Young Hegelians" and close associate of Marx and Engels, among the first German Jews to embrace communism, before becoming the first theoretician of Zionism—and Rosenzweig's political theology. Both reject Hegel's Christian political theology. Both question the traditional belief that between Greek and Roman "political philosophy" and Jewish "revealed religion" there is only radical opposition and incompatibility. The chapter then shows how in the philosophical system of the *Star of Redemption*, Rosenzweig follows Goethe's and Nietzsche's post-Christian attempts to recover paganism in a positive light. This allows him to re-politicize the understanding of the Jewish messianic ideal and its relation to the divine law, bringing it closer to neo-Roman republican constitutionalism.

squarely fall under the category of "religious constitutionalism" because they purportedly manifest a "subordination of the otherwise sovereign democratic polity to God" (Moyn 2015, 31). For different perspectives on this question, see (Cohen and Laborde 2015).

[6] Foucault's reading of the Iranian Revolution is criticized in (Afary and Anderson 2005) and in part in (Honig 2008), but see now (Ghamari-Tabrizi 2016) for a more sympathetic and historically accurate approach to Foucault's analysis.

[7] (Novak 2000, 29).

The conventional view is that Rosenzweig is a religious thinker who never quite rid himself of the Hegelian legacy and whose political ideas remained under the shadow of German nationalism.[8] His critique of political Zionism and his apparent claim that the Jewish people were somehow meant to live "outside" of history seemed to many hopelessly misguided after the Shoah and the foundation of the State of Israel.[9] In order to address these claims, this chapter discusses Rosenzweig's strategy to overcome the Hegelian philosophy of history that sidelines the historical existence of the Jewish people by analyzing the central role played by the problems of nationalism and imperialism and the emergence of a global perspective on constitutionalism in his thinking.[10]

In his recent and magisterial overview of "politics in the Hebrew Bible," Michael Walzer presents the party of the prophets as holding the belief that "social justice at home guarantees divine protection abroad: there is no need for citizen soldiers" (2012, 174). Walzer chastises this lack of realism on the part of the theocrats: "it denies what cannot be long denied: the autonomy of international politics and the dangers it poses" (2012, 108).[11] This chapter contests the

[8] On these claims, see (Mendes-Flohr 1991). Compare with a discussion of Rosenzweig in light of political theology found in (Rosenstock 2009; and Taub 2013). I am sympathetic to Bruce Rosenstock's (2009) attempt to recover in Rosenzweig a "democratic, redemptive politics" (ibid., 5) and an "anti-Schmittian political theology" (ibid., 263). This stands in contrast with the readings of Rosenzweig as an "apolitical" thinker put forward by (Batnitzky 2000; and Gordon 2003).

[9] See Rosenzweig's discussion of Cohen's *Deutschtum und Judentum* in (Rosenzweig 1984). On Cohen's critique of Zionism and Buber's reply, see now (Barash 2015). For a sensitive approach to this question in Cohen, Buber, and Rosenzweig, see (Hollander 2006). Dana Hollander discusses Rosenzweig's response to Cohen's *Deutschtum und Judentum* which turns on the danger of reducing Judaism to "peoplehood" (associated for him with "naïve vulgar Zionism") and of elevating "Germanism" to the status of a (national) religion—for Rosenzweig a contradiction in terms. Hollander points out that Rosenzweig denies in any case that Germans and Jews confront each other as antithetical "fixed substances" (Hollander 2006, 100–1). On the question of German-Jewish identity, see (Mendes-Flohr 1999).

For the reception of Rosenzweig before World War II, see (Meyer 2009). The traditional source of opposition to Rosenzweig's thought from a Zionist standpoint is forcefully restated in (Schweid 2012).

[10] See the "Concluding Remark" from 1920 of Rosenzweig's *Hegel and the State*, where Rosenzweig lucidly and critically deconstructs the transition from Hegel's idea of the state to Bismarck's realization of the "national state": "So it came about that the state that Bismarck created neither became merely something more than the state that Hegel conceived, nor did it become a mere fulfilment [of it]. In its national foundation, the new realm [*Reich*] had something that was foreign to or at least unnecessary for the Hegelian state-ideal" (Rosenzweig 2000, 80). However, judging by his political wartime writings, it may be going too far to claim that in Rosenzweig "the state is thus voided of all possible intrinsic worth in relation to the newly released power of revelation in history" (Rosenstock 2009, 18). In *Globus* (especially the sections dedicated to the "national state" and to the idea of the "Kaiser") the least that can be said is that for Rosenzweig there is an internal relation and tension between *demos* and *ethnos*, on the one hand, and empire and national state on the other (Rosenzweig 2003, 62–3). Likewise, in *Vox Dei?* Rosenzweig argues that the state and its representatives (elites) lead peoples into wars, moved by the principle of "reason of state" or of the conservation of the state, whereas these peoples fundamentally desire peace, yet are unable to "act" on this desire, for state-based political action is always of a representative and elitist nature (ibid., 107–9).

[11] Walzer argues that the political discourse of biblical prophets is a form of "anti-politics" which is based on the prophetic call to " 'be quiet,' 'stand still'—the message is the same, and in both cases it represents a radical denial of the doctrine of self-help. Indeed, it is a leitmotif of the Hebrew Bible that self-help is unnecessary" (Walzer 2012, 102).

belief that Rosenzweig's interpretation of biblical theocracy is "deaf" to the facts of war and imperialism or to the realities of a republican politics as Machiavelli understood it. To the contrary, I show that Rosenzweig was perhaps one of the first thinkers in the 20th century to realize that the development of European Christian imperialism was leading to a new global, post- and supra-national legal order, and his efforts were aimed at formulating an alternative theocratic basis for this new "nomos" of the earth.

Finally, this chapter addresses the widespread view that biblical theocracy gives divine sanction to violence and assigns to war a religious function. Gil Anidjar has put forward an influential reading of Rosenzweig as the spiritual father of a vision that characterizes the three Abrahamic faiths as enmeshed in relations of political and theological "enmity."[12] The reception of Rosenzweig's political theology has not been helped by the fact that his treatment of Islam in the *Star of Redemption* has been criticized as fundamentally flawed and prejudiced.[13] I end this chapter with a critical discussion of these claims, in particular Rosenzweig's understanding of the phenomenon of "wars of faith" or "holy wars" and the role that Islam plays in relation to the *agon* between Jewish and Christian messianic beliefs.

Moses Hess and the origins of German-Jewish republican thought

The initial impetus for theocratic republican constitutionalism comes from Moses Hess. Hegel's Christian political theology was the principal target of Hess's critique because of its ambivalent relation to the Jewish roots of the idea of "holy history."[14] While Hegel's mature political philosophy draws a close connection between God and national existence in history that has obvious roots in the Jewish tradition, his early writings infamously argue that the single-minded adherence to the Torah shows that the Jewish people remained an unfree people, trapped under the "yoke" of an absolute heteronomous authority. For Hegel, strict adherence to merely positive law, to legality per se, is not the core of legal legitimacy, which instead lie in the (modern) rights of subjectivity.[15] On this view, the fidelity of the Jewish people to their laws left them "stuck" in the past.[16]

[12] See (Anidjar 2003).

[13] See (Schwartz 2012).

[14] This ambivalence is clearly visible in Michelet's defense of Hegel against Hess and in Hess's response discussed in (Rotenstreich 1962).

[15] This trope has recently received much attention in (Honneth 2015; and Menke 2018).

[16] See the discussion in (Fackenheim 1973, 81–2). For a wide-ranging take on the debate on Hegel and Judaism, see (Mack 2003). For a recent view on Hegel's critique of "Jewish" juridicism, see (Loick 2014).

Hegel believed that Christendom had taken over from Judaism the task of realizing the Kingdom of God on earth. Hegel's *Phenomenology of Spirit* can be understood as translating the Christian *Gottesreich* [Kingdom of God] into a *Geisterreich* [Kingdom of Spirit] on the basis of St. John's claim that God is *Logos* or spirit (Löwith 1962, 161). For Hegel, Christianity climaxed in the ideal of the Johannine Age of Spirit, "a reality in which God reigns as the one and absolute spirit" (Löwith 1964, 46).[17] Hegel's philosophy of objective spirit argues that the realization of the Kingdom of God under modern conditions takes the form of a Protestant, "liberal" relation between Church and State, but always and only on the assumption that "religion and the state can and must come to agreement on the ground of the Christian spirit" (Löwith 1964, 46).

In his early work, *The Holy History of Mankind*, Hess advances a post-Hegelian political theology in which biblical theocratic constitutionalism is joined up with tenets of modern socialist republicanism. Hess offers an entirely different vision of how Jewish fidelity to the Mosaic law is linked with the Johannine Age of Spirit. Formulating a conception of theocratic republican constitutionalism, Hess writes that "*true religion*, the knowledge of God revealed in the holy history, *is the only foundation of states, the basic law*, out of which the other laws follow. Because the highest good of men is to be *bound socially to all* and not exclusively to one person . . . [they] create a great covenant, in order to support each other as brethren, as equal beings, in their pursuits" (Hess 2004, 94, emphasis mine). In an uncanny anticipation of Hermann Cohen's views, the constitution of the Hebrew Republic is for Hess at once the most ancient and the most futural or messianic model for republics.

Hess adopts a "narrative" style of philosophy that borrows, in equal measure, from Hegel's philosophy of spirit and Schelling's philosophy of nature. The philosophical consciousness of truth develops along a tripartite conception of "holy history" that schematizes the dimensions of Creation, Revelation, and Redemption into three "world ages," following Joachim of Fiore's model of divine dispensations. Employing a classic Hegelian image, Hess speaks of historical development as a progression through three stages, symbolized by "kernel, tree and fruit. This law [of 'holy' history] proceed[s] from the kernel . . . [and] return[s] to the kernel as fruit" (Hess 2004, 61). The original "kernel" is "the unity of humanity under the aegis of unconscious, unified life" revealed in Creation (with Adam and Eve), which itself first appears in history "as a visible root with Abraham, the ancestral father of the nation, in whose legislation the unity of life, or God, was unmistakeably revealed" (Hess 2004, 61). The Abrahamic faith already contains,

[17] On the idea of the Johannine Age, see (Altmann 1988). Johannine speculations have been the object of intense scrutiny in recent post-Marxist thought, from (Cacciari 1990) through (Gauchet 1999; and Vattimo 2002) to (Bielik-Robson 2013).

if only in potentiality, a global constitution for humanity "whose external form is equality, or liberty. . . . Therefore the [Mosaic] Law originally divided all goods equally among the people and saw to it that equality . . . would be maintained" (61). Much later, Rosenzweig will take up this kernel metaphor in its original formulation by Judah Halevi,[18] in order to bring the *Star of Redemption* to a close under the sign of the greatest *Teshuvah*, "the greatest return, the recognition of the seed [the 'teaching of Moses'] in the fruit ['the Messiah whom we await']."[19]

Hess gives a radical democratic formulation to the "kernel as fruit" of this holy history: "the interests of the rulers and the ruled . . . will blend into each other, the cooperation of all in the state machinery . . . will be so harmonious, and this harmony so manifest, that no patriotism of any states of antiquity would equal that of the new league of nations [*Völkerbund*]. In the new Holy Covenant religion and politics will be once again one—a unity of which the state of antiquity provide[s] us merely a weak example" (Hess 2004, 89). The unity of religion and politics in its republican form, which Spinoza and Rousseau identified in the civil religions of ancient republics (including the Hebrew Republic), is unfolded by Hess into a providential conception of history, driven by the requirement to realize the Kingdom of God as a radical democracy, exactly as postulated later by Hermann Cohen. "There will be three powers in the Kingdom of God: the people as a mass—or the body of the people; the people as the executor of laws—or the will of the people; and finally the people as legislator—or the spirit of the people" (Hess 2004, 91). The formulation is the same as the one later found in Abraham Lincoln's Gettysburg Address: democracy is the rule of the people, by the people, and for the people.

But the originality of Hess's Jewish democratic political theology lies in the adoption of Spinoza's philosophy as the crucial redemptive event in the "holy history of humanity." In choosing Spinoza over Jesus, Hess breaks with the Hegelian political theology that identifies the crucial historical event with the Crucifixion of Jesus and the Resurrection as Christ, the Incarnation of God as a human being.[20] Picking up from the complex debate on Spinoza in the German

[18] As Yossef Schwartz points out, the kernel metaphor is first found in Islamic and Jewish medieval thought. Rosenzweig employs the formulation found in Judah Halevi, according to which "the nations mainly serve to introduce and save the way for the expected Messiah, who is the fruition, and they will all become His fruit. Then is they acknowledge Him, they will become one tree" (Halevi 1964: IV, 23) and in Maimonides, *Mishne Torah*, "The Laws of Kings and Their Wars," ch. 11, cited in (Schwartz 2003, 134).

[19] (Rosenzweig 2005, 401–2). In this chapter, I use Barbara Galli's translation of *The Star of Redemption*. However, I have on occasion modified this translation and adopted some variants found in the William Hallo version (Rosenzweig 1985). For the original German version, I employ the Suhrkamp edition (Rosenzweig 1988).

[20] Roberto Esposito's discussion of Hegel's political theology has emphasized its reliance on the idea of personhood, which is itself construed in Trinitarian terms (Esposito 2015). By way of contrast, Hess employs Spinoza's philosophy in order to reject the very idea of personality, in particular as employed by the "Young Hegelians" and their "personalist theology of monotheism," which according to him underpins the importance given to the institution of inheritance. See the discussion

Enlightenment,[21] and anticipating the 20th-century debate on Spinoza's relationship to Judaism and Christianity started by Cohen, Hess boldly portrays Spinoza's philosophy as the *Aufhebung* of both the Jewish and the Christian revelations. "The old law [of Moses] was crucified with Christ only so far as it had been external, existing in time and space, but its divine content, its eternal spirit, continued to live. . . . The old law, whose body has been buried with Christ, has been clarified and resurrected in Spinoza" (Hess 2004, 92). Indeed, Spinoza's "third revelation" is not the start of a "new religion . . . which is contrary to the previous ones: there exists only one eternal religion, and it is this ancient religion which is being revealed here in the illuminated garment of the spirit [i.e., in Spinoza's philosophical system]' (Hess 2004, 50). Spinoza's philosophy is testament to the "eternal" life or afterlife of the Jewish law and its messianic realization in the modern age of democratic revolutions.[22]

While in his early work, Hess's recovery of Spinoza's political philosophy links a socialist republican content with the Jewish understanding of the messianic Kingdom, in his later work *Rome and Jerusalem: A Study in Jewish Nationalism* he employs Spinoza to ground his commitment to Zionism.[23] In both cases, Spinoza provides the philosophical support for what Nathan Rotenstreich calls Hess's "pantheistic interpretation of Judaism" according to which "the universality of Judaism . . . consisted in its assertion of a single law for the universe at large and a single destiny for mankind" (1962, 285). Spinoza's "pantheism" conjures up for Hess the old, Philonic Judeo-Hellenistic symbiosis of Jewish faith in the One God with the Greek philosophical conception of divine law as the *nomos* of the just or ideal state. It is on the basis of Spinoza's "pantheism" that Hess takes the first step to bring together Athens and Jerusalem in the form of Jewish political theology. This "pantheist" gesture perhaps explains why Hess was later moved to advocate for a political Renaissance of the Jewish people, analogous to Mazzini's successful struggle for the independence of Italy, itself nourished by the old dreams of Italian unity first proclaimed by Machiavelli. For Hess, "Rome" no longer simply stood for the destruction of the Jewish temple-state in ancient

in (Rose 2014, ch. 6). For a good treatment of the Left Hegelian critique of Christian personhood as basis of state sovereignty and German monarchy, see (Breckman 2011). On the polemics concerning Hegel's supposed "pantheism" and "Spinozism," see also (Stewart 2011).

[21] On the relation between the Enlightenment debate on Spinoza and Rosenzweig, see the crucial discussion in (Rosenstock 2009, 123–61).

[22] The historiographical basis for this claim is provided in works like (Vernière 1982; and Israel 2002).

[23] The crucial importance of Moses Hess for the development of modern Zionism is addressed at length in (Berlin 1982; and Avinieri 1987). See now (Margolin 2018), who claims that Buber's "spiritual Zionism" is deeply influenced by Hess's Zionist writings. I discuss Buber's reading of Hess in chapter 6 on Arendt.

times, but it had also become a model for the resurgence of the Jewish state in Palestine in modern times.[24]

The idea of historical eternity and Rosenzweig's philosophical system

Hegel believed that the Jewish constitution was left behind by the "progress" of history, conceived as the secularization of the Christian history of salvation [*Heilsgeschichte*]. In contrast, Hess argued that this very constitution is what assures the Jewish people an eternal or supra-historical life in and through history. "Every holy constitution proceeds from the unity of consciousness of society on which it then impacts by permeating it and thus ceases to act on it as an external law . . . the republic in which it [the holy constitution] reigns *rejuvenates itself, is being elevated to a higher life, which is detached from it in space and time*" (Hess 2004, 94, emphasis mine). In Hess, the theocratic constitution becomes the locus of the historical realization of an eternal or messianic life. As the end of the previous chapter argues, the idea of "historical eternity" is a fundamental aspect of Cohen's philosophical interpretation of Judaism. Cohen does *not* simply oppose the Jewish belief in a "creator of the world" to the pagan, philosophical idea of the eternity of the world. The concept of a "historical eternity" with which Cohen concludes the *Religion of Reason* becomes the starting point of Part Three of the *Star of Redemption*, the explicitly politico-theological section of the treatise, which presents the idea of the Kingdom of God, or the "Eternal Supra-World," and discusses the conditions of possibility for humankind to accede to eternal life.

Rosenzweig's "new thinking" has frequently been interpreted from the horizon of Martin Heidegger's hermeneutic of finitude and original temporality.[25] Alexander Altmann interprets the idea of eternity in Rosenzweig as somehow compatible with the priority of futurity in Heidegger: "They are existential terms . . . they do not deny and invalidate history. On the contrary, they seek to give meaning to history" (Altmann 1988, 134). But the project of the *Star of Redemption* is not the existential one of accounting for how human beings give meaning to history. The latter project, as Karl Löwith will later show, depends on the secularization of Christianity.[26] Rosenzweig himself confessed, "I am

[24] See the evocative essay on the symbolic meaning of Rome for both German-Jewish Zionist and non-Zionist thinkers in (Biemann 2012).

[25] See (Löwith 1942; Altmann 1988; Myers 2003; Gordon 2003; and Mosès 2009).

[26] See (Löwith 1957). Wolfgang Herzfeld argues that Rosenzweig was always critical of the Hegelian attempt to see "God in history" (Herzfeld 2013, 320, 342); similar considerations are also found in (Myers 2003). For Benjamin Pollock, Rosenzweig "suggests that the only true, ultimately secure fact is the Kingdom" (Pollock 2009, 232).

sure only of God and His Kingdom, not of the *Zwischenreich* [the intermediate realm]."[27] Yet this does not mean that for Rosenzweig "God must redeem man not through history but—there is no alternative—through religion" (Altmann 1988, 132). Altmann's interpretation downplays the internal relation between divine revelation and legal revolution proposed by Hess and by German-Jewish republican thinking.

For Rosenzweig, eternal life is the life of knowing God, and he follows Cohen in claiming that the possibility of eternal life for humankind is contained in the correlation between the love of the neighbor and the love of God. "Being created by God and being in the image of God are the foundation set down in him by Creation, and upon this foundation he can build the house of his eternal life in the temporal cross-currents of love of God and love of neighbor" (Rosenzweig 1985, 278). The distinction between humanity and world with respect to their potential eternity is that whereas the eternity of humankind is determined at Creation ("man was created to be a super-man"), the world becomes capable of becoming a "super-world" only in and through the revelation at Sinai.[28] Unlike humanity and world, God is always eternal, that is, He is always in Redemption. The fundamental problem of Part Three of the *Star* is, then, how human beings can establish God's Kingdom on earth and found "the house of their eternal life." This "house" is the same "holy constitution" that Hess describes. Rosenzweig calls it the "supra-world" of the Kingdom of God in which humankind realizes its destiny as "super-man."

For Rosenzweig, Judaism is focused on the "End" of history precisely because it suspects the senselessness of trying to find ultimate meaning in human history when contrasted to the transcendent reality of (created) nature. Rosenzweig's republican approach to law and revolution is made possible thanks to his philosophical system having repositioned Judaism far closer to the Greco-Roman assignation of priority to nature over history than interpreters have been willing to countenance. For Rosenzweig, the threshold between Hegel's Christian idea of world-history and the return to the biblical, but more precisely Judeo-Hellenistic, view of nature and history is symbolized by the proper name of Nietzsche. Rosenzweig argues that Nietzsche reopened the "question of faith" after Hegel while rejecting modern historicism through his adoption of the Greek doctrine of the eternal return. Together with Kierkegaard, Nietzsche "is he whom none who must philosophize can henceforth bypass" (Rosenzweig 2005,

[27] Altmann cites from *Briefe* (Rosenzweig 1935, 302, 316–7, 331–2). In this sense, Löwith's attempts to disentangle the meaning of divine revelation from the "meaning of history" is more faithful to Rosenzweig's mature thought.

[28] (Rosenzweig 1985, 260). Galli uses the term "supra-man," which misses the clear Nietzschean connotations in the original German: "während der Mensch zu Übermenschen geschaffen ward" (Rosenzweig 1988, 290).

15) because he is "the first real man among philosophers" and "also the first to see God face to face—even if only to refute Him" (Rosenzweig 2005, 25).[29] By opening a path of return to the Greeks, Nietzsche also reopened the question of "faith and knowledge" that Hegel sought to close: "Revelation taught us to recognize in these [pagan] gods the hidden God, the hidden one who is nothing other than the not yet manifest one. . . . The life of the pagan gods became God's hidden primordial life" (Rosenzweig 2005, 411–2). The decisive insight that Greek polytheism and pantheism are *not opposed* to the revelation of the One God, but represent His "hidden" life that runs like an undercurrent throughout the unfolding of "holy history," accounts for the crucial role played by Goethe and Nietzsche in Rosenzweig's anti-Hegelian interpretation of the Johannine Age of Spirit.

Hegel thought that by translating Christian revelation into a philosophy of absolute spirit, revealed religion could shed its authoritative form, its positivity, that it inherited from Judaism, and finally become what it always was meant to be: absolute knowledge of God (1977, 65). Hegel's philosophical system intends to show that revealed religion has the same content as true philosophy. "The outcome of this absorption of religion into philosophy is Hegel's philosophy of religion. In his lectures, he explicitly treats religion and philosophy as one. *True philosophy is itself worship*" (Löwith 1964, 327, emphasis mine). However, if revealed religion is true philosophy, this identity makes religion "superfluous" (Löwith 1962, 159). If the practice of philosophy (as subjective, objective, and absolute spirit) is the authentic meaning of *Gottesdienst* (service to God, liturgy), then there is no longer a need for all the positive, legal entrapments of revealed religion, for the study of the Bible, for churches, synagogues, and mosques. Hegel's philosophical justification of religion is at the same time its destruction: Hegel prepares the way for the explicit atheism of the neo-Hegelians.

The transmutation of true philosophy into worship is the crucial point of inflection for Rosenzweig's philosophical system as well: it is only once "true philosophy" becomes prayer in Hegel's system that the *path of return* from modern Idealism back to the "fact" or "facticity" of biblical revealed law (whose content is the belief in the given and distinct realities of God, humanity, and world), and also back to the authentic sense of pagan, Greek philosophy, can be undertaken. If for Hegel, modernity requires that Greek philosophy (based on "substance") become theological (viz. adopt Christianity and its principle of subjectivity) in order to become true knowledge of God, then one can say that for Rosenzweig post-modernity begins from the return to the biblical, politico-theological

[29] It is indicative that immediately after this eulogy of Nietzsche, Rosenzweig offers great praise to Hermann Cohen, as another thinker who managed to conceive of God out of the "nothing."

conception of prayer in conjunction with the attempt to *recover the pagan and true conception of philosophy*.[30]

Part One of the *Star* shows the impossibility of the Hegelian translation of theology into philosophy. For between faith and knowledge, or revelation and philosophy, there exists a mutual need that preserves each in their separate form, rather than (mis)translating one into the other. Only the individual "who receives Revelation and experiences the content of faith in his life" can be "the one who philosophizes at present and, even scientifically, is the only possible philosopher of the new philosophy" (Rosenzweig 2005, 117). Conversely, Revelation stands equally in need of the "new philosophy" in order to "throw a bridge from Creation to Revelation," without which theology is unable to effect the connection "between Revelation and Redemption." Philosophy can connect Creation to Revelation by doing the *opposite* of what Hegel called upon it to do. For Hegel, modern philosophy had to develop, as conceptual content, the form of what is revealed in Revelation (viz., subjectivity). For Rosenzweig, instead, the post-modern "new thinking" must show how pagan philosophy *already contains* the content of what Revelation reveals in a new, viz., subjective, form: "Revelation does not in the least destroy genuine paganism, the paganism of creation. Not at all. It only allows the miracle of return and renewal to happen to it."[31]

For Rosenzweig, divine revelation says "nothing," and certainly nothing "new"—its message is *purely performative*. What counts in Revelation is not "what" is revealed but "that" God is revealed. This is what Rosenzweig calls the "facticity" of Revelation. This "fact" of Revelation comes to "verify" the truth of (pagan) philosophy. Philosophy is the "before of Revelation": "in Creation, revelation is—'foreseen' in its entire content, exactly in accordance with today's notion of faith, hence also including Redemption. Philosophy, as the theologian practices it, becomes the prediction of Revelation, so to speak the 'Old Testament' of theology. But before our astonished eyes, Revelation then gains its character of authentic miracle—authentic, for it becomes wholly the fulfillment of the promise that took place in Creation" (Rosenzweig 2005, 117). For Rosenzweig, no true understanding of the Torah is possible without the mediation of Greek philosophy. He shares with Cohen this Philonic assumption.

[30] In "The New Thinking," Rosenzweig says: "Thus paganism is definitely no mere religio-philosophical bogeyman for adults. . . . Rather it is—no more and no less than the truth. The truth, to be sure, in an elemental, invisible and unrevealed form" (Udoff and Galli 1999, 80). For a different account of Rosenzweig's recovery of pagan philosophy, see (Bielik-Robson 2014).

[31] (Udoff and Galli 1999, 90). It would take me too far afield to show how close this insight of Rosenzweig's stands in relation to Simone Weil's hypothesis of Pythagorean and Platonic philosophy as a "pre-intuition" of Christian revelation. Pollock also acknowledges the vicinity of Rosenzweig's thought to pantheism: "In redemption . . . the very pantheistic error of reducing all things to God, which philosophy has carried out . . . here too becomes true" (Pollock 2009, 228).

The development of this hypothesis in Jewish political theology is discussed at greater length in the next two chapters dedicated to Gerschom Scholem and Leo Strauss, respectively.

Part Two of the *Star* applies the structure of this argument to a discussion of miracles and seeks to investigate the origins of their modern disappearance.[32] This disappearance of faith in modern times becomes the topic of Strauss's first book on Spinoza, which is therefore appropriately dedicated to Rosenzweig for having set the research agenda, if not solving the problem. For purposes of working out Rosenzweig's political theology in terms of the tension between Athens and Jerusalem, what is of interest here is the connection between miracle and divine providence in the *Star*. In accordance with well-established precedent in the Jewish tradition, Rosenzweig defines a miracle not as what diverges from "the course of nature predetermined by law, but on the fact that it was predicted. Miracle is essentially 'sign'" (Rosenzweig 2005, 104). Rosenzweig therefore rescues the possibility of miracle by remaining within the medieval Islamic Aristotelian framework, shared by Maimonides, that all explanation of the miracle in and of the revelation of the divine law should not entail the need to alter the normal "course of the world."[33]

The first step of Rosenzweig's demonstration is to show that the miracle is the sign that verifies a prediction, that is, a prophecy. Maimonides opposed the true prophet to the magician because the latter seeks to interfere with the course of the world and therefore "attacks God's Providence," whereas "the prophet . . . unveils by foreseeing that which is willed by Providence" (Rosenzweig 2005, 104). The prophet is the foreseer of God's providence or government of the world along the course set by Him, which remains unknown to human beings. Miracle, as verification of the prophecy, is then "the sign that proves God's Providence." Revelation is simply revelation of this Providence, of God as King of the world, and, in the last instance, of God as Creator. The connection between divine revelation or divine providence and the Jewish conception of tradition is that this tradition transmits eyewitness testimony to the predictions or prophecies, and "faith" consequently means "trust" in the accounts of these witnesses and in maintaining an unbroken chain of transmission of this witnessing (Rosenzweig 2005, 106). Hence, for Rosenzweig the real source of the attack on miracles in modernity is

[32] Recent interpretations of Rosenzweig's political theology take as their starting point the comparison between Rosenzweig's understanding of miracles and Schmitt's analogy between miracle and state of exception but do not fully appreciate the Hegelian and Nietzschean background of the question. See (Santner 2003; and Honig 2007). On modern "disenchantment" from miracles, see also (Yelle 2019).

[33] For a discussion of Maimonides' expression, see the essay in (Hartman 1998, ch. 10) dedicated to Maimonides' conception of miracles. I shall return to this question in relation to Strauss's reading of Maimonides.

the attack on the Jewish conception of tradition at the hands of what he calls the "Enlightenment" view of history (the Enlightenment denial of tradition).[34]

Rosenzweig's solution to the tension between faith and knowledge established by the Enlightenment is that true philosophy does not come "after" Revelation, as Hegel had it, but "before" Revelation. True pagan philosophy is the *prophecy* of divine Revelation. In this sense, pagan philosophy is nothing other than the true doctrine of Creation. If the truth of pagan philosophy consists in its prophecy of God as truth, and the fact of Revelation is the miracle that confirms this truth, then the bridge between pagan philosophy and revealed theology can only take the form of an account of God's Providence, that is, a doctrine of the actualization of God as truth in the form of His Kingdom on earth. Working out this doctrine is the content of Part Three of the *Star*. In this way, the organization of the *Star* formally maintains the structure of Maimonides' *Guide* according to which philosophy is a doctrine of Creation and theology is a doctrine of Revelation, while the transition from Revelation to Redemption is found in the politico-theological Account of the Chariot.

Goethe's prayer and Machiavelli's politics

Part Three of the *Star* begins with a discussion of prayer.[35] The discourse of political theology in the 20th century identifies liturgy or prayer as one of its fundamental themes.[36] The focus on prayer and its relation to political theology was already thematized by Cohen, who linked prayer to "God's government of the world" (Cohen 1995, 396).[37] Rosenzweig takes up and radicalizes Cohen's

[34] Rosenzweig identifies three phases of Enlightenment: Greek, Renaissance, and finally the rise of historical criticism with Lessing and Reimarus (2005, 107–8).

[35] Rosenzweig's discussion of Jewish and Christian liturgical calendars in this part of the *Star* has at times been interpreted as the clearest expression of his turn to an "apolitical" idea of "religion" and as a clear rejection of his wartime discourse on imperialism (Mosès 1998). Herzfeld claims that only the German defeat in World War I led Rosenzweig to turn to an an idea of Judaism "without state and without frontiers" as the new symbol of humanity (Herzfeld 2013, 336). Other interpreters, on the contrary, suggest that after the German defeat of 1918, Rosenzweig pinned his hopes for redemption on a "*völkisch*" construal of Judaism as a "community of blood," thus shifting his continuing belief in the "liberal-imperial" construal of the Reich onto the domain of religion. For this second line of interpretation, see (Kartheininger 2006; and Quélennec 2018). For a cruder version of these arguments, see (Lilla 2007).

[36] See (Agamben 2011). The political theology of prayer is a major theme that Rosenzweig shares with Rosenstock-Huessy. For the latter's understanding of prayer, consider the following: "Revelation is knowledge of God's will, after his 'No' to our will has become known. Only then is God pure future, pure act—only when all his former creations exposed as non-gods, as mere artifacts.... On this basis the Jews became prayer. Israel is neither a nation nor a state nor a race, but it is prayer.... This prayer of true faith, of 'amen,' was separated from spellbinding, from magic, by Israel's faith.... Hitler is a spellbinder" (Rosenstock-Huessy 2011, 182).

[37] Divine government is "identical with the concept of God as the guarantor of the realization of the ideal ethico-political association [*Sittlichkeit*] on earth. The government of the world is the setting

approach to prayer as a doctrine of eschatological government by making more explicit who the "political" subjects that pray are, and as a consequence also the different forms taken by the drive to actualize on earth the messianic Kingdom of God. For Cohen, the politics of prayer was "universal" in a still abstract sense: "the prayer is the universal means for the connection with God. Hence, it is universal humanity, the human community [*Gemeinschaft*] by virtue of which the individual is able to seek, and entreat for, his own connection with God" (1995, 385). In Part Three of the *Star*, Rosenzweig articulates the idea of a universal "human community" signified by the Kingdom of God by analyzing the concrete, historico-political elements that conform with its conditions of possibility. The first of these elements concerns the relationship between imperialism, republicanism, and messianism under conditions of globalization. The second element concerns the distinct conditions of belongingness to peoplehood and nationhood ("blood" versus "land," respectively). The third and last element thematizes the different historical communities of prayer (Gentile, Jewish, Christian, Islamic, Modern/Secular) and their contributions to the articulation of the messianic "human community" in view of its relation to politico-theological friendship and enmity. These elements are each discussed in the following sections.

The focus on liturgy announces this third part of the *Star* as a treatise on Jewish political theology. The explicitly politico-theological character of these texts is alluded to with the exergue *in tyrannos!*, which is a Latin military term that commands a charge against the tyrant. The exergue suggests that Part Three identifies the political question of tyranny with the theological question of how God should be glorified, or, put otherwise, how one should pray to God. The connection of both themes was standard in modern republican writings where Moses was figured as a republican political leader.[38] Commentators of the *Star* have not given much attention to this exergue and its relation to the discussion on prayer that follows it.[39]

Rosenzweig questions the secularist prejudice that, through prayer, humans are tempting or manipulating God, asking of Him things that are beneath His

of an end for the world and the realization of that end for the world in its double meaning, as nature and as the human world" (Cohen 1995, 396, translation slightly modified).

[38] One recalls Thomas Jefferson's motto that "rebellion to tyrants is obedience to God" placed on the Seal of the new American republic with an engraving of the parted Red Sea collapsing on the heads of the Pharaoh's army. See the discussion in (Tierney 1982; and Gish and Klinghard 2013).

[39] The two-volume collection of essays from the international Rosenzweig congress at Kassel in 2004 bears the subtitles of the exergues for the first and second parts of the *Star* ("in philosophos!" and "in theologos!") but there is no third volume dedicated to Part Three. See (Schmied-Kowarzik 2006a, 2006b). Also, the otherwise informative collection in (Brasser 2004) does not focus on the doctrine of prayer. The line-by-line commentary of (Samuelson 1999, 223–32) does not comment on the senses of tyranny.

majesty to grant. To the contrary, he proposes a conception of prayer as a discourse in which God tempts humans and tempts them into revealing themselves for who they really are: either free or slaves. The locus classicus for such divine temptation is the Book of Job. The God of Israel only wants to be worshipped by "free" human beings (Rosenzweig 2005, 284). In order to elicit human freedom, God "not only must hide His rule [*sein Walten*] over human beings: He must deceive them about it . . . so that they have the possibility of believing Him and trusting Him in truth, that is to say, in freedom" (Rosenzweig 2005, 284, translation modified). In this employment of the Platonic motif of the "noble lie," Rosenzweig's interpretation of the problem of prayer betrays one of its Platonic-Maimonidean traits. But it also reflects a republican conception of divine government insofar as the freedom that God wants to elicit in such an indirect way is expressed as the "fear of God," which is the one thing that is *not* commanded by God through the covenant at Sinai.

Rabbinic literature contains many reflections on the politico-theological interpretation of this motif, which traditionally centers on the legend of the "oven of Akhnai" and on the negotiations around God's descent to Mount Sinai, and who was permitted and who was prohibited from ascending the mountain, as alluded to in Exodus 19.[40] Zachary Braiterman has condensed the point of these negotiations into the rabbinical doctrine that God's "sovereign power seems not to threaten their [the rabbis] own place in the world as both subjects and shapers of law, a privileged and protected place that the rabbis reserve in the interim for themselves (and for themselves alone) as the place of freedom, not constraint."[41] Rosenzweig intervenes in this hierocratic interpretative tradition by offering a more modern and republican (perhaps one can say, Machiavellian) interpretation of the relation between fear of God and the freedom of the people as the conditions of possibility for constitutional government in a world characterized by a process of globalization.

Prayer is understood mythically when it wishes for the course of the world to change and beseeches God to realize His Kingdom before the time is "ripe." This is the prayer of "the zealot, the sectarian, in short all tyrants of the Kingdom of heaven" who, in trying to "force" their way up the mountain to God's presence, achieve the opposite of what they aim, viz., they delay rather than accelerate the messianic End of history (Rosenzweig 2005, 289). The "tyrants of heaven," on this first reading, are precisely those religious fanatics who through their prayers call forth the Anti-Christ. However, Rosenzweig's critique of fanaticism and fundamentalism (zealotry) covers up an esoteric sense in which prayer *succeeds* in

[40] See also my discussion of Scholem's interpretation of the "oven of Akhnai" in the next chapter.

[41] (Braiterman 2014, 251). Braiterman cites in this context Bonnie Honig's use of the rabbinic arguments to contrast Schmitt's construal of the state of exception (Honig 2009, 70–6).

accelerating the coming of the Messiah. This esoteric prayer must be delivered at "the right time" if it is to be met with God's grace, that is, with His sending the Messiah.

According to Rosenzweig's teaching, the "right time" to pray for the Messiah only comes "after" the prayer he attributes to Goethe, the prayer of "unbelief": "Give, oh labor of my hands, the great happiness that I can finish it!" (Rosenzweig 2005, 293). Goethe's prayer corresponds to "the great moment in the history of mankind where for the first time human beings raise their arms praying to their own destiny" (Rosenzweig 2005, 295). Goethe's prayer opens the Johannine Age of Spirit, announced by Napoleon's dictum that "politics is destiny." It is the prayer of human self-assertion, in which the human species becomes all that it can be on its own, giving full vent to its Promethean legacy (Rosenzweig 2005, 300–4).[42]

There is widespread agreement among commentators that Rosenzweig takes up Schelling's conception of the *Weltalter* [Ages of the World].[43] Schelling's cosmological speculations turn on the hypothesis that divine Creation has a hidden "ground" that corresponds to an always active mythical, pagan "Past" against which the "Present" opened up by Christian revelation struggles. On this view, European history is the result of this struggle between paganism and Christendom, and an eschatological pull exerted by the horizon of an equally—and continuously—active dimension of the "Future." This dimension of the Future corresponds to the Johannine Age of Spirit and it roughly overlaps with the modern secular age as the last phase of Christianity.[44] Rosenstock correctly indicates that in the *Star*, Rosenzweig names Goethe as the true, representative figure of the Johannine Age of Christianity, which promised a final, messianic denouement of the *agon* between paganism and Christianity.[45] Goethe's prayer

[42] In this text, Rosenzweig seems to allude to Goethe's role in the "pantheism controversy" unleashed by Jacobi (Blumenberg 1988). Goethe is absent in the otherwise excellent discussion on the recovery of this controversy in German Jewish thought in the early 20th century (Lazier 2008, 69–110). For opposing views on the political stakes of this controversy, compare (Altman 2011; and Vatter 2019b).

[43] See (Herzfeld 2013) for copious documentation. On the *Weltalter* see (Schelling and Žižek 1997) with an essay by Slavoj Žižek which, however, does not discuss the geopolitics of Christianity. On the influence of the *Weltalter* on the development of Marxism, yet without reference to their presence in Hess, see also (Habermas 2004). For another reading of Schelling that is deeply informed by geopolitical considerations on Europe and Christianity, see (Cacciari 1990).

[44] On the tension between paganism and Christianity as animating European history in Rosenzweig, see (Rosenstock 2009, 133–46). However, caution is needed to avoid accepting the widespread belief that Rosenzweig's philosophy of history is merely a Schellingian reading of the Jewish tradition.

[45] (Rosenstock 2009, 133–46). However, I disagree with his view that Rosenzweig opposes both Judaism and Christianity, as forms of neighborly love, to the resurgent paganism in Goethe: "Rosenzweig's *Star* is written to assist everyone to return to the existential choice of 1800" between the paganism of Hegel and Goethe and the awareness of "his or her radical particularity" in the face of death that allows one "to hear the word of God once more" (ibid., 144).

is the prayer of "unbelief" because it is the prayer uttered by the pagan remnant or remainder, the "living pagan," who can be found in every Christian: "Goethe is really at the same time the great pagan and the great Christian" (Rosenzweig 2005, 301–2).

The role of Goethe's prayer should be understood within the overall project of the *Star*, namely, that of turning around (*Teshuvah*) "the pagan in the Christian" toward the true conception of Redemption and of philosophy (Rosenzweig 2005, 303). Goethe's prayer is the prayer of the modern revolutions for "liberty, equality, fraternity" (Rosenzweig 2005, 305). This is the secular, political content of the Johannine Church (Lessing) that effectively brings the long arc of Roman Catholic imperialism to an end. Rosenzweig's thesis is that without these modern revolutionary political pre-conditions, there can be no Kingdom of God on earth. To mention only the most obvious reason, without these revolutions humanity is still enslaved and therefore incapable of taking up God's yoke in freedom.

For Rosenzweig, the right prayer is in all cases a prayer for revolution. It is so in the Goethean sense, but it is also revolutionary in a more esoteric sense of the messianic prayer, according to which "eternity must be hastened; it must always be capable of coming as early as 'today'" (Rosenzweig 2005, 306). The transition from Goethe's prayer of unbelief to the authentic prayer for the Kingdom discloses the novelty of Rosenzweig's political theology, which does not conceive of the secular revolutions that established modern states in terms of the "secularization" of messianic aspirations, but, to the contrary, envisages secular political and legal revolutions as *preparatory* for what can be appropriately termed a post-secular messianic form of constitutionalism.[46]

The connection between modern revolutions and religious constitutionalism was fashioned out of the intense exchanges that Rosenzweig carried out with Rosenstock-Huessy during World War I. In 1931 Rosenstock-Huessy published *Die Europäischen Revolutionen: Volkscharaktere und Staatenbildung* (republished in English in 1938 as *Out of Revolution* following his emigration to the United States), where he develops a conception of cycles of legal revolutions starting with the Gregorian Papal (legal) Revolution. Without mentioning the precedent of Moses Hess's *Holy History of Mankind*, Rosenstock-Huessy takes up its post-Hegelian Joachimian narrative of history in a Christian key and applies it to decipher modern Western history as a history of revolutions driven by a Christian conception of "love of neighbor." His claim is that with the Papal legal revolution, not only are eschatological hopes and energies poured into worldliness, eliciting

[46] This theologico-political reading of Rosenzweig's discussion of prayer is not found in other political readings of Part Three, for instance in (Rose 1993; Batnitzky 1999; and Gordon 2003). See also (Mack 2003; and Bouretz 2003), where the political reading of prayer is mentioned, but not further developed.

the renewal of interest in the *saeculum* and a definitive bidding farewell to millenarian hopes of an imminent arrival of the Messiah, but that human beings understand themselves as having a politico-spiritual task to accomplish in order to be finally redeemed: this is the task of revolutionizing society.[47] Rosenstock-Huessy's conception of secularization identifies it with the Christianization of world politics.

Harold Berman takes up this hypothesis in order to establish the Christian bases of Western constitutionalism. He argues that the Christian dogma of Incarnation allowed for the "release of an enormous energy for the redemption of the world" and gave it an institutional form that "split the legal from the spiritual, the political from the ideological," thereby establishing the idea of the rule of law (Berman 1983, 78). On this view, only Christian messianism is the true inner-worldly realization of "love of neighbor" that takes an autonomous legal form. Hauke Brunkhorst draws on Rosenstock-Huessy and Berman in order to argue that the paradigm of Western legal and democratic revolutions was the 12th-century clerical revolution against the Holy Roman Emperor.[48]

Rosenzweig was unwilling to tie the development of constitutionalism in the West to the destiny of Christendom. He shared with Rosenstock-Huessy the belief that the Christian dualism of Empire and Church harbors dialectical processes and unintended consequences that ultimately destroy the hegemony of the national state and push European history toward a post-national constellation. With respect to the Christian justification of Empire ("Render unto Caesar that which is Caesar's"), Rosenzweig emphasizes that the Christian Emperor is the harbinger of "the universal rule of law on earth" (2005, 373). Not unlike Kelsen's reading of Dante, Rosenzweig sees in the Christian Empire the promise of a post-sovereign "empire of law" strong enough to quell the monarchic "rebellion" of the national states "which in contrast to empire did not presume to contend for jurisdiction over the world, but only over themselves" (2005, 372, translation modified).[49] Likewise, the affirmative yet unintended role of the Christian Church

[47] For a recent comparative study of Rosenzweig and Rosenstock-Huessy, see (Cristaudo 2012). Wayne Cristaudo's discussion of *Out of Revolution*, however, abstracts completely from jurisprudence and is mainly based on his reconstruction of the Christian idea of love. "That is the very requirement of a revolution, and indeed of the Holy Spirit itself: that we must ceaselessly renounce the external forms, the institutions, habits and so on of the spirit in order to be true to the divine spirit and thus entre more deeply into God's love" (ibid., 238). Rosenstock-Huessy plays an important heuristic role now in (Diamantides 2012; and Diamantides and Schütz 2018), but the aim remains that of capturing the phenomenon of legal revolution strictly within the bounds of Christian political theology.

[48] See (Brunkhorst 2014) and for a related narrative (Thornhill 2013).

[49] Antonio Negri and Michael Hardt's conception of "empire" reflects this power of global systems of law that are intended to keep national sovereignty in check, and they correctly associate this idea with Kelsen's jurisprudence (Negri and Hardt 2001). Negri and Hardt are also correct to see that this "empire of law" generates a remnant, the "multitude," whose revolutionary aspirations it cannot satisfy. But they offer an interpretation of the multitude in terms of a Christian (Franciscan) conception of love which is far closer to Rosenstock-Huessy than to Rosenzweig's political theology.

consists in opening up a possibility for politics that is both supra-national and constitutional: the Church "cannot dispense with a legal constitution of its own. On the contrary, it is a visible system and of a sort which the state cannot tolerate—say because it were to limit itself to a particular sphere—but rather a system which claims not to be a whit less universal than the state. Church law, no less than Caesar's law, sooner or later applies to everyone" (Rosenzweig 1985, 353). However, Rosenzweig believed that modern constitutionalism did not receive its fundamental impulse from the Christian empire as much as from the end of its dream of world peace. This end was spelled by Machiavelli's approach to politics.

In the *Star*, following the guiding-thread of historical eternity, Rosenzweig argues that the formation of a world-history within the European context is characterized by the attempt of nations and peoples (*nationes et gentes*), which, unlike the Jewish people, have not always already considered themselves to be eternal, to gain eternity in time through the process of state-building. "For the State is the ever-changing form under which time moves step by step toward eternity. . . . For the nations of the world there is only pure temporality [*reine Zeitlichkeit*]. But *the State symbolizes the attempt, inevitably and always to be renewed, to give nations eternity within the confines of time. But the fact that the State does undertake it and must undertake it, makes the State the imitator and rival of the people which is in itself eternal*" (Rosenzweig 2005, 352, emphasis mine and translation modified).

Rosenzweig describes the attempt by *nationes et gentes* to attain eternity in history by employing the famous simile from chapter 25 of Machiavelli's *The Prince*, where the state is represented as a dam built to contain the river of Fortune:

> The peoples of the world are in themselves without cycle; their life rushes downstream in a wide river. If the state is to provide them with eternity, the river must be stemmed, dammed up to form a lake. The State must seek to make a cycle out of that pure flow of time to which the peoples in themselves are devoted; it must transform the constant changing alternation of their life into preservation and renewal and thus introduce a cycle that would in itself have the capacity to be eternal. (Rosenzweig 2005, 352, translation modified)

On this view, the modern state attempts to replicate, in the secular space of the cycles of constitutions, what the cycle of prayer already does for the people of Israel, namely, to turn the linear flow of time around, to give it the form of a recurring cycle, and thus to stabilize its flow into predictable patterns. This way of interpreting the function of a constitution is of Platonic origin and gets formalized by Polybius's idea of the Roman constitution as the *arche* or foundation of its empire, *imperium*.

Following Machiavelli's lesson, Rosenzweig writes that the modern state can bend the river of time into a cycle only through violence:

> Violence [*Gewalt*] provides life to its law [of the state] against the law [of the state] [*Die Gewalt lässt das Leben zu seinem Recht gegen das Recht kommen*]. Since the state is violent [*gewaltsam*] and not merely lawful [*rechtlich*], the state remains at life's heels. This is the meaning of all violence: that it founds new law. It is not a disavowal of the law, as one probably thinks, fascinated by its revolutionary conduct, but on the contrary its justification. But a contradiction is hidden in the idea of a new law. Law as regards its essence is old law. Now violence shows itself for what it is: the renewer of old law. In the violent act law constantly becomes new law. And the state is thus equally as much lawful and violent, refuge of the old law and source of the new. (Rosenzweig 2005, 353, translation modified)

Violence becomes the ground of constitutional law in modern states because this constitution stands in constant need to be changed and renewed in order to "subsume" the "pure life" of peoples under the form of the national state. Since the new law requires the destruction of the old (here there is an implicit citation of *Zarathustra*'s "Of Old and New Law Tables"), it follows that violence (over life) lies at the origin of constitutional law. Rosenzweig's insight stands in the closest proximity to the ideas advanced by Walter Benjamin in his famous 1921 essay "Critique of Violence" and its theory of the legality of the state as expression of the mythical violence over pure or bare life.[50]

Rosenzweig's main point is that the constitutional, egalitarian framework of the modern state cannot, on its own, bring about eternal life and true peace to its peoples because it is plagued by an irresolvable contradiction: "the state is therefore equally as much lawful and violent, refuge to the old law and source of the new." The circularity of state constitution is incapable of effectively reversing the flow of time. This is the ultimate reason why "war and revolution are the only reality that the state knows" (Rosenzweig 2005, 353). Jefferson, in his most Machiavellian moment, believed that every constitution needed to be renewed every twenty years, and that the tree of liberty had to be periodically watered by bloody revolts; all this was required to keep the freedom of the North American

[50] On Benjamin's essay, see (Agamben 2005a; and Butler 2006) and more recently (Martel 2012; and Loick 2015). The *Star* was finished in 1919 but was published only in 1921. Benjamin writes his text in January 1921, apparently spurred by Ernst Bloch's *Spirit of Utopia* (1920). It is unclear whether Benjamin had already access to Rosenzweig's book at that point. (Löwy 2005) seems to think so, while (Steiner 2001) discusses Bloch, Erich Unger, and Georges Sorel as influences but does not mention either Rosenzweig or Cohen. Butler touches on the possible relation to Rosenzweig but does not work it out (Butler 2014, 74, 230). For a different reading of these passages that does not draw out their constitutional implications, see (Gibbs 2004).

people alive. Lincoln, perhaps more faithful to the biblical exemplar, reversed Jefferson and called for strict adherence to the constitution (or to its founding moment, as captured by the *Declaration of Independence*) while he justified going to war against some of his citizens in order to abolish slavery and realize the messianic ideal of equality expressed in the *Declaration*'s doctrine of natural rights. In both cases, modern constitutionalism is born from revolution and ends with revolution.

Part Three of the *Star* thematizes the possibility of moving from "bare life" as a product of modern state sovereignty to what Rosenzweig calls eternal life. Bare life is entirely caught up in the empty flow of time that constantly eats itself up as a condition of possibility for generating more time and thus surviving.[51] The transition to eternal life must therefore consist in acting against time, in trying to turn the times around. Politically speaking, messianic life is only possible as a product of revolutionary political activity.[52] The first affirmative concept of revolution is the secular, pantheistic one associated with Goethe's prayer of unbelief. Yet Rosenzweig's point is that these political, republican revolutions cannot by themselves lead to eternal life unless there is "joined an accelerating force" (Rosenzweig 2005, 306, translation modified). This accelerating force is the post-secular prayer for the messianic.[53] When compared to "the true eternity of life" of the "eternal people," political revolutions can appear as "the worldly, all-too-worldly illusory eternity of their lies of world historical moments drawn up into states" (Rosenzweig 2005, 355). In other words, for Rosenzweig the circular relation between revolution and constitution, which in the last instance keeps politics tied to war, corresponds more to the form of the national state that contains and neutralizes the cosmopolitan and supra-national messianic ideal expressed by their constitutions.

Rosenzweig is known for his claim that "the true eternity of the eternal people must remain always foreign and annoying to the state and to world history" (2005, 354).[54] However, for Rosenzweig the teaching of Jewish messianism is not simply that the national state is the false God on earth. His cosmopolitan

[51] Here lies the connection between atheism and what Martin Hägglund calls "chronolibido." See (Hägglund 2008, 2012). Hägglund's own perspective remains entirely within the sphere of bare life whose futile resistance against mythical violence he attempts to "spiritualize" into a "desire for survival" based on the "atheistic" rejection of all aspirations to "immortality" (Hägglund 2008, 9). Viewed from Rosenzweig's standpoint, Hägglund is giving the latest form of Protestant "atheistic theology."

[52] I refer to (Vatter 2014) for an elaboration of this theme.

[53] The uncanny proximity of these thoughts to Benjamin's own interpretation of Goethe is discussed in (Vatter 2014). On Benjamin's notion of revolution and its relation to Goethe, see now (Ross 2018).

[54] See also the fragment "The Jew in the State": "In the Jew, the state is not living (unlike all other peoples) because something else, something superior to the state is living in him. . . . It is necessary that the Jew be in the state because the state cannot be in the Jew. This is the deepest reason for the impossibility of political Zionism" (Rosenzweig 2003, 179).

political theology is not a "negative political theology," as Jacob Taubes has argued. Rather, it identifies in the Jewish idea of messianism an affirmative ideal of politics to which all other states ought to aspire. The Jewish polity was not left behind by world history, as Hegel believes: it represents the End of world history that is both immanent and imminent. Features of the Hebrew Republic thus become a model for all states that pray Goethe's prayer of unbelief. The messianic ideal of a people who enjoys eternal life and peace in adherence to law, but without a state, is the historical unconscious of all national states. What this means more concretely can only be determined by traversing Rosenzweig's critique of the European process of state- and empire-formation.

Land and sea: Rosenzweig and Schmitt on imperialism and globalization

Recent interpretations of Rosenzweig's political thought draw attention to his early political writings, culminating in the unfinished work *Globus: Studies Towards the World-Historical Doctrine of Space.*[55] Generally speaking, these new interpretations claim that during the Great War, Rosenzweig put forward a theory of German imperialism, adopting the concept of *Mitteleuropa*, understood as a geopolitical space centered on the German and the Austro-Hungarian *Reichs* that would stretch down southeastern Europe, and achieve "a vital balance between the securing of the rights of individual nations—both majority and minority—and a unified overarching political community" (Pollock 2004, 338).[56] On my interpretation, more than proposing a new model of German imperialism, Rosenzweig is one of the first European thinkers to speculate on the process now generally known as "globalization" and on its politico-theological underpinnings.

Globus brings a *post-secular* conception of globalization together with the speculation of an "End" of history in both senses of the term, namely as history's purpose or aim, and its messianic interruption. This genre of post-Hegelian speculation received notoriety at the end of the 20th century with Francis Fukuyama's famous thesis that the neoliberal process of globalization established liberal democracy as the designated post-Christian goal of history.[57] Along with Antonio

[55] I refer to the French edition of these writings in (Rosenzweig 2003). Translations from the French are mine. See the treatment of this material in (Pollock 2004; Kartheininger 2006; Bensussan 2013; and Quélennec 2018). The most copiously documented treatment of Rosenzweig's wartime writings and correspondence remains (Herzfeld 2013). On Rosenzweig's political writings prior to the *Star of Redemption*, see the general sketch of (Mendes-Flohr 1988).

[56] See the text "Die neue Levante" on the emergence of Turkish nationalism in (Palmer and Schwartz 2003, 71–6).

[57] (Fukuyama 2006).

Negri and Michael Hardt's *Empire*, which countered Fukuyama's neoliberal "end of history" thesis from a post-Marxist perspective, Jacques Derrida and Jean-Luc Nancy construed the relation between Christendom and the process of globalization in terms of a tension between reason and faith, or technology and creation.[58] Compared with this literature, Rosenzweig's approach to the political theology of globalization is centered on the trajectory of Christian imperialism, its development into European nationalism, and its expansion of war to a planetary dimension.

Rosenzweig argues that with the foundation of the Petrine Church, the Christian religion came to understand itself as a geopolitical entity, as an ecumenical space that first "transforms the earth into a closed historical space" or "world" (2003, 39). The ecumenical space of the *res publica Christiana* was politico-theological from the start because it synthesized "the intimations of the [Hebrew] prophets" with regard to the ultimate political unity of the terrestrial globe (under the rule of the One God) with "the reality of [the Roman] Empire" in the age of Constantine (2003, 38). European history was thereafter determined by "the infinitely fruitful marriage between the Empire of the Christian Caesars and the Germanic peoples and national kingdoms" (2003, 39). This is the Christian ecumenical space of European public law (*jus publicum Europaeum*) that gives content to Schmitt's political theology.

One of the main reasons for the renewed interest in Schmitt over the last decades is that this Christian vision of Europe as ecumenical space has regained actuality with the project and gradual construction of the European Union as a post- and supra-national political space. European philosophers like Derrida, Nancy, and Habermas suggested that the "postnational constellation" inaugurated by the project of the United Nations gave rise to two forms of globalization, one propelled by the Anglo-American alliance, the other adopted by continental Europe. The former tied globalization with the imposition of a neoliberal free market world order.[59] The continental approach to globalization, instead, derives from the model of the Christian Empire "as a supranational political order, as the dynamic expression of the pact (*foedus*) among nations that make it up" (Cacciari 2016, 137). This Christian covenant or pact draws upon the Roman imperial ideal of a city (*urbs*) that grows over the earth (*orbis*) by providing "a safe haven for absolutely distinct peoples; it stands on its ability to renew the harmony (*concordia*) among the peoples and the groups who live in it" (Cacciari 2016, 137). This Roman idea of world peace is overlaid by a Christian understanding of the Trinity that rejects the Hellenistic idea of a world emperor as representative of the One God in favor

58 See (Derrida 1994b, 2000; Negri and Hardt 2001; and Nancy 2002).

59 For the construction of this neoliberal ecumenical space, see (Slobodian 2018), among others.

of the separation between the authority of the Church and the power of the Empire.

This Christian post-national global order underlies Schmitt's proposal to understand international law in the 20th century as a function of "great transnational spaces [*Grossräume*]."[60] Schmitt developed his account of Christian imperialism and its establishment of a Christian "*nomos* of the Earth" in two crucial books, the wartime *Land and Sea* and the post-war *Nomos of the Earth*. In 1955 Schmitt published an essay in Spanish with the title "The Planetary Tension between Orient and Occident and the Opposition Between Land and Sea" that updated his views.[61] In this article he explains why Christian European imperialism could be considered the "soul of the world," drawing from a passage in Hegel's *Philosophy of Right* where one finds the assertion that "the principle of family life is dependence on the soil, on land, *terra firma*. Similarly, the natural element for industry, animating its outward movement, is the sea."[62] Schmitt argues that "the house remains the nucleus and centre of terrestrial life, together with its concrete orders: house and property, matrimony, family and inheritance. All these concrete orders are born and grow upon the soil and under the stamp of terrestrial life, specifically agricultural life. The fundamental institution of law, *dominium* or property, receives its name from *domus*" (2014, section 5).

Anticipating Derrida's and Nancy's later description of globalization as an effect of the "technoscience" developed by the Anglosphere, Schmitt centers his discussion on what he calls the modern historical "challenge" brought about by "the freeing of technology as an autonomous force" that began with the Industrial Revolution. His well-known thesis is that the Anglo-American world was capable of fashioning the decisive "response" to this challenge in early modernity by embarking upon a "maritime existence": "faith in absolute progress is a sign of having accomplished this passage towards maritime existence. The reactions caught up in a continuous and limitless process of invention are born in the historical, social and morally infinite space of sea life. . . . The maritime image of the world is first and foremost technomorphic before being sociomorphic" (Schmitt 2014, section 5).

Schmitt opposes the Anglo-American maritime conception of empire to Spain's and Portugal's land-based imperial expansion that led to "the great territorial conquest [of the Americas]." As he says in *Nomos of the Earth*, "the last, great heroic act of the European peoples—the land-appropriation of a new world and of an unknown continent—was not accomplished by the heroes of the

[60] On Schmitt's understanding of globalized politics, see (Galli 2015), chapter 5, "Schmitt and the Global Era"; and on Schmitt's topology in comparison with Agamben, and Deleuze, and Guattari, see now (Simons 2016).

[61] (Schmitt 2015).

[62] (Hegel 1952, par. 257). The passage is cited in (Schmitt 2014, section 5).

conquista as a mission of the *jus commercii*, but in the name of their redeemed Christ and his holy mother Mary."[63] Christian European imperialism and colonialism, on this view, are the central instruments through which Christianity sought to rid the earth of paganism and polytheism, and thereby fashion one "world" or "globe" under the aegis of an account of divine love and grace for humankind, symbolized by the relation of the virgin Mother Mary to Christ as Son of God.[64]

Rosenzweig's history of Christian Europe in *Globus* contrasts starkly with Schmitt's later terrestrial political theology of globalization.[65] For Rosenzweig, globalization is driven by what could be called, borrowing a term from Stephen Holmes, "constitutional pre-commitments" that emerge in the Judeo-Hellenistic civilization preceding Christianity. Rosenzweig suggests that the European pre-commitment to a global constitutionalism does not stop at the frontiers of the *nationes et gentes* first united by the Roman Empire. Rather, global constitutionalism was initially figured by Alexander the Great's dream to extend the frontiers of the ecumenical space past the "internal sea" of the Mediterranean and across the entire globe through Asia and Africa. Alexander, not the Romans, pushed the idea of the Greek *polis* toward the form of a *cosmopolis* through the conquest of the open seas (Rosenzweig 2003, 82). In *Globus*, Rosenzweig argues that Alexander gave a Hellenistic form to the geopolitical vision expressed in Deutero-Isaiah, according to which the land-based empires are surrounded by a "limitless" sea that "prefigures the world's transnational unity" (2003, 80–1).[66] This transnational unity of humanity is what Rosenzweig refers to in the *Star* in terms of the properly messianic belief that "Creation, the work of divine omnipotence, is completed in the universal rule of law [*allgemeinen Rectszustand*] on earth" (Rosenzweig 2005, 373, translation modified).

Deutero-Isaiah envisages the establishment of God's Kingdom on earth, centered in Jerusalem, through the actions of a Messiah, identified as the Persian emperor Cyrus the Great, who allowed Jews to rebuild their Temple after the

[63] (Schmitt 2003, part V, ch. 2). In the 1955 article he writes: "The fact that the Reconquest of Spain was a conquest fought on behalf of the cults of the Virgin is not difficult to understand. But my own observation—that the discoverers and conquerors of the New World brought with them the sacred image of their historical deeds through the image of the Immaculate Virgin and mother of God Mary—does not seem to have been understood" (Schmitt 2014, section 1).

[64] For a discussion of this Christian project of world conquest from the perspective of the non-Christian peoples and nations, see (Hickman 2016).

[65] For a comparative reading of both texts, see now (Taub 2017), although Taub does not focus on the jurisprudential issues at stake.

[66] For a related meditation on the encounter of Alexander's Hellenism, Judaism, and globalization, see (Levinas 1996, 43–76). For Gérard Bensussan, Rosenzweig depicts Alexander as a "representative" of a third force at play in the formation of world history, the "biblio-prophetic or even oceanic, Jewish element" (Bensussan 2013, 121). The Roman-Christian ecumenical space, instead, proceeds by "a force for unification, an ecumenical force, and a force for world-formation through borders, war, and revolution" (Bensussan 2013, 129).

Babylonian captivity.[67] For Benjamin Pollock, this reference to the eschatological perspective of Isaiah allows Rosenzweig to open up the question as to the "meaning of history," that is, the question of its End, by identifying the historical process as simultaneously "imperialist" and "redemptive."[68] On Pollock's account, if Christianity is characterized by an "ecumenical" drive to empire-building by establishing the *nomos* of the earth, then the countervailing Jewish idea of messianism proposes that only "the ultimate realization of a global empire will mark the crowning event of the absolute history of the world between Creation and Redemption" (Pollock 2004, 352). In my opinion, Pollock's interpretation of Rosenzweig's reading of Isaiah as "an endorsement of imperialism" is too reliant on an orthodox doctrine of an omnipotent God who employs pagan emperors as "political guardians" of the Jewish people (Pollock 2004, 334), much like chess pieces working unconsciously to bring about an endgame of which they have no idea.[69] Such a reading is open to Walzer's objection that the prophetic text is at best idealistic, at worst naïve, about the realities of international politics. But Rosenzweig's wartime political writings cannot easily be accused of either shortcoming.

Rosenzweig's *Globus* seeks to clarify the relation between divine *nomos* and the problem of violent land appropriation. Schmitt had no compunction in pointing to the biblical idea of the "promised Land" conquered through a "holy war" to justify his imperial conception of European Christianity.[70] Drawing mainly from figures and motifs in the Book of Job, in *Land and Sea* he links the modern maritime form of imperialism represented by the Anglo-American "islands" with a negative, non-messianic interpretation of the biblical idea of the ocean: "According to the story of biblical creation, after land and sea were separated from one another man was assigned to land as a viable space. The ocean

[67] For the historical context of this attribution, see (Fried 2002). For Walzer, the rise of non-Jewish empires which threaten the existence of Hebrew monarchs gives rise to a prophetic discourse of "post-imperial international politics" whose ultimate aim is "a federation of peoples, each one free from all the others, united only by their mutual recognition of divine sovereignty" (Walzer 2012, 94–5). But for Walzer's philo-monarchic interpretation of biblical politics, this internationalist motif in prophetism is not in itself politically productive or affirmative: it simply reflects the fact that "the princes of Israel had already been brought to nothing" and the loss of sovereignty becomes radicalized in a denial of all agency to Israel on the international scene (Walzer 2012, 96–7).

[68] For Pollock, "it is God, according to Isaiah, who has 'subdued nations' for Cyrus. God has done so for the sake of his chosen people. . . . What appears as the battle for worldly powers . . . is in fact part of the divine plan to 'bare his holy arm in the eyes of all nations' so that 'all the ends of the earth shall see the salvation of our God' (52:10)" (Pollock 2004, 348).

[69] On the need of the Jewish people to stand in alliance with a non-Jewish political "guardian," see now the very interesting discussion in (Trom 2018) which intersects on many points with the themes of my interpretation of Rosenzweig. The discussion of our differences would merit further elaboration in a different context.

[70] In *Nomos of the Earth* Schmitt cites a passage in the book of Joshua (11:23), "So Joshua took the whole land, according to all that the Lord said unto Moses," as justification for the doctrine of conquest of the New World.

remained seen as something dangerous and bad" (Schmitt 2014, section 5). In effect, Schmitt reverses the polarities between land and sea that Rosenzweig established from the point of view of Deutero-Isaiah.

From the latter perspective, God's law is uprooting with respect to every *nomos* of the earth and demands a supra-national rule of law that covers humanity in its "oceanic" dimension. This is what in *Globus* Rosenzweig calls a "supranational organisation" under the aegis of the faith in "the God of whom it is written that He is a warrior created one heaven and one earth" (2003, 79). Rosenzweig's political theology is cosmopolitan because it argues that in order to unleash the "oceanic" messianic force of Deutero-Isaiah, constitutionalism needs to transcend the limits of the nation and structure the globe as such by dissolving the borders of *nomos* of the earth in the "oceanic," messianic idea of one humanity beyond all sovereign borders. If the Mediterranean Sea, encircled by land and conceived as the common space of free trade and commerce, is the maritime equivalent of the Roman Catholic *oikumene*, then Rosenzweig's messianic vision of the "ocean" opens an ou-topian perspective in which the multitudes of humanity that cross the European "inner" sea are not refugees and "illegal" migrants, but the new "vanguard" of a different global order beyond all Christianized forms of global imperialism, whether terrestrial or maritime, and where orientation is given by a new geopolitics of the star(s).

Geopolitics according to the star(s)

As discussed in the preceding, Schmitt claims that the concrete normative orders that compose the *nomos* of the earth "are born and grow upon the soil and under the stamp of terrestrial life, specifically agricultural life." The originary appropriation and division of land that is characteristic of this kind of *nomos* is ultimately for the sake of establishing a domestic, agricultural form of life.[71] Schmitt was aware that the European conception of "civilization," based on the "cultivation" of land, is from the start set off by a frontier beyond which lies "barbarism" or "savagery." The Romans distinguished clearly *limes* (frontier) from *terminus* (border), where the former term refers to the exterior frontier separating their empire and their civilization from the vast expanse of what they considered wilderness and savagery, and the latter term refers to the internal boundary that separated what is legally mine from yours, or property.[72] Whereas borders can

[71] For an alternative genealogy of *nomos* that is critical of Schmitt's pastoral account, see now (Zartaloudis 2019). A discussion of the extent to which this alternative genealogy is itself dependent on the Philonic interpretation of *nomos* as based on Greek Mystery religion and its Pythagorean philosophical translation would take me too far afield here.

[72] For a wide-ranging discussion of these terms, see (Dumezil 1968).

only be drawn from *within a common legal community*, and are consequently propped up by legality, frontiers function more like "fault-lines" drawn between a legal community and what lies outside its legal order.[73] The populations of subjects and citizens that fall within the common legal and land-based boundaries can engage in "civil" practices of war-making and diplomacy, according to the legal distinction between friend and enemy developed in the *jus publicum Europaeum*. Conversely, those populations that fall foul of these "amity lines" are considered "unjust enemies," to employ Schmitt's terms. Their killing is internally tied to fulfilling a religious duty, that is, they are an object of a "holy war."[74]

Rosenzweig's geopolitical and politico-theological interpretation of the Jewish divine *nomos* problematizes this Schmittian territorial logic. Rosenzweig begins his argument by developing a very different idea of agriculture and its relation to the divine *nomos* than the one presupposed by Schmitt. As discussed earlier, the messianic prayer requires understanding history as a process that is always open to its End, which must be "capable of coming as early as 'today.'" Rosenzweig's "today" refers to the *nunc stans*, or eternal moment which gives to the *aion* or life span of human life the symbolic form of a work week plus the Sabbath (Rosenzweig 2005, 307–9). The "week" stands for the "cultivation" of the human world, for the progress of culture, or *Bildung*. The Sabbath, on the other hand, stands for the day in which service is given here on earth to God's Kingdom by the "believing community" (Rosenzweig 2005, 310).

Rosenzweig's deconstruction of the concept of the *nomos* of the earth relies on the recovery of some controversial and obscure passages in the *Guide of the Perplexed* that Maimonides dedicates to the star worship of the Sabians, which is mentioned in an Arabic text on *The Nabatean Agriculture* (where the "Nabatean people" refers generically to populations in the ancient Near East, ranging from Egyptians to Canaanites).[75] Rosenzweig seems to refer to Maimonides' discussion when he writes:

> But not for nothing is the word for cultivation and worship, for the service of the earth and the service of God, cultivation of a field and cultivation of the Kingdom, one and the same in the holy tongue. The week is more than what it is as humanly established law of cultivation: it is an earthly simile of the eternal; as

[73] Schmitt's conception of *nomos*, minus its politico-theological assumptions, is thematized, formalized, and deconstructed as a "topology of legal orders" in (Lindahl 2013, 44–76). For a recent wide-ranging discussion of globalization and law, see now (Lindahl 2018).

[74] For critical discussions of Schmitt's topography of international law, see also (Legg 2011; and Minca and Rowan 2015).

[75] For a general treatment of the discussion on Maimonides' aims in his interpretation of the Sabians in *Guide* 2.26 and 3.29, see (Strousma 2009). Strousma argues that Maimonides understood the reason of the commandments that had no apparent purpose to lie in God's intention of weaning the Israelites from their pagan beliefs gradually; these beliefs were associated with the religion of the Sabians. On the traditions of the Sabians, see (Greene 1992).

divinely established law of worship, it draws the eternal into the today not only symbolically but in reality. (Rosenzweig 2005, 309)[76]

Agriculture is practiced by all "non-nomadic" nations and peoples as a condition of possibility not just for reproducing their lives, but also in order to assign culture and constancy to life amidst the flow of time. Agriculture is carried out in cycles, and the "cycles" of planets and stars (when considered from the earth as fixed point) form the center of religious life.

At the exoteric level, Maimonides seems to oppose the teachings of Abraham and Moses to those of the Sabians, whose pagan religion is described as if it were a compendium of Hellenistic, Neoplatonic beliefs, and duly excoriated. However, it is a well-rehearsed possibility in Maimonidean studies that the medieval Jewish philosopher may have esoterically employed the example of the Sabians to put forward a doctrine that is closer to his own mind.[77] In this sense, the reference to the Sabians in Maimonides, and by extension in Rosenzweig, is far richer in its significance. Following the hypothesis of Michel Tardieu and David Pingree, the Sabians may have been among the first people to develop the idea that a universal or natural religion (which later in the Renaissance receives the name of "ancient theology," *prisca theologia*) underlies the Abrahamic revealed religions.[78] On this hypothesis, their star worship in reality expressed the teachings brought to them by the Neoplatonist Simplicius, who seems to have settled and taught in Harran (Turkey/Syria)—the city-state of the Sabians—after the closure of the Athenian Academy by the Byzantine emperor Justinian. The Sabian religion would thus be a prophetic civil religion (the Sabians claimed Hermes as their prophet) based on the Pythagorean and Platonic teachings of ensouled stars and planets, forming the core of that religion of Mysteries which Goodenough claims was received by Philo and applied to the interpretation of the Torah.

These teachings were later transmitted through the Arab Hermetic corpus to the Italian Renaissance, where they were granted enormous resonance thanks to Ficino's translation of the *Corpus Hermeticum* and then in the aftermath

[76] On this topos in Jewish hermetic thought, see (Lelli 2007, 116ff), who follows indications by Moishe Idel on how and why Hellenistic Hermetic discourses were adopted within Judaism to give a philosophical yet not Aristotelian rational explanation of the Jewish faith. I discuss this point further in chapter 4 on Scholem.

[77] See Pines's "Translator's Introduction" in (Maimonides 1963; and Kreisel 2015) for examples.

[78] See the discussion in (Tardieu 1986). According to Pingree, the Sabians "pretended that they were practising an ancient universal religion of star and planet worship" (2002, 22). Jan Assmann identifies in Maimonides' reading of the Sabians the origin of the idea of a *duplex religio* (double but also duplicitous religion): one idea of religion based on faith and particularistic, the other idea of religion based on reason and universal (Assmann 2002). Assmann considers Maimonides' reading of the Sabians as a first instance of what he calls Enlightenment "paganology," according to which pagan polytheism cannot attain the "mystery" of oneness that is, instead, the "hidden" theology of Judaism. I propose here a different way in which Maimonides and then Rosenzweig attempt to harmonize paganism and monotheism.

of the Copernican Revolution.[79] For Pingree, the Sabians developed such a universal conception of religion out of necessity. They wanted to assure the survival of the Pythagorean-Platonic teaching through the different empires—Hellenistic, Persian, Christian, and Islamic—to which they were subjected. In this respect, it could be said that the Sabians shared a predicament analogous to that of the Jewish people with respect to the preservation of their Mosaic teachings.

One point about Pingree's interpretation of the Sabian religion is particularly important for my argument. The Sabian calendar assigned each day of the week the name of a planetary deity endowed with intelligence and agency, but their religion taught that over and above these planets and stars stands the "Oneness of God" who commands the movement of these astral souls. Thus, in the Sabian religion the pagan cycle of weekdays included a placeholder for the messianic Sabbath. Pingree cites al-Kindi to the effect that the Sabian religion transmits the (Judeo-)Hellenistic political theology according to which the One "undertook only the major task, leaving inferior matters to the mediators appointed by Him to administer the world."[80] In other words, it is likely that the Sabian religion mentioned by Maimonides was an esoteric reference to the Philonic understanding of the formula of Hellenistic political theology, "the king reigns but does not govern." The Sabian religion would then simply be a discursive construction intended to synthesize Platonic-Aristotelian philosophy and messianic monotheism in the form of a cosmopolitan political theology.

In the *Star*, Rosenzweig offers his own cosmopolitan interpretation of the agricultural metaphorology of the Sabian religion. On this interpretation, the earth is cultivated by all the nations of the world through their states and their arts, a process that is symbolized by the working week. Into this cultivated soil, the revealed monotheisms plant the "seed" of messianic politics, which corresponds to the cosmic Sabbath and its ideals of free, universal education and land redistribution. Rosenzweig's symbolism of the week, based on the astral-agricultural metaphor, suggests that there is an underlying unity between the Greek teaching of the Oneness of God and the revealed teachings on the messianic implications of this Oneness. The full week, symbolic of human history, comprises the days for the cultivation of pagan religion (and philosophy) together with the day(s) corresponding to the messianic Sabbath. The political meaning of the Sabbath is both revolutionary and cosmopolitan, thanks only to having its groundwork in the universality of agriculture and the (Sabian) cult of the stars that it gives rise to.

79 See (Yates 1991) and the subsequent debate on the sources and developments of the Copernican Revolution. For the Greek and Latin Hermetic corpus, see (Copenhaver 1992).

80 (Pingree 2002, 17–20).

For Rosenzweig, there can be no Star of Redemption without this astral theology because "the time which worship prepares for the visit of eternity is not the individual's time . . . it is everyone's time. Day, week and year belong to everyone in common; they are founded on the cosmic orbit of an earth which patiently bears them all, and in the law of the labor in it that is common to all. . . . 'In multitudes' he praises the Lord. The enlightenment which befalls the individual can here be none other than that which can befall all others too" (Rosenzweig 2005, 310, translation modified). Rosenzweig's post-secular messianic politics is ultimately addressed to the real universal multitude composed of all those people who cultivate and live from the land. The dynamics of capitalist globalization force them into wandering the face of the globe without a place of their own, kept outside national borders by walls or crowded into congested and polluted urban centers, turning every potential *polis* into a "megacity" that is the opposite of a messianic cosmopolis. For this reason there can be no post-secular messianic politics that does not begin with the demand to secure for all humanity the basic needs for water, shelter, food, and clean air, as well as access to hospitals and schools.

But the agricultural metaphor employed by Rosenzweig is crucial for another reason: it distinguishes the growth and development of the "trees" composed by the nations of the world from the messianic "seed" that gave rise to them but whose true "fruit" lies in the overcoming of national, religious, and ethnic divisions within humanity. The agricultural metaphor also frames Rosenzweig's critique of nationalism. The modern nation-state depends on a concept of the nation defined by a people's choice to "sink their roots into the night of the earth" for "they do not have confidence in the living community of blood which would not be anchored in the solid ground of the earth" (Rosenzweig 2005, 318). Whereas the cultivation of the earth is the basis of the division of the earth into separate nations, the world-historical Sabbath is carried by messianic peoples who do not divide up the common earth into property.

Leaving aside for the moment the elaboration of Rosenzweig's conception of a community of blood, and its relation to Judaism, the salient point is that for him messianic peoples cannot "live like the peoples of the world in a national life placed visibly in the world, in a popular language that expresses its soul resoundingly, in a national territory, solidly based and staked out on the soil" (Rosenzweig 2005, 323). Pursuing the agricultural metaphor to the point of paradox, Rosenzweig claims that "the seed of eternal life has been planted and can wait for the budding. The seed knows nothing of the tree that grows from it even if it overshadows the whole world. One day from the fruits of the tree there will come a seed like it" (2005, 355). In other words, the "seed" representing the messianic politics of revealed religions is meant to give rise to a different plant than the "trees" representing the nation-states: these trees grow on the land demarcated by their terrestrial *nomoi* but they do not correspond to the ultimate configuration of human geopolitics.

Biopolitics, racism, and the community of blood

Rosenzweig's post-secular political theology not only engages with the problem of nationalism and geopolitics, but also takes up the problem of modern racism and biopolitics. Rosenzweig was acutely aware of the biologization and racialization of politics in his age. As he writes in his early text on "Atheistic Theology": "He who is able to see through the pseudonaturalist wrappings of the race idea . . . recognizes here the striving to transform the concept of peoplehood in such a way that the people obtain the right to exist simply from their existence, independently of their factual achievements." [81] However, his belief that Jews constitute a "community of blood" is misconstrued if taken to mean that Jews should embrace the "apparent despiritualization of the people into a race, of the 'national' to the 'populist' notion [*zum völkischen Gedanken*]," which Rosenzweig explicitly rejects in the case of all other nations.[82] Indeed, "Atheistic Theology" is a text designed to criticize not only the Protestant "Life-of-Jesus theology" as legitimacy for racist nationalism, but also those attempts within Judaism to work out a "Judaism-of-the-people theology."[83] Rosenzweig's reconstruction of a messianic conception of "people" in Judaism and Christianity is aimed at opening a post-secular transition from nationalism based on "soil" to cosmopolitanism based on "blood."

Rosenzweig argues that the life of the Jewish people is not a "national life placed visibly in the world"; it is a form of life "released from the river of time, and since life is kept holy, it is no longer alive" (2005, 323). Instead, the "immortality of its life [consists] in the creating of its own eternity *out of the obscure source of blood*" (2005, 323). Rosenzweig's discourse on the community of blood is perhaps the single most controversial aspect of his political theology. While his critique of the nation-state form is rejected by advocates of political Zionism, who want to establish the "right" of the State of Israel to exist as a "normal" nation-state, his reference to a Jewish community of blood is often accused of harboring an ethnic particularism verging on racism and exhibiting an uncomfortable proximity to National Socialist *völkisch* ideology. However, I argue that

[81] (Rosenzweig 2000, 17); see the commentary in (Mack 2003).

[82] See the discussion in (Batnitzky 1999; and Mack 2003).

[83] For a defense of Rosenzweig in relation to the racism charge, see (Fackenheim 1994). For an excellent discussion of the problem of nationalism in Rosenzweig and the distinction between his conception of Jewish people as opposed to *völkisch* conceptions of Judaism in "Atheistic Theology," see (Hollander 2008, 170–6). For this complex of problems, where Christianity is linked to nationalism by way of "blood," see (Anidjar 2014).

the importance of Rosenzweig's political theology consists precisely in offering a way to engage these conceptual bases of modern nationalist populism and turn them against their *völkisch* articulation.

One interpretative strategy suggests that Rosenzweig's "notion of blood reacts only against philosophical concepts that set out to justify the shedding of blood for the political possession of land. He associated the earth with death and blood with life."[84] This line of thinking is found in Rosenzweig's text, but it does not go far enough to resolve the deeper dilemmas raised by the discussion of blood in the *Star*. The first problem is that, as shown earlier, the common possession of the earth and the basis of worship and cult in agriculture is the groundwork into which the messianic seed is planted. Thus, it is not correct to say that Rosenzweig stigmatizes the earth as such.

The second problem has been articulated by Slavoj Žižek: even if "Jews are constituted by the lack of land, of territory," their universalism or cosmopolitanism still remains partial, since "it reserves for itself a privileged position of a singularity with a direct access to the universal" (Žižek, Santner, and Reinhard 2013, 154). Emil Fackenheim already asked how Rosenzweig could avoid both "a natural determinism of the blood" and a "supernaturalist determinism of divine decrees," given that both imperil the freedom of Jews presupposed by their covenantal action. Fackenheim sees here a dilemma that Rosenzweig cannot resolve. Either the individual Jew is free to choose whether he or she remains a Jew, which means that the purported eternity of the "eternal people" is hostage to the choice of the individuals composing it, who could, after all, cease to follow the commandments of Moses or marry outside of the community of faith; or "Jewish existence" somehow precedes individual choice, but this would elevate Jewish "life" over Jewish "faith," a gesture that seems to turn Judaism into an *ante litteram* form of "identity politics."[85]

Eric Santner has shown that Rosenzweig's discussion of the foundations of Jewish "life" contains a form of biopolitics (Santner 2007, 19, 30). I would add that Rosenzweig's biopolitics adopts a republican idiom. Fackenheim's dilemma no longer appears quite as problematic if one looks at it from republican assumptions. From a republican perspective, a people can never be reducible to the aggregation of atomic individuals, just as the "will of the people" is not reducible to the sum of their choices. According to republican doctrine, the state of nature is not populated by a- or anti-social individuals prior to the establishment of human governments, as Hobbes taught, but by free peoples who have the right to assume "the separate and equal station to which the Laws of

[84] (Mack 2003, 130). This interpretative move was anticipated by (Cacciari 1985, ch. 1).

[85] (Fackenheim 1994, 83–4). The connection between Rosenzweig and "identity politics" is made by (Lilla 2016).

Nature and of Nature's God entitle them," as Jefferson stated in the *Declaration of Independence*.[86] Just like a republican conception of natural right sets out the natural yet legal conditions under which individuals can be considered citizens of a free people, so too Rosenzweig is after a natural yet legal condition for belonging to the Jewish people, understood as a people charged with harboring and transmitting the messianic ideal that all nations compose one humanity in the eyes of the One God.[87]

Rosenzweig finds this natural-yet-legal condition in the obligation of "procreation" (*Erzeugung*), understood as the demand to secure the transmission of the messianic "seed" by giving birth to future generations. The Jewish people are "preserved in the eternal self-preservation of the procreative blood [*der ewigen Selbsterhaltung des fortzeugenden Bluts*]" (Rosenzweig 2005, 362, translation modified). This form of biopolitics inscribed within the Jewish conception of filiation can be compared and contrasted with the biopolitics implicit in the Roman conception of filiation, where, as a condition for bearing legal rights, the child must be exposed to the absolute power of life and death held by the father.[88] In the case of the Jewish messianic community, the capacity to bear the law, or to have a *sui iuris* status, is given to the individual at birth and through natality itself. Since Rosenzweig argues that the Jewish divine *nomos* entails that those who partake of the covenant cannot be born "out of the earth," the transmission of "procreative blood" bypasses the distinction between natives and foreigners that is basic for the Schmittian "*nomos* of the earth." The same idea is also found in Cohen, for whom it is a trait of the Jewish conception of natural right that it denies the a priori validity of an essential distinction between natives and foreigners.

Rosenzweig distinguishes this biopolitical condition of the Jewish messianic peoplehood from the Christian condition of belonging to the messianic community, which requires that each individual, irrespective of his or her nationality, be "born again"—this time as witness (*Zeugnis*) to the "event" that God came on earth, died on the Cross, and was then resurrected (Rosenzweig 2005, 363). For Rosenzweig, no nationality as such can give access to a messianic community or peoplehood. No individual is born a Christian: the political body that gives rise to a Christian is the mystical one of Christ. That is why Christianity has as its destiny that of being a "missionary" religion: it must bear witness (*Zeugnis*) to the advent of the Messiah.

86 For this view, see (Skinner 2005; and Pettit 2005).

87 This approach does not require that "the blood community . . . marks the limit of philosophy itself" (Batnitzky 1999, 148). The "Laws of Nature" and "Nature's God" are, after all, both accessible to reason.

88 See the discussion of the Roman law formula *vitae necisque potestas* in (Agamben 1998, 87–90; and Esposito 2012).

But there is a sense in which no individual is born a Jew either, because being part of this people signifies having covenanted with God. As Elazer elucidates, the Sinaitic covenant has as its only purpose "to *actually create the new body politic* in which God assumes direct rule over Israel" (Elazer 1997, 8, emphasis mine). For Rosenzweig, this messianic political body is not a mystical body: belonging to its covenant is transmitted to each future generation merely through "begetting" (*Erzeugung*). That is why Rosenzweig says that, unlike the faithful Christian, the individual Jewish believer does not have "faith in something" but instead simply his or her life is itself "the having of faith" (2005, 363).[89]

Rosenzweig connects this account of natality as source of the Jewish sense of faith with the idea of the facticity of Revelation. That "God is the truth" can only be existentially demonstrated; that is, it must be "verified" by the individual in his or her own experience. This "verification" takes the form of a "rebirth" into a messianic form of life. Unlike in the Pauline interpretation of the messianic life, "the rebirth of the Jew . . . is not his personal one, but the re-creation of his people to freedom in God's covenant of the Revelation" (Rosenzweig 2005, 418). In other words, for the Jewish individual, the rebirth or verification of God as the truth occurs thanks to the people having covenanted with God on Mount Sinai: "the individual is from now on born into the Jew. . . . The decisive movement, the great now, the miracle of rebirth, lies before the individual life" (Rosenzweig 2005, 419). Through the covenant, and its tradition and authority, the individual is born into the Jewish people. It is not up to the individual's decision whether to be or not to be a Jew: "the Jew possesses in him and carries with him his being-Jewish before his own birth" (Rosenzweig 2005, 419). The freedom of choice, in this sense, is not an individual affair, but belongs to a people who freely chose to covenant with the One God and become His people. From Rosenzweig's perspective, an individual is free *because they are born* to such a people, and if so procreated, then they are also "re-born" to the original covenant. For the Jew, rebirth is a matter of birth, and birth is a matter of political freedom.[90]

Through this obscure politico-theological doctrine of natality, Rosenzweig tries to address a paradox that poses a difficult, perhaps insurmountable problem to the liberal belief in a social contract resting on individual freedom of choice. The problem is as follows: if a people is a function of the free choices that individuals make in order to join it, as per the liberal idea of the social contract, then no people can be free as a people. From the liberal perspective, to join a people, to covenant with others, is always a decision that cuts off some part of one's natural

[89] The distinction between the two kinds of faith is later formalized in (Buber 2003) and commented on in (Agamben 2005b).

[90] I discuss in chapter 6 on Arendt her analogous biopolitical conception of freedom that identifies natality as a condition for human freedom.

freedom.[91] That is why the choice of belonging to a people must be imposed on the individual at birth, prior to their conscious choice. No one chooses the country into which they are born, and everyone obeys its laws prior to being able to verify their legitimacy. Indeed, this verification can only be achieved counterfactually, through a thought experiment of the kind established by John Rawls's idea of the "original position."[92] The libertarian idea that the right to "exit" any community into which an individual has been cast is a fundamental individual right merely expresses the belief that belonging to any community whatsoever is by definition a limitation of one's freedom and thus the individual must have the right to withdraw from the community without thereby paying an undue cost.[93]

The problem with the liberal idea of the social contract also explains the sort of "evidence" on which rests the nationalist, populist, and racist refrain: "love it or leave it." This refrain reflects on the same "fact" that human beings are born "in chains." The refrain means to say that unless one comes to "love" these chains and accept that one has been unwillingly recruited into the community, then one cannot demand the right to willingly change its laws. Conversely, it also says that no matter how much one willingly changes these laws, this will only bind one all the tighter to the community, reasserting the initial, coerced fact of belonging to it. The refrain poses a paradox for the liberal individual: one cannot be a revolutionary unless one is a patriot first, but if one really becomes a patriot, then one will never be a revolutionary.

Rosenzweig's idea of a messianic community of blood tries to conceive of the possibility of a people whose fundamental reason for existing is to reverse the preceding paradox. On this view, the Jewish people is a people that identifies birth as the moment of maximal freedom, rather than an instance of sheer dependence and obedience to sovereign power, because in being born into this people, one is born into a covenant or agreement that not only permits but requires every individual to "break free" of any human source of domination. This would be one way to interpret the Hebrew expression for the covenant as *lichrot brit* ("to cut a covenant"): to become a part of the "Kingdom of God" on earth, one must have cut oneself off from the patriotic or nationalist demand to "love" one's nation above all. On this messianic view, one cannot be a patriot (in the sense of a member of the messianic community) unless one is a revolutionary first, but if one is truly a revolutionary first, then one will never be a patriot (in the sense of someone who lives in accordance to the dictum "love it or leave it").

[91] For discussion of this point from the perspective of justification of state coercion, see (Simmons 2001).

[92] See (Forst 2012).

[93] See (Kukathas 2003), and for recent discussion of the tensions between nationalism and liberalism, see (Levey 2014).

The problem of holy war and the messianic goal of peace

Hegel considered a people's right and capacity to engage in war against other nations the crowning point of a state constitution. In his early theological writings, he criticized Judaism and Christianity because as religions based on the "love of neighbor," and thus theoretically eschewing war-making, they also were incapable of giving their teachings a lasting constitutional form. Rosenstock-Huessy and Rosenzweig shared the opposite belief: the meaning of the revealed commandment to "love thy neighbor" provides the *revolutionary* foundation for the constitutionalization of the power of the state. However, Rosenzweig diverges from Rosenstock-Huessy by arguing that revealed religions of "love" are inseparable from the phenomenon of "wars of faith [*Glaubenskrieg*]" or "holy wars" (Rosenzweig 2005, 351).

For Rosenzweig, Christianity is essentially complicit with the rise of nationalism. Augustine had criticized the aspiration of pagan states to attain eternal life on earth, but he affirmed this aspiration for the representative of the "city of God," namely, the Apostolic Church. Rosenzweig identifies the Western origins of nationalism with the medieval adoption of the Christian belief in the eternity of the Church on the part of national states, such that every nation came to believe in its "chosenness" and "manifest destiny" (2005, 349–50).[94] The sacralization of the nation in early modernity made it possible for secular, political wars to be seen as "holy wars" (or "wars of faith" [*Glaubenskriegs*]) through the medieval device of "just wars." "The Holy War, war as a religious act, remained reserved for the Christian Era after the Jewish people had discovered it" (Rosenzweig 2005, 350, translation modified). This sanctification of secular, princely wars led to a radical divergence between the path of Western nationalism, now oriented toward "total" warfare (in the forms of colonialism, imperialism, and finally planetary war) and the Jewish people which "by living the eternal peace . . . stands outside of a warlike temporality [*kriegerischen Zeitlichkeit*]" (Rosenzweig 2005, 351).

The difference between Judaism and Christianity on this count is that whereas in the Jewish tradition the distinction between holy war and political war is "constitutionally distinguished," the Christian nations "cannot draw this fine distinction; they simply cannot know in how far a war is holy war, and in how far merely a secular war" (Rosenzweig 2005, 350). Furthermore, the Jewish people "has its war of faith behind it in a mythic past. Therefore all wars that it still experiences are purely political wars for it" (Rosenzweig 2005, 351). Since the Jewish people does not experience the dualism between "particularity and world-history," or between "earth and heaven," it lacks the motivation that enjoins going to war in

[94] This hypothesis is treated in an analogous way in Ernst Kantorowicz's text on *pro patria mori* (Kantorowicz 1984), and for commentary (Elshtain 1991).

the case of all other Christian nations: the Jewish people "does not know war" (349); "the Jew is really the only man in the Christian world who cannot take war seriously, and therefore is the only genuine 'pacifist'" (351).

The meaning of "war of faith" or "holy war" in the Bible is one of the most contested topics related to Jewish political theology. In Deuteronomy 20:15 a distinction is introduced as part of the Mosaic constitution between political wars engaged against faraway peoples and holy wars engaged in the "promised Land" of Eretz-Israel.[95] Why is this distinction introduced as part of constitutional law? Does this writing of war into the constitutional framework of the Hebrew Republic confirm Rosenzweig's point that modern constitutions emerge from revolution and war and end therein, or, to the contrary, does it somehow point beyond this internal relation between modern constitutions and war established from Machiavelli to Hegel?

Just like the opposition between blood and land, so too the opposition between "war of faith" and "war of politics" structures the difference between the Jewish people and the rest of the nations. Rosenzweig's discussion of holy war fits in with his response to the question of the relation between messianic politics and international war. My thesis is that Rosenzweig carries forward Cohen's interpretation of Jewish messianism as conducting a "war against [international] war." Rosenzweig gives a dialectical reading of this war-like opposition to war. The Jewish idea of "holy war" is a form of struggle against the "political war" employed by nations. This struggle leads the Jewish people, once their state is disbanded, to the prohibition from engaging in wars. However, the concept of holy war is later adopted without constitutional restrictions by Christianity in order to carry out political wars based no longer on pagan civil religion, but on a universalist messianic aim to realize Christ as *pantocrator*, as emperor of the world. How Islamic *jihad* fits into this picture adds an additional dimension to the problem of monotheism and war.

The conquest of Canaan as "promised Land" has been linked with a religious sanction for genocide and as the first conceptualization of an idea of "total war."[96] Walzer confirms that the Deuteronomists interpreted the *herem* or "ban" as requiring the complete destruction of the conquered cities and populations (Walzer 2012, 36–7). He hypothesizes that the constitutional inscription of holy war is because "the Deuteronomists insisted that all Israel's troubles had a single cause: the worship of Canaanite gods, the imitation of religious practices

[95] "Thus shalt thou do unto all cities which are very far off from thee, which are not of the cities of these [seven Canaanite] nations. But of the cities of these people, which the Lord thy God doth give thee for inheritance, thou shalt save alive nothing that breatheth: But thou shalt utterly destroy them. . . . That they teach you not to do after all their abominations" cited in (Walzer 2012, 43). Walzer calls this "the law of holy war."

[96] See the discussion in (Walzer 2012, 36ff), where he refers also to (Schwartz 1998).

abhorrent to Yahweh. And the reason for this endlessly reiterated sin was the continued presence of Canaanites in the land and the sexual intermixing of the two peoples. Hence the invention of the totalizing *herem* was probably a retrospective response to the dangers of miscegenation . . . making it [the *herem*] something like a functional equivalent of the ban on intermarriage" (Walzer 2012, 43–4). Maintaining his skeptical view of prophetic politics, Walzer points out that the warrior-kings of Israel did not always or perhaps ever put into practice such a holy war either in Canaan or elsewhere. Instead, they were content with adopting "a kind of international law" that sought to avoid "total war" (2012, 41). The idea of holy war, on Walzer's hypothesis, is merely the expression of the Jewish desire to distinguish its nation, based on a covenant with God, from that of all other nations, rather than to consider itself one nation among many, all of them submitted to the necessity of (limited) international war.

For Walzer, the "fantasy" of holy war and the banning of intermarriage are both, ultimately, a response to the perceived need to constitute the Jewish people into a "holy" community based on ritual purity: "holy community and holy war are related ideas. . . . The stronger the union, the greater the enmity" (2012, 48). The authors of Deuteronomy "retrospectively" imagined a total war having occurred against Canaanite tribes in order to assure a (counterfactual) degree of purity. The later prophetic narrative that requires Israel to trust in God's will and withdraw from all international politics follows from this opposition of "holy community" to a realist engagement with other nations in world history through the practice of secular wars.

The scholarly discussion on the biblical conception of the holy war was only developed in the beginning of the 20th century by German scholars. It was Friedrich Schwally who coined the term "holy war" (*heilige Krieg*) in relation to certain biblical texts, and the term was adopted by Max Weber in his book *Ancient Judaism* soon thereafter.[97] Weber's thesis is that the biblical "holy community" (*edah*) is in reality a conflation between a religious idea of *covenant* with God and a political idea of a *confederation or league* between distinct tribes (*Bund*, translation for *brit*, covers both meanings). The purpose of this confederation is the pursuit of war, but, because of its additional covenantal meaning, the war pursued by this Israelite confederation comes to be termed a "holy" war.

Unlike the reading proposed by Walzer, Weber's interpretation understands the covenant with God as functional for the constitution of a republican people-in-arms. The adoption of holy war is not the consequence of a "religious" ex post facto reconstruction of the "purity" or "holiness" of the *edah*, but exactly the opposite: it follows from the *political* need to establish in the Jewish people a constitution that allows them to engage successfully in war. Weber's interpretation

[97] See (Batsch 2004).

is far closer to Machiavelli than Walzer's because Machiavelli was the first, in modern times, to argue that a republic has more chances of survival if it fights with "arms of its own" rather than mercenary armies, and this in turn depends on trusting in a God "of one's own."[98]

In a later, influential interpretation, Gerhard von Rad explicitly draws out this republican connotation of the Jewish holy war by arguing that its constitutional inscription was introduced precisely in order to counter the royal or sovereign prerogative to engage in war with other nations.[99] For von Rad, technically speaking, a holy war can only be carried out by a republican people-in-arms, and must be led by YHWH Himself, in strict opposition to the royal wars that were initiated by the king and always relied on the aid of mercenary armies.[100] Even Walzer admits that the idea of holy war is a discursive, ideological reconstruction of historical events in Canaan whose intention was to resist the pro-monarchic ideology, but he gives a puritan and hierocratic explanation of this resistance to monarchy by seeing it as a religious drive to morally sanctify the *edah*, rather than understanding this resistance as an expression of a republican reading of the *edah*.[101]

This scholarly discussion on the meaning of holy war shows that the constitutional or republican delimitation of holy war supports Rosenzweig's hypothesis that Jewish messianism could *not* be imperialistic, whereas the Christian adoption of holy war, as my discussion of Schmitt shows, could *only* be imperialistic. If the Jewish idea of holy war is related to idea of the holiness or purity of the political body (*edah*), then it is only insofar as it aims to delimit and ideally put an end to discretionary wars initiated by kings and sovereigns. The distinction between holy war and political war is then best understood as contesting the principle that the fundamental characteristic of the human sovereign is the right to declare war at their own discretion (*jus belli*). With

[98] See (Vatter 2013).

[99] See the discussion in (Batsch 2004, 29).

[100] See the arguments in (Rad 1969). In chapter 6, I argue that Buber already suggested this interpretation of constitutional war in his discussion of YHWH as a military commander.

[101] Confirmation of the republican sense of "holy war" is given by the fact that this idea is recovered again at the time of the Maccabean Revolt, when a part of the Jewish people in Palestine identified itself as a "people in arms" leading a holy war against the Seleucid royal armies and their Jewish supporters (Batsch 2004, 31–2). I discuss the politico-theological significance of the Maccabean Revolt in 20th-century Jewish political theology in the next chapter. Batsch adopts the view on war found in the Book of Jubilees (probably written shortly after the Maccabean Revolt, and adopted by the Hasmonean dynasty), according to which war is to be considered "an anti-institution, a disorder" that undermines the pursuit of "purity" as fidelity to the divine Law (Batsch 2004). Far from a holy war resulting out of a drive toward purity, as Walzer claims, Batsch convincingly shows that this drive requires understanding all war as a form of pollution. It is therefore necessary to give up the practice of aggressive international wars—contra the ambitions of Jewish monarchs—and engaging in war is only permitted as a function of resistance to the human usurpation of the "place" of divine sovereignty.

respect to the ban on intermarriage, which Walzer links closely to the idea of the holy war, this should be understood, again, in republican terms. First, this ban serves to keep under control or resist the principle of intermarriage as formative of dynasties (which is the basis of European, Christian monarchies and empires). Second, the ban reflects the republican idea of a community of blood which rejects the belief that all human beings are necessarily born into a "nationality" and thus under the control of a state as opposed to being born to freedom. In sum, Walzer argues that human kingship is better than prophetic theocracy because the former "normalizes" the state of war that is characteristic of international relations and also opens up the possibility of regulating war through international law.[102] Rosenzweig, instead, is interested in the possibility of constitutionally inscribing the messianic task to "go to war against war," which in this case takes the form of pitting a constitutionally delimited idea of holy war against the discretionary capacity for warfare of sovereignty.

How does the Islamic conception of *jihad* figure in relation to the Jewish and the Christian ideas of holy war, particularly considering Walzer's hypothesis of "religious" purity leading to "total" war? Traditionally, in Islam *jihad* means to "strive" against a visible enemy, the devil, or certain unworthy aspects of oneself. Additionally, it means to promote "God's Kingdom on earth," which can also be undertaken in the form of a "*jihad* of the sword" that entails "defending Islam and propagating the faith," although mainly this "lesser *jihad*" of "warring in the path of God" is restricted to a fight against apostates.[103] The traditional interpretation of *jihad* is that with the first Mecca revelations, when the community of believers (the *umma*, the Islamic equivalent of the *edah*) was still weak, the prophet stressed the avoidance of conflict and an orientation toward peace. In this sense, the first sense of *jihad* falls in with the Jewish tendency toward the prohibition of all war after the Maccabean Revolt. Only after the first persecutions and the Medina revelations does Muhammad start to teach that war for defensive purposes is divinely sanctioned. As the *umma* continues to grow, further revelations seem to warrant that "war against non-Muslims could be waged virtually at any time.... God was, in effect, preparing and guiding his community for the role of world conquerors" (Firestone 1999, 50).

In his study on the Islamic *jihad*, Reuven Firestone rejects the traditional view and suggests a new hypothesis. The expansion of the *umma* required extending the revealed doctrine of brotherliness or solidarity beyond the boundaries of

[102] A similar "realist" or "monarchist" critique of the problem of holy war is developed by Suzanne Stone in her description of the Halakha as a rabbinical construction of "transnational legal culture" in the absence of a proper state, whose finality is to place war under international law (Stone 2012, 342).

[103] See (Firestone 1999, 16–7).

kinship relations. "Because kinship no longer functioned exclusively in defining mutual relationships within the innovative political *umma*, the members of the new community were able to—indeed were forced to—define relationships increasingly in ideological terms . . . the members of the *umma* . . . could easily view themselves as ideological comrades, even ideological 'brethren'" (Firestone 1999, 129). Here appears the first important difference with the Jewish model of the holy war. Rather than holiness (viz., adherence to God's revealed law) serving the political aim of constituting a free people-in-arms, in the Islamic case it is the absorption of foreigners into the *umma* that requires turning the content of the revelation into something like a (civil) "religion" for the new political community. This is also what Rosenzweig means when he claims that only Islam was consciously constituted as a "religion" for purposes of political "foundation" (of the *umma*). Despite this difference, the idea of Islamic *jihad*, just like that of Jewish holy war, lies at the antipodes of Walzer's hypothesis that holy war is a "religious" construal of war.

According to Firestone, because this new community of "brothers" no longer relied on economic relations of sustenance based on kinship, it had to resort to the institution of the "pre-Islamic tribal raid." In other words, the prophet had to make a place for aggression toward those who were not part of the *umma*: this corresponds to the "pagan" moment in Islam that Rosenzweig points out. The burning political question then became, who should be raided? According to Firestone, the answer given by the prophet turned out to be: the *umma* must raid their own Arabic kin and the Meccan tribe. "It was felt that some higher authority was required to justify violation of the prohibition against attacking one's own kin," and thus this kind of internecine raid became designated as a holy form of war (Firestone 1999, 131). If holy war in Judaism is intended to maintain the Jewish people apart from international wars, the Islamic *jihad*, on this reading, *internalizes international war* within the *umma* itself. It is an assertion of aggression, but still a limited one, because aggression is directed against those people who are of one's own kind, rather than complete strangers. Again, the pursuit of a "holy" community (*umma* or *edah*) is not intended to "totalize" and "export" the activity of war, pace Walzer. "The Muslim believers were fighting the pagan Meccans, whatever their kinship relation, because the latter represented an enemy bent on destroying the Muslims, God's prophet, and God's religion itself" (Firestone 1999, 133). If this hypothesis is correct, then the Islamic *jihad* is far closer in spirit to the Jewish holy war than to the Christian variant. Like the Jewish holy war, it is also a way to contain and eventually abolish the capacity to wage wars against other nations, compared with the Christian idea of the holy war, which ultimately entails the sanctification of international and imperial war against non-Christian peoples and nations.

Beyond Christianity: Islam, theological enmity, and the Jewish *katechon*

In the *Star of Redemption*, Rosenzweig does not assign an analogous politico-theological role to the Islamic prayer in the messianic logic of history, as he does the two other Abrahamic monotheisms. In the systematic structure of the *Star*, the discussion of Islam in six sections of Part Two plays a "mediating" role between the critique of pagan philosophy that occupies Part One and the account of redemption based on Jewish and Christian messianisms that occupies Part Three. Interpreters like Schwartz and Cristaudo claim that Rosenzweig situates Islam closer to pagan monotheism in order to reject it as a second-order religion, more "political" and "civil" than "theological" or "redemptive."[104] Schwartz relies on Shlomo Pines's hypothesis, in his famous essay on "Der Islam im Stern der Erlösung," according to which Rosenzweig's depiction of Islam is itself dependent on Hegel's interpretation of Islam.[105] The latter, in turn, relies on Maimonides' engagement with the Arabic *Mutakallimum* (Schwartz 2003, 127–8). The transmission of medieval Islamic philosophy to German Idealism brought "the classic legacy of pagan philosophy" back into modernity in the form of a "monistic paganism." Schwartz and Cristaudo assume that Rosenzweig rejects this proximity of Islamic and Greek philosophy. But their assumption is premised on holding on to a *linear and progressive* understanding of Redemption as being the farthest point from Creation. They believe that Islam and its messianic discourse do not fit with Rosenzweig's purported aim to prioritize the "sisterhood" of Judaism and Christianity, a dualism according to which the believer is either "on the way" to God, like in Christianity, or the believer is "always with" God, like in Judaism (Schwartz 2003, 146–7).

Yet, given Rosenzweig's affirmative understanding of the relation between Hellenistic cosmopolitanism and Jewish messianism that I discussed earlier, it makes little sense to think that he considers Islam's proximity to Hellenism as something in need of being criticized. Far from Redemption being about a

[104] Schwarz chastises Rosenzweig for his claim in *The New Thinking* that Judaism and Christianity "were originally something wholly 'unreligious,' the one a fact, the other an event. . . . Only their parody, Islam, is religion from the very start and does not want to be otherwise; it is consciously 'founded'" (Udoff and Galli 1999, 91–2). He also mentions Rosenzweig's infamous claims in the *Star* that Islam is "a remarkable case of world-historical plagiarism," cited in (Schwartz 2003, 138, 140). Cristaudo applauds Rosenzweig's supposed "critique" of Islam: "Yet the Muslim is . . . also and ever fundamentally the ally of the pagan—indeed, for the energies that Islam responds to and works with are never, for Rosenzweig, more than the energies of Creation. It is the pagan that the Jew must most stringently define himself in relation to; it is the pagan whom he most seeks to alert the Christian to seeing in his or her temptation. For what is redemptive in Christianity for Rosenzweig comes purely from the Jewish side, for the Jewish faith is the faith of the elect whose entire election is built on nothing less than the revealed promise of Redemption" (2012, 409).

[105] See (Pines 1987–9; and Lehmann 1993–4).

"reversal" of Creation through the miraculous irruption of the Revelation of Christian "love's salvaging power" (Cristaudo 2012, 407), my hypothesis is that Rosenzweig understands Redemption in far more Machiavellian, or neo-pagan, terms of turning around the process of modern secularization that Christianity has set off, and in so doing "returning to the beginning" of Creation.[106]

On my hypothesis, Greek philosophy and Islam acquire an entirely different value and location in Rosenzweig's system: far from being "excluded" or "left behind" by the Christian revelation, they become gateways to the true End, which is found at the Beginning. Reversing the historical direction that Christianity gave to Redemption turns out to be the real content of Jewish messianism and the role it plays in the Christianized world. The cosmic rotations of the starry heavens are internally related to the messianic teaching of the *Star*. Rosenzweig follows al-Gazali and Halevi in their belief that the retrieval and cultivation of Greek philosophy within medieval Arabic and Islamic thought posed the condition of possibility for the planting of the messianic seed in paganism. As a consequence, the transmission of Hellenistic "astral theology" by Arabic medieval philosophy, which played such a key role in the Renaissance and in particular in Machiavelli's republican critique of revealed religions, needs to be re-evaluated in a positive sense to understand the project and teaching of the *Star*. Rosenzweig simply does not understand the messianic role played by Christianity and Judaism in anti-pagan and supra-political terms.[107] If this hypothesis is correct, then the conventional claim according to which Rosenzweig "condemns" Islam must also be entirely reconceived.

Those interpretations that claim Rosenzweig assigns a messianic priority to the "sisterhood" of Judaism and Christianity over Islam often refer to the following passage:

> Before God, therefore, both Jew and Christian are workers on the same task. He cannot dispense with either. Between the two, he set an enmity for all time, and yet he binds them together in the narrowest reciprocity. To us he gave eternal life by igniting in our heart the first of the Star of his truth. He placed the Christians on the eternal way by making them hasten after the

[106] In construing the claim to universal love on the part of Judaism and Christianity in terms that exclude Islam and paganism, Cristaudo ends up accepting Anidjar's reading of Rosenzweig's philosophy as a discourse of theological (and political) enmity (Anidjar 2003). Ironically, Cristaudo stages a polemical rebuttal of Anidjar's reading, which he accuses of being "fascistic" (Cristaudo 2012, 138–40). Anidjar and Cristaudo share a common assumption that Rosenzweig's political theology is anti-pagan.

[107] Cristaudo claims that for Rosenzweig "modern representative states . . . have been Christianized—and thus for Rosenzweig touched by the living God of the Jews." These states support the individual whereas he compares ancient states with totalitarian ones in which "those individuals have disappeared" (2012, 165). This characterization of Christianity paradoxically transforms it into a universal form of political religion.

> rays of that Star of his truth into all time until the eternal end. (Rosenzweig 2005, 438)

This passage harkens to the Pauline idea in Romans 11:28, according to which Jews are "as regards the gospel . . . enemies of God." This idea plays an important role in Rosenzweig's articulation of the difference between Jewish and Christian messianisms.[108]

Despite its imbrication with modern nationalism and imperialism, despite its adoption of an aggressive interpretation of the holy war, Rosenzweig nevertheless argues that Christian messianism also harbors a post-national dimension thanks to its conception of brotherliness or solidarity that "takes men as it finds them and yet binds them together across differences of sex, age, class, and race. Brotherliness connects people in all given circumstances—*independently of these circumstances, which simply continue to exist*—as equals, as brothers 'in the Lord'" (Rosenzweig 1985, 344, emphasis mine).[109] In light of the problem of divine violence and holy war discussed earlier, the question emerges as to the relation between the Christian drive to universal brotherhood and the Jewish and Islamic discourses on holy war.

Jacob Taubes, in a well-known exchange with Schmitt, provided one possible connecting link by claiming that Paul's doctrine of the "enmity" set by God between Jews and Christians is the prototype of the "political" conception of the enemy.[110] Following Taubes's hypothesis, God's "enmity" toward Jews would be related to their refusal to pursue the messianic Kingdom through international wars. By the same token, the same Paulinian paradigm suggests that Christians ought to have recourse to the category of holy war in pursuit of their own messianic end of universal fraternity. Žižek's claim that the authentic messianic standpoint should adopt the principle of Christian love and universal fraternity but practice it with "excessive cruelty as its necessary obverse," where this "cruelty" is represented by the Jewish idea of holy war, develops further Taubes's hypothesis (Žižek, Santner, and Reinhard 2013, 189).

Gil Anidjar's critique of Rosenzweig's treatment of Islam offers another answer to the relation between Christian brotherliness and the problem of holy war. Anidjar argues that whereas Rosenzweig affirms the Pauline idea that places Christianity and Judaism in a relation of "theological" enmity, he places Islam and Judaism in a relation of "political" enmity: "enemies both, the Jew and the

[108] For discussions of Rosenzweig's messianism in relation to the contemporary debate on Saint Paul and Jewish messianism, see (Bielik-Robson 2014; and Palmer 2015).

[109] Rosenzweig is paraphrasing the basis of Paulinian universalism contained in the concept of the *hos me* ("as if not") in 1 Corinthians 7:29–32, later analyzed by (Taubes 2003; and Agamben 2005b).

[110] See the excellent discussion in (Rosenstock 2014). I address Taubes's claims on Jewish messianism in more detail in the next chapter on Scholem.

Arab receive distinct determinations, one military and political, the other theological" (2003, 35). This reading of Saint Paul sets the context for Anidjar's claim that Rosenzweig's political theology "made Islam the political enemy" of Jews (2003, 98) because it considers Islam to be "failing in its religious dimension, failing as a religion," and consequently Islam can only be "war, 'pure political' war" (2003, 88).

Anidjar's damning judgment relies on the assumption that Rosenzweig separates monotheistic "theology" (by which is meant a doctrine on suprapolitical doctrine of messianic redemption) from the pagan understanding of "politics" (based on the belief that the gods are always the gods of the city, and political enemies of the city are thereby also its religious enemies). Previously I showed that Rosenzweig does not share this assumption. Rather, he understands Judaism and Islam in far closer proximity to pagan understandings of republicanism and does so in order to place both in contrast with the Christian adoption of international warfare as the vector for its messianic aims.

It is not through the category of holy war that one can understand Rosenzweig's interpretation of Saint Paul's idea of a "theological enmity" between Jews and Christians. Instead, this enmity should be understood as a function of a struggle between two conceptions of the *katechon* or "restraining power" that keeps the Anti-Christ from manifesting itself in history.[111] Theological enmity is inherent in the idea of the Messiah because of the problem of its proximity to the Anti-Christ. Erik Peterson explains the katechontic or restraining function of the Catholic Church as a function of the non-arrival in secular history of the Parousia. For Peterson, the historical sign of the "not yet" of Redemption is none other than the fact or, better, the "mystery" of the ongoing historical existence of the Jewish people, despite their not having a state of their own to protect them, despite their rejection of international war, and despite their millennial history of exclusion and persecution. Thus, for Peterson there is "history" because the Jewish people *resist* converting to Christianity, because they refuse to recognize that "Jesus is the Messiah." Peterson's view on Jewish "stubbornness" is dialectical: the Jewish religion, in its very hoping for the arrival of the Messiah, is to be understood not so much in opposition to the Catholic Church but as an indication that the Church needs to open itself to those who have been excluded. Judaism forces the Church to become more universalistic, more messianic by taking up the critique of the state on the part of democracy, and especially of the poor. This part of Peterson's Catholic political theology is later developed by Liberation theology and by German political theologians like Jean-Baptiste Metz and Helmut Moltmann, and its echo is strongly felt in Jürgen Habermas's political theology. Having said that, Peterson's narrative of historical progress remains

[111] For a recent discussion of the Pauline idea of the *katechon*, see (Cacciari 2017).

"eliminationist" in the sense that it is only when the Catholic Church will have become truly universal, and in that sense will have absorbed all Jews into its mystical body, that "history" will come to its proper "End."[112]

Rosenzweig's political theology is katechontic in a parallel but inverse way to that of Peterson.[113] His main insight, which he experienced existentially in his rejection of conversion, is that "history" as *saeculum* exists only because Christians *resist the eternity of Judaism*, and that is why the messianic reality (when all humanity shall worship the One God) is "not yet."[114] Like Peterson, Rosenzweig also proposes an interesting dialectic between Judaism and Christianity. Christianity is the religion of the messianic "present" in history, whereas Judaism is the religion of the messianic sense of "future," that is, of eternal life. The continued existence of the Jewish people shows that Christians will never attain the End (viz., true knowledge and love of God) but are destined to remain "on the Way" to God. From this perspective, it is the Christian standpoint that somehow stands in the way of the coming of the Messiah.

Rosenzweig's discussion of the post-secular function of Christianity begins, significantly, with a citation from Maimonides, who distinguishes the "true Messiah" from the "great deception of worshipping another besides God," that is, from the faith in Jesus as Christ (2005, 357). Rosenzweig recovers the source of perplexity for Jews identified by Maimonides: the fact that after Jesus the "whole world has become full of the messianic idea." The "perplexity" that brings the Jewish tradition into crisis is constituted by the fact that a false messianism has been accepted universally by nearly all pagan peoples, thus sharpening the Pauline conflict between Christians and the "eternal people" on a world-historical level. It is crucial to note that Rosenzweig identifies the perplexity that led Maimonides to write his *Guide of the Perplexed* not with the recovery of pagan philosophy, nor with the growth of Islam, but with the success of Christian messianism, and, secondarily, with its influence on Judaism in the radical developments of the Kabbalah.[115]

For Rosenzweig, the universal spread of Jewish messianism in a spurious form takes two shapes: as Pauline theology and as Sabbatianism. In the former case, "our commandments are certainly true but no longer legally in force" (2005, 357). Here Rosenzweig also alludes to Spinoza's thesis that divine commandments are

[112] See here the critique of Peterson's views on Judaism in (Agamben 2011).

[113] For an attempt to address in parallel Jewish and Christian political theologies from Cohen to Metz and Moltmann, but without considering the problem of the *katechon*, see (Mittleman 2009, 202–56).

[114] Rosenzweig says that Yom Kippur, the Day of Atonement, is the only day that Jews kneel to God hoping that one day "every knee will bend before God, where all idolatry will have disappeared from the earth. . . . [And] everything takes up the yoke of His Kingdom"; to take up this yoke means nothing other than all peoples will make "one single covenant to do God's will with a whole heart" (Rosenzweig 2005, 343–4).

[115] These motifs are discussed at length in the next chapter on Scholem.

exclusively legal-political and that without a Jewish state, they are not applicable. In the case of Sabbatianism, the commandments are believed to hide secrets "and nothing can be understood in the plain literal sense, and that at one time the Messiah came and made manifest that which is secret" (2005, 357). Anticipating Scholem's rewriting of the history of Judaism from the perspective of spurious messianism, Rosenzweig suggests a messianic reading of Maimonides, seeking the key to understanding the role played by the "deception" of the Christian Messiah in attaining the true form of eternal life. He poses the question: how does the "deception" of the Christian Messiah further the aims of Jewish messianism, namely, "clearing the way for the royal Messiah who will establish the world upon the service of God" (2005, 357)? Anticipating Strauss's controversial political readings of Maimonides, Rosenzweig for a second time associates divine providence with a "deception" or "noble lie" on the part of God. Except that here it is Christianity as a whole (not, it is noteworthy, Islam) that serves as God's "noble lie."

Although spurious, Christian messianism serves the ultimate cause of messianic peace by breaking with the cyclical character of state government in order to "conduct through time" all nations toward the "End" of the true messianic age and eternal life. The post-secular significance of Christianity lies in that "it must master time" for the nations of the world because, unlike the eternal people, these nations cannot "create their own time and thus make themselves free from time" (Rosenzweig 2005, 357). The messianic function of Christianity consists in "mastering" the empty flow of time through its concept of the *saeculum* (Rosenzweig speaks of the "epoch"), which stretches the eternal moment of the *nunc stans* into the historical period following the first Coming of Christ and lasting until the End of times. "All the time that succeeds, from Christ's earthly sojourn to his second coming, is now that sole great present, that epoch, that standstill. . . . Time has become a single way, but a way whose beginning and end lie beyond time" (Rosenzweig 2005, 359).

In his famous discussion of secularization, Löwith blamed the reception of the Jewish idea of messianism and its orientation toward the Future for the rise of the modern historicist belief that salvation will come, not at the End of history, but in and through its indefinite progress. To modern philosophy of history based on unending progress into the future, Löwith opposed the orthodox Christian belief that the Christ already came once in history and the radical singularity of this event took away any redemptive force from whatever happened in history after that event. Rosenzweig's thesis on secularization is slightly different from Löwith's. He shares the belief that the utility of Christianity lies in its testimony that nothing historical can be saved from itself because the End of history is not in history, as Benjamin would later argue. But he rejects the claim that Christianity is, in any way, connected to the End of redemption. The End of redemption is certainly not the Second Coming of the Christ.

Rosenzweig understands Christianity as propelling a process of secularization that, although entirely disconnected from the End of history, nonetheless accelerates its coming insofar as it "eternalizes" the present by turning history into the "way" to redemption. Thus, every single historical event "stands in the center between beginning and end of the eternal way and through this central position in the temporal interval kingdom of eternity, every event is itself eternal" (2005, 360). In this sense, Christian messianism has the task of arresting the empty flow of time and bring the progression of time to a "standstill." Benjamin's interpretation of the Baroque Christian *Trauerspiel*, for which all of history becomes "natural history," works out one possible implication of Rosenzweig's hypothesis. Benjamin's later interpretation of Baudelaire and *la modernité* as "drawing out the eternal from the transitory" works out another implication of the same hypothesis. As paradoxical as it may sound, Rosenzweig's post-secular reading of Christian messianism understands it as a historical force that disabuses nations and peoples of their secular faith in progress.[116]

Thus, for Rosenzweig, the Christian Messiah only has an intermediary, not an eschatological role. It is one thing to say that Christianity seeks to bring history to a standstill, and an entirely different proposition to claim that in Judaism history and time are themselves reversed or revolutionized. This second, properly eschatological task is the one Rosenzweig assigns to the post-secular idea of Jewish messianism. Christianity will never attain the End of history: at best, it can prepare the nations of the world for this End, much in the same sense that for Marx capitalism brings pre-history to an "end" and is thus preparatory for authentic communism, in which everything will be, perhaps ever so slightly, reversed.

To conceive the unique character of Jewish messianism, Rosenzweig turns to Maimonides one last time, and tackles what is perhaps the thorniest question of all within a philosophical account of Judaism, namely, the question as to the esoteric meaning of the relation between the Account of the Beginning (Creation) and the Account of the Chariot (Redemption). Maimonides said that these two accounts stand to each other like physics (nature) to metaphysics (God). Picking up this suggestion, Rosenzweig advances the stunning hypothesis that "Creation is really already Redemption" (1985, 443). Redemption is only possible on the condition that God as Creator of Nature is also Nature's God.

[116] In contrast, Rosenzweig claims that the Sh'ia conception of the Twelfth Imam is more supportive of a conception of history as progress: "That the kingdom is 'among you,' that it is coming 'today,' is a notion of the future which eternalizes the moment. And it is this notion which expires in the concept of eras, the Islamic as well as the modern one. True, the ages form an endless sequence here, but endless is not eternal" (Rosenzweig 1985, 226). Compared with Christian messianism, Islamic messianism is a modernist variant.

In the "system" of the *Star of Redemption*, philosophy correlates to the doctrine of Creation, theology to the doctrine of Revelation, and political theology to the doctrine of Redemption. The *Star* begins with an initial anti-Hegelian motif, according to which it is not (Christian) theology that anticipates the truth of philosophy, as Hegel's system has it, but rather that true pagan philosophy is always already "prophetic" in that it announces the End, the messianic age. Rosenzweig concludes the *Star* with the reverse claim, namely, that the messianic End is attainable only in a "return to the beginnings" of pagan philosophy: this is the possibility preserved by Jewish messianism.

The Jewish *katechon* reveals its meaning most properly if understood as a "return to the beginning" of philosophy. In their community of learning and prayer, the Jewish people brings about a "strange inversion . . . of the temporal sequence" such that its ethico-political reality, by "constantly anticipating the End," turns this End of Redemption back onto the beginning of Creation: "in this reversal it [the life of the eternal people] *denies time as resolutely as possible* and places itself outside of time" (Rosenzweig 2005, 442–3). On this account, progress toward Redemption is achieved by *going against* historical "progress" and turning time around, deconstructing history backward toward Creation.[117] As Rosenzweig says: "to reverse a between [the Christian *saeculum*] means to make its after into the before, its before into the after, the end into the beginning, the beginning into the end. And the eternal people does that" (2005, 443). This formulation echoes Nietzsche's doctrine of eternal recurrence, and it provides the context for Strauss's critique of historicism and his question, Progress or Return?[118] The salient point is that Rosenzweig's Jewish political theology depends on this positioning of Redemption, not at the End of history, but at its very beginning (in Creation, so to speak), in order to actively deny meaning to "progress" (that is, to all secularized ideals of a *Heilsgeschichte*). For if Creation is already Redemption (and this may have been also Maimonides' teaching), then the very concept of historical progress is a contradiction in terms: progress only takes us away from Redemption, rather than bringing it about.

The Jewish conception of the messianic undoes Saint Paul's antinomianism because what is "temporally only a starting point, the [divine] law, this it sets up as the goal" (Rosenzweig 2005, 443). The divine law that is found at the beginning, in Creation, and that will be recovered equally by all creatures at the End of time, is a form of natural right. For Rosenzweig, just like for Cohen, a

[117] Benjamin will later adopt this thesis and radicalize its implications in his *The Concept of History*, where he speaks of *apokatastasis* and *reductio ad integrum*. In this sense, the "eternal life" of the messianic community must be understood as an "active denial" of the belief that historical distance is productive of truth.

[118] Both (Pollock 2009, 276–8; and Gibbs 1998) miss the movement of eternal return in Rosenzweig.

secret and mutual understanding between Greek philosophical conceptions of the law of nature and Jewish religious conceptions of divine law lies underneath the apparent division between Athens and Jerusalem. By itself, "Athens" is characterized by the worship of pagan gods, which signifies a worship of the state and of the arts, of "civilization." By itself, "Jerusalem" stands for the belief that "He who thrones in heaven mocks" both the state and the arts. But together, Athens and Jerusalem reveal how the all too human work of "civilization" is opposed by "the quiet effectiveness of created nature," or, what is the same, "divinely ruled nature" (Rosenzweig 2005, 444). Systematically speaking, for Rosenzweig, Islam is the way by which the authentic approach to Greek philosophy is brought back into modernity, and, for the same reason, it can also be the pathway for an inverse exodus from Christian modernity back to the truth of pagan philosophy. But "divinely ruled nature" grounds the conviction that all human beings are created equal and are endowed with inalienable or innate right. In this sense, the "reversal" of progress, the return to beginnings, suggests that the goal of all philosophical politics is the fulfillment of natural right. With these Rousseauian-sounding claims, Part Three of the *Star* literally rejoins the Third Book of the *Guide*, and God's government is seen to be most active in and through (created) Nature and its orders, and opposed to all (Gnostic) ideals of an absolutization of human progress and self-creation.

Rosenzweig prepares Strauss's project—which the latter will pursue on the path of return to Maimonides and then Plato—of showing the politico-theological meaning of the fact that divine truth operates through natural right:

> This truth because it has everything lying at its feet as one single vast nature, can show *his share to everyone and therefore put the universe in order.* As long as both state and art, each for itself, need to be regarded as omnipotent, just so long as they each also, and rightly, claim all of nature for themselves. They both know nature only as their "material." Only truth, because it circumscribed both, the state in eternal life [of Judaism], art in the eternal way [of Christianity] *could free nature from this twofold slavery and make it one again*, in which state and art might now receive their share, but not more. And truth—from where else should it draw its pillar of strength that bears the All of nature than from the God who gives himself configuration in it and only in it? (Rosenzweig 2005, 444, emphasis mine)

In this incredible passage, Rosenzweig gives one last formulation of the tension between philosophy and religion, or Athens and Jerusalem. The key *agon* between religion and philosophy, or between eternity and history, requires returning to a doctrine of natural law in which created nature, with its order, is recognized as the shape of God's providence. The conclusion to Part Three of the

Star makes explicit what is already implicit in the Maimonidean identification of Redemption with Creation, of metaphysics with physics, namely, that the redemption of humankind from war and poverty must also be the redemption of the All of Nature, that is, its emancipation from the slavery in which it has been placed by civilization, by the pretense of omnipotence brandished by the state and by technology, when it turned the creations of nature into mere material for the inventions of human beings.

In this last aspect, Rosenzweig's theory of redemption anticipates not only Benjamin's theory of the *restitutio in integrum* of nature (and Scholem's interpretation of this program in a Sabbatian direction), but also many of the leitmotifs of the Frankfurt School and its dialectic of the Enlightenment. It is thus fitting to conclude with an aphorism by Benjamin that seems to recapitulate the central points of the *Star of Redemption*, starting from its title, "To the Planetarium," passing through its initial reflection on star worship, and culminating in the vision of a new redemptive approach to nature: "technology is the mastery not of nature but of the relation between nature and man. Men as a species completed their development thousands of years ago, but the development of mankind as a species is just beginning. In technology, a *phusis* [nature] is being organized through which mankind's contact with the cosmos takes a new and different form from that which it had in nations and families. . . . Living substance conquers the frenzy of destruction only in the ecstasy of procreation."[119]

[119] In "One-Way Street," (Benjamin 1996, 487).

4
Gershom Scholem and the Mystical Foundations of Authority

Introduction

The significance of Jewish thought for political theology in the 20th century lies primarily in its thematization of the idea of messianism. There is no more imposing thinker of the messianic idea than Gershom Scholem.[1] Even a cursory look at the scope of Scholem's historiography of Judaism shows that it deals nearly exclusively with esoteric material related to Jewish mystical literature, from speculations on the mysteries of the Chariot, through Kabbalistic formulations of God's Nothingness, to the esoteric practice of breaking the commandments in Sabbatianism and Frankism, culminating in his late reflections on "religious anarchism." At first sight, it is not clear how this body of scholarship can receive a politico-theological interpretation. In this chapter, I argue that Scholem's abiding problem is the exploration of the mystical foundations of the authority of divine Law.[2]

No one doubts the importance of the relationship with Walter Benjamin for the development of Scholem's thinking.[3] Benjamin's messianic thinking has been at the center of the contemporary discussion on political theology at least since Jacques Derrida posed the problem of the "mystical foundations" of law (Derrida 1994a). Yet this problem has rarely been worked out in relation to Scholem's studies on Jewish mysticism. Scholem's "theological horizon" is determined by the Benjaminian motif of a "crisis of tradition."[4] The crisis of authority of the Torah as positive law is a widespread motif in 20th-century Jewish

[1] Jacob Taubes, in a rather mean quip, spoke of the "cult of personality . . . propagated in Germany (and not only here) with the researcher and scholar of Kabala for completely transparent reasons: a Jewish representative was needed and sought who could represent *the one* Judaism for the public after the death of Buber" (Taubes 2016, 169).

[2] In what follows I shall use capitalized "Law" to refer to divinely revealed law or Torah.

[3] *Major Trends in Jewish Mysticism*, published in English in 1946, was dedicated to Benjamin, and in 1975 Scholem published the autobiographical study, *Walter Benjamin: The Story of a Friendship* (Scholem 1981). On the meaning of Benjamin for Scholem, see (Biale 1982; Alter 1991; and Mosès 1992). For some of the more recent contributions to this discussion, see (Lebovic 2010; and Sharvit 2017).

[4] Daniel Weidner argues that "the question of tradition is decisive for Scholem's *entire* body of thought" (2006, 213).

Living Law. Miguel Vatter, Oxford University Press (2021). © Oxford University Press.
DOI: 10.1093/oso/9780197546505.003.0005

political theology from Rosenzweig and Buber through to Strauss and Arendt. The Rabbinical approach to the Torah is based on the claim that, as a matter of historical fact, God revealed the Written Law to His chosen people, and then to Moses on Mount Sinai, and, at the same time, He authorized an Oral Law to be developed and transmitted by "teachers of the law" (rabbis), whose purpose was to articulate the historical conditions of the "applicability" of this revealed Written Law (Scholem 1971, 50). "Tradition is concerned with the realization, the enactment of the divine task which is set in the revelation. It demands application, execution and decision. . . . It constitutes a living organism, whose religious authority was asserted with as much emphasis as is at all possible within this system of thought. Nothing demonstrates this authority, the authority of commentary over author, more triumphantly than the story of the oven of Akhnai which is told in the Talmud" (Scholem 1971, 291).[5] The essence of Rabbinical thought on the tradition is that the Torah is written law, and the Jewish people must strive, as befits a written law, to apply it always and everywhere, even in the Messianic age: oral law is the tradition of application.[6]

In *The Story of a Friendship*, Scholem intimates that Benjamin's life somehow embodied the idea of a crisis of tradition.[7] Recounting their time together in Switzerland in the period 1918–1919, Scholem says that "although Benjamin and Dora recognized the supremacy of the religious sphere of revelation (and for me this was still tantamount to the acceptance of the Ten Commandments as an absolute value in the moral world), they did not feel bound by it" (1981, 54). Although the "fact" of revelation was not to be denied in Benjamin's "household," its commandments were no longer applied. Scholem adds that Benjamin's disregard for the commandments was not motivated by cynicism, but rather flowed from "his deep-rooted messianic faith" and "his anarchism" (54–5). Benjamin develops both of these antinomian elements (Scholem specifies: "between 1915 and at least 1927") from out of his adherence to "the concept of *Lehre* [teaching] . . . which he interpreted in the sense of the original meaning of the

[5] The Talmudic aggadah of the oven of Akhnai culminates with this passage: "Thereupon a heavenly voice was heard saying: 'Why do you dispute with Rabbi Eliezer? The Halakhah always agrees with him.' But Rabbi Joshua arose and said (Deut 30:12): 'It is not in heaven.' What did he mean by that? Rabbi Jeremiah replied: 'The Torah has already been given at Mount Sinai [and is thus no longer in Heaven]. We pay no heed to any heavenly voice because already at Mount Sinai You wrote in the Torah' (Exod. 23:2): 'One must incline after the majority'" cited in (Scholem 1971, 291).

[6] Scholem links this view with what he calls the "conservative" version of the messianic idea, but aspects of this view also overlap with the "restorative" idea that he discusses in relation to Maimonides. For Maimonides, the Messiah is a human king "from the House of David who meditates on the Torah and practices its commandments like his ancestor David in accordance with Written and Oral Law, prevails upon all Israel to walk in the ways of the Torah and to repair its breaches and fight the battles of the Lord" (Scholem 1971, 28–9).

[7] The figure of a "crisis" of tradition, of an "end" of experience, is one of the earliest leitmotifs in Benjamin's thought: see (Agamben 1979) and Martin Jay's texts on this motif, "Is Experience Still in Crisis? Reflections on a Frankfurt School Lament" (2011).

Hebrew *torah* as 'instruction,' instruction not only about the true condition and way of man in the world but also about the transcausal connection of things and their rootedness in God. This had a great deal to do with his conception of tradition, which increasingly assumed a mystic note" (56).[8] Thus, for Benjamin and Scholem the "crisis" of tradition entails an unquestioned faith in the possibility of Redemption, together with the scholarly need to reactivate the Torah as a cosmological and mystical "teaching" rather than as a positive legal code, hence the internal relation between "crisis" and "anarchy."

Scholem's historiographical investigations into the mystical components of the Jewish tradition were oriented from the start by the desire to find a conception of messianism that is not seen as the "fulfillment" of the tradition (whether in the Orthodox or in the Pauline senses), but that emerges out of the tradition's own internal and ongoing "crisis." "Here we have a new concept of tradition: after all, the Hebrew word kabbalah means 'the receiving of the tradition'" (Scholem 1971, 293).[9] Scholem represents the Jewish tradition as a process that carries within itself a permanent "self-critique" in the Benjaminian sense of the term, according to which critique means the "destruction" of interpretation in view of allowing the un-interpretable "truth content" to emerge.[10] For Scholem, this self-critique or destruction of the tradition even invests the figure of the messiah. For with Sabbatai Zvi and the religious movement of Sabbatianism, the true messiah becomes an apostate to Islam. From this perspective, Redemption takes the form of "transcendence breaking into history, an intrusion in which *history itself perishes*" (Scholem 1971, 10, emphasis mine). Benjamin's and Scholem's conception of "authentic tradition" is but one more formulation of what Cohen and Rosenzweig call "historical eternity."

But this raises the further, and decisive question: if an alternative, "authentic" tradition is hidden in plain sight within the tradition, what is the ground, other than the Written Law, that sustains it? And what significance does this hidden root of the crisis of the tradition hold for the understanding of the authority of the Law? In his late essay, "Religious Authority and Mysticism," Scholem expounds the mystical idea of history that he developed from Benjamin.[11] He argues that

[8] In the preparatory notes to his *Theses on the Philosophy of History*, Benjamin works out a "mystical" idea of history based on "the idea of discontinuity as the foundation of the authentic tradition" (Benjamin 1991, I:3 1236, translation mine). See the discussion in (Mosès 1992, 158ff), (Greiert 2012) and (Kavka 2014b).

[9] More exactly, Kabbalah refers to a paradoxical, "hidden" tradition of what is anti-traditional; something not unlike what Arendt calls a "tradition of revolution" (where revolution means a paradoxical event in which one tradition comes to an end and another finds its beginning).

[10] On Benjamin's idea of critique, see "Language and History: Linguistic and Historical Categories in Benjamin's Thought" in (Agamben 2007, 48–61; and Steiner 2000).

[11] In a letter to Adorno from June 20, 1965, Scholem writes: "Last year I gave you my Eranos lecture on the concept of the tradition of commentary. There you will find my most precise formulations on revelation and tradition that I am capable of providing. They met with Walter Benjamin's full

mysticism "has two contradictory or complementary aspects: the one conservative, the other revolutionary" (Scholem 1996, 7). Much of the essay is dedicated to explaining how these two aspects work together dialectically. As conservative, mysticism functions as a way to "rediscover the sources of traditional authority" (Scholem 1996, 7). At the same time, the mystical experience recovers a revolutionary function because "a mystic may substitute his own opinion for that prescribed by authority, precisely because his opinion seems to stem from the very same authority" (Scholem 1996, 9, emphasis mine). The mystical experience allows for a return to the ground or *arche* of legal authority in order to give rise to new beginnings.

But, just as likely, these mystical returns to the *arche* can give rise to moments of radical destruction and loss in the case of "revolutionary mystics . . . [who] aspire to establish a new authority based on their own experience. In extreme cases, they may even claim to be above all authority, a law unto themselves. The formlessness of the original experience may even lead to a dissolution of all form, even in interpretation" as happens with "the borderline case of the nihilistic mystic" (Scholem 1996, 11). The mystical conception of tradition is therefore characterized by both anarchic *and* nihilistic moments: the Aristotelian-Philonic idea of a "living law" that is "a law unto itself" may embody both the Life that is source of Law as much as the lawless image of boundless tyranny. I expand on this point later in the discussion of Scholem's theory of the Sabbatian movement.

The mechanism that allows for a mystical and disruptive return on the foundation of legal authority is based on a theological theory of language: "the mystic transforms the holy text, the crux of this metamorphosis being that the hard, clear and unmistakeable word of revelation is filled with *infinite* meaning" (Scholem 1996, 12). More precisely, "the absolute word is as such meaningless, but it is *pregnant* with meaning. Under human eyes it enters into significant finite embodiments which mark innumerable layers of meaning. . . . Each man has his own unique access to Revelation. *Authority no longer resides in a single unmistakeable 'meaning' of the divine communication, but in its infinite capacity for taking on new forms*" (Scholem 1996, 13, emphasis mine). This extremely compressed and condensed formulation offers Scholem's answer to Hegel's challenge, viz., the problem of how the Torah can change in and through history not despite, but *because* it is tied back to its authoritative beginnings. The answer lies in the character of this "infinity" of the "divine communication"; or, better, in the abysmal "formlessness" or "meaninglessness" that the mystical tradition uncovers in the divine *arche*. This linguistic formulation of the crisis of tradition

agreement in 1932 when I first put them on paper in my response to Mr. Schoeps" (Scholem 1995, 141). All translations from German are mine.

contains a politico-theological doctrine whose decipherment is unfolded at the end of the chapter.

The antinomy of theocracy and pagan political philosophy

This chapter proposes to identify Scholem's politico-theological standpoint by attempting to triangulate with the positions held by Benjamin and Leo Strauss during the 1920s and 1930s. This constellation is somewhat unusual and so needs some justification.[12] There exists a letter by Scholem to Benjamin in which he signaled Strauss's 1935 book on Maimonides' political thought, *Philosophy and Law*, as "an unfeigned and copiously argued (if completely ludicrous) affirmation of atheism as the most important Jewish watchword."[13] This characterization must have raised Benjamin's interest, for Scholem later reported:

> I do not remember whether I wrote him [Benjamin] about Goldberg's book, one of the most outrageous polemics against Maimonides as the real corrupter of Judaism—that is, Judaism as Goldberg thought it should be. . . . In any case I recommended to him Leo Strauss' recently published important book *Philosophie und Gesetz: Beiträge zum Verständnis Maimunis. Benjamin even considered writing a review of this book*, which was a searching though problematical analysis of the central role of political philosophy for Maimonides' view of Judaism. *In such a review he could have put at opposite ends the two poles of 'political philosophy' of Judaism*, both of which aroused his interest and were bound to strike related chords in his own thinking: the liquidation of that magical element in a rational esotericism and on the other side the nurturing of a strictly magical, mythical view. (Scholem 1981, 201, emphasis mine)

This recollection is significant because it makes clear that Scholem saw in Strauss's book on Maimonides a possible way to reply to Oskar Goldberg's own critique of the great Jewish medieval philosopher.[14] As recently shown by Bruce Rosenstock, Scholem's treatment of Sabbatianism and mystical nihilism was influenced from the start by his polemical engagement with Goldberg's writings. Rosenstock is surely correct to point out that both Scholem and Goldberg sought in their recovery of Sabbatian messianism to counter the "decline of Judaism's

[12] See the letter of Strauss to Scholem from February 5, 1952, in which he asks about Scholem's publications "because it is true that extremes touch each other and even attract each other" (Scholem and Strauss 2008, 166, translation mine; Meier 2001). On the overlap between the two thinkers with regard to esotericism, see the preliminary considerations in (Smith 1993).

[13] Letter from March 29, 1935, in (Scholem 1989, 156–7).

[14] The reference is to Goldberg's book, *Maimonides: Kritik der jüdischen Glaubenslehre*, published in 1935. Strauss's *Philosophy and Law* is discussed at length in the next chapter.

vitality" (2017, 166). Goldberg's fundamental project was to revitalize Judaism by working out a new, biopolitical understanding of divine Life: "to lead humanity beyond races and folk groups to a unity grounded in the 'biologically-productive' principle of YHWH" (Rosenstock 2017, 172). In his autobiographical writings, Scholem makes no secret about the fact that Goldberg was his "bête noire" because of his "strictly magical, mythical" views on Judaism.[15] In his famous 1937 letter to his editor Schocken, Scholem implicitly places his approach to Judaism as a middle ground between Goldberg's mythical and Hermann Cohen's rationalist approach. Whereas Cohen wanted to purify Judaism as a "religion of reason" from myth and pantheism, Scholem believed that Judaism "attempted to raise them to a higher level *within which they would be negated*" (Scholem 1997b, 4, emphasis mine). Mythology and pantheism were features that the Jewish tradition identified with pagan religions. To "raise them to a higher level" meant, following in the tracks of Philo, to give of these religions a (Greek) philosophical or "mystical" interpretation. To then "negate" this philosophical or "mystical" element of paganism meant to determine how much, and what kind of "Athens" was to be included into "Jerusalem" as a protective measure.[16]

It seems that, from relatively early on, Scholem saw in Strauss a theoretical ally of sorts for this project, despite Strauss's vaunted "atheism" and their nearly opposite political standpoints with respect to Zionism.[17] But, if so, what was the basis of this emerging alliance between the scholar of Jewish medieval philosophy and the scholar of Jewish medieval mysticism? And why might Benjamin have been positively inclined toward both poles? This chapter argues that an answer to this question can be found in a common project to radicalize insights inherited ultimately from Cohen and Franz Rosenzweig that seek the politico-theological significance of Judaism by drawing from its (often hidden) conception of a groundless (an-archic), nihilist, even a/theist dimension of the One God found at work in the moments of Creation, Revelation, and Redemption.

15 "Between 1921 and 1923 I had many dealings, albeit indirect ones, with the group around Oskar Goldberg. . . . The Kabbala was highly regarded by them—not so much because of the religious and philosophical aspects that had prompted me to study it, but on account of its magical implications" (Scholem 1980, 146). Scholem cites his own opinion of Goldberg: "I am inclined to regard him as a representative of the devil in our generation" (ibid., 147). He recounts that after the publication of Goldberg's main work, *Die Wirklichkeit der Hebräer* [The Actuality of the Hebrews], in 1924, "I wrote a long, critical letter about the book; Benjamin and Leo Strauss disseminated copies of it in Berlin" (Scholem 1981, 98). The letter is now published as Letter 94 from August 23, 1928, addressed to Rosa Okun, in (Scholem 1994, 235–8). Scholem renders the content of the book as follows: "The actuality of the Hebrews, or why we should become Frankists?"

16 Harry Wolfson distinguishes between Hellenistic Jewish "apostates" who were "well versed in the arts and the sciences and philosophy, but devoid of any religious training—not only Jewish but also heathen" and other Hellenistic thinkers who did have that religious training and pursued "the application of philosophy to religion, either for the defense of Judaism or for the defense of heathenism" (Wolfson 1947, I:82).

17 About his own and Benjamin's religious beliefs, Scholem simply says: "Since we both believed in God, we never discussed His 'existence'" (1981, 56).

Undoubtedly, Benjamin and Scholem shared a fascination with "religious nihilism" and "religious anarchism."[18] Yet the proper significance of this religious nihilism and anarchism in their thinking becomes visible only when placed side by side with the most striking piece of evidence disclosed by Scholem's recollection, namely, Benjamin's intention to write something about the " 'political philosophy' of Judaism." The fact that Scholem places "political philosophy" in quotation marks shows his awareness of the paradox contained in the expression. For political philosophy, as Strauss and Arendt would not cease to repeat, has Greek and Roman, that is, pagan, roots. How could it be integrated into Judaism based on the Torah understood as a teaching of strict monotheism? Did Benjamin think that this could be done by bringing together, in however unlikely a synthesis, the "philosophical" approach of Strauss together with the "magical, mythical" aspects of Kabbalah revealed by Scholem's incipient research (and even perhaps Goldberg's own intuitions)?[19] And to what end?

Benjamin's *Theological-Political Fragment* and his essay *Critique of Violence* are often credited with introducing the term "theocracy" into the Weimar politico-juridical debate and making it the focal point of a possible " 'political philosophy' of Judaism." In the *Fragment*, Benjamin asserts that the Kingdom of God "is not the goal [*Ziel*] but the terminus [*Ende*]" of history, and that is why "theocracy has no political but only a religious meaning."[20] This distinction between "political" and "religious" meanings of theocracy has puzzled interpreters and has been interpreted in various ways.[21] In the *Fragment*, Benjamin gives credit to Ernst Bloch's *Spirit of Utopia* for this distinction.[22] In Bloch, it was meant to reject the facile identification—very widespread again during the Cold War—of Marxism as the latest example of a millenarian or chiliastic social movement. That said, Bloch was evidently interested to use the religious sense of theocracy

[18] For these terms, see "Der Nihilismus als religiöse Phänomen" in (Scholem 1984a, 129–88), discussed in the following. On Benjamin and nihilism, see (Wohlfarth 2002, 2005). Agamben's and Taubes's more influential discussions of Benjamin's and Scholem's nihilisms are addressed later.

[19] On Benjamin's fascination with Goldberg's disciple, Erich Unger, see, apart from Rosenstock, also (Steiner 2001; and Jennings 2012).

[20] (Benjamin 2002, 306).

[21] For Eric Jacobson the "religious" meaning of theocracy corresponds to "an anarchist kingdom of God," as opposed to a monarchic understanding of the Messianic Kingdom, where the Messiah is a human king of Davidic lineage (Jacobson 2003, 30–1). Taubes employs the *Fragment* to impugn Scholem's interpretation of the Jewish idea of messianism: "Benjamin divides the order of the profane from the order of the messianic in a way that runs contrary to the Jewish understanding of the messianic idea as promulgated by Scholem" (Taubes 2016, 167). For Scholem, Jewish messianism always had an inner-worldly orientation, whereas Taubes is claiming that in Benjamin, Jewish messianism was much more Gnostic in its repudiation of any worldly power. The Scholem-Taubes polemic is addressed later.

[22] (Rabinbach 1985, 27–65). In a late letter to Anson Rabinbach from January 25, 1977, who had asked him for details on the lost "long review on the 'Geist der Utopie,' " Scholem emphasized Benjamin's "strong reservations about the tenor of his writing" and also claims that "Benjamin's essay 'Kritik of Violence' [*sic*] was not concerned with Bloch" (Scholem 1999, 152). The latter assertion is difficult to sustain.

for a political thinking about revolutions.[23] In addition, given the German-Jewish context in which it was penned, Benjamin's distinction between a political and a religious meaning of theocracy also sought to preempt any appropriation of the messianic idea by political Zionism, a strategy that was generally shared by Buber and Scholem at the time, and that is reiterated by Taubes himself.[24]

Yet, the best way to understand the distinction between political and religious meanings of theocracy in Benjamin and Scholem is to go back to the origin of the term. Flavius Josephus coined the term in *Contra Apionem* 2:164–7, precisely in order to facilitate a comparison between Greek and Hebrew constitutional forms:

> Now there are innumerable differences in the particular customs and laws that are among all mankind, which a man may briefly reduce under the following heads: Some legislators have permitted their governments to be under monarchies, others put them under oligarchies, and others under a republican form; but our legislator [*nomothetes*] had no regard to any of these forms, but he ordained our government [*politeuma*] to be what, by a strained expression, may be termed a Theocracy, by ascribing the authority [*arche*] and the power [*kratos*] to God, and by persuading all the people to have a regard to him, as the author of all the good things that were enjoyed either in common by all mankind, or by each one in particular, and of all that they themselves obtained by praying to him in their greatest difficulties.... Moreover, he represented God as unbegotten and immutable through all eternity ... and, though known to us by his power, yet unknown to us as to his essence.[25]

From this definition, it is clear that the term "theocracy" is the most evident expression of an earlier, Judeo-Hellenistic attempt at working out something like a "political philosophy" of Judaism.[26] The Hebrew Republic with its

[23] "In this functional relationship between relief and spirit [*Entlastung und Geist*], Marxism and religion, united in their will to realize the Kingdom, all streams, the soul, the Messiah, the Apocalypse as the act of awakening to the totality, flow into the final system, giving the last impulse to action and knowledge. As such they constitute the a priori of all politics and culture" (Bloch 1985, 346).

[24] (Taubes 2016, 170–1). On the separation between Zionism and messianism in Benjamin, see (Eiland 2016). For a discussion of this separation in cultural Zionism, see (Ohana 2012). See also Amir Engel's claim that in his early approach to Sabbatianism, "Scholem argued polemically and powerfully against the unholy harnessing of religious thought to politics, and more specifically against what he perceived as the messianic delusions of Zionism in Palestine" (Engel 2017, 131). See Scholem's July 30, 1921, letter 82 to Robert Weltsch and Hans Kohn: "the systematic concept that I have of Zionism . . . considers the whole political sphere . . . as irrelevant if not as corrupt" (Scholem 1994, 216). "[T]he irredeemable 'modern' confusion between religious and political categories ... damages both spheres and may one day violently undermine them" (ibid., 217).

[25] (Josephus 1987, 803–4). On Josephus's contribution to Judaism, see (Momigliano 1994).

[26] Gabriele Guerra and Daniel Weidner have recently drawn attention to the influence exerted by the late 19th-century interpretation of Jewish theocracy found in the work of Julius Wellhausen. Wellhausen claimed that Moses introduced a political form of theocracy. However, once human kingship was adopted by Israel, theocracy took a "religious" form oriented toward the coming of the future Messiah, see (Guerra 2010; and Weidner 2014). I argue that the distinction between political

Mosaic constitution was comparable, politically speaking, to the Greco-Roman constitutions, while it was different from them, theologically speaking, because Moses's laws spoke to God's rule or sovereignty being divided between *arche* and *kratos*, as well as between His unknowable essence and His power.

The concluding passages of the *Critique of Violence* dedicated to "divine violence" betray the same Judeo-Hellenistic signature. Benjamin's dualistic distinction between "sovereignty" and "violence" within the Godhead follows directly from Josephus's dualistic approach to God's rule, which distinguishes between *arche* and *kratos* (Benjamin 1996, 252). Ever since the readings offered by Derrida's *Force of Law* and Agamben's *Homo sacer*, what Benjamin may have meant by his talk of divine "sovereignty" and divine "violence"—the two components of theocracy—and its relation to the idea of (bare) life, has been at the center of the current debate on political theology and its relation to Carl Schmitt's theory of sovereignty.[27] My hypothesis is that the kind of "political philosophy of Judaism" Scholem and Strauss try to develop is centrally concerned with how to conceive this distinction between authority (*arche*) and power (*kratos*) at the heart of Jewish political theology since Josephus.

Josephus introduced his discussion of theocracy as a fourth constitutional form by drawing on the frequent analogy between Moses and the other human lawgivers (*nomothetes*) honored by the Greeks and Romans. Both were understood as being divinely inspired *nomothetes*.[28] This understanding raises the "political problem of monotheism": what does it mean to subsume God's *Thora* under the Greek concept of *nomos*? I propose to approach this problem by delving deeper into the Jewish Hellenistic context within which Josephus developed his concept of theocracy. This context is the one framed by the Maccabean Revolt, the series of critical events in the history of the Jewish people represented in the apocalyptic text of *The Book of Daniel* as well as in *I Maccabees* and *II Maccabees*.[29] In his 1937 book *Der Gott der Makkabäer*, still published in Berlin by Schocken,[30] the great historian of this period, Elias Bickerman, put forward

and religious theocracy in Benjamin and Scholem is *not* to be understood in this way, but as the distinction between theocracy as a form of state and theocracy as a political way of life that is not dependent on state sovereignty.

[27] See the wide-ranging discussion in (Martel 2012).

[28] The Hellenistic discussion and context for Philo's and Josephus's depiction of Moses as "ideal leader" is treated in (Feldman 1996, 233–87) and in more general terms also in (Momigliano 1990, 74–96).

[29] For the connection of these biblical texts to Greek historiography and philosophy, with special attention given to Josephus and Jewish apocalyptic literature, see the essays in (Momigliano 1994).

[30] The author remarks in the Preface to the English translation that "I was surprised that my academic and even pedantic book (published by Schocken, Jüdischer Buchverlag) could offer some consolation to the persecuted Jews in Germany, as several letters I received from my readers told me" (Bickerman 1979, xii). Bickerman had already published his essential discoveries in 1928 and then in a more accessible book in 1935.

an interpretation of the Maccabean Revolt as a function of what he calls "the antinomy of the theocracy of Jerusalem, the paradox of this state of God, the foundation of which was the will of the godless foreign ruler" (Bickerman 1979, 91). It is this antinomy of theocracy that offers a new path toward the understanding of both Scholem's and Strauss's Jewish political theologies.

According to tradition, the Maccabean Revolt was primarily a struggle of the Jewish people in Jerusalem against the persecution at the hands of the Seleucid (Syrian) king, Antiochus IV Epiphanes, who in 167 BC rescinded the law of Moses and desecrated the temple on Zion. Bickerman's essential discovery, instead, is that the revolt was "a civil war, a religious struggle between reformers and orthodox" (Bickerman 1979, 90).[31] More precisely, it was "a religious war between two groups of Jews: between the polytheists who sacrificed God in order to save their people through assimilation to the surrounding world, and the monotheists, who were ready to give up their lives and that of the people in order to preserve the law of Moses" (Bickerman 1979, 91).[32] The basic intention of the Jewish Hellenizers seems to have been to facilitate the "assimilation" of the Jewish communities in Jerusalem, but also in the Diaspora, to the post-Alexandrian political universe of the Egyptian and Syrian monarchies, by applying the Sophistic distinction between nature and law (as convention), *phusis* and *nomos*, to the Torah itself. They wanted the Torah to be recognized as one "divine law" among others and sought to identify the nameless God with the "Lord of Heaven," or, for the Greeks, Zeus Olympus (Bickerman 1979, 109). The Maccabean Revolt led by Mattathias and his sons rejected this attempted appropriation of Hellenism by a part of the Jewish priestly elite.

Bickerman, however, also refutes the traditional picture of the Maccabees "as the bitter enemies and destroyers of Hellenistic culture." Rather, he sees them as the origin of a Jewish dynasty that succeeded "for the first time since the Exile" in having the Jewish people be "recognized as an independent power, and by the very people [the Romans] who ruled the world" (Bickerman 1962, 133).[33] Bickerman's fundamental insight captures concisely and elegantly the *complexio*

[31] See the text of 1 Maccabees 1:11–13 in which the aspect of civil strife is apparent: "In those days went there out of Israel wicked men, who persuaded many, saying, Let us go and make a covenant with the heathen that are round about us: for since we departed from them we have had much sorrow. So this device pleased them well. Then certain of the people were so forward herein, that they went to the king, who gave them licence to do after the ordinances of the heathen".

[32] The motivation for the Jewish people to come to terms with the various pagan empires during Hellenism is starkly put by Bickerman: "If Jerusalem had not been a part of a Gentile empire, the nomads would have driven the Jews into the sea or swallowed up Palestine, and the rock of Zion would have been the foundation of an Arabian sanctuary a thousand years before Omar's mosque" (Bickerman 1962, 10).

[33] "Judah's lifework had been to prevent the threatening Hellenization of Judaism and the surrender of the Torah. He succeeded, and gave his life to his success. Jonathan and his successors, his brother Simon and Simon's descendants, will now seek to accommodate Hellenism to Judaism. Under them Judea becomes a Hellenistic principality" (Bickerman 1962, 139).

oppositorum of Athens and Jerusalem within Hellenistic Judaism: "The reform party wished to assimilate the Torah to Hellenism; the Maccabees wished to incorporate Hellenic culture in the Torah" (Bickerman 1962, 156). Thus, the Maccabean Revolt, whose success was sealed by the introduction of the new festival of Hanukkah into the liturgy, in reality represented "the introduction of Hellenic usages into Judaism without making a sacrifice of Judaism" (Bickerman 1962, 121).[34] Hellenism was introduced all the better to protect the priority of the Torah and its distinction from (pagan) divine *nomoi.*

At the theoretical level, Hellenistic Judaism opened up two distinct avenues to "incorporate Hellenic culture in the Torah": the first consisted in a philosophical conception of revealed religion as first advanced by Philo; the other consisted in the understanding of the Torah as a religion of (pagan, both Greek and Persian) "mysteries."[35] The first path led to the development of the medieval Judeo-Arabic philosophical tradition studied by Strauss. The second path led to the development of the medieval Jewish mystical tradition of the Kabbalah studied by Scholem. Seen from this perspective, neither Strauss's turn to classical "natural right" nor Scholem's recovery of the mystical and the messianic traditions in Judaism are "heretical" in any obvious sense because both can be understood as intended to defend the priority of the Torah, to maintain "alive" its teachings against all threats of "assimilation," and to remain "faithful" to these teachings other than in the Rabbinical, institutional way.[36]

But what motivated these two German Jews in the early 20th century to return to the Hellenistic context? The autobiographical narratives of the two authors coincide remarkably on the general outlines of the "spiritual" dilemmas confronting them.[37] They were not orthodox Jews, but they also rejected assimilation in a period of virulent anti-Semitism in Germany that would bring Hitler

[34] "This accommodation of new elements to the Bible, this consideration for native tradition, characterizes the Hellenization carried through under the Maccabees, and differentiates it from the rationalistic assimilation which had been the aim of the reform party" (Bickerman 1962, 157).

[35] For a discussion of the Jewish Diaspora in Hellenism and the adoption of these two avenues, see (Collins 2000). I have discussed the significance of Erwin Goodenough's work for the approach to Judaism through the pagan "mysteries" in chapter 1. For the debate on Goodenough's later symbological approach to Judaism, and its relation to Scholem's symbolic analysis, see (Momigliano 1994, 48–57).

[36] In this sense, my interpretation departs from Benjamin Lazier's influential politico-theological reading of Scholem and Strauss in (Lazier 2008a, 2008b). The Judeo-Hellenistic context is also crucial in Lazier's attempt to conceptualize the connection between theocracy and heresy in both Scholem and Strauss. In his opinion, Strauss and Scholem are "heretical" because they no longer believe in the Torah as *nomos*, in the Rabbinic understanding of the Torah as legal "institution" and as a permanent demand to always strive to apply all the commandments. Instead, they "revived an ancient Greek distinction: they set law and convention (*nomos*) against teleological notions of nature (*physis*) and for the most part they adjudicated this contest in favor of the latter" (Lazier 2008a, 16).

[37] The literature on the "spiritual" situation of Jews in Weimar Germany is enormous. For two recent approaches, based on the work of Steven Aschheim, see (Aschheim and Liska 2015; and Mendelsohn, Hoffman, and Cohen 2014).

to power.[38] Both authors sought to avoid the extremes of an ultra-nationalist form of Zionism (à la Jabotinsky) and a misplaced concretization of the longing for a Messiah (à la Goldberg) to deliver the Jewish people from their world-historical predicament.[39] What was needed, they seemed to think, was a form of adherence to Judaism that was both "political" (viz., opposed to the Rabbinic "quietistic" option)[40] *and* also "theological" (viz., opposed to the secular turn toward nationalism and/or militarism, coupled with an oblivion of the Jewish tradition).

Instead of adopting the "modernist" paths opened up by the various kinds of Zionism, Scholem and Strauss argued that a way out of their predicament had first to be uncovered by *going backward* in history, back to the earlier Hellenistic context in which adherence to Judaism had been both "political" and "theological," where Jewish "theology" meant retaking up the two Hellenistic forms of "philosophical" or "mystical" Judaism. At this point, they both encountered the "antinomy of theocracy" pointed out by Bickerman, which appears as the greatest challenge faced on the path of "return" out of the theologico-political predicament of Weimar Germany. For the Maccabean Revolt was symptomatic of the fundamental problem of Exile, namely, that God's Torah was "applicable" in a fully or absolute political sense, that is, as the foundation of a truly autonomous or sovereign Jewish political community (as opposed to what would become the Rabbinic limited, political sense, following the idea of the medieval *kahal*), only thanks to the favor or "grace" of a non-Jewish human sovereign. In the lapidary sentence of Bickerman: "if Artaxerxes could force the law upon the people, Epiphanes could abolish it" (Bickerman 1979, 91). Since this human favor or grace can always be withdrawn, leaving a people at the mercy of the sovereign's arbitrary will, from a republican perspective the Jewish people remained in a status of slavery during their Exile.

In his best-known book on Judaism and the Western philosophical tradition, Emil Fackenheim adopts Scholem's standpoint that political existence in history is essential for Judaism, whereas this is not the case with authentic

[38] Scholem speaks of the "self-deception" of German Jews regarding "the German-Jewish relationship" (Scholem 1980, 26). "I no longer had any hope for the amalgam known as 'Deutschjudentum' i.e., a Jewish community that considered itself German, and expected a renewal of Jewry only from its rebirth in Eretz Israel" (Scholem 1980, 140).

[39] For a recent approximation of Strauss's and Scholem's youthful adherence to Zionism, see (Muller 2014; and Biale 2014).

[40] Scholem speaks of an "almost unanimous opposition of the rabbis" to an activist pursuit of the messianic utopia over a period of 1,500 years, from the Bar Kochba revolt to the Sabbatian movement. "There are many reaosns for this: the care for the stability of the community, the care for the destiny of the Jews after their disappointment, as the historical experience suggests, joined with a deep-rooted rejection of 'those who force the End' [*Bedränger des Endes*], the Hebrew expression for people who cannot wait for the arrival of the Messiah but who want to actively bring it about" (Scholem 1973, 164).

Christianity: "Jewish religious existence is between Creation (or Fall or Exodus) and the Messianic future . . . this religious self-understanding is world-historical" (Fackenheim 1973, 85).[41] Fackenheim considers that Hegel's philosophy of world history represents "the deepest modern philosophical challenge to Jewish religious existence today" because, on the one side, this philosophy views Jews as an ahistorical people, and, on the other, Hegel's general standpoint is that a people must prove its eternal significance in and through history (Fackenheim 1973, 85).[42] Against the Hegelian picture of a servile "service to the Law" bequeathed by Moses to his people—a picture that is clearly of Spinozist origin[43]—Fackenheim's strategy is to show that revealed Law is not simply positivistic and heteronomous because this Law permits changes and deviations in how the Jewish people interpret it. This freedom of interpretation, in turn, guarantees the continued existence of the Jewish people through history.[44] Crucially for my argument, Fackenheim draws the key illustration of his thesis from Bickerman's reading of the Maccabean Revolt.

The basic idea is that the Jewish notion of divine providence (i.e., divine grace) is operative in and through *transgressions* of divine Law on the part of God's chosen people. However, viewed from the perspective of the End, these transgressions are judged to be for the sake of maintaining the people's fidelity to the pact with God which is sealed by a conjoint rulership over God's Kingdom, viz., the Messianic reality. God's Kingdom engages the world historical struggle against "earthly power" by breaking the very Law of theocracy. In other words, a "religious" conception of theocracy breaks with a "political" conception of theocracy. Concretely stated, the Maccabees understood the necessity of *not observing* the Sabbath in order *to fight* the army of the Syrian (Seleucid) king. "Those who had abandoned their homes in order not to depart from the [Mosaic] law 'either to the right hand or to the left' were united by that very measure which infringed the Torah for the Torah's sake" (Bickerman 1979, 100).

Fackenheim here gives expression to one of the most fundamental motifs of Jewish political theology in the 20th century, namely, that the divine Law is broken, or more correctly, is placed in a state of exception, in order to assure

41 On the debate on Jewish historicity from Löwith to Taubes, see now (Gordon 2012b).

42 The argument is carried forward in (Yovel 1998).

43 For the historical background to Hegel's critique, namely, the relation of modern Judaism to political emancipation along Spinozist lines, see (Sutcliffe 2003). The question of Spinozism in German Enlightenment, discussed earlier in relation to Cohen, will be picked up again later in relation to Strauss.

44 According to Fackenheim, Cohen's shortcoming is mainly that he makes no room for Zionism within his account of Jewish messianism. Similarly, he objects to Rosenzweig's treatment of the "eternity" of the Jewish people because it draws Judaism out of history. For Fackenheim, by contrast, the events designated by the names of "Auschwitz" and the "rebirth of the Jewish State" demonstrate that there is no "eternity" of the Jewish people without understanding the inherent relation of Judaism to historicity (Fackenheim 1973, 121).

its continued validity.[45] I hope to show in this and the following chapter that this motif of "hypernomianism" (Wolfson) is worked out nowhere more radically than in Scholem and Strauss starting in the 1930s, and in strictly parallel ways: the former working through a recovery of Kabbalistic mysticism in the Jewish tradition; the latter through the recovery of Arabic philosophical precursors of Maimonides. What distinguishes both from Fackenheim is that they erect this principle as the foundation of a theocratic understanding of the legitimate authority of Law that places its rule above any of its regime-based, "political" realizations.

The central hypothesis of this chapter is that Scholem's wide-ranging historiographical investigations into the Jewish mystical tradition of the Kabbalah and its relation to the idea of messianism are all organized around the exploration of this antinomy of theocracy. If one understands the Jewish tradition as the sustained effort to apply the Torah as law, then Scholem is interested in disinterring a counter-tradition which recognizes the congenital "crisis" of the tradition because in Exile the divine Torah as constitutional framework of theocracy is always at the mercy of the human sovereign. This Western conception of human sovereignty was modeled on the Hellenistic conception of kingship and gave rise to the discourse of political theology. Given this situation, it follows that the sought-after "political philosophy" of Judaism is a theory that places at its very core the paradox of legal application: the concrete legal situation within which the divine Torah is applicable is *not* under the control of the Torah. The tradition of the Torah is thus placed in permanent crisis.

Awareness of this crisis situation inevitably leads Jewish political theology in an anti- or hyper-nomian, anarchist, and nihilist direction: for the Torah to become applicable in and of itself (without dependency on the human sovereign), it would first have to become "inapplicable." Or, put differently, the response to the paradox of theocracy, that is, that the constituent power of Moses's Law belongs to the Gentile emperor, must take the form of internalizing constituent power within the Law. This internalization of constituent power within the Law requires something like a nihilist or anarchist foundation of its legal authority.

45 Elliot Wolfson has appropriately called this motif "hypernomianism": "the apparent antinomianism contained in the prophet's request to break the law is, in truth, a means to fulfil the law, and hence it would be more appropriate to refer to this gesture as hypernomian—what seems to be blatantly transgressive is, in fact, a more profound expression of obedience to the law" (Wolfson 2006, 236). However, I disagree with Wolfson's suggestion that, somehow, Scholem misses this dimension of hypernomianism. Engel also mentions this principle in his interpretation of Scholem but understands its only valid application as being the Talmudic *mitzvah ha-Ba'a be-Avera*, ("a commandment fulfilled while committing a transgression"), while he thinks that Sabbatianism, with its idea of "redemption through sin," perverts the principle (Engel 2017, 142–3). Like Wolfson, Engel does not perceive Scholem's constructive bid to make hypernomianism the foundational principle of legal authority in the (crisis of) tradition. (Bouretz 2003) also discusses this idea in the context of Scholem but deprives it of its politico-theological significance.

What Scholem means by "religious anarchism" refers, then, to the following hypothesis: the Torah needs to be understood as if it contains an antinomian and anti-sovereign doctrine. The Torah would have to be conceived as a divine law that gives license to "take exception" to the given positive human legal order, while at the same time rejecting its conflation with the Hellenistic ideal of the human king as a "living law." Strauss and Scholem were all too aware that Hitler's employment of the "state of exception" as justified by the legal thought of Schmitt was the latest manifestation of this conflation.

Law and the mystical foundation of authority

Scholem considered that myth and pantheism were the elements that determined the repeated, internal tendency to crisis in the Jewish tradition. Scholem's historiography tries to answer Hegel's challenge by showing how Judaism could withstand and react critically to a history of persecution thanks to its internalization of the power of crisis in the form of gnosticism and pantheism. Scholem's main discovery is that the internal "crisis" of the Jewish tradition is not rooted in the idea of messianism, but rather comes from its internalized Hellenistic component. This internalized Hellenism works itself out in two basic forms. The first is identified with the Jewish gnosticism of the Merkabah and Hekhaloth mystical literature dedicated to the mystery of the Throne and Palace of God as Lord of the world. The second is identified with the pantheism/nihilism found in the Kabbalah's teachings on the mystery of Creation. Both forms of mystical discourses can be read as harboring a secret teaching on divine authority as something other than legality.

Scholem considers that the mystical interpretations of the Torah were from the start a way to politicize the interpretations of the Kabbalistic tradition by linking it to the politico-historical reality of a determined people.[46] What appear to be "mystical" visions, and therefore merely subjective limit-experiences, are in reality a way to place a determined historical group into contact with "divine Life" and its politico-theological structure. The mystical experience did not presuppose long years of study of the Law: it was thus an experience that was open to the "lay" public. Moshe Idel, instead, objects that by interpreting Judaism as a mystical religion from the very outset, Scholem fails to appreciate the historical (and political) reality of the Jews.[47] However, this objection misses the

[46] In my opinion, (Bouretz 2003) is the one who best expresses this point.

[47] Scholem transforms the "historical experience [of the Galut] into a mystical vision of reality . . . via a symbolic understanding of reality—'symbols of a very special kind, in which the spiritual experience of the mystics was almost inextricably intertwined with the historical experience of the Jewish people'" (Idel 2015, 22).

Hellenistic background of "mysteries" thanks to which it was possible to connect the symbolic, mystical interpretation of the Torah with the revival of more radical politico-theological teachings of pagan thought amidst Rabbinical culture.[48]

The Hellenistic tradition was familiar with the idea of philosophical legislators who claimed that their laws came from the mouth of a divinity.[49] Given this context, the problem for the Jewish community was how to address, philosophically, the difference between Moses's divinely revealed legislation and the legislation of, say, Minos. The divine origin of laws was often vouched for by the amount of power that these laws could generate for those who upheld them. Polybius reflects this widespread belief when he claims that the Roman (religious and military) constitution is the *arche* of Roman power and empire. Likewise, Thucydides recounts how the Athenians justified their claims to empire by adopting the Sophist idea that it was divine law for the stronger to rule over the weaker. This Sophistical interpretation of Pindar's formula *nomos basileus* has been read by Agamben to mean that sovereign power is the "force of law without law": it is law reduced to pure enforcement (Agamben 2005a, 39). In the Jewish tradition, where it was common to think of the Jewish God as a *Pantokrator* (omnipotent ruler of the All), it would have been possible to take up this pagan logic (which Benjamin calls "mythical violence," based on "bloody" power over mere life). But to do so would have meant that the claim of the Jewish God to omnipotence could be falsified by the course of historical events, such as the destruction of the Second Temple by the Romans.

The other path, instead, consists in finding a different, "mystical" foundation to the revealed Law: not in power, but in authority. To work out the distinction between power and authority became increasingly important in 20th-century Jewish political thought, from Buber to Arendt and Derrida. My hypothesis is that Scholem understood that what motivated the adoption of "gnostic" elements in Jewish mysticism was the necessity *to perceive the difference between authority and power*. The "gnostic" motif of a Hidden God is tied to the phenomenon of the authority of the Law, not to its power or violence. Scholem always emphasizes the distinction between *Jewish* gnosticism and Gnosticism "as such," as pointed out by Joseph Dan.[50] The Jewish gnostic rejects the crucial belief of the Gnostic

[48] Idel connects Scholem's symbolic approach to Jewish mysticism back to Pythagoreanism and the idea of *prisca theologia* through the Renaissance scholar of Kabbalah, Johannes Reuchlin (Idel 2014a). But he fails to see that Pythagoreanism played a crucial role in the narrative of Hellenistic kingship as a model of a philosopher-king adopted by Philo and the revival of these insights in the Italian Renaissance, as I indicated in my discussion of Goodenough.

[49] "According to the historical principles basic to Greek thought, Jewish law was the invention of Moses, enjoined by him upon is followers" (Bickerman 1979, 86). See also the wide-ranging discussion in (Momigliano 1990).

[50] (Dan 1987, 43). Dan goes on to explain why Scholem did not make claims regarding the origin of Gnosticism either as a Christian heresy, or as a "third religion" independent of Christianity, as being found in Jewish mysticism (ibid., 45).

doctrine according to which the Hidden God and the God of Creation (and of Revelation) are two different persons that stand in irremediable conflict one with another. For Scholem, Jewish gnosticism is an example of the introjection of Athens into Jerusalem as a supplementary "fence of the Torah." The Hidden God and the Creator God are not two distinct divine persons, but one and the same God for whom there obtains a radical distinction between His authority (*arche*) and His power (*kratos*).

In *State of Exception*, Agamben argues that the suspension of the validity of legal norms in a state of exception reveals an underlying juridical vacuum at the heart of all law. "The state of exception separates the norm from its application in order to make its application possible. It introduces a zone of anomie into the law in order to make the effective regulation of the real possible" (2005a, 36). Agamben derives this hypothesis from Scholem's description for the crisis of the tradition of the Jewish Torah in terms of the loss of applicability of revealed law found in his epistolary exchange with Benjamin over Franz Kafka and the "Nothingness of Revelation."[51] In so doing, Agamben identifies this crisis with the gradual but inevitable expansion of the "virtual" state of exception in and through systems of positive law, all the way to the point at which the state of exception is no longer exceptional but has become the rule.[52] For Schmitt, the state of exception that declares the "Nothingness" of positive law reveals the ground of a deeper "order" and "authority." According to his decisionist theory of sovereignty, whether the situation of order exists or not is a matter of decision; and he who has the authority to make this decision is sovereign.[53] For Agamben, instead, the space of authority is nothing but the space of anomie, a moment of rule-lessness ("anomie") and thus of "pure violence" (whether mythical or divine) antecedent to the application of law. The crisis of tradition sucks into it all authority in such a radical way that the very *authority* of law now becomes the source of a *Stillstand des Rechts*, a "kenomatic state, an emptiness and standstill of the law," an "anomic space" (Agamben 2005a, 45, 48).[54] By

[51] For a discussion of this exchange and Agamben's interpretation of it, I refer to (Vatter 2008a).

[52] "Being in force without significance [*Geltung ohne Bedeutung*]: nothing better describes the ban that our age cannot master than Scholem's formula for the status of law in Kafka's novel. What, after all, is the structure of the sovereign ban if not that of a law that is in force but does not signify? . . . All societies and all cultures today . . . have entered into a legitimation crisis in which law (we mean by this term the entire text of tradition in its regulative form, whether the Jewish Torah or the Islamic Shariah, Christian dogma or the profane nomos) is in force as the pure 'Nothing of Revelation.' But this is precisely the structure of the sovereign relation, and the nihilism in which we are living is, from this perspective, nothing other than the coming to light of this relation as such" (Agamben 1998, 51).

[53] "Here the decision separates itself from the norm, and, paradoxically, authority demonstrates that it does not need to be entitled in order to do justice [*Hier sondert sich die Entscheidung von der Rechtsnorm, und (um es paradox zu formulieren) die Autorität beweist, dass sie, um Recht zu schaffen, nicht Recht zu haben braucht*]" (Schmitt 1996a, 19, translation mine).

[54] It is fascinating that Agamben here cites Machiavelli's suggestion in the *Discourses* of " 'breaking' the order to save it" ["For in a republic where such a provision is lacking, one must either observe the orders and be ruined, or break them and not be ruined."] (Agamben 2005a, 46). But Agamben gives

mistakenly identifying Scholem's doctrine of the "Nothingness of Revelation" with Schmitt's standpoint, Agamben turns Scholem's account of messianism into a theory of a/legal violence rather than of the mystical foundation of legal authority.[55] In what follows, the question of authority in its distinction from power serves to contextualize Scholem's use of Jewish gnosticism to articulate a "political philosophy of Judaism" that is unwilling to accept the origin of its Law as coming from an antecedent juridical vacuum in the sense posited by Agamben.

The political theology of the throne and the problem of nationalism

Scholem's analysis of Merkabah and Hekhaloth mysticism brings out the role of the gnostic component in a Jewish teaching of the Law that does not base its legitimacy on its power (i.e., its capacity to govern empires), but rather on its authority. The guiding problem that motivates this mystical literature is to seek the answer to the question: who is the Author of the Law? As Bickerman shows, the "universalist" or "reformist" camp of Judaism took advantage of the fact that "the Jews named their Deity 'God of Heaven'" in order to then subsume the Mosaic revelation as exemplary of the "natural theology of mankind [that] had identified God with the heavens" (1962, 49).[56] The Jewish mystical tradition, instead, asked whether it was possible for the human soul to "ascend" beyond the spheres of the stars in order to approximate God as the One who is other than the "heavens." It also asked: what is required for this God to "descend" back to earth? In so doing, Jewish mysticism fashioned a response to the Trinitarian logic of

of Machiavelli's republican understanding of dictatorship a Schmittian interpretation that opposes it to the rule of law. This is a false reading, as can be seen now from (Geuna 2017). More importantly, Machiavelli's suggestion is much more in line with a Maccabbean reading of the Torah and its teachings, as I have shown in (Vatter 2013).

55 "The Scripture (the Torah) without its key is the cipher of the law in the state of exception, which is in force but is not applied or is applied without being in force (and which Scholem, not at all suspecting that he shares this thesis with Schmitt, believes is still law)" (Agamben 2005a, 63). Agamben opposes Benjamin's messianism to Scholem: "Confronted with the imperfect nihilism that would let the Nothing subsist indefinitely in the form of a being in force without significance, Benjamin proposes a messianic nihilism that nullifies even the Nothing and lets no form of law remain in force beyond its own content" (1998, 53). Contrary to Agamben, Stéphane Mosès interprets Scholem's formula of a law that is in force without signifying as a description of the "negative theology" that Scholem identifies in Kafka (Mosès 1999).

56 "For some time the Jews had been in the habit of calling their God 'Lord of Heaven' or even simply 'Heaven' as is the regular practice in the First Book of the Maccabees. But for the Greeks the Lord of Heaven was Zeus Olympios. In Aramaic the expression was probably *Baal Shemin*, under which title all the peoples of Syria worshipped the ruler of heaven. In this manner the 'God of the Jews' was now accepted into the general pantheon" (Bickerman 1962, 109).

divine government through the Son and its ecclesiastical or imperial representatives, while, at the same time, it avoided a purely Gnostic rejection of all Law as merely the expression of might and power. Put differently, in his reading of early Jewish mystical literature, Scholem is conceptualizing the distinction between God's *arche* and His *kratos* in Jewish theocracy along the lines of a distinction between the authority and the force of law. On this hypothesis, the Merkabah and Hekhaloth mysticism is geared toward leading a community toward divine authority in a situation in which the Law's enforcement or application is no longer possible. The introduction of gnostic motifs into Judaism injects crisis into tradition as a way to maintain the legitimacy of the Law within a historical reality that threatens or even denies its legality.

As is well known, Scholem posited a tripartite division of Jewish messianism into conservative, restorative, and utopian messianisms.[57] Whereas conservative messianism was linked with Rabbinic Judaism and centered on maintaining the conditions of possibility of applying/enforcing the Law in Exile, Scholem sought to revive the significance of the "dialectical" relation between the two other forms of messianism. The introduction of the gnostic component into Judaism is an example of re-establishing the dialectic between restorative and utopian messianisms.

The restorative form of messianism is characterized by an eschatology "of a *national* kind," in the sense that it upholds the belief that in the messianic age all *nations* on earth will come together in peace to worship the God of one nation, Israel, and will acquiesce to be ruled by a descendant of the House of David. On the contrary, the utopian or apocalyptic variant of messianism is far more revolutionary in character, in the sense that it envisages a fundamental change in the very structure of the world, and that means, essentially, a change in those power structures that make of this world a stage of permanent war between nations and peoples. The difference between the restorative and the utopian forms, politically speaking, seems to be that on the former view the Jewish Messiah will impose something akin to a real *pax romana* on all the nations of the world, by convincing them to worship the (true) One God [*eis theos*].[58] For apocalyptic or utopian messianism, however, the emphasis is placed on the unavoidability of "a final struggle between Israel and the heathens," a struggle in which the Christian

[57] (Scholem 1971, 3ff).

[58] This has some parallel to early forms of Christian political theology in Eusebius, according to which it is the Roman Empire that realizes the Messianic age. As Peterson says: "In this theory, the Roman Empire, which is at the same time the ideology of Constantine's reign, becomes the realization of the Messianic kingdom. . . . Jewish monotheism and not the Trinitarian God becomes the theological basis for the elevation of the Roman Empire into the worthiness of an eschatological kingdom" (1951, 87). Until the very end of his life, Peterson would hold the thesis that both heathen and Christian political theology had Jewish roots.

Pope represents the Anti-Christ, while the (hidden) Jewish Messiah bids his time, slumming at the gates of Rome (Scholem 1971, 12).[59]

Scholem always held on to the postulate that there exists a crucial difference between Jewish and Christian messianisms due to the "political" nature of the Jewish idea of redemption as opposed to the "spiritual," other-worldly character of the second.[60] His analysis of mystical Judaism seeks to identify that discourse within Judaism that most directly engages the politico-theological question of the priority of "enmity"—not only the "traditional" enmity between Jews and pagan peoples, but also (after Saint Paul) the new "enmity" between Jews and Christians. Looked at from this perspective, Scholem's studies of the Merkabah and Hekhaloth literature stand in close proximity with the themes of Part Three of Rosenzweig's *Star of Redemption*, from the political function of prayer to the political meaning of eschatology. Like Rosenzweig, Scholem also believes that the vision of the "Merkabah, the throne-world of God" drawn from *Ezechiel*, a vision of God as enthroned and crowned King of All, or *Pantokrator*, contains a teaching on the world historical dimensions of the *agon* against paganism as much as against Christianity.[61]

The Merkabah literature expresses the biblical teaching that each nation had an angelic guardian who pleaded their case to God in the heavenly court, on which depended the historical destiny of the given nation.[62] Peterson identifies in this angelology the original formulation of the "problem of nationalism" in Judaism and Christianity. He argues that pre-Trinitarian Christian political theology derives from Philo's idea of "divine monarchy" according to which "the invisible divine monarch . . . [who] abstractly 'reigns,' while the so-called national deities allocated to the different parts of the earth concretely 'govern' in his stead."[63] The Christian dualism between reign and government therefore adopts

[59] See (Momigliano 1994, 91), commenting on *Sanhedrin* 97b and 98a, where "the Messiah awaits his hour among the poor and the lepers at the gates of the city." There is a related legend of the Messianic banquet, often cited by Schmitt and Agamben, according to which in the Messianic age, the Jewish people will devour the body of the slain Leviathan (Scholem 1996, 60). On the importance of this apocalyptic legend for the contemporary discussion of political theology in Schmitt and Taubes, see (Rosenstock 2014).

[60] (Scholem 1971, 1). Taubes's entire critique of Scholem turns on the rejection of this postulate; see the 1983 essay "The Price of Messianism" in (Taubes 2010), and for documents related to the Taubes-Scholem polemic, see (Taubes 2000). The last, and certainly most important, exchange of letters is found in (Scholem 1999, 154, 387), which contains Scholem's definitive refusal to engage Taubes and Taubes's long, complex proposal to edit a book in honor of his eightieth birthday in which "Scholem would not only be treated as a 'Monument' but would be resurrected to *new life* through the 'mortification' of critique."

[61] "We are dealing with a Judaized form of cosmocratical mysticism concerning the divine King (or Emperor)" (Scholem 1977, 54).

[62] Peterson cites Deutoronomy 32 as the source of the idea that each nation was allotted their proper angel, except Israel whom God chose to relate to directly. "A nation is always more than the sum of its attributes; it is constituted through a spiritual principle and this principle is now, as the Jews say, either an angel or a god" (Peterson 1951, 82).

[63] (Heron 2018, 33), referring to (Peterson 2011, 70–2).

and adapts the distinction between *arche* (authority) and *dynamis* (power) in the Godhead, familiar from Philo and Josephus, and articulates it in the form of an angelology, whose ranks and dignities are meant to mimic the Persian kingly court, in which satraps "administer" the world for the Persian emperor.[64]

The genre of Merkabah mystical literature can be understood as a therapeutic discourse intended to come to terms with the "fear and trembling" elicited by the vision of the terrifying angels and archons surrounding the Throne in Ezechiel's prophecy, which symbolizes the dread and despair experienced by the Jewish nation when confronted with the destructive power of pagan empires. This Jewish mystical literature, on Scholem's reading, has two main foci of interest: the first concerns the nature of God's "majesty," or how God receives the attribute of the Crown; the second concerns the human ascent to and descent from the Godhead, and addresses the question of "fear and trembling."[65] Both themes are treated through a double reference, one internal to the Jewish tradition, the other linked with the tradition of Hellenistic kingship. The Jewish mystical literature can be understood as a running, internal critique of the Rabbinic teaching on God's rule in the age of exile, according to which the Torah itself was the heavenly Crown from which flowed the legitimate authority of the earthly crowns, belonging to the prince and to the priestly classes, respectively.[66] On the Hellenistic model of kingship, the crucial "mystical" foundation of regal authority consisted in the possibility of representing God on earth through a process in which the human sovereign "ascends" to the divine and the divine "descends" in and through the human sovereign.[67]

Arthur Green has explained the Midrashic background that is elaborated in the mystical treatment of the angelic guardians found in Ezechiel's vision of the wheel of the Throne. This wheel is itself composed by a gigantic angel, Sandalphon, who is "brother" to Enoch-Metatron: the two angels who stand behind and in front of God's Throne, respectively.[68] This gigantic angel is related to the figure of Adam Kadmon, the enormous Man, who was God's first,

[64] "The national gods have the role of satraps who stand by the side of the highest God, who is thought in analogy with the Persian emperor, in the administration of the world [*der Administration der Welt*]" (Peterson 1951, 85). Peterson cites a Talmudic text as origin of this analogy with the Persian emperor.

[65] "The aspects of God which are really relevant to the religious feeling of the epoch are His Majesty and the aura of sublimity and solemnity which surround Him" (Scholem 1977, 55). "Majesty, Fear and Trembling are indeed the key-words to this Open sesame of religion" (ibid., 57).

[66] On this Rabbinical discourse on the three crowns, see (Trigano 1991; and Cohen 2007).

[67] In his study of the mystic literature on the Crown, Arthur Green reiterates this Hellenistic context without registering Goodenough's pioneering studies: "Often a direct link between the two kingdoms [earthly and heavenly] is also provided by ancient myths and rituals, either in the descent of the gods into the person of the earthly ruler or in the ascent of the earthly kind, or his mythic ancestor, to the heavens. This link becomes the source of legitimation for the earthly ruler's authority, joining the domain of the sacred with the powers of the earthly realm" (Green 2014, 3).

[68] (Scholem 1977, 68–70).

yet unsuccessful creation, and whose body reached up from earth to heaven (Green 2014, pp. 22–3).[69] In one of the Midrashic collections, *Pesqita Rabbati*, the role of Sandalphon is to wreathe a crown from words. The crown then flies over the Godhead, effectively crowning God as King. Upon the Crown touching His head, so the story goes, "the creatures are silent and roar like a lion. Then they all respond and say: 'Holy holy holy is YHWH of Hosts; the whole earth is filled with His Glory.' . . . When the crown reaches His head, He strengthens Himself to receive the crown from His servants. All the creatures, seraphim, ofanim, chariot wheels and the throne of glory . . . say in unison: 'May YHWH rule forever, your God O Zion from generation to generation. Halleluyah!' (Ps. 146:10)."[70] Green comments that this story contains "the full group of *qedushah* [holiness] refrains—Isaiah 6:3, Ezekiel 3:12 and Psalm 146:10—in what is clearly a heavenly liturgy, recited amid great exultation in response to the (daily, as we shall see) coronation of the Creator."[71] Green does not comment on the possible relation between this Jewish heavenly liturgy and the Hellenistic coronation rituals.

It was in his early study *Eis Theos* (One God) on Hellenistic and Roman imperial acclamations and their transfer into Christian theology that Peterson suggests a Jewish source for them, possibly explained by the fact that "the acclamation expressing the desire for the eternal duration of the worldly messianic Kingdom is of oriental descent generally speaking" (Peterson 1926, 142).[72] In the previous chapter I showed the fundamental role that a political theology of liturgy plays in Rosenzweig's idea of the Kingdom. Scholem's analysis confirms that these insights have their historical ground in a mystical current of the Jewish tradition. The basis of the Jewish coronation hymns (*qedushah* liturgy) is the politico-theological belief that "the kingdom of earth is like the kingdom of heaven" (Green 2014, 33); more specifically, it turns out that the materials out

[69] Scholem discusses the passage in Ezekiel 1:26 that recounts the view of a "primordial man" on the Throne of the Merkabah (Scholem 1977, 63–6). Idel offers a discussion of Adam Kadmon as a crucial figure in working out the question of Hekhaloth literature concerning the sense in which the Torah (in Heaven) was an "image" or "icon" or even "body" of God. Here, the Torah is Adam Kadmon himself, and this Adam stands both for the necessity of giving the Torah to human beings, and also how adherence to its teachings will elevate human beings up to their humanity (Idel 2014b, 49–50).

[70] Cited in (Green 2014, 26).

[71] (Green 2014, 26). Scholem's discussion of the *qedushah* makes explicit reference to Rudolf Otto's "celebrated book *The Idea of the Holy*" and adopts from him the term "numinous hymns" (Scholem 1977, 57–60). Otto's conception of the numinous is crucial also for Strauss, and is therefore discussed in the next chapter.

[72] "It is certainly remarkable that the *eis aiouna* [for eternity] acclamation is also featured as refrain and acclamation in the Jewish cult. Obviously I am not thereby saying that the profane *eis aiouna* acclamation of the Roman Empire derives from Judaism. However, it seems to me that ultimately it is the Orient that has transmitted this acclamation to the West and that Egypt merely played the role of a mediator" (Peterson 1926, 143).

of which the Merkabah angel fashions God's crown are Israel's prayers.[73] "It is the community of Israel, as the liturgical sources clearly state, that offers a daily crown to God in prayer. This act, viewed from one side as a rite of submission to divine power, may also be seen from precisely the opposite point of view. Depicting themselves as the daily offerers of God's crown places Israel in a position of great mythic power, one that *makes them nearly equals in the economy of divine/human powers on which the world is based*" (Green 2014, 35, emphasis mine). The people's "great mythic power" refers to the theurgical function of prayer visible in the practice of glorification.[74] Scholem's hypothesis is that "the presentation of the crown to God is almost the only act through which the devotee can still bear witness to the religious destiny of man" (Scholem 1977, 61). For Scholem, the Merkabah literature suggests that it is God's *authority*, rather than His power, which has *both a mystical and a democratic basis* since it is a function of His people's prayers (acclamations).[75] Thus, for Scholem the "religious destiny of man" exemplified by Jewish mysticism takes the form of a *democratic political theology* because it refers to the "crowning" of the One God (of Israel) as the (true) King or Lord of the Heavens in and through the acclamations of His people. Prayer here expresses literally the idea of a divine democracy.

But what is the meaning of the democratic basis of God's Kingdom? Since Agamben hypothesized in *The Kingdom and the Glory* that Christian conceptions of government rest on the popular "acclamation" of Jesus as the Messiah to the Throne, there have been more studies connecting (direct) democracy to a conception of divine Glory.[76] Agamben's hypothesis relies on Peterson's *Eis Theos*, and its adoption by Schmitt in his own account of direct democracy in *Constitutional Theory*, for his claim that modern direct democracy is a secularized version of a Roman-Catholic interpretation of imperial acclamations.[77]

[73] Green argues that the repetition in the chant "Holy holy holy" refers to the three Crowns that are fashioned through Israel's prayers: one to be placed on God's head, the other two "upon the heads of Israel" (Green 2014, 34).

[74] Green claims that "the God who 'desires' the prayers of Israel or the righteous is in fact dependent on them for His very crown, symbol of God's *cosmic authority*" (2014, 36, emphasis mine). Agamben refers to the same "theurgical character of prayer" expressed in the Kabbalah, but does so in relation to Marcel Mauss's treatise on prayer and its development in Émile Durkheim (2011, 227–30).

[75] Green cites in this context the Rabbinical saying: "there is no King without a people," apparently based on *Pirqey rabbi Eliezer* 3: "if the king has no army and no camp, over what does he rule? And if there is no people praising the king, what is that king's glory" (Green 2014, 36). Note that these formulations are easily relatable to the use of the analogy between God and the commander of armies in Aristotelian theology as discussed by Goodenough and examined in chapter 1.

[76] See (Dean 2017), whose analysis of acclamation remains within Agamben's parameters of a Christian political theology that takes for granted the division between "sovereignty" and "governmentality." Dean consequently divides acclamations into three kinds, corresponding to the acclamation of an emperor or charismatic leader, to the more liberal idea of public opinion as a form of acclamation managed through the press, and lastly an acclamation that is operative in social media and constitutes a "public mood." See also (Guyette 2014).

[77] (Agamben 2011, 254–5).

But does this mean that Israel's acclamations play an "economic" role in God's plan for ruling the world?[78] Or, on the contrary, do these mystical texts work a quite distinct politico-theological interpretation of the *Shema* (Deutoronomy 6:4): "Hear O Israel, the Lord our God is One Lord"?[79]

Bickerman can again be helpful to contextualize the stakes of Scholem's interpretation of the mystical elaboration of the *Shema*:

> The Jews accepted the idea of the unpronounceable Divine Name only after the Exile. Their national God was now "the God in Jerusalem" or the "God of Heaven" a name which identified Him with the supreme deity of the Persians and the Syrian peoples. Accordingly, the pronunciation *Elohim* (God) and afterward *Adonai* (my Lord) was substituted for the tetragrammaton YHWH. When the Greeks came, the abstract term "God" perfectly corresponded to their philosophical conception of the Supreme Being, *ho Theos*, the God, or *to Theion*, the Divine. So they accepted this indefinite designation for the God of the Jews. By a kind of reverse attraction, the Greek speculative term then influenced the Hebrew writers. (Bickerman 1979, 66)

It is this "reverse attraction" that Scholem identifies as operative in Jewish gnostic mysticism: at stake is a complex politico-theological transition from a national God to the One God who is the true Lord of Heavens. In this transition, Jewish mysticism seems to *reverse* the Hellenistic conception of monotheism: as opposed to uniting a people around "one king" representing the "one god," the Jewish acclamation reverses the direction of glorification, so that it is only thanks to the democratic acclamation by One People—a unified people-in-arms—that the national God of the Hebrews is elevated over and above the universe and its governors/archons as the One God.

On Agamben's hypothesis, the democratic glorification of God is ultimately possible because the Throne is always already "empty": democracy is only the fuel on which the governmental machine runs.[80] All sovereign authority has

[78] Green's reference to the "economy of divine/human powers" would seem to lend support to Agamben's contention that the liturgy of God's Kingship is ultimately functional to a "governmental machine." "The economy is anarchical and, as such, has no foundation in God's being; and yet, the Father has generated the Son before the eternal times. This is the 'mystery of the economy,' whose darkness glory is not able completely to dispel in its light. . . . Government glorifies the Kingdom, and the Kingdom glorifies Government. But the center of the machine is empty, and glory is nothing but the splendour that emanates from this emptiness, the inexhaustible *khabod* that at once reveals and veils the central vacuity of the machine" (Agamben 2011, 211).

[79] See (Bruno 2013, 32ff) for a recent discussion of the Shema, and its four possible meanings: "YHWH is our God, YHWH is one"; "YHWH our God, YHWH is one"; "YHWH our God is one YHWH"; "YHWH is our God, YHWH alone."

[80] See the discussion of the "empty throne" in (Agamben 2011, 245). I return to this motif in the Conclusion.

been emptied out into government, and the legitimacy of this government is exclusively democratic (plebiscitarian). On Scholem's hypothesis, instead, only the democratic constitution of a people can elevate God (YHWH) above the plane of national deities and state governments, in their constant wars for power and influence, in order to place Him on the Throne of Glory. By internalizing gnostic motifs and Hellenistic acclamations, Jewish mystical literature articulates the priority of the Oneness or singularity of God over His attributes of power as Lord of Heavens, attributes that were still associated with the Persian image of God as King, helped in his administrative duties by the national angels or gods. This prioritization of God's Oneness or singularity corresponds to the Oneness of all the peoples on earth that is occasioned by their assumption of a republican political form in which the authority of the law is based on the consent of the people. Where the Rabbinical tradition understands the Oneness of God as a function of His power to manipulate kingdoms and empires in pursuit of His world-historical providential plan, the Jewish mystical tradition, on this interpretation, argues quite the opposite point: the Jewish national God will be able to become the One God of All only when power will become what is held by All together, that is, by peoples over their governments. The advance of monotheism is essentially tied up with the advance of democracy, not of imperialism.

If this hypothesis is correct, then it becomes clear why maintaining the *political unity* of the Jewish people as a people under a divine constitution became the central concern of Jewish mystical literature, for such a political, republican unity was constantly threatened or divided by the ascendancy of the priestly class as well as by the kingly hierarchies. This division is the fate that befalls the Christian peoples. Peterson argued that through their liturgical acclamations of Jesus as Christ, the community of Christian believers constituted themselves as a laity (*laos*), much like in the pagan *ekklesia*, "the *laos* signals its status through its right to express its *ekboesis* [acclaim] to the *despotes* [ruler or dictator]" (Peterson 1926, 179). Nicholas Heron shows that in Christianity the idea of *laos* is given a pastoral, anti-democratic interpretation in order to introduce a distinction "between the people insofar as it is the subject of sovereignty and the people insofar as it is the object of government" (2018, 55). Thus, in the Christian tradition "liturgy ceases once and for all to be a service performed by the people and for the people itself; rather, it becomes a service for the people . . . that is performed by the those who, in a very determinate sense, are not the people" but the clergy (Heron 2018, 50). In this way, direct democracy is thus subsumed under an "economical" rather than "political" logic of government, one based on the clergy rather than on the *demos*.

Scholem's reading of the Merkabah and Hekhaloth acclamations reveals a crucial departure of the Jewish from the Christian tradition because this Jewish mystical literature *resists* the Christian sublation of a politically self-organized people into an obedient group of believers led by its clergy. Indeed, the Jewish equivalent of the *laos* is not reducible to its Christian, Trinitarian, and governmental articulation. The Septuagint translation of *laos* does not have a "pastoral" sense as much as a civic-military one: *laos* refers to "the people insofar as they stand assembled and unified behind a [military] leader" (Heron 2018, 54, 57–60). [81] In other words, the Septuagint is simply following the biblical conception of God as *melekh*—or military leader—of a people-in-arms. Thus, for the Jewish mystical tradition, it is only the political unification of a people that grants prayer its constituent power and, in this sense, makes for a "priestly" or "holy" people.

Peterson identified the "essence of the acclamation" in the belief that the "acclaimed one was lifted and elevated by the acclamation towards an apotheosis."[82] Through the acclamation by his people, the political leader would be raised to the level of a deity (apotheosis) and so entered into communication with the Godhead. In an essay of 1944, Ernst Kantorowicz followed up this theme and focused in particular on the structure of the soul's "ascent" to God. His claim is that Christian imperial acclamations were based on a "very old" analogy between the acclamation of the Hellenistic king as he enters into the worldly city and the entry of the soul into the heavenly city (1944, 208). Kantorowicz does not mention that this analogy is also fundamental to the Hekhaloth mystical literature, which is related to the gnostic motif of the ascension of the soul from earth up to the divine resting place of God, represented by the symbol of Seven Palaces that stand above the heavens. The mystic pilgrim ascends past the planetary archons that guard the gates of the Palace and "are opposed to the liberation of the soul from its earthly bondage and whose resistance the soul must overcome" (Scholem 1977, 50). The origin of this symbol is found in Daniel 10:13, where the angel of Persia tries to prevent Daniel's prayer from reaching God.[83] Several Jewish legends attest to God's intervention on behalf of Moses against His angels, with some texts indicating that God offered Moses a place on His Throne of Glory, others simply stating that God told Moses to hold on to the Throne for protection. The motif of human enthronement turns out to be a decisive one in the Jewish mystical literature.

Joseph Schultz discusses the theme of angelic opposition to Moses's ascension to receive the Law. He argues that the angels objected to giving the Law to Moses because it contained certain "mysteries" that needed to remain in Heaven and

[81] Heron relies on Orsolina Montevecchi's claim according to which the Jewish use of *laos* refers to a people elected by God: "you are a holy people [*laos hagios*] for the Lord your God, and the Lord your God has chosen you to be for him a special people [*laos periousias*] as compared with all other nations [*para panta ta ethne*] to be found on the face of the earth" (Deuteronomy 7:6) (Montevecchi 1998) cited in (Heron 2018, 60).

[82] "It belongs to the essence of acclamation that the one who is acclaimed is lifted and elevated by the acclamation which can even lead to apotheosis" (Peterson 1926, 173).

[83] (Peterson 1951, 83).

were not to be disclosed to mere humans. These mysteries were not simply the practical commandments discussed in the Talmud, but consisted in "the mysteries of Tora . . . and all the depths of the perfect Law . . . and all the secrets of the universe and all the secrets of creation" as well as "the Gnosis of things above and the fear of heaven."[84] The point of the angelic opposition to Moses is to allude to the dual nature of the Torah: while the exoteric part was communicated to all of Israel in the form of commandments, the esoteric part remained in the possession of Moses and was transmitted by way of a (secret) tradition to the future commanders of the people. It is this secret tradition of a second, hidden Torah that forms the basis of the Kabbalah. The tradition stretching from Merkabah to Kabbalah is therefore concerned with the esoteric teachings of divine rule of the universe and not just with the legalistic ethic to be followed by Israel.

The appearance of the king at the gates of the city is technically called "epiphany" or "parousia." It seems likely that the Roman Catholic hymns and prayers that acclaim the advent of the king before the gates of the city in imitation of "the Lord's triumphant entry as king into Jerusalem on Palm Sunday" (Kantorowicz 1944, 210) were to be counter-balanced in the Merkabah and Hekhaloth literature by the acclamations of the true Messiah hiding *outside* the gates of Jerusalem (or Rome), and who would thereby bring God's Kingdom down to earth by appealing to the support of those who were excluded from the city. Hellenistic and Christian acclamations leading to the apotheosis focused on the element of "throne-sharing":

> throne-sharing in connection with an Adventus must have been likewise familiar concept and a trait well known in the Hellenistic world. Christ, after his Ascension and at his Adventus in heaven, becomes the *Synthronos* of God. He shares the throne sitting on the right of the Father, and this idea is repeated later on over and over again in benedictions for the medieval ruler who, it is hoped, may share in the afterlife the throne of Christ and rule in *condominium* with the Christus "cuius typum gerit in nomine [whose type he bears in name]." (Kantorowicz 1944, 213)

By contrast, the aim of this early Jewish gnostic mysticism of the Throne and the Palace may have been to persuade the Jewish people (*laos*) that *no throne-sharing between Father and Son has taken place* in the divine palaces of the One God, and that Moses's ascent to God on Mount Sinai confirmed this fact. That is why Moses brings down from Heaven the Written Torah as a legal constitution and does not set himself up as the earthly representative or vicar in the form of an Emperor or Pope of the Jews. For these sovereign authorities are based on the

[84] (Schultz 1971, 296), citing from 3 Enoch.

assumption of "throne-sharing," on the belief that Jesus is the Christ (Messiah) who rose up from death and is sitting at the right of the Father, with the Father and the Son dividing their power and authority into kingdom and government. The central politico-theological aim of the early Jewish mystical experience, by contrast, would be to offer a first-person and lay testimony to the whole Jewish people that there is no divine throne-sharing in Heaven.

Perhaps it would be more exact to say that the Merkabah mysticism is not opposed to a sharing of the Throne as such, but denies that the Son shares it with the Father. The legends surrounding Moses's ascension to the Throne find an echo in the anthropomorphic symbol for God the Creator as an enormously large human being (Adam Kadmon) found in the Merkabah and Hekhaloth literature. The gigantic Adam has a politico-theological function that Scholem addresses in his discussion of the idea of "communion" or *devekut* with God, which he distinguishes from the Hellenistic, philosophical idea of *homoiosis* ("unification") with the divine. As he explains: "if man casts off all earthly or material elements and ascends through all the worlds and becomes one with God to the degree of losing the feeling of separate existence, then will he be rightly called *adam*, Man, 'being transformed into the cosmic figure of the primordial man whose likeness upon the throne Ezekiel beheld' " (Scholem 1971, 226).

The figure of Adam Kadmon sitting on the Throne could be symbolic of the belief that the proper object of Redemption is all of humanity, as opposed to the Christian belief in a personal salvation. Put another way, only humanity as a whole could aspire to wearing the Crown. Consequently, God does not "descend" from the Throne in the form of another Person, as the Son. The image of Adam Kadmon undermines all vicarious representatives of the Son, whether in the form of Pope or Emperor. It also opens the possibility of an anarchic God who not only "descends" from His Throne but "abdicates" His Crown, not for the sake of His Son or His vicars, but for the sake of humanity as such. The possibility that humanity as a whole could be elevated to a dignity that is royal and divine is related to a gnostic-like division between the unknowable essence of God as King, an essence that is never realized in the world (and, for that reason, makes possible the Creation of the world as something apart and distinct from God), and the existence of God as Creator. This existence is characterized by His "descent" from the Throne and finding in His Creation the Shekinah, or place of rest, otherwise known as the glory or manifestation of God.

The empty throne and creation out of nothing

The transition from late Hellenistic and early medieval Merkabah literature to the late medieval and early modern Kabbalah in Scholem's historiography can be understood in terms of a shift of emphasis from the One God as King of All to the One God as Creator of All. This transition marks a shift from a Jewish political theology that is mainly expressed liturgically to a Jewish political theology that articulates itself in more philosophical terms of metaphysics and physics, such as Scholem finds in the Spanish and then Palestinian development of the Kabbalah starting with the *Zohar*. The shift marks a move from discussing the mystery of the Chariot to the mystery of the Creation as *creatio ex nihilo*, with emphasis on the Kabbalistic conception of Nothingness. These later interpretations shed a fundamental light on Scholem's earlier exchanges with Benjamin about Kafka and the "Nothingness of Revelation," remarks that were foundational for the renewal of interest in political theology in Derrida and Agamben.

If God is the King of All and has for all eternity sat on His Throne alone, then the question or "mystery" emerges as to why He "descended" from the Throne and was "moved" to create nature out of nothing. What does the introduction of movement at the heart of the unknowable and unmovable God mean for Jewish political theology? The mystery of Creation expresses one of the highest points of tension between Judaism and Gnosticism. Orthodox Judaism identifies God as Father/King with God as Creator (or the God of Israel), while Gnosticism radically distinguishes both divinities as two distinct persons. Gnosticism sees the Creator as a mere Demiurge and believes that God the Father had to send a Redeemer to save the world from the evil that was created by the Demiurge. Scholem investigates how a gnostic form of Judaism negotiates between these two antithetical views on the inner division within the Godhead.[85]

The question of the relation between God and His Creation raises the specter of pantheism. If Creation is somehow "essential" to who God is, then there exists the danger of identifying God with Nature's God; if it is not, there is the danger that Creation is only the work of a malevolent demiurge. According to Harry Wolfson's grand narrative of medieval philosophy, these dangers were realized only with Spinoza's defense of pantheism. Spinoza put an end to the Judeo-Hellenistic employment of philosophy (and mysticism) as shields for the Torah. Scholem's contribution to understand the response to the immanent threat of pantheism is his original interpretation of the Kabbalistic doctrine of *creatio ex nihilo* as a form of affirmative nihilism. Despite the fact that Jewish orthodoxy stands or falls on the belief in the Creation of Nature,[86] Rabbinical doctrine

[85] "We may ask whether there did not exist—at any rate among the Merkabah mystics . . . a belief in a fundamental distinction between the appearance of God the Creator, the Demiurge, i.e. one of His aspects, and His indefinable essence? . . . As is well known, the anti-Jewish gnostics of the second and third centuries drew a sharp distinction between the unknown, 'strange,' good God, and the Creator, whom they identified with the God of Israel" (Scholem 1977, 65).

[86] "No Jewish theology whatever can renounce the doctrine that the world is a creation—as a one-time event or as a continual always self-renewing process . . . the Jewish faith in God as Creator will maintain its place, beyond all images and myths" (Scholem 1976, 277–8).

generally tended to think that Creation emerges from a mythical representation of "not-being" as a primordial matter, "something chaotic," rather than out of a "pure Nothing" (Scholem 1970b, 64).[87] Scholem argues that only Jewish mysticism, and neither the Rabbinical nor the philosophical development of tradition, worked out a pure conception of Nothingness. Only the Kabbalah strengthened the conception of God as Creator in order to take Him definitively away from the Gnostic orbit. Only the Kabbalah defended the belief in *creatio ex nihilo* from the risk of turning into mere religious dogma, a point of blind faith that could not be rationally defended.

As argued so far, Scholem's central idea is that Judaism defends and renews itself all the better the more it internalizes the Greek philosophy that is nominally opposed to it. In the case of the Kabbalah, what is internalized as a defense against Gnosticism is Neoplatonic doctrine. Thus, it is not surprising that Scholem's presentation of the Kabbalah is framed within the context of a discourse on the encounter of Athens and Jerusalem: a Neoplatonist identification of God as the "impersonal" One or *Hen* meeting the biblical conception of a personal God as King (Scholem 1970a, 14–7). For Scholem this encounter has a politico-theological motivation: it is designed to work out an account of the relation between the unknowable and unrepresentable essence and the powers (attributes, *sefira*) of the personal God: only the latter "realizes itself in the world of emanation" (Scholem 1996, 145). The central intuition is to develop a conception of God that is critical of power while avoiding the Gnostic rejection of power. The key is the development of an alternative theory of the authority of the Law out of a conception of constituent power as *creatio ex nihilo*.[88]

The strict division between the hypostases of One and Mind, *Hen* and *Nous*, introduced by Plotinus, allowed mystical Judaism to work out a distinction and hierarchy between the unrepresentable God and the revealed God and His primary action, namely, Creation (Scholem 1970a, 20). Scholem is clear that by appropriating the philosophical duality *Hen*/*Nous*, mystical Judaism was able to deal with the problems caused by the priority assigned by Rabbinical Judaism

[87] Scholem follows Wolfson in claiming that Philo still had not developed such a pure concept of Nothingness, and, a fortiori, this pure concept was also absent in the subsequent medieval philosophical tradition of monotheism—only in Kabbalah does the required idea of Nothingness emerge (Scholem 1970b, 63).

[88] Joseph Ben-Shlomo, another authoritative interpreter of Scholem, misses the politico-theological significance of this distinction between God's power and its relation to God's substance. His reading is too centered on the anxiety of not confusing the Christian adoption of Neoplatonism in the figure of *unio mystica* as opposed to the Jewish idea of "communion [*devequt*] with Him" which preserves the radical difference between "the Creator and His creature" (1994, 60). However, Scholem's greater anxiety lies with not conflating the unrepresentable God with the revealed God: he is willing to go a long way with pantheism, and thus critically question the orthodox distinction between God as Creator and His creatures, in order to preserve the Neoplatonist point of the transcendence of the One with respect to its emanations, which includes the power of Creation.

to the revealed God of Israel, that is, to God as a function of His powers, even if these powers were thought to have been checked by the terms of the covenant with His people.

Considered in this light, the Rabbinic approach to the God of Revelation had at least three problematical features. First, it left Judaism open to the following objection: if the God of Israel was indeed omnipotent, how were the defeats of His people at the hands of stronger empires to be explained in and through history? The traditional Rabbinical answer, that historical defeat and exile and persecution were due to the "sins" of the Jewish people, to their non-application of all commandments, was not a satisfactory answer given that the conditions for the complete application of the Law would become a reality only with the indefinitely postponed advent of the true Messiah. Scholem argues that it became necessary for Judaism to counter this traditional view of sin with an entirely different conception of "sin as redemption," a view that, logically speaking, was only possible if the "true" Jewish Messiah had arrived in history and had himself "gone under," bringing down with him the entire messianic complex.

Second, the traditional fixation on the powers of God, on His revealed attributes, left unthematized the question of the *authority* of God's Law (as opposed to its powers). It left the Law at the mercy of the transmission from father to son of the "experience" of God's terrifying self-revelation on Mount Sinai and the "capitulation" of the people, even back then, to Moses's charisma and authority rather than to God's own authority. The political problem this raised was evident: if from the very start the people of Israel was unable to withstand the revelation of the true King, how would it be capable of this reception once the Temple was destroyed and the Diaspora generalized? No amount of aggadic reflection on these past events seemed to render back to all Jews the experience of this unrepresentable One. Neoplatonism held out another path, precisely the mystical path of *henosis*, or reunification with the One (*Hen*), as a *permanent* possibility to "return to beginnings" and, thus, as a source of new life for the Jewish people.

Third, the traditional emphasis on the revealed attributes of an anthropomorphized God was a source of permanent danger to the claim that the God of Israel was the unique Being, the source of all existence, without whom nothing at all could be. The danger, more precisely, was that God's powers could become autonomous, and the angels of nations become "independent." This situation could cast into question not only strict monotheism, but above all the goodness of Creation: it could offer a possible justification for the apotheosis of victorious human archons, and it could also fuel the Gnostic belief in the evil of this world that has been left up to the government of those who have most power.

Scholem's decisive historiographical intervention was to rehabilitate the Plotinian One or *Hen* as the main philosophical and mystical resource of the

Kabbalistic doctrine of God as the Infinite, *En sof* (Scholem 1970a, 22). Through this internalization of Neoplatonism, the Kabbalah could respond to the preceding perplexities raised by the crisis of the Jewish tradition. Perhaps the most important point was to effect a basic reorientation in the experience of history and its philosophy. The historical vicissitudes of the identification of God with its attributes oriented the Jewish people toward the future coming of a Redeemer, as if Creation and then the events on Mount Sinai conformed an unreachable "past" whose shadow extended indefinitely into a "future" along a straight line of progression. By way of contrast, the Neoplatonist focus on the primacy of the One over the Mind, and above all the Neoplatonist belief in the permanent possibility of a *return to the One*, allows history to be turned *around and back* toward its unfathomable origin.[89]

Furthermore, the Neoplatonist division between the "In Itself" and the emanations of the One makes it clear that all powers emerge from the "ur-wisdom" of the One: everything has its origin from the *En sof* and must return back to it (Scholem 1970a, 23, 26). Over and above the *powers* that determine the conditions of application of the Law stands its *authority*, which is linked to a conception of wisdom, or *Sophia*. The concept of *Sophia* is analogous to the Hellenistic idea of a providential world-spirit (*pronoia*) that "moves" around the world, and wherever it takes up residence, an empire flourishes, only to "fall" once it moves on. The tradition of this idea, found in the image of four empires described in the Book of Daniel, leads from Polybius to Machiavelli and finally to Hegel.[90] The Hellenistic idea of the world spirit or world soul links the divinity with a conception of historico-political movement that, as Fackenheim intuited, was problematic for the Jewish experience of history because it left it open to the Hegelian claim that Jews were no longer historically "actual," that world history had left the Jewish people "behind," as it had left behind other peoples in its inexorable progressive march. By positing the *En sof* as an unknowable origin of this historico-political wisdom, the Kabbalah introduces an archi-historical or counter-historical source of "movement" deep in the "In Itself" of God. This source functions as a standing possibility to "recall" or "call back" (to a more originary state) everything that has happened in history. From this perspective, nothing that occurs in history is ever in its "final" state of completion. To the contrary, the idea of the *En sof* as articulated in the Kabbalah gives rise to the image of history as a field of ruins, which receives its theological expression in the shattering of the "vessels" that were supposed to withhold God's wisdom (*Shevirat*

[89] I disagree with Ben-Shlomo's claim that for Scholem "the internal logic of the doctrine of [Neoplatonic] emanation leads to pantheism and it is therefore inherently antithetical to Jewish mysticism" for reasons set out in the following (Ben-Shlomo 1994, 61).

[90] See the essay "Daniel and the Greek Theory of Imperial Succession" in (Momigliano 1994, 29–35).

ha-Kelim).[91] Echoes of this conception are not difficult to find in the theological tropes used by Benjamin in his *Theses on the Philosophy of History*, like the idea of an *apokatastasis* or *restitutio ad integrum* [restitution to an original state], as well as the image of the Angel of history.

The thesis that lies at the heart of Scholem's new interpretation of the Kabbalistic *En sof* is that there must exist a distinction between God's wisdom, as second attribute, and the "movement" in the *En sof*. If God's wisdom is the plan He has developed for Creation, then the idea of God's movement in the *En sof* means that this plan is always already open to exceptions, to unexpected deviations, precisely because it is undergirded, even subverted, by what Scholem calls God's "thinking" or "willing" beyond any possible horizon of human and even divine knowability, and is thus radically unexpected and unannounceable.[92] In other words, if God as *En sof* has the monopoly of authority and decision, then this monopoly is in the function of attaining *freedom from history* rather than power over it.

For Scholem, the Kabbalah tends to side more with an idea of God's "will" rather than His "thought" because of its Neoplatonist affiliation: this allows it to take distance from the Aristotelian God as *unmoved* mover whose defining feature is thought (*Nous*) thinking itself, wherein there is no recourse to an anterior One, or *Hen*, that lies "beyond thought" (Scholem 1970a, 30–3).[93] At the same time, the Neoplatonist doctrine of the One understands the passage from God as *En sof* to God as Creator as a function of an emanation, a movement of "emptying out" or *kenosis* of the One that comes from its "overfullness" with itself.

These Neoplatonic motifs are immediately transposed and modified in the Kabbalistic theory of the Nothing. For the Kabbalah, the idea of God's "will" is identical with God's Nothing, and this Nothing is conceived not in terms of lack or absence or void, but in terms of an excess of being, as the *Übersein* (*hyper-on*; *super-esse*) of God qua *Ensof* (Scholem 1970a, 39–

[91] Bouretz argues that Scholem's interest in Kabbalistic speculations, especially the Kabbalah that is developed after the Jews were expelled from Spain and Portugal, is due to his belief that these speculations allowed Judaism to track the political experience of ongoing persecution and historical disasters, offering an incentive for the messianic development that will culminate with Sabbatianism. This is no doubt correct, but Bouretz misses the inherently productive view of history that, according to Scholem, the Kabbalah brings about in and through its account of history as a catastrophe, and that is not related to the Sabbatian messiah. The Kabbalistic doctrine of Nothingness is about Creation; Sabbatianism is part of a discourse on Redemption.

[92] "However, in the Kabbalists these two moments part ways. For them the will, the word and the wisdom of God will never be identical. . . . This is exactly the special position of the will at the threshold between the hidden and the revealed God, to which the Kabbalistic conception gives a particular emphasis" (Scholem 1970a, 38).

[93] Maintaining the difference between the God of Moses, as radically transcendent, and the God of Aristotle, as "unmoved mover" of the heavens, is thus only a first move in a complicated game. Scholem beliefs that the second move is for Kabbalah to adopt Plotinus under the guise of the Arabic Neoplatonic compendium called *Aristotle's Theology* as a way to counteract Aristotelianism from inside Greek philosophy itself. Compare with (Kreisel 2015) on Maimonides' relation to the Kabbalah.

40).[94] The doctrine of Nothingness in the Kabbalah is a doctrine of God's freedom. God does not freely will "the Nothing" from which Creation emerges, but, as Nothing, God decides to freely create some being other than itself. The Nothing of God is the condition of possibility of the freedom of what is created.[95] The Nothing permits, in a sense, the free Creation of more freedom: human freedom is based on nihilism, just as Cohen and Rosenzweig teach. This process of Creation is the veritable content of Scholem's account of divine sovereignty as constituent power. It accounts for the ultimate sense in which the God of Israel is King of All; and why the Nothing is designated as the Crown, the first of the divine sefiroth. This is also why God as King is not different from God as Creator: God is Crowned (by His people) insofar as He freely decides the Creation (of freedom) (Scholem 1970a, 47).

On a superficial view, Creation out of Nothing brings into play the conventional tension between Greek philosophy and biblical revelation, the former denying that something can be created from nothing, the latter affirming this possibility. Scholem believes that Jewish (but also Christian) mystics overturned the apparent meaning of the doctrine in order to see in Nothing the "fullness" of Being or God: "The creation out of nothing, as it emerges repeatedly in the mystical tradition, is the creation out of God itself" (1970b, 68). In other words, God is Nothing, or, better, the "Nothingness of the super-Being of God [*Nichts des Überseins Gottes*]" (68).[96] Creation out of Nothing then refers to the *kenosis*, or emptying out, that follows from the overfullness of God as Nothing.

In this context, Scholem makes use of Scotus Eriugena's conception according to which "the descent of God into its own originary grounds [*Urgründe aller Dinge*] where all things are archetypically developed, is the descent into His own Nothingness, out of which everything derives" (Scholem 1970b, 73). The wording here is crucial: Creation refers to a "descent" [*Hinabsteigen*] of God (from His Throne) into His Nothingness in order to create something that is other than God. There is a strong sense here of God's *abdication* from the Throne in order to make possible Creation (and thus the creation of freedom in His creatures). If

[94] Wolfson offers a Heideggerian reading of Scholem's reconstruction of the Kabbalah's doctrine of Nothing and hyper-essentiality which deserves a fuller discussion (Wolfson 2012). The main difference between our readings is that I offer a politico-theological discussion of God's nothingness and anarchy, whereas his treatment remains at the ontological level of the deconstruction of presence.

[95] "God is free. This freedom proves itself not in a leap from the En Sof to the first Sephiroth . . . but in the decision to emanate the area which is the thinking of God and His Sophia as the true beginning of the act of Creation. When we speak of Creation out of Nothingness we mean that God's freedom lies in the Creation and not in Nothingness" (Scholem 1970a, 43).

[96] There is unfortunately no room to pursue the similarities between Jewish mysticism and the discourse of Christian mystics like Meister Eckhart on the idea of the Nothingness of God. See (Schürmann 2005; and Flasch 2006) for two very different approaches to the latter. This discussion would lead to a complicated discourse on the overlap between Heidegger's appropriation of Christian mystical discourse and Scholem's idea of Jewish mysticism.

the Crown of God is God's Nothingness, then Creation emerges in and as God's emptying of, or abdicating from the Throne. Crucially, this abdication does not take the form of the co-substantiality of the Son with the Father as one finds in the Trinitarian scheme. In the Kabbalistic tradition, God's abdication from absolute rule is not equivalent to the creation of government, according to Peterson's formula of the "king reigns but does not govern." Nor is the Kabbalistic doctrine of Nothing as fullness put in the service of a Hellenistic theory of kingship, as happens, for instance, in Alfarabi's appropriation of the Plotinian scheme.

The Kabbalistic version of *kenosis* serves to undermine the Hellenistic idea of monarchy. The Kabbalistic teaching is that "Creation out of Nothing" refers to the Creation of the second sefiroth, wisdom (*Chochma*), from out of the first sefiroth, the Crown (*Keter*) of God. According to Scholem, Kabbalists are divided as to what this Crown is. Some claim that it is an emanation from the *En sof*, a kind of "aura around his Being" (Scholem 1970b, 76). The first sefiroth, or Crown, also takes the form of an "infinite abyss in God itself"—it is this abyss or *an-arche* that makes the *En sof* or Infinite into the Nothing (Scholem 1970b, 77). Others believe that the first sefiroth, the Crown, or infinite will of God, represents the essence of the *En sof*. "Thereby *En sof* and *Ajin*, the Infinite and Nothingness, are identical. From the point of view of the creature, the Infinite appears as a super-Being of Nothingness [*erscheint das Unendliche als ein Übersein des Nichts*], not as a determination of God but as Godhead itself [*die Gottheit selbst*]" (Scholem 1970b, 77). This latter interpretation, which Scholem links to the Spanish Kabbalah of Luria and Codovero, teaches "that the Nothing is Being, and Being is the Nothing [*dass das Nichts der Sein ist, und das Sein das Nichts*]" (Scholem 1970b, 78). Although in this context Scholem gestures toward Hegel's first movements of the Logic of Being, in reality his understanding of the Kabbalistic doctrine excludes the fundamental role of negation ("nicht") found in Hegel's doctrine of the passage from Being to Nothing, because it remains rooted in the Neoplatonist conception of the *Hen* as a *superesse*, an *excess* of Being, and it is this excess that "is" the Nothing.[97]

Scholem's apparently metaphysical explanation of the "Nothing of Revelation" can be understood in politico-theological terms as follows. Divine authority,

[97] "The Nothing is not the Nothing independent from God, but Its Nothingness. [*Das Nichts ist nicht das Nichts, das von Gott unabhangig ist, sondern sein Nichts.*] The transformation of Nothingness into Being is a process within God Himself, namely, the act in which the divine wisdom manifests itself and Nothingness and Being are both only aspects of the one, undifferentiated 'super-Being' [*des einen, ungeschiedenen 'Überseins'*] (*superesse*)" (Scholem 1970b, 79). These texts seem to contradict Idel's claim that "Scholem's understanding of Nothingness, which is correct semantically but wrong ontologically, reflects a Hegelian [*sic*] approach to negation found within divinity, whereas the intention of the Kabbalists is ontological plenitude even though they use the term Ayin" (Idel 2015, 26). As can be seen from the citations, Scholem insists repeatedly that the Nothing is God's *superesse*. Scholem explicitly states that "Nothingness out of which everything emerges represents God's hyperessentiality [*Überwesentlichkeit*] 'superessentia'" (1970b, 74).

tied to God's unforeseeable will, consists in the decision to ab-dicate from the Crown (of absolute sovereignty or *arche*), and descend from His Throne, thus establishing theocracy as a form of an-archy. The descent is not a movement of emanation, outside of God, but consists in an internal emptying out: it is a descent into God's own abyss or absence of ground (*an-arche*). This abdication into anarchy then gives rise to Creation as a work of divine wisdom. Scholem's reading of the Kabbalistic doctrine of Nothing employs a Nietzschean sense of "descent," rather than a Heideggerian idiom of *Gelassenheit*. God "overcomes" Himself (*Übersein*) by "going down" into Nothingness. God is in excess of Himself as *superesse* precisely by abdicating from His own powers in and through Creation. This abdication of God as the super-being (and super-Man) is symbolically captured by the image of Adam Kadmon, who symbolizes the self-overcoming of human beings, or "overman." The Kabbalistic teaching of God's Nothingness is that humanity can be "crowned" in its dignity only once all sovereignty is abdicated following the model of God's descent. Benjamin's image in the *Theological-Political Fragment* of the "eternity of downfall" corresponds quite closely to this Kabbalistic understanding of the Nothingness of God.

On this interpretation of the Kabbalah, Creation is no longer an expression of God's omnipotence, of God being only (and all) power and order, as much as of God's self-limitation as Only Being. However, this self-limitation is not a form of negation of this singularity: God remains the sole and unique Being, and everything else derives, not from God as an emanation from Him, but from the "Excess" of this One Being, which Excess of Being can only be designated as Nothing. In turn, Nothing denotes an abyss, "the place where all beings stand in their formless undifferentiation," that is, the place of the "formless and simple *causae primordiales*," perhaps a synonym for Chaos. Thus, God's Creation is a result of His Only Being self-contracting into Nothing. The central idea is that "only where God withdraws within Himself . . . can He create something that is not divine Essence and Being" (Scholem 1970b, 85). Luria's idea of *zimzum* is a "conception of God as self-contraction that makes space for Creation" (Scholem 1970b, 86).

If the crucial Kabbalistic step consists in changing "Creation out of Nothing into a Creation out of the Excess of Being of God" (Scholem 1970b, 84), the most difficult point that needs elaboration is the "identification of Creation out of Nothing with the Idea of Emanation." How does the introjection of a Hellenistic philosopheme, that is, the idea of emanation, get turned around in favor of a doctrine of Creation? Emanationism carries the danger of pantheism, understood as the belief that nothing other than God can exist, and thus God is Nature, God is everything and everywhere (Scholem 1970b, 84). Ultimately, in order to justify Creation and its goodness, it is necessary to show how a being that is not God can subsist outside of God: "how can things subsist if they are not God?" (Scholem

1970b, 85).[98] The Kabbalistic teaching of the "deep motility [*Bewegtheit*] in the Godhead [*Gottheit*] itself" clashes with both religious and philosophical orthodoxy, according to which God is the unmovable mover. For Scholem, the greatness of the later Kabbalah of Luria and Cordovero is that it clearly sees that "God as Living is incompatible with the belief in the immovability of God" (Scholem 1970b, 86). This Jewish appropriation of pantheism, paradoxically, is what saves the universalism of Jewish monotheism because it explains in what way "His Hidden Life pulsates in everything" (Scholem 1994, 223–4). Confirming my hypothesis, Scholem explicitly says that Luria's saving thought of *zimzum* was made possible because the "monotheistic biblical thought was overpowered [*Überwaltigung*] through the Greek thinking" (Scholem 1970b, 86).

For Scholem, the most important element of the doctrine of *zimzum* is its "continuous" nature: "Everything that exists derives from the dual movement through which God contracts within Himself and at the same time something of His Being emanates. . . . The process of emanation that communicates something divine to all beings, at each point and at every level returns to God's self-contraction" (Scholem 1970b, 87). Luria's Jewish reformulation of pantheism consists in arguing that God is, indeed, found "everywhere" and in "everything," but that His omnipresence takes the form of a self-contraction, a self-limitation of His own will or freedom.[99] If one compares Luria's conception of *zimzum* with the Christian medieval discussions of *creatio ex nihilo* that Schmitt took as basis of his theory of constituent power, then on Luria's model, God's *creatio ex nihilo* is a constituent power only insofar as it is also a "destituent" power, to employ a term recently used by Agamben.[100] The difference with Agamben's articulation

[98] In the central essay of *Major Trends* dedicated to the "Theosophical Doctrine of the Zohar," Scholem explains the doctrine of the relation between the "hidden" God, *En sof* or "Infinite," and the act of Creation. For the *Zohar*, this act of Creation is internal to the hidden God, and not a function of an "emanation" outward. This is the predecessor doctrine of the Lurian idea of *zimzum* whereby the hidden God withdraws inwardly and brings forth "Nothing" as the first and highest sefiroth, the "Supreme Crown" of the Hidden God. In the subsequent essay, dedicated to Luria's Kabbalah and the idea of *zimzum* as the process of divine contraction that leads to Creation, Scholem argues that Luria's philosophical invention is a response to the problem of pantheism inherent in the notion of God as *En sof*.

[99] Through his readings of Cordovero and Luria, Scholem is reflecting on the pantheist formula: *hen kai pan* (One and All), which played a decisive role in the German Enlightenment debate on Spinozism since Lessing made use of the formula. Ben-Shlomo argues that Scholem sees in Cordovero a "pan-entheist" middle ground between orthodox theism and philosophical pantheism: the Nothing allows for "a modified pantheism in which all reality is comprehended within the Godhead but is not identical with it" (Ben-Shlomo 1994, 64). With regard to Luria, instead, he claims that "only the doctrine of zimzum can provide a satisfactory explanation for the existence of anything that is not divine" (ibid., 65). Whether the Jewish form of pantheism is best described as "pan-entheist" is an open question. In this context what concerns me is the politico-theological significance of *zimzum* as a theory of legal authorization, about which Ben-Shlomo does not comment.

[100] For the Christian medieval conception, see (Oakley 1998), and for its use by Schmitt, see (Ojakangas 2012). On destituent power, see (Agamben 2014), but the idea of a "destituent" conception of constituent power is arguably older. I discuss its genealogy in (Vatter 2004a).

of destituent power, which is modeled on Heidegger's *Gelassenheit*, is that God's self-contraction into His Nothing is the expression of His authority as a function of a self-limitation of His Power that becomes manifest in and as Creation. Scholem therefore returns to the Schmittian analogy of constituent power as a power to create out of nothing, yet he offers a conception of constituent power that is not decisionist.

The Spanish Kabbalah of Cordovero and Luria was a reaction to the catastrophe of Spain's expulsion of its Jewish population. Here a sovereign decision had withdrawn the order that allowed for the application of the Torah. The account of Nothingness in Kabbalah reflects an attempt to think how the withdrawal of order allows for the constituent power of Law, for the giving of another Law that cannot be written, and thus also that cannot be suspended. If the Nothing, as Scholem says, is connected with God's wisdom (as basis of authority), then God's power is separate and distinct from Law's authority. In Kabbalah, on Scholem's reading, the authority of Law is tied to wisdom, rather than to decision. Conversely, if power is separate from, but emanating out of, the authority of the Law, then power comes to be tied up with a (historical) process in which divine Law is "animated" by divine Life.[101] From this follows Scholem's closing formula for redemption: "The continuous Creation derives from the repeatedly renewed contact with Nothingness, the *always new miracle of beginning* [*immer erneute Wunder des Anfangs*]" (Scholem 1970b, 89, emphasis mine). Scholem's formulation of divine anarchy (the Nothingness of God) harkens to a theory of natality and eternal return. Here what counts is that God's descent into Nature takes the form of an ever-repeating beginning or natality of Being, and, just as with Rosenzweig, one can find Redemption only in returning to the idea of Creation. This theme is equally retrieved by Arendt, as discussed in chapter 6.

At the opposite end of the interpretative spectrum, David Novak offers a liberal, contractualistic reading of the Kabbalistic teaching of *zimzum*. Citing a Rabbinic Midrash, Novak argues that the *zimzum* originates from the need to interpret the historical fact that the assembled people were not able to bear hearing God's voice in its "full strength" and thus God "only came upon them according to their strength" (Novak 1992, 301). For Novak, this means that "God limits His own power" so that all Israelites can receive God's message in their own way. It is as if Novak were punning on the word for contraction: the descent and self-contraction of God as Creation is done for the sake of "contracting with" the people. Scholem saw in the Lurianic *zimzum* a teaching that offered

[101] By way of contrast, Christoph Schmidt's reading identifies God's power with His unknowable substance, rather than seeing in His power (symbolized by the sefiroth) only the emanation from the Nothing of divine authority (2009, 171).

the metaphysical basis for disconnecting the authority of the Law from its application, and eventually it would also offer the basis for a radical utopian messianic teaching that identifies redemption with the non-observance of the revealed legal commandments. For Novak, instead, "God has descended to the human level by giving the Torah as a human possession, binding Himself to what is now humanly interpreted and adjudicated law" (1992, 302). In this way, the Torah is bound to a legalistic approach that subsumes it under positive law, exactly the opposite result sought by Scholem.[102] The clear contrast between Scholem and Novak brings up the following question: what is the relation between "the life of God" and the "life of the commandments" in the Jewish tradition and in the Kabbalah?

The Tree of Life and biblical antinomianism

Scholem's historical reconstruction of the Kabbalah is particularly interested in those junctures in the Jewish tradition in which the use of symbolic representation touches on, or draws from, a conception of divine "Life" that has the potential to overwhelm and undermine all (Rabbinic) institutional forms of life made possible by the Oral Torah itself. In this sense, mysticism fulfills the requirement of the transgression of the Law in order to maintain the Law. The mystical symbol locates in divine Life (rather than in applicable Law) the root of a continually productive crisis within tradition. However, the same mystical symbol is also the cause of a crisis that is not "productive" but radically "destructive" of the tradition.

> What interests us here is the way in which the mystical experience of man's contact with *the primal source of life* could find its expression in a symbol implying *the negation of all authority*. An illumination concerning Messianic freedom in redemption crystallizes around the symbol of Life. In his mystical experience the mystic encounters Life. This "Life," however, is not the harmonious life of all things in bond with God, a world ordered by divine law and submissive to His authority, but something very different. Utterly free, fettered by no law or authority, *this "Life" never ceases to produce new forms and to destroy what it has produced. It is the anarchic promiscuity of all living things.* . . . The nihilistic mystic descends into *the abyss in which the freedom of living things is born* . . . and not content with rejecting and abrogating all values and laws, he

[102] Novak, on the contrary, believes that Kabbalah helped the Rabbinic cause because "the doctrine that the life of the commandments involves a real participation in the life of God gave an enormous incentive to increase observance and deeper piety" (1992, 310).

tramples them underfoot and desecrates them, in order to attain the elixir of Life. (Scholem 1996, 29, emphasis mine)

The theme of divine Life is one of the main guiding-threads of Scholem's political theology. Scholem's discourse on divine Life and its relation to the revealed law is indicative of a more general feature found in 20th-century discourses on political theology, namely, their tendency to cross over into biopolitical discourses. Scholem attempts to address the same problems that motivated Rosenzweig's development of the idea of a community of blood as the basis of Jewish peoplehood. Schmitt also objected to the formalistic and legalistic approach to law that separates it from life, where by "life" he means the sovereign decision on the miracle or state of exception.[103] An antinomian conception of divine life is also present in both Benjamin's and Bloch's formulations of theocracy in a "religious" sense. In *Spirit of Utopia*, Bloch argues that eternal, divine life cannot be satisfied by a mere economical reorganization of the world as described in "abstract-utopian socialism . . . as secularized form of the Thousand Year Kingdom." For these socialist utopias are unable to dispatch "the original religious wish [*der religiose Urwünsch*] . . . *to clear a space for Life to present itself as divine* [*dem Leben Raum schaffen wollte, um sich göttlich zu verwesentlichen*], in order to finally install itself chiliastically in Goodness, Freedom and as Light of the End" (Bloch 1985, 305, emphasis mine). Bloch's "religious" idea of theocracy based on a divinization of life comes very close to a pantheistic viewpoint.

Apart from Rosenzweig, Schmitt, Bloch, and Benjamin, another relevant crossing of biopolitics and political theology is found in Goldberg's thought. For Goldberg, God's Revelation contained a biopolitical teaching on how it was possible "to reconcile God's omnipotence (*Allmacht*) with the imperfections of the world, imperfections that are felt as injustices" (Rosenstock 2017, 185). Goldberg adopts the Kabbalistic idea of divine self-contraction and gives it a biopolitical interpretation which is neither the Rabbinical legalistic (contractual) one advanced by Novak, nor the symbolic/allegorical interpretation it receives in Scholem, but is rather closer to a Schmittian sense. By limiting His power, the manifest God becomes dependent on His capacity as a military leader of His people: YHWH Elohim is the God who leads Israel into "the wars of YHWH" against the cults of other gods (polytheism). Here the distinction between *laos* as people of the One God and *ethnos* as racially and ethnically distinct peoples, each with their own divinities, becomes operative again in a biopolitical and politico-theological form because, according to Goldberg, God enters into war and

103 "In the exception, the force of true life breaks through the crust of the repetition of a fixed mechanism [*In der Ausnahme durchbricht die Kraft des wirklichen Lebens die Kruste einer in Wiederholung erstarrten Mechanik*]" (Schmitt 1996a, 21).

history by creating for Himself a "transcendental organism"—viz. His people or *laos*—that He can occupy and thus come into manifestation. This divine organism "must contain the virtual power of all biological functions" in order to transcend the "merely" biological order that, purportedly, lies at the basis of other ethnic groupings (*ethne*). God's Revelation takes the form of a "continuous production of the divine organism" (possibly symbolized by Adam Kadmon) that "can be considered a continuous miracle, but it is better understood as the production of a new natural order in the midst of the old one" (Rosenstock 2017, 187). These descriptions suggest that Goldberg's conception of "transcendental organism" adopts the Christian idea of a *corpus mysticum* and applies it to the Jewish people as a product of the covenant: "the people correspond to the organism of God. Both together—God and people—constitute the *Brit*, the covenant, in other words, a system of mutual exchange" (Rosenstock 2017, 190). Perhaps it was this unconscious Christian ecclesiology at work in Goldberg that accounted for Scholem's deep rejection, and, conversely, may explain Schmitt's interest in his thought.

Like Goldberg, Scholem also identifies the force that moves against law and order in an unredeemed world as God's divine life, eternal life. In his historiographical works, Scholem always associates the possibility of a second Torah of the Messiah (or *'azilut*) with the mythical conception of the Tree of Life that stood together with the Tree of Knowledge in Paradise.[104] Whereas Adam's eating from the Tree of Knowledge led to the expulsion from the paradisiacal condition and to the idea of an "original sin," Scholem argues that in Jewish mysticism, the Tree of Life "represents the pure, unbroken power of the holy, the *diffusion of the divine life through all worlds* and the *Communications of all living beings with their divine source*" (1971, 21, emphasis mine).[105]

The mythology of the Tree of Life as it appears in the mystical writings of the Kabbalah leads Scholem to his dialectical discussion of messianism and the politico-theological problem of the "forcers" of the End. The Kabbalisitic developments on the Tree of Life associate the Halakhah, based on its description as mere "positivistic" law, with the Tree of Knowledge (of good and evil), but not with the Tree of Life in Redemption. From the perspective of utopian messianism, Halakhic laws are seen as "obstructions to the stream of life," and these obstructions need to be cast away so that "a world in which *only the pure life still reigns* [*das reine Leben waltet*]" may advene (Scholem 1971, 23). The employment of the term *walten* in conjunction with the almost verbatim citation of Benjamin's words from the *Critique of Violence* is remarkable. The claim that

[104] On the symbolism of the tree in the Kabbalah, see also (Wolfson 1995, ch. 2).

[105] I refer to (Vatter 2014) for a reading of this "divine life" motif in Benjamin. See now also the wide-ranging discussion in (Bielik-Robson 2019).

the (Oral) Torah has become itself, qua condition of applicability of the Written Torah, a "fence"—in the sense of impediment—to attain the true Torah (understood not as positive law but as true teaching and as true way of life) orients the idea of divine life in a clearly antinomian direction.[106]

Although Scholem's antinomian formulations echo Schmitt's "pure life" as a force capable of breaking through the "crust" of positive law and its legal machinery, Scholem does not identify pure life with sovereign decision. In the place of sovereignty, Scholem inserts a conception of "anarchy." The conception of an anarchic divine life predates its development into "nihilism," for the mystical development of the idea of the Tree of Life is already found in the 13th-century text of the *Zohar*, thus well before what Scholem calls the "nihilistic" deviation, or perhaps climax, of Sabbatianism and Frankism. Scholem specifies that in these mystical works thematizing the Two Torahs, "Halakhah and Kabbalah are very closely intertwined" (1971, 22). The author of this mythology of divine Life "is not motivated in the least by an interest in the catastrophic aspect of the redemption . . . [but solely by] an *anarchic vision of liberation from the restrictions which the Torah* has laid upon the Jew in an unredeemed world" (Scholem 1971, 22, emphasis mine).

Jewish messianism questions the orthodox understanding of the legitimacy of Mosaic Law because it rejects "the idea of a *law which obligates the living*, or of *a tradition regarding its applicability*" (Scholem 1971, 51, emphasis mine). Utopian messianism enacts the tension between (divine) life and (human) law and articulates a doctrine of divine authority that legitimates the *dis-application* of the Torah. This position is not the same as questioning the authority of the Torah as such. Rather, Scholem's critique of application starts from a strict distinction between the authority of law and its enforcement or application. In contrast to the orthodox conception of legitimacy, which is based on the conditions of application of the given revealed law, the messianic form of legitimacy brings up, or accelerates, in the present, the perspective of the future Redemption, in order to think the dis-application of the Mosaic Torah for the sake of the Torah of divine life. Messianism moves in a direction that is counter to the tradition based on the transmission of the past into the future. Messianism is internally related to another, counter-tradition that brings the future to bear back on to the past.

The temporal tension between Revelation and Redemption explains the emergence of the two decisive antinomian movements that are crucial for Jewish political theology, namely, Saint Paul's messianism and Sabbatianism (Scholem 1971, 52, 57–8). Both movements are characterized by the fundamental idea that the "real" Messiah (Jesus, Zvi) has both *arrived* and *failed* by the standards

[106] I discuss Scholem's interpretation of the nature of divine *walten* in relation to the dialectic between Oral and Written Torah in the last section of this chapter.

of traditional, Maimonidean ideas of messianism. Jewish messianism, whether in its Pauline or Sabbatian form, is a doctrine of the necessary failure of the Messiah. On this point, Scholem and Taubes see eye to eye. They differ more radically on the reasons and consequences of this necessary failure of the Messiah. Both messianic movements are antinomian in the sense that they both reject the claim to trans-historical duration of Moses's law. They seek to replace it by the Messiah as "a Moses of the new aeon" who brings a new Torah (Scholem 1971, 53). This Messiah as new Moses comes to "release the prisoners" (Psalm 146:7) by announcing that what was forbidden by Mosaic law is now permitted in the Kingdom of the new Messiah. It is this dimension of "everything is permitted" that Scholem, technically speaking, calls "nihilistic."

Redemption through sin: or, the Sabbatian crisis of the crisis of tradition

Scholem works out his political theology of Redemption through his historiography of Sabbatai Zvi and the religious-social movement of Sabbatianism. Sabbatianism not only exemplifies the most radical expression of the utopian variant of Jewish messianism, but it also portrays the self-overcoming of the messianic complex, not unlike Nietzsche's Anti-Christ stages a self-overcoming of Christianity. Scholem's earliest and most famous formulation of the Sabbatian phenomenon is contained in the essay titled "Redemption through Sin," completed by 1935. However, as pointed out by Amir Engel, Scholem gave several, distinct reconstructions of Sabbatianism and its meaning for the Jewish tradition throughout his life.[107] Sabbatianism is thus an overdetermined object of study for Scholem. First, it illustrates a radicalization of the Judeo-Hellenistic idea of transgressing the Torah as a way of defending its authority. Second, it is also exemplifies a radicalization of the idea of a "secret" tradition that, in its Frankist, "religiously nihilist" spin-off represents a moment of exhaustion of the Jewish tradition and its crossover into modern secularism. Third and last, Sabbatianism also serves Scholem to carry out his critique of the temptation to unify messianism and Zionism after the founding of the State of Israel.

How does Kabbalistic nihilism become Sabbatean nihilism? The "utopian" form of messianism develops out of the Lurianic Kabbalah (Scholem 1971, 43–5). The central symbol of this Kabbalah is the idea of a world that has been created by "breaking the vessels" (i.e., commandments) that were thought to contain the emanations of God resulting from His contraction in Creation (*zimzum*). With the breaking of the vessels, the "sparks of divine light" got mixed up with the

[107] (Engel 2017, 124–67).

"shells" that contain the forces of evil. Thus, the first idea on the way to utopian messianism is that Creation generates an imperfection because "light" is mixed up with "darkness": in the unredeemed world, good and evil are not easily discernable or separable. The second idea that results from this imperfect Creation is that Redemption will have to be sought by stepping outside of the relative comfort of the traditional pursuit of the application of Torah as law. Since the Mosaic commandments have something not quite right about them, being themselves like broken vessels, applying them "mechanically" will not bring about the restoration (*Tikkun*) of the original state. The third idea that feeds into utopian messianism is that the restoration of the vessels requires a human, collective effort to gather in all the divine sparks of light. For Luria, this can be done on condition that Israel as a whole "amends" its ways (*Teshuvah*) and acts in accordance with the commandments (Scholem 1971, 46).

Given the problem of the imperfection of the created commandments, or of the commandments in the epoch of Creation, the Lurianic teaching is ripe for the dialectical reading it receives at the hand of Sabbatai Zevi's prophet and theologian, Nathan of Gaza. What commandments are to be obeyed in order to recollect the scattered lights? Is it the commandments of the Torah of Creation, or of the Torah of the Messiah? Does *teshuvah* mean to "return" to the traditional ways of worship? Or, does it mean to "re-verse," to "turn against" the current of Rabbinic tradition and "turn" the commandments "against themselves," thereby neutralizing or suspending their effects? Lastly, in the Lurianic teaching, the Messiah is not a human king from the lineage of David, but "the people of Israel as a whole [that] prepares itself to amend the primal flaw" (Scholem 1971, 48). This means that Redemption must be the work of a "democratic" process; it must be spurred by the *laos* or lay individuals, and not by the ranks of priests.

These are the Kabbalistic pre-conditions for any possible "utopian" form of messianism. They pose the questions that all subsequent utopian developments of the messianic idea will try to answer. They open up the possibility of a utopian messianism that can be either anarchic or catastrophic/nihilist. In Sabbatianism and then Frankism, Scholem analyzes the second possibility that happened to be realized historically in Central Europe. But he never reduces utopian messianism to Sabbatianism. He leaves open the possibility of an anarchic utopian messianism that does not get caught up in mystical nihilism. He gives the name of "religious anarchism" to this affirmative idea of utopian messianism.

For the Sabbatian movement, the Kabbalistic principle of the two Torahs (or, what is the same, the fidelity to the original and secret Torah in the Messianic age) and the priority of divine life over Mosaic law gets articulated through the belief that the Messianic age is characterized by a cosmic Sabbath in which the "workdays" (i.e., history under Moses's law) come to an end and "what was commandment becomes downright prohibition . . . acts that had previously been prohibited now become not only permissible but are even considered holy" (Scholem 1971, 72). The secret transgression of all outwardly valid commandments is justified by the belief that "in the world of redemption there can be no such thing as sin, therefore all is holy and everything is permitted" (Scholem 1971, 113).[108] Scholem's vocabulary is that of Nietzsche's Anti-Christ who will lead to a radical "revaluation of all values."[109] In both the Jewish and the Christian messianic traditions, there exists the idea that the Anti-Christ or Anti-Messiah appears to be indistinguishable from the true Messiah. In the essay on "Redemption through Sin," this Nietzschean element of Jewish messianism is emphasized by Scholem in the figure of the necessary apostasy of the true Messiah. The true Jewish Messiah needs to convert to Islam (or, in the case of the Frankist movement, to Catholicism) and descend into the realm of evil and impurity in order "to rescue the divine sparks still imprisoned there" (Scholem 1971, 94). This moment of apostasy of the true Messiah, his/her going down and going under, signals the crisis of the messianic idea in Judaism.

Scholem's reading of Sabbatianism seeks to present Jewish messianism as caught in an unresolvable aporia. This aporia could already be evinced in Benjamin's illustration of the relation between secular order and messianic age in the *Theologico-Political Fragment*. If, as Benjamin says, the arrow of History and that of Redemption point in opposite directions, then any historical realization of the messianic will not be the true Messiah. Conversely, the Kingdom of the true Messiah will not be a historical kingdom.[110] The necessary "failure" of the messianic idea, as shown by Sabbatai Zvi's conversion to Islam, uncovers the first feature of Scholem's theory of Sabbatianism as a self-overcoming of messianism. It indicates exactly the process through which "messianism was transformed into nihilism," namely, in the idea that "true faith" in the Messiah cannot be observed outwardly by Jews, but must become entirely "inward" and "esoteric" (Scholem 1971, 109–10). For Scholem, this necessary *internalization or esotericism* of utopian messianism in Sabbatianism and Frankism represents the lived reality of a "revolution of values, what was formerly sacred has become profane and what was formerly profane has become sacred" (Scholem 1971, 110). But such "internalization" of the messianic also mimics the "end" of Jewish messianism already declared by Saint Paul. In this sense, for Scholem the development of the

[108] For Scholem, the symbol of this practice of "redemption through sin" is the restoration of the "promiscuity" that characterized Paradise, where "Eve might, at least in principle, have belonged to several men while she was still in Paradise," and which he believes was ritualistically enacted in Sabbatian sects through the "orgiastic exchange of wives" (Scholem 1971, 75). For a comparative analysis of the essay "Redemption through Sin," which contextualizes it within the Eranos Circle as well as the speculations on religion of the Collège de Sociologie in pre–World War II Paris, see (Wasserstrom 1997).

[109] On Scholem's earliest reception of Nietzschean themes, see (Lazier 2002), but this text does not discuss Scholem's mature writings and their Nietzschean strains.

[110] Variants of this aporia of messianism are discussed in (Mosès 1992) and (Macho 2014).

messianic idea in Sabbatianism leads Judaism toward Protestantism, or, perhaps, more accurately, towards the Johannine, "nihilist" form of Christianity.[111]

By way of contrast, Taubes saw in Sabbatianism an exemplary case of how the messianic community needs to be maintained united, despite the historical failure of the Messiah, by bringing into play the Pauline dimensions of "conviction" and "faith." Thus, for Taubes, the messianic only becomes politically effective *after* its historical "failure" (Macho 2014, 32–3). Unlike Scholem, Taubes sees this necessary failure of historical realization of the messianic as proof that there is a need for a Christian Gnostic interiorization of messianism, represented for him by Marcionism. On his view, Saint Paul was the true Jewish messianic thinker. For Scholem, instead, neither Sabbatianism nor Pauline theology represents the quintessence of Jewish messianism. From his perspective, the "revolution" of Sabbatianism only had the consequence of overturning Judaism into its opposite, that is, into Christian political theology.

Other interpreters argue that by unleashing the crisis of the messianic idea, Sabbatianism modernized Judaism and finally "redeemed" it from its own messianic complex.[112] On this reading, Scholem's contribution is said to consist in his principled separation of Jewish messianism from Zionism because messianism was "invented as a kind of spiritual recompense" by the Jewish people for the "lack of their vital resolve to live as a people" (Scholem 1997b, 116).[113] Scholem is presented as a critic of those forms of (religious, proprietary) Zionism that seek to give a theological justification for the political and legal provisions that followed the establishment of the State of Israel.[114] By the same logic, Scholem appears as a critic of any revolutionary applications of messianic motifs against the state. In sum, he is depicted as upholding a rather liberal distinction between

[111] For a Nietzschean elaboration of the "nihilist" idea of Johannine Christianity based on the infinity of interpretation, see (Vattimo 1997, 1999).

[112] "Sabbatai Zwi hereby becomes the incarnation of a postmodern political theology that Walter Benjamin describes in his famous Fragment as the act that 'redeems' history from the messianic" (Schmidt 2009, 202). In a similar vein, Noam Zadoff also argues that "Scholem presented the powers of renewal of the Sabbatean movement as breaking the traditional framework of Jewish society and heralding new forms of Jewish life such as Hasidism, the Haskala, and secularization" (Zadoff 2017, 51).

[113] At the end of the late lecture (1977) "Messianism—A Never Ending Quest?" Scholem concludes his conference by citing his own closing words to the famous essay "The Messianic Idea in Judaism" and its claim that Messianism and Zionism should not infiltrate one with the other since "the Messianic idea is the real anti-existentialist idea," whereas Zionism "is bound to history itself and not to meta-history" (Scholem 1997b, 112–3). See also his essay "What Is Judaism?" of 1974 in which he claims two main things: first, that "the real mission of the Jews" is not to act as the "light of nations" but to "face history in a social way as a people seeking to order their affairs" (ibid., 116). Second, "Zionism is not to be regarded as a species of messianism. It is a great error, therefore—for which Zionism may have to pay dearly—if the movement attributes to itself messianic significance. Messianic movements are apt to fail. Zionism is rather a movement within the mundane, immanent process of history; Zionism does not seek the end of history, but takes responsibility within the history of an unredeemed and unmessianic world" (ibid., 116).

[114] See the classic discussion in (Ravitzky 1996).

politics (Zionism) and religion (Jewish messianism) where each is legitimate as long as they keep to their own autonomous spheres of validity.

However, these liberal readings of Scholem fail to appreciate the dialectic of a secular Zionism that profanates everything sacred, all the better to realize its inner messianic aspirations. Scholem was not unaware of something that Idel pointed out much later, namely, that most secular advocates of Zionism were reluctant to give up the discourse of messianism once the State of Israel was founded.[115] Indeed, there is a different way to interpret Scholem's analysis of Sabbatianism as a discourse on the necessary failure of the Messiah and the secular overcoming of the tradition if one heeds the central image found in Benjamin's *Theologico-Political Fragment*, namely, the possibility that, in any given historical event, the arrow of the secular pursuit of happiness may not only touch with the arrow of messianism pushing in the opposite direction, but actually *cross over one into the other*. When this happens, the most zealous pursuit of the Messianic age becomes *indistinguishable* from the most profane pursuit of individual happiness. For Scholem, Zionism stands in the middle point of this perilous crossover between the secular and the messianic.

The phenomenon of Sabbatianism allowed Scholem to test the hypothesis of Benjamin's secular-messianic *complexio oppositorum*. In his eyes, Frankism became exemplary of the social movement that best corresponds to the destructive "task of world politics . . . whose method must be called nihilism," to cite Benjamin's famous formulation in the *Theologico-Political Fragment*. For Scholem, "Frank was a nihilist, and his nihilism possessed a rare authenticity" (1971, 127). With Frankism, messianism inflects into secularism, with the failed Messiah becoming the harbinger of a new Jewish figure of state sovereignty. Thus, at the end of one of his essays, Scholem speaks of "a messianic, anarchic Judaism" that gets configured as an "overthrowing the values of all positive religions" and is based on the idea of the Messiah as new *melekh* or commander of "mystical 'soldiers' . . . [and] '*soldiers are not allowed to have a religion.*' "[116]

The Frankist concept of "mystical soldiers" is perhaps the key point of inflection for Scholem in which the affirmative nihilism of the Kabbalah turns into a nihilism that is destructive of Judaism. Scholem was passionate about his antimilitarism, and it remains one of the reasons of his permanent critique of political Zionism, especially the kind advanced by Ze'ev Jabotinsky's Revisionist movement.[117] In the early 1920s Scholem joined the *Brit Shalom* group that

[115] (Idel 2012). On Ben-Gurion and messianism see also (Ohana 2012).

[116] (Scholem 1971, 77, emphasis mine). The cited phrases come from Frank.

[117] Zadoff cites from a 1923 article by Jabotinsky prophetically entitled "On the Iron Wall": "our colonization should either stop or continue against the will of the native population. And this is why it may continue and develop only under the protection of a force, independent of the local population—an iron wall, though which the local population cannot break" (2017, 48).

rejected the creation of a Jewish army in Palestine: "all of our efforts must be directed at uprooting from ourselves the military spirit and illusions promulgated in the name of heroism and national pride."[118] Zadoff also cites from a little known letter to Werner Kraft in 1924 in which Scholem writes: "The hour has come when hearts must decide *whether Zionism—whose meaning is preparation for the eternal—will succumb to the Zionism of the Jewish state, which is a catastrophe*. The theocracy has proven to be too weak, and the nation's priests have not placed themselves in the breach. Now the worldly political Zionism of yesterday seeks to fill the vacuum left by the theocracy" (Zadoff 2017, 45). Inexplicably, Zadoff says that in this passage Scholem "calls the Jewish state a 'theocracy,' referring to the nationalist tendency in Zionism—which claimed that the Bible was the source of the Jewish people's right to the entire Land of Israel and held that this right was to be asserted by force of arms" (Zadoff 2017, 46). But Scholem clearly opposes, in strict Benjaminian fashion, his idea of theocracy to the legitimation discourse of "proprietary" Zionism that sees in the Jewish nation-state the "realization" of the biblical messianic utopia on the land of Palestine.[119] At this stage, at least, Scholem argues for a conception of *theocracy against the state*, or an "anarchic" conception of theocracy, that can somehow replace the failure of the Rabbinic institutions to stand in the way of Zionism's self-interpretation as a settler colonial project.[120] Unlike the proponents of a clear distinction between a "successful" Zionist project and a "failed" Jewish messianism, Scholem suggests that the "success" of political Zionism may just be an expression of the Sabbatean faith that the "failed" messiah is "successful" in and through its "failure." Behind the call to "normalize" the status of the state of Israel as just "one nation among other nations" there always lurks, for Scholem, the specter of Frankism.

Sabbatianism faded into a nominally secular Zionism because of a convergence of the secular pursuit of happiness with the realization of messianic aims. From the side of Sabbatianism, the doctrine of "redemption through sin" easily converts into a message to pursue dominion and hedonism freed from the yoke of the divine law. From the side of Zionism, on the other hand, Scholem liked to say that the "most profound statement that an opponent of Zionism ever made of the movement" was uttered by Hermann Cohen, who once complained to Rosenzweig that the main problem with Zionists was simply the fact that "these lads just want to be happy!"[121] While Cohen probably meant to say that,

[118] Scholem cited in (Zadoff 2017, 39).

[119] In his reading of Scholem's early diaries, Lazier points out that the Zionism of Scholem turns on the concept of "Zion" that is irreducible to the project of resettling the Jewish people either in some part or in the whole of Palestine (2002).

[120] For a typology of different kinds of Zionism and post-Zionism at issue in the contemporary debate, see (Gans 2016). Scholem's "religious" conception of theocracy seems to be in tension with all forms of Zionism, whether proprietary, hierarchical, or egalitarian.

[121] Cited in (Scholem 1980, 69).

in its wish to make of Israel a nation like other nations, Zionism had given up all higher, noble ideals of redemption linked with the tradition, for Scholem the quip revealed the danger that the Zionist pursuit of political happiness accelerated the realization of messianism in the world as its own downfall.

The Oral Torah in the state of exception and religious anarchism

Judaism's embrace of secularism, and the consequent turn to political forms of Zionism, on the basis of the "failure" of the messianic complex exemplified in Sabbatianism and Frankism, did not prevent Scholem from seeking to draw an antidote from the "poison" developed in both the Kabbalistic and Sabbatean forms of nihilism.[122] He called this antidote by the name of "religious anarchism." Although David Biale claims that Scholem made a clear "a distinction between nihilism—which he rejected—and anarchism" (2015, 63), this is not borne out by his texts, and for good reason.[123] For such a distinction between nihilism and anarchism runs the danger of missing the underlying difference between a destructive sense of nihilism, which he associates with Frankism, and an *affirmative sense of nihilism* which he uncovers through the "destruction" of the tradition. It is this affirmative nihilism that he designates through the term of religious anarchism.

Scholem claims that to be anarchic in religious matters means to have "a religious understanding of Jewish continuity [that] goes beyond the principle of Torah from heaven" (1997b, 16). Biale gives three meanings to Scholem's religious anarchism as a function of fidelity to the Jewish tradition. The first entails "the rejection of a nationalist politics that turned the nation-state into a messianic goal" (2015, 68). Religious anarchism, on this reading, is a defense of a cultural as opposed to political, viz. nationalist Zionism.[124] The second sense of religious anarchism is tied to the crisis of the Jewish tradition. It refers to the claim that the authority of this tradition is no longer translatable into legal (Halakhic) force. "As a result, all that can be learned from the study of history is the struggle for absolute values among conflicting voices of authority" (Biale

[122] Scholem's last text on the tradition ends with a citation from *Yebamot* 21a, as interpreting Leviticus 18:30, where the saying to "set a watch upon the watch" is found. By which is meant to watch over the multiplication of prohibitions intended to ward the poison of temptation or evil.

[123] In "Redemption through Sin," Scholem speaks both of a "nihilistic" Torah of *atzilut* (the highest emanation) and of "a messianic, anarchic Judaism" (1971, 77).

[124] Zadoff speaks of the idea of *kinus* as being fundamental to Scholem's historiographical work: "the essence of this Zionist idea . . . was to collect the treasures of Jewish culture and present them in modern editions to create a cultural continuum between the nation's past and present" (2017, 19).

2015, 69). Third, and last, religious anarchism for Biale refers to "the infinitude of possible interpetations of revelation that one finds in both Talmudic and Kabbalistic sources—what might be called in modern terms the 'anarchy' of interpretation" and that illustrates Scholem's claim that "the word of God is 'meaningless itself but meaning bestowing'" (Biale 2015, 69).

These different senses of religious anarchism stand in tension one with the other. On the one hand, religious anarchism is understood by Biale to mean that the *legal authority* of the tradition is exhausted. On the other hand, for Biale the appeal to the *legal authority* of the tradition is necessary precisely in order to avoid "nihilist" interpretations of God's revelation in the world like the ones illustrated by Frank and Goldberg. However, this authority "is, by definition, inaccessible, a mystery wrapped in an enigma . . . grounding these sources in an ultimate source means that we are not dealing with a nihilistic denial of authority but rather the denial of a single, dogmatic interpretation" (Biale 2015, 69).[125] The only way to navigate this tension is to hypothesize that for Scholem there exists an authority of revealed law that is counter to human legal authority and human institutional interpretation (and in this sense is "anarchic"), yet it is very much a divine ("religious") authority and it subtends the possibility of a Jewish life, as opposed to the adoption of a secular form of life.[126] It is this idea of divine anarchic authority that I seek to further determine by way of conclusion.

"Apocalypticism, as a doubtlessly anarchic element, provided some fresh air in Judaism; it provided a recognition of the catastrophic potential of all historical order in an unredeemed world" (Scholem 1971, 323). The formulation is strictly Benjaminian: "all historical order in an unredeemed world" is potentially a catastrophe that needs to be addressed by apocalyptic messianism and its anarchy. Like Sabbatianism and Frankism, Scholem's conception of nihilism

[125] By way of constrast, Willem Styfhals follows Agamben in arguing that "the fulfillment of genuine messianic thinking" is to show the absence of God as *arche*, the absence of divine authority, from which follows that "religious claims have no ontological ground" at all (2018, 199). Zadoff's position is closer to Biale's: "the essence of this anarchism is the rejection of existing religious authorities coupled with belief in the existence of God. To phrase this in the terms that Scholem used here, it is belief in pure Torah—as it is—but not in Oral Torah, or the authority of existing commentary" (2017, 67).

[126] This is why William Altman's reading of Scholem is questionable. For Altman, Scholem is representative of "atheistic Judaism—what Klein has called 'Judaism without God'" (Altman 2011a, 304). Altman follows Lazier in thinking that Jewish gnosticism "is the last word in heresy: a rebellion against the God of Israel staged by his chosen people" (ibid., 305). But Altman also believes that there is a direct relation between Jewish gnosticism and Nazism: "If National Socialism aimed at the annihilation of Israel as a means to annihilating God, Christianity (understood as *Verjudung*) and all other traces of 'modernity,' then it too must also be understood as a Jewish heresy, complete with its own nihilist Messiah" (ibid., 305). The argument seems to be: (a) only Jewish heresy (Gnosticism, Sabbatianism, etc.) can fight against the Jewish God; (b) Nazism also fights the Jewish God; thus, (c) Nazism (aka "Judaism without God") is a form of Jewish heresy. See also Altman's bizarre twisting of Scholem's words to make him say that Nazism was "among the freest" of movements in which "the messianic idea lived on in a disguised—and given the Jewish origin of the idea horribly inverted—form" (ibid., 307).

depends on the claim that in the messianic time the revealed Mosaic Torah will cease to apply. However, for Scholem, messianic nihilism is compatible, and indeed requires, the idea of a new Torah to replace the old Torah, as opposed to a situation in which there is no Torah, a situation of anomie, as Agamben calls it. If, as discussed earlier, Scholem believes that messianic nihilism depends on the tension between divine Life and the life that is made possible under the yoke of Mosaic law, this does not entail that divine Life rejects *all* law. The new Torah is a form of "living law": it is, literally speaking, the Law of divine Life. The idea of a new Torah stands in continuity with the Philonic idea of the Torah as *nomos phuseos*, as a living divine law. Furthermore, Scholem believes that the affirmative lesson of Sabbatianism is that the new King or *basileus* who brings the new *nomos* of divine Life must necessarily be a *failed sovereign*—or, exhibit the necessary failure of sovereignty—because the Law of divine Life is structurally inapplicable.

To understand Scholem's affirmative nihilism, one needs to appreciate his key insight that the Written Torah is in reality not a positive law at all because its content is as such inapplicable or was never intended to be applied as law. Citing the later Sabbatian theologian Miguel Cardoso, Scholem writes: "Following the mystics, the written Torah, the revelation as such, is seen as *not calling for concrete execution in any realm of application whatever*. The Torah becomes applicable only through the medium of the Oral Torah in which the word of God is appropriated to the contingencies of its fulfilment" (1971, 67, emphasis mine). It is only the tradition in the form of Oral Torah that "legalizes" the Written Torah retroactively, starting with Moses's second set of law tables, by seeking to "apply" the Torah differently in different historical conditions. The "nihilistic" practice of dis-applying the Written Torah (by "neutralizing" the Oral Torah) is one side of an affirmative practice of making a return (*teshuvah*) to the real Written Torah, which is not the one brought down by Moses from Mount Sinai, but what Scholem identifies with the *aleph* of God's Voice heard by all of Israel. Scholem's affirmative nihilism is a way to "destroy" the claims of human interpretations of the *aleph* that legalize its teaching, in order to defend (to erect a "fence") around the true, anarchic authority of the Written Torah as divine *aleph*.

Scholem's affirmative, nihilistic version of messianism, although antinomian, follows the same principle of Jewish political theology according to which the transgression of the Torah (or: the non-accomplishment of the commandments) is for the sake of the Torah. This is the reason why Scholem goes out of his way to show that the *setting-out-of-force or the dis-application* of the Oral Torah does not, as such, mean a surrender of the Written Torah. Utopian, apocalyptic messianism "forces" the crisis of tradition only as a crisis of legitimation for the Oral Torah, but not for the Torah as such: it is a crisis of legitimacy of the Torah as (positive) law, not of the Torah as God's life and wisdom. Scholem's explanation of this apparent paradox is contained in his interpretation of the Kabbalistic reading of the Written Torah as the Name of God, and of God's Voice as the *aleph* heard on Mount Sinai.

Whose Voice did the people of Israel hear on Mount Sinai, and what did they hear in this Voice? No question is more crucial to the development of the Jewish tradition of Oral Torah. Idel claims that Scholem shares with Rosenzweig and Buber the belief that what counts about the revelation at Mount Sinai is the "experience" of God's presence rather than the "content" of what God "said" to or through Moses (i.e., the commandments themselves) (2015, 27).[127] Famously, Scholem writes that "to hear the alef is to hear next to nothing: it is the preparation for all audible language but in itself it conveys no determinate, specific meaning . . . the revelation on Mount Sinai into a mystical revelation, pregnant with infinite meaning, but without specific meaning" (1996, 29).[128] Interpreters like Idel have assumed that by defining the *En Sof* as a "nothingness that is replete with meaning," Scholem intends to reject the "content" of the revealed, Written Torah. "By introducing the concept of an infinity of meanings of revelation—not only of the canonical text, Scholem, and his contemporaries, attempted to relativize or even to circumvent one single specific meaning—the Rabbinic, or institutional one" (Idel 2015, 32).[129] In other words, Scholem is placed on the philo-Hellenic "reformist" side, rather than on the side of the Macabbees.

This chapter has pursued exactly the opposite hypothesis: that Scholem's Hellenistic ("universalist") approach to Jewish mysticism is employed to build a "fence" against the attack on the Torah in Christianity. Scholem's "negative dialectics" of the Torah can be schematized as follows. The Rabbinic or Talmudic principle is that the Oral Torah is as old as the Written Torah. "For rabbinic Judaism . . . every religious experience after revelation is a mediated one. It is the experience of the voice of God rather than the experience of God. But all

[127] Idel cites a 1924 letter by Rosenzweig to Buber in which he says that "revelation is certainly not lawgiving. The only immediate content of revelation—is revelation." Idel then refers to late and unpublished remarks by Scholem: "the Alef of Anochi was the only thing which Israel at Mount Sinai got directly without interpretation, without all oral Torah. Everything besides the Alef was an oral Torah" (2015, 30).

[128] For similar formulations, see also (Scholem 1971, 120, 295). Idel claims that Scholem's attribution of the latter sentence to "rabbi Mendel," a Hasidic source, is a historical falsehood, since the actual source of the sentence is a 1901 book on the Kabbalah written by Ahron Marcus, a German Jewish scholar of Hasidism (Idel 2015, 30ff). Idel and Schmidt both think that Scholem's reading of the *aleph* is a consequence of his having sublated the *nihil* of the Kabbalists into the debate on the "nothingness" of Revelation with Benjamin. Idel puts it this way: "modern research on Kabbalah" experiences "the impact of the German cultural tradition" [*sic*] (ibid., 24).

[129] Idel places Rosenzweig and Scholem on the side of a Christian, Pauline "universalist" sense of Redemption against which Idel sets the Rabbinical "particularistic" view of Redemption. For Idel these Jewish-German thinkers wanted to preserve "a strong universalist valence [to Jewish revelation]. Jewish mysticism is thus but one mode of interpreting a larger phenomenon: the transition from the inchoate and meaningless, the 'nothingness of revelation'—which includes, nevertheless, all possible meanings—to a specific language and tradition" (Idel 2015, 33).

reference to the 'voice of God' is highly anthropomorphic—a fact from which theologians have always carefully tried to escape" (Scholem 1971, 292). On this Rabbinic reading of God's self-contraction, God's revelation in the form of a covenant with His people means that all further human interpretations of the Written Torah are as legitimate as the Sinaitic revelation of God to the whole people, first, and then, due to their weakness, to Moses himself. Through Halakhah, therefore, the Jewish people would be living in a "perpetual present" with the Mosaic revelation throughout all historical periods and tribulations. One may call this a paradoxical "Hegelian" negation of Hegelian world-history which corresponds to Fackenheim's standpoint. It is a conservative reading of what Rosenzweig means with his famous formula that the Jewish people are "outside" of history and lead an "eternal" life.

Scholem criticizes this Rabbinic solution to the problem of legal application and proposes a Kabbalistic interpretation of the "eternal life" carried by Judaism. Against the backdrop of the Rabbinic insistence on the mediate character of divine revelation, he thinks of the possibility of an "immediate" experience of God found not on Mount Sinai but in "the mystical concept of tradition" (1971, 293). From this Kabbalistic perspective, divine revelation is not at all mediated by tradition as Oral Torah. This is so because the revelation of God—for the Kabbalah—is composed exclusively of the divine Name and its actional attributes such that the Written Torah is made up only out of these names, as a "hieroglyph of hieroglyphs," as the "final signature of all things" (1971, 293ff), which correspond to God's "abyss" or "primordial causes" into which He "descends."[130] This is a writing that cannot be "read" or "understood" by any given human interpretation, nor by their concatenation, as claimed by the orthodox conception of tradition. In other words, the Written Torah does not *signify* anything; it contains no communication that can be "interpreted," and so applied as law, by the Oral Torah.

This Kabbalistic notion of the Written Torah as non-signifying *aleph* lies at the heart of his religious anarchism. The first consequence is that there never was "such thing as a Written Torah in the sense of an immediate revelation of the divine word" on Mount Sinai (Scholem 1971, 294). Such immediate revelation is only the Wisdom of God, an "Ur-Torah," the second sefiroth, and it is not identifiable with Mosaic law. Mosaic law is already a human interpretation of the Ur-Torah, of God's Wisdom (Scholem 1971, 295). This means that Moses's "Written Torah" (the tablets of the law that he brings down from the mountain) is always

130 "Thus, the Torah is a texture (Hebrew: *arigah*) fashioned out of the names of God and . . . out of the great, absolute name of God, which is the final signature of all things. It constitutes a mysterious whole, whose primary purposes is not to transmit a specific sense, to 'mean' something, but rather to express the force of the divinity itself which is concentrated in this 'name' " (ibid., 294). For a discussion of Scholem's and Benjamin's theory of language in relation to divine names, see (Weidner 2003).

already Oral Torah. On Scholem's reading, then, Kabbalah gives an *inversion* of the Talmudic principle according to which Oral Torah is always already Written Torah. This is what is meant by "dis-applying" the commandments in the sense of a practice of *teshuvah* as turning the commandments against themselves or twisting free the Torah from its legalistic form. But this does not do away with the significance of the Written Torah; it does not mean that according to "Scholem's theology" Moses "invents the content he revealed," as Idel suggests (2015, 29). The aim of this inversion is not to make a definitive break with the Written Torah, but of recovering in it the original source of authority, a conception of authority that precedes and is irreducible to the idea of legal enforcement.

If the Written Torah is already Oral Torah, then, historically speaking, it is impossible to assign a priority to the Sinaitic revelation, to Moses, over and above any other moment in the history of the Jewish people: all moments are open to the irruption of the Ur-Torah in the messianic interruption. This corresponds to Scholem's take on Rosenzweig's leading idea that eternal life "must always be capable of coming as early as 'today.'" In this way, the continuity of the Rabbinical conception of tradition (viz., the handing down of the testimony of the events that occurred on Mount Sinai from generation to generation) is completely shattered, because it loses its meaning of being the main avenue of transmission of God's Torah.

But this does not mean that all continuity is broken, that all tradition and thus all authority is given up. To understand this decisive point, it is necessary to engage now Scholem's second point with regard to the divine *aleph* as source of an infinity of interpretations. It is important to recover the way in which Scholem adopts Nietzschean philosophemes in order to build a new fence around the Written Torah. God's self-withdrawal into the *aleph* of His Wisdom turns His Voice into a source of terror in His people. "There is no immediate, undialetical application of the divine word. If there were, it would be destructive" (Scholem 1971, 296). The full and immediate revelation of His Wisdom (the Truth) would entail the destruction of His people—hence, the need to reveal Himself symbolically in the Pentateuch. This symbolic revelation of the Written Torah is already in itself a "fence" that God erects. Present in this line of thought is a Nietzschean, more than Hegelian, understanding of the symbol: the cultivation of the human being through the learning of the Torah requires a level of "stupidity," or Apollinian illusion, which Rosenzweig referred to in terms of the "narrowness" of the student of Torah. To know the whole truth—or absolute knowledge—is overwhelming for individuals and for groups. This absolute, not mediated access to divine Wisdom would lead human beings to adopt Silenus's wisdom, according to which it is better never to have been born; or, what amounts to the same, it could lead to a desire for unification (*unio mystica*) with the One and thus to the destruction of all individuality, a kind of enactment of the death drive.

Scholem's suggested path to deal with the nihilism of Revelation adopts the Nietzschean strategy to insist that the Mosaic law does *not* represent a set of "moral facts." The Torah is *not* a symbol for a moral truth that lies beyond interpretation. Rather, its mystical symbols teach that "there are no facts but only interpretations" with regard to morality. "God's word is infinitely interpretable; indeed, it is *the* object of interpretation par excellence. . . . Here revelation, which has yet no specific meaning, is that in the word which gives an infinite wealth of meaning. Itself without meaning. [*Hier ist die Offenbarung, die keinen spezifischen Sinn hat, das unendlich reichen Sinn Verleihende im Wort. Selber bedeutungslos, ist sie das Deutbare schlechthin*]" (Scholem 1971, 295). Given the meaninglessness of God's Wisdom, this Wisdom can only be withstood if it is radically opened to all interpretations: "God's wisdom . . . is the very essence of interpretability" (Scholem 1971, 297). In other words, there can never be a final interpretation of the Written Torah, nor is any interpretation superior to that of others, because there is no "original text" which can serve as criterion for the correctness of any interpretation.

From Scholem's principle that all application of the Ur-Torah must be "mediated" or "reflected," there follows a rejection of the claim that the only "reflection" on the Written Torah can come from priestly authorities. But there also follows a rejection of a "liberal" reading of the mediation according to which one can simply dispense with the idea of a divine source of authority. To the contrary, Scholem seems to think that the proper Nietzschean consequence to the "fence" of divine wisdom that correlates with the "stupidity" of each individual is the idea that "the Torah turns a special face to every single Jew, meant only for him and apprehensible only by him" (1971, 297). The infinite reflexivity in the application of the Ur-Torah refers to a law that is living only for the singular, and thus not as a universal with respect to the particular.

The third and last consequence of Scholem's Kabbalistic political theology under its Nietzschean interpretation is the following: given this mystical nature of the Ur-Torah, and the reversal of the Written Torah into the Oral Torah (as opposed to the Rabbinical interpretation of Oral Torah as another Written Torah), it follows that for Scholem the Oral Torah cannot be an exclusive human achievement. This is the opposite conclusion to the one arrived at by Idel and Schmidt, according to which Scholem's thesis of the infinity of interpretations is reducible to secularism, to the end of Rabbinical institutionalism, to a liberal reading of the Torah, and so on. But Scholem also rejects Fackenheim's claim that the Oral Torah is the equally legitimate, because divinely inspired, human contribution to the Covenant with God, a contribution that corresponds to human free will and, in turn, is met by God's grace.[131]

[131] "Either mere man arrogates himself the right of radical interpretation; but then the law of God becomes a mere pious fiction if indeed not a swindle; or else that law is and remains genuinely

For Scholem, instead, the Oral Torah is itself the "re-sounding" of the Voice, the *aleph*, of God in history.[132] Thus, it is not as if the *aleph* of the divine Voice ceases immediately to resound and is replaced by human interpretation, sempliciter. In a performative gesture that expresses what Scholem means, he ends his essay on tradition and authority by *stopping his own writing* and *begins to cite* a Kabbalistic source on the mystical meaning of the tradition. The first citation comes from a 1531 work by Meir ben Gabbai, *Avodat ha-Kodesh*, that states: "all words that can ever be said in a new way have thus been placed into this fundament which is the divine voice; the Master of the world desired that they receive actuality through men of this earth who form and fulfill God's name. That great voice is the gate and portal for all other voices, and that is [the meaning] of 'fence of unity' and the reference of the verse in the Psalms: 'This is the gate of the Lord,' the gate representing the Oral Law which leads to God, who is the Written Torah, guarded by the Oral Torah" (Scholem 1971, 299). The *aleph* itself is both a "fence" that keeps away from the Written Torah any moralistic and legalistic interpretation of God's Wisdom, while at the same time it opens up God's Wisdom to human "communion" in the form of Oral Torah as "re-sounding" of the Voice through the infinity of its interpretations, Jewish and non-Jewish equally (Scholem 1971, 298).

More importantly, God's Wisdom, or God as the Ur-Torah, is the living Law itself, but understood not as the paroxysm of human sovereignty, but as Life's law. This divine Life is Law as received in the form of the words of the "sages" from the school of Shammai and Hillel that compose the Oral Torah. As mentioned before, the Talmudic teaching opposes both schools, usually taking the interpretation offered by the school of Hillel as the one that can be "applied."[133] However,

divine: but then the interpretation is not merely human but rather itself divinely inspired. The rabbis embarked firmly on the second course: an oral Torah, additional to the written, had been given at Sinai itself. And the whole, vast unique world of the Talmud is in the end nothing but the creative tension between the two Torahs" (Fackenheim 1973, 117).

[132] Citing from Ben Gabbai: "This is what Onkelos meant when he interpreted the Hebrew text of Deutoronomy 5:19 on the voice of God at the revelation . . . as a 'great voice that did not cease speaking.' That great voice sounds forth without interruption; it calls with that eternal duration that is its nature" (Scholem 1971, 299).

[133] "In Jewish tradition the views of the schools of Hillel and Shammai, two teachers who lived shortly before Jesus, play an important part. Their mutually contradictory attitudes toward theoretical and practical problems are codified by the Talmud with great thoroughness, although in the application of the law the views of Hillel's school are decisive. But the rejected views are stated no less carefully than the accepoted ones. . . . It was only one of the latest kabbalists who formulated the daring and, at first blush, surprising thesis, which has since been often reiterated, that the Halakhah would be decided according to the now rejected view of the school of Shammai in the Messianic era" (Scholem 1971, 290). Levinas adds that the disagreement between the schools of interpretation "are not a sign of the finitude of divine wisdom. They signify the life of the Thora, which the Talmud calls war-between-sages or between the 'disciples of wisdom.' The infinite aspects of the absolutely True live amidst the rabbinical debates and disputations, avoiding dogmatism and heresies" (1996, 54).

the speaker for the mystical concept of tradition cited by Scholem takes up the opposite conceit, namely, that the content of the Ur-Torah is reflected in the coincidence of opposite interpretations. "It appears to me that the expression of the Talmud 'These and those are the words of the living God' is justified prima facie only where it is possible to hold that the words of both parties are valid at the same time" (Scholem 1971, 302). Here one has dis-application of the Written Torah due to an excess of authority or legitimacy. Once again, the distinction between Written Torah and Halakhah is operative: as Halakhic law, only one interpretation can be valid due to the need for legal decision; but as expression of the "living God," both incompatible meanings of the Written Torah are legitimate at once. On the mystical view, the Oral Torah has become the living Law of God, or, more precisely, the philosophical discussions and contradictions of the sages act as the Life of Law in the sense that through their disputations and exchange of arguments and opinions, whose truth is ultimately undecidable, they become the "mouthpiece" of God's Voice. At the same time, these thinkers and poets are the vessels of God's Voice only because of the contradictions between their interpretations of the Oral Torah. Not a "divinely inspired" human interpretation, but the coincidence of their opposition is the form of the true that cannot be understood by the human intellect without the aid of divine grace.

Adopting a Philonic gesture, the text cited by Scholem goes on to say:

> If this is so [if the text contradicts itself and both interpretations are legitimate], how can I study the Law? Therefore Scripture continues: "They are given by one shepherd; One God gave them, one spokesman [*ein Gott hat sie gegeben, ein Walter*] said them out of the mouth of the Lord of all actions, praised be He, as is said (Exod. 20:1)": "And God spoke all these words" . . . We have here the affirmation that all differences of opinion and viewpoint that contradict one another were given by one God and said by one spokesman [*ein Walter*]. (Scholem 1971, 303)

The one-to-one analogy between God and legislator (*ein Walter*) in this passage is Judeo-Hellenistic: it brings together the idea of prophetic revelation with the Pythagorean-Platonic belief that truth is harmony as unity of contraries, unity of one and many, of creator and created.[134]

Significantly, Scholem concludes his famous essay by citing Goethe: "It [the Kabbalistic sense of tradition] is the living contact in which man takes hold of ancient truth and is bound to it, across all generations, in the dialogue of giving

[134] Simone Weil shows that the idea of truth as "unity of contraries" is fundamental for Pythagorean-Platonic thinking, but is also shared by Judaism: "The principle of all limitation is God. Creation is the putting order into matter by God and this ordering action of God consists in setting limits. This is also the conception found in Genesis" (1951, 129–30).

and taking. Goethe's word applies to it: 'The truth that long ago was found/ Has all noble spirits bound/ The ancient truth, take hold of it' " (Scholem 1971, 303). The citation of Goethe at this high point of his treatment of Judaism might seem odd for the author who has become, perhaps, best known as the most ardent critic of the "Judeo-German symbiosis." However, the Goethe citation makes perfect sense if placed in context with the reading of Goethe and Nietzsche first advanced by Rosenzweig and carried out by Benjamin, namely, a reading of these two German philosophers that harkens back to a common, shared "ancient truth" that in binding Athens and Jerusalem together and indissolubly, "has all noble spirits bound."

5

Leo Strauss and the Concrete Order of Law

Introduction

The "spiritual situation of German Judaism as a whole" during the Weimar period left Leo Strauss in a "theologico-political predicament."[1] He rejected the project of assimilation with a German nation characterized by its rising hatred against Jews; and his professed atheism stood at odds with the Rabbinic, institutional path to safeguard the Jewish people in Exile and to lead them to Zion. Last, but not least, he had increasing reservations about the Zionist movement to which he adhered in his youth.[2] By the early 1930s, Strauss's analysis of the shortcomings of Zionism with respect to the Jewish tradition, coupled with the critique of modernity he developed through his early works on Spinoza and Hobbes, led him to consider the possibility and necessity of a *backward-looking* possibility to deliver the Jewish people from their world-historical predicament and *return* to "the community established by the Jewish faith and the Jewish way of life—*T'shuvah* (ordinarily rendered by 'repentance') in the most comprehensive sense."[3]

Strauss came across this possibility of Return as Repentance nearly by chance in the early 1930s when he recognized "the necessary relation between politics and theology" in Maimonides' thought and articulated "the interpretation of medieval Jewish philosophy issuing out of Platonic politics."[4] The path toward this politico-theological conjunction of Platonism and Judaism was disclosed to

[1] (Strauss 1997c, 7). A long-ranging and complex discussion of his early "predicament" is given in the autobiographical 1965 "Preface to the English edition" of *Spinoza's Critique of Religion* (Strauss 1968). The reference to "spiritual situation" is found in (Strauss 2002, 75) and is further developed by Strauss in a series of essays in the early 1930s.

[2] One of these reservations is captured in an exchange that Strauss voiced in a late lecture entitled "Why We Remain Jews." There he recounts: "I was myself (as you might have guessed) a political Zionist in my youth, and was a member of a Zionist student organization. In this capacity, I occasionally met Jabotinsky, the leader of the Revisionists. He asked me, 'What are you doing?' I said, 'Well, we read the Bible, we study Jewish history, Zionist theory, and, of course, we keep abreast of developments, and so on.' He replied, 'And rifle practice?' And I had to say, 'No' "(Strauss 1997a, 319).

[3] (Strauss 1997c, 7). The idea recurs twice more in the same text: "in favor of the unqualified return to biblical revelation. In fact, Rosenzweig's return was not unqualified" (Strauss 1968, 237), and "whether an unqualified return to Jewish orthodoxy was not both possible and necessary" (239). In my opinion, (Bouretz 2003) is the author who is most sensitive to the implications of this *Teshuvah* in Strauss's development, but see also (Green 1993).

[4] "The necessary connection between politics and theology (metaphysics), on which we stumbled as if by accident, vouches for the fact that the interpretation of medieval Jewish philosophy beginning from Platonic politics (and not from the *Timaeus* or from Aristotelian metaphysics) does not have to lose sight of the metaphysical problems that stand in the foreground for the medieval philosophers

Living Law. Miguel Vatter, Oxford University Press (2021). © Oxford University Press.
DOI: 10.1093/oso/9780197546505.003.0006

him through a statement of the Islamic philosopher Avicenna: "what has to do with kingship is contained in the book of Plato and of Aristotle on the state, and what has to do with *prophecy* and the *religious law* is contained in both of their books on the *Laws*."[5] The discovery that "a Greek philosophy of divine law lies at the basis of the Jewish and Muslim philosophy of the Torah and Shari'a," as one commentator aptly puts it, "hit him, the first time he read it (when he was a young man in his thirties) as a bombshell."[6]

But as "a young man in his thirties" Strauss was also occupied with Carl Schmitt's Hobbesian political theology and its critique of liberalism's perceived ills of atomism, relativism, and economicism. In the long review essay on Schmitt which he wrote at the time, Strauss argued that Schmitt's advocacy of a "total" conception of politics based on the sovereign decision to impose a state of exception to law remained caught up in a common modern framework shared with liberalism that was based on the separation of politics from religion initially advanced by Hobbes and Spinoza.[7] Much later, Strauss would date the "change of orientation" that led him to defend the case of the Ancients against the Moderns to this review essay on Schmitt.[8] Having already emigrated

themselves" (Strauss 1995, 78; 1997b, 66). As late as 1970, in a joint appearance with Strauss entitled "A Giving of Accounts," Jacob Klein (one of his oldest and closest friends) said that starting from his student years Strauss only ever had two interests in his philosophical studies: God and politics (Strauss 1997a, 458). Klein does not say "Being and politics" or "*phusis* and politics."

[5] (Strauss 1995, 122; 1997b, 112). The statement is found in Avicenna's text *On the Parts of Science*. The great importance that Strauss gave to this statement by Avicenna is confirmed by the fact that he uses it as an epigraph to his last published book, *The Argument and the Action of Plato's Laws* (Chicago: University of Chicago Press, 1975). Strauss's other utterances of a similar statement are documented in (Green 1993, 62).

[6] See Thomas Pangle's essay "Platonic Political Science in Strauss and Voegelin," in (Emberley and Cooper 1993, 347). In "Quelques remarques sur la science politique de Maimonide et de Farabi" (1936) Strauss writes: "c'est bien une philosophie grecque de la loi divine qui est à la base de la philosophie juive et musulmane de la Tora ou de la Chari'a: selon Avicenne, les *Lois* de Platon sont l'oeuvre classique sur la prophétie et la Chari'a" (Strauss 1997b, 126).

[7] (Green 1993) highlights the centrality of Maimonides for Strauss's political and theological thought but fails to address the key role played by Schmitt's political theology in Strauss's "turn" to Maimonides. In this early work, Green also relativizes the importance of Cohen's Maimonides interpretation for Strauss's development. He has since rectified this problem in (Green 2013). Conversely, the detailed commentary of Strauss's review essay on Schmitt found in (Meier 1995) hardly mentions Maimonides or medieval Jewish philosophy.

[8] See the "Preface to the English Translation" in the 1965 edition of (Strauss 1997c). As has been often noted, the text of the "Preface" contains entire passages that are nearly identical to ones found thirty years before in *Philosophy and Law*. The "Preface" thus provides an account of why Strauss was led to the standpoint that found expression in the earlier book and which remained his in the post-emigration years. Strauss wrote to Kojève that this "Preface" "comes as close to an autobiography as is possible within the bounds of propriety." Letter of May 26, 1962, cited in (Strauss 1963, 309). See also his response to Scholem's remark that Strauss had never been so bold in expressing his position as in the "Preface," cited in (Smith 1991, 76). For two attempts at Strauss's intellectual biography, see (Sheppard 2007) and (Tanguay 2003). One of the earliest diagnostics of this "change of orientation," and still among the best readings of it, is found in (Janssens 2000, 2008). For a more recent collection of essays on this question, see (Yaffe and Ruderman 2014).

from Nazi Germany, in 1935 Strauss published a book entitled *Philosophy and Law* that formulated his new standpoint: given human laws are always open to exception, a "unitary, total order of human life [*einheitlichen, totalen Ordnung des menschlichen Lebens*]" is only possible if it is established on the basis of divine law imposed by a prophet who is both a philosopher and a political leader.[9] This is the meaning of his claim made in a 1930 letter according to which the Arab and Jewish medieval philosophers "through the link to the ancient idea of the concrete *nomos* [law] and *nomothetes* [lawgiver], [offer] a much greater possibility than does the natural right which preoccupied [the] 18th century of *accepting the concrete order of revelation.*"[10] In other words, the Islamic and Jewish medieval philosophers find a way to adopt a Platonic understanding of divine law and apply it to develop a political theology based on prophetic revelation. Strauss inherits from Hermann Cohen's political theology the project to conceptualize together Plato and the Jewish prophets, and he does so in line with the philosophical approach to prophetology inaugurated by Philo.[11] In this chapter my aim is limited to working out how Strauss makes use of this medieval canon to fashion a Jewish political theology, and why this return to medieval political philosophy indicated to him a way out of the modern "theologico-political predicament."

[9] (Strauss 1995, 73; 1997b, 61). He argues that for Alfarabi and Maimonides "the prophet is therefore proclaimer of a law directed to the specific perfection of human beings. But the law aims at making possible life in common [*die Ermöglichung des Zusammenslebens*]. Hence the prophet is the founder of a society [*Gesellschaft*] directed towards the specific perfection of human beings" (Strauss 1995, 121, translation modified; 1997b, 110).

[10] Letter of June 26, 1930, to Gerhard Krüger as cited in (Pangle 2014, 63, emphasis mine). Strikingly, Pangle does not comment on what "concrete order of revelation" means in this context, nor does he signal that "concrete order" is a term also employed during the same years by Schmitt; see (Schmitt 1995) and for commentary (Herrero 2015). See also Strauss's claim: "It is only in their political doctrine that medieval philosophers discuss the basis of their thought, the deepest presupposition by which they distinguish themselves from the ancient as well as the modern thinkers: the belief in Revelation" (1997b, 125). William Altman believes that the source of "divine laws" in Strauss is "not the God of Abraham through Moses nor even Zeus through Minos, but rather the Athenian Stranger intent on securing divine sanction for *phusis*" (Altman 2011b, 480). For Altman, "Plato's *Laws* is the first document that shows how a legalistic tyrant can abolish the very possibility of that separation [of Church and State] by means of an atheistic re-enactment of religion. This book has attempted to show why such a project was of paramount interest to the German Stranger and why it holds the key to the true relationship between Leo Strauss and National Socialism" (ibid., 479). In my opinion, Strauss does not oppose in this way the God of Moses to Platonic philosophy. Also, Strauss seems to see a continuity between Plato's *Republic* and Plato's later political dialogues like *Statesman* and *Laws*: "Summarizing the analysis of the political given by Xenophon's Socrates, we may say that there is a fundamental agreement between that analysis and the analysis given in the Platonic dialogues, especially the *Republic* and the *Statesman*" (Strauss 1986, 145).

[11] "Prophetology" is a term employed by Strauss throughout *Philosophy and Law*. During the 1930s Strauss seems unaware of Goodenough's interpretation of Philo. Strauss does not discuss Philo at any length in his writings. However, he was aware of his founding role for medieval Arabic and Jewish philosophy. At the end of *Philosophy and Law* he writes: "The doctrine of the prophet's direct knowledge, by which he differs from the philosopher, is anticipated especially by Philo" (Strauss 1995, 129; 1997b, 120).

Strauss's approach to Arabic and Jewish medieval philosophical and political thought has been much questioned by later specialists. Contrary arguments range from the claim that political philosophy was a minor concern of medieval Arab and Jewish philosophers to the claim that Arabic *falasifa* understood revealed religion as a form of *theologia civilis* or civil religion, that is, as an *instrumentum regni* for whoever happened to be in power.[12] At the opposite side of the spectrum, one finds a number of Straussian interpreters who argue the thesis according to which Arabic *falasifa* and their Jewish followers apply Greek philosophical concepts in order to develop an interpretation of revealed religion as a "tool" of the philosophers to protect them from their "conflict" with political power and social opinions or conventions.[13] It is only quite recently that the suggestion that Arabic *falasifa* might be formulating a "political theology" has been taken up by some scholars of Islamic and Jewish medieval thought.[14]

Political theology does not mean the translation of a theological construal of God (as King) into the political rule by way of revealed law. For Strauss, "theology" does not get to determine either the essence of God or the essence of law, and therefore it does not determine political science. His hypothesis is exactly the opposite: Arabic and Jewish philosophical teachings on the prophet (viz., prophetology) is "political, not metaphysical." He clearly states that "the foundation of a perfect nation, and as a consequence, the proclamation of a perfect law that must serve as a constitution for the perfect nation, this is, according to Maimonides, the purpose of prophecy."[15] This means that prophecy is not an "instrument" or a tool of an already constituted political power, because it is the legitimate constituent power of the ideal society. At the same time, prophetic religion is also not an instrument or tool of philosophy because "the founding of the perfect society is not possible for the human being who is only a philosopher. That is why the philosopher is also dependent on the law that is given by the prophet; the philosopher must also obey the prophet . . . [because] his theoretical insight would not make him capable of legislation; and the human being, as a political being, can only live under law."[16]

[12] For the former view, see (Gutas 2002); for the latter, see (Crone 2004).

[13] For some examples, see (Mahdi 2001; Butterworth 2011; and Parens 2016).

[14] See, for example, (Campanini 2011), but this approach was pioneered by the Spanish scholarship on medieval Arabic philosophy found in (Hernández 2011). Ironically, Campanini identifies Strauss's interpretation with that of his Straussian followers, and thus believes that his own politico-theological reading of the Arabic thinkers does not correspond to Strauss's reading, but this is due to his ignorance of Strauss's writings.

[15] (Strauss 1995, 143). "The purpose of prophecy is political, the supreme practical role of the prophet is not mantics, but political leadership [*politische Leitung*]" (Strauss 1995, 122, translation modified; 1997b, 111). The political character of philosophy found in Maimonides' prophetology is expressed most clearly in Maimonides' belief that the pinnacle of prophecy is the Mosaic legislation (*Guide* 2.39) and not the belief in a Messiah that is to come in the "future time": "the peak of prophecy is therefore legislation" (Strauss 2013, 214). On the tradition of divine law, see the wide-ranging discussion in (Brague 2005).

[16] (Strauss 1995, 121, translation modified; 1997b, 111).

Strauss could hardly be more explicit: an authentic or legitimate politics is possible only on condition of a prophetically given divine law. True politics is neither philosophical nor civil: it can only be theological. Knowledge of the divine law is a kind of knowledge that is accessible to the prophet alone, not to the philosopher because the philosopher qua philosopher does not have direct access to God's mind or will, to God's essence, which remains forever "hidden" in its inscrutable darkness, only to be on occasion, and in punctual manner, "enlightened [*erhellt*]" through "lightning flashes from on high [*durch Blitze aus der Höhe*]" (Strauss 1995, 126; 1997b, 117). For Strauss, the only thing that can pierce through the Platonic cave in which humankind resides "by nature" are the "lightning flashes from on high, by direct knowledge of the upper world" granted the prophets (but not the philosophers) (Strauss 1995, 127; 1997b, 118).

Making the case for Leo Strauss as a Jewish political theologian is a complicated exercise due to the highly contested and polemical terrain of Straussian interpretation in the last decades.[17] This conflict of interpretation has cemented the impression that Strauss stands firmly planted in the "city" of philosophy, Athens, and addresses the "city" of faith, Jerusalem, from a point of view external to it. Counter to the Judeo-Hellenistic framework I have proposed so far to make sense of the discourse of Jewish political theology in the 20th century, this reigning interpretation assumes that for Strauss the relation between the two cities is one of mutual exclusion and radical antagonism.[18]

Strauss's thought is characterized by the overlap of two basic problems around which all his writings circle. In the lecture "Why We Remain Jews," given in Chicago in 1962, he states "without any exaggeration, that since a very, very early time the main theme of my reflections has been what is called the 'Jewish Question.' "[19] Elsewhere he refers to the "theologico-political problem" posed

[17] See the account of Straussianism in (Zuckert 2006). The literature on Strauss's anti-liberalism spans from (Drury 1988) to (Altman 2011b), among many others.

[18] Some of Strauss's texts lend superficial support to this Straussian view. See the following citations for some examples: "Generally stated, I would say that all alleged refutations of revelation presuppose unbelief in revelation, and all alleged refutations of philosophy presuppose already faith in revelation. There seems to be no ground common to both" (Strauss 1997a, 131); "We speak, and we speak rightly, of the antagonism between Jerusalem and Athens, between faith and philosophy.... The whole history of the West can be viewed as an ever repeated attempt to achieve a compromise or synthesis between these two antagonistic principles.... Philosophy is made, against its meaning, the handmaid of theology, or faith is made, against its meaning, the handmaid of philosophy. The Western tradition does not allow of a synthesis of its two elements, but only of their tension: this is the secret of the vitality of the West" (Strauss 1989, 72–3). For a balanced discussion of this antagonism in Strauss's later writings, see (Ranieri 2009). However, like most of the Straussian reception, from (Pangle 2006) to (Tanguay 2003), Ranieri also argues that Strauss decidedly sides with Athens or philosophy against the claims based on biblical revelation. For doubts relating to this point, asserting the central place of Arabic medieval philosophy for Strauss, see (Brague 1989). A nuanced discussion of Strauss's adherence to both Athens and Jerusalem is found in (Bernstein 2015). For my discussion of Bernstein's claims, see (Vatter 2017b).

[19] (Strauss 1997a, 312).

by the tension between human reason and divine revelation as ultimate sources for the guidance of human life: "No alternative is more fundamental than this: human guidance or divine guidance" (Strauss 1953, 74). In *Philosophy and Law*, Strauss argues that this tension between knowledge and faith was resolved by medieval Arabic and Jewish political thought through the claims that philosophy both stands in need of revealed divine law and is itself enjoined by divinely revealed law.

The second main problem that characterizes Strauss's thinking is the tension between the philosophical life and the political life: "there is a necessary conflict between philosophy and politics if the element of society necessarily is opinion" because philosophy attempts to replace opinion by knowledge (Strauss 1988, 229). At least since the "change of orientation" that takes place in his thinking in the early 1930s, Strauss believed that the resolution to this problem was to be found in what he called "Platonic political philosophy."[20] "Platonic political philosophy" is a technical term of art that covers what Strauss also calls the teaching of "classical natural right" on the "problem of law and legitimacy" (Strauss 1963, 76). "Classical natural right" covers essentially the same ground as what Erwin Goodenough called the theory of "Hellenistic kingship." The "problem of law and legitimacy" refers to the fateful debates on legality and legitimacy that involved Max Weber, Hans Kelsen, Carl Schmitt, and other jurists and philosophers of law in Weimar Germany.[21] Weber and Kelsen argued that modern democratic revolutions equated legitimacy with legality, viz., the legal procedures guaranteeing the supremacy of equal individual rights over the ideas of the good life.[22] Their argument was that the validity of law could not be based on morality because moral judgments are ultimately relative. Schmitt contested this liberal viewpoint by pointing out that human law cannot apply itself but is always applied by a representative person who is authorized to decide the meaning of the law in any given situation.[23] This representative person must be endowed with a supra-legal source of "legitimacy" that ultimately has Christian theological foundations. In *Philosophy and Law*, Strauss argues that the "problem of law

[20] For the standard Straussian view on what the terms means: "His understanding of ancient philosophy has to do with the political problem of philosophy or the issue of the philosophical life and not a philosophy of politics, as it is usually understood.... Strauss makes clear that the philosophical life is to be understood as a form of zetetic questioning. This is the meaning of 'Platonic political philosophy' in its original sense" (Smith 2011, 77). See also the long discussion of "Platonic political philosophy" found in (Zuckert 2014). In what follows I shall refer to Platonic political philosophy without citation marks, but the reference is always to Strauss's technical sense of this expression. For an excellent recent discussion of the origins of Strauss's interest in "Platonic political philosophy," see (Meyer 2014). For another narrative of Strauss's development that minimizes the impact of the "Jewish Question" in his oeuvre, see (Meier 2014).

[21] For a good overview of the different debates and stakes, see (Dyzenhaus 1998).

[22] For this debate on legality and legitimacy in German philosophy of law, see (Habermas 1996).

[23] See (Schmitt 2004).

and legitimacy" can only be tackled if the representative is understood to be a prophet who applies divine law like a philosopher-king. His central thesis is that "the Islamic and Jewish philosophers of the Middle Ages are 'more primitive' than the modern philosophers because they are guided not, like them, by the derived idea of natural right but by the *original, ancient idea of law* as a unified, total order of human life [*sondern von der* ursprünglichen, antiken Idee des Gesetzes *al seine einheitlichen, totalen Ordnung des menschlichen Lebens*]; in other words, because they are pupils of *Plato* and not pupils of Christians" (Strauss 1995, 73; 1997b, 61). In this chapter I show that Strauss's reconstruction of the medieval discourse of prophetology in *Philosophy and Law* offers an answer to the crucial hermeneutic challenge of explaining how the "theologico-political problem" relates to "Platonic political philosophy" in the development of his thinking.[24]

From atheism to faith in the fact of divine revelation

In the secondary literature, there exist two plausible arguments drawn from Strauss's early writings that seek to cast doubt on the authenticity of his *Teshuvah*. The first and most common argument appeals to the biographical fact that Strauss understood himself as an atheist. In his early writings on Judaism he seems to have adopted the Nietzschean stance of intellectual probity—"this new fortitude, being the willingness to look man's forsakenness in its face, being the courage to welcome the most terrible truth" (Strauss 1968, 257).[25] If this is so, then how could an atheist and "free thinker" seriously consider the validity of the claims made by the Jewish Torah, its tradition, and the Jewish faith?

An initial response to this objection is provided by the philosophical context in which Strauss moved. Already in the 1920s, Martin Heidegger argued for the necessity of philosophy to adopt a form of methodological atheism which at the same time would recognize the legitimacy of theology as a positive science.[26] Theology is a positive science insofar as it presupposes a givenness or *Faktum* to which there corresponds faith as a "way of existing of human Dasein [*Existenzweise der menschlichen Daseins*]" (Heidegger 1978, 52). This *Faktum*, for Christian theology, is the "crucified God." "Only in faith can this Faktum

[24] Whereas (Meier 2006) proposes to read the "theologico-political" problem starting from the question of Platonic political philosophy, and (Janssens 2008) leaves both problems next to each other but fundamentally unrelated, in (Vatter 2004b) I suggested that the turn to Platonic political philosophy was part and parcel of Strauss's attempt to reverse the "theologico-political problem" of the moderns by developing a discourse on political theology which drew its foundations from the understanding of "divine law" in Arabic and Jewish medieval philosophy.

[25] On Strauss's atheism, among many others, see (Lampert 2009).

[26] In his lecture "Phänomenologie und Theologie," Heidegger argues that "theology is a positive science and as such completely different from philosophy [defined as 'the science of Being']" (Heidegger 1978, 49, translation mine).

come to be 'known'" (51). As shown in the following, Strauss adopts a similar way of conceiving Jewish "theology," where the *Faktum* is the divine revelation of law. However, unlike Heidegger, he does not assume a priori that philosophy is anterior and superior to the "fact" of religion.

Similarly, Rosenzweig argued in the *Star of Redemption* that any post-secular return to the Jewish faith necessarily would have to traverse Nietzsche's thought about the "death of God." Additionally, the scholarly literature has documented extensively on the adoption of Nietzsche's thought by many currents of Zionism in the 1920s.[27] This context helps to explain why Strauss could understand the adoption of Nietzschean probity already in the "Introduction" to *Philosophy and Law*—the very text that led Scholem to suggest its reading to Benjamin in virtue of its paradoxical defense of Judaism through atheism—as being *fundamentally compatible* with the assertion of an "unqualified return" to biblical virtue. "Not only was Biblical morality as veracity or intellectual probity at work in the destruction of Biblical theology and Biblical morality; not only is it at work in the questioning of that very probity . . . Biblical morality will remain at work in the morality of the overman. . . . And, as we have learned from Nietzsche, Biblical morality demands the Biblical God."[28] In other words, intellectual probity—the virtue of Nietzsche's "free thinkers"—is traversed through and through by biblical morality and cannot possibly, in Strauss's mind, be the ground on which to give up the possibility of a return to the Torah.[29]

The second general objection found in the literature is that in his youth Strauss was a political Zionist who considered Jewish Orthodoxy as a "Jewish enemy."[30] According to a recent treatment of his early Zionist views, Strauss is said to have rejected out of hand all of Cohen, Rosenzweig, and Buber. He is said to have agreed with the Herzlian formula for Zionism as seeking a "normal historical existence" for the Jewish people. He is believed to have uncritically adopted the theories of German nationalists and anti-Semites like Julius Wellhausen and Paul de Lagarde as well as those of "good Europeans" like Theodor Mommsen and Nietzsche, according to which post-exilic Judaism generated a "prophetic, apolitical" interpretation of the Pentateuch that depoliticized the religion of the

[27] Among the many works now dedicated to this overlap between Nietzscheanism and Zionism, see (Golomb 2004), which remains among the best. Scholem's attachment to Nietzsche was discussed in the previous chapter.

[28] (Strauss 1997a, 151).

[29] (Miner 2012) goes through the entire debate on Strauss and Nietzschean probity, but without paying attention to the context of German-Jewish philosophy. He argues, contra Janssens, that Strauss did not believe in his own criticism of Nietzschean probity. This is not the place to engage Strauss's complex reading of Nietzsche, which lies at the heart also of (Lampert 1996).

[30] "Zionism has a single Jewish enemy and that enemy is Orthodoxy" (Strauss 2002, 127). Since it was thematized by (Sheppard 2007), the literature on Strauss's early engagement with political Zionism and right-wing political thought has increased. For some interesting contributions, see also (Kartheininger 2006; Dotti 2009; Muller 2014; and Quélennec 2018).

Jewish people. Lastly, he is said to uphold "the validity of the critique of revelation developed in the modern critique of religion."[31] A careful reading of Strauss's early, purportedly "Zionist" writings show that none of these claims stands up to scrutiny.

There is no doubt that the young Strauss also wrote in order to "épater le bourgeois." Hence his provocative call to "understand the internal legitimacy, the Jewish necessity, of a Jewish development that is influenced by and learns from European nationalism and anti-Semitism" (Strauss 2002, 86–7). Yet far from agreeing with Herzl's and Nordau's definition of political Zionism as satisfying "the need for a normal existence under normal conditions" by giving up the "*galut* existence" in which "Zionism and Messianism coincide" (Strauss 2002, 85), Strauss finds that "the more Herzl's original will now comes alive, *the more distinctly we perceive the will to normality as unmotivated*" (Strauss 2002, 128, emphasis mine). To Nordau, Strauss objects that "Zionism continues and heightens the de-Judaizing tendency of assimilation [*entjudende Tendenz der Assimilation*]" (Strauss 1997b, 319; 2002, 87). What he means is that "in Zionist matters, theology has no say; Zionism is purely political . . . this is the voice of a science that is free of presuppositions!" (Strauss 2002, 87). The exclamation mark suggests Strauss's disagreement with the uncritical secularism of political Zionism. A brief perusal of Strauss's writings at all times indicates his rejection of the Weberian ideal of "value free" science.[32] As discussed in the following, Strauss identified the great shortcoming of political Zionism precisely in its total disregard for what he calls the "fact of religion" or the "fact of revelation."

In his early writings, Strauss often refers to "the power and depth of the religious notion of transcendence" (2002, 114) in terms of the "uncanny" that the Hebrew prophets employed in order to reject "pre-prophetic religion . . . for being canny, for being all too canny" (2002, 113). Strauss believes that political Zionism's wish for "normality" is thwarted by the "uncanny" harbored by Jewish religion. This standpoint comes to expression in his essay on Freud's *The Future of an Illusion* that some commentators inexplicably consider a defense of atheism. Actually, Strauss uses Freud to argue *against* the claim of political Zionism that "in the age of atheism, the Jewish people can no longer base its existence on God but only on itself alone" (2002, 203). Strauss employs Freud dialectically, in order to manifest the insufficiency of the basis in "unbelief" adopted by political Zionism. Freud and Strauss both agree that modern science cannot refute belief in religious doctrines, but at most can raise questions as to the "rational" justifications given for this belief. Through his early study on *Spinoza's*

[31] For all these claims, see (Muller 2014, 18, 23, 26–7). Muller's reading of Strauss is hard put to explain a text like *Philosophy and Law* where Strauss advances none of these claims.

[32] On the critique of Weber in Strauss, see (Behnegar 2003).

Critique of Religion, Strauss came to the conclusion that "if orthodoxy claims to know that the Bible is divinely revealed, that every word of the Bible is divinely inspired . . . [then] Spinoa has refuted orthodoxy." However, Strauss immediately adds: "But the case is entirely different if orthodoxy limits itself to asserting that it believes the aforementioned things. . . . For all assertions of orthodoxy rest on *the irrefutable premise that the omnipotent God, whose will is unfathomable, whose ways are not our ways, who has decided to dwell in this thick darkness, may exist*" (Strauss 1997c, 254, emphasis mine). In other words, the modern Enlightenment had "laughed orthodoxy to death" by recourse to the basis of modern science only because it had failed to *refute* philosophically the standpoint of orthodoxy (Strauss 2002, 132).

This leaves open the question as to the non- or extra-rational support of the "irrefutable" belief in the transcendent God. Here Strauss departs from Freud. For the latter, belief in God emerges from the experience of "human misery and helplessness" (Strauss 2002, 207). Freud's point is that, insofar as belief in God is employed to provide comfort and help, this God can only be an "illusion." Strauss, though, rejects Freud's assumption that belief in God is only employed to provide comfort: "is it not in truth the case that *the* danger from which the believer hopes to be saved is beyond all the dangers that can be known to the unbeliever, that therefore belief brings just as much, and much rather, *despair* than comfort and help?" (2002, 208). Strauss makes a distinction between two kinds of primal scenes or "states of nature," out of which the religious belief in God is supposed to provide guidance. The first, attributed to Freud's argument, is a situation in which "life without God appears to him [the believer] hopeless, stale and shallow." In this case, the belief that God brings "meaning" and "sense" to the life of the believer is misleading. However, Strauss considers another situation or "state of nature" in which the *reality* of God as *numen* encountered in faith generates in the believer the awareness of the "lack of comfort, hopelessness, staleness and shallowness of life without God" (2002, 208). This second form of faith is entirely justified.

Strauss's construal of Jewish theology in his early writings is heavily reliant on the work of the German Protestant theologian, Rudolf Otto. Otto's thesis is that the term "holy" does not originally refer to an idea of moral perfection, or something entirely good, but rather to something that is anterior to the "gradual shaping and filling in with the ethical meaning." This anterior being of God is an undefinable "X" for which Otto adopts the Roman term of *numen*, "numinous" (Otto 1950, 5–6). The numinous is characterized by a wholly in- and extra-human *mysterium tremendum* that has three signal characteristics: it is "aweful"; it is "majestic" or "overpowering"; and it is "urgent" or "wrathful" (Otto speaks also of "energy" and "vitality") (1950, 13, 19, 23). Confronted with the numinous in these three manifestations, the "fear of God" is the most fundamental and appropriate response by those who are subject to it. Strauss argues that Otto's concept of the *numen* had the merit of shifting attention away from the discussion of the "rational" attributes of God and toward God's essence or substance as it is represented in the "Old Testament and from Jewish liturgy" (2002, 76–7). Evidently, through his engagement with Otto, Strauss is intent on working with a primordial and "irrefutable" conception of the Jewish God as Lord and "Father of the world" (2002, 131). Whereas Freud only considers the misery of the human being prior to the civilizational, redemptive, and hence also illusory belief in God, Strauss also considers "*the* misery" posterior to the revelation of the numinous God whose content is precisely this "civilized" condition.

By the early 1930s, Strauss becomes convinced that modern liberalism and political Zionism share the mistaken assumption that the "Jewish problem" is "a merely human problem" that can receive a civilizational solution. For Strauss, the highest expression of this solution is found in Spinoza's *Theologico-Political Treatise*.[33] Both liberalism and political Zionism presuppose that the Jewish faith and way of life organized around the Torah are one civilizational human achievement among others. In so doing, they disregard the fundamental tension between divine revelation and civilization. For Strauss, "the rock bottom of any Jewish culture are the Bible, Talmud and Midrash. And if you take these things with a minimum of respect or seriousness, you must say they were not meant to be products of the Jewish mind. They were meant to be ultimately 'from Heaven,' and this is the crux of the matter: *Judaism cannot be understood as a culture.... The substance is not culture, but divine revelation. Therefore the only consistent solution, clear solution,* is that which abandons, which goes beyond, cultural Zionism and becomes clearly religious Zionism. *Return to the Jewish faith, to the faith of our ancestors.*"[34]

The key to Strauss's Jewish political theology is contained in the idea that "Judaism cannot be understood as a culture" because divine revelation (the "substance" of Judaism) is a "fact of religion as such" irreducible to culture.[35]

[33] "In providing for the liberal state, Spinoza provides for a Judaism that is liberal in the extreme. The 'assimilationist' 'solution to the Jewish problem' which Spinoza may be said to have suggested was more important from his point of view than the 'Zionist' one which he likewise suggested" (Strauss 1997c, 20–1).

[34] See the essay "Why We Remain Jews" in (Strauss 1997a, 52, emphasis mine).

[35] "It is striking, however, that in spite of his unmistakeable inclination towards philosophy of culture... [Guttman] already suggests *the suspicion that religion cannot be rightly understood in the framework of the concept of "culture"*.... The claim to universality on the part of 'culture,' which in its own view rests on spontaneous production, *seems to be opposed by the claim to universality on the part of religion*, which in its own view is not produced by man but given to him.... But in any case he [Guttmann] finds himself driven to a remarkable distancing from philosophy of culture by *the fact of religion as such*, which thereby proves to be one crux of philosophy of culture" (Strauss 1995, 42, emphasis mine). The first chapter of *Philosophy and Law* is dedicated to an interpretation and critique of Julius Guttman's *The Philosophy of Judaism*. For the most detailed and best discussion of the Strauss-Guttmann polemic, see (Meyer 2009). In distinction to my interpretation, Meyer does not

To appreciate the reality of the Jewish tradition it is necessary to translate oneself back to a "state of nature" that is not the liberal, Hobbesian "state of nature" which is merely functional to the establishment of human laws, and also that is not characterized by a condition of absolute "freedom." The sought for "state of nature," best described by Plato and Aristotle, turns out to be characterized by the givenness of divine law, and by the natural human "need for guidance."

Strauss questions both modern liberalism and political Zionism on the grounds that they misunderstand the fundamental *theological* feature of Judaism and fall short of giving Judaism its adequate *political* articulation. Liberal democracy cannot resolve the "Jewish problem" because "liberalism stands or falls by the distinction between state and society, or by the recognition of a private sphere, protected by the law but impervious to the law, with the understanding that, above all, *religion as particular religion belongs to the private sphere*. Just as certainly as the liberal state will not 'discriminate' against its Jewish citizens, so it is constitutionally unable and even unwilling to prevent 'discrimination' against Jews by individuals or groups. *To recognize a private sphere in the sense indicated means to permit private 'discrimination,' to protect it and thus in fact to foster it.*"[36]

By privatizing religion, modern liberalism simply shifted the source of persecution from the state to civil society. Similarly, political Zionism assumes that the "Jewish problem" can be solved "politically" through the foundation of a Jewish nation-state which, obviously, falls far short of establishing the Kingdom of God on earth.[37] Strauss argues that "the Jewish state will be an empty shell without a Jewish culture which has its roots in the Jewish heritage," thus political Zionism requires cultural Zionism. But cultural Zionism is itself caught up in a pragmatic contradiction, for it understands "the Jewish heritage itself as a culture, i.e., as a product of the national mind, of the national genius," rather than as a "divine gift, as divine revelation."[38] As is clear from the discussion so far, Strauss criticizes both contemporary Jewish orthodoxy and secularist Zionism on the basis that neither recognizes the revealed divine law as a "fact" that can only be met with

address the idea of a "claim to universality" based on the "fact of religion" as opposed to the viewpoint of culture. The division, indeed opposition, between divine revelation and culture (understood as the highest form of human self-assertion) problematizes the reduction of Strauss's idea of the prophet to a Nietzschean "genius of culture," as claimed by (Drury 1997) and (Lampert 2013).

[36] (Strauss 1997a, 143; and the same idea is reiterated at 314).

[37] (Strauss 1997a, 141). On why Strauss considers the State of Israel not to be a solution to the "infinite, absolute" nature of the "problem" posed by Judaism, see the discussion in (Bouretz 2003, 639–41).

[38] (Strauss 1997a, 143). In a text of 1925, "Ecclesia militans," Strauss is scathing against those advocates of cultural Zionism who argued that the "affirmation of the nation" required the affirmation of the "national culture" which is in turn claimed to be centered on the Torah. Strauss's sarcastic response: "As if the fundamental question of religion could be decided by a national decree!" (2002, 125).

the acknowledgment of the authority its teachings have over human reason and by following its absolute commands.[39]

In the autobiographical "Preface," Strauss acknowledges that his own early thinking about the "fact" of revelation was influenced by the "radical empiricity" of the *Neues Denkens* of Buber and Rosenzweig, on one side, and of Heidegger, on the other.[40] Characteristic of the "new thinking" of Buber and Rosenzweig is the idea that divine revelation "*is the only awareness of something absolute which cannot be relativized in any way as everything else, rational or non-rational, can; it is the experience of God as the Thou, the father and king of all men; it is the experience of an unequivocal command addressed to me here and now as distinguished from general laws and ideas which are always disputable and permitting of exceptions*. Only by surrendering to God's experienced call which calls for one's loving Him with all one's heart, with all one's soul and with all one's might can one come to see the other human being as one's brother and love him as oneself" (Strauss 1997a, 146, emphasis mine). From this Buberian description of the "absolute experience" of a divine commandment, Strauss safeguards the intuition that the possibility of genuine ethics is connected to the legal order that issues from the radical transcendence of the biblical God: an order that permits of no exception, and whose validity is trans-historical.

Like Scholem, Strauss was also critical of Rosenzweig and Buber, but his criticisms are all *internal* to the debate about the features of the revealed divine *aleph*. Buber worried that to determine in any way the "absolute experience" of God's Voice is to fall into "mere interpretation," that is, to substitute a human authority for divine authority. Strauss responds that Buber's concern is illegitimate because it rejects the possibility that "any one interpretation is the simply true interpretation." As a consequence, Buber is also forced to reject the idea that "the Jewish fate is the outcome of one particular interpretation of

39 "No one can oversee the fact that with Jewish culture things stand differently than with the culture of other peoples. The Jewish culture is identical with the study and compliance of the law.... The Jewish law according to the Jewish tradition is a law given by God." In "Die geistige Lage der Gegenwart" (Strauss 1997b, 444). In *Philosophy and Law*, he defends Ibn Daud's view that it is only "because [revealed law] is not accessible to reason, [that] it has the advantage of making complete obedience to God possible for man.... The realization of this highest virtue—the virtue established by Abraham in the binding of his son—is wholly dependent on the existence of revealed commandments inaccessible to thought" (Strauss 1995, 68). In the "Preface" he defends the reading given by Spinoza of Maimonides' teaching according to which "Gentiles who perform the seven Noahidic commandments because reason decides so are not wise men," on the grounds that Maimonides "denied that there are any rational commandments" (Strauss 1997c, 24). In "Progress or Return?" he again points out Abraham's obedience to a humanly incomprehensible commandment as the crucial example of the majesty of moral obligations in the Bible, compared to the secondary status of such obligations in the tradition of classical philosophy.

40 (Strauss 1997a, 147–8). For an excellent study of the category of facticity in Heidegger and its theological presuppositions, see (Savarino 2001). For another pertinent philosophical developments of the category of facticity, see (Agamben 1988).

the absolute experience" (Strauss 1997a, 150). In *Philosophy and Law*, Strauss defends Maimonides' claim that Moses might offer "the simply true interpretation" of God's *aleph*.

Similarly, Strauss faults Rosenzweig for speaking about the Jewish experience of divine revelation not "from what is primary or authoritative for the Jewish consciousness," that is, the fact of the Torah, but from "the primary condition of possibility of the Jewish experience," that is, the Jewish nation. In so doing, Rosenzweig continues to make of the fact of divine revelation something that is relative to a human condition of possibility, namely, to the prior existence of the Jewish nation. By way of contrast, Strauss defends the belief that "if the Jewish nation did not originate the Torah but is manifestly constituted by the Torah, it is necessarily preceded by the Torah which was created prior to the world and for the sake of which the world was created" (Strauss 1997a, 152). In *Philosophy and Law*, he provides a politico-theological justification for the belief in Creation.

Strauss's criticism of the positions of Buber and Rosenzweig in the end boils down to pointing out that their construals of the "fact of religion as such" do not take sufficiently into account the "fact of the political" that is internally related to the facticity of divine revelation:

> The other crux of philosophy of culture is *the fact of the political* (see my "Anmerkungen zu Carl Schmitt, Der Begriff des Politischen," *Archiv für Sozialwissenschaft und Sozialpolitik*, Vol. 67, pp. 732ff). If "religion" and "politics" are the facts that transcend "culture" or, to speak more exactly, are the original facts, then the radical critique of the concept of "culture" is possible only in the form of a "theologico-political treatise," which must, however, if it is not to lead again to the foundation of "culture," *take exactly the opposite direction from the theologico-political treatises of the seventeenth century, especially those of Hobbes and Spinoza*. The first condition for this would be, of course, that these seventeenth-century works no longer be understood, as they almost always have been up to now, within the horizon of the philosophy of culture. (Strauss 1995, 138)

Strauss owes to and shares with Schmitt the claim that liberalism and its philosophy of culture are unable to come to grips with these two "facts" of religion and the political, as he explains in his 1932 review of *The Concept of the Political* to which he draws attention in the preceding passage.[41]

[41] I have previously argued that when Strauss calls for a "theologico-political treatise" that must "take exactly the opposite direction from . . . those of Hobbes and Spinoza," he is referring to the possibility of a treatise of political theology whose signal feature would be the critique of the neutrality of the modern state with respect to positive revealed religions which Hobbes and Spinoza were the first to advocate. See (Vatter 2004b).

Both liberalism and Zionism mistakenly assume that the modern ideal of culture offers "a safe middle ground between politics (power politics) and divine revelation, between the sub-cultural and the supra-cultural" (Strauss 1997a, 143). In contrast, for Strauss the political and the theological, the sub-cultural and the supra-cultural dimensions of human existence exceed the domain of human culture and autonomy because they characterize the human being in a "state of nature" that is more fundamental than any civilizational ideal. Strauss could hardly express himself in clearer terms. Only a discourse that understands the political and the theological in their most direct connection, that is, only a political theology, can hope to offer a correct presentation of this "state of nature" and thereby offer a standpoint from which to engage in a "fundamental critique of at least the prevailing concept of culture."[42]

The Torah as Aristotelian political science

The real novelty of Strauss's work in the 1930s is his claim that it was Aristotle who made possible the adoption of Plato's philosopher-king into medieval prophetology, precisely because the prophet, unlike the philosopher-king, has knowledge of "political science," the discipline that Aristotle invents, and consequently the prophet has the skill in using the imagination and rhetoric to communicate successfully with the masses. "The prophet is therefore more than a philosopher" because, by way of "actualizing of the imaginative faculty" and of rhetoric, he also belongs to the class of "statesmen, legislators, soothsayers, magicians" (Strauss 2013, 213).[43] The prophets stand higher than the Platonic philosopher because, through their prophetic "capability to lead the multitude" with their imaginative faculty and their rhetorical powers (2013, 213), they become actual "founders of the ideal state" that Platonic political philosophy had argued for in philosophical speech, that is, only rhetorically (Strauss 1997b, 114, 122).[44] Thus, Strauss's thesis is that God governs

[42] "Notes on Carl Schmitt, *The Concept of the Political*," cited in (Meier 1995, 95). Much of the literature dedicated to Strauss and Schmitt either understands his reading of Schmitt in continuity with his early adherence to political Zionism (Dotti 2009; Altman 2011b), or claims that through his reading of Schmitt, Strauss abandoned his early adherence to political theology (McCormick 1998; Meier 1998; and Howse 2014). Michael Zank admits that the early Strauss shows many traits of "decisionism" (Strauss 2002, 26–7). He speaks of "the alliance of Strauss with Schmitt," as well as "Strauss' agreement on principle with Schmitt's concept of the political" (ibid., 35). Yet Zank also thinks Strauss abandons Zionism and political theology simultaneously. This is to presuppose that political Zionism is a form of political theology, which is a misunderstanding.

[43] "We may conclude that the prophet must be philosopher/statesman/seer/(miracle-worker) in one *in order that* he may be the founder of the society [*Gesellschaft*] directed to the specific perfection of human beings, the perfect society" (Strauss 1995, 121; 1997b, 111).

[44] It is indicative that Strauss associates Maimonides' conception of prophecy, as the joining of philosophy with rhetoric, with Cicero's high praise of rhetoric in his account of the founders of cities. In "Cohen and Maimonides," Strauss cites a passage from *De divinatione* I 40, 89: "Generally among

human beings through the prophet as a legislator of a perfect political community.[45] Viewed from this standpoint, then, the biblical prophet is more Aristotelian than Platonic: true political science is actualized by Jerusalem.[46] It is through his new approach to the medieval reception of Aristotle's political thought that Strauss responds to Schmitt's political theology.

Strauss adopts Cohen's fundamental teaching that "enlightened Judaism" is "a Judaism understood within Plato's horizon" (Strauss 2013, 179; 1997b, 396). Like Cohen, Strauss also seeks to defend Maimonides by showing that he is a Platonic political philosopher.[47] Despite their explicit use of Aristotelian physics and metaphysics, Arabic medieval philosophers did not employ Aristotle's *Politics* in their political treatment of prophetology. The *Politics* was never translated into Arabic, although there are indications that this text may have been known by some Arab philosophers, perhaps even by Alfarabi.[48] Strauss asks himself whether this omission is just a coincidence (Strauss 2013, 218; Strauss 1997b, 426). His answer is that it is not a coincidence. Rather, the omission is meant to indicate that, for the

the ancients who were in control of things, the same men held the auguries. For both wisdom and divining alike guided rulership, as our city is witness" (Strauss 2013, 220). For an excellent review of the Aristotelian and Ciceronian discourses on the founders of cities, see (Syros 2011).

45 This is ultimately the reason why Strauss holds that particular providence belongs to political science. Joshua Parens seems to think that for Maimonides, the particular providence of God is expressed in the fact that the revealed law favors the intellectual perfection of the philosopher (2014, 163–5). I defend the opposite claim, namely, that for Strauss, Maimonides holds that the intellectual perfection of the philosopher is necessary insofar as this philosopher is called to act as God's stand-in in history. The historical action of philosophy is representative of God's particular providence. The philosopher must be sovereign—this is the only reason why Strauss also argues that Maimonides was always pro-monarchic. Ultimately, as he argues in *On Tyranny*, a philosopher can exercise particular providence best by capturing the "ear" of a monarch or tyrant or sovereign.

46 By way of contrast, in his study on the political thought of medieval Rabbinic Judaism, Menachem Lorberbaum argues that Maimonides adopted Aristotelian politics in an attempt to neutralize and secularize the idea of divine law rather than establish theocracy. On Lorberbaum's reading, Aristotle's dictum that "man is by nature political" provides Maimonides with a "naturalistic" basis of human politics into which he inscribes, through his prophetology, the functioning and meaning of the divine law as Torah (Lorberbaum 2002, 30ff). On this view, the Torah "is not law because it is God's positive command but because it applies to human beings who need political rule. According to Maimonides all legal systems are based on the same presupposition about human beings' political nature, namely, that people must live in a society ordered by a ruler," which ruler is the political government of the *kahal*, shared by the human monarch (executive branch) and the Sanhedrin (the judiciary branch) (ibid., 31). Thus, his thesis is that Maimonides adopts Aristotelianism in order to think about the Torah as one naturalistic "legal system" among others (hence, as a form of what the ancients call *theologia civilis*) with the supplementary proviso that the Torah, unlike other divine *nomoi*, also seeks to guide human beings to exercise a contemplative life that is extra-political because "religious." The guide of this religious life is offered by the Rabbinical interpretation of the *halakhah* (the set of ordinances derived by the written and Oral Torah through tradition).

47 For other approaches to Strauss's debt to Cohen, see (Batnitzky 2006a; and Hollander 2014a; 2014b). Against the prevalent opinion that Strauss sought to destroy Cohen, see the discussion in Bouretz. Janssens acknowledges the influence of Cohen but does not offer a reading of his thought as a form of Platonic political philosophy.

48 For this discussion, see Shlomo Pines's "Translator's Introduction" in (Maimonides 1963, lxxvii), and now (Melamed 2003, 2012).

Arabic *falasifa* and their Jewish followers, Platonism offers the ultimate horizon because Plato "compels" philosophers "to care for others and to guard them so that the Republic becomes in reality a state, a true state [*damit der Staat in Wirklichkeit Staat, wahrhafter Staat sei*] (*Republic* 519D–520C)" (Strauss 1995, 132, translation modified; 1997b, 122). Plato requires philosophers to become leaders of the multitude, whereas Aristotle keeps philosophers separate from political activity.

However, Strauss departs from Cohen by arguing that Aristotle's political thought does not stand in opposition to Platonic political philosophy but is instrumental to it. In particular, Aristotle's political thought serves to connect the figure of the Socratic philosopher to the Greek conception of the noble individual, the "gentleman" (*spoudaios*).[49] In *Politics* III, 4 Aristotle discusses the distinction between the virtue of the good citizen, relative to a given constitution, and the virtue of the noble man (*andros spoudaios*) which is not relative in the same way. Later in the text, Aristotle discusses the possibility that these two figures may coincide in the "good ruler [*ton archonta ton spoudaion*] [who] is a good [*agathon*] and wise man [*phronimon*]" whereas "the citizen need not be wise" (*Pol.* 1277a15).[50] Thus, the "gentleman" for Strauss does not simply refer to a virtuous citizen, but to a potential or actual political ruler endowed with practical wisdom or *phronesis*.[51] Strauss considers that Aristotle offers the source of an alternative political theology that is not Christian. Aristotelian political science offers a way to conceive of religion as a form of politico-philosophical rhetoric that is employed by Arabic and Jewish medieval philosophers in their attempt to reunite Athens with Jerusalem at the politico-theological level of *a unified system of law*, rather than establish a political theology based on the division between Church and State found in the Christian tradition.

Cohen argued that Maimonides understood Platonic political philosophy to mean the principle that there exists no real separation between true philosophy and true politics. Already in his 1931 lecture "Cohen and Maimonides," Strauss explicitly agrees with him on this point.[52] He maintains the same idea

[49] On the exoteric employment of Aristotle's "gentlemen" in Strauss, see (Rosen 2003, 134–7) and for the uses of Xenophon, see (Altman 2011b, 447–92). For a clear discussion of "gentlemen" in Platonic political philosophy, see the "Third Lecture" in "The Problem of Socrates" (Strauss 1989, 133–50).

[50] I employ Barnes's revision of the Jowett translation of the *Politics* (Aristotle 1998). Aristotle later emphasizes that "practical wisdom [*phronesis*] is the only excellence peculiar to a ruler [*archontos*].... The excellence of the subject [*archomenon*, the one who is ruled] is certainly not wisdom [*phronesis*], but only true opinion [*doxa alethes*]" (*Pol.* 1277b25–30).

[51] "We must beware of mistaking Aristotle's man of moral virtue or 'good man' who is the perfect gentleman for the 'good man' who is just and temperate but lacks all other virtues, like the members of the lowest class in Plato's *Republic*" (Strauss 1964, 28).

[52] It is often claimed in the Straussian literature that Plato never seriously endorsed the model of the philosopher-king discussed in the *Republic*, and that in the *Laws* Plato took a "turn" toward realism and moderation. See, among many others, the discussion in (Zuckert 2014, 79–80, 119–43; and Tanguay 2003). This view rests on several texts by Strauss in which the *Laws* is presented as Plato's

in a late work like *The City and Man*: for Socrates and Plato, "*political philosophy* [the concern with 'what is by nature right and noble or with the nature of justice and nobility'] broadly understood *is the core of philosophy or rather 'the first philosophy*'" (Strauss 1964, 20, emphasis mine). Strauss holds that Socrates and Plato considered philosophizing to be a form of life that is in itself political, but it is not, precisely, the same form of life that characterizes the citizen within the *polis*, the form of life of the city *qua* city. This is what Socrates could be taken to mean by his paradoxical saying in *Gorgias* : "I think that I am one of the very few Athenians, not to say the only one, engaged in the true political art, and that of the men of today I alone practice statesmanship" (Plato 1985, 531D).[53]

The Socratic "ascent" to the "idea of the Good" denotes neither a metaphysical nor a mystical experience that lies beyond politics; rather it is an expression of the identity of "first philosophy" with "political philosophy."[54] When Strauss says that "man's true excellence or virtue exists beyond the political, or is transpolitical,"[55] he refers to the possibility of governing or ruling over political things from a standpoint that is not bound by the limits of the city and its regimes. It does not refer to a standpoint that would lie "beyond" politics, that is, beyond the problem of ruling by some over others. Since Socratic philosophizing is already political (for why else would Socrates have been put on trial in democratic Athens?), the standpoint of Socrates and Plato does not permit them to think about the inferior form of life found in the city as city from a "pure" philosophical or "scientific" perspective, that is, to study objectively political phenomena. That is why in *The City and Man* Strauss argues that Aristotle, not Plato, is the true founder of "political science" as a discipline which is strictly separated from metaphysics or "first philosophy."[56]

"real" political thought. For instance: "Hence Plato devoted his most extensive work, the *Laws*, which is *the* political work of Plato, to politics. And the *Laws* presents the best city which is possible for beings who are not gods nor sons of gods" (Strauss 1989, 162). But for a persuasive counterargument to the view commonly held by Straussian interpreters, and one that does not contradict Strauss's texts, see now (Horn 2013), who argues that Plato's *Laws* do not reject the identity of philosophy with true politics, but simply gives a different form to such identity, namely, one that makes possible constitutional government. It is noteworthy that Christoph Horn speaks of the *Laws* as containing Plato's "political theology."

[53] For an excellent discussion of the meaning of this famous and much-discussed claim made by Socrates, see (Horn 2008).

[54] "If Socratic philosophizing is in itself political, then for Aristotle politics moves into second place" (Strauss 2013, 202).

[55] "Man's true excellence or virtue exists beyond the political, or is transpolitical. Xenophon's Socrates is the representative of man's transpolitical existence, whereas his Cyrus is the representative of that life which is highest if the principle which is characteristic of the political is adhered to and thought through. The polarity of Socrates and Cyrus corresponds to the fundamental tension between philosophy and the polis" (Strauss 1989, 148).

[56] By way of contrast, the orthodox Straussian reading of the discussion of Aristotelian political science in *The City and Man* claims that "like Aristotle, then, Socrates does not unqualifiedly transcend the sphere of opinion, yet more clearly than Aristotle, he shows the necessary directedness of

If this is the case, then for Strauss the Aristotelian proposal to separate radically the philosophical life from the political life, metaphysics from political science, must be understood as a "rhetorical" gesture, in at least two distinct senses. In a first sense, it means that the Aristotelian distinction between metaphysics and political science does not say the whole truth about philosophy. Aristotle's claim that philosophers, like Epicurean divine beings, are entirely separate from or uninterested in political matters, merely serves to shield the Platonic philosopher's true political aspirations and actions. Seen in this way, when in *The City and Man* Strauss argues that Aristotle, not Plato, discovered political science, what he means thereby is that Aristotelian political science is a sublime exercise in rhetoric.[57] But Strauss also sees in the rhetorical function of Aristotelian social science a positive development and achievement. Aristotle's "political science" perfected Platonic political philosophy by showing the necessity of rhetoric for the philosophical life. Platonic philosophers find it necessary to indulge in science, and above all in the social sciences, in order to govern (perhaps even to fabricate or manipulate) the element of "consent" of the people that Aristotle (and Strauss) considers to be a fundamental requirement of any stable political form of government or regime.

In *Natural Right and History*, Strauss explicitly argued that the ideal Platonic society in which justice ("what is good in each case for the soul") is realized because "wise men are in absolute control"[58] turns out to be impracticable.[59] All

this sphere to the philosophic life, understood as the search for wisdom in the face of the elusive or mysterious character of the whole about which and within which the philosopher seeks wisdom" (Collins 2015, 458). As indicated, this is to turn upside down the way in which Strauss understands the relation between Platonism and Aristotelianism. For Strauss, Socrates is not a "better" philosopher than Aristotle, somehow possessing a better metaphysics than the Stagirite, but rather Aristotelian metaphysics is functional to a Socratic teaching about the philosophical life that is inherently "political, not metaphysical."

[57] My hypothesis about Strauss's understanding of the distinction between Platonism and Aristotelianism reverses Stanley Rosen's rhetorical reading of Strauss's teaching in (Rosen 2003, 87–140). There he argues that Plato's "political philosophy is the public appearance of philosophy" (ibid., 109) which hides the "contradiction between the true interests of the philosopher and those of the city" (ibid., 109). For me, Aristotelian political science is the actual rhetorical, careful, moderate self-presentation of philosophy in the city: a self-presentation that is intended not to stir the hatred of the city towards the putative "non-political" character of the philosophical life.

[58] "If justice is to remain good, we must conceive of it as essentially independent of the law. We shall then define justice as the habit of giving to everyone what is due to him according to nature. . . . Just as only a physician truly knows what is good in each case for the body, only the wise man truly knows what is good in each case for the soul. This being the case, there cannot be justice, i.e., giving to everyone what is by nature good for him, except in a society in which wise men are in absolute control" (Strauss 1953, 146).

[59] "This solution, which at first glance seems to be the only just solution for a society in which there are wise men, is, as a rule, impracticable. The few wise cannot rule the many unwise by force. The unwise multitude must recognize the wise as wise and obey them freely because of their wisdom. But the ability of the wise to persuade the unwise is extremely limited. . . . This being the case, the natural right of the wise must be questioned, and the indispensable requirement for wisdom must be qualified by the requirement for consent" (Strauss 1953, 140).

of Strauss's post-emigration writings on "classical natural right" discuss the hypothesis according to which Plato was aware that the philosopher-king was an "unrealistic" solution to the question of the best regime, and that he decided to opt for a second-best form of regime tied to constitutional rule (by which is meant: the rule of a regime or *politeia*). In these texts, Strauss presents this second-best solution as if the late Plato had become Aristotelian, or was always already an Aristotelian philosopher. In reality, Strauss simply maintains his initial insight that Aristotle "urbanizes" Platonic political philosophy, making what he calls Socratic "tyrannical teaching" more palatable under democratic conditions.[60]

However one understands the meaning of the expression "Platonic political philosophy" in Strauss, one thing is certain: the fundamental and constant question for him concerns the true nature of the relation between Platonism and Aristotelianism.[61] The question of the harmony or contradiction between Plato's and Aristotle's teachings was from the beginning a burning question. For Hellenistic and Judeo-Hellenistic philosophers it seemed to be a life-and-death question, *the* political issue. It was no less so for medieval Islamic and Jewish philosophers. For the young Strauss the problem of the harmony of Plato and Aristotle had become an extremely live question after decades of relative indifference.[62] This was due to the near simultaneous irruption of Werner Jaeger's philological discoveries with respect to Aristotle's development and Heidegger's novel "phenomenological" approach to Aristotle (and Plato).[63] Jaeger's developmental hypothesis pointed to the exact opposite thesis that Strauss later upheld in *The City and Man*. Jaeger believed that the more empirical, that is, the more "scientific" Aristotle's thinking became, the further he distanced himself from Plato.[64] Conversely, Aristotle's metaphysical works, because they stood closer to Plato in time and resented his influence, were for Jaeger ultimately no more than

[60] For a discussion of this claim, I refer to (Vatter 2010). The most recent Straussian scholarship on *On Tyranny* admits that Strauss is putting forth a "tyrannical teaching" as the substance of Platonic political philosophy while avoiding any reference to the contemporary discussions on tyranny, sovereignty, and dictatorship (Buzzetti 2014). For reasons of space I cannot engage more fully with Strauss's post-emigration readings of Aristotle.

[61] "What does the opposition between Socrates and Aristotle signify? Whereby we understand by Socrates the Socrates of the Platonic dialogues" (Strauss 2013, 198).

[62] For an alternative narrative that does not thematize the political stakes in the return to Platonism in German-Jewish thought, see (Kajon 2012).

[63] The first edition of Jaeger's fundamental work on Aristotle (Jaeger 1962) dates to 1923 and overlaps with the years in which Heidegger was giving his phenomenological interpretations of Aristotle (Heidegger 2003). Heidegger refers critically to Jaeger's discoveries throughout his lectures. Strauss mentions both Heidegger and Jaeger together in the unpublished lecture "Living Issues of German Postwar Philosophy" found in (Meier 2006, 134–5). According to Meyer, Strauss attended the lectures of both in the early 1920s.

[64] For example, Jaeger believes books I–III of the *Politics* were entirely written under the influence of Plato's *Statesman*, whereas the later, more empirical, books signal a break with Platonism (Jaeger 1962, 262–6).

youthful rhetorical and dramatic exercises. For Jaeger, Plato is the poet, Aristotle is the scientist.[65] In his lectures on the *Sophist*, Heidegger also defended Aristotle as the true scientist compared with Plato, but, contra Jaeger, Heidegger identified the "scientific" advances made by Aristotle with his metaphysics (including the *Physics*), not with his more "empirical" analysis of animal parts or city-state constitutions.[66] For that reason, in his lectures on *The Sophist*, Heidegger upheld as absolutely valid and decisive Aristotle's distinction between metaphysics and political science, between philosophical life and political life, ranking the former higher than the latter.[67]

Despite the importance of Jaeger's and Heidegger's contributions to the question of the harmony between Plato and Aristotle, they pale in comparison to the importance recovered by Cohen's interpretation of Platonism for the young Strauss. Cohen gives the clearest statement before Strauss on the importance of the question as to the priority of Platonism or Aristotelianism for Judaism and its standing in the modern world. Thus, the politico-theological matrix of Platonic political philosophy was clear to Strauss from the start of his engagement with Cohen's philosophy, and it is only abstractly that one can divide both questions.[68]

Cohen famously argued that as Judaism's foremost interpreter of the Torah, Maimonides could not have been an Aristotelian deep down. For Cohen, Plato is the philosopher of a strict or pure monotheism; Aristotle remains a pantheist.[69] Strauss was not entirely unsympathetic to Cohen's critique of Aristotelianism from a Jewish viewpoint. The reception of Aristotle's *Politics* in the Christian West strengthened the hand of republicanism against monarchism, and Strauss—here following tradition—always considered Maimonides to be a monarchist.[70] Additionally, it was by applying, in more or less creative ways,

65 For a critique of Jaeger's approach from a roughly Straussian perspective, see (Lachterman 1990).

66 See (Heidegger 2003, 59, 122, 154). The best treatment of the role played by Heidegger's interpretation of Aristotle on Strauss's development is found in (Chacón 2010). Chacón believes that Heidegger's Aristotle is more fundamental to Strauss than Cohen's Plato, and he also understands the role of Aristotle in Strauss's construal of Platonic political philosophy entirely differently from what I propose, not the least because the problem of revelation falls outside of his discussion. Furthermore, Chacón's claim is premised on his arguing that Heidegger's Aristotle subverts the theory/practice distinction. A thorough engagement with Heidegger's interpretation of Aristotle is beyond the scope of this chapter.

67 (Heidegger 2003, 119–21).

68 Here I disagree with the hypothesis put forward by Meyer, cited earlier, according to whom Strauss approached the "theologico-political problem" always already armed with his idea of Platonic political philosophy. For an argument that Strauss and Cohen were entirely at odds, see (Altman 2011b, 106–13, 281–300, 466–70).

69 For another account of Cohen's reading of Maimonides and Strauss's critique thereof, see now (Yaffe 2014). In my opinion, Yaffe does not appreciate the extent to which Strauss agrees with Cohen's interpretation of Platonic political philosophy, or, said otherwise, he does not see that Strauss's critique of Cohen's reading of Plato is an *internal* critique.

70 For the basic history, see (Baron 1988; Ullmann 1980; Nederman 2009; and Melamed 2012). For Strauss's early statement on the reception of Aristotelianism in the Christian West, see his critique of Abravanel's republicanism in "On Abravanel's Philosophical Tendency and Political Teaching" (Strauss 1937).

Aristotelian and Latin Averroist political categories that Dante and Marsilius of Padua attacked the legislative pretensions of the Roman Catholic Church and gave a blow against Papal theocracy from which Christianity would never fully recover.[71] Aristotle's radical distinction between the contemplative life and the political life could be construed to give rise to the "double truth" doctrine that divorced true knowledge from religious faith.[72] If radicalized, a version of the same doctrine could eventually be used to separate the real science of nature from all theological claims, thus making of religion not only a private affair but a cultural prejudice, as occurs later with Galileo, Spinoza, and Hobbes.[73] Strauss began his academic career attempting to understand this decline and fall of the belief in divine revelation in the modern age: how could religion pass from its status as repository of divine knowledge in the ancients to its status as human prejudice in the moderns?[74]

Strauss seems to blame this story of decline and fall, in the last instance, on the medieval Christian reception of Aristotle.[75] In the 1930s he came to believe that medieval Islamic and Jewish philosophers like Alfarabi, Avicenna, Averroes, and Maimonides did not follow this Christian path toward secularization.[76] According to Strauss, these philosophers did not accept the idea that divine revelation contained only (supernatural) truths accessible to faith but not to natural reason; they did not separate religious authority from political power. The crucial piece of evidence that Strauss employs to support this claim was the discovery that these Islamic and Jewish medieval thinkers treated prophetology as a branch of political science and not of metaphysics.[77]

[71] See (Syros 2012) and (Mulieri 2019). For a long discussion of Strauss's reception of Marsilius, see (Zuckert 2014, 167–95).

[72] On the history of "double truth," see now (Bianchi 2008).

[73] For this development, see now (Gatti 2015).

[74] See the account of the correspondence between Strauss and Gerhard Krüger on the crisis of Christianity in late modernity given in (Pangle 2014).

[75] See the discussion of Averroism in (Strauss 1953), and the discussion of modern Epicureanism in (Strauss 1997c). By Averroism in this context, Strauss means Latin Averroism, not the philosophy of Averroes himself.

[76] For an argument as to how prejudice against Judaism in Christianity was instrumental to the idea of "secularization" see (Yelle 2011). For a Straussian construal of the turn toward Arabic-Jewish medieval thought, see now (Parens 2016).

[77] "This specific problem of prophecy is a subject matter of *politics*. But since politics stands in the last place in the system of sciences, this answers the question of the positon occupied by the philosophical foundation of the law in the system of medieval philosophy. It stands not at the beginning and not at the center, but it is the end and conclusion, or if you like, the crown and seal of metaphysics" (Strauss 1995, 70; 1997b, 58). As Parens puts it: "According to Strauss, the theme of the *Guide* is the Law, and the Law is analysed from within the philosophic discipline of political science" (Parens 2014, 163). However, Parens's interpretation does not thematize whether political science as "philosophic discipline" is to be understood along Platonic or Aristotelian lines. Second, Parens adheres to the orthodox Straussian belief that the "Law is the highest expression of the city's way of life" and furthermore that "through the lens of the city, the philosopher appears to be a renegade" (ibid., 160) so that a "philosophic" analysis of the Divine Law is for Parens necessarily one that is anti-theological or irreligious. But Strauss nowhere makes such claims.

In order to show the real implications of this claim, Strauss had to determine that this "political science" is a Platonic one, and thus he had to show that the Aristotelianism of the teachers of the teachers of Aquinas, that is, the Aristotelianism of Averroes and Maimonides, was a "rhetorical" device. This "rhetorical" reading of Aristotle had already been suggested by Cohen's interpretation of Maimonides. Cohen does not think that Maimonides' exclusion of the belief in Creation from the Thirteen Principles of Faith found in the *Guide of the Perplexed*, which correspond to the (Aristotelian) general conventional ethics, proves that he was an Aristotelian.[78] For these principles of faith had to be rational in an Aristotelian, not in a Platonic, sense: they are principles that must be able to be based on Aristotelian science, that is, Aristotelian physics and metaphysics, which excludes belief in Creation. However, this does not mean that belief in Creation cannot be rational in a higher, Platonic sense. By excluding Creation from the domain of what follows from Aristotelian physics and metaphysics, Maimonides gives Creation a central place within his version of Platonic political philosophy. Creation is now related to the idea of God's providence and to the messianic purpose of nature, which is also entailed in the fourth Maimonidean principle of faith, that "the Creator is the first and *the last*" (Cohen 2004, 60, emphasis mine). This argument illustrates Cohen's thesis that Maimonides speaks like an Aristotelian philosopher without being one: Aristotelianism is Maimonides' rhetoric, not his philosophy. In other words, Maimonides employs Aristotle's philosophy as rhetoric because Aristotle deifies cognition as the ultimate purpose of human life and is therefore a useful weapon "against the suspicions of obscurantists and the scoffing of the skeptics" (Cohen 2004, 63). Cohen concludes that Aristotle is employed by Maimonides to defend Judaism as a "religion of reason," not to undo the rational or philosophical basis of Judaism.[79]

The true, politico-theological role of the belief in Creation is also the central preoccupation of Strauss's *Philosophy and Law*, as discussed in the following. However, Strauss does not link Creation with the messianic idea, as Cohen does. While Cohen projected a messianic ideal onto Plato's Idea of the Good, thus turning him into a proto-socialist, Strauss sees in Plato the possibility of thinking about politics from the idea of an "eternal order" beyond the distinctions of Left and Right, progressive and conservative (Strauss 2013, 197; 1997b, 397).[80] Cohen

[78] Similarly, Cohen does not believe in Maimonides' apparent agreement with Aristotle's debasement of ethics as a teaching composed of *endoxa* (widely shared opinion, rather than true knowledge). Cohen argues that in *Guide* 1.2 the term "conventional" is not opposed to reason because it means the same thing as "self-evident," that is, axiomatic. For an excellent treatment of this question, see (Dobbs-Weinstein 1995, 150ff).

[79] This point is missed by both (Yaffe 2014; and Parens 2014).

[80] Strauss here refers to Cohen's last public lecture, "The Social Ideal in Plato and in the Prophets." But see the closing words of the essay in which Cohen's "defining political position" is "his passionate support for the politics of 'the great Left of humanity' . . . this idea sets the limits of his understanding

and Strauss agree that Maimonides developed a Bible science that is at the antipodes of Spinoza's Bible science: whereas the latter is intended to show that at its core, the Bible is not science, is not knowledge, but mere faith, Maimonides' allegorical interpretation of the Bible is intended to show the core identity of the Bible with Greek science.[81] As Strauss puts the question in an early essay: for Spinoza "it is possible, in principle, for the theorist to lead his life in disregard of revelation," whereas Maimonides "demands caution and distrust of human thought and refers to the tradition founded on prophecy" (Strauss 2002, 181). According to this Maimonidean Bible science, the prophets were philosophers, and more than philosophers because they couched science in a language that non-scientists could also grasp (Strauss 1997b, 400). The decisive question then becomes what kind of Greek "science" or philosophy is best apt to show the rational core of the Bible: is it Aristotelian science or Platonic science? Strauss believes that Cohen "did not do justice to Aristotle" (1997b, 409). The ultimate meaning of Platonic political philosophy is not graspable if Aristotle is opposed to Plato in the way that Cohen does.

In "Cohen and Maimonides," Strauss says that Aristotle makes two fundamental contributions to Platonic political philosophy. First, Aristotle offers a scientific conception of the world that can be a match to the modern scientific picture of the world.[82] This is clearly a nod toward the Husserlian-Heideggerian conception of the life-world, which Heidegger had read back into Aristotle in his famous phenomenological interpretations of Greek philosophy that Strauss refers to obliquely in this text: "If Phenomenology has meanwhile become an all-prescribing power . . . then this signifies a decisive step toward the re-establishment of Aristotelianism" (Strauss 2013, 197). As I discuss next, in *Philosophy and Law* the synthesis of Heideggerian and Cohenian readings is expressed by the dialectical relation between the "legal foundation of philosophy" and the "philosophical foundation of the law," respectively.

Strauss's appropriation of Husserl's attempted recovery of the experience of life-world underneath all scientific abstractions and formalizations on the basis

of Plato, and thereby also of his understanding of Rambam. We will not be able to understand Plato, and thereby also not Rambam, until we have acquired a horizon beyond the opposition progress/conservatism, Left/Right, Enlightenment/Romanticism . . . not until we again understand the idea of the *eternal* good, the *eternal* order, free from all regard for progress or regress" (Strauss 2013, 222).

[81] "For Maimonides . . . the truths of revelation are identical with the truths of reason, that is, they are accessible to human reason. This is not to say that unguided human reason left to its own resources could have discovered all fundamental truths" (Strauss 2002, 181). See also the crucial letter cited by Meier (2006, 29, n.29) where Strauss admits that he later came to hold Guttmann's view of the "identity of reason and revelation" in the Middle Ages [letter of June 22, 1952, to Scholem]—which he had criticized previously—but that he has "radicalized" this medieval rationalism and at the same time "moderated" it. Whether Strauss also changed his mind about Spinoza, interpreting him as closer to Maimonides, is a question that is too complex to discuss here.

[82] See also (Strauss 1995, 33).

of noetic self-evidences was strategic. It served Strauss to question the validity of the "modern world-picture" introduced by Galileo, for this "world-picture" had made belief in miracles something "impossible" to uphold, on pain of ridicule.[83] By way of contrast, Aristotle's conception of the world fits better with the "common sense" view of nature (not nature as an abstract, scientific construction of the moderns) that is reconcilable with the reception of divine revelations by prophets.[84] Strauss identifies in Cohen's anti-Aristotelian fervor an over-eagerness to destroy ancient science in favor of modern science. Such a modernizing reading of the Greeks, so Strauss claims already in 1931, may do the moderns a disservice because it is only the "unidealized, unmodernized Greek philosophy [that] shows us a way out of the modern anarchy" (Strauss 2013, 197; 1997b, 410). Ancient Greek science recognizes the "eternity" of the natural order, and it also offers the background against which both the tension and the secret unity between Greek philosophy and Jewish revelation can be meaningfully recovered.[85]

The recovery of Aristotle's conception of natural science has a second, more political finality that follows from the desideratum of seeking the true basis of political order. Cohen argued that in the Torah, God had revealed His ethical or political ways or attributes to Moses, and that these ways pointed toward an ideal, messianic condition of peace and equality among human beings (Strauss 2013, 205–9). Strauss, instead, argues that Maimonides believed God to have revealed *all* His attributes to Moses, not just His ethical ones (2013, 209). The Bible only speaks of ethical actions because these are to serve as models for "every leader of human beings" and are "necessary for the leadership of states" (2013, 209). The rest of God's actions are physical, not moral, and refer to His general, rather than particular, providential ordering of the world.[86] Because Cohen does not take into account God's physical actions, but only His ethical ones, it seems to him that ethical action as prescribed in the Mosaic Law is the external *telos* of nature, and that is why he takes Maimonides to be a Platonist. But for Strauss this

[83] See the discussion of Lessing in the "Introduction" to (Strauss 1995).

[84] "The highest knowledge is knowledge of the highest being. And both Jews and Greeks call the highest being: God. The idea of *theorein* becomes the ideal of *knowledge of God*. The highest science is theology. From this point of view it becomes intelligible how the Jews and non-Jews of the Middle Ages could avail themselves of Aristotelian philosophy: what matters for man is designated in Scripture too as knowledge of God" (Strauss 2013, 204). By way of contrast, Hobbes and Spinoza construed a conception of nature in which "unbelieving science and belief no longer have, as in the Middle Ages, the common ground of natural knowledge, on which a meaningful quarrel between belief and unbelief is possible" (Strauss 1995, 31).

[85] Meyer correctly points out that Löwith believed Strauss's critique of modern science does not touch the validity of the ancient belief in the eternity of nature (Meyer 2009, 82). But Löwith misses Strauss's point, which seeks to preserve the Aristotelian conception of nature as compatible with the "state of nature" depicted in the biblical revelation.

[86] To support this claim, Strauss cites *Guide of the Perplexed* 1.54 and 3.54.

is not Maimonides' belief. Strauss concludes that Cohen's thesis on Maimonides' purported anti-Aristotelianism needs to be "moderated."

The reason for such moderation is strictly political: as Strauss says much later in *The City and Man*, "for Aristotle political inequality is ultimately justified by the natural inequality among men. *The fact that some men are by nature rulers and others by nature ruled points in its turn to the inequality which pervades nature as a whole:* the *whole as an ordered whole consists of beings of different ranks*" (1964, 38, emphasis mine). In this context, Strauss argues that since the belief in natural inequality depends on the science of nature as articulated by Aristotle's *Physics*, Maimonides' adoption of Aristotle's physics allows him to explain why God reveals His Ways just as much in the natural inequality between human beings as in the (tendentially) egalitarian norms of the Decalogue and the virtues they foster: charity, kind-heartedness, forgiveness, fairness. As Maimonides says, "some (beings) achieve perfection to an extent that enables them to govern others, whereas others achieve perfection only in the measure that allows them to be governed by others" (*Guide* 2.37). Maimonides' ending the *Guide* by referring to the biblical moral virtues was the ultimate justification adduced by Cohen for his Platonic reading of the Jewish philosopher.[87] Strauss believes that exclusive attention to these virtues at the expense of their underlying substance could also imperil the understanding of the essence of a true divine *nomos*.

Strauss holds that Maimonides teaches the same as Aristotle: namely, that the world has no end outside of itself (*Guide* 3.13). Strauss therefore identifies a major difference between Maimonides' view and the traditional Jewish view about Creation: Maimonides rejects the belief in Creation (at least at the level of physics). "If therefore man is *not* the purpose of the world, if there is something greater than he in the world, then he cannot be what [ultimately] matters; then politics cannot be the highest and most important science; then the highest thing is: contemplation of existing [things] and understanding of Being" (Strauss 2013, 210). Aristotle's ranking between philosophical and political life must be reasserted: dianoetical virtues (*sophia*) stand above ethical virtues (*phronesis*).

It is in the context of rehabilitating Maimonides' Aristotelianism, and the priority of contemplation over ethics, that Strauss adds a side remark to the manuscript: "Distinguishing the wise from the multitude [is] fundamental: esotericism" (Strauss 2013, 211). This seems to be one of the first times in his work that Strauss addresses the question of esotericism. Strictly speaking, what is

[87] Cohen is referring to the passages in *Guide* 3.53–54 where Maimonides offers the interpretation of *hesed* (loving-kindness or *charis*), *mishpat* (judgment), and *sedaqah* (righteousness or justice) to clarify the fact that "it is My purpose that there should come from you loving-kindness, righteousness, and judgment in the earth [*Jer.* 9:23] in the way we have explained with regard to the thirteen attributes: namely, that the purpose should be assimilation to them and that this should be our way of life" (Maimonides 1963, 3:54).

esoteric in Maimonides, what cannot be taught to the many *for politico-theological reasons*, is the superiority of physics (based on the claim of the eternity of nature) over ethics (based on the belief in Creation). In so doing, Strauss rejects Cohen's central belief regarding Maimonides' Platonism, namely, that the knowledge of Israel's God as found in the Torah is higher than "pure understanding" (2013, 211; 1997b, 421). And yet, Strauss maintains that Cohen remains in the right with his claim that for Maimonides, Platonism stands higher than Aristotelianism, and also for the correct basic reason, namely, because Israel's God is superior to Aristotle's God: "one must recall Cohen's guiding insight: 'All honor to the God of Aristotle; but he is not the God of Israel.' This fundamental fact, thus expressed by Cohen, can surely not remain without consequences for Rambam and the understanding of Rambam. *Cohen's fundamental insight is so evident that in fact it remains unshaken*" (2013, 211, emphasis mine).

Strauss's internal critique of Cohen's construction of Platonic political philosophy leads to the following result. Through the idea that the biblical prophet is modeled after the Platonic philosopher king, Cohen's belief in the superiority of the transcendent God of Israel can be joined together with Aristotle's claim that theory stands above ethics, or the philosophical life stands above morality, because this philosophical life is the bringer of the true divine *nomos*.

> I sum up: the Cohenian starting point, "All honor to the God of Aristotle, but He is not the God of Israel" leads no further if one interprets the God of Israel as the God of morality. *Instead of morality, one must say: Law.* The idea of law, of *nomos*, is what unifies Jews and Greeks: *the idea of the concrete, binding order of life*, which is covered over for us by the Christian and natural right tradition, this idea [is the one] under whose spell at least our philosophical thought moves. (Strauss 2013, 221, emphasis mine)[88]

Interpreters of Strauss have found it difficult to hold on to this Judeo-Hellenistic coincidence of opposites. Thus, they have either read Strauss as a defender of the God of Israel on ethical grounds, pointing to the limits of philosophy, or they have seen in Strauss a wholesale rejection of Judaism in the name of adhering to the superiority of the supra-moral or supra-political philosophical life.[89] In reality, Strauss's teaching is that the prophet of the God of Israel should be understood as being not only a superior legislator or politician, but also an

[88] I need not emphasize how in this text Strauss reasserts the correctness of Cohen's basic viewpoint once again and in the strongest possible terms, as well as clearly states that the idea of divine *nomos* as "concrete, binding order of life" allows one to link together Athens and Jerusalem, which is the Philonic, Judeo-Hellenistic viewpoint.

[89] For the first possibility, see (Green 1993; and Batnitzky 2006b), for the second, see (Meier 2006; Pangle 2006; and Lampert 2013).

Aristotelian philosopher. For that reason, Jerusalem not only ought to remain open to the claims of Athens, but it must learn how to adopt them as a "gate" to the true teaching of the Torah. In this sense, one can say that Strauss interprets the Torah as the opposite of a pagan civil theology, that is, as a religion of the (human) city.[90] For Strauss, the Torah is better conceived as a politics of God legislated by an Aristotelian philosopher. In this sense, Strauss is squarely situated within the Philonic tradition of the philosopher as living law, first uncovered by Goodenough.

On divine violence and the state of exception

The Jewish political theology that Strauss develops in *Philosophy and Law* retains its interest for contemporary political science and philosophy of jurisprudence for at least two reasons. First, Strauss provides one of the most articulate responses from outside the horizon of liberalism and Christianity to the challenge posed by Schmitt during those years. Schmitt's challenge consists in the claim that the liberal rule of law necessarily presupposes a sovereign authority to decide on the state of exception to its laws as a condition for these laws to be kept in force.[91] Strauss's early writings betray an awareness of the conditional nature of the citizenship status that the German state afforded German Jews, and the incumbent possibility of their being placed in a state of exception.[92] As Arendt feared, and Agamben and others have pointed out more recently, the phenomenon of placing human beings in a legal state of exception has by no means abated in our own times.

Philosophy and Law was published in Germany only months before the passage of the Nuremberg racial laws that deprived all German citizens of Jewish descent of their German nationality, turning them into "stateless people" without civil or human rights. Strauss's text responds to this challenge by recovering an idea of (divine) law for which there is no exception because such a law recognizes, in the form itself of the law, universal validity to what is heterogeneous or singular. Singularity here denotes not only the fundamental feature of the monotheistic

[90] In this context it is useful to recall that in the early modern tradition, starting with Machiavelli and going through Hobbes, Spinoza, Rousseau, Montesquieu, Kant, and Hegel, the Torah was understood as a civil religion of the Jewish people, in principle no different than the civil religions of pagan nations.

[91] On this challenge, see (Mouffe 1999; Agamben 2005a; and Dyzenhaus 2006), among many others.

[92] In a 1923 article for the *Jüdische Rundschau*, Strauss already mentions the possibility of a state of exception: "The fateful hour of German Jewry has arrived. The Jews can no longer feel secure about their physical safety in Germany: legal equality, always praised as fundamental to Jewish existence, has been shaken to its core; the possibility of a special status for them [*Ausnahmegesetzgebung*] . . . appears to be on the horizon"; cited in (Muller 2014, 20).

God worshipped by Judaism and Islam. It also refers to that feature of human existence in virtue of which every individual comes to stand outside of the particular and historically determined politico-cultural attachments that make up an individual's identity or selfhood.[93] Opposed to the concept of identity, singularity refers to the individual considered in their radical "solitude," "foreignness," or "otherness." On Strauss's reading, the Torah (and Shari'a), as conceived by Arabic and Jewish medieval philosophers, speaks to this singular existence of individuals because "not the city, not civilization, but the desert, is the place in which the Biblical God reveals himself."[94]

The discussion of prophetology in *Philosophy and Law* represents Strauss's first explicit treatment of what he came to call after his emigration "the problem of the law and legitimacy" in a clear allusion to the polemic between Kelsen and Schmitt over decisionism and political theology during the Weimar years (Strauss 1963, 76). In 1934 Schmitt published *Über die drei Arten des Rechtswissenschaftlichen Denkens* [On the Three Types of Jurisprudential Thinking] in which he announced his turn from decisionism toward understanding law as a "concrete order," that is, as *nomos*, and proceeded to offer a long discussion of the Platonic understanding of the formula *nomos basileus*.[95] *Nomos basileus* was the ancient formula for absolute sovereignty. On October 10, 1934, Strauss wrote to Jacob Klein asking whether he had read Schmitt's latest work: "he now is against Hobbes' decisionism and for a 'thinking of order' on the basis of the argument in my review essay, which he naturally does not cite."[96] Strauss exaggerates the impact of his review essay on Schmitt's adoption of the idea of a "concrete order" and the long analysis of *nomos basileus* found in *Über die drei Arten*, for the simple reason that there was no explicit discussion of Plato's conception of the *nomos* in Strauss's review essay.[97] It is much more likely that Schmitt went back to the classical sources of natural law (*nomos phuseos*) in an effort to counteract Kelsen's own critique of all "natural right" doctrines, whose origins he drew back to Plato and Aristotle.[98] However, Strauss's admission may indicate an awareness that both he and Schmitt approached the "problem of law and legitimacy" through the discourse of political theology.

[93] See the distinction between selfhood and singularity in (Derrida 2005).

[94] In "Progress or Return?" (Strauss 1997a, 251).

[95] On Schmitt's understanding of *nomos*, see now (Ojakangas 2009; Herrero 2015; and Loughlin 2015). On the influence of Catholic institutionalism linked with Maurice Hariou and Romano Guardini on Schmitt's turn, see (Bates 2006).

[96] "Er ist jetzt gegen den Dezisionismus von Hobbes, für 'Ordnungsdenken' auf Grund der Argumentationen in meiner Rezension, die er natürlich nicht zitiert" (Strauss 2008, 524).

[97] In his detailed discussion of this review essay, Meier does not mention the problem of concrete order shared by Strauss and Schmitt (Meier 1995).

[98] For the early formulations of this critique of natural right, see (Kelsen 1928); for a later, more precise formulation, see (Kelsen 1957).

In the 20th-century discourse of political theology, the idea of legitimacy is connected to the "authority [*Gewalt*]" of the concrete order that offers those who follow positive laws the assurance or security that these laws will be applied, that is, that they will be "in force." Without order and rule, the law would have no "facticity" or "force," although it could still retain its (purely formal) legality. The practice of ruling is both necessary to the rule of law, because order is necessary to this rule, yet falls outside of the form of law, because the practice of ruling is not exercised in such a legal form. Derrida acknowledges this "problem of the law and of legitimacy" when he states that "there is no law that does not imply *in itself*, a priori, *in the analytic structure of its concept*, the possibility of being 'enforced,' applied by force" (2001, 233).

However, the expression "force of law" chosen by Derrida to translate *Gewalt* is in many respects unfortunate and lends itself to confusion because it is all too often equated with the concept of "enforcement," that is, with the kind of force or violence associated with the police. The dual meaning of *Gewalt*, on the one hand as authority of the law, on the other as institutionalized use of violence, is obviously the crucial issue in Benjamin's "Critique of Violence" and in Derrida's commentary of that essay. However, one misunderstands Benjamin's essay if one does not, at the same time, keep in mind that from the perspective of Jewish political theology, the term "force," when applied to the divine law, refers to the *numinous* essence of God, thematized by Strauss and Scholem. Ultimately, it refers to God's "energy" or "life" and has nothing to do with the action of the police. Derrida, however tentatively, is onto this possibility insofar as he draws attention to the idea of a "*mystical* foundation of authority." The expression comes from Montaigne, who writes that "laws are now maintained in credit, not because they are just, but because they are laws. It is the mystical foundation of their authority; they have none other. . . . Whosoever obeyeth them because they are just, obeys them not justly the way as he ought."[99] As Derrida goes on to insist: "the authority of the laws rests only on the credit that is granted them. *One believes in it; that is their only foundation*" (2001, 240, emphasis mine). This "act of faith" has neither "an ontological or rational foundation" and that is why it is best termed "the mystical foundation" of legal authority.[100] More specifically, the

[99] (Montaigne 1962, III, 13, "De l'expérience").

[100] Unfortunately, in the very same text Derrida goes on to refer to "the mystical" in terms of a "violence without ground" (2001, 242). This leap from an idea of authority based on an "act of faith" to violence is never justified by Derrida. It merely represents his transitioning to Benjamin's unfolding of his analytic of *Gewalt* into the famous distinction between *rechtsetzende* and *rechtserhaltende Gewalt* where both are modeled not on conditions for law-following but on phenomena of law-breaking: the "great criminal" as a potential giver of a new law, on the one hand, and the extra- and infra-legal character of modern police action, on the other. The idea of a "mystical foundation" of legal authority need not contain a necessary relation to violence. In *State of Exception*, Agamben formalizes and radicalizes Derrida's conflation of authority and violence, as discussed in the previous chapter, when he argues that the polemical point of Benjamin's essay is to unveil that behind Schmitt's discourse on

term "mystical" refers to the politico-theological foundation of the law in an "act of faith" that cannot be provided with a rational justification.

Strauss's contribution to this debate is centered on giving a complex interpretation of the "act of faith" required for rule-following in light of the Arabic and Jewish medieval rationalism and political theology. My hypothesis is that Strauss's political theology rejects the identification of authority with violence later articulated by Derrida and Agamben. Strauss is after a "legal" concept of constituent power, not a "sovereign" one as formulated by Schmitt. He believes that Alfarabi's and Maimonides' prophetology provides the model for a constituent power that, unlike Schmitt's, does not take exception to law because it is founded on the "fact" of divine law coupled with a Greek, philosophical conception of natural right. Faith in the *fact* of revealed law leads to the determination that the order and ruling which, according to the requirements of legal authority, is presupposed by all rule-following behavior that is uncoerced, can be provided in a manner that is felt to be "natural" by those subject to law, that is, in accordance to the Platonic and Aristotelian doctrine, which he later calls "classical natural right." In this way, *Philosophy and Law* works out an account of God's rule or theocracy that resolves the problem of the application of its law without relying on the goodwill of the "absolute" sovereigns of the nations. Prophetology is Strauss's solution to the "paradox of theocracy." Short of this Maimonidean solution, Strauss believes that divine law is bound to remain inapplicable and thus without force: at most, it will retain a "nomic" validity that is tied to legal formalisms (associated with Rabbinical institutionalism) but not a politico-theological validity tied to real political legitimacy.

Strauss's *Philosophy and Law* lays the ground for the following hypothesis: what best corresponds to the singular being of each individual is not a dualistic system of law divided between public morality and private ethics, but a *unitary legal order* whose source is the singularity of God. *Philosophy and Law* proceeds to argue for this claim in two parts.[101] Under the heading of "the legal foundation of philosophy," Strauss provides a justification for the claim that divine law is always addressed to everyone; the standpoint of faith in revelation has a radically democratic character. Under the heading of "the philosophic foundation of the law," Strauss justifies the claim that divine law, despite being a particular unitary legal order, can nonetheless be considered to be both universal and necessary: "universal" because it satisfies the most "natural" understanding of

authority and legitimacy in reality there lies an idea of "anomic violence" as sole content of the "force of law."

[101] Meyer has pointed out the complex and also fortuitous story behind the publication of this "book" out of four more or less independent essays written by Strauss from 1931 to 1935. This fact does not take away from the hypothesis that the essays make up a systematic argument.

what it means to be a human individual, and "necessary" because it satisfies the need for integrity in the legal order. It is only jointly that these arguments address the desideratum of a picture of Judaism as a rational faith (as distinct from a "religion of reason" in the Enlightenment sense) and give consistency to Philo's idea of Judaism as a divine democracy.

Harry Wolfson famously claimed that Philo inaugurated the medieval epoch of philosophy by making the teachings of divine revelation into the content of philosophy. Strauss agrees that for medieval philosophers, "revelation is *constitutive* for this philosophy."[102] For Strauss this general claim entails two distinct theses. First, it means that for Maimonides and his Arabic precursors, philosophy itself begins from the acceptance of a *Faktum*, which in this case is the *givenness* of divine law and the "extra-rational" or "mystical" foundation of its authority: "there may be debate about what must be considered the *content* of revelation . . . but *no debate is possible about the reality of the revelation and the obligation to obey it. And it also means: the recognition of the authority of revelation is 'self-evident.'* The medieval philosophers do indeed strive to demonstrate the philosophic possibility of the revelation and the historical reality of the revelation, but these arguments only confirm what was already established *before* argument, what was 'evident of itself.' "[103] The "legal foundation" of philosophy refers to the idea that the divine law manifests itself to human experience as a "pre-theoretical fact [*vorphilosophischen Voraussetzung des Faktum der Offenbarung*]" (Strauss 1997b, 67, 68).

Strauss employs Husserlian and Heideggerian phenomenology to "bracket" the universal validity claims of the modern scientific "picture of the world." But he also applies the Husserlian phenomenological language of originary givens or self-evident presentations to consciousness (intentionality) prior to any theoretical interpretation of them in order to make sense of the claim that prophets have "unmediated" access to "suprarational" truths.[104] Strauss articulates phenomenologically the Jewish tradition of the divine *aleph* heard at Mount Sinai.[105]

[102] (Strauss 1995, 57). "It is in prophetology that the revelation, as the *law* given by the *prophet*, becomes the subject matter of philosophy" (Strauss 1995, 104; 1997b, 90).

[103] (Strauss 1995, 58, emphasis mine). See also an early formulation of this point in "Ecclesia militans," where contemporary Orthodoxy is chastised because it seeks acknowledgment of the "existence of God" without "first having to obtain the acknowledgment of its dogmatic presuppositions" that "could never be obtained from the majority of contemporary Jewry," and it does this by arguing that "there are no dogmas in Judaism" (Strauss 2002, 125). Strauss's response to this "trick" is that it destroys "any seriousness of the religious decision," "as if what mattered was not rather the simple fact of the self-evidence with which our prayers refer to the existence and actions of God" (ibid.).

[104] "To summarize, the prophet is a man of perfect intellect and perfect imaginative faculty, who is completely controlled by the desire for knowledge of the upper world. Only such a man can be in *direct* union with the upper world, can directly know 'God and the angels.' This knowledge, superior to all human knowledge, qualifies him to be a *teacher* of human beings, *even* a teacher of *philosophers*" (Strauss 1995, 111; 1997b, 97).

[105] See the long development of Maimonides' theory of prophecy in (Strauss 1995, 105–10; 1997b, 91–6), culminating in the claim that "the prophet [is] unconditionally *superior* to the philosopher,

Strauss is emphatic in denying that this *Faktum* is the same as a *factum brutum* that is of no inherent interest to philosophy. "Whomever 'believes' in revelation in this manner actually, as Lessing puts it, keeps only the names and repudiates the thing itself [*Wer so an Offenbarung "glaubt" behält wirklich, wie Lessing sagt, nur den Namen bei und verwirft die Sache*]" (Strauss 1995, 64; 1997b, 51). The "fact" of revelation exceeds and underlies all schemas of experience (every disclosure of a "world" or "horizon" of sense); and access to it can be had through faith (Abraham's faith) alone. But this "fact" is not a mere figment of the human imagination. Spinoza suggested that, given the employment by prophets of imaginative or poetic language to communicate what they had "seen" or "heard," this meant that prophets were subject to hallucinations that have no basis in reality. Strauss rejects this inference "*because* the prophet knows more and more directly than the philosopher, *because* he is blinded by the all-too-dazzling, unfamiliar light, that he presents the known figuratively, the known fills him *completely*, seizes him completely, thus including his imaginative faculty" (Strauss 1995, 110; 1997b, 96).

More importantly, the "self-evident," pre-theoretical character of the fact of revelation makes divine law accessible to all human beings. As Strauss formulates this idea: "The *possibility of the revelation follows from its reality, but its reality is known immediately*. . . . That the revelation is real is *seen* by the seeing Jew in the superhuman wisdom and justice of the Torah, is *seen* by the seeing Muslim in the superhuman beauty of the Qur'an" (1995, 59, emphasis mine). The "superhuman" wisdom, justice, and beauty of what is revealed to the prophet is not a construction of human reason or interpretation.[106] This argument of Strauss reappears nearly verbatim in Charles Taylor's post-secular discourse. Taylor also argues that the unbeliever "sees less" than the believers because they "shut" themselves to the "self-evidence" of the divine revelation (Taylor 2007, 768–9). Without citing Strauss, Taylor shares his claim that the "immanent" or "secular" social imaginary of modernity is the intentional result of the modern mind "closing" itself off to the fact or evidence of divine transcendence (2007, 546, 556). Just like Strauss, Taylor argues that it is modern epistemology, which rests on the problematic assumption of a "value-free" idea of modern science (i.e., the idea that only facts, not values, are objective) that is ultimately responsible for this self-closing of the modern mind to the absolute "fact" of inherent value (2007, 562ff).

and a fortiori to all other men. But he is superior to the philosopher even in the philosopher's own sphere, as a knower: he can know *immediately*, 'without premises and conclusions' what all other men can know only mediately; consequently he can have at his disposal insights that could not be attained by the individual whose knowledge is merely philosophic" (Strauss 1995, 106; 1997b, 92).

[106] For analogous considerations, see the discussion of revelation in Barth and Rosenzweig in (Rashkover 2005).

The politico-theological outcome of this claim is that, if divine revelation is real, then it is possible in principle for everyone to access its content, irrespective of their cultural prejudices and paradigms, and as long as one is willing to bracket, or suspend, the validity of these prejudices and paradigms. Because divine revelation is factical, if it is experienced, it can only be experienced equally by all: "The universally binding revelation is addressed to all" (Strauss 1995, 57; 1997b, 91). The standpoint of faith in revelation is "universal," in this sense, because it is possible for "every human being [to adopt this standpoint] if he does not refuse himself to it."[107] Unlike the exercise of reason or even of common sense, the fact of revelation cannot give rise to any difference and so discrimination between the few who know and the many who are ignorant. This is the real ground for Alfarabi's and Averroes's claims that the one divine truth must be able to be communicated in ways that makes it accessible to all, and thus both through rational demonstration and through poetic images and parables, both as "philosophy" and as "religion."[108]

Strauss's "legal foundation" of philosophy contains a radical democratic teaching: only that divine law which allows individuals to live under law independent of their cultural, national, ethnic, and racial identifications can claim to be universally binding. Or, put another way, the authority of divine law cannot be employed as ground for any discrimination between human beings whatsoever. This is but the other side of what Strauss will claim is the "philosophical foundation" of divine law, namely, the idea that all human beings, by nature and independent of their intelligence, stand in need of the guidance of law (though what this guidance is will depend on what kind of individual one is). The very *facticity* of revelation denies the possibility of establishing a distinction between "orthodox" and "heretic," "believer" and "unbeliever." All these distinctions are but the results of an unregulated because unphilosophical *interpretation* of the universal fact of revelation.

[107] (Strauss 1997c, 8). Strauss defends the idea of the universal accessibility of the standpoint of faith already in his earlier Spinoza book: "Yet what is the significance of this limitation, self-imposed on the positive mind, to a field which is open to accurate observation and strict analysis? Is that limitation not a deed of human defiance, of convulsive closing-in on itself? Is not the insensitivity to the command and the grace, to the Law and the blessing, a matter of will? The defensive attitude in face of (real or alleged) revelation is then not a matter of course. It is called in question again and again by belief in revelation. If the positive mind denies that it closes itself in defiance against revelation, it must confess that it does not itself experience revelation. In so doing, does it not admit that it lacks an organ, that it is blind? This is not a reproach that can be volleyed back against the opponent, for the believer sees everything that the unbeliever sees, sees it also more exactly as the opponent sees it, and yet nevertheless sees more" (ibid., 145).

[108] In the *Attainment of Happiness*, Alfarabi, in this followed by Averroes, claims that "according to the ancients, religion is an imitation of philosophy" (2001, I:55). In another section, Alfarabi says that "the legislator" (viz., the prophet) receives revealed truths in two ways: through the intellect and through the imagination, by way of dialectical arguments and by way of images and persuasive arguments (rhetoric). When formulated through images and rhetoric, these truths "are a religion for others," while when grasped intellectually, "they are philosophy" (2001, I:59).

The democratic implications of the philosophical approach to the *Faktum* of divine law are threatening for established institutions of *human* learning and rule. Jewish and Islamic political and religious leaders saw the entry of Greek philosophy into the game of leadership as a threat to their authority. The Orthodox complaint against the Arab *falasifa* and their Jewish followers sounded something like this: "there were many who broke the fences of the Law, who destroyed the covenant and who regarded the study of the Torah as secondary to the alien sciences, which were their true delight. They filled volumes with their farfetched philosophic homilies. They were steeped in the study of logic and physics and in the works of Averroes and Aristotle."[109] For this reason, the *falasifa* saw it as their task to demonstrate that the Shari'a *commanded* the pursuit of philosophy. This was the second task of the "legal foundation of philosophy." "Philosophy stands *under the law* but in such a way that it is *commanded* by the law. And indeed it is not merely commanded as one among many human activities, but rather its proper end is identified with the end of the law" (Strauss 1995, 83; 1997b, 70).[110]

The divine law authorizes philosophy to freely interpret the *Faktum* that can be experienced by everyone pre-philosophically as the divine Voice.[111] The "right to interpretation" defended by the Arab *falasifa* is the way in which philosophy seeks to determine the kind of guidance that human beings, by nature, need. This will turn out to be the guidance offered by Platonic political philosophy. But the philosophical interpretation of the divine law is not absolutely "free." It cannot deny the existence of the *Faktum* that assigns philosophy the task of human guidance. Hence the philosophical interpretation "must not lead to the disavowal of the *existence* of the things belonging to the principles of the law; only with regard to the *quality* of these things is interpretation possible" (Strauss 1995, 85). Paraphrasing the results of Averroes's *Decisive Treatise*, Strauss concludes that:

> the results [of philosophy as authorized by revealed law] are known from the outset precisely through the law, and error with regard to these results is declared to it from the start to be unforgivable. This bondage of philosophy is

[109] Reported words of Abba Mari ben Moses, cited in (Horowitz 1960, 704).

[110] This is the point of Averroes's famous claim in the *Decisive Treatise* that "'truth does not disagree with truth, but is in harmony with it and testifies to it' (*Facl-ul-maqal*, 7:6–9). Philosophy and law cannot conflict with one another since they are both truth and both go back to the same source of truth, to God, the giver of the Law and the Creator of reason" (Strauss 1995, 84; 1997b, 70). Strauss reads *Guide* 2.40, 3.25–7, 3.52, 3.54 as making the same point as Averroes: "the purpose of the law is identical to the purpose of philosophy" because both aim at the perfection of the human being in the form of knowledge of God. "Since the recognition of the authority of revelation is prior to philosophizing and since the revelation lays claim to man totally, philosophizing is now possible only as commanded by the revealed law" (1995, 63).

[111] For Avicenna, the prophet "hears the word of God and he sees God's angel in visible form" (Strauss 1997b, 104). "That philosophy as authorized by the law is free with respect to that law is proved in the right of interpretation" (Strauss 1995, 85).

> expressed in its definition: it is nothing other than knowledge of God derived from creation. In the end philosophy does no more than to deepen and demonstrate the knowledge accessible to all Muslims through the law. Philosophy owes its authorization, its freedom, to the law; its freedom depends on its bondage. Philosophy is not sovereign. (Strauss 1995, 88; 1997b, 74)

Philosophy, in other words, cannot call into question the dogmas (the "true opinions" on God and His angels) revealed in the divine law. The fundamental dogma is that of Creation which is internally correlated to the singularity or unicity of God the Father of All. For philosophy to refute these dogmas (which according to Maimonides are not rationally refutable) is equivalent to deny that the Torah is also a teaching that guides the human mind to its perfection. It is equivalent to deny the difference between the Torah and the civil religions of particular cities or nations. This denial would mean giving up the internal connection between philosophy and the pursuit of the good or just life. Denying the dogma of createdness, philosophy would have no claim to guide individuals, and it would become merely a teaching about how reason is the "slave" of their passions and interests, just as in Hobbes and Hume.

As discussed earlier, Strauss believes that the Arabic *falasifa* and Maimonides were convinced that philosophy, in its study of the lower world or the natural world, could not but arrive to Aristotle's result that this world is eternal, that the dogma of Creation has no justification from physics. But they did not allow themselves to discuss this finding publicly. This precaution was not just taken out of fear of persecution. Rather, these philosophers were aware that if it were not for the fact of its authorization through divinely revealed law, philosophers would be tempted to draw universal norms from the results of their free investigation of nature and in so doing they would reduce political philosophy to a science of nature.[112] This is the same as permitting philosophy to abdicate its duty to guide human beings so that they may become who they ought to be. Strauss's research into Spinoza and Hobbes indicated to him that early modern philosophers pursued modern science beyond the sublunary limits imposed by the physics of the ancients because they wanted to "emancipate" philosophy from the responsibility that the yoke to the divine law imposes upon philosophy, namely, to guide and incentivize all individuals to seek out what is the right life for them.

The distinction between Maimonides' and Spinoza's conceptions of the freedom to philosophize is crucial to understand Strauss's own project. Like Spinoza and Kant after him, Maimonides also attempted a "critique" of pure

[112] Alfarabi calls them "the counterfeit philosopher, the vain philosopher, or the false philosopher is the one who sets out to study the theoretical sciences without being prepared for them" (2001, I, 60).

reason. He, too, set out to rationally demonstrate the limits of human reason.[113] From a Spinozist or Kantian perspective, however, a rational critique of reason means that reason must accept as universally valid *only* what results from its rational critique of itself, and nothing more—certainly nothing that transcends reason. Instead, Strauss argues that "Maimonides *demonstrates* that reason has a limit and *must therefore accept the suprarational doctrines of revelation without being able to understand or demonstrate them.* Maimonides' rational critique of reason shows that philosophy knows, strictly speaking, only the 'lower' world and that, starting from this, it can demonstrate the existence, unity and incorporeality of God. Contemplative knowledge of the 'upper world' is possible only for prophets and this is denied philosophers" (Strauss 1995, 54, emphasis mine). The insufficiency of human reason to obtain knowledge of the absolute or divine truth is for Maimonides reason enough to accept the "suprarational doctrines" and "supranatural truths [*übernatürliche Wahrheiten*]" revealed to prophets, and in the first place the doctrine of the createdness of the world.[114] For Spinoza and Kant, on the contrary, if an individual believes these dogmas and thereby transgresses the self-discovered limits of reason, its claim to have attained "true opinion" loses all universal and necessary validity and becomes mere prejudice or subjective opinion. For Strauss, Maimonides' rationalism preserves the possibility, denied by modern critical philosophy, that faith may transcend reason and, at once, also claim for itself universal and necessary validity.[115] "Maimonides's assertion of the insufficiency of human intellect takes its concrete meaning as an assertion of the insufficiency of human intellect to answer the question: 'created world or eternal world.' Indeed for Maimonides it is known that Scripture teaches the Creation of the world and—what is even more important for him—that Judaism forfeits its foundation if the assertion of Creation is abandoned" (Strauss 1995, 91; 1997b, 78). By way of contrast, Spinoza's *Deus sive natura* is the exemplary result achieved by a modern freedom to philosophize that has broken with the bondage to revealed law.

Is the divinely revealed authorization to philosophize in freedom merely a "noble lie," an exoteric teaching designed to protect philosophical freedom from persecution at the hands of fundamentalist adherents of the divine law in its literalness? Some interpreters have claimed that, starting with *Persecution and the Art of Writing*, Strauss adopts the view that the yoke of divine law is merely a shackle to philosophy, an exterior impediment to the "natural" freedom of

[113] (Strauss 1997b, 54).

[114] For a thorough discussion of the problem of the insufficiency of human reason in Maimonides, see (Dobbs-Weinstein 1995).

[115] Maimonides, according to Strauss, teaches that "through the prophets, the philosopher like all other human beings gets to know the truth that transcends philosophy, viz. that the world is not eternal but created" (Strauss 1997b, 54).

inquiry and philosophy supposedly espoused by Socrates. On my hypothesis, Strauss's reading of medieval philosophy is actually quite republican insofar as it reflects the belief common to Athens and Jerusalem that human political freedom is only understandable as a function of following civil rules or laws. The same principle applies to philosophy: here the law that "frees" philosophy is the divine one. However the case may stand with Strauss's post-emigration writings on medieval thought, in *Philosophy and Law*, at least, he vigorously rejects the "pedagogical" idea of religion, according to which revelation is a lower form of expression used to communicate purely philosophical truths to the philosophically uninitiated. Strauss rejects this argument as being "not only objectively untenable . . . but above all unintelligible in itself" (1995, 63). It is "unintelligible" because for Strauss these Arabic and Jewish medieval philosophers were convinced that philosophy stands in *need* of revelation. It lies in the deepest *interest* of philosophers to subject themselves to divine law. "There can be an *interest* in revelation only if there is a *need* for revelation. The philosopher needs revelation if he knows that his capacity for knowledge is in principle *inadequate* to know *the truth*" (Strauss 1995, 64; 1997b, 51). Why this is the case is the topic of the second argumentative strategy, which Strauss calls the "philosophical foundation of law."

From philosophy to biopolitics of divine law

The second main reason why Strauss's account of divine law recovers significance today is because it offers a diametrically opposite strategy to the one pursued by Scholem's "mystical" foundation of divine authority, which as discussed in the previous chapter theorizes the necessary inapplicability of the divine law as basis for a critique of state sovereignty. For Strauss, the Arabic and Jewish medieval philosophers interpreted the divine law from the Platonic model of the concrete order of *nomos* and thus defended the possibility that divine law, unlike human positive law, is *radically applicable in all life situations*. When considered in light of the discussion on biopolitics that traverses Jewish political theology in the 20th century, as I have shown in previous chapters, Strauss's viewpoint on divine law intervenes in the debate on the sacredness of life and on what the proper relation between life and law ought to be. When considered in light of the fundamental problem of the relation between Athens and Jerusalem, Strauss's viewpoint on divine law ultimately calls into question the distinction between Jewish life and philosophical life.

According to Strauss, the "philosophic foundation of the law" is an argument made by Arabic and Jewish medieval philosophers that justifies the claim that the "supranatural truths" about God communicated to the prophet stand higher than the "knowledge of God" that philosophy can discover through its investigation of (created) nature. The most important of these supranatural truths is the doctrine that God is the Creator of nature. It is a prophetic truth because, for Strauss, these philosophers were convinced that Aristotle demonstrated that the scientific investigation of (sublunary) nature offers no evidence for the createdness of the world, but on the contrary presupposes its eternity.[116] Strauss's main point in *Philosophy and Law* is to argue that this "philosophic foundation" of the law is not based on a physical or metaphysical argument, but is of one piece with Islamic and Jewish political theology, that is, it technically belongs with the treatment of prophecy within political science. The argument has three components: (a) by nature human beings need the guidance of divine law; (b) philosophers are also subject to this unitary code of law; (c) prophets are superior to philosophers because the code of law contains stipulations that must be divined and cannot be deduced from general principles or axioms about law.

On the first point that philosophy stands in "need" of the revealed law, Strauss says the following. "The philosopher needs the revelation if he knows that his capacity for knowledge is in principle inadequate to know the truth. Maimonides, the classic author of medieval Jewish rationalism, is filled with this conviction. The decisively important doctrine, the doctrine on whose truth the possibility of being a Jew depends absolutely, that is, the doctrine of createdness of the world, is, according to his explicit and emphatic statement, not demonstrable."[117] The Socratic or zetetic "conviction" that human reason is demonstrably inadequate to grasp "the truth" is of one piece with the claim that the most important of these "supernatural" truths is the prophetically communicated "doctrine of the createdness of the world."[118] This doctrine, additionally, happens to be the condition for the existential "possibility of being a Jew." The so-called tension between "philosopher and Jew," on which so much ink has been spilled in Straussian literature, is resolved by Strauss with the claim that the doctrine that is essential to Judaism *is also essential* for philosophy understood as a Socratic or zetetic activity, that is, as an activity carried on in full awareness of the limits or insufficiency of the human, unguided pursuit of knowledge.

How does Strauss demonstrate that philosophy needs revelation? "The truth transcending philosophy [*die der Philosophie transzendente Wahrheit*] . . . the

[116] For a philosophical discussion of the Arabic and Jewish medieval proofs related to Eternity and Creation, see the classic works (Davidson 1987; and Sorabji 2006).

[117] (Strauss 1995, 64; 1997b, 51). The argument is anticipated in (Strauss 1997b, 182) where Strauss speaks of the "the human correlate of a superhuman revelation, namely, with the fact of man's inadequacy for the guidance of his own life"; "the interest in revelation grounded in the conviction, or in the insight, that human life in itself is either completely directionless or lacks adequate direction."

[118] In his *Early Writings*, Strauss speaks of "the theological conception of biblical history, which presupposes the rigorous notion of God as the Ruler of the world rather than merely as the Ruler of the human world" (Strauss 2002, 134).

truth that the world is not eternal but created . . . has in principle *the feature that it is absolutely necessary for life* [*dass sie für das Leben schlechthin notwendig ist*]: for on the truth of creation there depends not, to be sure, the possibility of revelation in general, but certainly the truth and the possible absoluteness of the one particular revelation" (Strauss 1995, 66–7, emphasis mine; 1997b, 54). The revealed doctrine of Creation that is philosophically undemonstrable is nevertheless "absolutely necessary for life." Strauss's claim that the revealed truth of Creation, which he describes as "truths necessary for life [*lebensnotwendigen Wahrheiten*]" (Strauss 1995, 67; 1997b, 54), is somehow "absolutely necessary for life" sounds odd at first. After all, those human beings who do not believe that the world is "created" by the One God do not thereby cease to live.[119] With the expression "absolutely necessary for life," Strauss does not mean that the concrete legal order of divine revelation is necessary for biological life, nor does he mean that it is necessary for the ideal of civilization. Instead, Strauss means the same thing that Cohen, Rosenzweig, and Buber also meant: namely, that the doctrine of the Creation of the world is a doctrine whose "truth" must be assumed in order to establish a *just* social life.

In *Philosophy and Law*, divine law is said to be "absolutely necessary for life" for two reasons. The first is that the *non-application of divine law* has fatal consequences. As Strauss reiterates in a much later text: "it is impossible to suspend judgment regarding matters of utmost urgency, regarding matters of life and death. Now the question of revelation is evidently of utmost urgency. If there is revelation, unbelief in revelation or disobedience to revelation is fatal."[120] Unbelief in revelation is fatal only if the possibility of leading a just life in accordance to the legal order of divine law is linked, from the start, to a condition in which biological life stands in mortal peril. This condition is what Schmitt terms the "state of exception." The legal order of divine law requires that individuals take exception to human, conventional laws in order to show their "obedient

[119] In a note, Strauss adds: "since the end of revelation is the transmission of teachings necessary for life [*lebensnotwendigen Lehren*], the revelation proclaims also such teachings as are not properly true but are nevertheless necessary to make human life, that is, community life, possible" (1995, 140). Eve Adler takes this to mean that, according to Strauss, "the revelation presents rational and supra-rational teachings which, while not strictly true, are necessary for life, while philosophy presents rational teachings which, while true, are not strictly necessary for life" (ibid., 18). Yet, nowhere in *Philosophy and Law* does Strauss say that philosophy presents teachings that are "true, but not strictly necessary to life." Instead, Strauss claims that the rational and supra-rational teachings of revelation are "true" and their "truth" has the characteristic of being, at the same time, "absolutely necessary for life." "Now the revelation, to be sure, communicates not only those truths necessary for life that are suprarational, but *all* truths necessary for life that are not self-evident" (Strauss 1995, 67; 1997b, 54). In addition, along with the "strictly true" teachings which are necessary for life, revelation also provides teachings that are strictly necessary for human life in a political community, but which are also not "strictly true," that is, convenient ideology. But to believe that Strauss simply equates revelation as such with convenient ideology is a misrepresentation of his point.

[120] In "Mutual Influence of Theology and Philosophy" (Strauss 1997a, 222). This motif of urgency is taken up in (Derrida 1994a, 57–8).

love" of God—as the exemplarity of Abraham's life indicates. On Strauss's interpretation, prophecy brings along with it a state of exception to human laws precisely because the prophet is the founder of a "complete order of human life [*vollkommen Ordnung des menschlichen Lebens ist ihm durch einen Propheten gegeben*]" (Strauss 1997b, 123).[121]

To be in a position of having to choose for or against such a "unified, total order of life" (Strauss 1997b, 61) brought forward by the political, "state-founding" figure of the prophet (Strauss 1995, 71–2) is equivalent to being situated in a state of nature where the protection of the individual's biological life and the form of legal life made possible by divine law do not overlap. Divine law threatens "life pure and simple" in a sense that recalls the possibility of "divine violence" that Benjamin identifies as the necessary manifestation of divine justice in *Critique of Violence*. Benjamin linked this divine violence to the actions (purges) undertaken by Moses against those members of Israel who revolted against the revealed law.[122] For Strauss, only from this existential position or standpoint can the individual pose the question as to what gives absolute value or meaning to life, that is, what "saves" life absolutely. But what saves life absolutely is not the preservation of mere life—as in Hobbes—but the possibility of leading a just life—as in Plato.

In these passages, Strauss seems to be after something analogous to what Derrida, in the context of his interpretation of Benjamin's essay, calls "the awakening of a Jewish tradition" contained in the idea that "what is sacred in one's life is not life itself but the justice of one's life" (Derrida 2001, 289).[123] Benjamin and Strauss agree that this justice is harbored by the possibility of an ethico-political concrete order that is not mercenary because it is based on the principle that "the reward for [the fulfillment of] the commandment is the commandment."[124] Like Benjamin's text on divine violence, Strauss's reading of Jewish and Islamic Platonic political philosophy thus stands in close proximity with the categories of Schmitt's political theology, while being extremely distant from the latter's Christian interpretation of political theology. For in Schmitt the political (the sovereign decision on the state of exception) calls upon a sacrifice of life for the sake of asserting the "sacredness," the "absolute dignity" of mere life; whereas in Strauss the political, viz., the prophetic interpretation of the state of exception,

[121] (Strauss 1995, 73). See also the expression: "a unified, total order of human life [*einer einheitlichen, totalen Ordnung des menschlichen Lebens*]" (Strauss 1997b, 61).

[122] See, apart from Derrida, the discussion on divine violence in Benjamin found in (Martel 2012).

[123] The idea is already voiced by Emmanuel Levinas: "That dying may lead to living, is no doubt to affirm that life, within the human being, has meaning only beyond the egoism of its biological reality, that life is immediately life with others, always already beyond the perseverance to exist, beyond the 'at any cost' of the *conatus essendi*" (1996, 61, translation mine).

[124] (Strauss 1997a, 171). See Derrida's comment on Benjamin's analysis of divine commandments in *Critique of Violence*: " 'Thou shall not kill' remains an absolute imperative once the principle of destructive divine violence commands the respect of the living being . . . for this imperative is followed by no judgment" (2001, 288). On this point, see also the considerations in (Fenves 2011, 187–226).

calls upon a sacrifice of life through "divine" violence manifested in the action and words of the prophet only for the sake of defending the "holiness" of a "just" or "examined" life.

The second reason for why the belief in Creation is "absolutely necessary to life" is that divine law applies to all situations of human life. In this sense as well, divine law disregards the distinction between private and public that structures modern law. While Agamben argues that human positive law gains its condition of application by capturing "life pure and simple" in a state of exception where it is completely vulnerable to being killed (Agamben 1998), for Strauss, once the concept of divine law as *nomos* is understood as "a unified, total regimen of human life" it becomes possible to think of a rule of law that secures this life by permitting no aspect of it to be excluded from the jurisdiction of its law. Unlike human law, divine law must be a law that covers in principle all circumstances of human life without exception.

It is at this point of the argument that Strauss appeals most directly to the foundation of divine law in the political philosophy of Plato and Aristotle. The unexceptionality of the divine law, the fact that in its form it covers all circumstances of life, addresses the fundamental Platonic belief that the human being is "by nature a political living being [who] is in need of laws and therefore of a lawgiver" (Strauss 1995, 70). Here it becomes clear why, for Strauss, Maimonides' appeal to Aristotle's definition of the human being as "by nature a political animal" is by no means a "secularization" or "naturalization" of divine law, viz., an opening for granting lawmaking powers to the human sovereign, but, on the contrary, it is an argument for granting constituent power (the power to make constitutions) only to an authority that can act as "guide" for human beings and lead them toward their physical and intellectual perfection.[125] This kind of guidance can only be given by a prophet.

Divine law singularizes individuals by drawing them out of their apparent sense of security provided by civilized modes of life and returning them to a state of nature in which their biological life is threatened while simultaneously disclosing the horizon of a higher form of security or salvation. Adherence to divine law in its radical difference from human law is life-threatening because it can lead to persecution at the hands of believers as much as unbelievers. In

[125] "The highest perspective acknowledged in common by Plato and the medieval philosophers . . . [is] the idea of a rational law, that is, a law directed to the specific perfection of man. But such a law—and only such a law deserves the name of "law"—can only be of divine origin. The idea of the divine law is the required highest perspective" (Strauss 1995, 76). "There are two kinds of leadership [*Leitung*]: legislation and government [*Gesetzgebung und Regierung*]. The legislator lays down the norms for actions, the ruler [*Herrscher*] enforces compliance with them; the governing leadership [*regierende Leitung*] already presupposes therefore the legislative leadership [*gesetzgebende Leitung*]. . . . The law directed to the specific perfection of human beings is *divine* law, and its proclaimer is a *prophet*" (Strauss 1995, 121; 1997b, 111).

the modern tradition of natural right, the state of nature denotes a situation in which human life is radically insecure and threatened because it lacks civil law and civilization as such. The state of nature to which faith in divinely revealed law "returns" any individual who acts in accordance with it, is not the same state of nature described by Hobbes and Spinoza, nor is it reducible to the concept of "nature" (*phusis*) of Greek philosophizing. The state of nature that corresponds to prophetology looks more like the "desert" of Abrahamic religions—to which the human being was exiled after eating from the Tree of Knowledge of good and evil—than the Epicurean "garden." From the viewpoint of the prophetic state of nature it is possible to assert that "grace [Torah] perfects nature [*phusis*], it does not destroy nature."[126]

Strauss discusses the exchange of views between Heidegger and Buber on the fundamental features of the state of nature that best describes the true human condition. In his *Nietzsche* book, Heidegger polemicized against the biblical prophets who "announce immediately the God upon whom the certainty of salvation is a supernatural blessedness."[127] Heidegger distinguished the prophetic announcement of the Messianic age from the "foretelling" of "the word of the Holy" that he links with Nietzsche and the return of Greek gods. The point is that Heidegger denies "supernatural" grace: "for Heidegger there is no security, no happy ending, no divine shepherd" (Strauss 1968, 235). Buber, in turn, rejected Heidegger's characterization of prophets because "the prophets of Israel . . . have always aimed to shatter all security and to proclaim in the opened abyss of the final insecurity the unwished for God who demands that His human creatures become real, they become human."[128] Strauss retorts to both existentialist thinkers, ironically, that "the controversy can easily degenerate into a race in which he wins who offers the smallest security and the greatest terror and regarding which it would not be difficult to guess who will be the winner" (Strauss 1968, 235). He takes issue with Buber's conception of the prophet, tellingly, by saying that "Buber's protest would be justified if the biblical prophets were only, as Wellhausen may seem to have hoped, prophets of insecurity, not to say an evil end" (235). The rebuke is uncharacteristically sharp: Buber comes too close to the anti-Jewish image of the prophets propounded by Wellhausen.

[126] In "Progress or Return?" Strauss asserts that "not the city, not civilization, but the desert, is the place in which the Biblical God reveals himself" (1997a, 251). Jerusalem or Zion is not a "city" like Athens or Rome: for Strauss, it represents the permanent tension in the West between ideals of human civilization marked by a belief in the progress of human laws and technological development in the arts and sciences, which are made possible by life in the cities or states or empires, and the ideal of fidelity and obedience to the prophetically revealed Law (or teachings) that structure the Tradition(s) of Abrahamic monotheisms (but perhaps not only them).

[127] (Strauss 1968, 234) referring to (Heidegger 1961b, II:320).

[128] Cited from the 1952 edition of (Buber 2016, 97) in (Strauss 1968, 234).

Strauss's own standpoint seeks to maintain an equilibrium between nature and grace, Athens and Jerusalem: "the biblical experience is not simply undesired or against man's grain. . . . *Not every man but every noble man is concerned with justice or righteousness and therefore with any possible extra-human, supra-human support of justice, or with the security of justice. The insecurity of man and everything human is not an absolutely terrifying abyss if the highest of which a man knows is absolutely secure. Plato's Athenian Stranger does not indeed experience that support, that refuge and fortress* [which comes not from putting one's 'trust in flesh and blood but in God alone'] *as the Biblical prophets experienced it, but he does the second best: he tries to demonstrate its existence*" (Strauss 1968, 235, emphasis mine). These words correspond very closely to the spirit of Philo's philosophy. They reflect a conception of the human condition for which the Platonic ideal of true nobility of spirit is profoundly compatible with the biblical revelation.

The state of nature to which Strauss seeks to return is not simply characterized by the insecurity that prophets alert to, which Strauss also calls in the same text "a deeper understanding of the power of evil in man," but also by what is "the second best" thing beside trust in "God alone," namely, the Platonic, philosophical attempt "to demonstrate" the existence of "any possible extra-human, supra-human support of justice, or with the security of justice." Strauss does not in this instance cite any passages from Plato's dialogues featuring the Athenian Stranger, but it is likely that he may have been thinking of those passages in Plato's *Laws* according to which: "where the [divine] law is despot [or 'tyrant'] over the rulers and the rulers are slaves of the law, there I foresee safety and all good things which the gods have given to cities" (*Laws* 715D).

Rosenzweig's epigraph at the start of Part Three of the *Star of Redemption* was an invitation to enter into the discussion of the tyrannical rule of God's law in relation to human systems of law. Strauss picked up this invitation wholeheartedly. His first American book, *On Tyranny*, addressed what he calls the "tyrannical teaching" of Platonic political philosophy as a way of treating the problem of the prophet as a living law "*in corpore vili*, thus with respect to some strategically favorable, non-Jewish object. I chose Xenophon."[129] For the prophet as a giver of the divine law has the characteristics of a living law, and from the perspective of constitutional rule, the prophet-legislator-state founder appears also as a "tyrant." Thus, Strauss engages Schmitt on his terrain, but he does so, in the last instance, by remaining faithful to Rosenzweig's standpoint.

Strauss and Schmitt both hold the belief that a law which cannot be applied is not, factically speaking, a law. Both hold the belief that whether a law applies to a given situation is not something that can be determined by reference to the form

[129] Letter of May 20, 1949, to Julius Guttmann, cited in (Meier 2006, 24).

of law, and thus by reference to a rational principle, but requires an extra-legal decision that reveals what Derrida calls a "mystical" foundation of law. According to Strauss, the philosopher, in fact, "cannot give this [divine] law either to himself or to others; for while he can indeed, qua philosopher, *know* the principles of a law in general and the principles of the rational law in particular, he can never *divine* the concrete individual ordinances of the ideal law, whose precise stipulation is the only way the law can become effectual, or simply, can become—law" (Strauss 1995, 62–3; 1997b, 59). To always do the right thing at the right time is not something that human beings can determine without divine guidance. A tyrannical teaching necessarily follows from the belief that the applicability of the law to the situation ultimately makes reference to decisions ("stipulations" in Strauss's language) of authoritative persons who represent the "mystical" authority of the law. If both prophets and sovereigns can be said to be "tyrannical," only prophets are at the same time the instruments of divine "justice," and, as such, the sole political agents capable of providing integrity to the legal order. If the decisions or stipulations of the prophet are necessarily extra-legal, they are so in view of articulating the necessary difference between human legality and divine justice, a difference that is absent in the case of Schmittian sovereigns who suspend the law in a state of exception that carries no reference to divine justice. The very *facticity* of revelation indicates the impossibility of a rational conception of justice. Strauss's conclusion is not so distant from what Derrida alludes to, in his reading of Benjamin, when he states that "justice remains *to come*" (2001, 236): "There is an *avenir* for justice and there is no justice except to the degree that some event is possible which, as event, exceeds calculation, rules, programs, anticipations and so forth. Justice, as the experience of absolute alterity, is unpresentable, but it is the chance of the event and the condition of history" (236).

Philosophy and Law gives an original interpretation of Rosenzweig's paradoxical claim that Greek philosophy is the prophecy of Jewish revelation. Strauss's final thesis is that the Arabic *falasifa* and Maimonides, although they sided with Aristotle's philosophy over Plato's at an exoteric level, they esoterically chose Plato over Aristotle, because in Plato "the philosopher stands under the state, under the law. Philosophy has to be responsible before the state, before the law: it is not absolutely sovereign" (Strauss 2013, 219; 1997b, 426). From here comes the crowning formula of Strauss's thought in the years of his "re-orientation" or "turn" away from the Moderns and toward the Ancients: "What was required by Plato, that philosophy stand under the law, is fulfilled in the age of the revealed religions" (Strauss 2013, 219, translation modified; 1997b, 426). "The prophet is the founder of the Platonic state. He fulfills what Plato required, what he foretold. But this means that revelation, the Law, is understood in light of Plato [*der Prophet ist der Stifter des Platonischen Staats. Er erfüllt, was Plato gefordert, was er geweissagt hat. Das heisst aber die Offenbarung, das Gesetz wird im Licht Platos verstanden*]" (Strauss 2013, 220). It is clear that for Strauss the belief in divine revelation as concrete legal order is *entirely compatible* with Platonic political philosophy because it fulfills the Platonic requirement that an ideal regime will be ruled by philosophers. Athens and Jerusalem are thus united at the highest level. But this coincidence of opposites, as is evident, can only receive a paradoxical formulation, which in Strauss's formulation is this: Plato, in reality, is more like a biblical prophet because he "foresees" the proper form of redemption, and Moses, in reality, is more like a Platonic philosopher king because he "realizes" the true Republic in the stipulations of the divine law.[130] Either way, to admit that Maimonides was a Platonic political philosopher is *not* an argument against Maimonides' fidelity to the core tenets of Judaism. "Maimonides pursued the philosophic approach up to its end because he was . . . animated by that intrepid piety which does not shrink from the performance of any duty laid upon us in the prayer 'Purify our heart so that we can serve Thee in truth.' If he had not brought the greatest sacrifice, he could not have defended the Torah against the philosophers as admirably as he did in his Jewish books" (Strauss 1988, 169). In this sense, Strauss's interpretation of Maimonides out of Platonic and Aristotelian sources remained very much within the outlines of a philosophical conception and defense of the Torah as living law, pioneered by Philo and revived by his German-Jewish contemporaries.

130 "Their un-Platonic premise—the fact of revelation—were at bottom not so un-Platonic as it seems at first glance" (Strauss 1995, 129).

6
Hannah Arendt and Federalism

Introduction

Two major political challenges in the 20th century are crystallized in the struggle for a Jewish state in Palestine. The partition of the globe at the hands of expansionist territorial sovereign nation-states through imperialism, colonialism, and world war gave rise to the demand by all dominated peoples that their "right to be 'a people like all peoples' and human beings among our fellow human beings" be legally and politically recognized (Arendt 2007, 162). Since their expulsion from Spain in the 15th century, this fundamental right was not recognized for the Jewish people, whose members became instead conceived purely as the embodiment of a particular religion that brought upon them discrimination, persecution, and finally genocide. The second challenge emerged when it became clear that recognizing the right to self-determination in the form of territorial and national sovereignty, especially when state-building occurs on territories carved up by imperial and settler colonial powers, did not prevent the fate of statelessness, persecution, and forced migration to be visited on other peoples and on millions of individuals who are not treated by states as "fellow human beings." The Israeli-Palestinian conflict and the tension between rights to national self-determination and the politics of human rights have become among the most evident symbolic indicators of the difficulty of addressing both challenges simultaneously.[1]

The driving motivation of Arendt's political thought is to find an answer to these twinned challenges. Arendt's analysis of the Jewish political experience since the Enlightenment led her to propose the substitution of a multinational and multiethnic federalism for national sovereignty as a basic principle for global political life. Her early *Jewish Writings*, composed during the 1930s and 1940s, reveal that decades before her reconstruction of neo-Roman constitutionalism in *On Revolution* (1963) Arendt had already cast her die in favor of federalism as the most appropriate form not only for Jewish politics under conditions of anti-Semitism, but for all peoples who form permanent minorities within nation-states.

[1] From the Palestinian perspective, see (Said 1995), and in relation to the Zionist versus post-Zionist debate, see now (Gans 2016).

Living Law. Miguel Vatter, Oxford University Press (2021).
DOI: 10.1093/oso/9780197546505.003.0007

Arendt's understanding of the Jewish political experience as a "pariah" people after the Enlightenment struggle for Jewish Emancipation also led her to reformulate the problem of human rights. According to Arendt, the German Enlightenment, as represented by Gotthold Lessing, Moses Mendelssohn, and Christian Dohm, symbolizes the idea of "human rights" through the condition of European Jews—their "liberation a symbol of man's liberation"—but it disregarded the struggle for "equal rights for fellow citizens of a faith different from that of the Christian state and the world around him" (2007, 62). This is one of the first formulations of her famous critique of the "Rights of Man" in *The Origins of Totalitarianism* and her constructive proposal to rethink human rights in terms of a "right to have rights . . . and a right to belong to some organized community" (1973, 297) based on the conditions of natality and plurality, shared by all human beings without exception.

This chapter argues that Arendt's contribution to Jewish political theology in the 20th century rests in the way she conceptualizes together Roman and Jewish theologico-political motifs to lend support to her republican conception of federalism and human rights. My claim is that Arendt recovers the widely held belief by modern republicans that Romans and Jews, during their republican periods, both held a "civil" conception of religion.[2] By a "civil" conception of religion, I refer to the idea that the meaning and limits of religion follow from the requirements of republican constitution-making in a context of natural equality, as opposed to the belief that civil laws follow from or rest on the theological presupposition of a transcendent, trans-mundane absolute.[3] By contrast, Judith Butler's post-secular reading of Arendt claims that "what is finally Jewish about Arendt's political thought" lies in an ethical and religious exigency of cohabitation on earth with the stranger or foreigner.[4] Samuel Moyn, instead, believes that Jewish theology enters into Arendt's discussion of politics because "the sanction with which the absolute provides politics" is required even

[2] "The Gods of the Pagans were in no sense jealous Gods; they divided the empire of the world between them; even Moses and the Hebrew people sometimes countenanced this idea by speaking of the God of Israel" (Rousseau 1968, 177).

[3] For this idea of civil religion, see (Vatter 2017a). For a wide-ranging discussion of the concept and problem of civil religion, see (Beiner 2011).

[4] (Butler 2014, 122). She recapitulates her thesis on Arendt's Jewish thought as follows: "1) a conception of cohabitation that emerges in part from a condition of exile; 2) an affinity with that Benjaminian version of the messianic . . . by giving priority to the "wandering" and "scattered" character of Jewish life (resonant with Rosenzweig as well) . . . 3) as scattered and diasporic, Jewish life becomes concerned with the ethical relation to the non-Jew and considers cohabitation to be not only a historical exigency, but a fundamental task of Jewish ethics; 4) a relation between Jewish ethics and Kant profoundly influenced by the work of Hermann Cohen . . . the ethical demand to negotiate relationship with alterity, the signature piece of a certain Jewish cosmopolitanism. . . . Finally 5) the historical condition of the refugee . . . established a critical perspective on the nation-state" (Butler 2014, 153).

in "modern and revolutionary politics" (2008, 75). For Moyn, Arendt was in the business of finding "nonreligious versions" of the old theological absolutes and the American Revolution was "the experiment of discovering a secular proxy for religion" (2008, 77).

The first half of the chapter reconstructs Arendt's early understanding of Jewish politics. I show how she changes the terms of the so-called Jewish Question from an identitarian to a political question by reformulating the ethico-religious teaching of the Torah into new principles of federalist politics.[5] I suggest that Arendt finds in Martin Buber's politico-theological recasting of Jewish politics in the 1930s and 1940s a crucial impetus for her new thinking. This impetus is given by Buber's "anarchical" interpretation of the Hebrew Republic, on the one hand, and by his non-territorial conception of the Homeland, on the other. In this context I also discuss the affinities and differences between Buber's and Heidegger's approaches to the question of the Homeland and, more generally, to their spatial conception of the political. Heidegger's supposed influence on Arendt's political thought has been much discussed in the literature, but the connection between Arendt, Buber, and Heidegger has yet to be analyzed in terms of their approaches to the question of the Bible's relation to political philosophy (both in relation to the Hebrew Bible as well as in relation to the New Testament).[6]

In the second half of the chapter I show that Arendt's transition from Jewish to Greco-Roman politics is motivated by the need to give an answer to the problem of the "foundation" or "constitution" of freedom. Stated in biblical terms, this is the problem of the transition from the covenant of Exodus to that of Sinai. Like Machiavelli, Spinoza, and Rousseau, Arendt also reads Moses as providing a civil religion, whose exemplary lessons are reactivated in modern republicanism and in the specificity of modern republican revolutions. The fundamental lesson is the need to separate the power of the people from the authority of the laws in order to avoid the so-called problem of the absolute, that is, the projection of God's omnipotence onto political relations between human beings. Arendt's unique contribution to this problem consists in turning to the Roman poet Virgil as source of an idea of civil religion based on the "divinity of birth" that preserves her idea of freedom as beginning, while resolving the problem of authority

[5] For Butler, "being a Jew implies taking up an ethical relation to the non-Jew" (2014, 117). Julie Cooper has criticized Butler for her "identitarian" rather than "political" approach to the question of sovereignty in Judaism based on the debate on Zionism prior to the war (2015). However, she does not refer to Arendt's theologico-political discussion of federalism in this context.

[6] For Buber and the binational solution to the Israeli-Palestinian conflict, see the texts collected in (Mendes-Flohr 1983) and now the discussion in (Mendes-Flohr 2019). Mendes-Flohr has also recently come to a reading of Buber in terms of political theology (2008, 32). See in this context the politico-theological readings of Buber in (Lebovic 2008; and Schmidt 2009).

without absolutes. Additionally, Arendt recovers a republican understanding of Jesus as the teacher of a "divine natural right" who illustrates the possibility of universalizing the Judeo-Roman synthesis in the form of a modern republicanism of human rights.

Zionism and federalism in Arendt's Jewish writings

The early *Jewish Writings* leave no doubt that Arendt considers Jews as a nation, but a nation that was inherently a minority in any of the established nation-states on earth. In this sense, the Jewish people are said to lack a "motherland" (Arendt 2007, 126). For Arendt, the so-called Jewish Question refers to the fact that "all politics dealing with minorities, and not just with Jews, have foundered on the existent and abiding fact of state sovereignty" (Arendt 2007, 126). The problem is that state sovereignty gives rise to "a new class of people in Europe, the stateless . . . modern pariahs. That minority rights could not apply to them was an immediate hallmark of the failure of such rights—they foundered on this most modern of phenomena" (127). The pariah signals the limits of a system (in this case, the nation-state system) that has given rise to it. The existence of "pariah" peoples points to the failure of any of the possibilities offered by the system to incorporate what it must necessarily exclude from itself.

Thus, Arendt rejected in principle all "individual" solutions (i.e., all liberal solutions) that turn on assimilation to, or naturalization in, a given nation-state, for these are "solutions" that require abandoning the Jewish nationality. Likewise, she rejects minority rights because they either give rise to the identification of the minority as "a state within a state [of the majority]" or because they lead to the depoliticization of the minority nation. "Even in an ideal situation minorities can demand no more than cultural autonomy" (Arendt 2007, 128), which means that they cannot demand precisely what they most want, namely, an equal right to participate in the political life of the state. The crucial point for Arendt is that "the Jews are a people," whereas from the assimilationist standpoint "Jews are all sort of things—a religion, the salt of the earth, world citizens par excellence—but not a people" (Arendt 2007, 49). At the same time, Arendt rejected the Zionist "abstraction" of Jews as a "natural substance" which is opposed to another "natural substance," namely, the German nation, as if "we are totally foreign to and despised by that other people [the German] on the basis of its inalterable substance. Such a schematic generalization appears to conform perfectly to the National Socialists who crystallize their worldview of a *Volksgemeinschaft* in anti-Semitism" (2007, 55). In both cases, Zionists and anti-Zionists miss the central point, namely, that to be a people is to have a common *inter-esse* that is independent from any identity, whether it is constructed along national or ethnic or racial lines.[7] In her later political thought, she would conceive of this *inter-esse* through the experience of covenanting as the mode of generating a *res publica* based on the "federal principle, the principle . . . according to which constituted political bodies can combine and enter into lasting alliances without losing their identity" (1990, 171). Already in 1940, two decades before *On Revolution*, Arendt conceives of the republican demand for equal "participation in the government of affairs" (1990, 127) as a *human right*. Arendt's republicanism always seems to have been intended to address the problem of permanent minorities and pariah peoples.

Assuming the existence of a human right to equal participation in political life, what kind of political association can fulfill this demand for minority nationalities? Arendt's insight is the following:

> The notion that nations are constituted by settlement within borders and are protected by their territory is undergoing a crucial correction. Spaces that can truly be maintained economically and politically are constantly expanding. *There may soon come a time when the idea of belonging to a territory is replaced by the idea of belonging to a commonwealth of nations whose politics are determined solely by the commonwealth as a whole.* That means European politics—while at the same time all nationalities are maintained. (Arendt 2007, 130, emphasis mine)

Already at this early stage, Arendt thinks about political questions in *spatial or topological* terms. The issue for her was how to conceive of a political space that did not map onto a "territory" or require "settlement within borders." In the next section I argue that this way of approaching the problem of political space was prefigured by the discussion in the 1930s in Buber and Heidegger on the way peoples "situate" themselves historically, viz., the *Da-sein* (being-there) of peoples.

In 1940, when the outcome of the war was far from being decided, Arendt proposed resolving what she called "the minority question" through the creation of a new federal Europe. "Within such a commonwealth we could be recognized as a nation and be represented in a European parliament. For this 'solution' of the Jewish question, the conundrum of a people without land in search of a land without a people—practically speaking, the moon, or a folktale free of politics—would finally have become meaningless" (2007, 131). She placed her hopes for the resolution of the Arab-Jewish conflict in the Middle East in terms

[7] Her usage of the term "interest" is also neo-Roman: she understands it already as *inter homini esse*, as the in-between of a public space that defines the political life of a people. "The language of the Romans, perhaps the most political people we have known, used the words 'to live' and 'to be among men' (*inter homini esse*) . . . as synonyms" (Arendt 1958, 7).

of a federal project of European Union based on the unity of the diverse peoples and civilizations facing the Mediterranean basin: Christian, Arabic, and Jewish. As she writes in 1943:

> In a model of this sort the Arabs would be strongly represented and yet not in a position to dominate all others. . . . For Jews it would mean the restoration of both their dignity and their place among the nations of the Mediterranean, to the cultural glory of which region they have contributed so much. . . . It is clear that both the Near East and North Africa would have to belong to such a system. . . . Under such roughly sketched plans, the Arabs would be brought into union with European peoples. And surely this ought to frighten no one who is aware of the great and lasting achievements that the Arab people once passed on to Western civilization. If they are given the opportunity to overcome feudal, backward conditions and terrible poverty, then there is really no reason why they cannot be in that same situation again. (Arendt 2007, 197)

For Arendt, federalism was always a counter-concept set against imperialism and colonialism.

Arendt calls for a "Jewish politics in general" (2007, 59) that she carefully distinguishes from political Zionism. "Jewish politics in general" means for Arendt a return to "the original, national revolutionary slogans. . . . Self-emancipation means: equal rights for a people who by the work of their own hands make this earth richer and more beautiful; freedom for a people who in their struggle have proved that they prefer death to slavery" (2007, 144). The task of formulating a politics based on the *inter-esse* of different nationalities not based on territorial conquest, division, and resettlement; the attention to federalism as the only political form capable of solving the problem of national minorities: all these features point Arendt toward thinking about the possibility of Jewish politics in and through a radical rethinking of the Western political tradition initiated by the Greek but especially the Roman peoples.[8] At the same time, this turn toward the tradition never loses sight of the peculiar challenges that emerge from the modern "Jewish" condition, which is captured by the condition of statelessness, the status of the pariah, and the human or natural right to political participation, wherever one finds oneself on the terrestrial globe.

Dirk Moses has argued that Arendt's appeal to Roman political thought in order to think through the predicament of Jewish politics after the Second World War has nothing to do with a republican discourse on the co-implication of liberty and power, but is in reality a covert endorsement of "war, conquest, and reason of state" (2013, 874). Arendt's turn to Roman political thought would be

[8] On Arendt's idea of tradition and its crisis, see (Arendt 2005) and the discussion in (Forti 1996).

a symptomatic expression of the settler colonial mentality that the State of Israel required to legitimate its occupation of Palestine.[9] Arendt admits that Jewish refugees "know of course that only the area of settlement in Palestine can guarantee them their rights in the future; but they have also learned that the security of Palestine will depend on them and their status in a liberated Europe" (2007, 146). However, this statement does not equate to a defense of the State of Israel and its expansionist policy of occupation. It is one thing to say that the State of Israel defends the rights of those Jews who happen to be citizens of that state (as other states do with their citizens), but it is entirely a different claim to say that this state thereby represents a definitive answer to the problems encountered by the Jewish people in their modern history. Evidently, the Jewish state in Palestine cannot be such a definitive answer because of the concurrent expulsion from political community of another people.[10] I take it to be a misreading of Arendt's republicanism to separate it from her concurrent development of a new conception of human rights as the right to have rights which are opposed to state sovereignty and are equally applicable today to Palestinians as they were yesterday to Jews: "the idea of a fundamental, natural inequality of peoples, which is the form of injustice has taken in our time, can only be defeated by *the idea of an original and inalienable equality among all who bear a human countenance*" (2007, 157 emphasis mine).

It is precisely under this new conception of equal human rights, which are no longer rights as gifts granted by nation-states but are conceived as the right of peoples to live politically in a space organized by themselves, that Arendt connects Jewish politics to neo-Roman republican politics. This connection occurs in a federalist key that is *opposed* to both an imperialist notion of expansion and a colonial notion of settlement. "As long as the Passover story does not teach the difference between freedom and slavery, as long as the Moses legend does not call to mind the eternal rebellion of the heart and mind against slavery, the 'oldest document of human history' will remain dead and mute to no one more than the very people who wrote it" (Arendt 2007, 150). Arendt's point here is that republicanism (freedom

[9] "To revive rather than reject the civilization that produced fascism and the Holocaust, Arendt embraced an ideology of civilization modeled on the Roman republic and justified through its progressive incorporation of diverse peoples into a federated international order. . . . Rome's mythic foundation in colonial conquest and settlement and its spread of civilization by violent expansion was, she thought, an acceptable, indeed necessary, theodicy that could be distinguished from modern imperialism" (Moses 2013, 876).

[10] Gil Rubin has claimed that Arendt's federalism has a similar motivation to the position worked out by her friend Salo Baron, who saw federalism as the solution to Jewish statelessness, not to assimilation (Rubin 2015, 408). I think Rubin conflates two points that Arendt always kept apart. Jews ought not to be excluded from the possibility of political community because they are a people. But this access to political life on an equal basis to other peoples need not, for Arendt, require "state protection" for its peoplehood in order to be realized for the very reasons Rubin mentions when he recalls that Arendt "emphasized that while the creation of a Jewish state would solve the problem of Jewish refugees it would inevitably create a new category of refugees, Palestinian Arabs" (ibid., 414).

as living as political equals, as being *sui iuris* by nature not by convention) has its oldest document in the Bible: "there is paradoxically a growing number of those who believe they must replace Moses and David with Washington or Napoleon. Ultimately this attempt to forget our past and to find youth again [i.e., re-naissance] at the expense of strangers will fail—simply because Washington's and Napoleon's heroes were named Moses and David" (2007, 150). At this early point in her career, this statement is more promissory than anything else: the implied symbiosis or cross-fertilization of Jewish and (neo-)Roman political traditions needed to be accounted for, both on the side of "Jerusalem" and on the side of "Rome." In her mature political thought she would work toward a symbiosis of Judaism and Greco-Roman political thought at two distinct levels. The first level requires showing the Jewish origins of federalist political thinking, the idea of a political space not rooted in a sovereign demarcation of territory and borders. This entails an engagement not only with Buber's theo-politics, but also with Heidegger's turn to a topology of Being in the 1930s. The second level requires engaging the republican idea of civil religion and its function in the constitution of freedom.

The problem of the homeland in Buber and Heidegger in the 1930s

If Jews "have the right to be 'a people like all peoples' and human beings among our fellow human beings" (Arendt 2007, 162), then it stands to reason that Jewish politics should be viewed from the republican Greco-Roman standpoint that begins from the existence of politically organized peoples and not from separate individuals in an apolitical state of nature. By 1935, Arendt discerned in Buber's "theo-political" approach to the Bible a possible ally. Buber seeks to bring about the "renaissance of the Jewish people" which, like the Renaissance of other European peoples, required the recovery of an ancient political wisdom, "the seeds of the future in the past" (Arendt 2007, 32).[11] Buber's "turning" toward the biblical past in order to project a new political future for the Jewish people is part of a new "Jewish science" that "seeks to make the most distant aspects of the biblical past alive and relevant to our present-day existence" (2007, 32).[12] Arendt

[11] Arendt rejects the identification of Jews as an "Oriental" people found in the discourse of anti-Semitism: "we enter this war [against Hitler] as a European people, who have contributed as much to the glory and misery of Europe as any other of its peoples" (Arendt 2007, 143).

[12] "Buber has always known how to infuse Zionism with a distinctive spirit. He has an unparalleled way of combining the preservation of the past with the struggle for the future. Now and always, he has reiterated that the renaissance of the Jewish people can only come about through a radical return to its great past and its living religious values" (Arendt 2007, 32). After the war, Buber uses the expression "the turning," which can translate both the idea of *teshuvah* (repentance) and resonates with the Heideggerian idea of a *Kehre* (turn). See (Buber 1952). For Arendt, this new "Jewish science"

explicitly names Buber's "fundamental work *The Kingdom of God*" as an exemplary product of this new scientific approach to the study of Judaism.

What makes Arendt's short 1935 text on Buber, written from exile in Paris, particularly significant is that it shows why the recovery of the biblical past is at once a religious and a political move: "It is only by listening to these very ancient voices and learning to understand them that *we will know how to fulfill the mission God gave to this, his people*" (2007, 32, emphasis mine). For any interpretation of Arendt that wishes to see her as a purely secular thinker, utterances like these pose a stumbling block. But they should be read in the same spirit with which Michael Walzer presents "the story of Israel's deliverance from Egypt" as a story of "this-worldly redemption, liberation, revolution" (1986, ix), the very themes of *On Revolution*. There is a deep continuity between what Arendt said in 1935 and what she said to Scholem in the 1960s when, to his infamous accusation that she did not love her people, she recalled something Golda Meir once confessed to her: "You will understand that, as a Socialist, I, of course, do not believe in God; I believe in the Jewish people." Arendt then comments to Scholem: "I found this a shocking statement, and being too shocked, I did not reply at the time. But I could have answered: The greatness of this people was once that it believed in God, and believed in Him in such a way that its trust and love toward Him was greater than its fear. And now this people believes only in itself? What good can come out of that?—Well, in this sense I do not 'love' the Jews, nor do I 'believe' in them; I merely belong to them as a matter of course, beyond dispute or argument" (Arendt 2007, 467).

Arendt's statement echoes Buber's conception of Jewish faith as the "trust" placed by a people in God's guidance. In her 1929 dissertation on Augustine, written under the supervision of Heidegger, Arendt had queried after the political meaning of the "love of God." She found that Augustine's Christian theology was incapable of serving as the basis for a true republic because it could not find a satisfying mediation that leads from the "love of God" to the "love of the neighbor."[13] Clearly, by 1935 she thought that Buber's investigations into the Bible's "theopolitics" were more promising. Indeed, like Buber, Arendt was also invested in the idea that God's relation to His People is fundamentally a political relation, more than an ethical one or a religious one. But what political role does God have to play in a "Jewish politics in general" that would not reduce the

is intended to replace the 19th-century German discourse on the "science of Judaism" judged to be too liberal and assimilationist in outlook.

[13] Arendt's conclusion was that for Augustine, "although we can meet the other only because both of us belong to the human race, it is only in the individual's isolation in God's presence that he becomes our neighbor" (Arendt 1996, 112). The internal relevance of the neighbor for all human beings is therefore *not* "tied to Christianity."

political life of the Jewish people to the function of bearing a Jewish religion? To answer this question, it is necessary to consider the political theology of Buber and its resonance with Heidegger's turn to a discourse of political theology in the 1930s.

In 1944 Buber wrote an article on Moses Hess as the founding father of modern Zionism. Buber begins by asking the question: "What brought the Socialist Hess to the glorification of nation and land in their relation to one another?"[14] This question had become an existential one for him as well, at least since the failure of the Bavarian soviet republic of 1919 and the assassination of his political hero, the anarchist Gustav Landauer, which spurred Buber's project of establishing socialist settlements in Eretz-Israel.[15] Buber valorizes Hess's attempt to "fit socialism into a vast, super-social, cosmic interrelationship . . . along the lines of that Spinoza whom he had esteemed since his youth" (Buber 1945, 139). But in *Rome and Jerusalem* Hess moved toward Zionism because he also considered "the natural forces of 'race' and the spiritual force of 'tradition'" (Buber 1945, 140). Buber immediately suggests that "race" should be substituted by "nationality" and "tradition" by the idea of "constructive faith": in this way Hess's thinking could be seen to lead to modern Zionism.[16] Above all, in *Rome and Jerusalem*, Hess tried to work out these elements of his political thought within a framework that recognized the fundamental unity of religion and politics within Judaism: "the Jews saw no difference between religious and political injunctions, between duties to God and duties to Caesar" (Buber 1945, 140).

According to Buber, the key advance of *Rome and Jerusalem* was to connect the historical reality of Jewish nationality with the ideal or utopia of Zion, "the Holy Land and the Eternal City" (Buber 1945, 142). For Hess, "the Jewish people will participate in the great historical movement of present-day humanity [i.e., "abolishing class and race rule. . . by the cooperation of all the forces of production"] only when it will have its own fatherland" (Hess 1918, 165–67). Buber, for his part, claimed that "our religion, that is . . . the religion that is inseparably bound up with politics, can be no isolated sphere of cult and theology, but the universe of a faith whose aim and object is to be transformed into the social vital activity of a people" (1945, 144).[17] Buber thus represents Hess as a precursor of his

[14] (Buber 1945, 137). Buber often articulates his (political) understanding of "Jerusalem" in opposition to "Rome" (and "Moscow"). However, a closer reading of his more politico-theological texts tells a different story. For this anti-Roman picture of Buber's political thought, very tied to the figure and exemplarity of Gandhi as "peaceful resistance," see (Susser 1981, 112–36).

[15] On the Buber-Landauer relationship, apart from (Mendes-Flohr 2019), see also (Löwy 2014; and Yassour 2011).

[16] Buber cites an early letter by Hess in which he speaks of having "strangled the thought of his nationality within his breast forever." Buber takes this to mean that for Hess the Jewish "race" refers to the Jewish "nationality."

[17] Buber cites Hess: "the faithful Jews, he says, require *earth* 'in order to realize the historical ideal of our people, an ideal which is neither more nor less than the reign of God upon earth'" (Buber 1945, 143).

own belief that the "rebirth" of the Jewish people passes through the rebuilding of "the Homeland, *wherein the productive forces of the Jewish People are rooted* and from which alone they can renew themselves" (1945, 143, emphasis mine).[18]

This new description of the Holy Land as the "Homeland" of the Jewish people signals a fateful movement past the standpoint of Rosenzweig, for whom the peculiarity of the Jewish people was not to be "rooted" in the earth as other nations. Unlike Rosenzweig, Buber translates the messianic task of realizing the Kingdom of God on Earth into the idea that the Jewish people need a "place" on earth in order to live out their fidelity to their traditional constitution, the divine law. Rosenzweig's "oceanic" viewpoint on the Kingdom of God appears to have been left behind for the sake of a land-based conception of the Kingdom. In order to make sense of Buber's contribution to Jewish political theology in the 20th century, it is necessary to understand the way in which he conceptualizes the Homeland as the "place" (ou-topia, eu-topia, or dys-topia, as the case may be) in which to give new life to the ancient constitution.[19]

The first edition of Buber's *Kingship of God* appeared in Germany in 1932, the same year as Schmitt's second edition of *The Concept of the Political*. Current scholarship identifies in Buber's book a Jewish politico-theological response to Schmitt's political theology, even though Schmitt is not explicitly mentioned in this work.[20] Nitzan Lebovic claims that by 1942 "Buber took on the air of a decisionist prophet" and fell into a wholesale "adoption of Schmitt's theory" (2008, 105). Other interpreters argue the opposite point: Buber's conception of God's Kingdom "declares human authority itself to be usurpation," whereas Schmitt's "political theology is a form of idolatry" (Brody 2015, 83).[21] These

[18] Buber's problematization of land is a constant from early on. For two examples, see his 1916 response to Hermann Cohen's critique of Zionism: "We do not want Palestine 'for the Jews': we want it for humanity, because we want it in order to actualize Judaism" (Buber 1963, 299). Compare with his discussion of Pinsker and Herzl and their thoughts on a Jewish "fatherland": "Of course one could 'create' and 'build' settlements and if one wanted, one could also give them biblical names, as the Christian settlers did in America. However, the term 'Promised Land' should be dealt with care, acknowledging that once a people was 'promised' a land, a very particular land" (Buber 1963, 422).

[19] For a recent intervention in the debate with respect to the question of land in Arendt's early Jewish writings, see (Honig 2016). For Bonnie Honig, "when in 1958, Arendt bars cultivated land from object-hood in *The Human Condition*, she might well be undercutting the promise of the Promised Land" (Honig 2016, 320). Arendt was reacting, according to Honig, against mistaking "land cultivation for actual politics." There is no reference in Honig to Hess's or Buber's theopolitical discourse on land. For a more traditional take on the question of land occupation in the Jewish political tradition, see (Novak 2006), although this treatment also does not discuss either the Buber-Schmitt or the Buber-Heidegger nexus.

[20] For recent articles opposing Buber's "theopolitics" to Schmitt's "political theology" see (Brody 2015; Schaefer 2017; Lesch 2019; and Scharf 2019). The comparison of Buber with Schmitt goes back at least to (Lebovic 2008), who claims that the origin of "Jewish political theology" is to be found in Buber's work on the "theopolitical hour," but see also (Mendes-Flohr 2008; and Schmidt 2009). The issue of Buber's political theology was also thematized by Taubes and his circle in the late 1970s and early 1980s.

[21] Similarly for Schaefer, "theology points to the absolute and exclusive authority of God in the realm of politics and therefore renders conditional, even heretical, all human forms of sovereignty"

readings do not problematize the connection between divine law and promised land that lies at the heart of Buber's "theopolitics" (*Theopolitik*). For Buber, "the Jewish nation may fulfil its function in the establishment of the Kingdom of God" only under two related conditions: first, "*it must have earth under its feet; earth of its own*"; second, it must "establish *its independent, self-determined life according to the will of God*" (Buber 1945, 143, emphasis mine).

I argue that in *Königtum Gottes*, Buber offers a *republican interpretation* of these two conditions of Biblical "theopolitics." His book anticipates Arendt's own project during the war years to develop a "Jewish politics in general" around the ideas of federalism and republicanism. For Buber, the "first and last" concerning Jewish political life is "the realization of an all-encompassing rule of God [*allumfassende Gottesherrschaft*]" (1964, 538). If Schmitt's Christian political theology is centered on a conception of human sovereignty, then Buber's central claim is that the Bible's theo-political teaching is ultimately best expressed by Gideon's *renunciation* of human sovereignty in Judges 8:23 because only YHWH can "rule" (*walten*) over His people.[22] Biblical "theopolitics" is republican because it rejects sovereignty.

But what kind of "rule" is entailed by the *walten* of God? [23] As the secondary literature has remarked time and again, Buber was profoundly affected by the experience of the failed German soviet revolution of 1919 and by the transition to the Weimar Republic that led Max Weber to formulate his two most famous political theses. The first of these Weberian theses on politics is that all democracy in modern times must be a *Führerdemokratie*. The second political thesis is that the fundamental decision is whether democratic legitimacy comes from a charismatic leader (whom Weber models on the figure of the Jewish prophet),

(2017, 243). The thesis is repeated by Lesch's more "ethical" reading of Buber's theopolitics: "when we live the spirit of theopolitics in all our relationships, we effectively restore a condition of divine sovereignty" (2019, 206). Only Scharf suggests that Buber's theopolitics is not Schmittian because the former reflects "the necessity of collaboration [that] arises from the division of power between two parties—God and human leadership" (2019, 256). Here Buber's theopolitics is contextualized within a broader, constitutionalist view on biblical politics.

[22] "Then the Israelites said to Gideon, 'Rule over us—you and your son and grandson—for you have saved us from the hand of Midian.' But Gideon replied, 'I will not rule over you, nor will my son. The LORD shall rule you.'" (Judges 8:22–3).

[23] How to translate the German verb *walten* employed by Buber to designate the political role of God with respect to the Jewish people is a complicated question. Buber employs this term because it resonates with Weber's idea of *Gewalt* as legitimate violence and possibly also with Benjamin's earlier *Critique of Violence* [*Gewalt*]. I have chosen to keep the German term because its meaning can only be discerned by taking into consideration all aspects of Buber's discourse in *Kingdom of God*. However, in an approximative sense, one can say that *walten* could be here better rendered by terms like "direct" or "overlook" than by "rule." Elazer will also have a problem in his translation. He chooses the less felicitous term "management." The problem is that God's "rule" as *walten* cannot be a form of *Herrschaft* or *legitimate use of violence* in the Weberian sense. It is an an-archic form of rule, whose employment of violence is also sui generis (related to the problem of "divine violence" in Benjamin).

or from a bureaucratic, rational form of legality.[24] In *Kingdom of God*, Buber reconstructs the political meaning of Exodus in terms of the establishment of a *Führerdemokratie*, where God is the *Führer* or *melekh*, the charismatic leader of His people. In *Political Theology II*, Schmitt identified Weber's theory of charisma as his affirmative conception of political theology. But Schmitt did not mention that already back in 1932, Buber had employed Weber's conception of "a Yahwe certified war hero or war prophet" in order to construct Jewish political theology around the idea of God's *walten* as a divine democracy.[25]

Buber explicitly understands Gideon's renunciation of human kingship as a recognition of the impossibility of routinizing charisma and thus as the impossibility of attaining a "legitimate" form of *Herrschaft*. The new reading of biblical theocracy that Buber advances is based on the idea that God's rule or *walten* is essentially characterized by *not* determining a specific form of state or form of legitimate government between human beings.[26] In other words, God's "rule" is, literally, a form of no-rule or *an-archein*: it establishes no-rule as the horizon of all human politics. This is what Buber calls "the anarchic soul of theocracy [*dem anarchischen Seelengrund der Theokratie*]" (1964, 686).

The "leadership" function of YHWH presupposes a people that is constituted into an army, following closely Weber's sociological interpretation of the Jewish covenant as the constitution of an armed people that acclaims God as its leader in the making of "holy war."[27] However, Buber does not understand this divine leadership of a people-in-arms, either purely or primarily in antagonistic terms, as a call to war against polytheistic religions. He does not identify the political movement enjoined by God as *melekh* in terms of a war against other gods, or idolatry.[28] Such a reading of the Jewish idea of "holy war" as a war against idolaters, as I showed in chapter 3, was rejected by both Weber and Rosenzweig, and Buber follows suit (Buber 1964, 692). The idea of a "holy war" against idolaters, rather, emerges with the "apocalyptic" mindset that supervened the Roman destruction of the Second Temple in Jerusalem at the end of the Jewish Wars. I discuss Arendt's critique of this mindset later in some detail.[29]

24 See the essay "Zum Begriff der 'plebiszitären Führerdemokratie'" in (Mommsen 1974, 44–71).

25 "As far as can be determined this unstable Israelite confederation till the time of kings had no permanent political organs at all. . . . Confederate unity found expression in that a Yahwe certified war hero or war prophet regularly claimed authority also beyond the boundaries of the tribe. People came to him from afar to have him settle their legal disputes or to seek instruction in ritual or moral duties" (Weber 1952, 83).

26 Again, Elazer follows here Buber: "the covenant does *not dictate or establish the form of regime. . . .* The form of regime is taken from human sources on the basis of necessity and convenience" (Elazer 1997, 8, emphasis mine).

27 (Weber 1952, 90–146).

28 In this sense, Buber does not share James Martel's Benjaminian reading of the struggle against idolatry as the highest form of political struggle (Martel 2014).

29 For the classic account of Jewish apocalyptic political thought see (Taubes 2009, 43–65). "Two world principles clashed in this tenacious, even desperate, struggle between the Zealots and the

In the 1930s, both Buber and Arendt judge that an apocalyptic interpretation of Jewish politics leads to political quietism. On Arendt's reckoning, it was of utmost urgency that some part of the Jewish people enter the war against Nazi Germany, by any means necessary.[30] For Arendt, this meant drawing a bridge between Judaism and the Roman understanding of politics and the role that religion plays in the Roman Republic. For Buber, Israel is a "holy nation" to the extent that it chooses God as leader of a particular struggle or *agon*, what he calls "der *innere Kampf* um JHWH" (1964, 630, emphasis mine). The term "inner struggle" is the usual rendition of the Islamic *jihad*, but in Buber "inner" does not refer to a subjective space of interiority, but to the internal space of no-rule that a people needs to disclose within its society in order to be free. Interestingly, given Rosenzweig's discussion of Islam in the *Star*, Buber illustrates the meaning of Gideon's renunciation of rule by drawing a comparison with the Shi'ite conception of messianism. According to Buber, the Shi'a belief in the hidden Imam posits that "the unity of the community of believers is represented by the field commander," and the commander is chosen by the spirit (*Ruah*) and proves this chosenness through the success of his actions.[31] Buber argues that Jewish *Theopolitik* is even more anarchic than Shi'ite messianism insofar as the gift or grace (*hesed*) of God's *walten* does not fall upon the imam as charismatic field commander, but rather designates the disclosure of a space of no-rule in which no person rules over other human beings.

The second, major innovation in Buber's reading of Biblical theopolitics concerns the interpretation of "holy land" or "homeland" that was the object of God's promise to Abraham. *Königtum Gottes* intervened on three opposed fronts: in reaction to Schmitt's concept of the political and his idea of law as *nomos*, that is, as a "concrete order" based on the violent appropriation and enclosure of land; in response to Rosenzweig's claims that the Jewish people, unlike other nations, was constituted by transmission of blood rather than by occupation of a territory; and, last but not least, in parallel with Heidegger's incipient questioning about the ideas of *Heimat* and Fatherland.

In *The Nomos of the Earth*, Schmitt provocatively gives as the exemplar of a law-founding land appropriation [*Landnahme*] the acts of Joshua, quoting from the Bible: "Joshua took the whole land, according to all that the Lord said onto

Romans. This may not have been their first confrontation but it was the first time they were fully aware of the nature of the conflict: the global empire of masters against a world revolution of the oppressed" (ibid., 45).

[30] See many of the articles written for *Aufbau* (Arendt 2007, 134–240).

[31] Brody also speaks of "a charismatic leadership in which the recipient of the temporary *charis* is recognized to hold a commission to some limited and particular task" (Brody 2015, 78). However, for him the people can only "wait" for divine grace, or otherwise supplant it by "deciding" that a state of emergency exists and requires a human sovereign (ibid., 81).

Moses."[32] Understanding the differences between Schmitt's and Buber's readings of Joshua is important if only because of their implications to the case of the settlement of Eretz-Israel. For Buber, God is the sole possessor of the entire earth: "For the land shall not be sold in perpetuity, since the earth is Mine; hence you are sojourners and tenants with Me [*gerim ve-toshavim immadi*]" (Leviticus 25:23). Since human beings are merely "sojourners" on an earth that does not belong to them, God presents Himself to them as their *melekh*, the "leader" or "guide" who accompanies His people to their "promised" portion of this Earth. "JHWH is He who Is by them, He who Stays presently by them, that is, He who Accompanies them (Ex. 33:16; Deut. 20:4; 31:6), He who Precedes them (Ex. 13:21; Num. 14:14; Deut. 1:30–3), the leader, the *melekh* [*JHWH ist der bei ihnen Seiende, der ihnen gegenwärtig Bleibende, also der Mitgehende, der Vorangehende, der Führer, der Melekh*]" (Buber 1964, 618). Walzer says that the biblical conception of the "promised Land" is articulated in two registers: as the land of "milk and honey," and as "a kingdom of priests and a holy nation." Using a Buberian expression, Walzer explains that "a kingdom of priests would be a kingdom without a king (God would be king)" (1986, 107). But if this is so, then the question of what is the "promised land" can only be answered by working backward from the biblical conception of God as *melekh.*

In *Kingdom of God*, Buber's first point is that the God of Israel is not rooted to a specific territory. This God is not a Baal, a local divinity of the land, because He is precisely the One that "leads" a people out of their autochthony and promises them another (kind of) place on earth.[33] Before addressing the characteristics of this other place or space, it is useful to consider that Buber prioritizes, to use the terms of Soloveitch and Hartman, the covenant of Exodus over and above the covenant of Sinai (Buber 1964, 610–5). The priority given to Exodus shows that Buber's theopolitics of Homeland, whatever else it may be, entails in any case an understanding of the kind of politics that is fitting for a people for which its "motherland" and "fatherland" are both in question. To this extent, Buber retains Rosenzweig's intuition of the opposition between Torah and the control over a determined territory exercised by the nation-state. God qua *melekh* does *not* call for a people that has been made possible by the violent appropriation and settlement of land, but, rather, for a people that is willing to embark on the contrary "oceanic" movement of an exodus from the land in which they were born.

Walzer argues that if one constructs a conception of political freedom out of the experience of Exodus, then freedom becomes internally linked with the idea

[32] (Schmitt 2001, 84). See also the discussion in (Ojakangas 2009, 46; Gross 2005, 98–113; and Loughlin 2015). Interestingly, Gross does not cite or comment on Schmitt's use of the biblical citation, and Loughlin also ignores it.

[33] Arendt later says that "Abraham . . . shows such a passionate drive toward making covenants that it is as though he departed from his country for no other reason than to try out the power of mutual promise in the wilderness of the world, until eventually God himself agreed to make a Covenant with him" (1958, 243–4).

of a (political) movement initiated by a people: "change of position is a common metaphor for change of regime . . . progressive parties, advanced ideas, vanguard politics, revolution . . . movement itself, as in 'the labor movement' " (1986, 15). In Weimar Germany, this association of Exodus with the movement of an entire people was not only linked with parts of the Zionist program to resettle European Jews in Palestine. The Communist and the National Socialist parties also understood themselves as giving political direction to the revolutionary "movement" of society itself. Right-wing intellectuals like Schmitt, Jünger, and Heidegger, for a short period of time and with different strategies, believed they could "oversee" the direction in which the official leader of the movement of the German "conservative revolution" took the German *Volk*. The idea was "to lead the leader" [*der Führer führen*].[34]

To Schmitt's conception of divine law as a function of the violent appropriation of land, Buber responds through his conception of YHWH as *melekh* of His people who leads them not in a war against other nations for territorial expansion, but in the conquest of a *political space of no-rule* within society. The primary sense in which YHWH leads His people to the "promised Land" is by "overseeing" (*walten*) the *whole* ethical and political life of a people. YHWH rejects His localization within a specific social sub-system or sphere: YHWH should be "restricted" neither to the place of the sacred (i.e., a Church) nor to the place of the private (i.e., individual conscience), for both reduce Him to being merely a "religious" (as opposed to also a political and social) reality.[35] Schmitt understood the concept of "the political" as referring to a process of politicization that can happen anywhere and everywhere in society, whenever an issue is converted into a matter of "life-and-death" for a group within society.[36] For Buber, YHWH is the vector of a politicization of a people that seeks to establish society on principles of non-domination.

By comparison with Schmitt, Buber's engagement with and response to Heidegger's discourse in the 1930s is a more complicated and ambiguous affair. In explaining the sense in which YHWH is "the Lord of History, the 'King' " (Buber 1964, 624), Buber employs idioms related to the existential discourse on *Da-sein*. For Buber, YHWH is He who says "I am who I am" [Exodus 3:14, *ehyeh asher ehyeh*] in the sense that He is "here" where his people are [*da (hier) sein*]

[34] (Pöggeler 1985).

[35] "He is not satisfied with being 'God' in a religious sense because He does not want to give over to one human being what is not 'God's', namely, the regime over the whole actuality of worldly life [*das Regiment über die ganze Tatsächlichkeit des weltlichen Lebens*]" (Buber 1964, 647).

[36] For a discussion of this point that is especially pertinent in the discussion between Schmitt and Strauss, see (Meier 1995). On the concept of the "political" in Schmitt, see (Vatter 2008b). This idea of "the political" is then taken up by contemporary political theory under the rubric of "post-foundational" or "agonistic politics." For a discussion of its origins in post-Marxist thought, see (Marchart 2007).

but also He will also be "there" in ways that will be always unexpected for them [*ich werde da sein*].[37] As Buber explains, for YHWH to be understood as "He who is there [*Der* da *ist*]" means that He is never at the disposal of His people, magically recallable at will. YHWH is neither something "ready at hand" nor something "present to hand," to employ Heidegger's categories for the kind of presence of beings. On Buber's description, YHWH's modes of showing and hiding are closer to the ontological dimension of what Heidegger will call in the 1930s, Beyng [*Seyn*] as Event [*Ereignis*].

Conversely, Heidegger's attempts in the 1930s to connect Beyng with the historical existence of peoples and in particular with the question of the Fatherland, employ a language that is uncannily similar to that employed by Buber in *Kingdom of God*. Thus, in the *Beiträge zur Philosophie*, Heidegger writes: "a people is a people only if it receives its history as allotted to it through finding its god, the god that compels this people beyond itself and thus places the people back amid the beings. Only then does a people escape the danger of circling around itself and of idolizing, as its unconditioned, what are merely conditions of its subsistence. . . . The essence of a people is grounded in the historicality of those who belong themselves through their belonging to the god" (1989, 398). Given my argument that Buber's theopolitics plays a role in the development of Arendt's conception of a "Jewish politics in general," and given the well-known debate on Heidegger's influence on the development of Arendt's political thought, it seems important to address here, if only partially, the question of Heidegger's political theology in the 1930s.

Among the very few Jewish individuals that Heidegger actively sought out after the war, the best known are Arendt, Celan, and Buber. Heidegger adhered to National Socialism in the early 1930s and he maintained a much decried and discussed "silence" after the war with respect to the Shoah until his death. After the illusion of being able to offer a philosophical "leadership" to the German *Führer* vanished in 1934, Heidegger's thinking undertook a "turn" [*Kehre*] in which the task to "oversee" the possibility of a political life of a people was seen to reside principally in poetry rather than in philosophy. In the lectures of 1934 dedicated to Hölderlin's hymn *Germania*, Heidegger seeks an answer to the burning political question of the "Dasein of the peoples." His central hypothesis is that "the Dasein of the peoples in each case springs from poetry" rather than from philosophy or politics (2014, 22). Setting aside for a moment the question of the

[37] See also Buber's formulation of the two types of faith: "Of course 'faith' should not be understood in the same way as in the Epistle to the Hebrews (11,6): believing that God is. This was never in doubt for the soul of Israel [*die Jakobseele*]: when they confess their faith, their *Emuna*, they confess only that they trust an existing God [*dem seienden Gott*] that He, just like the forefathers had experienced, (Genesis 28:20; 35:3) will be with Israel [*bei ihr da sei*], and they entrust themselves to He who exists by them [*dem bei ihr Daseienden*]" (Buber 1963, 202). See also the commentary in (Mendes-Flohr 2019, 141ff).

similarity and distinction between poetry and prophecy in Jewish thought and in Heidegger, there is an evident sense in which the discourse of Jewish political theology in the 20th century also seeks the answer to the question of the *Dasein* of the Jewish people from the poetic and prophetic books of the Bible. Additionally, Heidegger sought to determine the question of the *Da-sein* of peoples in relation to Hölderlin's meditations on the Homeland and the Fatherland.[38] But he was preceded by Buber's introduction of the politico-theological problem of finding a land of one's own, a "homeland" for the revival of the Jewish Torah. It was Buber who thematized the problem of *Heimat* in relation to the sovereignty of God, *Gottesherrschaft*, before Heidegger began to speak of the *Herrschaft des Seyns* in connection with Hölderlin's meditations on *Heimat* and the hidden God.

Buber's connection between God's leadership of His people and the opening of a political space alternative to national sovereignty anticipates by a few years Heidegger's simultaneous "politicization" and "spatialization" of the discourse on *Da*-sein in his *Introduction to Metaphysics* of 1935, where he claims that the *Da-* of *Dasein* refers to the space of the *polis* which does not designate a state as much as "the historical site [*Geschichtsstätte*], the 'there' in which, out of which, and for which history happens [*Geschichte geschieht*]."[39] The extant scholarship on the Buber-Heidegger exchanges mainly focuses on their early discussions on the intersubjective dimension of human existence in relation to Buber's 1923 classic work *I and Thou* and Heidegger's conception of *Mitsein* in *Being and Time*, or they treat their postwar discussion of the relation between thinking, acting, and language.[40] The relation between Buber's theo-political formulation of the *Da-sein* of God with Heidegger's contemporaneous turn to political theology and to a topological approach to ontology remains an outstanding task.

The secondary literature that has focused on the "topological" turn in Heidegger has so far mostly ignored his discourse of political theology.[41]

[38] "The 'fatherland'" is Beyng itself, which from the ground up bears and configures the history of a people as an existing [*daseienden*] people" (Heidegger 1980, 109). But Peter Fenves suggests that this theo-political reading of the German poet is already found in Benjamin's text *Two Poems by Friedrich Hölderlin* of 1916 (Fenves 2011, 18–43). Of particular significance is Scholem's remark that Hölderlin "lived the Zionist life among the German people" (ibid., 40).

[39] (Heidegger 1961a, 151–2). On the *Introduction to Metaphysics*, see now the essays in (Polt and Fried 2001), which, however, do not mention Buber or other contemporary Jewish thinkers. For a similar definition, see also: "The polis is *polos*, that is, the pole, the swirl or vortex in which and around which everything turns" (Heidegger 1996, 100); and "[the polis] is neither merely state [*Staat*] nor merely the city [*Stadt*] rather in the first instance it is properly "the stead" [*die Statt*]: the site [*die Stätte*] of the abode of human history.... From which all human relations toward beings ... are determined" (ibid., 102–3). See the discussion in (Elden 2000).

[40] The vicissitudes of the "dialogue" between Buber and Heidegger has been treated several times, from (Theunissen 1984; to Novak 2013; and Mendes-Flohr 2014). To my knowledge there is no discussion of Buber's engagement with the question of *Da-sein* in relation to *Kingdom of God*. The comparison between Heidegger's and Buber's ideas of nationalism discussed in (Hadad 2017) remains within the focus of the problem of language and dialogue.

[41] Judith Wolfe points to the internal connection between Heidegger's political theology and his turn to a topology of Beyng: in 1934 Heidegger characterized the German people by their

Some interpreters have used the topology of Beyng to distinguish Heidegger's discourse on the Fatherland both from the "politics" of the Hitler regime and from the "political" of Schmitt.[42] Others see in Heidegger's idea of the *polis* as a "space of appearing" a source for Arendt's later discussion of the Greek polis in the *Human Condition*.[43] My interest here is to indicate a different constellation through which Buber's and Heidegger's parallel investigations into the idea of "Homeland" may have suggested to Arendt the need to rethink the commonality between Jerusalem and Rome, not in the Zionist sense inaugurated by Moses Hess, but in the direction of a republican civil religion. Roman civil religion is polytheist, Jewish political theology is strictly monotheistic: how is a bridge between these at all conceivable? Heidegger's interpretations of Hölderlin suggest a possible path, even though it is one not taken up by Heidegger himself.

Heidegger's turn to a topology of Beyng in relation to his interpretation of Hölderlin's poetry occurs at the same time as he develops a discourse on political theology in the *Black Notebooks* culminating in his unpublished book of 1936, *Beiträge zur Philosophie*. The publication of these *Notebooks* has given a crucial impetus to the ongoing polemical discussion of Heidegger's involvement with National Socialism. According to Donatella di Cesare's in-depth account of the *Notebooks*, Heidegger's political theology in the 1930s is characterized by a "metaphysical anti-Semitism." The *Notebooks*, on her reading, have as their central theme the idea of "a political conflict between the dominance of machination, the *Macht der Machenschaft*, and the sovereignty of Being, the *Herrschaft des Seyns*." But "the violent, metaphysical power of machination is the Jewish power . . . devoid of roots and of land" (Cesare 2018, 97–8).[44] There is no doubt that Heidegger's discussions of "Jews," "Judaism," and "world-Jewry" in the *Notebooks* reflect typical anti-Semitic tropes linking the historical existence of the Jewish people with "rootlessness." However, this fact leaves untouched the

godlessness, requiring that "it [the German people] . . . empty itself through 'complete conversion' and 'silent waiting' [GA 94, 170] to prepare a space into which the radically other 'god' can descend. Unlike death, this god determines the people's essence not by negation but by donation: the god 'must already have arrived if a people is to find its essence' " (Wolfe 2017, 39).

42 See the discussions in (Elden 1999; Malpas 2012; and Phillips 2005).

43 On Arendt's purported debt to Heidegger's (political) ontology or (political) existentialism, and whether her notion of plurality is more or less comparable to his conception of *Mitsein*, see (Taminiaux 1985; Villa 2008) and more recently (Flakne 2012; and Menga 2018).

44 Citing (Heidegger 2017), sections 24 and 37, in which Heidegger claims that "the power of Judaism" understood as an "empty rationality and calculative capacity" was "expanded" in modern times by attaching itself to metaphysics, and "thereby [Jews] created for themselves an abode in the 'spirit' without ever being able, on their own, to grasp concealed decisive domains." Jeffrey Malpas acknowledges what he calls the "extreme thinking" of Heidegger in this period, but believes the anti-Semitism remains "contingent": "they arise out of the obsessive attempt to think being, and only being, and to do so in a way that also reads the contemporary state of the world in the light of that obsession" (2018, 111). Malpas does not see any relation between Heidegger's simultaneous "focus on place" and his discourse on political theology.

question of what Heidegger may have thought about the Zionist path taken up by Jewish thinkers like Buber who argued for a Jewish homeland as an essential aspect of the theopolitical teaching of the Torah.

In a recent discussion of the similarities between Heidegger's discourse in the 1930s and Jewish political theology, Michael Fagenblat suggests that Heidegger's way of reading Hölderlin's idea of the "fatherland" somehow corresponds with "the *land* of Israel or Zion—not Zionism but Zion—[which] is the mythopoetic political ground of being Jewish historically" (2017, 257, emphasis mine). More particularly, Heidegger's discourse on the "Fatherland" would share an affinity with the "Zion traditions"[45] that bring about a shift in the way that YHWH dwells among His people from "an extraterritorial no man's land . . . [and] the anarchistic tendencies associated with the Sinaitic traditions" to a "territorialization of YHWH into political form and place" beginning with the Davidic kingdom (Fagenblat 2017, 259). Perhaps more than drawing motifs from the discourse of political Zionism, as Fagenblat's interpretative hypothesis suggests, Heidegger's discourse on the topology of Beyng may have applied to the German *Volk* features that are already found in Buber's cultural and anarchistic thematization of the "Homeland."[46]

Other interpreters argue that Heidegger's turn to Hölderlin is part of his overarching aim to oppose "Jewish-Christian monotheism as a political system of sovereign power based on the metaphysical-technological subject from the perspective of a mythotheology of Greek and poetical polytheism of being."[47] This anti-Christian polemic is also underwritten by a "radical anti-Judaism" because "Judaism is the source of monotheism and its logos."[48] However, the texts of Hölderlin's poems *Germania* and *Der Rhein* that are cited and commented by Heidegger in his 1934/1935 lectures cast into question such a binary opposition between Jewish monotheism and Greek polytheism. There is a straightforward sense in which Hölderlin's poetry is itself infused by a strict monotheism as well as by a doctrine of the divine Logos. For instance, Heidegger repeatedly stresses that Hölderlin always has in view "the essence of the uniqueness of the divine being [*das Wesen der Einzigkeit des Gottwesens*]" (Heidegger 1989, 406). This emphasis on the singularity of

[45] Fagenblat refers to the hypothesis in (Levenson 1987, 91).

[46] Fagenblat says that "Heidegger's Germans of 1934/35, then, are not properly rooted in the fatherland. Perhaps for this reason they resemble the malevolent portrait of the Jews in the *Black Notebooks* whose 'emphatic talent for calculation' likewise results from their 'absolutely unbound' type of humanity" (2017, 262).

[47] (Schmidt 2017, 132). Schmidt follows Habermas's conviction that Heidegger rejected Judeo-Christian monotheism because he sought to retrieve pagan polytheism (Habermas 1989).

[48] (Schmidt 2017, 146). The key opposition here is between "the monotheistic God" and, even more precisely, Christ as Logos, "who through his calculating reason represents nature in its objectivity and who is model of man's own sovereign power" and the "gods of the Physis [which] are names for a non-instrumental relation between man and nature" (Schmidt 2017, 140).

the divinity as the sole, unique, true Beyng is typical of Jewish philosophical monotheism developed by Philo's reading of the biblical God as equivalent to the *to on* of Greek Pythagorean-Platonic philosophy and its associated Mysteries. Even the belief claim that Judaism is reducible to the "logos" of "monotheism" is too coarse a representation of the Jewish tradition: it would not apply to *the mystical approach of the Kabbalah*, nor would it fit the *philosophical approach of Philo*, as discussed in previous chapters.[49]

The discussion of monotheism and polytheism in Hölderlin's poetry, and in Heidegger's interpretation of this poetry, is highly complicated and overdetermined.[50] The complex interplay between Heidegger's 1934 interpretation of Hölderlin's *Germania* and the texts from the German poet that Heidegger refers to but does not always interpret in his lectures indicates both where he rejects the Jewish tradition and where he may borrow from it. For example, in order to justify the privilege assigned to poetry in relation to the manifestation of Beyng, Heidegger cites a passage from *Hyperion* in which Hölderlin says that the Greeks understood the One as divine beauty which begets art, from art comes religion, and from religion comes the state.[51] For Hölderlin, it was the poetic approach to the One—that is, the Orphic formulation of the divine Mysteries—that made the Greeks into a philosophical people, not vice versa. Hölderlin's thesis coincides with the thesis defended by Philo, if one follows Goodenough's interpretation. It resonates with the belief of the Jewish tradition according to which the revealed Torah is a "teaching" that provides a poetic, philosophical, and political education into the ways of the One God.

In *Hyperion*, Hölderlin follows this parallelism between Greek Mysteries and Jewish Torah, long established by Philo, when he claims that the divine Light emanating from the One is first taken up by poetry and only subsequently transmitted to the intellect in the form of philosophy. Hölderlin believed that for the Greeks, the religious and poetic Mysteries took priority over the development of Greek philosophy. Again, this mirrors the priority of revelation over philosophy in Judaism. Heidegger accepts this priority without question: "the

49 This point seems to be borne out in the recent interpretation of Heidegger's theological discourse proposed by Eliot Wolfson, the well-known scholar of Kabbalah. Wolfson compares Heidegger's discourse on the "last god" to the Jewish belief in the Messiah: "god is not to be found in beings but only in beyng. Heidegger thereby undermines the theistic idea of the immanence of the divine in the world: the trace of god shows itself nowhere. But it is precisely this nonshowing that the essence of the godship shows itself. In a way intriguingly reminiscent of the Jewish belief that the possibility of the Messiah's coming is predicated on the impossibility of the Messiah's arrival" (2017, 215).

50 See (Haar 1989) for the argument that Heidegger reverses the order of priority between the God and the Holy that is found in Hölderlin's poems.

51 The passage runs: "The first child of divine Beauty is art. . . . Beauty's second daughter is religion. Religion is love of Beauty. . . . Without such a love of Beauty, without such a religion, every state is a dry skeleton without life and spirit" (Hölderlin 1984, 91–2).

poet harnesses the lightning flashes of the God, compelling them into the word, and places this lightning-charged word into the language of his people" (2014, 30). Adopting a Jewish prophetic vocabulary, Heidegger goes on to say that "the poet does not process the lived experiences of his psyche but stands 'under God's thunderstorms'—'with naked head' left without protection and delivered from himself. Dasein is nothing other than the exposure to the overwhelming power of Beyng" (2014, 30). For Heidegger, the German poet takes up the role of the Jewish prophet in giving "word" to the light (Logos) of the divine.

Heidegger and Buber share the idea that the answer to the question of the Dasein of peoples has to do with the meaning given to the "historicity of peoples." Rosenzweig had given a decisive impulse to this question by claiming that the historicity of Western nations sought to imitate the mode of dwelling on earth pioneered by the Jewish people: a dwelling that is oriented by an idea of "eternal life" and by the redemption of nature. Heidegger pursues the problem of the temporality of peoples through Hölderlin's belief that "this originary, historical time of the peoples is therefore the time of the poets, thinkers, and creators of the state—that is, of those who properly ground and found the historical Dasein of a people" (2014, 49). Now, in Hölderlin's poem *Germania* there is a clear reference to this "originary, historical time of the peoples" as being one that is determined or figured by a "prophetic mountain" and in reference to the "eternity" of "the God." These are allusions to Mount Sinai, the mountain where Moses the prophet/poet/founder receives the divine Light from the eternity of the One God and transmits it into the space of history in the symbolical form of the Holy Ark of the Torah.

Not surprisingly, in his lecture on *Germania*, Heidegger never gives a reading of the expression "prophetic mountain." However, he cannot avoid a discussion of "eternity" in relation to Hölderlin's conception of "der Gott [*to on*]". It is here where a real divergence with the contemporary discourse of Jewish political theology can be identified. For Heidegger simply *applies* to Hölderlin's text his own *earlier* discussion of temporality in *Being and Time* which was not developed in relation with an engagement with the German poet. Thus, Heidegger makes the totally unfounded claim that for Hölderlin "the God himself is 'time' " [as opposed to "eternity"]. From this claim he goes on to posit that "the definition of eternity is not itself self-contained: rather, our representation of what we call eternity and its concept are in each case determined in accordance with our guiding representation of time" (Heidegger 2014, 52). This is clearly false in the case of Hölderlin but is a key doctrine of Heidegger's.

Heidegger then proceeds to argue that the concept of eternity is merely the hypostatization of "a particular experience of time, namely, time as the pure sequential flowing of nows."[52] Leaving aside whether Heidegger's account of eternity is tenable, it is undeniable that it stands in direct contradiction with the text by Hölderlin (*Fragment 13*, IV, 246) that Heidegger cites as proof of the validity of his own reading. In fact, in this fragment Hölderlin says: "And for this reason free will and the higher power to command and to accomplish have been given to the godlike, that most dangerous of goods, language has been given to the humans so that, creating, destroying, and perishing, and *returning to the eternally living*, to *the mistress and Mother*, that they may bear witness to what they are, their heritage, learnt from her, *the most divine of her attributes, all-sustaining love*."[53] In his interpretation, Heidegger provides an anthropocentric and historicist reading that omits reference to the "eternal life" and "all-sustaining love" of Mother Earth.

It is difficult to judge the significance of Heidegger's reticence to speak of the Greek Mysteries and the relation between "the god," *to on*, and the cult of Demeter, even as these ideas are reflected in Hölderlin's poetry. However, in his interpretation of the coming into being of a homeland, Heidegger speaks of "a nurturing of the Earth for the gods, in which the Earth is held open for an encounter with the prevailing of the gods in the course of the changing seasons of the year and their festivals" (2014, 95) that can be taken as a reference to the doctrine of intelligible matter as *khora*, which in the Greek Mysteries is often associated with the cult of Demeter and Dionysus.[54] Here there remains a trace of the ancient connection between the cultivation of the earth and religious cult that plays such a central role in Rosenzweig's analysis of the Jewish calendar of festivals. As discussed in chapter 1 on Philo and in chapter 4 on Scholem, it is precisely the Eleusinian Mysteries in relation to Demeter and Dionysus that prepared the ground for the reception of a Jewish discourse on the "redeemer God" in Hellenism. In this sense, Hölderlin's poetic text is a testament to a reception within German philosophy of the paradoxical phenomenon of *Greek* monotheism and of *Jewish* panentheism (by which is meant a gnostic form of Judaism) that problematizes the simplistic opposition of Jewish *monotheism* and Greek *polytheism*. Scholem employed the resources of this paradoxical crossing of the Jewish with the Greek in his own reconstruction of the relation between the idea of messianism and its relation to the question of a Jewish Homeland (Zion). As it turns out, Scholem was not alone in this venture, since Arendt would also turn toward this crossing in her thinking about "Jewish politics in general" in relation to Roman civil religion (Virgil) and in relation to the political teaching of Jesus.

[52] *Sempiternitas* simply refers to "a never-ending sequence of nows" while *aeternitas* refers to "an encompassing now" (Heidegger 2014, 52).

[53] Cited in (Heidegger 2014, 56, emphasis mine).

[54] Heidegger mentions *khora* in (Heidegger 1961).

From biblical charisma to Roman constitutionalism: The legal problem of the absolute

Buber's *Kingdom of God* can be read as a discourse on the relation between revolution and constitution. Buber reconstructs God's "rule" as a function of *hesed* (God's "convenantal faithfulness and kindness" as Walzer translates it, but which is better rendered as "grace" or, more politically, as "charisma") that cannot be fully institutionalized or stabilized by any arrangement of human offices or division of power (by any form of *brit* or covenant between people and God).[55] In this sense, Buber's treatise shows that the introduction of the "absolute" (represented by YHWH's *walten*) into politics grounds the superiority of constituent power (*hesed*) over constituted power (*brit*), and is thereby tied to the possibility of revolutions and new beginnings.[56] This claim opens the central problem faced by Arendt's mature political theory: how can the revolutionary principle of no-rule or principle of anarchy become the ground or foundation of a constitutional government or rule of law?

Arendt thought that modern revolutions are caught up in "Sieyes's vicious circle: those who get together to constitute a new government are themselves unconstitutional, that is, they have no authority to do what they have set out to achieve. . . ." (1990, 184). In order to address this predicament, secular modern revolutions felt "the need for a divine principle, for some transcendent sanction in the political realm" (1990, 186). Moyn argues that Arendt's conception of the biblical covenant is her answer to the problem of the authority of the law on the basis of a revolutionary break with the law.[57] My interpretation is different in that I claim that Arendt employs the biblical covenant model to think about power in anarchic terms, but her solution to the problem of the authority of the law does not depend on the biblical covenant model. Rather, Arendt draws on an entirely different religious paradigm which has pagan and philosophical origins.

Arendt appeals to an account of covenants to establish her republican conception of power. She famously argues that "power comes into being only if and when men join themselves together for the purpose of action, and it will disappear when, for whatever reason, they disperse and desert one another" (1990, 175). This echoes the way in which Buber describes how YHWH as *melekh* "accompanies" His people. Arendt distinguishes "two kinds of 'social contract'" (1990, 169): the one is based on "consent" to the command of a sovereign, the other on

[55] See here Weber: "As far as can be determined this unstable Israelite confederation till the time of kings had no permanent political organs at all. . . . Confederate unity found expression in that a Yahwe certified war hero or war prophet regularly claimed authority also beyond the boundaries of the tribe. People came to him from afar to have him settle their legal disputes or to seek instruction in ritual or moral duties" (Weber 1952, 83).

[56] Andreas Kalyvas has picked up this problem in relation to Weber and Arendt in (Kalyvas 2009).

[57] (Moyn 2008). See also (Klusmeyer 2009) who shares this thesis.

the "mutual promise" between the members of a people in view of generating their power (1990, 177). Arendt's interpretation of the biblical covenant is clearly drawn from Buber's an-archic interpretation of the *brit*: she distinguishes the covenant that generates government from the contract that generates the power of the people. Only the latter makes it possible for a people "to be free . . . neither to rule nor to be ruled. . . . To be free meant to be free from the inequality present in rulership and to move in a sphere where neither rule nor being rule existed" (Arendt 1958, 32–3).[58]

Perhaps the central achievement of *On Revolution* is the principled separation of the concepts of power and authority: whereas power is synonymous with freedom, authority is related to the legitimacy of law.[59] It is a central hypothesis of *On Revolution* that the American Revolution kept the power of the people distinct from the authority of the law, whereas the French Revolution united power and authority in a concept of the sovereignty of the nation.[60] That is why Arendt claims that "the chief problem of the American Revolution . . . turned out to be the establishment and foundation *not of power but of authority*" (1990, 178, emphasis mine).

If Arendt's appeal to the biblical covenant was meant to replace the Schmittian politico-theological conception of authority, as Moyn suggests, then he would be correct to claim that she engages in a self-contradiction because "the notion of the covenant is one of the hoariest theological concepts there is . . . the final paragraph of the *Declaration of Independence*, which features the mutual-pledge language, also appeals to 'the Supreme Judge of the world' and to 'the protection of divine providence.' How could the covenants be an answer to Schmitt when, as a matter of historical fact, they would seem to perfectly exemplify his claims?" (Moyn 2008, 87). But given the principled separation of power from authority in Arendt, the answer to Moyn's question is that Arendt's response to Schmitt's political theology is not found in her theory of power or covenant, but only in her own account of authority, which does not rely on the idea of divine commandments at all, thus separating in principle the role of religion and churches from the substance of secular law.

Arendt does acknowledge the influence of the Christian Church in the political tradition of the West, which meant that "secular laws were understood

58 The novel application of the biblical covenant in the American Revolution, unlike in the Puritan compact, entails "a political body in which rulers and ruled would be equal, that is, where actually the *whole principle of rulership no longer applied*" (Arendt 1990, 172, emphasis mine). Her point, if one can put it so paradoxically, is that the American revolutionaries were far more "Jewish" (in the Buberian, anarchic reading of the *brit*) than the Puritan Pilgrims.

59 I have defended this interpretation of Arendt in (Vatter 2005, 2007). Recent discussions like that in (Wilkinson 2012) and (Volk 2016) still tend to confound the question of political power with that of legal authority.

60 In the French case, "both power and law were anchored in the nation, or rather in the will of the nation, which itself remained outside and above of all government and all laws" (Arendt 1990, 163).

as the mundane expression of a divinely ordained law" (1990, 186–9). But she does not accept that this belief was also held by the authors of the republican tradition. For Arendt, laws can be understood independently of this divine command structure inherited from Christian religion, as shown by the Greek and Roman conceptions of the law which, despite their differences, do not rely on religious sanction because they are not conceived in analogy with a divine command (1990, 189ff). Arendt's recovery of Greek and Roman conceptions of the law is done in full awareness that for "ancient nations" religion is an outgrowth of what Rousseau calls "divine natural right" or divine *nomoi* (laws), in the sense that religion is a phenomenon that depends on the primacy of law, and not conversely as is the case in Christianity. The problem of the absolute manifests itself only when a conception of law is subsumed under the model of a divine command. But in those theologico-political traditions where law is not conceived as a divine command, as occurs in the Greek and Roman traditions,[61] and then again in modernity (not only with Montesquieu but already since Marsilius and Machiavelli), the problem of the absolute need not be resolved by finding an adequate secular proxy, as Moyn suggests.

Arendt's alternative solution turns on a pre-Christian, civil-religious connection between piety and the idea of a "return to beginnings." Arendt's appeal to pagan civil religion is evident in her famous interpretation of the U.S. Constitution: "If their [the American people] attitude towards Revolution and Constitution can be called religious at all, *then the word 'religion" must be understood in its original Roman sense*, and their piety would then consist in *religare*, in binding themselves back to a beginning, as Roman *pietas* consisted in *being bound back to the beginning* of Roman history, the foundations of the eternal city" (Arendt 1990, 189, emphasis mine). Here one can say that the law (viz., the constitution) comes before religion, and not religion before the law.[62] Arendt's

[61] See here the long discussion of Greek versus Roman ideas of law in (Arendt 2003, 108–22).

[62] The crucial role played by the ancient idea of civil religion in Arendt is easily missed because she herself does not properly thematize the civil conception of religion on which her own arguments nonetheless rely. Thus, in a key passage, she cites John Adams's appeal to the civil religion of the ancients and misconstrues his intentions: "It is all more noteworthy that John Adams . . . should have believed that 'it was the general opinion of ancient nations that the Divinity alone was adequate to the important office of giving laws to men.' For the point of the matter is that Adams was in error, and that neither the Greek *nomos* nor the Roman *lex* was of divine origin, that neither the Greek nor the Roman concept of legislation needed divine inspiration" (Arendt 1990, 186). In reality, Arendt and Adams, in this as in many other points, are actually in agreement, because Adams was referring to a pagan conception of the relation between divinity and law, according to which god's "rule" over human beings finds expression in constitutional, rather than monarchical, rule and was the opposite of the Christian concept of law derived from Paul. Another example is Arendt's citation of Machiavelli to the effect that the highest exemplars of humanity are those individuals "who have reformed republics and kingdoms with new laws and institutions" (Arendt 1990, 202): if read in its proper context, Machiavelli is referring to the ancient figure of the givers of religion as law, that is, to founders of civil religions. It is highly likely that Adams may have been inspired by Machiavelli's discussion of civil religion.

concept of authority, then, depends on a civil religion that takes as its starting point the political constitution: "one is tempted to conclude that it was the authority which the act of foundation carried within itself, rather than the belief in an Immortal Legislator . . . that assured stability for the new republic" (1990, 199). The act of foundation as the source of the authority of the laws of the republic clearly bears no resemblance to a substitution for any absolute, e.g. for the act of Creation. That is why she can claim that "it would be the act of foundation itself, rather than an Immortal Legislator or self-evident truth or any other transcendent, transmundane source, which eventually would become the foundation of authority in the new body politic" (1990, 204).

The "act of foundation" contains both a political and a legal meaning: it refers both to "the constituting act . . . by which a people constitutes itself into a body politic" and to "the result of this act, the Constitution as written document" (Arendt 1990, 203). After all, the "worship" of the American Constitution referred to "at least as much the act of constituting as it was the written document itself" (1990, 204). But how does political power get transmuted into legal authority? And what role does civil religion play in this transformation? The civil-religious basis of legal authority shows that such authority has the structure of a "return to beginnings":

> To remain tied back to the beginning of the ancestors in pious remembrance and conservation meant to have Roman *pietas, to be "religious" or "bound back" to one's own beginnings*. . . . The very coincidence of authority, tradition, and religion, all three simultaneously springing from the act of foundation, was the backbone of Roman history from beginning to end. . . .To the Romans, at least, the conquest of Italy and the building of an empire were legitimate to the extent that the conquered territories enlarged the foundation of the city and remained tied to it. (Arendt 1990, 201, emphasis mine)

This Roman conception of *re-ligio* as source of legal authority is distinct from the belief in a Creator God who begins Creation only once, and whose absolute sanction is needed for laws, because it is internally tied to a moment of repetition, and is based on the requirement to *begin anew* or to engage in a *re-naissance* of the foundations through their "conservation and augmentation" (1990, 201). One meaning of legal authority as *re-ligio* is that the legal order must be self-authorizing: what authorizes laws is that they can be "led back" to the constitution (in the last instance of judicial review), viz., that they can be seen to derive from the first constitution, and not from the first moment of generation of power. However, if the return to beginnings is the authorizing mechanism of laws, it is also the case that the legitimacy of the constitution is tested or verified if and only if actual beginnings (i.e., moments of popular empowerment) occur in and through the returns to constitutional principles. If a return to constitutional principles does not empower the citizens, the constitution will fail to root itself in the people. Thus, legal authority for Arendt is only possible if it is understood in terms of the inherent iterability of revolution: beginning and return to beginning, revolution and authority, must be internally related.[63]

In a recent book, Andrew Arato has offered an interpretation of Arendt's dualism of power and authority that distinguishes a concept of "constituent authority" from that of Schmitt's "constituent power."[64] Arato takes "authority" to refer to a legal continuum that makes possible a discontinuity, for instance the authoring of a new Constitution, without having to appeal to a Schmittian idea of "absolute" constituent power. However, Arato's separation of power and authority is dissimilar from Arendt's because for her the whole point is that legal authority is a continuity that is fashioned as a function of the *repetition* of revolutionary beginnings. For Arendt these beginnings are discontinuous—she speaks of the "problem of the beginning, of an unconnected, new event breaking into the continuous sequence of historical time" (1990, 205)—and do not themselves rely on a preexisting legal continuum. Notwithstanding, these beginnings also carry with them their own principle of continuity, on which legal authority comes to rest. Arendt's systematic point is that, precisely because the beginning is not absolute (since it is founded on covenants and is therefore contingent), it can and must be *repeated*; and it is through this iteration that the beginning becomes a source of legal authority. Authority therefore does not presuppose an absolute foundation. But it does require an account of how beginning and repetition are internally connected. The question of civil religion, which gets concretized in her interpretation of Virgil, is designed to explain such a paradoxical account of beginnings as both discontinuous and continuous, as both revolutionary and legally authorized.

Arendt's Virgil: civil religion and natality

The question of why Virgil comes to occupy such an inordinate importance in the overall system of Arendt's political thought has rarely been posed and remains unanswered. Her two main works of maturity, *On Revolution* and *The Life of the Mind*, both effectively conclude on a nearly identical reading of Virgil, as if this repetition underscored the significance of the Roman poet for the Jewish

[63] So much is clear from previous debates on the iterability of constituent power, which, however, fail to acknowledge the civil-religious origins of this conception. See the debate started from Habermas's response to Rawls on constitutional iterations, from (Honig 2001; to Frank 2010; and Lindahl 2007).

[64] See (Arato 2016, 22ff).

political thinker. Dean Hammer is correct to say that the Roman aspect of Arendt's thought has not been fully appreciated in the secondary literature when compared to the tendency to see her as advocating a renewal of Greek political thought and in particular as a form of neo-Aristotelianism (Hammer 2002). Arendt's turn to the exemplar of Roman politics is, in the first instance, determined by her belief that a republican politics depends on the principled separation of the power of the people from legal authority, where such a separation seeks to provide the generation of political power with a legal stability that it would otherwise lack.

But why does Arendt need the reference to Virgil's poetry over and above a generic adoption of the Roman idea of *auctoritas*? Arendt may have conceived of her interpretation of Virgil as a response to Heidegger's own 1930s interpretations of Hölderlin's idea that it is the poet who is the true founder of a people's "homeland." As mentioned earlier, Heidegger turns to political theology after 1933 because he wanted to preserve the "spirit" of the German conservative revolution alive despite his belief that Hitler's regime had put an end to that movement. Analogously, Buber sought to preserve within the Zionist movement the "spirit" of the anarchic and socialist revolution of the Bavarian soviet republic that failed in 1918. *Mutatis mutandis*, Arendt turns to Virgil's poetry in order to find a solution to this general problem: how can the "spirit" of republican revolutions live on once they have established a new constitution?[65] Like Heidegger's focus on the "temporality of peoples," Arendt speaks of this problem in terms of the temporality of revolution, caught between a "no longer and not yet," which in the Jewish political tradition finds its analogy in the problem of the transition from Exodus to Sinai.[66]

As I discussed earlier, Hölderlin's republican sympathies were given expression in his poetry in terms of elaborating a civil conception of religion that contained both pagan and biblical conceptions of the One God. Similarly, Arendt turns

[65] Antonio Negri argues that every legal constitution has the function of bringing to an end the revolutionary process. The establishment of a constituted power spells the end of constituent power; the institutionalisation of *potestas* (understood as identical with legal *auctoritas*) puts an end to *potentia* (understood as identical with the power of the people) (Negri 1999). For another equivalent idea, see (Brunkhorst 2012, 225): "The idea of a revolution that is permanent is the right idea, Arendt argues in accordance with Jefferson and Trotzki, but the problem is that one can avoid the tendency of totalitarian self-destruction of the revolution then and only then, if it is possible to constitutionalize the permanence of the revolution (and to include the reflexive operation of a permanent revolution of the constitution itself)."

[66] Partial confirmation for this hypothesis comes from Austin Harrington's finding that Arendt's preoccupation with beginnings, with the "gap between past and future," seems to have started only *after* her reading of Hermann Broch's *The Death of Virgil* published in 1946. "Again and again after 1946—and at no time before—Arendt wrote fervently of the 'abyss of freedom,' of the 'gap between past and future,' of the 'turning point of history,' of the order and rupture of the ages, of the act of beginning and the founding of principles, of "new generations" and of the inaugurating and reestablishing of a new-old world order of law" (Harrington 2008, 84).

to Virgil as the poet of the ideal of republicanism because she is receptive to the Weimar scholarly discovery that Virgil's political poetry may have contained a much closer correlation to the Jewish political experience than nearly all other works of pagan literature. At stake here is, in the first instance, the common experience by Romans and Jews of a crucial difference between liberation and freedom, on which build the analogies that she draws between Aeneas and Abraham. Thus, in *On Revolution*, as soon as Arendt leaves behind the problem of the absolute and starts to speak about the beginning as alternate source of authority, she turns to the parallelism between the stories of Exodus and "Virgil's story of the wanderings of Aeneas" (1990, 205). This is indication enough that Virgil's *Fourth Eclogue* will be interpreted by Arendt considering the problem of Jewish politics. What both narratives about political beginnings have in common is the presupposition of a wandering in the wilderness prior to the establishment of a new polity, "the eventual conquest of a promised land or the foundation of a new city" (1990, 205). Thus, the turn to Virgil belongs within the Judeo-Roman parallel with which Arendt began her political theorizing of a "Jewish politics in general" during the late 1930s. The phenomenon of revolution designates that spatial and temporal "stretch" or *durée* that happens after the event of liberation and before the event of foundation: "the legends unanimously tell us of great leaders [Moses and Aeneas] who appear on stage of history precisely in these gaps of historical time" (1990, 205).

But there is a far more crucial parallelism between Roman and Jewish political experiences that Arendt seeks to recover through Virgil, and this has to do with her original identification of natality as the solution to the paradox of the absolute, a solution which in Arendt is formalized in the claim that each new beginning contains its own principle [*arche*] within it (1990, 212). The concept of natality crowns her theoretical attempt to think political freedom as a function of the paradoxical coincidence of revolution and authority, of an-archy and stability. My claim is that Virgil's *Fourth Eclogue* is the "basic text" in which Arendt tries to show the inner relation between natality and legal authority. This in turn requires her to recover Jewish elements within the Roman conception of religion and authority.

It is often forgotten that Arendt's reflections on Virgil address natality just as much, if not more, than her well-known citation from Augustine's *City of God*: "*[Initium] ut esset, creatus est homo, ante quem nemo fuit. . . .* God created man in order to introduce into the world the faculty of beginning: freedom" (Arendt 1977, 167). Virgil is chosen by Arendt as the crucial textual resource for this audacious enterprise because of the messianic language found in the *Fourth Eclogue* that has given rise to the debate between so-called Westerner and Easterner readings of Virgil.[67] In short, Virgil is a text that lends itself to thinking about the translation of Rome into Judea and Judea into Rome, in a way that

[67] On this debate, see (Nisbet 1978).

reference to the *Iliad* (otherwise employed in the discussion of *archein* in the *Human Condition*) would not have helped. Arendt's theorizing of Jewish politics needed Virgil's subversive repetition of Homer.

In *Europe, la voie romaine* Rémi Brague describes the "Roman structure" or "spirit" in terms of its capacity to absorb materials coming from both "Athens" and "Jerusalem," the two more original roots of the Western tradition. The experience of Rome is that of an epigone: it is born after a more original source (Hellenism or Judaism), which it first adopts, then changes, and finally transmits to the future (1993, 56). Echoing the words of Arendt, he writes: "If Aeneas, the roman hero par excellence, is at the antipodes of Ulysses, who in the end returns home, then perhaps he is the best pagan analogue of Abraham, who leaves his land, his country and his father"s home. Similarly, one can put in parallel the foundation of Rome with the absence of a fatherland in the Jews [*la non-autochtonie des Hébreux*]" (1993, 73, translation mine). Yet, it is not Arendt whom Brague cites in this context. Interestingly, he refers this view to Theodor Haecker's *Vergil, Vater des Abendlandes*, published in 1931 in Weimar Germany.

Brague seems to be unaware of the ideological effect of this work in Weimar Germany and, more generally, of the political usage made of Virgil in the transition from Weimar to Nazi Germany. Haecker converted to Catholicism in the early 1920s and was at the forefront of a "Christian" appropriation of Virgil which, in its claim that the *imperium romanum* survives in modern Europe through the Roman Catholic Church, could easily be co-opted by Fascist interpretations of Virgil.[68] Indeed, as Richard Faber has shown, in the 1920s and 1930s, the Roman exemplar and standard was primarily raised by Fascist ideologues; it was a central discursive trope of the German "conservative revolution"; and the Third Reich, just like the Italian Fascist regime, eagerly sought parallels with the Roman Empire, in particular adopting Virgilian themes as the highest expression of a Roman "political theology."[69] It is this context that explains Schmitt's citation of Virgil at the close of *The Concept of the Political*, and this is also the crucial element if one is to understand Arendt's own recovery and "redemption" of Virgil out of this particular German reception.[70]

[68] On Haecker's conflictual relation with the Nazi Reich, see now (Tomko 2017). On Heidegger's not unsympathetic references to Haecker, see (Cesare 2018).

[69] On all these themes, see (Faber 1975, 1981).

[70] Dirk Moses believes that he has identified a Fascist and colonial core in Arendt's philo-Roman approach to the problem of Jewish politics. But the reason for this belief is simply that he collapses, without any evidence, Arendt's reading of Virgil onto these other, Christian and Fascist readings. Thus, he reads the *Aeneid* as an epic of colonial settlement: he claims that Arendt's "sympathies lie with the Trojans who were civilizing the natives by founding a political community with a temporal sense of origins . . ." (Moses 2013, 883). On his reading, Virgil and Arendt are both motivated by the principle that "civilization is spread by imperial conquest and settlement and justified by appeals to the cultural superiority of the colonists—exiles and migrants—with their settled agriculture over the autochthonous with their bare life" (ibid.). This claim implies that the Romans saw the Etruscans, and

That Roman beginnings are never absolute has important political consequences when it comes to thinking about the revolutionary character of beginnings. There are two political threats that such a conception of an iterable (hence, not ab-solute) beginning is meant to ward off for Arendt. The first is the temptation to link the collective act of beginning with the singular act of Creation. Arendt calls this option the "Hebrew solution" to the problem of the absolute: "the assumption of a Creator God who is outside his own creation in the same way as the fabricator is outside his fabricated object" (1990, 206). This solution is tied to the "age-old thought-customs of Western men, according to which each completely new beginning needs an absolute from which it springs and by which it is 'explained' " (1990, 206). But for Arendt, Creation is not itself a political or collective act like beginning. Indeed, even attributing the "Hebrew solution" to the Jewish tradition as such is not entirely unproblematic since the problem with setting up Creation in this role was already identified by Cohen and Rosenzweig. Both of them, and for the same reason, argued for a secret compatibility between the true meaning of Judaism and the doctrine of the eternity of the world.[71] What matters for Arendt is that the Founding Fathers of the American Republic avoided appeals to the Hebrew-Christian idea of a *creatio ex nihilo* when they tackled the problem of how to justify a beginning, and instead turned to Roman antiquity (1990, 206).

However, Roman thought harbors a threat of its own to a political conception of beginnings, namely, the temptation to recur to a dictatorial model of constituent power, much like Cicero called on Scipio to become the "*dictator rei publicae constituendae*" in the context of the Roman civil wars.[72] Arendt associates this temptation to rely on dictatorship in order to exercise constituent power with a belief she finds in Machiavelli and Robespierre: that "to found a new republic . . . must be the work of one man only."[73] The belief that political beginnings had to be "dictatorial" was based on imagining the founder as a builder who exercises violence on the pre-given human "material" in order

other Latin peoples, as "savages" in need of being "civilized." Moses does not provide any evidence of this claim, which is indeed difficult to find because, ultimately, they contradict basic beliefs of Roman civil religion and one of the central themes of classical culture, especially prevalent in Roman letters, namely, the belief that "first" peoples were more civilized and happier than subsequent civilizations. On classical "primitivism," see (Lovejoy and Boas 1997).

[71] See the argument in the preceding chapters dedicated to these thinkers.

[72] On the current discussion on the republican conception of dictatorship, compare (Kalyvas 2007; and Geuna 2017).

[73] Arendt refers to *Discourses on Livy* I:9 (Arendt 1990, 207). Here Arendt does not mention that Machiavelli had already recognized the "secondary" nature of Roman foundations that was linked with Numa's introduction of religion and law after Romulus. For Machiavelli, the figure of Numa is more important for the Roman becoming than Romulus.

to build a new polity. For Arendt, this need to be "alone" in the moment of foundation is due to the mistaken analogy between acting and making that has plagued the Western political tradition, as she argues extensively in the *Human Condition.*

The significant point in this discussion of Roman dictatorship is that Arendt does *not* abandon the Roman model for the Athenian one. To the contrary, from the start Arendt argues that Roman political thought has the resources to avoid both the Creationist and the Dictatorial models of fabrication: it is "because of the inner affinity between the arbitrariness inherent in all beginnings, and human potentiality for crime that the Romans decided to derive their descendants not from Romulus, who had slain Remus, but from Aeneas" (1990, 209). To avoid the Romulean beginning and its logic of violence, while remaining within the tradition of Roman republicanism, Arendt shifts her attention to Virgil's "second" narrative of foundation. From this Virgilian perspective, "all decisive political changes in the course of Roman history were reconstitutions . . . even this first act [of foundation] had been already a re-establishment, as it were, a regeneration and restoration" (1990, 208). Virgil becomes crucial to Arendt because the Roman poet articulates a conception of Rome as "second" Troy.[74] Anticipating much later analyses of Virgil's employment of catachresis,[75] she puts forward a reading of the *Aeneid* according to which the poem stages a repetition of the Trojan war that would reverse its outcome for the defeated and exterminated side: "the Trojan war *must be repeated* once more, and this meant to *reverse the order of events* as it was laid down in Homer's poem. The *reversal of Homer* is deliberate and complete in Virgil's great poem: there is again an Achilles possessed by indomitable rage. . . . Aeneas is obviously another Hector" (1990, 209, emphasis mine).

In the first instance, Arendt saw in Virgil's poetry a way to disconnect the beginning from the absolute, and instead link beginnings with a logic of repetition which is also one of subversion of the original model. The burden of the demonstration of this fundamental point is given over to her reading of the *Fourth Eclogue* which shows why "even the foundation of Rome was not understood as an absolutely new beginning" (Arendt 1990, 210). Arendt interprets the *Fourth Eclogue* as showing "constitution and foundation in terms of restoration and re-establishment. For in the reign of Augustus 'the great cycle of periods is born anew' . . . . *Magnus ab integro saeclorum nascitur ordo* . . . precisely because the 'order of periods' is not the American *novus ordo saeclorum* in the sense of an

[74] "The fable of Troy served Rome in two fundamental ways: it gave her a place in the cultural milieu of the Greek world—and, by the same token, it announced her distinctiveness in that world. Roman intellectuals welcomed incorporation in the cultural legacy of Hellas, but utilized it to sharpen a sense of their own identity" (Gruen 1990, 20).

[75] On Virgil's employment of catachresis, see the definitive (Quint 2011).

'absolutely new beginning'" (1990, 210). Much is at stake in unpacking this well-known claim.

Arendt's first point is that the *Fourth Eclogue* is not about an "absolutely new beginning." This last phrase is not a citation from any of the American Founding Fathers, but it comes from Eduard Norden's path-breaking interpretation of the *Fourth Eclogue* during the 1920s in Weimar Germany.[76] Norden was the first to argue not only that Virgil was influenced by "Oriental" (Jewish and Persian) messianic notions, but also that his poetry was prophetic with respect to the "absolute" break in history occasioned by the irruption of the Son of God into history, represented by Jesus Christ.[77] I will discuss Arendt's stance with respect to this "Oriental" hypothesis on Virgil in the following.

Arendt's second point in the preceding passage concerns the difference between the Roman idea of a re-constitution and the North American idea of an original constitution of freedom. Moyn cites the previous distinction between Roman and North American ideas of foundations as crucial evidence for his claim that Arendt's recovery of the Romans occurs only within the context of the North American "postreligious founding," a context that is both revolutionary and secular. After all, Arendt does say that the American Revolution was interested in "founding a new Rome" rather than "rebuilding Rome anew" (1990, 208). On Moyn's interpretation, Virgil's poem does not contain anything that is essential for Arendt's political thought. Rather, she would be employing Virgil merely in order to shed light on the important shift in the idea of *saeculum* from the Roman to the North American usage: the North Americans change the Roman "great order of the ages [*magnus ordo saecolorum*]" into "new order of the ages [*novus ordo saecolorum*]." With this substitution of *novus* for *magnus*, according to Moyn, Arendt wants "to stress not just the novelty but also the secularity of the modern enterprise. . . . Her reading of how the Americans updated Virgil . . . thus provides in miniature Arendt's overall interpretation of the place of revolution in modern politics: a classical revival at its best . . . but one in new and changed circumstances that were crucially post- and anti- or at least non-religious" (Moyn 2008, 89–90). Moyn believes that Arendt's repudiation of the myth of the virgin birth of a new god who arrives on earth from a "transcendent, transmundane" place means that she must adhere to a purportedly modern and "non-religious" understanding of the *novus saeclorum*. But such a reading does not account for the presence of a civil religious meaning in Virgil's poem.

[76] Arendt refers to Eduard Norden's *Die Geburt des Kindes: Geschichte einer religiösen Idee* of 1924. She adds: "I follow Norden's translation and commentary, but I doubt the religious significance of the poem" (1990, 318, n. 53). By which I take Arendt to mean "Christian" religion, not all forms of religion.

[77] A conception of "absolute novelty" that is still maintained by Schmitt's "Christian" conception of history in his late text, "Drei Möglichkeiten eines christlichen Geschichtsbildes" (Schmitt 2007, 161–6).

One of Taubes's students, Richard Faber, has drawn attention to the complex crossing of civil religions at work in the Virgilian text. In his reconstruction of the Jewish and Roman religious motifs that flow into the *Fourth Eclogue*, Faber adopts the so-called Easterner approach to the Eclogue first proposed by Norden, which identifies in Virgil a reception of the Judeo-Christian *Third Sibylline Oracles*.[78] These *Sibylline Oracles*, not to be confused with the original Roman oracles tied to the Sibyl from Cumae,[79] reflected an anti-Roman apocalyptic literature centered on the rebellion of the zealots in Bar Kochbas.[80] Following Alfons Kurfess's suggestions from his 1951 edition of the *Oracles*, Faber argues that the *Oracles* employ the pagan idea of a Golden Age in order to inscribe within it a messianic, social utopia. On this reading, the *Oracles* depict the Roman Empire as the main culprit of social and political decadence and prophesy Rome's eventual destruction. Faber then rehearses the hypothesis that Virgil applied his penchant for catachretic readings also to the Judeo-Christian *Sibylline Oracles*, turning their anti-Roman affect into a prophecy of Roman "eternal" greatness.[81] In my opinion, Faber's interpretation remains captive to Taubes's own construal of Jewish apocalypticism and does not shed light on what Arendt is ultimately trying to say through her reading of Virgil. The main fault with Faber's reading is that it collapses Roman republican civil religion onto a Roman imperial political theology.

Moving to Arendt's interpretation of the *Fourth Eclogue*, one notices that, contra Faber, she sees in Virgil both a *symbiosis* of Roman and Jewish elements *and* a clear separation between Roman civil religion and imperial political theology. Arendt can support this interpretation only because she operates with a reading of Jewish religion as a civil religion (rather than as an apocalyptic or messianic discourse), which is characteristic of the modern republican approach to biblical politics. For Arendt, the possibility of Judeo-Roman symbiosis is not premised on the future-orientedness of apocalyptic literature, but rather on its opposite: a civil-religious sense of "piety" toward beginnings. This shared

[78] On the Judeo-Christian Sibylline Oracles, the definitive treatment is now found in (Lightfoot 2007).

[79] On the original Roman Sibylline oracles and their importance in republican Rome, see "The Advent of the Magna Mater" in (Gruen 1990, 7): "Adoption and incorporation of foreign deities held a long and honoured place in those practices [Roman religious practices]. Hellenic influence permeated the religious scene, and the 3rd century BC witnessed some of the most prominent instances of alien cults welcomed in Rome. The Sibylline Books supply a significant link in the chain. As sacred verses that contained Greek oracles, they were consulted regularly by a priestly college of *decemviri* to obtain elucidation of prodigies. Legend has it that Tarquinius Superbus bought the *libri Sibyllini* from an elderly foreign woman, the Sibyl from Cumae, thus attesting an early and Hellenic origin."

[80] See (Faber 1994, 142ff). For the original hypothesis, see (Norden 1913; and Kurfess 1934). It is taken up again in (Taubes 2009, 45–7) from where Faber, in all probability, first picked it up.

[81] "[Virgil] did not only translate this Jewish-Alexandrian prophecy into the Roman language, but he also made out of this entire (Jewish) oracle a '*Carmen Cumaeum*, viz. a state oracle'" (Faber 1994, 144).

valorization of the "return to beginnings" is premised as much on the myth of the Reign of Saturn (the Golden Age) as on what Buber characterizes as the fundamental gesture of Jewish prophetism, namely, the action of "turning" back to beginnings.

Thus, commenting on the key phrase *magnus ordo saecolorum*, Arendt explains that "the order of the fourth *Eclogue* is great by virtue of *going back to and being inspired by a beginning* which antedates it: 'Now *returns* the Maid, *returns* the reign of Saturn' as the next line explicitly states" (1990, 211, emphasis mine). This statement is of crucial importance to my argument: for Arendt, "greatness" is not opposed to "novelty" as Moyn would have it, but it is tied to "a beginning which antedates it" and to which it seeks to return, or which it tries to repeat. The Jewish usage of the pagan Golden Age motif (originally of Hesiodic-Platonic provenance) is therefore retained by Arendt, but deprived of its apocalyptic, anti-Roman pathos by being turned backward toward a beginning, rather than forward toward an end of history.

Having established this fundamental point of hermeneutics, Arendt proceeds to take a stance against Norden's (and Nisbet's) "Oriental" or messianic interpretation of the *Fourth Eclogue* by rejecting the assumption that the *nascens puer* refers to a "virgin birth" of the Son of God.[82] She argues that, given the context of the eternal return that frames the *Fourth Eclogue*, "it follows, of course, that the child to whose birth the poem is addressed is by no means a *theos soter*, a divine savior descending from some transcendent, transmundane region. This child, most explicitly, is *a human child born into the continuity of history . . . far from being the prediction of the arrival of the divine child and savior, it is, on the contrary, the affirmation of the divinity of birth as such, that the world's potential salvation lies in the very fact that the human species regenerates itself constantly and forever*" (Arendt 1990, 211, emphasis mine).

Interpreters have paid scarce attention to the exact words employed by Arendt. Arendt not only rejects the identification of the child in the *Fourth Eclogue* with the prophecy of the birth of Jesus the Christ ("a divine savior descending from some transcendent, transmundane region"). She does not simply substitute for the Christian belief another belief in "the affirmation of the divinity of birth as such," that is, her theory of beginning as natality (as opposed to Creation). Most radically, perhaps, is the fact that she inscribes the "divinity of birth as such" within a belief in the eternity of the world ("the human species regenerates itself constantly and forever") that is based on pagan religion. In other words, by rejecting the Christian interpretation of the *birth of a divine child* (the Son of

[82] Nisbet argues that it is very difficult not to associate the *nascens puer* (newborn boy) with messianic doctrines like that of Isaiah 7:14: "Behold, a virgin shall conceive, and bear a son, and shall call his name Immanuel." He also speaks of "near-Eastern worship of divine infants" (Nisbet 1978, 65).

God) in favor of the *divinity of birth as such*, Arendt rejects the conflation of absoluteness and beginning, and replaces it by the idea of an unending iterability of beginnings.[83] It is incorrect to say that the *Fourth Eclogue* has no reference to the idea of a *novum saeculum*, as Moyn states, since that phrase occurs also in the *Eclogue* and not just in its "American" appropriation. The point is that the true effect of "secularization" that Arendt recovers from Virgil is one connected to the pagan affirmation of the eternity of the world and of the eternal return of everything worldly.[84]

Most interesting of all, given my previous discussion of Mother Earth and the cult of Demeter and Dionysus in Hölderlin's poetry, is the fact that Arendt, contrary to Heidegger, emphasizes the Dionysian motifs of the poem since she reads the figure of the child in terms of the eternal rebirth of all things.[85] This insight is now confirmed by Helene Whittaker's identification of the child with Ploutos, the son of Demeter, associated with plenty and with the non-discriminatory distribution of goods, whose birth is central to the cult of the goddess Demeter at Eleusis, which is "first and foremost associated with the fertility of the earth" (Whittaker 2007, 67). Not surprisingly, Whittaker suggests that the motif of the "return of the Virgin" in the *Fourth Eclogue* should not be interpreted as a reference to the goddess of justice, *Dike*, but rather "one might remember that a virgin who does return and whose return is re-enacted every year in ritual is Persephone," who is the sister of Ploutos (2007, 70). Persephone is connected to the Renaissance iconology of the Spring, or *Primavera*, as evidence of the eternal rebirth of Nature.

With these elements in hand, one can attempt another approximation to the significance of the *Fourth Eclogue* for Arendt's political thought. The *Eclogue* is dedicated to the "divinity of birth," and its reappearance within a modern revolutionary context signals that modern revolutions enact the political principle of natality: "what matters in our context is less the profoundly Roman notion that

[83] For a recent discussion of natality in Arendt and its relation to Christian ideas of nativity, and for the distinction between Arendt's child and the infant (as dependent on maternal care) see (Cavarero 2014). With respect to Caverero's reading, I emphasize the pagan civil-religious, Dyonisian elements of Arendt's child or *puer*, on the one hand, and the connection of the "divinity of birth" with an idea of the eternity of the world, on the other.

[84] Arendt's intuitions have recently received more philological support in Helène Whittaker's critique of Nisbet (Whittaker 2007). Whittaker has suggested that the references to divine children in Virgil's *Fourth Eclogue* can be interpreted exclusively through reference to pagan religious contexts, without having to appeal to any of the Judeo-Christian sources employed since Norden.

[85] This is entirely opposed to the thrust of Taubes's reading, for whom "history is the project of the spirit; it surpasses the bounds of nature. . . . The *novum* exceeds the cycle of origin. The *novum* is the element of history. Seen from the perspective of history, origin becomes the *beginning*, followed by the middle and the end" (Taubes 2009, 12). Taubes explicitly opposes "the eternal return of the same is dominated by eros, which draws together what is above and what is below, and completes nature's cycle" to "the realm of time moving irreversibly in one direction, it is the spirit that rules, as it presses forward. Therefore the spirit is strictly bound up with time" (ibid.).

all foundations are re-establishments and reconstructions than the somehow connected but different idea that *men are equipped for the logically paradoxical of making a new beginning because they themselves are new beginnings and hence beginners, that the very capacity for beginning is rooted in natality, in the fact that human beings appear in the world by virtue of birth*" (Arendt 1990, 211, emphasis mine). Thus, contra Moyn's hypothesis, on Arendt's republican conception of modern revolutions, these are not defined by the attempt to find a substitute for an absolute. These revolutions are misinterpreted if they are seen to replace God with the People, or to take down old churches in order to set up new romantic cults of novelty; or, lastly, if they are seen as grounding politics on an anti-religious or non-religious basis. Unlike Taubes, Arendt does not understand modern revolutions along messianic lines: for her, modern revolutions do not seek an apocalyptic end to all power, nor do they seek to bring eternal peace in the name of the realization on earth of the Kingdom of the Son of God. But this does not mean that she thinks that modern revolutions have no relation whatsoever to divinity, for at a minimum they have a relation to the divinity of natality.

To resume, I have shown so far that in Arendt's reading of Virgil, the "greatness" of the "order of periods [*magnus saeclorum ordo*]" is not separated from its "novelty" because the crucial meaning of the *saeclorum* turns on the idea of the "eternal" return to and of beginnings. On my hypothesis, the basic meaning of secularism in republican political thought, then, has little to do with the secularization of divine absolutes or with finding secular proxies for these absolutes, and much more with re-establishing the idea of the eternity of the world and the eternal return of the same as the proper context in which the internal relation between beginning and repetition, so essential to a republican conception of revolution and authority, can be thought. I have also shown that Arendt's solution to the problem of the absolute is not "post- and anti- or at least non-religious" because it is rooted in a civil-religious idea of the "divinity of birth."

The last open question is whether Arendt privileges the American model over the Virgilian one? Does she hold onto "absolute novelty" as the key category for her republican politics? Or is it not rather the case that Arendt warns hagiographers of the American Revolution of the *hubris* of thinking that the American Age somehow transcends the *magnus ordo saeclorum*, the eternal return of all things? It is of course true that by changing the Virgilian *magnus ordo saeclorum* into *novus ordo saeclorum* "they [the American Founders] had admitted that it was no longer a matter of founding 'Rome anew' but of founding a 'new Rome'" and the "thread of continuity" between the new republic and the Roman one was "broken and could not be renewed" (Arendt 1990, 212). Nonetheless, Arendt believes that *despite* this break with the Roman tradition, the American revolutionaries nevertheless returned to the Roman model:

> And yet, *when reading Virgil's fourth Eclogue*, they might have been faintly aware that *there exists a solution for the perplexities of beginning which needs no absolute to break the vicious circle in which all first things seem to be caught.* What saves the act of beginning from its own arbitrariness is that it carries its own principle within itself, or, to be more precise, that beginning and principle, *principium* and principle, are not only related to each other, but are coeval. The absolute from which the beginning is to derive its own validity and which must save it, as it were, from its inherent arbitrariness is the principle which, together with it, makes its appearance in the world. (1990, 212, emphasis mine)

This is Arendt's last word on the subject, and it is a sufficiently obscure passage to have given rise to a number of different interpretations as to the *anarchic* character of her political thought.

The Virgilian frame within which Arendt inscribes her doctrine of beginnings links every beginning unavoidably to the possibility of its repetition or of a return to beginning. This makes it impossible for the beginning to be posited as an ab-solute. This is one sense in which beginnings are *an-archic*, without absolute foundations (*arche*).[86] But Arendt does not seem to want to leave it there: beginnings are also "acts of foundation," they have a positive relation to a conception of *archein*, which she expresses by saying that the beginning is "saved" because it has "its own principle (*arche, principium*) within itself." Again, the Virgilian frame helps to see that this internal principle or *arche* of beginnings is the *principle of natality*. Interpreted in this way, Arendt's point is that the republican *constitutio libertatis* must have as its highest principle that of allowing every biological individual to become a beginner, and thus to grant them access to a political or public space in which they can be both actors and judges of actions. This reading seems to be confirmed when she adds that "the principle inspires the deeds that are to follow and remains apparent as long as the action lasts" (1990, 213).

For my purposes in this chapter, what is most fascinating in Arendt's last word on beginnings is that she feels compelled to translate her intuition back into Greek terms to confirm the validity of her construal: "the Greek word for beginning is *arche* and *arche* means *both beginning and principle*" (1990, 213, emphasis mine). In so doing, Arendt corrects the translation that she had given of *archein* in the *Human Condition*, where it recovers primarily the meaning of "leading" and is conjoined with the verb *prattein*, "following through, finishing" (1958, 189). In *On Revolution*, by way of contrast, beginnings are, as it were, complete

[86] For this reading of the Arendtian enterprise see (Schürmann 1990, 1996). With regard to her reading of Augustine, see (Vatter 2006). For other developments of this Arendtian motif, see (Agamben 2011, 2014; and Lindahl 2015).

in themselves: they do not stand in need of being "followed through" or "finished" because and to the extent that they carry or reveal their own "principles" of action, which are accessible and shared by all those who join in the action. Unlike in *The Human Condition*, *archein* in *On Revolution* does not serve as the foundation of a form of government or management: one can say that for Arendt beginning as *archein* remains a form of no-rule and is not the basis of rule or of government, in this sense it is inherently an-archic, while at the same time, beginnings as containing (constitutional) principles, also offer a ground for legal authority.

A confirmation of these hypotheses is given by the presence of the most unlikely gesture for Arendt: in order to support her new reading of *arche* she appeals to a passage in Plato's *Laws* VI:775, to which she provides a translation herself. Citing Plato's *Laws* in the context of a discussion of natality, beginning, and principle is striking enough, especially if one recalls that previously Arendt had charged Plato with inventing a political use of "theology" when introducing the idea of Hell and the similar introduction of transcendent "standards according to which cities may be founded and rules of behavior laid down for the multitude" (1977, 131). Here, by way of contrast, the Platonic text is employed for *the exact opposite purpose*. Arendt's translation runs as follows: "for the beginning, because it contains its own principle, is also a god who, as long as he dwells among men, as long as he inspires their deeds, saves everything." I have found no explanation in the secondary literature why Arendt feels the need to appeal to Plato's theology to uphold her own political philosophy of beginnings.

Arendt's translation reiterates the belief in the "divine" nature of beginnings. In particular, Arendt must have been aware that this passage comes in the middle of Plato's discussion of marriage, wedding parties, drunkenness, and the conception of children. Indeed, in the standard translations, Plato refers to the god in the feminine, and later in *Laws* 782b it is a question of Demeter and her daughter Persephone.[87] Arendt was surely aware of the fact that the one passage that she cites of Plato in an entirely affirmative sense contains a reference to the goddess Demeter and her children (Persephone and Ploutos) who were called upon in Virgil's *Fourth Eclogue* and in her discussion of the "divinity of birth" itself. In confirmation of my central thesis in this chapter, Arendt's translation changes the gender of the god so that Plato's text adopts

[87] For purposes of comparison, Pangle's translation of the passage runs as follows: "For the beginning, which among human beings is established as god, is the savior of all things—if she receives the proper honor from each of those who make use of Her" (Plato 1980, 775e). Bury's translation runs as follows: "for the Beginning that sits enshrined as a goddess among mortals is the Savior of all, provided that she receives the honor due to her from each one who approaches her." Morrow also identifies the goddess in question with Demeter (1960, 452–3).

a decidedly Jewish tone. For Arendt seems to be saying through Plato's words that, as long as human beings are beginners and dwell politically, then God "dwells among men [and] as long as he inspires their deeds, saves everything." This is as close as possible to the meaning of YHWE as *melekh* given by Buber in his *Kingship of God*.

Most in line with her claim that natality lies at the root of political freedom, Arendt extracts Plato's discussion of *archein* from its familial context and transposes it to a constitutional, political level. Thus, to seal the complete symbiosis of Jewish and neo-Roman motifs, she claims to find the same Platonic (and Jewish) idea of the divinity of natality in Polybius's claim that the constitution is the beginning (*arche*) of the *res publica*, and then also in Harrington, the republican nemesis of Hobbes. This combination of Jewish and Roman republican motifs is, finally, reflected in a second possible reading given by Arendt of what it means for the beginning to have "its own principle within itself": for here this internal principle of beginning is identified with the power-making covenant for which Arendt did recognize a biblical provenance. "The principle which came to light during those fateful years when the foundations were laid—not by the strength of one architect but by the combined power of the many—was the interconnected principle of mutual promise and common deliberation; and the event itself decided indeed, as Harrington had insisted, that men 'are really capable . . . of establishing good government from reflection and choice,' that they are not 'forever destined to depend for their political constitutions on accident and force' " (Arendt 1990, 214).

Heine, a republican Jesus, and human rights

In *The Human Condition*, Arendt anticipated the complicated nexus of natality, the "principle of mutual promise," and the figure of the savior-child, in her famous discussion of Jesus as a political genius:

> The miracle that saves the world, the realm of human affairs, from its normal, natural "ruin" is ultimately the fact of natality, in which the faculty of action is ontologically rooted. It is, in other words, the birth of new men and the new beginning, the action they are capable of by virtue of being born. Only the full experience of this capacity can bestow human affairs faith and hope, those two essential characteristics of human existence which Greek antiquity ignored altogether. . . . It is this faith and hope for the world that found perhaps its most glorious and most succinct expression in the few words with which the Gospels announced their "glad tidings": "A child has been born unto us." (Arendt 1958, 246–7)

The passage is well-known and has been commented untold times, and yet it can easily lead to misinterpretation if it is abstracted from Arendt's commitment to the ideal of civil religion as something shared by Roman and Jews that I have uncovered in the previous sections.[88]

Most interpreters of Arendt's reading of Jesus assume the existence of an unbridgeable gulf between Roman and Judeo-Christian political motifs.[89] For these interpretations, the figure of Jesus represents a caesura in Arendt's own thought with respect to the Greco-Roman horizon. In my opinion, these readings are correct to indicate that the political thought of "Jesus of Nazareth" has a systematic role to play in Arendt's overall political philosophy because it brings a crucial supplement to both Roman and Jewish civil religion. However, in my opinion these interpretations have not correctly identified the salient political element that "Jesus of Nazareth" brings into play (which I shall argue is related to an idea of natural equality and of human rights), nor have they grasped that the role played by this figure, politically speaking, is one that sets him in continuity with the (Roman and Jewish) republican traditions, not in opposition to them.

Arendt's recovery of "Jesus of Nazareth" for the political tradition emerges out of her interpretative strategy with respect to the Virgilian *Fourth Eclogue*, but this does not mean that he is to be identified with the Christ that later Christian readers would read into the Eclogue. This is clear insofar as Arendt, in the long passage cited in the preceding, indisputably states that the "miracle that saves the world" is *nothing other* than "the fact of natality": the miracle is therefore *not* the belief that "Jesus is the Christ." According to Arendt, Jesus's own original contribution as a political thinker was to show that forgiveness was an inherent articulation of natality, in the sense that it is that (re-)action which permits actions and so beginnings to be *repeated*: "Forgiving, in other words, is the only reaction which does not merely re-act but acts anew and unexpectedly, unconditioned by the act which provoked it and therefore freeing from its consequences both the one who forgives and the one who is forgiven" (Arendt 1958, 241). Thus forgiveness is instrumental to maintaining the effective truth of natality as the repeated "birth of new men and the new beginning," which is how Arendt interprets the fundamental sense of the "glad tidings": not as the arrival of the Savior-child or

[88] For a recent treatment, see (Diprose and Ziarek 2017).

[89] Moyn argues that Arendt is at her least secular and falls into political theology when speaking of natality and of the introduction of miracles into politics by way of Jesus. Danielle Celermajer and Christopher Irwin both take the position that Arendt turns to Judeo-Christian motifs in order to complement or supplement something, namely, the ideas of faith and hope, that she cannot get from the Greco-Roman tradition. For Irwin, "forgiveness gives the individual an opportunity to be released from the burden of unpredictable and unknowable consequences of action and so is vital to the survival of community" (2015, 559). Similarly, Celermajer sees in Arendt's category of natality "an orientation to a future in which hope abides as possibility, and it is this orientation that imbues the present with the capacity for freedom" (2011, 8).

Son of God, but, in the expression she employs fully only in *On Revolution*, as a function of the "divinity of birth" itself.[90]

Arendt's point is that to become a follower of Jesus means to engage in new beginnings, which in turn means to participate in generating constituent power through the mutuality of promising and acting in common. Arendt therefore puts forward a picture of Jesus of Nazareth as a republican hero. There are two possible sources for such a republican conception of Jesus: the most proximate one is none other than Buber's reading of Jesus in his famous book on *Two Concepts of Faith*. Arendt does not cite this book; however, she may very well be alluding to his interpretation of the distinction between Jewish and Christian ideas of faith in the footnote which closes the chapter dedicated to "action" in *The Human Condition*: "Jesus himself saw the human root of this power to perform miracles in faith—which we leave out of our considerations. In our context, the only point that matters is that the power to perform miracles is not considered to be divine—faith will move mountains and faith will forgive" (Arendt 1958, 247, n.84). Arendt's "secular" reading of faith as a political act is far more reminiscent of Buber's discussion of faith than of any of the Pauline variants since discussed in the literature by Badiou, Agamben, and others because the Buberian idea of faith as trust (*Emunah*) in what God *does*, as opposed to belief (*pistis*) in what God *is*, fits much better with the Arendtian idea of power based on the mutuality of promise.

The second source for Arendt's reading of Jesus of Nazareth may well be the tradition of modern republican thought, which always sought a continuity between Jesus's teaching and the tradition of Roman, republican political thought. The first one to openly consider this possibility was none other than Machiavelli, in both of his well-known theses: first, that the end of the Roman Republic was not due to advent of Christianity but had internal political reasons; and more surprisingly, in his claim that Jesus did not preach against the civil religion of the Romans. In fact, in a passage in *Discourses on Livy* I:12, Machiavelli says that "if such a religion [the Roman one of Numa] had been maintained by the princes of the Christian republic as was ordered by its giver [Jesus], the Christian states and republics would be more united, much happier than they are." In other words, Machiavelli suggests that the religion of the early "Christian republic" founded by Jesus was more similar to the Roman civil religion than to the "imperial" religion of the Catholic Church after the so-called Donation of Constantine led to the development of Christian political theology. If Arendt's "republican" Jesus is indeed taken from this modern republican reading of the founder of Christianity, then Arendt's treatment of Jesus has nothing to do with the tradition of Christian

[90] Compare and contrast with the interpretation of the "life of Jesus" given by Taubes: "The good news of the Gospel is the promise that the Kingdom is now also coming on earth" (2009, 50).

political theology ultimately taken up by Schmitt, where Jesus the Christ serves as representative of God on earth by way of the earthly sovereign, but, instead, belongs to a tradition that offered a "secular" reading of Jesus as political revolutionary, a tradition that begins with Spinoza and leads up to Rousseau, Kant, and Jefferson. This tradition sees in Jesus a particularly radical and innovative representative of republican civil religion.

My second claim is that the function of this "republican" Jesus in Arendt's discourse is to open the possibility for a new discourse on human rights as the "right to a place" on earth where every individual can lead a political, republican life. In so doing, Arendt took a page from the Spinozist and Rousseauian development of the idea of civil religion. According to both of them, Jesus of Nazareth supplemented the civil religion of ancient republics because he proposed a form of "natural divine right" that elevated the love of the stranger *above* the love for one's *polis*. The fundamental question faced by modern, republican civil religions was how to integrate the "love of the world" (that is, of the city) with the "love of the stranger."

The solution that was offered by modern republicanism took the form of integrating the "rights of Man" with the "rights of the Citizen." That is, Jesus's charity (of which the principle of forgiveness is but one formulation) was both adopted and transformed in the form of a doctrine of "natural" rights that every human being, in virtue of birth, is endowed with, and whose recognition has to be inscribed in all republican constitutions. In Arendt's political philosophy, the systematic role played by Jesus of Nazareth's political teaching consists in linking the condition of natality with the new foundation of human rights, such as can be found in the following passage: "The fact that man is capable of action means that the unexpected can be expected from him, that he is able to perform what is infinitely improbable. And this again is possible only because each man is unique, so that with each birth something uniquely new comes into the world" (Arendt 1958, 178). Human rights in Arendt vouchsafe for this uniqueness and equality in dignity carried forth by each birth.[91]

Butler identifies the theoretical problem that Arendt's new conception of human rights is meant to resolve: on the one hand, the existence of human rights ought to deny any legal priority to nationalism or communitarianism (the very forces that generate "pariah people"), but, on the other hand, a valid conception of human rights ought to somehow figure the reality that equal rights have preconditions that include "place and political belonging . . . the human as a social being, as one who requires place and community in order to be free" (Butler

[91] The debate on Arendt as a thinker of human rights, and in particular her attempt to frame them through the idea of a "right to have rights" is very extended nowadays. For recent approaches, see (Barbour 2012; Besson 2012; and Gündoğdu 2015, 164–202), which cover the French, German, and English-speaking reception of the debate.

2014, 147). Arendt's famous essay "The Jew as Pariah" (1944) is one of the first attempts to confront at the level of theory the horns of the dilemma and avoid a "parting of ways" between an exclusionary nationalism and an impotent cosmopolitanism. To do so, she employs a conception of human dignity as a kind of status and rank held by any individual in virtue of being born which gives access to a right to treatment as political equals without requiring incorporation into a state characterized by majorities and minorities.[92] Thus, she begins the essay by asking which Jewish authors "did most for the spiritual *dignity* of their people" and at the same time were not simply "assimilated" into the nations that hosted them. She refers to "those bold spirits who tried to make of the emancipation of the Jews that which it really should have been—an admission of Jews as Jews to the *rank of humanity*, rather than a permit to ape gentiles or an opportunity to play the parvenu" (2007, 275, emphasis mine). The first of these exemplary pariahs is Heinrich Heine (the others are Bernard Lazare, Charlie Chaplin, and Franz Kafka).

Heine is not chosen by chance. He was a German Jewish poet who converted to Christianity only in order to "return" to his Jewish roots later in life.[93] Heine represents in poetry perhaps the highest symbol of the "symbiosis" between Germans and Jews that so spectacularly fell apart in Weimar Germany. Above all, Heine was a radical democratic thinker, invested in the project of turning the German Reich into a republic, much like his contemporaries Marx, Ruge, and Hess, all of whom he knew well. In a fragment entitled "On the Democratic Principle," Heine gives expression to a conception of human dignity and human rights that is very close to the one that Arendt was seeking:

> We fight for the principle according to which all the *human beings on earth are born equal and noble*, and no individual ought to be privileged in the state depending on their birth. The partisans of this principle are those who we call democrats, and their party is called democracy. The adversaries of this principle who affirm *against all dignity and all reason* that "a man born more noble than another must in virtue of this merit have more rights than others" we call them aristocrats and their party aristocracy. (Heine 1994, 400–1, translation mine)

Although at this date, Arendt had not yet developed her conception of natality as root of political freedom, it is striking that Heine draws a direct connection between human dignity as a status concept and the equality of rights that the fact of birth on earth grants all individuals.

92 See (Waldron 2015) for a contemporary defense of human dignity as a status concept, and for my critique and new approach to human dignity, see (Vatter 2019a).

93 For an excellent treatment of Heine's understanding of Jesus in the context of his revolutionary commitments, see (Goetschel 2012).

The strange connection between the pariah, the earth, and children is the focus of Arendt's interpretation of Heine as a "schlemiel," an innocent and clumsy or unfortunate character (a "loser or fool"):

> For the pariah, excluded from the formal society and with no desire to be embraced within it, turns naturally to that which entertains and delights the common people. . . . He turns, in fact, from the world of men and the fashion thereof to the open and unrestricted bounty of the earth. And this is precisely what Heine did. Stupid and undiscerning critics have called it materialism or atheism, but the truth is that there is only so much of the heathen in it that it seems irreconcilable with certain interpretations of the Christian doctrine of original sin and its consequent sense of perpetual guilt. It is indeed no more than that simple joie de vivre which one finds everywhere in children and in the common people. (Arendt 2007, 278)

The exclusion of the pariah from a national territory propitiates a turn toward the "earth" and its "unrestricted bounty." Arendt contrasts such a turn toward the earth with the "turn" toward Heaven characteristic of those who understand Judaism as a messianic and even apocalyptic religion. However, she also does not accept that Heine, in turning downward to earth, is simply adopting a materialist or atheist attitude. In a surprising anticipation of the hypothesis I defended earlier, Arendt points to this turn toward the earth as non-Christian, yet as not being divorced from religion entirely, that is, not divorced from a pagan sense of religion associated with the cult of the earth, fertility, birth, and children, to which she dedicates so much attention in her interpretations of Virgil.

The perspective of the "earth" that comes from the experience of the pariah has immediate political connotations: "The bare fact that the sun shines on all alike affords him daily proof that all men are essentially equal. In the presence of such universal things as the sun, music, trees, and children—things which Rahel Varnhagen called 'the true realities' just because they are cherished most by those who have no place in the political and social world—the petty dispensations of men which create and maintain inequality must necessarily appear ridiculous" (Arendt 2007, 279). Thus, the turn taken by the pariah away from recognition within national borders goes hand in hand with a conception of "natural equality" that can be called a republican conception of natural right.[94] It diverges in the

[94] For an extended reading of "The Jew as Pariah" and of the treatment of Heine, see (Honig 2015). However, Honig believes that Arendt criticizes Heine for his "illusory promise of nature" (ibid., 463) and shows herself "sceptical of Heine's naturalism" (ibid., 464). In my opinion, Arendt's text gives no grounds for such claims, but is precisely intent on rescuing the democratic dimensions of this "naturalism" in Heine. For a defense of Arendt's theory of human rights as having a crucial relation to her conception of nature as *phusis*, see (Birmingham 2006).

starkest possible terms from Heidegger's attempts to read in Hölderlin's poetry a doctrine of the homeland that denies a place for the human rights of Jews and other minorities. "Confronted with the natural order of things, in which all is equally good, the fabricated order of society, with its manifold classes and ranks, must appear a comic, hopeless attempt of creation to throw down the gauntlet to its creator. It is no longer the outcast pariah who appears the schlemiel, but those who live in the ordered ranks of society and who have exchanged the generous gifts of nature for the idols of social privilege and prejudice" (2007, 279). In my opinion, this reading of Heine is compatible, if not identical, with one possible, affirmative interpretation of the reference to "Nature's God" and to the "self-evidence" of natural rights as they appear in the *Declaration of Independence.*

In her celebrated discussion of the "End of Rights of Man," Arendt clearly distinguished three issues: the first is the artificial character of legal equality which "is not given to us, but is the result of human organization insofar as it is guided by the principle of justice" (1973, 301); the second is the idea of human rights as "right to have rights" (1973, 296), as "the right of every individual to belong to humanity" (1973, 298); and the third issue, which produces the "perplexities" of the category of human rights, is the phenomenon of "a deep resentment against the disturbing miracle contained in the fact that each of us is made as he is—single, unique, unchangeable; the 'dark background of mere givenness'; the fact that 'the alien' is a frightening symbol of the fact of difference as such" (1973, 301). The great challenge of any theory of human rights is that of connecting the "right to have rights" to this "dark background of mere givenness." To this end, Arendt argues that it is necessary to move beyond the categories of freedom and equality (or justice) in order to reach to the more fundamental categories of natality and plurality. For if human rights are merely a function of our will, that is, "our decision to guarantee ourselves mutual rights" (1973, 301) then they are doomed to founder on the distinction between "civilized" and "savage" peoples that upholds modern colonialism, imperialism, and racism. Everything about Heine, the Jew as pariah, speaks against this distinction. Hence Arendt's insistence that in order to realize the radically egalitarian ideals of the *Declaration of Independence* it is just as important not to mistake liberation through civil rights with freedom through political rights, as it is to recognize the ground of natural freedom on which a concept of political equality that will not generate "pariah people" ultimately stands.

Conclusion

The Empty Throne: From Theocracy to Anarchy

The principle of anarchy

Claude Lefort is the contemporary democratic theorist who has most insisted on the close connection between democracy and anarchy. Democracy is defined by the fact that sovereignty is an "empty place." As a consequence, "no one holds the formula for democracy and that it is most profoundly itself by being savage democracy."[1] But as with Hannah Arendt's conception of republicanism, for Lefort the principle of law provides the normative order within which democratic politics seeks to abolish the difference between those who rule and those who are ruled.[2] This situation brings with it a paradox: on the one hand, democracy is meant to be anarchical in the sense of lacking a commanding principle that legitimates the ruling power (*arche*); on the other, democracy requires that some principle of law be transcendent with respect to government and the political struggle for power.

Abensour notes that this democratic paradox finds expression in Reiner Schürmann's formula of a "principle of anarchy," where anarchy itself seems to be tied to a principle of law.[3] However, Abensour cannot make way into the meaning of this formula because of his assumption that "anarchy destroys the idea of principle" (2002, 717). He reasons that if law is to be coupled with anarchy, as called for by Lefort, then law must itself somehow "be considered 'anarchic,' devoid of an *arche* in the sense of being without an origin, without a beginning" (2002, 722). But this solution is unacceptable since it deprives law of precisely the attributes that allow for its transcendence from power and social conflict, namely, the reference to principle and authority, that is, to the question of origin and beginnings (*arche*). In this book I have shown that Jewish political theology in the 20th century can be understood as a long, complex exploration of

[1] (Lefort and Thibaud 1979, 34; cited in Abensour 2002, 707).

[2] Miguel Abensour formulates Lefort's point as follows: "haunted by its recognition of a being that is indeterminate par excellence, democracy is that form of society in which law, by its external relationship to power, proves to be always in excess of what is established, as if the instituting instance, once posited, re-emerges in order to reaffirm the existing rights and to create new ones" (2002, 709).

[3] (Schürmann 1987, 2019).

Living Law. Miguel Vatter, Oxford University Press (2021). © Oxford University Press.
DOI: 10.1093/oso/9780197546505.003.0008

the principle of anarchy, one that keeps faith to both the normative demands of a principle (*arche*) and of anarchy (*an-arche*). Short of this exploration, one is left with the traditional, even metaphysical opposition between anarchy and principle, and is consequently unable to further comprehend the paradoxical unity of law and anarchy that is essential to democracy.

Giorgio Agamben has recently critically engaged with Schürmann's principle of anarchy. They both start by drawing attention to the dual meaning of the term *arche* as "origin" (or "principle") and "command." But whereas Schürmann argues that it is possible to disconnect the idea of principle from the grip of command, for Agamben principle is ultimately indistinguishable from command, just as law is ultimately indistinguishable from violence. "In our culture, the *arche*, the origin, is *always already in command*; the beginning is *always also* the principle that governs and commands. . . . The origin is what commands and governs not only the birth, but also the growth, development, circulation and transmission—in a word: the history—of that to which it has given origin" (Agamben 2019, 52, emphasis mine). Indeed, Agamben's theological genealogy of modern ideas of the economy and of government claims that the liberal practice of government is a way of establishing order in and through the interiorization of disorder or "anarchy."[4] Elsewhere, he speaks of "the anarchy internal to power" (Agamben 2016, 275).

The intuition that lies behind Schürmann's paradoxical expression of principle of anarchy is that all origins are internally riven and *this* is the condition that makes possible both the univocity of command and its inherent impotence.[5] For Agamben, instead, it is the sphere of command that is internally riven according to a Trinitarian model that divides and unites sovereign and government, constituent and constituted powers, into a "machine of government," and *this* is the condition of its power.[6] For Schürmann, the origin or principle is always a principle of legislation *and* of transgression.[7] Ultimately, his insight is that the metaphysical idea of *arche* contains within itself its own contrary, *an-arche*, because

[4] "The apparatus of glory finds its perfect cipher in the majesty of the empty throne. Its purpose is to capture within the governmental machine that unthinkable inoperativity—making it its internal motor—that constitutes the ultimate mystery of divinity" (Agamben 2011, 244). And: "The divine government of the world is so absolute and it penetrates creatures so deeply, that the divine will is annulled in the freedom of men. . . . At this point, theology can resolve itself into atheism, and providentialism into democracy because God has made the world just as if it were without God and governs it as though it governed itself" (ibid., 286).

[5] Schürmann has a rather Arendtian reading of Foucault's conception of power according to which power exists in and through difference and multiplicity, and withers away when it is concentrated in a point of command (be this sovereignty or government).

[6] See the essay "Archeology of Command" in (Agamben 2019). For the "machine of government" see also (Esposito 2015).

[7] In an early essay, he speaks of a "formal transgression at the very heart of transcendental legislation" (Schürmann 2019, 79). Later he defines transgression as "the co-normativity of the law's disparate other under the very *reign of the law*" (ibid., 136).

they are both comprehended by the One (*Hen*) that is beyond Being (*epekeina tes ousias, hyper-on, hyper-ousia*).[8] Thus, Schürmann's work points to the Pythagorean, Platonic, and Neoplatonist philosophical tradition as the source of a possible way to reconnect principle and anarchy. Similarly, the insight that the One is principle for both legislation and transgression is perhaps best captured in the Jewish tradition by what I have called the paradox of theocracy: the idea that the Torah can be protected and maintained only by transgressing it. In this book I have tried to show how this fateful conjunction of Pythagoreanism-Platonism and Judaism is the fundamental source that nourishes the discourse of Jewish political theology.

Divine government between order and revolution

The empty Throne is a biblical image for the paradoxical unity of law and anarchy derived from the mystical Account of the Chariot. In his genealogy of the modern economy, Agamben associates the image of the empty Throne with the Christian economic theology that underpins, on his hypothesis, liberal governmentality. This form of government is the secularized version of the Christian, Trinitarian view that sees in Jesus Christ's government the determinate negation of the sovereignty of the divine Father and Creator. The Father's sovereignty withdraws from the world in order to give place to the an-archy of the Son's government. In modernity, this divine *oikonomia* becomes the "mystery of the economy," thanks to which the equilibrium of demand and supply is achieved as if by the workings of an "invisible hand," allowing free markets to self-regulate, thereby limiting the intervention of the government and making its citizens freer. Agamben considers that the modern hegemony of political economy over politics is simply the index of a constitutive emptiness of divine sovereignty: God's Kingdom is, always already, characterized by an "empty throne" (2011, 242).

Agamben's hypothesis of Trinitarianism as an economic theology carries serious implications for the republican conception of the rule of law and constitutionalism. For Rousseau, popular sovereignty can only be expressed in the form of a general, non-discriminatory law, viz., it can only be constitutional. Rousseau believes that republics depend on a clear distinction between the sovereign rule of law, which he calls "general will," and the practice of government based on particular decrees or commands. However, on Agamben's reading, Rousseau's distinction between constitution and government is burdened by a "theological inheritance" that effectively undoes it (2011, 276). This inheritance is the

[8] For henology as anti-metaphysical, see (Schürmann 1983). For the systematic exposition of this idea in the history of metaphysical principles, see (Schürmann 2003).

Judeo-Hellenistic tradition of the law of nature that makes its way to Rousseau's notion of a "general will" through Malebranche, who conceived of God's "general will" as the sum total of eternal and unbreakable natural laws.[9] However, Agamben thinks that Malebranche's conception of the law of nature incorporated the Christian idea of divine *oikonomia*, whereby Christ "executes and renders effective in its particulars the grace that God established through general laws. . . . Christ acts, in other words, as the chief of the executive of a *gubernatio* of which God is the supreme legislator" (2011, 266). In this way, Malebranche is said to turn the idea of the law of nature as expression of divine sovereignty into its opposite: a sign that God has relinquished His sovereignty in favor of the (economic) government of His Son and His ministers. The republican attempt to distinguish popular sovereignty from government, general laws from particular decrees, collapses because it fails to see that "the real problem, the central political mystery of politics is not sovereignty, but government; it is not God, but the angel; it is not the king, but ministry; it is not the law, but the police" (2011, 276).

By "police," Agamben follows Foucault's derivation of its meaning from a practice of Christian pastoral power that supervises and controls *omnis et singulatim* (all and one), not against but in and through everyone's consent.[10] Unlike sovereign power, that works through inspiring majesty, awe, and fear, pastoral power is far more "liberal" and "peaceful." According to Agamben's theological genealogy of modern government, Christianity resolved the "political problem" of monotheism posed by the potential for tyranny of an omnipotent but distant God through the Thomistic idea of divine government "out of the nature of things themselves." As the *dispositio* of natural things such that out of their own unplanned interaction a providential order emerges in spontaneous fashion, the Aristotelian conception of nature based on a fundamental separation of substance and accident, necessity and contingency, is made to fall under a Christian idea of divine *oikonomia* in which "the good of order" emerges in and through the contingent unfolding of events by secondary causes (Agamben 2011, 132–4). "Government defines itself as a very particular form of activity, which is necessarily not violent . . . and articulates itself by means of the very nature of governed things. Divine government and the self-government of the creature coincide; governing can only mean . . . knowing the nature of things and letting it act" (2011, 132). The "good of order" that the pastoral power of the police enacts presupposes the consent of those who are thereby ordered: this becomes the model for the liberal conduct of human conduct.[11]

[9] For another interpretation of this inheritance in Malebranche, Rousseau, and Sieyès, see (Frank 2011).

[10] The reference is to "'Omnes et singulatim': Toward a Critique of Political Reason" in (Foucault 2000), where Foucault establishes the genealogy of liberalism in the Christian idea of pastoral power.

[11] On the idea of a "government of things" as key to modern governmentality, see (Lemke 2014).

The third-century BC Greek philosopher Alexander of Aphrodisias was one of the key thinkers who offered a bridge between the Greek philosophical worldview and Christian providence. Alexander came up with an idea of the nature of things that does not conform to a deterministic order because it is subject to fate (*Heimarmene*), but in virtue of a kind of "divine power" inherent in nature such that things are ordered without deliberation and without choice yet also not by accident (Agamben 2011, 116–9). However, Alexander of Aphrodisias's idea of a divine or creative power inherent in nature is not a one-way street leading to the idea of spontaneous order that is operative in Christian political theology and then, in secularized form, in liberal governmentality. As indicated in previous chapters, Alexander's notion of a creative power within nature, as received by Maimonides through his Islamic predecessors and also as received by Kabbalistic authors, was employed to bridge together the Platonic-Pythagorean idea of a law of nature found in Philo with Aristotle's conception of natural causality. This bridge between Philo and Aristotle, fashioned through Alexander, allows for the divine or creative power of nature to be identified with the conception of a *living law*.

The main political implication of this alternative inheritance of the idea of natural law was that the realization of the transcendent Good does not take the shape of an immanent *disposition* of things generating a spontaneous order, but, on the contrary, of the *disruption* of the "good of order" and the *restitutio ad integrum* of things by returning them to their original state at Creation. Rosenzweig's idea of a return to created nature as a moment of anarchic beginnings; Arendt's connection between the idea of natality as ground of human freedom and Platonic conception of the divinity; Scholem's interpretation of the Merkabah and Hekhaloth mysticism according to which, contrary to Trinitarian discourse, the moment of anarchy is *internalized* within the Godhead, with the consequence that divine providence does *not* unfold in an "economical" fashion—these are all attempts to think the same basic idea, namely, that the sovereignty of the Father is not merely functional to the economical government of the Son, but requires that nature be ruled through a law whose principle is that of radical equality of each with all. In this way, the return to created nature as a source of law has anti-governmental effects because it requires that order follow from equal law, as opposed to from the economic disposition of things. In short, the incorporation of Platonism and Neo-Platonism into the Jewish mystical and philosophical tradition allowed for an idea of divine government that is not oriented by the *omnis et singulatim* of pastoral power as much as by the *hen kai pan* [One and All] of pan(en)theism, the presence of God in all of nature and perhaps even as the all of nature.

This way of envisaging the relation between God and nature also affects the other aspect of the solution of the political problem of monotheism, namely, the question of consent to what is natural or necessary. Here too the discourse of Jewish political theology offers an alternative to Christian pastoralism. According to Cohen, the biblical concept that best captures the relevant idea of consent is the principle that "the fear of God remains outside the sphere of divine omnipotence" (1924, III:134). This omnipotence is visible in Creation, in the fact that nature is an overwhelming play of forces or, in Nietzschean terms, will to power. Cohen suggests that the book of Job may contain the secret of the Account of the Chariot, that is, of the (empty) Throne of God, because of the way it thinks together divine power with the only thing that this power cannot command, viz., the "fear of God" itself. This fear is the limit of His omnipotence, the source of His relation to anarchy, and the other side of the "love of God," the beginning of wisdom. For Cohen, absent this "fear of God" there can be no truly free relation between human beings because its teaching contains the key to offset the compulsion that makes human beings obey human sovereigns.

The political significance of prayer corresponds to the element of consent tied to the experience of the fear of God. In this book I have shown that for the discourse of Jewish political theology, prayer has the function of empowerment. The glorification of God, by virtue of the paradigm of *homoiosis*, translates into the power that the opinions of all individuals have in propping up governments, or, should their opinion change, in bringing them down. Jewish political theology upholds the revolutionary experience that all governments rest not on a sovereign decision, but on public opinion and public elections. Likewise, the discussion of prayer in Rosenzweig showed that Jewish political theology strengthens the case for democratic election, as long as these secular prayers are understood as Goethe's prayer for human autonomy and human dignity, which accelerate the prayers for the coming of a messianic age, understood as a post-sovereign and cosmopolitical political and legal institutionalization of the rule of law that rejects all rule of persons. Lastly, in Scholem's treatment of Jewish prayers, their theurgical power serves to elevate a human being past the angelic ministers up to the divine Throne, but only in order to verify that no Son of God sits on it, and thus all claims by sovereign representatives to rule by divine right are empty. The empty Throne in this Jewish political theology at once signifies that God's essence is invisible and unrepresentable and that the realization of His Kingdom on earth cannot occur until human sovereigns bend their knees before the dignity of humanity itself.

Simone Weil and a Pythagorean solution to the problem of divine omnipotence

The relation between God, natural necessity, consent, and anarchy is at the heart of one of the most dense and provocative texts of political theology in the 20th century: Simone Weil's "Descente de Dieu" [Descent of God]. Weil is one of the great thinkers of anarchism in the 20th century and, arguably, puts forward her own "materialist" political theology.[12] "Descent of God" is such an intriguing text because it suggests a hidden harmony between Pythagoreanism and Platonism, on the one side, and Trinitarianism, on the other. Even though Weil is known for her critiques of Judaism and her proximity to Catholicism (albeit she refused to convert), I suggest that "Descent of God" is her unique contribution to the discourse of Jewish political theology, understood as the attempt to capture the unity of law and anarchy.

Weil's intention is to show that Greek mystical and philosophical spirituality is best captured by Pythagoreanism and Platonism, and in turn these teachings constitute the basic content of the Christian Mysteries and of the Trinity in particular.[13] Weil's thesis is remarkably similar to the one defended by Erwin Goodenough a decade or so before she formulated independently her interpretation of Pythagoreanism. This suggests that Weil's interpretation of Platonism can be used to *retrace backward* the path from Trinitarianism to Pythagoreanism and at the same time to the Jewish conception of the One God.

Like Goodenough, Weil believes that "Pythagoreanism is for us the great mystery of Greek civilization. One finds it everywhere . . . above all in Plato. . . . Plato's political thought (in its authentic form, that is, as exposed in the *Statesman*) follows from Pythagoreanism."[14] Weil's hypothesis is that the "assimilation to God" with which Plato identifies justice in the *Thaetetus* is given by a "mediation" that takes the form of geometric proportionality (1951, 120–1). The Greek idea of a mathematical function or *logos* captures this idea of geometric proportionality, and Weil thinks that it also explains the sense in which Christ as mediator is named *Logos* by Saint John (1951, 166). Indeed, her hypothesis is that Jesus's teaching of love of neighbor derives from the Pythagorean idea of harmony and friendship: "The Christ is the harmony or the unity of contraries, the mean proportional [*Moyenne proportionelle*]" (1951, 133). That is the reason why the "Pythagorean definition of friendship applies marvellously both to our friendship with God as to the friendship between human beings" (1951, 132).

[12] For attempts to work out a materialist and Christian political theology in Weil which does not rely on her interpretations of Pythagoreanism or Platonism, see now (Lloyd 2011; and Radzins 2016) and Agamben, who wrote his dissertation on Weil. See the discussion of the reception of Weil in Agamben and Esposito in (Ricciardi 2009).

[13] "Descent of God" is a text that was first published in a posthumously edited volume, *Les Intuitions Pré-chrétiennes* (Weil 1951). As Michel Narcy concludes his discussion of the misleading nature of the title of the edited volume, "for S. Weil it is not that Antiquity, or any other prior civilization to the Roman Christian West, is rich in 'pre-Christian intuitions' as much as Christianity is rich with truths known much before and independent of it" (2009, 580, translation mine). On Weil's Platonism and its relation to Christianity, see also (Doering and Springsted 2004).

[14] (Weil 1951, 108–9). All translations from the French are mine.

The Pythagorean idea of *logos* explains, for Weil, the constitution of the world as the necessary, mathematical relation of contraries: "Necessity is always in the form of laws of variation determined by relations that are fixed and invariant. . . . The reality of the universe is for us nothing other than necessity, whose structure is given by number [*gnomon*]" supported by unlimited or indeterminate materiality [*khora*] (Weil 1951, 142–3). The key to Weil's political theology is her belief that mathematical necessity is the "intermediary" between the indeterminate materiality of nature and what is supernatural, viz., the Oneness of God. Necessity is but another name for the force that governs all nature.

The human mind (*nous*) can understand, or better, contemplate, the world of forces in terms of mathematical functions. It thereby comes to know force as what is mathematically necessary. However, Weil does not consider that the human intellect is transcendent with respect to the natural world. The only aspect of human life that *is transcendent* with respect to necessity or force is the faculty of "consent" (*consentement*): "The human being is free to consent or not to consent to necessity" (Weil 1951, 147). Not unlike Cohen, who sees that the fear of God expresses one side of human freedom whose other side is love of God, that is, obedience to God's commands, and very much in line with the Kabbalah as interpreted by Scholem, Weil believes that God's consenting to create something other than Himself correlates with the human capacity to consent to necessity: both are actions of the love of God (in their subjective and objective senses of the genitive) (1951, 148).

Because God is "mediated" by a mathematical conception of the law of nature, Weil can explain the love of God by the formula *amor fati*, love of necessity (1951, 149). Her Platonism joins up with the pantheism of Spinoza and the atheism of Nietzsche, not unlike the crucial role that these two thinkers play in 20th-century Jewish political theology. In an explicitly Nietzschean reading of Jesus's teaching, Weil believes that the Christ teaches *amor fati* as the "indifference" to good and evil in the world. This "indifference" is exemplified in the Father's Creation: "To imitate this indifference is simply to consent to it, to accept the existence of everything that is, including evil, with the sole exception of that portion of evil which we have the possibility and the obligation to prevent" (1951, 150). Thus, mathematical necessity is not only the mediation between God and nature, but also between all natural things because necessity "constitutes an order through which each thing, having its place, allows all other things to exist" (1951, 151). This is analogous to what allows each human being to consent to the existence of another, namely, love of neighbor.

Taking up an Orphic motif that understands natural necessity as the "world soul" or Dionysus, Weil understands natural necessity as the "obedience of matter to God" (1951, 152). "In this way, the pair of contraries constituted by necessity in matter and by freedom in us finds its unity in obedience, because to be free, for us, is nothing other than to desire to obey God" (1951, 152). Here Weil's meditation comes as close as possible to the interpretation of the mystical and philosophical tradition of Judaism offered by the authors treated in this book. It is no surprise, therefore, that she refers both to Spinoza and to the book of Job in order to express her fundamental thesis according to which "necessity is for matter the intersection between the obedience to God and the brutal force that subjects all creatures" (1951, 154).

In sum, natural necessity is the absence of choice; it corresponds to the divine indifference of creation that allows for the harmonious coexistence of all creatures, and the denial of which is simply the meaning of evil. But the harmonious coexistence of creatures endowed with *conatus* or the desire to persevere in life is the formula for natural right. Above natural right stands the Platonic idea of the Good as supreme justice. This Good is nothing other than "the acceptance of the coexistence between us and all other beings and all other things that exist in fact" (1951, 156). Recovering the conception of the Stream of Light that is central to the Pythagorean and then Philonic idea of the divine *logos*, Weil concludes: "One must never forget that *light shines equally* on all beings and things. This light is the image of the creative will of God that upholds equally all that exists" (1951, 157). The neo-Pythagorean image of the Stream of Light whose form is the equality of natural right is joined here with a pantheist conception of the *conatus* and the *hen kai pan*, and then brought back to what is, in the last instance, a Jewish conception of divine sovereignty: "All obeys God, and for that reason all is perfectly beautiful. To know this, to really know it, is to be perfect like the heavenly Father is perfect" (1951, 162).

Weil ends her discussion with an affirmation of divine sovereignty as the only path that leads to the consent to necessity that affirms the world in all its plurality, and thus to human freedom from force, or anarchy. Through a return to Platonism and Pythagoreanism, the Trinitarian conception of divine government is deconstructed back to its Jewish theocratic premises that were sidelined or forgotten once Christendom set about conquering the secular world. Perhaps nothing shows the proximity of Weil's thinking of anarchy to the motifs of 20th-century Jewish political theology, as I have attempted to sketch them in this book, as much as her concluding meditation on *amor fati* as the formula for the divine aleph which resounded on Mount Sinai. Given the lack of a final end or purpose to the eternity of nature,[15] the human cry for an explanation of its sufferings ("why?") will never meet with answer. However, Job comes to understand that this realization need not be a source of infinite despair as long as the human being "does not give up on loving" despite the lack of finality or purpose

[15] "All this universe is empty of purpose" (Weil 1951, 168).

in existence because "one day she will hear, not an answer to the question that she cries, because there is none, but the very silence as something infinitely more full of significance than any answer could have, a silence that is God's very word" (Weil 1951, 168). This is perhaps the best account of the meaning of the empty Throne that we can hope to rise ourselves up to.

References

Abensour, Miguel. 2002. "'Savage Democracy' and 'Principle of Anarchy.'" *Philosophy & Social Criticism 28*(6): pp. 703–26.

Afary, Janet, and Kevin B. Anderson, eds. 2005. *Foucault and the Iranian Revolution: Gender and the Seductions of Islamism*. Chicago: University of Chicago Press.

Agamben, Giorgio. 1979. *Infanzia e Storia*. Turin: Einaudi.

Agamben, Giorgio. 1988. "La passion de la facticité." In *Heidegger: Questions ouvertes*, edited by Eliane Escoubar, pp. 63–81. Paris: Osiris.

Agamben, Giorgio. 1998. *Homo sacer: Sovereign Power and Bare Life*. Translated by Daniel Heller-Roazen. Stanford: Stanford University Press.

Agamben, Giorgio. 2000. *Means without End: Notes on Politics*. Translated by Vincenzo Binetti and Cesare Casarino. Vol. 20, *Theory out of Bounds*. Minneapolis: University of Minnesota Press.

Agamben, Giorgio. 2005a. *State of Exception*. Chicago: University of Chicago Press.

Agamben, Giorgio. 2005b. *The Time That Remains: A Commentary on the Letter to the Romans*. Stanford: Stanford University Press.

Agamben, Giorgio. 2007. *Profanations*. New York: Zone Books.

Agamben, Giorgio. 2011. *The Kingdom and the Glory: For a Theological Genealogy of Economy and Government*. Stanford: Stanford University Press.

Agamben, Giorgio. 2014. "For a Theory of Destituent Power." *Critical Legal Thinking. Law and the Political.* Accessed July 7, 2015, https://criticallegalthinking.com/2014/02/05/theory-destituent-power/.

Agamben, Giorgio. 2016. *The Use of Bodies*. Stanford: Stanford University Press.

Agamben, Giorgio. 2019. *Creation and Anarchy: The Work of Art and the Religion of Capitalism*. Stanford: Stanford University Press.

Alfarabi. 2001. *Philosophy of Plato and Aristotle*. Translated by Muhsin Mahdi. Chicago: University of Chicago Press.

Alter, Robert. 1991. *Necessary Angels: Tradition and Modernity in Kafka, Benjamin, and Scholem*. Cambridge: Harvard University Press.

Altman, William. 2011a. "Disturbing Proximity." *The Jewish Quarterly Review 101*(2): pp. 292–308.

Altman, William. 2011b. *The German Stranger: Leo Strauss and National Socialism*. Boulder: Lexington Books.

Altmann, Alexander. 1988. "Franz Rosenzweig on History." In *The Philosophy of Franz Rosenzweig*, edited by Paul Mendes-Flohr, pp. 124–37. Hanover: University Press of New England.

Anidjar, Gil. 2003. *The Jew, the Arab: A History of the Enemy*. Stanford: Stanford University Press.

Anidjar, Gil. 2014. *Blood: A Critique of Christianity*. New York: Columbia University Press.

Arato, Andrew. 2016. *Post Sovereign Constitution Making*. Oxford: Oxford University Press.

Arendt, Hannah. 1958. *The Human Condition*. Chicago: University of Chicago Press.

Arendt, Hannah. 1973. *The Origins of Totalitarianism*. New York: Harcourt, Brace.

Arendt, Hannah. 1977. *Between Past and Future: Eight Exercises in Political Thought*. New York: Penguin Books.

Arendt, Hannah. 1990. *On Revolution*. New York: Penguin.

Arendt, Hannah. 1996. *Love and Saint Augustine*. Edited by Joanna Vecchiarelli Scott and Judith Chelins Stark. Chicago: University of Chicago Press.

Arendt, Hannah. 2003. *Was ist Politik? Fragmente aus dem Nachlass*. Edited by Ursula Ludz. Muenchen: Piper.

Arendt, Hannah. 2005. *The Promise of Politics*. Edited by Jerome Kohn. New York: Schocken Books.

Arendt, Hannah. 2007. *The Jewish Writings*. Edited by Jerome Kohn and Ron H. Feldman. New York: Schocken Books.

Aristotle. 1998. *Politics*. Translated by C. D. C. Reeve. Indianapolis: Hackett.

Aschheim, Steven E., and Vivian Liska, eds. 2015. *The German-Jewish Experience Revisited*. Berlin: De Gruyter.

Assmann, Jan. 1998. *Moses the Egyptian: The Memory of Egypt in Western Monotheism*. Cambridge: Harvard University Press.

Assmann, Jan. 2002. *Herrschaft und Heil. Politische Theologie in Altägypten, Israel und Europa*. Frankfurt: Fischer.

Assmann, Jan. 2009. *The Price of Monotheism*. Stanford: Stanford University Press.

Avinieri, Shlomo. 1987. *Moses Hess: Prophet of Communism and Zionism*. New York: New York University Press.

Badiou, Alain. 2003. *Saint Paul: The Foundation of Universalism*. Stanford: Stanford University Press.

Barash, Jeffrey Andrew. 2015. "Politics and Theology: The Debate on Zionism between Hermann Cohen and Martin Buber." In *Dialogue as a Trans-Disciplinary Concept: Martin Buber's Philosophy of Dialogue and Its Contemporary Reception*, edited by Paul Mendes-Flohr, pp. 49–59. Berlin: De Gruyter.

Barbour, Charles. 2012. "Between Politics and Law: Hannah Arendt and the Subject of Rights." In *Hannah Arendt and the Law*, edited by Christopher McCorkindale, pp. 307–20. Portland: Hart.

Baron, Hans. 1988. *In Search of Florentine Civic Humanism*. Princeton: Princeton University Press.

Bates, David. 2006. "Political Theology and the Nazi State: Carl Schmitt's Concept of the Institution." *Modern Intellectual History* 3(3): pp. 415–42.

Batnitzky, Leora. 1999. "The Philosophical Import of Carnal Israel: Hermeneutics and the Structure of Rosenzweig's *Star*." *Journal of Jewish Thought and Philosophy* 9: pp. 127–53.

Batnitzky, Leora. 2000. *Idolatry and Representation: The Philosophy of Franz Rosenzweig Reconsidered*. Princeton: Princeton University Press.

Batnitzky, Leora. 2006a. "Hermann Cohen and Leo Strauss." *The Journal of Jewish Thought and Philosophy* 13: pp. 187–212.

Batnitzky, Leora. 2006b. *Leo Strauss and Emmanuel Levinas: Philosophy and the Politics of Revelation*. Cambridge: Cambridge University Press.

Batnitzky, Leora. 2012. "Political Theory: Beyond Sovereignty?" In *The Cambridge History of Jewish Philosophy*, edited by Zachary Braiterman Martin Kavka, and David Novak, pp. 579–605. Cambridge: Cambridge University Press.

Batsch, Christophe. 2004. *La guerre et les rites de la guerre dans le judaisme du deuxième Temple*. Leiden: Brill.

Behnegar, Nasser. 2003. *Leo Strauss, Max Weber, and the Scientific Study of Politics*. Chicago: University of Chicago Press.

Beiner, Ronald. 2011. *Civil Religion: A Dialogue in the History of Political Philosophy*. New York: Cambridge University Press.

Bell, Duncan. 2019. *Reordering the World: Essays on Liberalism and Empire*. Princeton: Princeton University Press.

Ben-Shlomo, Joseph. 1994. "Gershom Scholem on Pantheism in the Kabbala." In *Gershom Scholem: The Man and His Work*, edited by Paul Mendes-Flohr, pp. 56–72. Albany: State University of New York Press.

Benhabib, Seyla. 2004. *The Rights of Others*. Cambridge: Cambridge University Press.

Benjamin, Walter. 1991. *Abhandlungen*. Edited by Hermann Schweppenhaeuser and Rolf Tiedemann. Vol. I.3, *Gesammelte Schriften*. Frankfurt: Suhrkamp.

Benjamin, Walter. 1996. *Selected Writings. Volume 1: 1913–1926*. Edited by Marcus Bollock and Michael W. Jennings. Cambridge: Harvard University Press.

Benjamin, Walter. 2002. *Selected Writings. Volume 3: 1935–1938*. Translated by Howard Eiland and Edmund Jephcott. Edited by Howard Eiland and Michael W. Jennings. Cambridge: Harvard University Press.

Bensussan, Gérard. 2013. "Rosenzweig and War. A Question of 'Point of View': Between Creation, Revelation and Redemption." *CR: The New Centennial Review 13*(1): pp. 115–36.

Berlin, Isaiah. 1982. "The Life and Opinion of Moses Hess." In *Against the Current: Essays in the History of Ideas*, edited by Henry Hardy, pp. 213–51. New York: Penguin Books.

Berman, Harold. 1983. *Law and Revolution: The Formation of the Western Legal Tradition*. Cambridge: Harvard University Press.

Bernstein, Jeffrey Alan. 2015. *Leo Strauss on the Borders of Judaism, Philosophy, History*. Albany: State University of New York Press.

Bertolino, Luca. 2013. "Die Frage 'Was ist?' bei Hermann Cohen und Franz Rosenzweig." *Journal of Jewish Thought and Philosophy 21*: pp. 57–71.

Besson, Samantha. 2012. "The Right to Have Rights: From Human Rights to Citizens' Rights and Back." In *Hannah Arendt and the Law*, edited by Christopher McCorkindale and Marco Goldoni, pp. 335–56. Portland: Hart.

Biale, David. 1982. *Gerschom Scholem: Kabbalah and Counter-History*. Cambridge: Harvard University Press.

Biale, David. 2014. "Gershom Scholem, *Einst und Jetzt*: Zionist Politics and Kabbalistic Historiography." In *Against the Grain: Jewish Intellectuals in Hard Times*, edited by Ezra Mendelsohn, Stefani Hoffman, and Richard I. Cohen, pp. 51–63. New York: Berghahn Books.

Biale, David. 2015. "Gershom Scholem on Nihilism and Anarchism." *Rethinking History 19*(1): pp. 61–71.

Bianchi, Luca. 2008. *Pour une histoire de la "double verité."* Paris: Vrin.

Bickerman, Elias. 1962. *From Ezra to the Last of the Maccabees*. New York: Schocken Books.

Bickerman, Elias. 1979. *The God of the Maccabees: Studies on the Meaning and Origin of the Maccabean Revolt*. Leiden: E. J. Brill.

Bielik-Robson, Agata. 2013. "Modernity: The Jewish Perspective." *New Blackfriars 94*: pp. 188–207.

Bielik-Robson, Agata. 2014. *Jewish Cryptotheologies of Late Modernity: Philosophical Marranos*. London: Routledge.

Bielik-Robson, Agata. 2019. *Another Finitude: Messianic Vitalism and Philosophy*. London: Bloomsbury.

Biemann, Asher D. 2012. "'Thus Rome Shows Us Our True Place': Reflections on the German Jewish Love for Italy." In *German-Jewish Thought between Religion and Politics: Festschrift in Honour of Paul Mendes-Flohr on the Occasion of His Seventieth Birthday*, edited by Christian Wiese and Martina Urban, pp. 241–61. New York: de Gruyter.

Bienenstock, Myriam. 2009. *Cohen face à Rosenzweig: Débat sur la pensée allemande*. Paris: Vrin.

Bienenstock, Myriam. 2012. "Hermann Cohen on the Concept of History: An Invention of Prophetism?" *Journal of Jewish Thought and Philosophy 20*(1): pp. 55–70.

Birmingham, Peg. 2006. *Hannah Arendt and Human Rights: The Predicament of Common Responsibility*. Bloomington: Indiana University Press.

Björk, Marten. 2018. "Life Outside Life: The Politics of Immortality, 1914–1945." PhD thesis, University of Gothenburg.

Bloch, Ernst. 1985. *Geist der Utopie*. Frankfurt: Suhrkamp.

Blumenberg, Hans. 1985. *The Legitimacy of the Modern Age*. Cambridge: MIT Press.

Blumenberg, Hans. 1988. *Work on Myth*. Cambridge: MIT Press.

Blumenfeld, Bruno. 2001. *The Political Paul: Justice, Democracy and Kingship in a Hellenistic Framework*. London: Sheffield Academic.

Böckenfoerde, Ernst-Wolfgang. 2006. *Recht, Staat, Freiheit*. Frankfurt: Suhrkamp.

Borda, Mara. 2005. "Political Theology and the Politics of Conversion. Hermann Cohen's Religion of Reason as Alternative to Reason." *Leipziger Beiträge zur Jüdischen Geschichte und Kultur 3*: pp. 255–72.

Borgen, Peder. 1996. "Philo of Alexandria: A Systematic Philosopher or an Eclectic Editor?" *Symbolae Osloenses 71*: pp. 115–34.

Bouretz, Pierre. 2003. *Témoins du Futur: Philosophie et messianisme*. Paris: Gallimard.

Brague, Rémi. 1989. "Athènes, Jérusalem, La Mecque: L'inteprétation 'musulmane' de la philosophie grecque chez Leo Strauss." *Revue de Métaphysique et de Morale 94*(3): pp. 309–36.

Brague, Rémi. 1993. *Europe, la voie romaine*. Paris: Criterion.

Brague, Rémi. 2005. *La loi de Dieu. Histoire philosophique d'une alliance*. Paris: Gallimard.

Braiterman, Zachary. 2014. "The Patient Political Gesture: Law, Liberalism, and Talmud." In *Judaism, Liberalism, and Political Theology*, edited by Randi Rashkover and Martin Kavka, pp. 241–68. Bloomington: Indiana University Press.

Brasser, Martin, ed. 2004. *Rosenzweig als Leser: Kontextuelle Kommentare zum Stern der Erlösung*. Tübingen: Max Niemeyer Verlag.

Breckman, Warren. 2011. "Politics, Religion, and Personhood: The Left Hegelians and the Christian German State." In *Politics, Religion, and Art: Hegelian Debates*, edited by Douglass Moggach, pp. 96–117. Chicago: Northwestern University Press.

Brody, Samuel Hayim. 2015. "Is Theopolitics an Antipolitics? Martin Buber, Anarchism, and the Idea of the Political." In *Dialogue as a Trans-Disciplinary Concept: Martin Buber's Philosophy of Dialogue and Its Contemporary Reception*, edited by Paul Mendes-Flohr, pp. 61–88. New York: De Gruyter.

Brown, Wendy. 2008. *Regulating Aversion: Tolerance in the Age of Identity and Empire*. Princeton: Princeton University Press.

Brunkhorst, Hauke. 2011. "Critique of Dualism: Hans Kelsen and the Twentieth Century Revolution in International Law." *Constellations 18*(4): pp. 496–512.

Brunkhorst, Hauke. 2012. "Power and the Rule of Law in Arendt's Thought." In *Hannah Arendt and the Law*, edited by Christopher McCorkindale and Marco Goldoni, pp. 215–28. Portland: Hart.

Brunkhorst, Hauke. 2014. *Critical Theory of Legal Revolutions: Evolutionary Perspectives*. London: Bloomsbury.

Bruno, Christopher R. 2013. *"God is One": The Function of Eis ho Theos as a Ground for Gentile Inclusion in Paul's Letters*. London: Bloomsbury.

Buber, Martin. 1945. "Moses Hess." *Jewish Social Studies 7*(2): pp. 137–48.

Buber, Martin. 1952. *At the Turning: Three Addresses on Judaism*. New York: Harper and Row.

Buber, Martin. 1963. *Der Jude und sein Judentum*. Köln: Joseph Melzer Verlag.

Buber, Martin. 1964. *Königtum Gottes*. In his *Werke. Zweiter Band. Schriften zur Bibel*, pp. 489–64. München: Kösel Verlag.

Buber, Martin. 1980. "Zion, the State, and Humanity: Remarks on Hermann Cohen's Answer." In *The Jew: Essays from Buber's Journal Der Jude 1916–1928*, edited by Arthur A. Cohen, pp. 85–96. Tuscaloosa: University of Alabama Press.

Buber, Martin. 2003. *Two Types of Faith*. Syracuse: Syracuse University Press.

Buber, Martin. 2016. *Eclipse of God: Studies in the Relation Between Religion and Philosophy*. Princeton: Princeton University Press.

Butler, Judith. 2006. "Critique, Coercion, and Sacred Life in Benjamin's 'Critique of Violence.'" In *Political Theologies: Public Religions in a Post-Secular World*, edited by Lawrence E. Sullivan and Hent de Vries, pp. 201–19. New York: Fordham University Press.

Butler, Judith. 2014. *Parting Ways: Jewishness and the Critique of Zionism*. New York: Columbia University Press.

Butterworth, Charles E. 2011. "Alfarabi's Goal: Political Philosophy, Not Political Theology." In *Islam, the State, and Political Authority*, edited by Asma Afsaruddin, pp. 53–74. New York: Palgrave Macmillan.

Buzzetti, Eric. 2014. "A Guide to the Study of Leo Strauss' *On Tyranny*." In *Brill's Companion to Leo Strauss' Writings on Classical Political Thought*, edited by Timothy W. Burns, pp. 227–57. New York: Brill.

Cacciari, Massimo. 1985. *Icone della Legge*. Milan: Adelphi.

Cacciari, Massimo. 1990. *Dell'Inizio*. Milan: Adelphi.

Cacciari, Massimo. 2016. *Europe and Empire: On the Political Forms of Globalization*. New York: Fordham University Press.

Cacciari, Massimo. 2017. *The Withholding Power: An Essay on Political Theology*. London: Bloomsbury Academic.

Campanini, Massimo. 2011. "Alfarabi and the Foundation of Political Theology in Islam." In *Islam, the State, and Political Authority*, edited by Asma Afsaruddin, pp. 35–52. New York: Palgrave Macmillan.

Canning, Joseph. 1987. *The Political Thought of Baldus de Ubaldis*. Cambridge: Cambridge University Press.

Caverero, Adriana. 2014. "'A Child Has Been Born Unto Us': Arendt on Birth." *philoSOPHIA 4*(1): pp. 12–30.

Celermajer, Danielle. 2011. "Hebraic Dimensions of Hannah Arendt's Thought." *Journal of Modern Jewish Studies 10*(1): pp. 3–22.

Cesare, Donatella di. 2018. *Heidegger and the Jews: The Black Notebooks*. London: Polity.
Chacón, Rodrigo. 2010. "Reading Strauss from the Start: On the Heidegerrian Origins of 'Political Philosophy.'" *European Journal of Political Theory* 9(3): pp. 287–307.
Cohen, Hermann. 1904. *Ethik des Reinen Willens*. Berlin: Bruno Cassirer.
Cohen, Hermann. 1915. *Deutschtum und Judentum*. Giessen: Verlag Alfred Töpelmann.
Cohen, Hermann. 1924. *Jüdische Schriften*. Edited by Bruno Strauss. 3 vols. Berlin: C. A. Schwetschke & Sohn.
Cohen, Hermann. 1993. *Reason and Hope: Selections from the Jewish Writings of Hermann Cohen*. Edited by Eva Jospe. Cincinnati: Hebrew Union College Press.
Cohen, Hermann. 1995. *Religion of Reason Out of the Sources of Judaism*. Atlanta: Scholars Press.
Cohen, Hermann. 2004. *Ethics of Maimonides*. Edited by Almut Sh. Bruckstein. Madison: University of Wisconsin Press.
Cohen, Jean, and Cécile Laborde, eds. 2015. *Religion, Secularism, and Constitutional Democracy*. New York: Columbia University Press.
Cohen, Stuart. 2007. *The Three Crowns: Structures of Communal Politics in Early Rabbinic Jewry*. Cambridge: Cambridge University Press.
Collins, John J. 2000. *Between Athens and Jerusalem: Jewish Identity in the Hellenistic Diaspora*. Grand Rapids: William B. Eerdmans.
Collins, Susan D. 2015. "Aristotle's Political Science, Common Sense, and the Socratic Tradition in *The City and Man*." In *Brill's Companion to Leo Strauss' Writings on Classical Political Thought*, edited by Timothy W. Burns, pp. 443–72. Leiden: Brill.
Cooper, Julie. 2015. "A Diasporic Critique of Diasporism: The Question of Jewish Political Agency." *Political Theory 43*(1): pp. 80–110.
Cooper, Julie. 2016. "The Turn to Tradition in the Study of Jewish Politics." *Annual Review of Political Science 19*: pp. 67–87.
Cooper, Julie. 2017. "Reevaluating Spinoza's Jewish Legacy for Jewish Political Thought." *The Journal of Politics 79*(2): pp. 473–84.
Copenhaver, Brian P. 1992. *Hermetica: The Greek Corpus Hermeticum and the Latin Asclepius in a New English translation*. Cambridge: Cambridge University Press.
Cristaudo, Wayne. 2012. *Religion, Redemption, and Revolution: The New Speech Thinking of Franz Rosenzweig and Eugen Rosenstock-Huessy*. Toronto: University of Toronto Press.
Crone, Patricia. 2004. *God's Rule, Government and Islam: Six Centuries of Medieval Islamic Political Thought*. New York: Columbia University Press.
Dan, Joseph. 1987. *Gershom Scholem and the Mystical Dimension of Jewish History*. New York: New York University Press.
Davidson, Herbert. 1987. *Proofs for Eternity, Creation and the Existence of God in Medieval Islamic and Jewish Philosophy*. Oxford: Oxford University Press.
Dean, Mitchell. 2013. *The Signature of Power: Sovereignty, Governmentality and Biopolitics*. London: Sage.
Dean, Mitchell. 2017. "Three Forms of Democratic Acclamation." *Telos 179*: pp. 9–32.
Delatte, Armand. 1922. *Essais sur la politique pythagoricienne*. Liège: Vaillant-Carmanne, Bibliothèque de la Faculté de philosophie et lettres de l'Université de Liège.
Delatte, Louis. 1941. *Les Traités de la royauté d'Ecphante, Diotogène et Sthenidas*. Paris: Librairie E. Droz.
Derrida, Jacques. 1991. "Interpretations at War: Kant, the Jew, the German." *New Literary History 22*: pp. 39–95.
Derrida, Jacques. 1994a. *Force de la loi*. Paris: Galilée.

Derrida, Jacques. 1994b. *Specters of Marx*. London: Routledge.

Derrida, Jacques. 2000. *Foi et Savoir: Les deux sources de la "religion" aux limites de la simple raison*. Paris: Seuil.

Derrida, Jacques. 2001. "Force of Law: The 'Mystical Foundation of Authority.'" In *Acts of Religion*, edited by Gil Anidjar, pp. 230–98. New York: Routledge.

Derrida, Jacques. 2005. *Rogues: Two Essays on Reason*. Stanford: Stanford University Press.

Deuber-Mankowsky, Astrid. 2000. *Der frühe Walter Benjamin und Hermann Cohen: Jüdische Werte, Kritische Philosophie, vergängliche Erfahrung*. Berlin: Vorwerk 8.

Deuber-Mankowsky, Astrid. 2015. "Explizite und implizite Bezugnahmen auf Hermann Cohens *System der Philosophie* in Benjamins *Wahlverwandtschaften*-Aufsatz." In *Benjamins Wahlverwandtschaften: Zur Kritik einer programatischen Interpretation*, edited by Uwe Steiner, Helmut Hühn, and Jan Urbich, pp. 195–220. Frankfurt: Suhrkamp.

Diamantides, Marinos. 2012. "On and Out of Revolution: Between Public Law and Religion." *Law, Culture and the Humanities 10*(3): pp. 336–66.

Diamantides, Marinos, and Anton Schütz. 2018. *Political Theology: Demystifying the Universal*. Edinburgh: Edinburgh University Press.

Diprose, Rosalyn, and Ewa Ziarek. 2017. *Arendt, Natality and Biopolitics*. Edinburgh: Edinburgh University Press.

Dobbs-Weinstein, Idit. 1995. *Maimonides and St. Thomas on the Limits of Reason*. Albany: State University of New York Press.

Doering, E. Jane, and Eric O. Springsted, eds. 2004. *The Christian Platonism of Simone Weil*. Notre Dame: University of Notre Dame Press.

Dotti, Jorge. 2009. "Jahvé, Sion, Schmitt. Las tribulaciones del joven Strauss." *Deus Mortalis: Cuaderno de Filosofía Política 8*: pp. 147–240.

Drury, Shadia. 1988. *The Political Ideas of Leo Strauss*. New York: St. Martin's Press.

Drury, Shadia. 1997. *Leo Strauss and the American Right*. New York: St. Martin's Press.

Duhem, Pierre. 2015. *To Save the Phenomena: An Essay on the Idea of Physical Theory from Plato to Galileo*. Chicago: University of Chicago Press.

Dumezil, Georges. 1968. *Mythe et épopée: L'idéologie des trois fonctions dans les épopées des peuples indo-européenes*. Paris: Gallimard.

Dumézil, Georges. 1988. *Mitra-Varuna: An Essay on Two Indo-European Representations of Sovereignty*. New York: Zone Books.

Dvornik, Francis. 1966. *Early Christian and Byzantine Political Philosophy. Origins and Background*. 2 vols. Washington: Dumbarton Oaks Center for Byzantine Studies.

Dyzenhaus, David, ed. 1998. *Law as Politics: Carl Schmitt's Critique of Liberalism*. Durham: Duke University Press.

Dyzenhaus, David. 2006. *The Constitution of Law: Legality in a Time of Emergency*. Cambridge: Cambridge University Press.

Eiland, Howard. 2016. "Walter Benjamin's Jewishness." In *Walter Benjamin and Theology*, edited by Colby Dickinson and Stéphane Symons, pp. 113–43. New York: Fordham University Press.

Elazer, Daniel J., ed. 1997. *Kinship and Covenant: The Jewish Political Tradition and Its Contemporary Uses*. Piscataway: Transaction.

Elden, Stuart. 1999. "Heidegger's Hölderlin and the Importance of Place." *Journal of the British Society for Phenomenology 30*(3): pp. 258–74.

Elden, Stuart. 2000. "Rethinking the Polis: Implications of Heidegger's Questioning the Political." *Political Geography 19*: pp. 407–22.

Elshtain, Jean Bethke. 1991. "Sovereignty, Identity, Sacrifice." *Social Research 58*(3): pp. 545–64.
Emberley, Peter, and Barry Cooper, eds. 1993. *Faith and Political Philosophy: The Correspondence between Leo Strauss and Eric Voegelin, 1934–1964.* University Park: Pennsylvania State University Press.
Engel, Amir. 2017. *Gershom Scholem: An Intellectual Biography.* Chicago: University of Chicago Press.
Esposito, Roberto. 2008. *Bios: Biopolitics and Philosophy.* Minneapolis: University of Minnesota Press.
Esposito, Roberto. 2012. *The Third Person.* London: Polity.
Esposito, Roberto. 2015. *Two: The Machine of Political Theology and the Place of Thought.* New York: Fordham University Press.
Esposito, Roberto. 2020. *Pensiero instituente: Tre paradigmi di ontologia politica.* Torino: Einaudi Editore.
Faber, Richard. 1975. *Die Verkündigung Vergils. Reich-Kirche-Staat. Zur Kritik der "Politische Theologie."* Hildesheim: Georg Olms Verlag.
Faber, Richard. 1981. *Roma Aeterna: Zur Kritik der 'Konservativen Revolution.'* Würzburg: Königshauen+Neumann.
Faber, Richard. 1994. "Vergil und Novalis: Das Ende der interpretatio christiana." In *Messsianismus zwischen Mythos und Macht*, edited by Eveline Goodman-Thau and Wolfdietrich Schmied-Kowarzik, pp. 141–63. Berlin: Akademie Verlag.
Fackenheim, Emil. 1973. *Encounters Between Judaism and Modern Philosophy: A Preface to Future Jewish Thought.* New York: Schocken Books.
Fackenheim, Emil. 1994. *To Mend the World: Foundations of Post-Holocaust Jewish Thought.* Bloomington: Indiana University Press.
Fagenblat, Michael. 2017. "Of Dwelling Prophetically: On Heidegger and Jewish Political Theology." In *Heidegger and Jewish Thought: Difficult Others*, edited by Elad Lapidot and Micha Brumlik, pp. 245–67. London: Rowman & Littlefield International.
Feldman, Louis H. 1996. *Jew and Gentile in the Ancient World: Attitudes and Interactions from Alexander to Justinian.* Princeton: Princeton University Press.
Fenves, Peter. 2011. *The Messianic Reduction: Walter Benjamin and the Shape of Time.* Stanford: Stanford University Press.
Fiorato, Pierfrancesco. 2004. "Voraussetzung des Denkens bei Cohen und Rosenzweig." In *Franz Rosenzweigs "neues Denken." Band I. Selbstgrenzendes Denken—in philosophos*, edited by Wolfdietrich Schmied-Kowarzik, pp. 126–39. Freiburg: Karl Alber Verlag.
Firestone, Reuven. 1999. *Jihad: The Origin of Holy War in Islam.* Oxford: Oxford University Press.
Flakne, April N. 2012. "Beyond Banality and Fatality. Arendt, Heidegger and Jaspers on Political Speech." *New German Critique 86*: pp. 3–18.
Flasch, Kurt. 2006. *Meister Eckhart: Die Geburt der "Deutschen Mystik" aus dem Geist der arabischen Philosophie.* Munich: C. H. Beck.
Forst, Rainer. 2012. *The Right to Justification: Elements of a Constructivity Theory of Justice.* New York: Columbia University Press.
Forti, Simona. 2006. "The Biopolitics of Souls. Racism, Nazism, and Plato." *Political Theory 34*(1): pp. 9–32.
Foucault, Michel. 2000. *Power: Essential Works of Foucault 1954–1984.* Edited by James Faubion. Vol. 3. New York: The New Press.
Foucault, Michel. 2001. *Dite et Écrits II: 1976–1988.* Paris: Quarto Gallimard.

Foucault, Michel. 2009. *Security, Territory, Population: Lectures at the Collège de France 1977–1978*. New York: Picador.

Fraenkel, Carlos. 2011. "Integrating Greek Philosophy into Jewish and Christian Contexts in Antiquity: The Alexandrian Project." In *Vehicles of Transmission, Translation, and Transformation in Medieval Textual Culture*, edited by Robert Wisnovsky, Faith Wallis, Jamie C. Fumo, and Carlos Fraenkel, pp. 23–48. Turnhout: Brepols.

Fraenkel, Carlos. 2012. *Philosophical Religions from Plato to Spinoza. Reason, Religion, and Autonomy*. Cambridge: Cambridge University Press.

Frank, Jason. 2010. *Constituent Moments: Enacting the People in Postrevolutionary America*. Durham: Duke University Press.

Frank, Stephanie. 2011. "The General Will beyond Rousseau: Sieyès' Theological Arguments for the Sovereignty of the Revolutionary National Assembly." *History of European Ideas* 37(3): pp. 337–43.

Frick, Peter. 1999. *Divine Providence in Philo of Alexandria*. Berlin: Paul Mohr Verlag.

Fried, Lisbeth S. 2002. "Cyrus the Messiah? The Historical Background to Isaiah 45:1." *The Harvard Theological Review* 95(4): pp. 373–93.

Fukuyama, Francis. 2006. *The End of History and the Last Man*. New York: The Free Press.

Galli, Carlo. 2015. *Janus's Gaze: Essays on Carl Schmitt*. Durham: Duke University Press.

Gans, Chaim. 2016. *A Political Theory for the Jewish People*. New York: Oxford University Press.

Gastaldi, Silvia, and Jean-Francois Pradeau, eds. 2009. *Le philosophe, le roi, le tyran*. Sankt Augustin: Academia Verlag.

Gatti, Hilary. 2015. *Ideas of Liberty in Early Modern Europe: From Machiavelli to Milton*. Princeton: Princeton University Press.

Gauchet, Marcel. 1999. *The Disenchantment of the World*. Princeton: Princeton University Press.

Geuna, Marco. 2017. "Extraordinary Accidents in the Life of the Republic: Machiavelli and Dictatorial Authority." In *Machiavelli on Liberty and Conflict*, edited by Nadia Urbinati, David Johnston, and Camila Vergara, pp. 280–308. Chicago: University of Chicago Press.

Ghamari-Tabrizi, Behrooz. 2016. *Foucault in Iran: Islamic Revolution after the Enlightenment*. Minneapolis: University of Minnesota Press.

Ghobadzadeh, Naser. 2015. *Religious Secularity: A Theological Challenge to the Islamic State*. New York: Oxford University Press.

Gibbs, Robert. 1998. "Lines, Circles, Points: Messianic Epistemology in Cohen, Rosenzweig, and Benjamin." In *Toward the Millenium: Messianic Expectations from the Bible to Waco*, edited by Peter Schäfer and Mark Cohen, pp. 363–82. Leiden and Boston: Brill.

Gibbs, Robert. 2004. "Gesetz in *The Star of Redemption*." In *Rosenzweig als Leser. Kontextuelle Kommentare zum "Stern der Erlösung,"* edited by Martin Brasser, pp. 395–410. Tübingen: Max Niemeyer Verlag.

Gibbs, Robert. 2005. "Jurisprudence Is the Organon of Ethics." In *Hermann Cohen's Critical Idealism*, edited by Reinier Munk, pp. 193–230. Amsterdam: Springer.

Gigante, Marcello. 1956. *Nomos Basileus*. Naples: Edizioni Glaux.

Gilson, Etienne. 1938. *Reason and Revelation in the Middle Ages*. New York: Charles Scribner's and Sons.

Gish, Dustin, and Daniel Klinghard, eds. 2013. *Resistance to Tyrants, Obedience to God: Reason, Religion, and Republicanism at the American Founding*. Lanham: Lexington Books.

Goetschel, Willi. 2012. "Reciting Jesus: Heine's Nazarene Family Relations." In *Christian-Jewish Thought between Religion and Politics: Festschrift in Honour of Paul Mendes-Flohr on the Occasion of His Seventieth Birthday*, edited by Christian Wiese and Martina Urban, pp. 43–58. New York: De Gruyter.

Golomb, Jacob. 2004. *Nietzsche and Zion*. Ithaca: Cornell University Press.

Goodenough, Erwin. 1928. "The Political Philosophy of Hellenistic Kingship." *Yale Classical Studies 1*: pp. 55–104, New Haven: Yale University Press.

Goodenough, Erwin. 1938. *The Politics of Philo Judaeus: Practice and Theory*. New Haven: Yale University Press.

Goodenough, Erwin. 1948. "Wolfson's Philo." *Journal of Biblical Literature 67*: pp. 87–109.

Goodenough, Erwin. 1949. "Review of L. Delatte, *Traités de la royauté d'Ecphante, Diotogène et Sthenidas*." *Classical Philology 44*: pp. 129–31.

Goodenough, Erwin. 1962. *An Introduction to Philo Judaeus*. New Haven: Yale University Press.

Goodenough, Erwin. 1969. *By Light, Light: The Mystic Gospel of Hellenistic Judaism*. Amsterdam: Philo press. Original edition, Yale University Press, 1935.

Gordon, Peter Eli. 2003. *Rosenzweig and Heidegger: Between Judaism and German Philosophy*. Berkeley: University of California Press.

Gordon, Peter Eli. 2012a. *Continental Divide: Heidegger, Cassirer, Davos*. Cambridge: Harvard University Press.

Gordon, Peter Eli. 2012b. "Jacob Taubes, Karl Löwith, and the Interpretation of Jewish History." In *German-Jewish Thought between Religion and Politics: Festschrift in Honour of Paul Mendes-Flohr on the Occasion of His Seventieth Birthday*, edited by Christian Wiese and Martina Urban, pp. 349–70. Berlin: De Gruyter.

Green, Arthur. 2014. *Keter: The Crown of God in Early Jewish Mysticism*. Princeton: Princeton University Press.

Green, Kenneth Hart. 1993. *Jew and Philosopher: The Return to Maimonides in the Jewish Thought of Leo Strauss*. Albany: State University of New York Press.

Greene, Tamara M. 1992. *The City of the Moon God: Religious Traditions of Harran*. Brill: Leiden.

Greiert, Andreas. 2012. "Geschichte als Katastrophe: Zu einem theologisch-politischen Motiv bei Walter Benjamin." *Zeitschrift für Religions- und Geistesgeschichte 64*(4): pp. 359–76.

Gross, Raphael. 2005. *Carl Schmitt und die Juden*. Frankfurt: Suhrkamp.

Gruen, Erich S. 1990. *Studies in Greek Culture and Roman Policy*. Leiden: E. J. Brill.

Guerra, Gabrielle. 2010. "Die Theokratie als Idee, die Anarchie als Anstalt. Religionsgeschichtliche Überlegungen zu Julius Wellhausen und Walter Benjamin." In *Profanes Leben: Walter Benjamin's Dialektik der Säkularisierung*, edited by Daniel Weidner, pp. 287–300. Frankfurt: Suhrkamp.

Gündoğdu, Ayten. 2015. *Rightlessness in an Age of Rights*. New York: Oxford University Press.

Gustavsson, Gina, and David Miller, eds. 2020. *Liberal Nationalism and Its Critics: Normative and Empirical Questions*. Oxford: Oxford University Press.

Gutas, Dimitri. 2002. "The Study of Arabic Philosophy in the 20th Century: An Essay on the Historiography of Arabic Philosophy." *British Journal of Middle Eastern Studies 29*(1): pp. 5–25.

Guttmann, Julius. 1973. *Philosophies of Judaism: The History of Jewish Philosophy from Biblical Times to Franz Rosenzweig*. New York: Schocken Books.

Guyette, Fred. 2014. "Agamben and the Migrations of Glory." *Political Theology 15*(5): pp. 438–53.

Haar, Michel. 1989. "Heidegger and the God of Hölderlin." *Research in Phenomenology 19*: pp. 89–99.

Habermas, Jürgen. 1989. "Work and Weltanschauung: The Heidegger Controversy from a German Perspective." *Critical Inquiry 15*(2): pp. 431–56.

Habermas, Jürgen. 1996. *Between Facts and Norms*. Cambridge: MIT Press.

Habermas, Jürgen. 2004. "Dialectical Idealism in Transition to Materialism: Schelling's Idea of a Contraction of God and Its Consequences for the Philosophy of History." In *The New Schelling*, edited by Judith Norman and Alistair Welchman, pp. 43–89. London: Continuum.

Hadad, Yemima. 2017. "Fruits of Forgetfulness: Politics and Nationalism in the Philosophies of Martin Buber and Martin Heidegger." In *Heidegger and Jewish Thought: Difficult Others*, edited by Elad Lapidot and Micha Brumlik, 201–20. London: Rowman & Littlefield International.

Hägglund, Martin. 2008. *Radical Atheism: Derrida and the Time of Life*. Stanford: Stanford University Press.

Hägglund, Martin. 2012. *Dying for Time: Proust, Woolf, Nabokov*. Cambridge: Harvard University Press.

Halevi, Judah. 1964. *The Kuzari*. Translated by Hartwig Hirschfeld. New York: Schocken Books.

Hammer, Dean. 2002. "Hannah Arendt and Roman Political Thought: The Practice of Theory." *Political Theory 30*(1): pp. 124–49.

Hammill, Graham. 2012. *The Mosaic Constitution: Political Theology and Imagination from Machiavelli to Milton*. Chicago: University of Chicago Press.

Hammill, Graham, and Julia Reinhard Lupton, eds. 2012. *Political Theology and Early Modernity*. Chicago: University of Chicago Press.

Hardt, Michael, and Antonio Negri. 2019. *Assembly*. New York: Oxford University Press.

Harrington, Austin. 2008. "1945: A New Order of Centuries? Hannah Arendt and Hermann Broch's 'The Death of Virgil.'" *Sociologisk Forskning 45*(3): pp. 78–88.

Hartman, David. 1998. *A Living Covenant. The Innovative Spirit in Traditional Judaism*. Woodstock, VT: Jewish Lights.

Hegel, G.W.F. 1952. *Philosophy of Right*. Translated by T.M. Knox. Oxford: Oxford University Press.

Hegel, G. W. F. 1977. *Faith and Knowledge*. Albany: State University of New York Press.

Heidegger, Martin. 1961a. *Introduction to Metaphysics*. Translated by Ralph Manheim. New Haven: Yale University Press.

Heidegger, Martin. 1961b. *Nietzsche*. Pfullingen: Neske.

Heidegger, Martin. 1978. *Wegmarken*. Frankfurt: Vittorio Klostermann.

Heidegger, Martin. 1980. *Hölderlins Hymnen "Germanien" und "Der Rhein."* Vol. 39. Frankfurt: Vittorio Klostermann.

Heidegger, Martin. 1989. *Beiträge zur Philosophie: Vom Ereignis*. Vol. 65. Frankfurt: Vittorio Klostermann.

Heidegger, Martin. 1996. *Hölderlin's Hymn 'The Ister.'* Bloomington: Indiana University Press.

Heidegger, Martin. 2003. *Plato's Sophist*. Edited by R. Rojcewicz and A. Schuwer. Bloomington: Indiana University Press.

Heidegger, Martin. 2014. *Hölderlin's Hymns 'Germania' and 'The Rhine.'* Translated by William Mcneill and Julia Ireland. Bloomington: Indiana University Press.

Heidegger, Martin. 2017. *Ponderings XII–XV: Black Notebooks 1939–1941.* Bloomington: Indiana University Press.

Heine, Henri. 1994. *De la France.* Edited by Gerhard Höhn and Bodo Morawe. Paris: Gallimard.

Heinemann, Felix. 1965 [1942]. *Nomos und Physis: Herkunft und Bedeutung einer Antithese im griechischen Denken des 5. Jahrhunderts.* Darmstadt: Wissenschaftliche Buchgesellschaft.

Hernández, Miguel Cruz. 2011. *Historia del pensamiento en el mundo islamico.* 2 vols. Madrid: Alianza.

Heron, Nicholas. 2018. *Liturgical Power: Between Economic and Political Theology.* New York: Fordham University Press.

Herrero, Montserrat. 2015. *The Political Discourse of Carl Schmitt: A Mystic of Order.* Lexington: Rowman & Littlefield.

Herzfeld, Wolfgang D. 2013. *Rosenzweig, "Mitteleuropa" und der Erste Weltkrieg.* Munich: Verlag Karl Alber.

Hess, Moses. 1918. *Rome and Jerusalem. A Study in Jewish Nationalism.* Translated by Meyer Waxman. New York: Bloch Publishing Company.

Hess, Moses. 2004. *The Holy History of Mankind and Other Essays.* Edited by Shlomo Avinieri. Cambridge: Cambridge University Press.

Hickman, Jared. 2016. *Black Prometheus: Race and Radicalism in the Age of Atlantic Slavery.* New York: Oxford University Press.

Hirschl, Ran. 2010. *Constitutional Theocracy.* Cambridge: Harvard University Press.

Hölderlin, Friedrich. 1984. *Hyperion, or The Hermit in Greece.* Translated by Willard R. Trask. New York: Frederick Ungar.

Hollander, Dana. 2006. "Buber, Cohen, Rosenzweig and the Politics of Cultural Affirmation." *Jewish Studies Quarterly 13*(1): pp. 87–103.

Hollander, Dana. 2008. *Exemplarity and Chosenness: Rosenzweig and Derrida on the Nation of Philosophy.* Stanford: Stanford University Press.

Hollander, Dana. 2014a. "'Plato Prophesied the Revelation': The Philosophico-Political Theology of Strauss's *Philosophy and Law* and the Guidance of Hermann Cohen." In *Judaism, Liberalism and Political Theology*, edited by Randi Rashkover and Martin Kavka, pp. 66–107. Bloomington: Indiana University Press.

Hollander, Dana. 2014b. "Understanding Law ('Gesetz' and 'Recht') in Hermann Cohen, with Help from the Early Strauss." *Idealistic Studies 44*(2–3): pp. 263–79.

Holzhey, Helmut. 2006. "Ethik als Lehre vom Menschen. Eine Einführung in Hermann Cohens *Ethik des reinen Willens.*" *Journal of Jewish Thought and Philosophy* 13: pp. 17–36.

Honig, Bonnie. 2001. "Dead Rights, Live Futures." *Political Theory 29*(6): pp. 792–805.

Honig, Bonnie. 2003. *Democracy and the Foreigner.* Princeton: Princeton University Press.

Honig, Bonnie. 2007. "The Miracle of Metaphor. Rethinking the State of Exception with Rosenzweig and Schmitt." *diacritics 37*(2–3): pp. 78–102.

Honig, Bonnie. 2008. "What Foucault Saw in the Revolution: On the Use and Abuse of Theology for Politics." *Political Theory 36*(2): pp. 301–12.

Honig, Bonnie. 2009. *Emergency Politics.* Princeton: Princeton University Press.

Honig, Bonnie. 2015. "The Laws of the Sabbath (Poetry): Arendt, Heine, and the Politics of Debt." *UC Irvine Law Review* 5: pp. 463–82.

Honig, Bonnie. 2016. "What Kind of a Thing Is Land? Hannah Arendt's Object Relations, or: The Jewish Unconscious of Arendt's Most 'Greek' Text." *Political Theory 44*(3): pp. 307–36.

Honneth, Axel. 2015. *Freedom's Right: The Social Foundations of Democratic Life*. New York: Columbia University Press.

Horn, Christoph. 2008. "Socrates on Political Thought: The Testimonies of Plato and Xenophon." *Elenchos. Rivista di studi sul pensiero antico 29*(2): pp. 279–301.

Horn, Christoph. 2013. "Politische Philosophie in Platons *Nomoi*—Das Problem von Kontinuität und Diskontinuität." In *Gesetze—Nomoi*, edited by Christoph Horn, pp. 1–21. Berlin: Akademie Verlag.

Horowitz, Irving. 1960. "Averroism and the Politics of Philosophy." *The Journal of Politics 22*(4): pp. 698–727.

Howse, Robert. 2014. *Leo Strauss: Man of Peace*. New York: Cambridge University Press.

Hunter, Ian. 2017. "Secularisation: Process, Program, and Historiography." *Intellectual History Review 27*(1): pp. 7–29.

Hunter, Ian. 2018. "Public Law and the Limits of Philosophy: German Idealism and the Religious Constitution." *Critical Inquiry 44*: pp. 528–53.

Idel, Moshe. 2012. "Messianic Scholars: On Early Israeli Scholarship, Politics, and Messianism." *Modern Judaism 32*(1): pp. 22–53.

Idel, Moshe. 2014a. "Johaness Reuchlin: Kabbalah, Pythagorean Philosophy and Modern Scholarship." In *Moshe Idel: Representing God*, edited by Hava Tirosh-Samuelson and Aaron W. Hughes, pp. 123–48. Leiden: Brill.

Idel, Moshe. 2014b. "Torah: Between Presence and Representation of the Divine in Jewish Mysticism." In *Moshe Idel: Representing God*, edited by Hava Rosh-Samuelson and Aaron W. Hughes, pp. 31–70. Leiden: Brill.

Idel, Moshe. 2015. "Transfers of Categories: the German-Jewish Experience and Beyond." In *The German-Jewish Experience: Contested Interpretations and Conflicting Perceptions*, edited by Steven E. Aschheim and Vivian Liska, pp. 15–41. Berlin: De Gruyter.

Igor, Héctor Oscar Arrese. 2011. "El exilio como metáfora hermenéutica. Una relectura del al teoría del Estado como ideal moral en la ética de Hermann Cohen." In *Políticas del Exilio. Orígenes y vigenica de un concepto*, edited by Fabián Ludueña Romandini, Marcello Burello, and Emmanuel Taub, pp. 85–94. Buenos Aires: Eduntref.

Irwin, Christopher. 2015. "Reading Hannah Arendt as a Biblical Thinker." *Sophia 54*: pp. 545–61.

Israel, Jonathan. 2002. *Radical Enlightenment: Philosophy and the Making of Modernity 1650–1750*. New York: Oxford University Press.

Jacobson, Eric. 2003. *Metaphysics of the Profane: The Political theology of Walter Benjamin and Gershom Scholem*. New York: Columbia University Press.

Jaeger, Werner. 1962. *Aristotle: Fundamentals of the History of His Development*. Oxford: Oxford University Press.

James, Susan. 2012. *Spinoza on Philosophy, Religion and Politics: The Theologico-Political Treatise*. Oxford: Oxford University Press.

Janssens, David. 2000. "Questions and Caves: Philosophy, Politics, and History in Leo Strauss's Early Work." *The Journal of Jewish Thought and Philosophy 10*: pp. 111–44.

Janssens, David. 2008. *Between Athens and Jerusalem: Philosophy, Prophecy, and Politics in Leo Strauss's Early Thought*. Albany: State University of New York Press.

Jay, Martin. 2011. *Essays from the Edge: Parerga and Paralipomena*. Charlottesville: University of Virginia Press.

Jennings, Michael. 2012. "Towards Eschatology: The Development of Walter Benjamin's Theological Politics in the early 1920s." In *Walter Benjamins anthropologisches Denken*, edited by Carolin Duttlinger, Ben Morgan, and Anthony Phelan, pp. 41–57. Freiburg: Rombach.

Josephus, Flavius. 1987. "Against Apion." In *The Works of Josephus*, edited by William Whiston, pp. 773–812. Peabody: Hendrickson.

Kahn, Victoria. 2014. *The Future of Illusion: Political Theology and Early Modern Texts*. Chicago: University of Chicago Press.

Kajon, Irene. 2012. "The Discovery of the 'True Plato' in Some Twentieth-Century German Jewish Thinkers." In *German-Jewish Thought between Religion and Politics: Festschrift in Honour of Paul Mendes-Flohr on the Occasion of His Seventieth Birthday*, edited by Christian Wiese and Martina Urban, pp. 133–49. Berlin: De Gruyter.

Kalyvas, Andreas. 2007. "The Tyranny of Dictatorship: When the Greek Tyrant Met the Roman Dictator." *Political Theory 35*(4): pp. 412–42.

Kalyvas, Andreas. 2009. *Democracy and the Politics of the Extraordinary: Max Weber, Carl Schmitt and Hannah Arendt*. New York: Cambridge University Press.

Kantorowicz, Ernst. 1944. "The 'King's Advent' and the Enigmatic Panels in the Doors of Santa Sabina." *The Art Bullettin 26*(4): pp. 207–31.

Kantorowicz, Ernst . 1984. *Mourir pour la patrie et autres textes*. Paris: PUF.

Kartheininger, Markus. 2006. *Heterogenität: Politische Philosophie in Frühwerk von Leo Strauss*. Munich: Fink.

Kavka, Martin. 2014a. "What Do the Dead Deserve? Toward a Critique of Jewish 'Political Theology.'" In *Judaism, Liberalism and Political Theology*, edited by Randi Rashkover and Martin Kavka, pp. 108–26. Bloomington: Indiana University Press.

Kavka, Martin. 2014b. "Reading Messianically with Gershom Scholem." In *Rethinking the Messianic Idea in Judaism*, edited by Michael L. Morgan and Steven Weitzman, pp. 404–18. Bloomingon: Indiana University Press.

Kavka, Martin, and Randi Rashkover, eds. 2014. *Judaism, Liberalism, and Political Theology*. Bloomington: Indiana University Press.

Kelsen, Hans. 1928. *Die philosophischen Grundlagen der Naturrechtslehre und des Rechtspositivismus*. Berlin: R. Heise.

Kelsen, Hans. 1957. *What Is Justice? Justice, Law and Politics in the Mirror of Science*. Berkeley: University of California Press.

Kervégan, Jean-Francois. 2005. *Hegel, Carl Schmitt: La politique entre spéculation et positivité*. Paris: PUF.

Kets, Gaard, and James Muldoon, eds. 2019. *The German Revolution and Political Theory: Marx, Engels, and Marxisms*. New York: Palgrave Macmillan.

Klatzkin, Jacob. 1980. "Germanism and Judaism: A Critique." In *The Jew: Essays from Martin Buber's Journal Der Jude 1916–1928*, edited by Arthur A. Cohen, pp. 63–84. Tuscaloosa: University of Alabama Press.

Klusmeyer, Douglas. 2009. "Hannah Arendt's Case for Federalism." *The Journal of Federalism 40*(1): pp. 31–58.

Kreisel, Howard. 2015. *Judaism as Philosophy: Studies in Maimonides and the Medieval Jewish Philosophers of Provence*. Boston: Academic Studies Press.

Kukathas, Chandran. 2003. *The Liberal Archipelago: A Theory of Diversity and Freedom*. Oxford: Oxford University Press.

Kurfess, Alfons. 1934. "Horaz, Vergil und die jüdische Sibylle: Zum grossen Horazjubiläum." *Pastor bonus 45*: pp. 414–25.

Laborde, Cécile. 2017. *Liberalism's Religion*. Cambridge: Harvard University Press.

Lachterman, David R. 1990. "Did Aristotle 'Develop'? Reflections on Werner Jaeger's Thesis." *Revue de Philosophie Ancienne 8*(1): pp. 3–40.

Lacoue-Labarthe, Philippe, and Jean-Luc Nancy. 1990. "The Nazi Myth." *Critical Inquiry 16*: pp. 291–312.

Lampert, Laurence. 1996. *Leo Strauss and Nietzsche*. Chicago: University of Chicago Press.

Lampert, Laurence. 2009. "Strauss's Recovery of Esotericism." In *The Cambridge Companion to Leo Strauss*, edited by Steven B. Smith, pp. 63–92. Cambridge: Cambridge University Press.

Lampert, Lawrence. 2013. *The Enduring Importance of Leo Strauss*. Chicago: University of Chicago Press.

Lazier, Benjamin. 2002. "Writing the Judenzarathustra: Gershom Scholem's Response to Modernity, 1913–1917." *New German Critique 85*(3): pp. 33–65.

Lazier, Benjamin. 2008a. *God Interrupted: Heresy and the European Imagination between the World Wars*. Princeton: Princeton University Press.

Lazier, Benjamin. 2008b. "On the Origins of 'Political Theology': Judaism and Heresy between the World Wars." *New German Critique 35*(3): pp. 143–64.

Lebovic, Nitzan. 2008. "The Jerusalem School: The Theopolitical Hour." *New German Critique 35*(3): pp. 97–120.

Lebovic, Nitzan. 2010. "Benjamins 'Sumpflogik': Ein Kommentar zu Agambens Kafka- und Benjamin-Lektüre." In *Profanes Leben: Walter Benjamins Dialektik der Sekularisierung*, edited by Daniel Weidner, pp. 191–212. Frankfurt: Suhrkamp.

Lefort, Claude, and Paul Thibaud. 1979. "La communication démocratique." *Esprit 9*(10): pp. 34–44.

Legg, Stephen, ed. 2011. *Spatiality, Sovereignty, and Carl Schmitt*. London: Routledge.

Lehmann, Matthias. 1993/4. "Franz Rosenzweigs Kritik des Islams im 'Stern der Erlösung.'" *Jewish Studies Quarterly 1*(4): pp. 340–61.

Lelli, Fabrizio. 2007. "Hermes among the Jews: *Hermetica* as *Hebraica* from Antiquity to the Renaissance." *Magic, Ritual, and Witchcraft 2*(2): pp. 111–35.

Lemke, Thomas. 2014. "New Materialisms: Foucault and the 'Government of Things.'" *Theory, Culture & Society 32*(4): pp. 3–25.

Lesch, Charles H. T. 2019. "Theopolitics Contra Political Theology: Martin Buber's Biblical Critique of Carl Schmitt." *American Political Science Review 113*(1): pp. 195–208.

Leshem, Dotan. 2016. *The Origins of Neoliberalism: Modelling the Economy from Jesus to Foucault*. New York: Columbia University Press.

Levenson, Jon D. 1987. *Sinai and Zion: An Entry into the Jewish Bible*. San Francisco: Harper & Row.

Levey, Geoffroy Brahm. 2014. "Liberal Nationalism and the Australian Citizenship Tests." *Citizenship Studies 18*(2): pp. 175–89.

Levinas, Emmanuel. 1996. *Nouvelles lectures Talmudiques*. Paris: Les Éditions de Minuit.

Libera, Alain de. 1998. "Introduction." In *Averroès. L'intelligence et la pensée. Grand commentaire du De anima Livre III (429a10–435b25)*, pp. 7–45. Paris: Flammarion.

Lightfoot, J. L. 2007. *The Sibylline Oracles: With Introduction, Translation, and Commentary on the First and Second Books*. New York: Oxford University Press.

Lilla, Mark. 2007. *The Stillborn God: Religion, Politics, and the Modern West*. New York: Alfred A. Knopf.

Lilla, Mark. 2016. *The Shipwrecked Mind: On Political Reaction*. New York: New York Review Books.

Lindahl, Hans. 2007. "Constituent Power and Reflexive Identity: Towards an Ontology of Collective Selfhood." In *The Paradox of Constitutionalism*, edited by Martin Loughlin and Neil Walker, pp. 9–24. New York: Oxford University Press.

Lindahl, Hans. 2013. *Fault Lines of Globalization: Legal Order and the Politics of A-Legality*. New York: Oxford University Press.

Lindahl, Hans. 2015. "Possibility, Actuality, Rupture: Constituent Power and the Ontology of Change." *Constellations 22*(2): pp. 163–74.

Lindahl, Hans. 2018. *Authority and the Globalisation of Inclusion and Exclusion, Global Law Series*. New York: Cambridge University Press.

Lloyd, Vincent. 2011. *The Problem with Grace*. Stanford: Stanford University Press.

Loick, Daniel. 2014. "Terribly Upright: The Young Hegel's Critique of Juridicism." *Philosophy and Social Criticism 40*(10): pp. 933–56.

Loick, Daniel. 2015. *Kritik der Souveranität*. Frankfurt: Campus.

Lorberbaum, Menachem. 2002. *Politics and the Limits of Law: Secularizing the Political and Medieval Jewish Thought*. Stanford: Stanford University Press.

Losurdo, Domenico. 2004. *Liberalism: A Counter-History*. London: Verso.

Loughlin, Martin. 2010. *Foundations of Public Law*. New York: Oxford University Press.

Loughlin, Martin. 2015. "Nomos." In *Law, Liberty and State: Oakeshott, Hayek, and Schmitt on the Rule of Law*, edited by David Dyzenhaus and Thomas Poole, pp. 65–95. Cambridge: Cambridge University Press.

Lovejoy, Arthur O., and George Boas. 1997. *Primitivism and Related Ideas in Antiquity*. Baltimore: The Johns Hopkins University Press.

Löwith, Karl. 1942. "M. Heidegger and F. Rosenzweig on Temporality and Eternity." *Philosophy and Phenomenological Research 3*: pp. 53–77.

Löwith, Karl. 1957. *Meaning in History*. Chicago: University of Chicago Press.

Löwith, Karl. 1962. "Hegels Aufhebung der Christlichen Religion." In *Einsichten. Gerhard Krueger zum 60. Geburtstag*, edited by Klaus Oehler and Richard Schaeffler, pp. 156–203. Frankfurt: Klostermann.

Löwith, Karl. 1964. *From Hegel to Nietzsche*. Garden City: Anchor Books.

Löwy, Michael. 2005. *Fire Alarm: Reading Walter Benjamin's "On the Concept of History."* London: Verso.

Löwy, Michael. 2014. "Utopia and Revolution: The Romantic Socialism of Gustav Landauer and Martin Buber." In *Jewish Thought, Utopia, and Revolution*, edited by Jayne Svenungsson, Alana M. Vincent, and Elena Namli, pp. 49–64. Amsterdam: Editions Rodopi.

Löwy, Michael. 2017. *Redemption and Utopia: Jewish Libertarian Thought in Central Europe*. London: Verso.

Lucchese, Filippo Del. 2014. "Machiavelli and Constituent Power: The Revolutionary Foundation of Modern Political Thought." *European Journal of Political Theory 16*(1): pp. 3–23.

Macho, Thomas. 2014. "On the Price of Messianism: The Intellectual Rift between Gershom Scholem and Jacob Taubes." In *Messianic Thought Outside Theology*, edited by Anna Glazova and Paul North, pp. 28–42. New York: Fordham University Press.

Mack, Michael. 2003. *German Idealism and the Jews: The Inner Anti-Semitism of Philosophy and German Jewish Responses*. Chicago: University of Chicago Press.

Mahdi, Muhsin S. 2001. *Alfarabi and the Foundation of Islamic Political Philosophy.* Chicago: University of Chicago Press.

Mahmood, Saba. 2005. *Politics of Piety: The Islamic Revival and the Feminist Subject.* Princeton: Princeton University Press.

Maimonides, Moses. 1963. *The Guide of the Perplexed.* Translated by Shlomo Pines. Edited by Leo Strauss. 2 vols. Chicago: University of Chicago Press.

Malpas, Jeff. 2012. *Heidegger and the Thinking of Place: Explorations in the Topology of Being.* Cambridge: MIT Press.

Malpas, Jeff. 2018. "Assessing the Significance of Heidegger's *Black Notebooks.*" *Geographica Helvetica 73*: pp. 109–14.

Maraviglia, Massimo. 2006. *La penultima guerra: Il concetto di "katechon" nella dottrine dell'oridine politico di Carl Schmitt.* Milan: LED Edizioni Universitarie.

Marchart, Oliver. 2007. *Post-Foundational Political Thought: Political Difference in Nancy, Lefort, Badiou and Laclau.* Edinburgh: Edinburgh University Press.

Margolin, Ron. 2018. "Moses Hess as a Prophet of Spiritual Zionism: The Origins of Messianic Jewish Humanism." *Modern Judaism 38*(1): pp. 75–95.

Martel, James. 2012. *Divine Violence: Walter Benjamin and the Eschatology of Sovereignty.* London: Routledge.

Martel, James. 2014. *The One and Only Law: Walter Benjamin and the Second Commandment.* Ann Arbor: University of Michigan Press.

McCormick, John. 1998. "Political Theory and Political Theology: The Second Wave of Carl Schmitt in English." *Political Theory 26*: pp. 830–54.

McLoughlin, Daniel. 2015. "On Political and Economic Theology. Agamben, Peterson and Aristotle." *Angelaki 20*(4): pp. 53–68.

Meeks, Wayne. 1968. "Moses as God and King." In *Religions in Antiquity: Essays in Memory of Erwin Ramsdell Goodenough*, edited by Jacob Neusner, pp. 354–71. Leiden: E. J. Brill.

Meier, Heinrich. 1995. *Carl Schmitt and Leo Strauss: The Hidden Dialogue.* Chicago: University of Chicago Press.

Meier, Heinrich. 1998. *The Lesson of Carl Schmitt.* Chicago: University of Chicago Press.

Meier, Heinrich, ed. 2001. *Korrespondenz Leo Strauss—Gerschom Scholem.* Stuttgart: J. B. Metzler.

Meier, Heinrich. 2006. *Leo Strauss and the Theologico-Political Problem.* Cambridge: Cambridge University Press.

Meier, Heinrich. 2014. "How Strauss Became Strauss." In *Reorientation: Leo Strauss in the 1930s*, edited by Martin D. Yaffe and Richard S. Ruderman, pp. 13–32. New York: Palgrave Macmillan.

Melamed, Abraham. 2003. *The Philosopher-King in Medieval and Renaissance Jewish Thought.* Albany: State University of New York Press.

Melamed, Abraham. 2012. *Wisdom's Little Sister: Studies in Medieval and Renaissance Jewish Political Thought.* Brighton: Academic Studies Press.

Mendelsohn, Ezra, Stefani Hoffman, and Richard I. Cohen, eds. 2014. *Against the Grain: Jewish Intellectuals in Hard Times.* New York: Berghahn Books.

Mendes-Flohr, Paul, ed. 1983. *A Land of Two Peoples: Martin Buber on Jews and Arabs.* Oxford: Oxford University Press.

Mendes-Flohr, Paul. 1988. "Rosenzweig and the Crisis of Historicism." In *The Philosophy of Rosenzweig*, edited by Paul Mendes-Flohr, pp. 138–61. Hanover: University Press of New England.

Mendes-Flohr, Paul. 1991. "'The Stronger and the Better Jews': Jewish Theological Responses to Political Messianism in the Weimar Republic." *Studies in Contemporary Jewry 7*: pp. 159–85.

Mendes-Flohr, Paul. 1999. *German Jews: A Dual Identity*. New Haven: Yale University Press.

Mendes-Flohr, Paul. 2008. "The Kingdom of God: Martin Buber's Critique of Messianic Politics." *Behemoth: A Journal on Civilisation 2*: pp. 26–38.

Mendes-Flohr, Paul. 2014. "Martin Buber and Martin Heidegger in Dialogue." *The Journal of Religion 94*(1): pp. 2–25.

Mendes-Flohr, Paul. 2019. *Martin Buber: A Life of Faith and Dissent*. New Haven: Yale University Press.

Menga, Ferdinando G. 2018. *Ausdruck, Mitwelt, Ordnung: Zur Ursprünglichkeit einer Dimension des Politischen im Anschluss an die Philosophie des frühen Heidegger*. Paderborn: Wilhelm Fink.

Menke, Christoph. 2018. *Kritik der Rechte*. Frankfurt: Suhrkamp.

Meuter, Günter. 1994. *Der Katechon: Zu Carl Schmitts fundamentalisticher Kritik der Zeit*. Berlin: Duncker & Humblot.

Meyer, Thomas. 2009. *Zwischen Philosophie und Gesetz: Jüdische Philosophie und Theologie von 1933 bis 1938*. Leiden: Brill.

Meyer, Thomas. 2014. "The Origins of Leo Strauss's Political Philosophy." *Idealistic Studies 44*(2–3): pp. 209–23.

Miller, David. 1997. *On Nationality*. Oxford: Oxford University Press.

Minca, Claudio, and Rory Rowan. 2015. *On Schmitt and Space*. London: Routledge.

Miner, Robert C. 2012. "Leo Strauss's Adherence to Nietzsche's 'Atheism from Intellectual Probity.'" *Perspectives on Political Science 41*(3): pp. 155–64.

Mittleman, Alan. 1996. *The Politics of the Torah. The Jewish Political Tradition and the Founding of Agudat Israel*. Albany: State University of New York Press.

Mittleman, Alan. 2009. *Hope in a Democratic Age: Philosophy, Religion and Political Theory*. Oxford: Oxford University Press.

Momigliano, Arnaldo. 1990. *Alien Wisdom: The Limits of Hellenization*. Cambridge: Cambridge University Press.

Momigliano, Arnaldo. 1994. *Essays on Ancient and Modern Judaism*. Edited by Silvia Berti. Chicago: University of Chicago Press.

Mommsen, Wolfgang. 1974. *Max Weber: Gesellschaft, Politik und Gechichte*. Frankfurt: Suhrkamp.

Montaigne, Michel de. 1962. *Essais*. Paris: Bibliothèque de la Pléyade.

Montevecchi, Orsolina. 1998. "LAOS: Linee di una ricerca storico-linguistica." In *Scripta Selecta*, edited by S. Daris, pp. 401–19. Milan: Vita e Pensiero.

Moore, George Foot. 1924. "The Rise of Normative Judaism. I. To the Reorganization at Jamnia." *Harvard Theological Review 17*(4): pp. 307–73.

Morrow, Glenn R. 1960. *Plato's Cretan City: A Historical Interpretation of the Laws*. Princeton: Princeton University Press.

Moses, Dirk. 2013. "*Das römische Gespräch* in a New Key: Hannah Arendt, Genocide, and the Defense of Republican Civilization." *The Journal of Modern History 85*: pp. 867–913.

Mosès, Stéphane. 1992. *L'Ange de l'histoire*. Paris: Seuil.

Mosès, Stéphane. 1998. "Rosenzweig et Levinas: Au-delà de la guerre." *Rue Descartes 19*: pp. 85–98.

Mosès, Stéphane. 1999. "Gerschom Scholem's Reading of Kafka: Literary Criticism and Kabbalah." *New German Critique 77*: pp. 149–67.

Mosès, Stéphane. 2009. *The Angel of History: Rosenzweig, Benjamin, Scholem*. Stanford: Stanford University Press.

Mouffe, Chantal, ed. 1999. *The Challenge of Carl Schmitt*. London: Verso.

Moyn, Samuel. 2008. "Hannah Arendt and the Secular." *New German Critique 35*(3): pp. 71–96.

Moyn, Samuel. 2015. *Christian Human Rights*. Philadelphia: University of Pennsylvania Press.

Mulieri, Alessandro. 2019. "Against Classical Republicanism: The Averroist Foundations of Marsilius of Padua's Political Thought." *History of Political Thought 40*(2): pp. 218–45.

Muller, Jerry Z. 2014. "A Zionist Critique of Jewish Politics: The Early Thought of Leo Strauss." In *Against the Grain: Jewish Intellectuals in Hard Times*, edited by Ezra Mendelsohn, Stefani Hoffman, and Richard I. Cohen, pp. 17–31. New York: Berghahn Books.

Myers, David N. 1992. "The Fall and Rise of Jewish Historicism: The Evolution of the *Akademie für die Wissenschaft des Judentums* (1919–1934)." *Hebrew Union College Annual 58*: pp. 107–44.

Myers, David N. 2003. *Resisting History: Historicism and Its Discontents in German-Jewish Thought*. Princeton: Princeton University Press.

Nancy, Jean-Luc. 2002. *La création du monde ou la mondialisation*. Paris: Galilée.

Narcy, Michel. 2009. "Intuitions Pré-Chrétiennes: Un Malentendu." *Archives de Philosophie 72*(4): pp. 565–80.

Nederman, C. J. 2009. *Lineages of European Political Thought: Explorations along the Medieval/Modern Divide from John of Salisbury to Hegel*. Washington: Catholic University of America Press.

Nederman, Cary J. 1991. "Aristotelianism and the Origins of 'Political Science' in the Twelfth Century." *Journal of the History of Ideas 52*(2): pp. 179–94.

Negri, Antonio. 1999. *Insurgencies: Constituent Power and the Modern State*. Minneapolis: University of Minnesota Press.

Negri, Antonio, and Michael Hardt. 2001. *Empire*. Cambridge: Cambridge University Press.

Nelson, Eric. 2010. *The Hebrew Republic: Jewish Sources and the Transformation of European Political Thought*. Cambridge: Harvard University Press.

Neusner, Jacob, ed. 1968. *Religions in Antiquity. Essays in Memory of Erwin Ramsdell Goodenough*. Leiden: E. J. Brill.

Newman, Saul. 2019. *Political Theology: A Critical Introduction*. Cambridge: Polity Press.

Ng, Julia. 2012. "Walter Benjamin's and Gershom Scholem's Reading Group Around Hermann Cohen's *Kants Theories der Erfahrung* in 1918." *MLN 127*: pp. 433–9.

Nietzsche, Friedrich. 1994. *On the Genealogy of Morals*. Edited by Keith Ansell-Pearson. Cambridge: Cambridge University Press.

Nisbet, R. G. M. 1978. "Virgil's Fourth Eclogue: Easterners and Westerners." *Bulletin of the Institute of Classical Studies 25*(1): pp. 59–78.

Norden, Eduard. 1913. *Josephus und Tacitus uber Jesus Christus und eine messianische Prophetie*. Leipzig: B. G. Teubner.

Novak, David. 1992. "Self-Contraction of the Godhead in Kabbalistic Theology." In *Neoplatonism and Jewish Thought*, edited by Lenn E. Goodman, pp. 299–318. Albany: State University of New York Press.

Novak, David. 2000. *Covenantal Rights: A Study in Jewish Political Theory*. Princeton: Princeton University Press.

Novak, David. 2005. *The Jewish Social Contract: An Essay in Political Theology*. Princeton: Princeton University Press.

Novak, David. 2006. "Land and People." In *Law, Politics, and Morality in Judaism*, edited by Michael Walzer, pp. 57–82. Princeton: Princeton University Press.

Novak, David. 2013. "Buber's Critique of Heidegger." In *David Novak: Natural Law and Revealed Truth*, edited by Hava Tirosh-Samuelson and Aaron W. Hughes, pp. 53–69. Dordrecht: Brill.

O'Meara, Dominic J. 2003. *Platonopolis: Platonic Political Philosophy in Late Antiquity*. New York: Oxford University Press.

Oakley, Francis. 1998. "The Absolute and Ordained Power of God and King in the 16th and 17th Centuries: Philosophy, Science, Politics and Law." *Journal of the History of Ideas* 59(4): pp. 669–90.

Oakley, Francis. 2006. *Kingship: The Politics of Enchantment*. Oxford: Blackwell.

Oakley, Francis. 2010. *Empty Bottles of Gentilism: Kingship and the Divine in Late Antiquity and the Early Middle Ages (to 1050)*. New Haven: Yale University Press.

Ohana, David. 2012. *Modernism and Zionism*. London: Palgrave Macmillan.

Ohana, David. 2018. *Nietzsche and Jewish Political Theology*. London: Routledge.

Ojakangas, Mika. 2009. "Carl Schmitt and the Sacred Origins of Law." *Telos* (147): pp. 34–54.

Ojakangas, Mika. 2012. "*Potentia absoluta et potentia ordinata Dei*: On the Theological Origins of Carl Schmitt's Theory of Constitution." *Continental Philosophy Review* 45: pp. 505–17.

Ostwald, Martin. 1986. *From Popular Sovereignty to the Sovereignty of Law*. Berkeley: University of California Press.

Otto, Rudolf. 1950. *The Idea of the Holy: An Inquiry into the Non-Rational Factor in the Idea of the Divine and Its Relation to the Rational*. Oxford: Oxford University Press.

Palélogue, Théodore. 2004. *Sous l'oeil du Grand Inquisiteur: Carl Schmitt et l'héritage de la théologie politique*. Paris: Les Éditions du Cerf.

Palmer, Gesine. 2015. *Angriff und Verteidigung: Paulus zwischen Juden und Christen*. Vol. 5, *Konversionen und andere Gesinnungsstörungen. Zur bleibenden Relevanz des Jüdischen Denkens nach Hermann Cohen und Franz Rosenzweig*. Berlin: epubli Gmbh.

Palmer, Gesine, and Yossef Schwartz, eds. 2003. *Franz Rosenzweig: "Innerlich bleibt die Welt eine." Ausgewählte Texte zum Islam*. Berlin: Philo.

Pangle, Thomas. 2006. *Leo Strauss: An Introduction to His Thought and Intellectual Legacy*. Baltimore: Johns Hopkins University Press.

Pangle, Thomas. 2014. "The Light Shed on the Crucial Development of Strauss's Thought by His Correspondence with Gerhard Krüger." In *Reorientation: Leo Strauss in the 1930s*, edited by Martin D. Yaffe and Richard S. Ruderman, pp. 57–68. New York: Palgrave Macmillan.

Parens, Joshua. 2014. "Leo Strauss on Farabi, Maimonides et al. in the 1930s." In *Reorientation: Leo Strauss in the 1930s*, edited by Martin D. Yaffe and Richard S. Ruderman, pp. 157–70. New York: Palgrave Macmillan.

Parens, Joshua. 2016. *Leo Strauss and the Recovery of Medieval Political Philosophy*. Rochester: University of Rochester Press.

Peterson, Erik. 1926. *Eis Theos: Epigraphische, formgeschichtliche und religiongeschichtliche Untersuchungen*. Göttingen: Vandenhoek & Ruprecht.

Peterson, Erik. 1951. "Das Problem des Nationalismus in alten Christentums." *Theologische Zeitschrift 7*: pp. 81–91.
Peterson, Erik. 2011. *Theological Tractates*. Translated by Michael Hollerich. Stanford: Stanford University Press.
Pettit, Philip. 2005. "Rawls's Political Ontology." *Politics, Philosophy and Economics 4*(2): pp. 157–74.
Phillips, James. 2005. *Heidegger's Volk: Between National Socialism and Poetry*. Stanford: Stanford University Press.
Philo. 1993. *The Works of Philo*. Translated by C.D. Yonge. Peabody: Hendrickson Publishers.
Pines, Shlomo. 1987–89. "Der Islam im 'Stern der Erlösung': Eine Untersuchung zu Tendenzen und Quellen Franz Rosenzweigs." *Hebräische Beiträge zur Wissenschaft des Judentums 3–5*: pp. 138–48.
Pingree, David. 2002. "The Sabians of Harran and the Classical Tradition." *International Journal of the Classical Tradition 9*(1): pp. 8–35.
Pinker, Steven. 2019. *Enlightenment Now: The Case for Reason, Science, Humanism, and Progress*. New York: Penguin.
Pitts, Jennifer. 2006. *A Turn to Empire: The Rise of Imperial Liberalism in Britain and France*. Princeton: Princeton University Press.
Plato. 1980. *The Laws of Plato*. Edited by Thomas Pangle. Chicago: University of Chicago Press.
Plato. 1985. *The Collected Dialogues of Plato*. Edited by Huntington Cairns and Edith Hamilton. Princeton: Princeton University Press.
Plato. 1992. *The Republic*. Translated by G.M.A. Grube. Indianapolis: Hackett.
Pocock, J. G. A. 1975. *The Machiavellian Moment: Florentine Political Thought and the Atlantic Republican Tradition*. Princeton: Princeton University Press.
Pöggeler, Otto. 1985. "Den Führer führen? Heidegger und keine Ende." *Philosophische Rundschau 32*(1–2): pp. 26–67.
Pollock, Benjamin. 2004. "From Nation State to World Empire: Franz Rosenzweig's Redemptive Imperialism." *Jewish Studies Quarterly 11*(4): pp. 332–53.
Pollock, Benjamin. 2009. *Franz Rosenzweig and the Systematic Task of Philosophy*. Cambridge: Cambridge University Press.
Polt, Richard, and Gregory Fried, eds. 2001. *A Companion to Heidegger's "Introduction to Metaphysics."* New Haven: Yale University Press.
Poma, Andrea. 2007. "Hermann Cohen: Judaism and Critical Idealism." In *The Cambridge Companion to Modern Jewish Philosophy*, edited by Michael L. Morgan and Peter Eli Gordon, pp. 80–101. Cambridge: Cambridge University Press.
Prozorov, Sergei. 2009. "Giorgio Agamben and the End of History: Inoperative Praxis and the Interruption of the Dialectic." *European Journal of Social Theory 12*(4): pp. 523–42.
Quélennec, Bruno. 2018. *Retour dans la caverne: Philosophie, politique et religion chez le jeune Leo Strauss*. Paris: Hermann.
Quint, David. 2011. "Virgil's Double Cross: Chiasmus and the *Aeneid*." *American Journal of Philology 132*: pp. 273–300.
Rabinbach, Anson. 1985. "Between Enlightenment and Apocalypse: Benjamin, Bloch and Modern German Jewish Messianism." *New German Critique 34*: pp. 78–124.
Rad, Gerhard von. 1969. *Der Heilige Krieg im alten Israel*. Göttingen: Vanderhoek & Ruprecht.

Radzins, Inese. 2016. "Simone Weil's Political Theology." *Political Theology 17*(3): pp. 226–42.

Rancière, Jacques. 2009. *Hatred of Democracy*. London: Verso.

Ranieri, John. 2009. *Disturbing Revelation: Leo Strauss, Eric Voegelin, and the Bible*. Columbia: University of Missouri Press.

Rashkover, Randi. 2005. *Revelation and Theopolitics: Barth, Rosenzweig and the Politics of Praise*. London: Continuum.

Ravitzky, Aviezer. 1996. *Messianism, Zionism, and Jewish Religious Radicalism*. Translated by Michael Swirsky and Jonathan Chipman. Chicago: University of Chicago Press.

Ricciardi, Alessia. 2009. "From Decreation to Bare Life: Weil, Agamben, and the Impolitical." *Diacritics 39*(2): pp. 75–93.

Rosanvallon, Pierre. 1998. *Le peuple introuvable*. Paris: Gallimard.

Rose, Gillian. 1993. *Judaism and Modernity: Philosophical Essays*. Oxford: Blackwell.

Rose, Sven-Erik. 2014. *Jewish Philosophical Politics in Germany, 1789–1848*. Waltham: Brandeis University Press.

Rosen, Stanley. 2003. *Hermeneutics as Politics*. New Haven: Yale University Press.

Rosenstock, Bruce. 2009. *Philosophy and the Jewish Question: Mendelssohn, Rosenzweig, and Beyond*. New York: Fordham University Press.

Rosenstock, Bruce. 2014. "Palintropos Harmonie: Jacob Taubes and Carl Schmitt 'im liebenden Streit.'" *New German Critique 41*(1): pp. 55–92.

Rosenstock, Bruce. 2017. *Transfinite Life: Oskar Goldberg and the Vitalist Imagination*. Bloomington: Indiana University Press.

Rosenstock-Huessy, Eugen. 2011. "Hitler and Israel, or On Prayer." In *Judaism Despite Christianity: The 1926 Wartime Correspondence between Eugen Rosenstock-Huessy and Franz Rosenzweig*, edited by Eugen Rosenstock-Huessy, pp. 178–94. Chicago: University of Chicago Press.

Rosenzweig, Franz. 1935. *Briefe*. Berlin: Schocken Verlag.

Rosenzweig, Franz. 1984. "Deutschtum und Judentum." In *Gesammelte Schriften III: Zweistromland. Kleinere Schriften zu Glauben und Denken*, pp. 169–75. Dordrecht: Martinus Nijhoff.

Rosenzweig, Franz. 1985. *The Star of Redemption*. Translated by William Hallo. Notre Dame: University of Notre Dame Press.

Rosenzweig, Franz. 1988. *Der Stern der Erlösung*. Frankfurt: Suhrkamp.

Rosenzweig, Franz. 2000. *Philosophical and Theological Writings*. Edited by Paul W. Franks and Michael L. Morgan. Indianapolis: Hackett.

Rosenzweig, Franz. 2003. *Confluences. Politique, Histoire, Judaisme*. Edited by Marc Crépon, Gérard Bensussan, and Marc de Launay. Paris: Vrin.

Rosenzweig, Franz. 2005. *The Star of Redemption*. Translated by Barbara Galli. Madison: University of Wisconsin Press.

Ross, Alison. 2018. *Revolution and History in Walter Benjamin: A Conceptual Analysis*. London: Routledge.

Rotenstreich, Nathan. 1962. "Moses Hess and Karl Ludwig Michelet: On the Occasion of the Centenary of *Rome and Jerusalem*." *Leo Baeck Institute Year Book 7*(1): pp. 283–6.

Rousseau, Jean-Jacques. 1968. *The Social Contract*. Translated by Maurice Cranston. London: Penguin Books.

Rubin, Gil. 2015. "From Federalism to Binationalism: Hannah Arendt's Shifting Zionism." *Contemporary European History 24*(3): pp. 393–414.

Runia, David T. 1988. "God and Man in Philo of Alexandria." *Journal of Theological Studies 39*(1): pp. 48–75.
Runia, David T. 1990. *Exegesis and Philosophy: Studies on Philo of Alexandria*. Aldershot: Variorum.
Said, Edward. 1995. *The Politics of Dispossession: The Struggle for Palestinian Self-Determination, 1969–1994*. New York: Vintage.
Samuelson, Norbert. 1999. *A User's Guide to Franz Rosenzweig's Star of Redemption*. Richmond: Curzon Press.
Santner, Eric L. 2003. "Miracles Happen: Benjamin, Rosenzweig, Freud, and the Matter of the Neighbor." In *The Neighbor: Three Inquiries in Political Theology*, edited by Slavoj Žižek, Eric L. Santner, and Kenneth Reinhard, pp. 76–133. Chicago: University of Chicago Press.
Santner, Eric L. 2007. *On the Psychotheology of Everyday Life: Reflections on Freud and Rosenzweig*. Chicago: University of Chicago Press.
Santner, Eric L. 2011. *The Royal Remains: The People's Two Bodies and the Endgames of Sovereignty*. Chicago: University of Chicago Press.
Savarino, Luca. 2001. *Heidegger e il cristianesimo 1916–1927*. Naples: Liguori.
Schaefer, Yoav. 2017. "Between Political Theology and Theopolitics: Martin Buber's *Kingship of God*." *Modern Judaism 37*(2): pp. 231–55.
Scharf, Orr. 2019. "A Tale of Love and Darkness: Martin Buber's Gnostic Canon and the Birth of Theopolitics." *Religions 10*: pp. 242–60.
Schelling, F. W. J. von, and Slavoj Žižek. 1997. *The Abyss of Freedom/Ages of the World*. Ann Arbor: University of Michigan Press.
Schmidt, Christoph. 2009. *Die theopolitische Stunde*. Muenchen: Wilhelm Fink.
Schmidt, Christoph. 2017. "Monotheism as a Metapolitical Problem: Heidegger's War against Jewish Christian Monotheism." In *Heidegger's Black Notebooks and the Future of Thelology*, edited by M. Björk and J. Svenungsson, pp. 131–57. London: Palgrave Macmillan.
Schmidt, Dennis J. 2001. *On Germans and Other Greeks: Tragedy and the Ethical Life*. Indianapolis: Indiana University Press.
Schmied-Kowarzik, Wolfdietrich, ed. 2006a. *Franz Rosenzweigs "neues Denken." Band I. Selbstbegrenzendes Denken—in philosophos*. Freiburg: Verlag Karl Alber.
Schmied-Kowarzik, Wolfdietrich, ed. 2006b. *Franz Rosenzweigs "neues Denken." Band II. Erfahrene Offenbarung—in theologos*. Freiburg: Verlag Karl Alber.
Schmitt, Carl. 1988. *Political Theology: Four Chapters on the Concept of Sovereignty*. Cambridge: MIT Press.
Schmitt, Carl. 1995. *Les trois types de pensée juridique*. Paris: PUF.
Schmitt, Carl. 1996a. *Politische Theologie*. Berlin: Duncker & Humblot.
Schmitt, Carl. 1996b. *Politische Theologie II: Die Legende von der Erledigung jeder Politische Theologie*. Berlin: Duncker&Humblot. Schmitt, Carl. 2001. *Le Nomos de la terre dans le droit des gens du jus publicum europaeum*. Paris: PUF.
Schmitt, Carl. 2003. *The Nomos of the Earth in the International Law of Jus Publicum Europaeum*. New York: Telos Press.
Schmitt, Carl. 2004. *Legality and Legitimacy*. Durham: Duke University Press.
Schmitt, Carl. 2008. *Political Theology II: The Myth of the Closure of any Political Theology*. Cambridge: Polity Press.
Schmitt, Carl. 2014. "The Planetary Tension between Orient and Occident and the Opposition Between Land and Sea." *Política Común 5. Carl Schmitt and the Early Modern World*. Coordinated by John D. Blanco and Ivonne del Valle.

Schmitt, Carl. 2015. *Land and Sea: A World-Historical Meditation*. Edited by Russell A. Berman and Samuel Garrett Zeitlin. Candor: Telos Press.

Schmitt, Carl, and Hans Blumenberg. 2007. *Hans Blumenberg, Carl Schmitt Briefwechsel 1971–1978 und weitere Materialen*. Edited by Alexander Schmitz and Marcel Lepper. Frankfurt: Suhrkamp.

Scholem, Gershom. 1963. "Wissenschaft vom Judentum einst und jetzt." In his *Judaica 1*, pp. 147–64. Frankfurt: Suhrkamp.

Scholem, Gershom. 1970. "Juden und Deutsche." In his *Judaica 2*, pp. 20–46. Frankfurt: Suhrkamp.

Scholem, Gershom. 1970a. "Das Ringen zwischen dem biblischen Gott und dem Gott Plotins in der alten Kabbala." In his *Über einige Grundbegriffe des Judentums*, pp. 9–52. Frankfurt: Suhrkamp.

Scholem, Gershom. 1970b. "Schöpfung aus Nichts und Selbstverschränkung Gottes." In his *Über einige Grundbegriffe des Judentums*, pp. 53–89. Frankfurt: Suhrkamp.

Scholem, Gershom. 1971. *The Messianic Idea in Judaism*. New York: Schocken Books.

Scholem, Gershom. 1973. *Judaica 3: Studien zur jüdischen Mystik*. Frankfurt: Suhrkamp.

Scholem, Gershom. 1976. *On Jews and Judaism in Crisis: Selected Essays*. New York: Schocken Books.

Scholem, Gershom. 1977. *Major Trends in Jewish Mysticism*. New York: Schocken Books.

Scholem, Gershom. 1980. *From Berlin to Jerusalem: Memories of My Youth*. New York: Schocken Books.

Scholem, Gershom. 1981. *Walter Benjamin: The Story of a Friendship*. New York: Schocken Books.

Scholem, Gershom. 1984a. *Judaica 4*. Edited by Rolf Tiedemann. Frankfurt: Suhrkamp.

Scholem, Gershom. 1984b. "Zur Sozialpsychologie der Juden in Deutschland 1900–1930." In *Judaica 4*, edited by Rolf Tiedemann, pp. 229–61. Frankfurt: Suhrkamp.

Scholem, Gershom. 1989. *The Correspondence of Walter Benjamin and Gershom Scholem, 1932–1940*. Edited by Gary Smith and Andre Lefevere. New York: Schocken Books.

Scholem, Gershom. 1994. *Briefe I: 1914–1947*. Edited by Itta Shedletzky. Munich: C.H. Beck.

Scholem, Gershom. 1995. *Briefe II: 1948–1970*. Edited by Thomas Sparr. Munich: Verlag C. H. Beck.

Scholem, Gershom. 1996. *On the Kabbalah and Its Symbolism*. New York: Schocken Books.

Scholem, Gershom. 1997a. *Judaica 6. Die Wissenschaft vom Judentum*. Edited by Peter Schäfer. Frankfurt: Suhrkamp.

Scholem, Gershom. 1997b. *On the Possibility of Jewish Mysticism in Our Time and Other Essays*. Philadelphia: The Jewish Publication Society.

Scholem, Gershom. 1999. *Briefe III: 1971–1982*. Edited by Itta Shedletzky. Munich: C. H. Beck.

Scholem, Gershom, and Leo Strauss. 2008. *Lettere dall'esilio. Carteggio (1933–1973)*. Edited by Carlo Altini. Florence: La Giuntina.

Schultz, Joseph P. 1971. "Angelic Opposition to the Ascension of Moses and the Revelation of the Law." *The Jewish Quarterly Review 61*(4): pp. 282–307.

Schürmann, Reiner. 1983. "Neoplatonic Henology as an Overcoming of Metaphysics." *Research in Phenomenology 13*: pp. 25–41.

Schürmann, Reiner. 1987. *Heidegger on Being and Acting: From Principles to Anarchy*. Bloomington: Indiana University Press.

Schürmann, Reiner. 1990. *Heidegger on Being and Acting: From Principles to Anarchy*. Bloomington: Indiana University Press.

Schürmann, Reiner. 1996. *Des hégémonies brisées*. Mauvezin: Trans-Europ-Repress.

Schürmann, Reiner. 2003. *Broken Hegemonies*. Indianapolis: Indiana University Press.

Schürmann, Reiner. 2005. *Maitre Eckhart ou la joie errante*. Paris: Rivages.

Schürmann, Reiner. 2019. *Tomorrow the Manifold: Essays on Foucault, Anarchy, and the Singularization to Come*. Edited by Malte Fabian Rauch and Nicolas Schneider. Berlin: Diaphanes.

Schwartz, Regina M. 1998. *The Curse of Cain: The Violent Legacy of Monotheism*. Chicago: University of Chicago Press.

Schwartz, Yossef. 2003. "Die entfremdete Nähe. Rosenzweigs Blick auf den Islam." In *Franz Roenzweig. "Innerlich bleibt die Welt eine." Ausgewählte Texte zum Islam*, edited by Gesine Palmer and Yossef Schwartz, pp. 111–47. Berlin: Philo.

Schwartz, Yossef. 2012. "From Religious Pluralism to the Clash of Civilizations: The Contemporary Dimension in Rosenzweig's Philosophy." In *Faith, Truth, and Reason: New Perspectives on Franz Rosenzweig's Star of Redemption*, edited by Yehoyada Amir, Yossi Turner, and Martin Brasser, pp. 573–90. Freiburg: Verlag Karl Alber.

Schwarzschild, Steven. 1956. "The Democratic Socialism of Hermann Cohen." *Hebrew Union College Annual 27*: pp. 417–38.

Schwarzschild, Steven. 1979. "'Germanism and Judaism':Hermann Cohen's Normative Paradigm of the German-Jewish Symbiosis." In *Jews and Germans from 1860 to 1933*, edited by David Bronsen, pp. 129–72. Heidelberg: Carl Winter Universitätsverlag.

Schwarzschild, Steven. 1990. *The Pursuit of the Ideal: Jewish Writings of Steven Schwarzschild*. Albany: State University of New York Press.

Schweid, Eliezer. 2012. "Is Franz Rosenzweig's Thought Relevant to Our Time?" In *Faith, Truth, and Reason: New Perspectives on Franz Rosenzweig's Star of Redemption*, edited by Yohayada Amir, Yossi Turner, and Martin Brasser, pp. 553–71. Freiburg: Verlag Karl Alber.

Shanks, Andrew. 1991. *Hegel's Political Theology*. Cambridge: Cambridge University Press.

Sharvit, Gilad. 2017. "Exile and Tradition: Benjamin's *Fichu* Dream, Scholem's Divine Law, and Kafka's Village." *The Germanic Review: Literature, Culture, Theory 92*(3): pp. 280–300.

Sheppard, Eugene. 2007. *Leo Strauss and the Politics of Exile: The Making of a Political Philosopher*. Waltham: Brandeis University Press.

Simmons, A. John. 2001. *Justification and Legitimacy: Essays on Rights and Obligations*. Cambridge: Cambridge University Press.

Simon, Ernst. 1935. "Zu Hermann Cohens Spinoza-Auffassung." *Monatsschrift fuer Geschichte und Wissenschaft des Judentums 79*(2): pp. 181–9.

Simons, Oliver. 2016. "Carl Schmitt's Spatial Rhetoric." In *The Oxford Handbook of Carl Schmitt*, edited by Jens Meierhenrich and Oliver Simons, pp. 776–802. New York: Oxford University Press.

Skinner, Quentin. 1978. *The Foundations of Modern Political Thought*. Vol. II: *The Age of Reformation*. Cambridge: Cambridge University Press.

Skinner, Quentin. 2005. "Hobbes on Representation." *European Journal of Philosophy 13*(2): pp. 157–84.

Slobodian, Quinn. 2018. *Globalists: The End of Empire and the Birth of Neoliberalism*. Cambridge: Harvard University Press.

Smith, Steven B. 1991. "Leo Strauss: Between Athens and Jerusalem." *The Review of Politics 53*(1): pp. 75–99.

Smith, Steven B. 1993. "Gerschom Scholem and Leo Strauss: Notes toward a German-Jewish Dialogue." *Modern Judaism 13*(3): pp. 209–29.

Smith, Steven B. 2011. "Philosophy as a Way of Life: The Case of Leo Strauss." In *Political Philosophy in the Twentieth Century: Authors and Arguments*, edited by Catherine Zuckert, pp. 61–79. New York: Cambridge University Press.

Sorabji, Richard. 2006. *Time, Creation and the Continuum: Theories in Antiquity and the Early Middle Ages*. Chicago: University of Chicago Press.

Spinoza, Baruch. 2002. *Spinoza. Complete Works*. Translated by Samuel Shirley. Indianapolis: Hackett.

Stacey, Peter. 2007. *Roman Monarchy and the Renaissance*. Cambridge: Cambridge University Press.

Stefou, K. C. 2015. "Nomos o panton basileus: Pindar, Callicles and Plato's Treatment of Nomos in the *Gorgias*." *Akroterion* (60): pp. 1–11.

Steiner, Uwe. 2000. "Kritik." In *Benjamins Begriffe*, edited by Michael Opitz and Ermudt Wizisla, pp. 479–521. Frankfurt: Suhrkamp.

Steiner, Uwe. 2001. "The True Politician: Walter Benjamin's Concept of the Political." *New German Critique 83*: pp. 43–88.

Stewart, Jon. 2011. "Hegel's Philosophy of Religion and the Question of 'Right' and 'Left' Hegelianism." In *Politics, Religion, and Art: Hegelian Debates*, edited by Douglass Moggach, pp. 66–95. Evanston: Northwestern University Press.

Stier, Hans Erich. 1928. "Nomos Basileus." *Philologus* LXXXIII (3): pp. 225–58.

Stimilli, Elettra. 2019. "Religion and the Spontaneous Order of the Market: Law, Freedom, and Power over Lives." *European Journal of Social Theory 22*(3): pp. 399–415.

Stone, Suzanne Last. 2012. "The Jewish Law of War: The Turn to International Law and Ethics." In *Just Wars, Holy Wars, and Jihads: Christian, Jewish, Muslim Encounters and Exchanges*, edited by Sohail H. Hashmi, pp. 342–82. New York: Oxford University Press.

Strauss, Leo. 1937. "On Abravanel's Philosophical Tendency and Political Teaching." In *Isaac Abravanel*, edited by J. B. Trend and H. Loewe, pp. 93–109. Cambridge: Cambridge University Press.

Strauss, Leo. 1952. *Persecution and the Art of Writing*. Chicago: University of Chicago Press.

Strauss, Leo. 1953. *Natural Right and History*. Chicago: University of Chicago Press.

Strauss, Leo. 1963. *On Tyranny*. New York: Free Press.

Strauss, Leo. 1964. *The City and Man*. Chicago: University of Chicago Press.

Strauss, Leo. 1968. *Liberalism Ancient and Modern*. Chicago: University of Chicago Press.

Strauss, Leo. 1986. *Studies in Platonic Political Philosophy*. Chicago: University of Chicago Press.

Strauss, Leo. 1988. *What Is Political Philosophy and Other Studies*. Chicago: University of Chicago Press.

Strauss, Leo. 1989. *The Rebirth of Classical Political Rationalism*. Edited by Thomas Pangle. Chicago: University of Chicago Press.

Strauss, Leo. 1995. *Philosophy and Law: Contributions to the Understanding of Maimonides and His Predecessors*. Albany: State University of New York Press.

Strauss, Leo. 1997a. *Jewish Philosophy and the Crisis of Modernity: Essays and Lectures in Modern Jewish Thought*. Edited by Kenneth Hart Green, *SUNY Series in the Jewish Writings of Leo Strauss*. Albany: State University of New York Press.

Strauss, Leo. 1997b. *Philosophie und Gesetz—Fruehe Schriften*. Edited by Heinrich Meier. Stuttgart: Verlag J. B. Metzler.

Strauss, Leo. 1997c. *Spinoza's Critique of Religion*. Chicago: University of Chicago Press.

Strauss, Leo. 2002. *Leo Strauss: The Early Writings (1921-1932)*. Edited by Michael Zank. Albany: State University of New York Press.

Strauss, Leo. 2008. *Hobbes' politische Wissenschaft und zugehoerige Schriften—Briefe*. Edited by Heinrich Meier. Vol. 3, *Gesammelte Schriften*. Stuttgart: Verlag J. B. Metzler.

Strauss, Leo. 2013. *Leo Strauss on Maimonides: The Complete Writings*. Edited by Kenneth Hart Green. Chicago: University of Chicago Press.

Strousma, Sarah. 2009. *Maimonides in His World: Portrait of a Mediterranean Thinker*. Princeton: Princeton University Press.

Styfhals, Willem. 2018. "Deconstructing Orthodoxy: A Failed Dialogue between Gerschom Scholem and Jacob Taubes." *New German Critique 45*(1): pp. 181–205.

Susser, Bernard. 1981. *Existence and Utopia: The Social and Political Thought of Martin Buber*. Teaneck: Fairleigh Dickinson University Press.

Sutcliffe, Adam. 2003. *Judaism and Enlightenment*. Cambridge: Cambridge University Press.

Syros, Vasileios. 2011. "Founders and Kings versus Orators: Medieval and Early Modern Views on the Origins of Social Life." *Viator 42*(1): pp. 383–408.

Syros, Vasileios. 2012. *Marsilius of Padua at the Intersection of Ancient and Medieval Traditions of Political Thought*. Toronto: University of Toronto Press.

Taminiaux, Jacques. 1985. "Arendt, disciple de Heidegger?" *Etudes phénoménologiques 2*: pp. 111–36.

Tamir, Yael. 1995. *Liberal Nationalism*. Princeton: Princeton University Press.

Tanguay, Daniel. 2003. *Leo Strauss: Une biographie intellectuelle*. Paris: Grasset.

Tardieu, Michel. 1986. "Sabiens coraniques et Sabiens de Harran." *Journal Asiatique 274*: pp. 1–44.

Taub, Emmanuel. 2013. *Mesianismo y redención. Prolegómenos para una teologia política judía*. Buenos Aires: Miño y Dávila Editores.

Taub, Emmanuel. 2017. "Historia universal y apocalipsis: Un comentario sobre el estado del mundo en Franz Rosenzweig y Carl Schmitt." *Ratio Juris 12*(24): pp. 343–62.

Taubes, Jacob. 1993. *Die Politische Theologie des Paulus*. Munich: Wilhelm Fink Verlag.

Taubes, Jacob. 2000. *Il prezzo del messianismo*. Edited by Elettra Stimilli. Macerata: Quodlibet.

Taubes, Jacob. 2003. *The Political Theology of Paul*. Stanford: Stanford University Press.

Taubes, Jacob. 2009. *Occidental Eschatology*. Stanford: Stanford University Press.

Taubes, Jacob. 2010. *From Cult to Culture*. Stanford: Stanford University Press.

Taubes, Jacob. 2016. "Walter Benjamin—A Modern Marcionite? Scholem's Benjamin Interpretation Reexamined." In *Walter Benjamin and Theology*, edited by Colby Dickinson and Stephane Symons, pp. 164–78. New York: Fordham University Press.

Taylor, Charles. 2004. *Modern Social Imaginaries*. Durham: Duke University Press.

Taylor, Charles. 2007. *A Secular Age*. Cambridge: Harvard University Press.

Theunissen, Michael. 1970. *Hegels Lehre vom absoluten Geist als Theologisch-Politischer Traktat*. Berlin: De Gruyter.

Theunissen, Michael. 1984. *The Other: Studies in the Social Ontology of Husserl, Heidegger, Sartre, and Buber*. Cambridge: MIT Press.

Thornhill, Chris. 2013. *A Sociology of Constitutions: Constitutions and State Legitimacy in Historical-Sociological Perspective*. New York: Cambridge University Press.

Tierney, Brian. 1982. *Religion, Law and the Growth of Constitutional Thought 1150–1650*. Cambridge: Cambridge University Press.

Tomko, Helena. 2017. "The Reluctant Satirist: Theodor Haecker and the Dizzying Swindle of Nazism." *Oxford German Studies 46*(1): pp. 42–57.

Trigano, Shmuel. 1991. *Philosophie de la loi: Origine de la politique dans la Tora*. Paris: Le Cerf.

Trom, Danny. 2018. *Persévérance du fait juive: Une théorie politique de la survie*. Paris: EHESS Gallimard Seuil.

Udoff, Alan, and Barbara E. Galli, eds. 1999. *Franz Rosenzweig's "The New Thinking."* Syracuse: Syracuse University Press.

Ullmann, Walter. 1980. *Jurisprudence in the Middle Ages: Collected Studies*. London: Variorum Reprints.

Urbinati, Nadia. 2019. *Me the People*. Cambridge: Harvard University Press.

Vatter, Miguel. 2004a. "Machiavelli after Marx: The Self-Overcoming of Marxism in the Late Althusser." *Theory and Event 7*(4).

Vatter, Miguel. 2004b. "Strauss and Schmitt as Readers of Hobbes and Spinoza: On the Relation between Liberalism and Political Theology." *The New Centennial Review 4*(3): pp. 161–214.

Vatter, Miguel. 2005. "Pettit and Modern Republican Political Thought." In *Political Exclusion and Domination. NOMOS XLVI*, edited by Melissa Williams and Stephen Macedo, pp. 118–63. New York: New York University Press.

Vatter, Miguel. 2006. "Natality and Biopolitics in Hannah Arendt." *Revista de Ciencia Política 26*(3): pp. 137–59.

Vatter, Miguel. 2007. "Resistance and Legality: Arendt and Negri on Constituent Power." In *The Philosophy of Toni Negri*, Vol. 2, edited by Tim Murphy and Abdul-Karin Mustapha, pp. 52–86. London: Pluto Press.

Vatter, Miguel. 2008a. "In Odradek's World: Bare Life and Historical Materalism in Agamben and Benjamin." *Diacritics 38*(3): pp. 45–70.

Vatter, Miguel. 2008b. "The Idea of Public Reason and the Reason of State. Schmitt and Rawls on the Political." *Political Theory 36*(2): pp. 239–71.

Vatter, Miguel. 2010. "Natural Right and State of Exception in Strauss' Teaching on Tyranny." In *Crediting God: Sovereignty and Religion in the Age of Global Capitalism*, edited by Miguel Vatter, pp. 190–206. New York: Fordham University Press.

Vatter, Miguel. 2012. "The Quarrel between Populism and Republicanism: Machiavelli and the Antinomies of Plebeian Politics." *Contemporary Political Theory 11*(3): pp. 242–63.

Vatter, Miguel. 2013. "Machiavelli and the Republican Conception of Providence." *The Review of Politics 75*: pp. 605–23.

Vatter, Miguel. 2014. *The Republic of the Living: Biopolitics and the Critique of Civil Society*. New York: Fordham University Press.

Vatter, Miguel. 2016. "Law and Life Beyond Incorporation: Agamben, Highest Poverty and the Papal Legal Revolution." In *Agamben and Radical Politics*, edited by Daniel McLoughlin, pp. 234–62. Edinburgh: Edinburgh University Press.

Vatter, Miguel. 2017a. "Machiavelli, 'Ancient Theology,' and the Problem of Civil Religion." In *Machiavelli on Liberty and Conflict*, edited by Nadia Urbinati, David Johnston, and Camila Vergara, pp. 113–38. Chicago: University of Chicago Press.

Vatter, Miguel. 2017b. "Must God Be a Conversation-Stopper for the Political Philosopher? Leo Strauss on Philosophy, Religion and Legality." *Theory & Event 20*(1): pp. 238–59.

Vatter, Miguel. 2017c. "Nationality, State and Global Constitutionalism in Herman Cohen's Wartime Writings." In *Crisis and Reconfigurations: 100 Years of European Thinking since 1914*, edited by Matthew Sharpe and Rory Jeffs. New York: Springer.

Vatter, Miguel. 2017d. "The Political Theology of Carl Schmitt." In *The Oxford Handbook of Carl Schmitt*, edited by Jens Meierhenrich and Oliver Simons, pp. 245–68. Oxford: Oxford University Press.

Vatter, Miguel. 2018. "Neoliberalism and Republicanism: Economic Rule of Law and Law as Concrete Order (*nomos*)." In *The SAGE Handbook of Neoliberalism*, edited by Melinda Cooper, Damien Cahill, Martijn Konings, and David Primrose, pp. 370–83. London: Sage.

Vatter, Miguel. 2019a. "Dignity and the Foundation of Human Rights: Toward an Averroist Genealogy." *Politics and Religion 13*(2): pp. 304–32.

Vatter, Miguel. 2019b. "'Only a God Can Resist a God': Political Theology between Polytheism and Gnosticism." *Political Theology 20*(6): pp. 472–97.

Vatter, Miguel. 2020. *Divine Democracy. Political Theology After Carl Schmitt*. New York: Oxford University Press.

Vattimo, Gianni. 1997. *Beyond Interpretation: The Meaning of Hermeneutics for Philosophy*. Stanford: Stanford University Press.

Vattimo, Gianni. 1999. *Belief*. Stanford: Stanford University Press.

Vattimo, Gianni. 2002. *After Christianity*. New York: Columbia University Press.

Vegetti, Mario. 2009. *"Un paradigma in cielo": Platone politico da Aristotle al Novecento*. Roma: Carocci.

Vernière, Paul. 1982. *Spinoza et la pensée francaise avant la Révolution*. Paris: PUF.

Villa, Dana. 2008. *Public Freedom*. Princeton: Princeton University Press.

Voegelin, Eric. 1952. *The New Science of Politics*. Chicago: University of Chicago Press.

Voegelin, Eric. 1998. *History of Political Ideas*. Vol. V: *Religion and Rise of Modernity*. Edited by James Wiser. Columbia: University of Missouri Press.

Volk, Christian. 2016. "Towards a Critical Theory of the Political: Hannah Arendt on Power and Critique." *Philosophy and Social Criticism 42*(6): pp. 549–75.

Vries, Hent de. 2001. *Religion and Violence: Philosophical Perspectives from Kant to Derrida*. Baltimore: Johns Hopkins University Press.

Waldron, Jeremy. 2015. *Dignity, Rank, and Rights*. Oxford: Oxford University Press.

Walther, Manfred. 2004. "Gestalten und Implikationen Politischer Theologie—mit Blick auf Althusius." In *Jurisprudenz, Politische Theorie, und Politische Theologie*, edited by Heinz Schilling, Dieter Wyduckel, and Frederick S. Carney, pp. 143–67. Berlin Ducker & Humblot.

Walzer, Michael. 1986. *Exodus and Revolution*. New York: Basic Books.

Walzer, Michael, ed. 2006. *Law, Politics, and Morality in Judaism*. Princeton: Princeton University Press.

Walzer, Michael. 2012. *In God's Shadow. Politics in the Hebrew Bible*. New Haven: Yale University Press.

Walzer, Michael, Menachem Lorberbaum, and Noam J. Zohar, eds. 2000. *The Jewish Political Tradition. Volume I: Authority*. New Haven: Yale University Press.

Wasserstrom, Steven M. 1997. "Defeating Evil from Within: Comparative Perspectives on *Redemption through Sin*." *The Journal of Jewish Thought and Philosophy 6*: pp. 37–57.

Weber, Max. 1952. *Ancient Judaism*. Edited by Hans Gerth and Don Martindale. New York: The Free Press.

Weber, Max. 1968. *On Charisma and Institution Building*. Edited by S. N. Eisenstadt. Chicago: University of Chicago Press.

Weidner, Daniel. 2003. *Gershom Scholem: Politisches, esoterisches und historiographisches Schriften*. Koln: Fink.

Weidner, Daniel. 2006. "Reading Gershom Scholem." *The Jewish Quarterly Review 96*(2): pp. 203–31.

Weidner, Daniel. 2014. "The Political Theology of Ethical Monotheism." In *Judaism, Liberalism and Political Theology*, edited by Martin Kavka, and Randi Rashkover, pp. 178–96. Bloomington: Indiana University Press.

Weil, Simone. 1951. *Les Intuitions Pré-Chrétiennes*. Paris: Éditions du Vieux Colombier.

Whittaker, Helène. 2007. "Virgil's Fourth Eclogue and the Eleusinian Mysteries." *Symbolae Osloenses 82*(1): pp. 65–86.

Whyte, Jessica. 2014. *Catastrophe and Redemption: The Political Thought of Giorgio Agamben*. Albany: State University of New York Press.

Wiedebach, Hartwig. 2010. "Logic of Science vs. Theory of Creation: The 'Authority of Annihilation' in Hermann Cohen's Logic of Origin." *Journal of Jewish Thought and Philosophy 18*(2): pp. 107–20.

Wiedebach, Hartwig. 2012. *The National Element in Hermann Cohen's Philosophy and religion*. Vol. 16, *Supplements to The Journal of Jewish Thought and Philosophy*. Dordrecht: Brill.

Wilkinson, Michael. 2012. "Between Freedom and Law: Hannah Arendt on the Promise of Modern Revolution and the Burden of 'The Tradition.'" In *Hannah Arendt and the Law*, edited by Christopher McCorkindale and Marco Goldoni, pp. 35–62. Portland: Hart.

Winter, Eggert. 1980. *Ethik und Rechtswissenschaft: Ein historisch-systematische Untersuchung zur Ethik-Konzeption des Marburger Neukantianismus im Werke Hermann Cohens*. Berlin: Duncker & Humblot.

Wohlfarth, Irving. 2002. "Nihilistischer Messianismus: Zu Walter Benjamins *Theologisch-politischem Fragment*." In *"Judische" und "christliche" Sprachfigurationen im 20. Jahrhundert*, edited by Ashraf Noor and Josef Wohlmuth, pp. 141–214. Paderborn: Ferdinand Schöningh.

Wohlfarth, Irving. 2005. "Nihilismus contra Nihilismus. Benjamins 'Weltpolitik' aus heutiger Sicht." In *Theologie und Politik. Walter Benjamin und ein Paradigma der Moderne*, edited by Mauro Ponzi and Bernd Witte, pp. 107–36. Berlin: Erich Schmidt Verlag.

Wolfe, Judith. 2017. "Religion in the Black Notebooks: Overview and Analysis." In *Heidegger's Black Notebooks and the Future of Theology*, edited by M. Björk and J. Svenungsson, pp. 23–48. London: Palgrave Macmillan.

Wolfson, Elliot R. 1995. *Along the Path: Studies in Kabbalistic Myth, Symbolism, and Hermeneutics*. Albany: State University of New York Press.

Wolfson, Elliot R. 2006. *Venturing Beyond: Law and Morality in Kabbalistic Mysticism*. New York: Oxford University Press.

Wolfson, Elliot R. 2012. "Nihilating Nonground and the Temporal Sway of Becoming." *Angelaki 17*(3): pp. 31–45.

Wolfson, Elliot R. 2017. "*Gottwesen* and the De-Divinization of the last God. Heidegger's Meditation on the Strange and Incalculable." In *Heidegger's Black Notebooks and the Future of Theology*, edited by M. Björk and J. Svenungsson, pp. 211–55. London: Palgrave Macmillan.

Wolfson, Harry Austryn. 1947. *Philo: Foundations of Religious Philosophy in Judaism, Christianity, and Islam*. Cambridge: Harvard University Press.

Yaffe, Martin D. 2014. "Strauss on Hermann Cohen's 'Idealizing' Appropriation of Maimonides as a Platonist." In *Reorientation: Leo Strauss in the 1930s*, edited by Martin D. Yaffe and Richard S. Ruderman, pp. 69–78. New York: Palgrave Macmillan.

Yaffe, Martin D., and Richard S. Ruderman, eds. 2014. *Reorientation: Leo Strauss in the 1930s*. New York: Palgrave Macmillan.

Yassour, Avraham. 2011. "Topos and Utopia in Landauer's and Buber's Social Philosophy." https://lib.anarhija.net/category/author/avraham-yassour. Accessed June 23, 2019.

Yates, Frances. 1991. *Giordano Bruno and the Hermetic Tradition*. Chicago: University of Chicago Press.

Yelle, Robert A. 2011. "Moses' Veil: Secularization as Christian Myth." In *After Secular Law*, edited by Robert A. Yelle, Winnifred F. Sullivan, and Mateo Taussig-Rubbo, pp. 23–42. Stanford: Stanford University Press.

Yelle, Robert E. 2019. *Sovereignty and the Sacred: Secularism and the Political Economy of Religion*. Chicago: University of Chicago Press.

Yovel, Yirmiahu. 1998. *Dark Riddle: Hegel, Nietzsche, and the Jews*. University Park: Pennsylvania State University Press.

Zadoff, Noam. 2017. *Gershom Scholem: From Berlin to Jerusalem and Back*. Waltham: Brandeis University Press.

Zank, Michael. 2006. "The Ethics in Hermann Cohen's Philosophical System." *Journal of Jewish Thought and Philosophy 13*: pp. 1–15.

Zartaloudis, Thanos. 2019. *The Birth of Nomos*. Edinburgh: Edinburgh University Press.

Žižek, Slavoj, Eric L. Santner, and Kenneth Reinhard. 2013. *The Neighbor: Three Inquiries in Political Theology*. Chicago: University of Chicago Press.

Zuckert, Catherine H. 1996. *Postmodern Platos*. Chicago: University of Chicago Press.

Zuckert, Catherine, and Michael Zuckert. 2006. *The Truth about Leo Strauss: Political Philosophy and American Democracy*. Chicago: University of Chicago Press.

Zuckert, Catherine, and Michael Zuckert. 2014. *Leo Strauss and the Problem of Political Philosophy*. Chicago: University of Chicago Press.

Index

For the benefit of digital users, indexed terms that span two pages (e.g., 52–53) may, on occasion, appear on only one of those pages.

Abensour, Miguel, 285n.2, 285–86
Abraham
  Arendt on, 250, 251n.33, 265–66, 267
  Cohen on, 48
  Hess on, 85–86, 109
  as living natural law, 31
  Philo on, 29–30
  Strauss on, 203n.39
absolute, legal problem of, 260–64
acclamation, 154–58, 154n.72, 155n.76, 158n.82, 159
Adams, John, 262n.62
Adler, Eve, 229–30n.119
Agamben, Giorgio, 4–5
  on anarchy, Schürmann's principle, 286–87, 286n.4
  anomie, 19, 149–50, 182–83
  on divine government, 287–89
  economic theology, 24–25, 287–88
  on emancipatory politics and Saint Paul's messianism, 39
  on Hitler, 21, 93n.36
  Homo sacer, 19–20, 19n.22, 20n.23, 141
  inoperativity, 42n.24
  Kingdom and the Glory, The, 155–56, 155n.76
  living law, 11n.3, 18, 19–20, 21, 23–25, 26n.34
  on *nomos basileus,* 20n.23
  on *oikonomia,* 23–24, 31, 31n.38, 287–88
  on prayer, political theology, 93n.36
  on Saint Paul and the Messiah, 39, 39n.15
  State of Exception, 149–50, 149nn.52–55, 220–21
  Trinitarianism, 18, 23, 287–88
Akhenaton, 25
Akhnai, oven of, 95, 95n.40, 133–34, 134n.5
aleph, 183–84, 184n.128, 185–86, 188, 203–4, 222–23, 293–94
Alexander of Aphrodisias, 51, 289
Alexander the Great, 18–19, 105, 105n.66
Alfarabi, 166–67, 193n.9, 206–7, 226n.112
  Attainment of Happiness, 224, 224n.108
Al-Ghazali, 124
Altman, William, 182n.126, 193n.10
Altmann, Alexander, 88–89, 89n.27
an-arche
  God as, 1, 1n.4, 46–47, 51–52, 52n.33, 167–68, 249, 285–87
  Mosaic principle, 56
anarchism, religious, 133, 134–35, 139, 146–47, 176, 181–90, 182n.125, 285–87
  Levinas, Emmanuel, 2n.6, 188n.133
  oral Torah in state of exception and, 181–90
  political theology, 56n.41
  Scholem, Gershom, 133, 134–35, 139, 146–47, 176, 181–90, 182n.125
  Weil, Simone, 2n.6, 189n.134, 290–91
Ancient Judaism (Weber), 119–20
angelic guardian, nation's, 152–53, 152nn.62–64
Anidjar, Gil, 84, 124n.106, 125–26
animate law *(nomos empsychos),* 11n.3, 14, 15, 20–23
anomie, 19, 149–50, 182–83
Anti-Christ, 8, 43–44, 95–96, 126–27, 151–52, 175, 176–77, 256–57

antinomy, 134–35, 172
biblical, Tree of Life and, 171–75
of theocracy, 146
of theocracy, pagan political philosophy and, 137–47
anti-Roman affect, 28–33
anti-Semitism, 3–4, 59, 65, 143–44, 199, 237, 240–41, 244n.11, 255–56, 255n.44,
apocalypticism, 182–83, 249–50n.29, 271
Aquinas, Thomas, Saint, 31, 100, 288
Arato, Andrew, 264
arche
anarchy and, 285–87
Arendt on, 266, 275–76, 277
Cohen on, 46–47, 52n.33, 56
Ecphantus on, 26
Polybius on, 99
Scholem and mystical foundations of authority, 135–37, 140–41, 148–49, 150–51, 152–53, 167–68, 182n.125
Arendt, Hannah
anarchy, principle of, 56n.41
on Buber, 239
civil conception, religion, 238–39, 238n.3
dignity, human, 280–81, 281n.92
freedom, 115, 115n.90
God's guidance, trust in, 245–46
Heidegger, Martin, 239
Imperialism, 242–44
Jesus, divine natural right, 239
"The Jew as Pariah," 280–81, 282n.94
Jewish Question, 239, 240, 241–42
on land, 247–48, 247n.19
revolution, temporality of, 265, 265n.66
On Revolution, 237, 240–41, 245, 261, 261nn.59–60, 265–66, 275–76, 278–79
Roman civil religion, Judaism and, 60n.50
Arendt, Hannah, and federalism, 237–83
Abraham, 250, 251n.33, 265–66, 267
absolute, legal problem of, 260–64
charismatic leader, 250, 250n.31
civil religion, 210n.63, 262–64, 262n.62
Da-sein, 239, 252–54, 254n.40
on dictatorship, 268–69, 268n.72
Heine, republican Jesus, and human rights, 277–83
homeland, in Buber and Heidegger, 244–59
Human Condition, 247n.19, 254–55, 266–67, 268–69, 275–76, 277, 279
human rights, 280, 280n.91
inter-esse, 240–41, 242
Jesus of Nazareth, 278–80, 278n.89
Jewish apocalyptic politic thought, 249–50, 249–50n.29
Jewish politics in general, 242, 245–46, 248, 253, 259, 265–66
Jewish science, 244–45, 244–45n.12
minority question, 241–42
natality, 272–74, 273n.83
res publica, 240–41, 277
revolutions, modern, 260
right, equal participation in political life, 240–41
Roman political thought, 242–43, 243n.9
on social contract, 260–61, 261n.58
Virgil, civil religion and natality, 264–77
Zionism and federalism, 240–44
Aristotelianism, 20–21, 48–49, 50, 165n.93
Rabbinic Judaism and, 206n.46
double truth doctrine, 212, 212n.72
Platonism and, 210–14
political science, Torah as, 205–18
Aristotle, 21
divine law, 232
gentlemen, 206n.48, 207
God of, 165, 165n.93, 217
monarch as head of household, 31, 31n.38
Aschheim, Steven, 143n.37
Assmann, Jan, 26n.33, 52–53, 54n.36, 109n.78
atheism, 49–52, 90, 137, 182n.126, 282, 292
chronolibido and, 101, 101n.51
Strauss, Leo, 138, 197–98, 197n.25
Atheist Theology, 112
Athens, Jerusalem and, 12–13, 44–45, 87–88, 92, 130–32, 162, 189–90, 195n.18, 217n.88, 227–28, 234, 235–36
Augustine, 36, 117, 245n.13, 245–46, 266–67

authority
  charismatic, 5–6, 11–12
  Church, 103–4, 212
  crisis of, 133–35, 149–50
  law and mystical foundations of, 147–50
  legal, 6, 7, 135–37, 146–47, 156–57, 220–21, 220–21n.100
  revelation of, 12–13, 14, 84, 115, 122, 135–37, 202–4
  revolution and, 263–64
  Scholem and mystical foundations, 133–90 (*see also* Scholem, Gershom, mystical foundations of authority)
  theocracy and, 140–41, 146
  totalitarian, 30
Averroes, 212–13, 212n.75, 224, 225–26, 225n.110
  Decisive Treatise, 225–26
Averroism, 67n.66, 212, 212n.75
Avicenna, 191–92, 192n.5, 225n.111

Badiou, Alain, 39
Baron, Salo, 243n.10
Bartolus de Saxoferrato, 63n.59
Batnitzky, Leora, 59n.47, 114n.87
Bauer, Bruno, 67n.64
ben Gabbai, Meir, *Avodat ha-Kodesh*, 188, 188n.132
Benjamin, Walter, 39, 39n.16, 54n.36, 100, 100n.50, 101n.53, 128–29, 134–35
  Critique of Violence, 95n.40, 100, 101n.53, 139–40, 139n.22, 141, 173–74, 220–21, 231–32, 231n.124, 248n.23
  eternal life, 130n.117
  Gewalt, 100, 220–21, 220–21n.100, 248n.23
  nature, *restitutio in integrum*, 132
  Scholem, Gershom (*see* Scholem, Gershom, mystical foundations of authority)
  Theological-Political Fragment, 139–40, 139n.21, 167–68, 177–78, 178n.112
Ben-Shlomo, Joseph, 162n.88, 164n.89
Bensussan, Gérard, 105n.66
Bergson, Henri, 69n.71
Berman, Harold, 98
Bernstein, Jeffrey, 195n.18
Beyng, 252–53, 254n.38, 254–58, 254–55n.41, 257n.49
Biale, David, 181–82
Bible science, (science of Judaism) 40n.17, 40–41, 52–53, 213–14, 244–45n.12
Bickerman, Elias, 141–43, 141n.30, 142nn.32–33, 144
  Der Gott der Makkabäer, 141–42, 141n.30
  on *Shema*, 156n.79, 156
Bielik-Robson, Agata, 91n.30, 125n.108
biopolitics, 81n.2, 112–16, 228–36
Björk, Marten, 81n.2
Bloch, Ernst, 39n.15
  Spirit of Utopia, 95n.40, 100, 139–40, 139nn.22–23, 172
blood, community of, 93n.35, 111–16
Blumenberg, Hans, 3–4, 96n.42
Bouretz, Pierre, 58n.45, 165n.91, 191n.3, 202n.37
Brague, Rémi, *Europe, la voie romaine*, 267
Braiterman, Zachary, 95, 95n.41
Broch, Hermann, 265n.66
Brody, Samuel Hayim, 250n.31
Brunkhorst, Hauke, 98, 265n.65
Buber, Martin, 1
  on absolute, 203, 260
  Arendt on, 239
  charismatic leader (*melekh*), 248–49, 250n.31, 250–51
  Cohen, Hermann, and, 59, 60, 60n.49, 61–62
  facticity, 203–4
  faith, two types, 252–53, 253n.37
  Führerdemokratie, 6, 248–49, 249nn.24–25
  God's rule *(walten)*, 94–95, 173–74, 174n.106, 248–49, 248n.23, 250, 252, 260
  on government, form, 249, 249n.26
  Heidegger, dialogue with, 254, 254n.40
  on Hess, 246–47
  Holy Land as homeland, 244–59, 246n.15, 247n.18
  holy war, 249, 249nn.27–29
  Jewish apocalyptic politic thought, 249–50, 249–50n.29

Buber, Martin (*cont.*)
Jewish race as nationality, 246–47, 246nn.16–17
Kingdom of God, The, 244–45, 247–49, 251, 253, 254n.40, 260
on land appropriation, violent, 252, 252n.35
Landauer and, 246, 246n.15
on "the political," 252, 252n.36
radical empiricity, 203–4
on prophets, 233, 247–48
on theocracy, 31n.39
theopolitics, 245–46, 247–48, 250, 251, 253
theopolitics, *vs.* Schmitt's political theology, 247n.20
Two Concepts of Faith, 278
on YHWH, 1, 248, 252–53, 260–61
on Zionism, 244–45, 244–45n.12, 246, 247n.18
Butler, Judith, 100n.50, 238–39, 238n.4, 239n.5, 280–81

Caesaro-Papism, 7n.20
Cacciari, Massimo, 103–4, 113n.84
Cardoso, Miguel, 183
Campanini, Massimo, 194n.14
Celermajer, Danielle, 278n.89
Chacón, Rodrigo, 211n.66
Chariot, Account of, 93, 129, 133, 160–61, 287, 289–90
charisma (*hesed, charis*), 5–6, 6n.16, 7, 29–30, 163, 260
Christianity. *See also specific topics*
Trinitarianism, 18, 36, 36nn.4–5, 56–57, 287–88, 290–91
world conquest, 104–5, 105n.64
Christian messianism, 98, 123, 125, 127, 128, 129, 129n.116, 152
City and Man, The (Strauss), 207–9, 208–9n.56, 210–11, 216
civil religion, 30, 36, 60, 60n.50, 121–22, 194
Arendt on, 210n.63, 262–64, 262n.62
Arendt on, natality and, 264–77
civil theology, 59–60, 217–18
Cohen, Hermann, 4, 83n.8, 289–90
culture wars, 38–39
ethico-political actions, 41
Ethik des reinen Willens, 62–63, 63n.59, 65, 68n.70
"God and His Kingdom," 39–40
Jewish political theology, 35
Jewish Question, 59–60, 61–62, 65, 67n.64, 71
Judaism, purifying, 137–38
Jüdische Schriften, 37–38, 37n.8, 54–55
Korrelation, 38–39, 38n.11, 57
as neo-Kantian, 37–38, 38n.9
on Platonism, 211–12, 211nn.68–69
religion, conception, 52–53, 52n.34
Religion of Reason Out of the Sources of Judaism, 37, 79, 88
on Sabbath, 42
Sittlichkeit, 38–39, 38n.12, 40, 40n.18, 41, 43, 53–54, 62–63
on Torah study, 40–41, 40n.19
on Zionism, 58–59, 60–62
Cohen, Hermann, socialist democracy and, 35–79
Germanism and Judaism, 39–40, 59–72
Maimonides, atheism, nihilism, and, 49–52
Maimonides, Platonist and radical democrat, 45–49, 46n.26
messianic political theology, 39–45
messianism and eternity of world, 76–79
monotheism as political problem, 35–39
nationality problem, *Germanism and Judaism,* 39–40, 59–72
natural right and Noachite laws, 72–76
on Plato and Jewish prophets, 52–59
community of blood, 93n.35, 111–16
Concept of the Political, The (Schmitt), 205, 205n.42, 247–48, 267
concrete order of law, Leo Strauss and, 191–236. *See also* Strauss, Leo, and concrete order of law
constitutionalism 63
global, 71, 85–86, 107
Greek and Roman, 82, 97–99, 140–41, 207, 207–8n.52, 209–10, 260–64
liberal, 81
religious (*see* religious constitutionalism)

constitutional theocracy, 81n.4, 81–82
Contra Apionem (Josephus), 140
Cooper, Julie, 239n.5
Cordovero, Moses ben Jacob, 169n.99, 170
Cosmopolitanism 41, 58n.45, 70, 71–72, 82, 113, 123–24, 167, 238n.4, 280–81
Creation, 8, 29–30, 138, 144–45, 147, 148–49, 153–54, 160, 176, 263–64, 268
belief in, 73–74, 204, 213–14, 216–17, 232
creatio ex nihilo, 160–71
Redemption and, 105–6, 131–32, 175–76
revealed doctrine of, 78, 78n.85, 229–30
Creator, God as, 76, 92–93, 129, 160–62, 161n.86, 162n.88, 165–66
crisis of tradition, 134n.7, 175–81
Cristaudo, Wayne, 98n.47, 123–24, 124nn.106–107
Critique of Violence (Benjamin), 95n.40, 100, 101n.53, 139–40, 139n.22, 141, 173–74, 220–21, 231–32, 231n.124, 248n.23
Crowņ (crown, *keter*), 58, 153–55, 153nn.66–67, 155n.74
Three Crowns, model of, 56–57, 56n.42, 155n.73
culture,
agriculture and, 108–9, 110, 267–68n.70
Jewish, 140n.23, 143, 147–48, 181n.124, 201–2, 203n.39
as *kinus*, 181n.124
liberal conception of, 204–6
culture wars, 38–39, 38n.10, 61–62

Dan, Joseph, 148–49, 148n.50
Da-sein, 42, 239, 252–54, 254n.40
David, 134n.6, 139n.21, 151–52, 176, 243–44
Dean, Mitchell 155n.76
Decisive Treatise (Averroes), 225–26
Delatte, Armand, *Essai sur la politique pythagoricienne*, 17, 17n.16
democracy
divine, 18, 31, 32, 32n.42, 154–55, 218n.91, 221–22, 248–49
intellectual capacity of everyone, 58, 58n.44
liberal, 4–5, 63n.58, 102–3, 202
plebiscitarian leadership (*Führerdemokratie*), 6, 248–49, 249n.24
socialist, 3–4, 9, 38n.13, 50–51, 85, 87–88, 172,
theocracy and, 1, 6–7
true, of nature, 32–33
democratic political theology, Jewish, 86–87
Derrida, Jacques 32, 43, 148–49
force of law, 141, 220–21, 220–21n.100
on *Germanism and Judaism*, 61–62, 62n.52, 68–69, 68nn.68–69, 70n.72
on globalization, 103–4
law and legitimacy, 220
mystical foundation of law, 133–34, 234–35
"Descent of God" (Weil), 290–91, 291n.13
destituent power, 169n.100, 169–70
Deutero-Isaiah, 105–7
dialectic of Enlightenment, 54, 54n.36
Diamantides, Marinos, 7n.20
Di Cesare, Donatella, 255–56
dictatorship
Arendt on, 268–69, 268n.72
Diotogenes on, 22–23
Machiavelli on, 149–50n.54, 268–69, 268n.73
dignity, human, 65–66, 68–69, 160, 167–68, 280–81, 281n.92, 290
Diotogenes, *On Kingship*, 22–23
Discourses on Livy (Machiavelli), 268n.71, 279–80
dispositio, 31, 288, 289
divine democracy, 18, 31, 32, 32n.42, 154–55, 218n.91, 221–22, 248–49
divine dispensation, 85–86
divine government, 4–5, 8, 26–27, 26n.34, 31, 41, 93–95, 93–94n.37, 150–51, 286n.4. *See also specific topics and types*
De Mundo, 23
between order and revolution, 287–90, 293–94
divine life, 137–38, 147–48, 170, 171–74, 173n.105, 176–77, 182–83, 188–89
divine providence, 7–8, 24–25, 26–27, 86, 92–93, 145, 206n.45, 213, 261, 289

divine revelation. *See* revelation (Revelation)
divine sovereignty (kingship), 2–8, 11–12
Dumezil, Georges, 22n.29

Ecphantus, 25, 26–27
Eis Theos (Peterson), 154–56, 154n.72
Eckhart, Meister, 67n.66, 166n.96
Elazar, Daniel, 40–41, 248
empire (Empire)
  Christian, 11–12, 36, 40, 98–99, 103–4, 105–6
  intermarriage, 120–21
  land-based, 105
  of law, 98–99
  maritime, 104–5
  Negri and Hardt on, 98n.49, 102–3
  non-Jewish, 106n.67, 142n.32, 153, 163, 164–65, 233n.126
  Persian, 23, 26–27, 152–53, 153n.64
  Polybius on Roman constitution and, 99
  Roman, 28, 104–5, 105n.63, 107–8, 148, 154n.72, 249–50n.29, 263, 267, 270
empty throne, 156–57, 156n.80, 286n.4, 287, 289–90, 293–94
  creating out of nothing (Scholem), 160–71
Engel, Amir, 140n.24, 146n.45, 175
Enlightenment
  critique of orthodoxy, 89
  dialectic of, 54, 54n.36
  German, 145n.43, 169n.99, 238
  paganology, 109n.78
enmity
  theological, 82, 84, 93–94, 119, 124n.106, 124–27
  traditional, 152
En sof, 163–65, 166n.95, 167, 169n.98
equality, 16, 16nn.12–13, 71–72, 75–76, 85–86, 97, 100–1, 218, 238–39, 242–43, 261n.58, 280, 281, 282–83, 289, 293
equal rights, Arendt on, 240–44
Esposito, Roberto, 86–87, 86–87n.20
eternal life, 77–79, 89, 100–2, 111–12, 117, 124–25, 127, 185, 186, 258–59
eternity
  historical, 8, 79, 88–93, 99, 135
  of nature, 214–15, 228–29
  world, Messianism and, 76–79
ethico-political association. See *Sittlichkeit*
ethics
  Maimonides, 45, 46–47
  as science, 46–49
  Sittlichkeit, 38–39, 38n.12, 40, 40n.18, 41, 43, 53–54, 62–63
Ethik des reinen Willens (Cohen), 62–63, 63n.59, 65, 68n.70
Eusebius, 11, 28, 151n.58
exception, state of
  divine violence, 218–28
  German Jews, 218, 218n.92
  oral Torah, 181–90
Exodus (exodus), 50, 50n.29, 144–45, 251–53, 265–66

Faber, Richard, 271
Fackenheim, Emil, 2–3, 2n.7, 12–13, 113, 144–46, 145n.44, 187–88n.131
facticity
  Rosenzweig, Franz, 90–92, 115
  Strauss, Leo, 203–4, 203n.40, 220, 224, 234–35
Fagenblat, Michael, 256
falasifa, 194, 206–7, 225, 226, 235–36
fatherland, 59, 60–61, 246–47, 247n.18, 250, 251
  and Beyng, 252–53, 254n.38, 254–58, 254–55n.41, 257n.49
federalism
  Arendt, Hannah, 237–83 (*see also* Arendt, Hannah, and federalism)
  Zionism and, 240–44
Fenves, Peter, 254n.38
Fichte, Johann Gottlieb, 69, 71–72
Firestone, Reuven, 121–22
Flasch, Kurt, 67n.66
Foucault, Michel, 4–5, 288, 288n.10
  on Iranian Revolution, 81–82, 82n.6
  Security, Territory, Population, 16–17, 16nn.14–15
Fourth Eclogue (Virgil), 265–67, 270–75, 273n.84, 276–77
Fraenkel, Carlos, 12–13, 12n.7, 13nn.8–9, 14–15, 17n.15, 75n.80
Frankism, 66, 133, 174, 176, 177–78, 179–80, 181, 182–83

Freedom, 7, 10, 94–95, 97, 100–1
  Arendt on, 115, 115n.90, 242, 243–44, 260–61, 265n.66, 266–67, 275, 283
  as purity of heart, 44
  Cohen on, 35, 42, 55–56, 75–76
  covenant and, 113, 115–16
  of Creation, 165–66, 166n.95, 167–68, 169–70
  exodus and, 251–52
  of intellect, 12–13, 27, 53, 76, 225–28
  of interpretation, 144–45, 225
  paradox of liberal, 115–16
  of religion, 6–7, 76
  Saint Paul on, 44
  Weil on, 292–94
Freud, Sigmund, *Moses and Monotheism*, 25
  The Future of an Illusion, 199–201
Fukuyama, Francis, 102–3

Galli, Carlo, 89n.28, 89
geopolitics, 81n.2
  Rosenzweig and Schmitt on, 102–7
  cult of stars, and, 107–12
German Enlightenment, 145n.43, 169n.99, 238
German Idealism, 42n.22, 69–70, 71–72, 123
Germanism, Idealism and, 66–67, 67n.66, 69
Germanism and Judaism (Cohen), 39–40, 59–72
  Derrida on, 64nn.60–71, 68–69, 68nn.68–69
  Hollander on, 60n.49, 62n.52
  Klatzkin on, 59, 60–62
  political Zionism, 58–59, 60, 61–62
  Schwarzschild on, 65–67, 65n.61
German-Jewish republican thought, 84–88
Gierke, Otto von, theory of legal personality, 62–63, 62n.56
Globus: Studies Towards the World-Historical Doctrine of Space (Rosenzweig), 83n.10, 102–3, 106–7
Gnosticism, 147, 148–49, 148n.50, 161, 162, 182n.126
God as Creator, 76, 92–93, 129, 160–62, 161n.86, 162n.88, 165–66
God as King, 92–93, 153–54, 156–57, 160–61, 165–66, 252–53
God in Jerusalem, 156
God of Aristotle, 165, 165n.93, 216–17
God of Heaven, 150–51, 150n.56, 156
God of Israel, 38–39, 94–95, 161, 161n.85, 162–63, 165–66, 182n.126, 216–18, 238n.2, 251
majesty of, 153–54, 153n.65
God of Moses, 165, 165n.93, 193n.10
Goethe, 82, 89–90, 93–102, 189–90
Goldberg, Oskar, 137–38, 137nn.14–15, 172–73
Goodenough, Erwin, 3, 3n.8, 7, 18–19, 55–56, 143n.35, 193n.11, 291
  king as living law, 21–23
  on living law, 18–28
  on Philo, 11–12, 11nn.1–3, 13–15
Gordon, Peter, 59n.47
government. *See also specific topics*
  divine, 4–5, 8, 23, 26–27, 26n.34, 31, 41, 93–95, 93–94n.37, 150–51, 286n.4, 287–90, 293–94
  pastoral, 4–5, 16–18, 157–58, 288
  vs. sovereignty, 4–5
governmentality, Foucault on, 16, 16n.14, 288n.11
government of things, 288n.11
Green, Arthur, 153n.67, 153–55, 155nn.73–75, 156n.78
Green, Kenneth, Hart, 192n.7
Gross, Raphael, 251n.32
Gruen, Erich, 271n.79
Guerra, Gabriele, 140–41n.26
Guide of the Perplexed (Maimonides), 45, 108–9, 108n.75, 127, 213, 213n.78, 216, 216n.87
Guttman, Julius, 201–2, 201–2n.35, 213–14n.81

Habermas, Jürgen, 126–27, 241n.7, 263–64n.63
Haecker, Theodor, *Vergil, Vater des Abendlandes*, 267–68, 267n.68
Halakha, 121n.102, 134n.5
Halevi, Judah, 85–86, 86n.19, 124
Hammer, Dean, 264–65
Harrington, Austin, 265n.66

Hartman, David, 2–3, 2n.7, 251
Hegel, Georg Wilhelm Friedrich, 7–8, 42, 42n.22, 71–72
  Christian revelation and philosophy, 90, 93, 130
  God in history, 88–89, 88n.26
  Hess, Moses, 84–87, 84n.14, 84n.16, 86–87n.20
  historicism, 89–90
  Islam, 123
  on Jewish constitution, 88
  Jewish polity and world history, 101–2
  Johannine Age of Spirit, 85, 85n.17
  Judaism and, 84–85, 84nn.14–16
  miracles, 92, 92n.32
  paganism, 96–97, 96n.45
  pantheism, 86–87n.20
  personhood, Trinitarian, 86–87, 86–87n.20
  philosophy from theology, 90–91
  Rosenzweig, Franz, 83, 83n.10, 89–90
  on Spinoza and modern Judaism, 144–45, 145n.43
  true philosophy as worship, 50n.30, 90–91
  war, 117
  Young Hegelians, 82, 86–87n.20
Hegel and the State (Rosenzweig), 71–72, 83n.10
Heidegger, Martin, 51–52, 88–89, 197n.26, 197–98
  anarchy, principle of, 56n.41
  anti-Semitism, 255–56, 255n.44
  Arendt on, 239
  Beiträge zur Philosophie, 253, 255–56
  Beyng, 252–53, 254n.38, 254–58, 254–55n.41, 257n.49
  Black Notebooks, 255–56, 256n.46
  Buber, dialogue with, 254, 254n.40
  facticity, 203–4, 203n.40
  on Hölderlin's poems, 257, 257nn.50–51
  homeland, 244–59
  on Jaeger, 210nn.63–64, 210–11
  Jewish political theology and, 256, 256nn.45–46
  on monotheism, Judeo-Christian, 256–57, 256nn.47–48
  post-war thinking, 253–54
  on biblical prophets, 233
  temporality of peoples, 88–89, 258, 265
  topological turn, 238–55, 254–55n.41
  and Zionism, 256
Heine, Henri, 277–83
  on Jesus, 281n.93
  naturalism, 282–83, 282n.94
  "On the Democratic Principle," 281
Hekhaloth mysticism, 147, 150–51, 152, 154n.69, 157–58, 159–60, 289
Hellenism, 13–14. *See also specific topics*
  kingship and living law, 18–28, 20n.24
  sun king, 21–22, 25–26, 26n.34
Hellenistic Judaism, 140–44, 141n.28, 142n.32, 142n.33, 143n.34, 143nn.35–36, 146–48, 184–85
  emanation, 168–69
  law and mystical foundation of authority, 147–48, 148n.48
  political theology of throne, 153–55, 153n.67, 156–57, 158, 159, 160
  providential world-spirit, 164–65
  throne and monarchy, 166–67
hen kai pan (One and All), 169–70, 169n.99, 289–90, 293
Hen/Nous, 162–64, 162n.88, 165
henology, 287n.8
Heron, Nicholas, 157, 158n.81
Herzfeld, Wolfgang, 81, 81n.2, 93n.35
Herzl, Theodor, 199
Hess, Moses, 82
  Buber, Martin, on, 246–47
  German-Jewish republican thought, 84–88
  Holy History of Mankind, The, 85
  Holy Land, 246–47
  Jewish democratic political theology, 86–87
  Jewish race as nationality, 246, 246n.16
  Rome and Jerusalem: A Study in Jewish Nationalism, 87–88, 246
  on Spinoza, 86–87, 86–87n.20
  Zionism, 87–88, 87n.23
Hillel, 188–89, 188n.133
historical eternity, 8, 79, 88–93, 99, 135
history. *See also specific topics*
  mystical, 134–35, 135n.8
  as providential, 7–8, 8n.22

Hitler, Adolf, 21, 93n.36, 143–44, 146–47, 244n.11, 254–55, 265
Hobbes, Thomas, 41, 44, 113–14, 215n.84, 232–33
Hölderlin, Friedrich, 265–66
  Demeter and Dionysus, 273
  Germania, 258
  Heidegger on poetry of, 257–59, 257nn.50–51
Hollander, Dana, 60n.49, 62n.52, 83n.9
Holmes, Stephen, 104
Holy Land
  God's promise to Abraham, 250, 251n.33
  as homeland, 244–59, 246n.15, 247n.18
holy war, 107–8
  Canaan, conquest of, 118–19, 118nn.95–96
  Maccabean Revolt, 120n.101
  messianic goal of peace and, 117–22
homeland
  Buber and Heidegger, 244–59
  Holy Land as (Buber), 244–59, 246n.15, 247n.18
homoiosis, 24, 27, 160, 290
Homo sacer (Agamben), 19, 19n.22, 141
Honig, Bonnie, 95n.41, 247n.19, 282n.94
Horn, Christoph, 207–8n.52
Human Condition (Arendt), 247n.19, 254–55, 266–67, 268–69, 275–76, 277, 279
human rights, 64–65
  Christian, 72–73, 73n.75
  Heine, republican Jesus and, 277–83
Husserl, Edmund, 214–15
  life-world and, 214
  intentionality and, 222–23
hypernomianism, 146n.45
hypotheses
  genealogical, 1–4
  Platonic ideas as, 67–68

Idealism
  German, 42n.22, 69–70, 71–72, 123
  Plato's, 55–56
  Plato's, Germanism and, 66–67, 67n.66, 69
Idea of the Good, God as, 37–39, 293
  Cohen, Hermann, 37–45, 46–47, 47n.27, 50, 53–55, 57, 68–69, 213–14
  concept of nature, absence, 54–55, 55n.37
  Plato on, 46–47, 47n.27
  Socrates, 208
Idel, Moishe, 109n.76, 147–48, 147nn.47–48, 184nn.127–129
imitatio dei, 24–25, 27, 50n.29
imperialism, 81, 93n.35, 125, 156–57, 242, 243n.9, 283
  European Christian, 83–84, 97, 104–5
  Rosenzweig and Schmitt on, 102–7
inter-esse, 240–41, 242
Irwin, Christopher, 278n.89
Islam, 123–26, 123n.104
Isocrates, 14n.10, 18–19
Israeli-Palestine conflict, 237, 237n.1

Jabotinsky, Ze'ev, 179–80, 179n.117, 191n.2
Jacobson, Eric, 139n.21
Jacobi, Friedrich, Heinrich, 96n.42
Jaeger, Werner, 210nn.63–64, 210–11
Jay, Martin, 134n.7
Janssens, David, 206n.47
Jefferson, Thomas, 94n.38, 100–1, 113–14, 265n.65, 279–80
Jerusalem, Athens and, 12–13, 44–45, 87–88, 92, 130–32, 162, 189–90, 195n.18, 217n.88, 227–28, 234, 235–36
Jesus, 174–75, 270, 272–73, 291, 292
  Arendt on, 278–80, 278n.89
  divine natural right, 239
  Heine, Henri, on, 281n.93
  Life-of-Jesus theology, 112
  republican, 277–83
  Taubes, Jacob, on, 279n.90
Jewish Messiah, 27–28, 151–52, 152n.59, 163, 176–77
Jewish messianism, 11–12, 28
  Cohen, Hermann, 39, 42, 56, 68–69, 71n.74, 78
  restorative, 151–52
  Rosenzweig, Franz, 82, 101–2, 118, 120–21, 123–24, 125n.108, 125n.110, 127–31
  Scholem, Gershom, 130–31, 135, 139n.21, 145n.44, 151, 174–75, 176–80
  tripartite, 151

Jewish messianism (*cont.*)
utopian, 151–52
Zionism and, 145n.44
Jewish political theology, 1–10, 35, 35n.2, 86–87, 220–21, 253–54
See also specific topics
as anarchic, 1, 1n.4, 2n.6, 285–87
anarchist theories and, 7, 7n.20
Arendt on, 238–39
biopolitics and, 228–29
Cohen, Hermann, on, 35
divine sovereignty to pastoral government and return, 2–8
existence and meaning, 1–2, 2n.6
fundamental motif of, 145–46
genealogy, 2–3, 247n.20
Heidegger and, 256
Messiah and, 174–75
metaphysics and, 160–61
methodological precautions and genealogical hypothesis, 1–4, 2n.7
pastoral government, 4–5
prayer and, 290
as republican, 1, 1n.3
as response to Schmitt, 218, 247–48
Scholem on, 133–34, 141, 146–47
secularization, 3–4, 7
Strauss on, 192–93, 195, 201–2,
throne of, 150–60
Weil on, 290–91, 292, 293–94
Jewish Question
Arendt, Hannah, 239, 240, 241–42
Cohen, Hermann, 59–60, 61–62, 65, 67n.64, 71
Strauss, Leo, 195–96, 196n.20
Jews, as pariah people, 237–38
jihad, 121–22
Joachim of Fiore, 85–86
Job, book of, 94–95, 106–7, 289–90, 292–94
Johannine Age of Spirit, 85, 85n.17, 89–90, 96–97
Johannine Christianity, 97, 177–78, 178n.111
Josephus, Flavius, 140, 140n.25, 141n.29
Judaism. *See also specific topics*
political thought, 40–41, 41n.20
political tradition, 81, 81n.1
politics in general, 242, 245–46, 248, 253, 259, 265–66
science of (see Bible science), 244–45, 244–45n.12
tradition, 2, 2n.7
Judaism-of-the-people theology, 112
justice, 16, 16n.12, 19–21, 22–23, 26, 45, 48–49, 64, 74, 83–84, 149n.53
divine violence and, 231–32
Plato on, 207–8, 209–10, 234
Torah of, 223, 231–32, 234–35

Kabbalah. *See also* Scholem, Gershom, mystical foundations of authority
aleph, 183–84, 184n.128, 185–86, 188, 203–4, 222–23, 293–94
En sof, 163–65, 166n.95, 167, 169n.98
Scholem, Gershom, 135, 135n.9, 139, 143, 146, 147, 148n.48, 151n.58, 155n.74, 158–59, 160–62, 163–66, 165n.91, 165n.93, 167–70, 171n.102, 185–86
Spanish, of Cordovero and Luria, 137n.12, 167, 168–69, 169n.98, 170, 175–76, 179–80
Tree of Life, 171–75
will, word, and wisdom, 165, 165n.92
zimzum, 168–71, 169n.98, 169n.99, 175–76
Kadmon, Adam, 153–54, 154n.69, 160
Kafka, Franz, 149–50, 280–81
Kalyvas, Andreas, 260n.56
Kant, Immanuel, 37, 71n.73, 238n.4
neo-Kantianism, 37–38
categorical imperative, 62–63
critique, 227–28
progress, 76–77
Kantorowicz, Ernst, 11, 117n.94, 158–59
katechon, 8, 8n.23, 43–44, 126–27, 127n.113, 130
Kavka, Martin, 52n.34
Kelsen, Hans, 74, 74n.78, 196–97, 219
king (King)
God, communion with, 25, 25n.32
God as, 92–93, 153–54, 156–57, 160–61, 165–66
imitatio dei, 24–25, 27, 50n.29
law as, 4, 4n.10

as living law, 21–23
philosopher-king, 24, 32–33, 55–57, 56n.39, 74, 148n.48, 196–97, 205–6, 207–8n.52, 209–10
sun king, 21–22, 25–26, 26n.34
Kingdom of God, 3–4, 39–45, 85
Benjamin on, 139–40
Buber on, 247–48
Jacobsen on, 139n.21
Rosenzweig on, 85, 86, 88, 89, 93–94, 97, 116
Strauss on, political Zionism and, 202–3
Kingdom of God, The (Buber), 244–45, 247–49, 251, 253, 254n.40, 260
kingship
divine, 2–8, 11–12
sacred, 11, 11n.1, 74, 74n.77
Kjellén, Rudolf, 81, 81n.2
Klatzkin, Jacob, 59, 60–62
Klein, Jacob, 182n.126, 191–92n.4, 219
Krüger, Gerhard, 193n.10, 212n.75
Kojève, Alexandre, 43

Landauer, Gustav, 246, 246n.15
Lange, Friedrich, 66–67
language, theological theory, 136–37
laos, 157–58, 158n.81, 159–60, 172–73, 176
law (Law). *See also specific topics*
concrete order, Leo Strauss and, 191–236 (*see also* Strauss, Leo, and concrete order of law)
as king, 4, 4n.10
Mosaic, 12–13, 27, 72, 75, 85–86, 145, 174–75, 185–86, 187, 215–16
mystical foundations of authority, 147–50
philosophical foundation, 212n.77, 214, 221–22, 224, 227–31, 229nn.117–118, 230n.119, 230n.120 (*see also* *Philosophy and Law* (Strauss); Strauss, Leo)
Law of Nature (*nomos tes phuseus*), 3, 4, 14–15, 289, 292
as justice, 16, 19–20
Moses and, 18, 21, 31–32
as natural right, 25-26, 75, 192–93, 196–97, 261–62, 287–88
Laws (Plato), 276–77, 276n.87
Lazier, Benjamin, 56n.41, 143n.36
Lebovic, Nitzan, 247–48
Lefort, Claude, 6–7, 285–86, 285n.2
legality and legitimacy, 7, 35, 84, 150–51, 183–84, 196–97, 196n.22, 261
legal personality, theory of, 62–63, 62n.56
Lemke, Thomas, 288n.1111
Lesch, Charles, 247–48n.21
Lessing, Gotthold, Ephraim, 93n.34, 215n.83, 222–23, 238
Levinas, Emmanuel, 1–2, 2n.6, 51–52, 105n.66, 231n.123
liberal constitutionalism, 81
liberal imperialism, 81, 81n.3
liberalism
modern, political Zionism and, 201–3, 202nn.37–39, 205
modern, Spinoza, 36, 36n.6
nationalism and, 115–16, 116n.93
Life-of-Jesus theology, 112
Life of the Mind, The (Arendt), 264–65
Light, Light: The Mystic Gospel of Hellenistic Judaism (Goodenough), 12
liturgical calendars, 93n.35
living law (*lex animata*), 7, 14, 21, 28, 48, 136, 182–83, 217–18, 234, 289
Ecphantus, 25, 26–27
idea of, 18–28
imitatio dei, 24–25, 27, 50n.29
nomos empsychos, 11n.3, 14, 15, 20–23
as *nous,* 23, 24, 26–27, 26n.34, 46n.26, 292
Logos, 14–15, 44–45, 45n.25
Logos-Nomos, 14–15, 17–18, 20, 31
Lorberbaum, Menachem, 206n.46
Lord of Heavens, 142, 150n.56, 156–57
Löwith, Karl, 42, 42n.23, 56–57, 88–89, 128–29, 215n.85
Loughlin, Martin, 251n.32
Luria, Isaac, 167, 168–71, 169n.98, 169n.99, 175–76

Maccabean Revolt, 120n.101, 142–43
Maccabees, 141–43, 142n.31
Machiavelli
breaking order to save it, 149–50n.54
on Jesus 279–80
politics, 93–102
state, dam and river analogy, 99

Mack, Michael, 84n16, 113
Maimonides, 27
  Aristotelianism, 46, 48–49, 215–17, 216n.87
  atheism, nihilism, and, 49–52
  Bible science, 213–14, 214n.81
  Chariot, account of, 131–32
  on God's singularity, 39–40
  God's thirteen actional attributes, 50, 50n.29
  Guide of the Perplexed, 45, 108–9, 108n.75, 127, 213, 213n.78, 216, 216n.87
  human reason, insufficiency, 226–27, 227n.114
  Jewish messianism, 129
  Messiah, 127, 134n.6
  messianic reading, 127–28
  Mishneh Torah, 73, 73n.76
  negative theology, 39–40, 44–45, 49–52, 50n.30, 51n.31, 58n.44
  as Platonist, 38–39
  as Platonist and radical democrat, 45–49, 46n.26
  prophecy, 205–6nn.44–46
  rationalism, 226–27, 227n.115
  Sabians and star worship, 108–10
  Spinoza and, 50, 73–74, 226–27
Malebranche, 287–88, 288n.9
Malpas, Jeffrey, 255n.44
Martel, James, 141n.27, 249n.28
Marx (and Marxism) 39, 42–43, 66–67, 66–67n.64, 77–78, 82, 85n.17, 96–97, 96n.43, 139–40, 252n.36, 281
Mary, Virgin, 104–5, 105n.63
Mazzini, Giuseppe, 87–88
Melamed, Abraham, 35n.2
melekh, 50n.29, 157–58, 179, 248–49, 250–51, 252, 260–61, 276–77
Mendelssohn, Moses, 238
Mendes-Flohr, Paul, 82n.6, 102n.55, 239n.6
Merkabah mysticism, 147, 150n.56, 152–55, 152n.61, 154n.69, 157–59, 160, 161n.85, 289
Messiah
  Jewish, 27–28, 151–52, 152n.59, 163, 176–77
  Maimonides on, 127, 134n.6
Messianic age, Christian, 151n.58
messianic political theology, 39–45
  goal of peace, holy war and, 117–22
messianic utopia, 143–44, 144n.40
messianism. *See also* Scholem, Gershom
  Christian, 98, 123, 125, 127, 128, 129, 129n.116, 152
  democratic, 32–33, 43–44, 83n.8, 85–86, 155–56
  future time and eternal life, 76–79, 77n.83
  Jewish (*see* Jewish messianism; Rosenzweig, Franz, religious constitutionalism and)
  Jewish, *vs.* Christian, 152
  Jewish, Zionism and, 145n.44
  Maimonidean, 77
  prophetic, 58–59
  Rosenzweig, Franz, 125, 125n.108, 127–32
  Saint Paul, 125–27, 174–75
  conservative, 134n.6, 151
  utopian, 144n.40, 151–52, 170–71, 173–74, 175–76, 177–78, 179–80, 183–84
  world eternity, 76–79
  vs. Zionism, 140n.24
Meier, Heinrich, 219n.97
Metz, Jean-Baptiste, 126–27
Meyer, Thomas, 63n.59, 201–2n.35, 211n.68, 215n.85, 221–22, 221n.101
Michelet, Karl, Ludwig, 84n.14
minority question, 241–42
Moltmann, Helmut, 126–27
monotheism, 53–54
  Heidegger, Martin, on, 256–57, 256nn.47–49
  Hellenism and, 16, 141–42, 156, 168–69, 256–57
  as political problem, 23–24, 31, 141–42, 163, 285–87, 288
  and Platonism 68–69
  star worship and, 25, 109n.78, 110
  war and, 118
Montaigne, Michel de, 220–21
Montevecchi, Orsolina, 158n.81
Mosaic Law, 12–13, 27, 72, 75, 85–86, 145, 174–75, 185–86, 187, 215–16
Moses
  Freud on, 25
  God of, 165, 165n.93
  as ideal leader, 141n.28, 141–42

Jewish Torah and law, 20, 31–32, 148, 148n.49
law of Nature, 18
living law, 14, 28, 29–30
logos tou onto (voice), 15
monotheistic religion, 27
natural law, application, 31
as *nomos empsychos* (ideal king), 21, 21n.27, 25–26, 26n.33, 28–29
Philo on, 29–30
Plato as student of, 11n.1
political theology, 27
Spinoza on, 72–73
sun symbolism, 25–26
Moses, Dirk, 242–43, 267–68n.70
Moyn, Samuel, 73n.75, 81–82n.5, 81–82, 238–39, 260, 261, 270, 278n.89
Muller, Jerry, 199n.31
Mystery of Being (Mystery of God, *to on*), 14–15, 18, 256–58
Hellenistic mysteries and Judaism, 13–14, 28–29, 107n.71, 259, 291
Jewish mysteries, 147, 160–61, 182
mystery of economy, 156n.78, 287
mysticism
conservative and revolutionary aspects, 135–36, 135–36n.11
Hekhaloth, 147, 150–51, 152, 154n.69, 157–58, 159–60, 289
Merkabah, 147, 150n.56, 152–55, 152n.61, 154n.69, 157–59, 160, 161n.85, 289

Nabatean Agriculture, The, 108–9
Nancy, Jean-Luc, 102–4
Narcy, Michel, 291n.13
natality, civil religion and, 264–77
nationalism, 13, 59–61, 64–72, 199
German, 59–60, 65, 82, 83n.10
human rights and, 280–81
liberalism and, 115–16, 116n.93
throne, political theology of, 150–60
natural rights, 18–19, 31n.39, 36–37, 53–54, 58–59, 62–63, 64, 71–72
Kelsen's critique, 219, 219n.98
Noachite laws problem and, 72–76
Strauss, Leo, 192–93, 196–97, 209–11, 209n.59, 217, 219, 219n.98
theocracy, 31n.39
nature, state of
Arendt, Hannah, 244–45
Cohen, Hermann, 57, 62–63, 64, 65, 72
Plato, 57
republican doctrine, 113–14
Strauss, Leo, 200, 201–2, 205, 215n.85, 231, 232–34, 233n.126
Nazism
biophilosophy, 68n.68
and Gnosticism, 182n.126
Heidegger and, 253–54, 255–56
and Platonism, 21–22, 22n.29, 193n.10
war against, 250
negative theology, 39–40, 44–45, 49–52, 50n.30, 51n.31, 58n.44
Negri, Antonio, 98n.49, 265n.66
neoliberal ecumenical space, 103–4, 103n.59
Neoplatonism, 25, 109, 162, 162n.88, 163–66, 164n.89, 165n.93, 167, 286–87
Nietzsche, Friedrich, 89n.28, 89–90, 90n.29
Anti-Christ, 175, 176–77
death of God, 198
eternal recurrence, 130
nihilism, Johannine Christianity, 178n.111
Nietzscheanism, Zionism and, 198, 198n.27, 198n.30
nihilism, 49–52
affirmative, 161–62, 179–80, 181, 183
Kabbalistic, 175–76
methodological, 51–52, 52n.32
religious, 139, 139n.18
Sabbatean, 175–76
Nisbet, R. G. M., 272–73, 272n.82
Noachite laws, natural right and, 72–76
nobility, 28–29, 44, 189–90
noble lie, 94–95, 127–28, 227–28
nomos, 14, 219, 219n.95
alternative genealogy, 107n.71
Delatte, Armand, on, 17n.16, 17
Schmitt, Carl, on, 83n.10, 102–3, 106–8, 108n.73
nomos basileus, 4, 4n.10, 18–21, 19n.22, 20n.23, 148, 219
nomos empsychos, 11n.3, 14, 15, 20–23
Nomos-Logos, 14–15, 17–18, 20, 31
Nomos of the Earth (Schmitt), 106–7, 106n.70, 250–51

nomos phuseos. *See* Law of Nature
nomothetes, 141–42
Nordau, Max, 199
Norden, Eduard, 178, 270, 270n.76, 272
normative Judaism, 14, 14n.10
Nothingness, 166n.95
  En Sof as, 184, 184nn.128–129
  Ekhart, Meister, 166n.96
  God's, 133, 149–50, 160–61, 166
  Kabbalah, 160–62, 162n.87, 165n.91, 165–68, 166n.95, 166n.96, 167n.97, 170
  of Revelation, 149–50, 160–61
nous, 23, 24, 26–27, 26n.34, 46n.26, 292
  in *Hen/Nous*, 162–63, 165
Novak, David, 170–71, 171n.102
Numa, 268n.73

oikonomia, 23–24, 30–31, 287–88
omnipotence, divine, 131–32, 148, 163, 168, 172–73, 239–40, 288, 289–90
  Pythagorean solution, Simone Weil and, 290–94
One and Mind, 162–64, 162n.88
One God, 15, 16, 23, 32n.42, 291
  Hölderlin, Friedrich, 257, 258, 265–66
  Rosenzweig, Franz, 87–88, 89–90, 103–4, 113–14, 115, 127
  Scholem, Gershom, 138, 151–52, 154–55, 156–57, 159–61, 172–73, 189
  Strauss, Leo, 229–30
One God, One People and, 32n.42
On Revolution (Arendt), 237, 240–41, 245, 261, 261nn.59–60, 265–66, 275–76, 278–79
Oral Torah, 2n.7, 171, 173–74, 185n.130, 187–88n.131, 206n.46
Ortega y Gasset, José, 68n.70
Otto, Rudolf, 153–54, 154n.71, 200–1
oven of Akhnai, 95, 95n.40, 133–34, 134n.5

pagan political philosophy, 90–91, 96–97
  Enlightenment, 109n.78
  theocracy and, antinomy, 137–47
Palestine, Jewish state in, 237, 237n.1, 242–44, 243n.10
  Pangle, Thomas, 192n.6, 193n.10
pantheism, 91n.31, 137–38, 161–62, 168–70, 292
  emanationism and, 168–69, 169n.98
  Goethe, 96n.42
  Greek, 90
  Hegel, 86–87n.20
  Hess, Moses, 87–88
  Philo, 16
  Rosenzweig, Franz, 91n.31
  Scholem, 147, 161–62, 162n.88, 169n.99
  Spinoza, 63n.59, 78, 86–87n.20, 87–88, 292
  Stoic, 24–25
Pantokrator, 148, 152
Parens, Joshua, 212n.77
pastoral government, 4–5, 16–18
Paul, Saint, 8, 32n.41
  Jewish messianism, 39, 39nn.14–16
  katechon, 126n.111
  political theology, post-Marxist, 35, 35n.3
  theological enmity, 82, 84, 93–94, 119, 124n.106, 124–27
  universalism, 125, 125n.109
peace, holy war and messianic goal, 117–22
Pentateuch, 3–4, 13–14
Persia, 21, 25–27
Peterson, Erik, 3–4, 3n.9, 11, 11n.2, 23, 56–57, 126–27, 152n.62
  acclamation, 154–58, 154n.72, 155n.76, 158n.82, 159
  Eis Theos, 154–56, 154n.72
Philo and political theology origins, 11–33. *See also* political theology, origins
  Nothingness, 162n.87
  prophetology, 193n.11, 222
Philo Judaeus, 3, 11–18, 21, 23n.30, 25–26, 27
  anti-Roman affect, 28–33
  Goodenough, Erwin, on, 11, 11nn.1–3, 13–15
  historiography, 12, 12nn.4–7
  Logos, 44–45, 45n.25
  revelation, 222
  on theocracy, 31–32
  On Virtues, 28–29
  Wolfson on, 12–13, 12n.5

philosopher-king, 24, 32–33, 55–57, 56n.39, 74, 148n.48, 196–97, 205–6, 207–8n.52, 209–10
philosophical foundation, of law, 212n.77, 214, 221–22, 224, 227–31, 229nn.117–118, 230n.119, 230n.120. *See also Philosophy and Law* (Strauss); Strauss, Leo
philosophical religion, 13
philosophy. *See also specific topics and philosophers*
  of history, 7–8
  Platonic, Christian revelation and, 91–92, 91n.31
  religion and, 12–13, 44–45, 87–88, 92, 130–32, 162, 189–90, 195n.18, 217n.88, 227–28, 234, 235–36
  revelation and, 12–13
  revelation and, Hegel on, 90, 93, 130
Philosophy and Law (Strauss), 137, 192–93, 193n.9, 195–97, 198, 204, 213–14, 218–19, 221–22, 221n.101, 227–31, 230n.119, 235–36
Pines, Shlomo, 123, 206n.48
Pingree, David, 109–10, 109n.78
Plato (Platonism), 17–19, 17n.15
  Cohen, Hermann, on, 211–12, 211nn.68–69
  Cohen, Hermann, on, internal critique, 52–59
  divine law, 232, 232n.125
  Ecphantus and living law, 26–27
  Enlightenment dialectic, 54, 54n.36
  on Good, 46–47, 47n.27
  ideas as hypotheses, 46–47, 67–68
  imitatio dei, 24–25, 27, 50n.29
  Judaism and, 38–39
  Laws, 276–77, 276n.87
  living law and cosmic rulership, 21–22
  Nazis on, 21–22, 22n.29
  noble lie, 94–95, 127–28, 227–28
  philosopher-king, 24, 32–33, 55–57, 56n.39, 74, 148n.48, 196–97, 205–6, 207–8n.52, 209–10
  realism, 55–56
Platonic philosophy, 13
  Christian revelation, 91–92, 91n.31
  political, 56, 56n.41, 196–97, 196n.20, 197n.24, 207–8, 207–8n.52, 210nn.61–62, 210–11, 235–36
political guardians, 105–6, 106n.69
political philosophy, 140–41
  of Judaism, 139, 140, 140–41n.26
  Torah as, 40–41
political theology, 27
  anarchism and, 56n.41
  anti-Trinitarian, Cohen's, 36–37
  Christian Trinitarianism, 18, 36, 36nn.4–5, 56–57, 287–88, 290–91
  democratic, 154–55, 155n.75
  Jewish democratic, 86–87
  Judaism as, 35, 41, 41n.21
  messianic, 39–45
  Moses, 27
  origins, 1, 1n.2, 1n.5
  Pauline, post-Marxist, 35, 35n.3
  prayer, 93–94, 93n.36
  Schmitt, Carl, 247–48, 247n.20, 247–48n.21
political theology, origins, 11–33
  genealogy, 11–18
  living law, 18–28
  Philo and anti-Roman affect, 28–33
Pollock, Benjamin, 91n.31, 105–6, 106n.68
Polybius, 99, 148, 164–65, 277
polytheism, 16, 42–43, 89–90, 104–5, 172–73, 256–57, 256n.47, 259
positive law, 20, 21, 31, 64–65, 74, 74n.78, 84, 133–34, 149–50, 170–71, 173–74, 183–84, 220, 228, 232
prayer
  Cohen on, 93–94
  coronation prayers (*qedushah*), 153–55, 154n.71
  Goethe's and messianic, 93–102
  Hegel and, 90
  Hellenistic kingship, 24–25
  Jewish, 93–94n.36, 290
  political theology, 93–94, 93n.36
  Zion as House of, 61–62
prophetology, 192–95, 193n.11, 194n.14, 205–6, 205nn.43–46, 212, 212n.77, 219, 221–23, 222nn.102–103, 222n.104

Pythagorean philosophy, 11–12, 15, 17, 25–26, 28–29, 91n.31, 107n.71, 109–10, 148n.48, 256–57, 286–87
  Weil and divine omnipotence, 290–94

qedushah (Jewish coronation hymn), 153–55

Rabbinic Judaism, 2, 2n.7, 14, 14n.10, 95, 121n.102, 133–34, 143n.36, 143–44, 147–48, 151, 153, 156–57, 161–63, 184–85, 187, 191, 206n.46
Rabinbach, Anson, 139n.22
racism, 112–16
Rancière, Jacques, 58n.44
Ranieri, John, 195n.18
Rawls, John, 115–16
realism, 55–56
  Star of Redemption, 152
reason, religion of, 3–4, 27, 36–38, 40–41, 44–45, 47–48, 54, 76–77, 137–38, 213, 221–22
Redemption (redemption), 85–86, 91–92, 123–24, 123n.104, 129–30
  Account of the Chariot, 129, 153–54, 287
  Cohen, Hermann, on, 78–79
  community of blood, 93n.35
  Creation and, 105–6, 131–32
  End of, 128, 130
  God in, 89
  Goethe's prayer, 97
  Incarnation, 98
  Israel's deliverance from Egypt, 245
  messianic, 126
  of nature, 258
  "not yet" of, 126–27
  object of, 160
  philosophy and, 91, 91n.31
  Plato, 235–36
  Rabbinical particularist view, 184n.129
  Revelation and, 91, 93
  Sabbatianism, 165n.91
  Scholem, Gershom, on, 170
  sin as, 163
  through sin, 146n.45, 175–81, 177n.108, 181n.123
  Tree of Life, 171–72, 173–74
  of Virgil, Arendt's, 267
  zimzum, 168–71, 169n.98, 169n.99, 175–76
religion. *See also specific topics*
  conception, 52–53, 52n.34
  philosophy and, 12–13, 44–45, 87–88, 92, 130–32, 162, 189–90, 195n.18, 217n.88, 227–28, 234, 235–36
  of reason, 3–4, 27, 36–38, 40–41, 44–45, 47–48, 54, 76–77, 137–38, 213, 221–22
  true, 36, 54, 76, 85
  true and untrue, Mosaic difference, 52–53, 53n.35
religious constitutionalism, 72–73, 81–82n.5, 81–82
  revolution and, 97–98, 97n.46
  Rosenzweig, Franz and, 81–132 (*see also* Rosenzweig, Franz, religious constitutionalism and)
religious constitutionalism, Franz Rosenzweig and, 81–132. *See also* Rosenzweig, Franz, religious constitutionalism and
religious nihilism, 139, 139n.18. *See also* nihilism
repentance. See *T'shuvah (teshuva)*
republicanism
  constitutionalism, neo-Roman, 82
  German-Jewish, 84–88
  Hebrew Republic, 56–57, 59–60
  Judaism and, 82
  Socialist, 66
  theocracy and, 81–82 (*see also* Rosenzweig, Franz, religious constitutionalism and)
republican Jesus, 277–83
res publica, 103, 240–41, 277
return. See *T'shuvah (teshuva)*
Return as Repentance, 191–92, 191n.3, 191–92n.4
revelation (Revelation), 88–90, 91–92, 91n.31, 134–35
  Altmann, Alexander, 88–89, 89n.27
  fact of (*Faktum*), 197–205, 222–23, 225
  Hess, Moses, 85–86
  vs. law giving, 184n.127
  meanings, 184, 184n.127

Philo, 222
philosophy and, 12–13
philosophy and, Hegel on, 89–90, 93, 130
Rosenzweig, Franz, 91–93
Spinoza, 86–87
revolution
Copernican, 109–10, 110n.79
Iranian, 81–82, 82n.6
modern, Arendt on, 260
religious constitutionalism and, 97–98, 97n.46
temporality, 265, 265n.66
rights
Arendt, Hannah, 238
equal, Arendt's, 240–44
natural (*see* natural rights)
rights, human, 64–65
Christian, 72–73, 73n.75
Heine, republican Jesus and, 277–83
Roman civil religion, Judaism and, 60, 60n.50
Roman political thought, Arendt, 242–43, 243n.9
Fascism and, 30, 243n.9
Rosen, Stanley, 209n.57
Rosenstock, Bruce, 83n.8, 96–97, 96n.45, 117
Rosenstock-Huessy, Eugen, 93n.36, 117
Die Europäischen Revolutionen: Volkscharaktere und Staatenbildung, 97–99, 98n.47
Rosenzweig, Franz
Akademie für die Wissenschaft des Judentums, 40n.17
on Cohen's oeuvre, 37–38, 60n.49
on Cohen's turn to Platonism, 61
democratic, redemptive politics, 83n.8
eternal return, 130n.118
facticity, 90–92, 115, 203–4
faith in something *vs.* having faith, 115, 115n.89
Globus: Studies Towards the World-Historical Doctrine of Space, 83n.10, 102–3, 106–7
God and His Kingdom, 88–89, 88n.26
Hegel and the State, 71–72, 83n.10
identity politics, 113, 113n.85
on Jewish nationality, 82
Korrelation, 38n.11
miracles, 92
natality, 114, 115–16, 116n.91
New Thinking, 88–89, 91n.30
on Nietzsche, 89–90
prayer, 93–97
racism, 112–13, 112n.83
radical empiricity, 203–4
Star of Redemption, 79, 82, 84, 85–86, 86n.19, 88–89, 91–93, 102n.55, 111, 123, 130, 132, 152, 198, 234
Taubes, Jacob, on, 39, 39n.15
Time and history, 128–31
violence, 100
Rosenzweig, Franz, religious constitutionalism and, 81–132
biopolitics, racism, and community of blood, 93n.35, 111–16
constitutional theocracy, 81–82
geopolitics, star(s) on, 107–12
Goethe's prayer and Machiavelli's politics, 93–102
Hegel and State of Israel, 83, 83n.10
Hess, Moses and German-Jewish republican thought, 84–88
historical eternity, 8, 88–93
holy war and messianic goal of peace, 117–22
on imperialism and globalism, 102–7
Islam, theological enmity, and Jewish *katechon,* 123–32
republican thought, German-Jewish, 84–88
theocracy and republicanism, 81–82
Rotenstreich, Nathan, 87–88
Rousseau, Jean-Jacques, 30, 239–40, 241n.7, 280, 287–88
Rubin, Gil, 243n.10

Sabbath, 42, 43–44, 108
Sabbatianism, 127–28, 133, 135, 137–38, 140n.24, 146n.45, 165n.91, 174–81, 182n.126, 182–83, 186
Sabians, 108–10, 108n.75, 109n.78
sacred kingship, 11, 11n.1
West, 74, 74n.77
Santner, Eric, 39, 113–14
on Saint Paul and the Messiah, 39, 39n.15

Schaefer, Yoav, 247–48n.21
Scharf, Orr, 247–48n.21
Schelling, F. W. J. von, 85–86, 96–97, 96n.43
Schmidt, Christoph, 170n.101, 256nn.47–48
Schmitt, Carl, 1–2, 1n.5. *See also specific topics*
anti-Christ, 43–44
Christian post-national global order, 103–4
Concept of the Political, The, 205, 205n.42, 247–48, 267
constituent power, 264
globalized politics, 104, 104n.60
Hobbesian political theology, 192–93
on imperialism and empire, 104–5
on imperialism and globalism, 102–7
on *katechon,* 8, 8n.23
on *nomos,* 83n.10, 102–3, 106–8, 108n.73, 219, 219n.95
on Peterson, 3–4
political theology, 248, 248n.22
political theology, *vs.* Buber's theopolitics, 247n.20
renewed interest in, 103–4
sovereignty, 141, 141n.27
Scholem, Gershom, 39
divine Life, 147–48, 170, 171–74, 173n.105, 176–77, 182–83, 188–89
Hekhaloth mysticism, 147, 150–51, 152, 154n.69, 157–58, 159–60, 289
Judeo-German symbiosis, 65n.61, 144n.38, 189–90, 281
Merkabah mysticism, 147, 150n.56, 152–55, 152n.61, 154n.69, 157–59, 160, 161n.85, 289
Redemption, 134–35, 138, 152, 163, 165n.91, 170–72, 173–74, 184n.129, 219
tradition, crisis of, 133–35, 133n.4, 134n.7
Walter Benjamin: The Story of a Friendship, 133n.3, 134–35
Scholem, Gershom, mystical foundations of authority, 133–90
anarchism, religious, 133, 134–35, 139, 146–47, 176, 181–90, 182n.125
authority, law and mystical foundations of, 147–50
empty throne, creating out of nothing, 160–71
Frankism, 133, 174, 176, 177–78, 179–80, 181, 182–83
oral Torah in state of exception, religious anarchism and, 181–90
redemption through sin, 146n.45, 175–81, 177n.108, 181n.123
Sabbatianism, 133, 135, 137–38, 140n.24, 146n.45, 165n.91, 174–81, 182n.126, 182–83, 186
theocracy and pagan political philosophy, antinomy of, 137–47
throne, political theology and nationalism, 150–60
Tree of Life and biblical antinomianism, 171–75
Schultz, Joseph, 158–59
Schürmann, Reiner, 285–87, 286nn.5–7
Schütz, Anton, 7n.20
Schwally, Friedrich, 119
Schwartz, Yossef, 85–86, 86n.18, 123, 123n.104
Schwarzschild, Steven, 62n.54, 65–67, 65n.61, 71n.73, 72, 74
science of Judaism, 40, 40n.17, 244–45, 244–45n.12
secularization, 7, 7n.21
Security, Territory, Population (Foucault), 16–17, 16nn.14–15
Shammai, 188–89, 188n.133
Shema, 156n.79, 156
Sibylline Oracles, 271, 271n.78, 271n.81
Sittlichkeit, 38–39, 38n.12, 40, 40n.18, 41, 43, 53–54, 62–63, 93–94n.37. *See also* ethics
social contract
Arendt's two kinds, 260–61, 261n.58
Rosenzweig, Franz, 115–16
socialist democracy, Hermann Cohen and, 35–79. *See also* Cohen, Hermann, socialist democracy and
Socrates, 18–19, 207–8, 208nn.53–54
imitatio dei, 24–25, 27, 50n.29
Soloveitch, Joseph, 2–3, 2n.7, 251

Sophia and Sophia, 13–14, 164–65, 166n.95, 216
sovereignty
  divine, 2–8, 16, 26–27, 81, 140–41, 165–66, 252–53
  as heretical, 247–48, 247–48n.21
  vs. federalism, 240–44
  vs. government, 4–5, 17–18, 287–90
  nomos basileus, 19–20, 219
  Schmitt, Carl, 19, 22–23, 32n.42, 43, 63, 141, 141n.27, 144
Spinoza, Baruch, 12–13, 27, 30, 58–59, 161–62
  on Christian Trinitarianism, 36
  Cohen's criticism of, 72–76
  divine commandments, 127–28
  in *Ethik des reinen Willens* (Cohen), 63n.59
  Hegel's critique of, 144–45, 145n.43
  on Judaism, 59–60, 60n.48
  liberalism, modern, 36, 36n.6
  Maimonides and, 50, 73–74, 226–27
  pantheism, 63n.59, 78, 86–87n.20, 87–88, 292
  revelation, 86–87
  Theologico-Political Treatise, 199n.31, 200–1, 201n.33, 204
Star of Redemption (Rosenzweig), 79, 82, 84, 85–86, 86n.19, 88–89, 91–93, 102n.55, 111, 123, 130, 132, 152, 198, 234. *See also* Rosenzweig, Franz, religious constitutionalism and
state of exception
  divine violence, 218–28
  German Jews, 218, 218n.92
  oral Torah, 181–90
State of Exception (Agamben), 149–50, 149nn.52–55, 220–21
state of nature
  Arendt, Hannah, 244–45
  Cohen, Hermann, 57, 62–63, 64, 65, 72
  Plato, 57
  republican doctrine, 113–14
  Strauss, Leo, 200, 201–2, 205, 215n.85, 231, 232–34, 233n.126
Stone, Suzanne, 121n.102
Strauss, Leo, and concrete order of law, 131, 143n.36, 191–236
  Agamben on, 20n.23
  anti-liberalism, 195, 195n.17
  antinomy, of theocracy and pagan political philosophy, 137–47
  Arabic and Jewish medieval thought, 192–94, 193n.11, 228–29, 229n.116
  Aristotle's gentlemen, 206n.48, 207
  atheism, 197–98, 197n.25
  on Averroism, 212, 212n.75
  background, 191–97
  Bible science, Maimonides, 213–14, 214n.81
  City and Man, The, 207–9, 208–9n.56, 210–11, 216
  on Cohen, 215–17
  concrete order, law as, 219–20, 219n.97
  Creation, 213–14, 215–16, 229–30
  Creation, belief in, 204, 213–14, 216–17, 232
  divine law, philosophy to biopolitics, 228–36
  divine revelation, fact of, 197–205
  divine violence and state of exception, 218–28
  enlightened Judaism, Cohen's, 206–8, 206n.47
  Faktum of revelation, 197–98, 222–23, 225
  falasifa, 194, 206–7, 225, 226, 235–36
  on Freud, 199–200
  Gewalt and force of law, 220–21, 220–21n.100
  Jerusalem and Athens antagonism, 195, 195n.18
  Jewish Question, 195–96, 196n.20
  law, philosophical foundation, 212n.77, 214, 221–22, 224, 227–31, 229nn.117–118, 230n.119, 230n.120
  legality and legitimacy, 196–97, 196n.22
  liberalism and political Zionism, 201–3, 202nn.37–39, 205
  on Maimonides, 31n.39, 31, 192n.7
  on Maimonides, insufficiency of human reason, 226–27, 227n.114

Strauss, Leo, and concrete order of law (*cont.*)
on Maimonides, rationalism, 226–27, 227n.115
on Maimonides' Aristotelianism, 215–17, 216n.87
on modern science, critique, 214–15, 215nn.84–85
natural right, 192–93, 196–97, 209–11, 209n.59, 217, 219, 219n.98
nature, state of, 200, 201–2, 205, 215n.85, 231, 232–34, 233n.126
Nietzscheanism, 198–99, 198nn.27–29, 198n.30
philosophical life and political life, 196–97
philosophy, legal foundation of, 222–23, 222n.103
on Plato, 57n.43
Platonic political philosophy, 196–97, 196n.20, 197n.24, 207–8, 207–8n.52, 210nn.61–62, 210–11, 235–36
Platonism, Cohen on, 211–12, 211nn.68–69, 213–14, 213–14n.80
Platonism, political science and, 212–13, 212n.77, 213n.78
on positive law, 220, 228, 232
prophet as philosopher and political leader, 192–93, 193n.9
prophetology, 192–95, 193n.11, 194n.14, 205–6, 205nn.43–46, 212, 212n.77, 219, 221, 222n.102
Return as Repentance, 191–92, 191n.3, 191–92n.4
revelation, faith in, 195n.18, 197–205, 221–22, 224, 224nn.107–108
revelation, medieval philosophers, 222, 222nn.102–103
Schmitt and Hobbes, 192–93, 204–5, 218–19, 234–35
on secularization, Christian *vs.* Islamic, 212, 212n.76
Socrates and "idea of the Good," 207–8, 208nn.53–56
on Spinoza, 191n.1, 203n.39
theologico-political problem, 191, 192–93, 195–97, 197n.24, 199n.31, 204
Torah as Aristotelian political science, 205–18
transcendence and uncanny, 199
transcendent God, 200
T'shuvah, 191, 191n.3, 197
tyrannical teaching, 18n.19
Zionism, political *vs.* cultural, 198–99
Strauss, Leo, *Philosophy and Law,* 137, 192–93, 193n.9, 195–97, 198, 204, 213–14, 218–19, 221–22, 221n.101, 227–31, 230n.119, 235–36
Stream of Light *(Logos),* 12, 14–15
Strousma, Sarah, 108n.75
Styfhals, Willem, 182n.125
sun king, 21–22, 25–26, 26n.34
ideal *(nomos empsychos),* 21, 21n.27, 25–26, 26n.33, 28–29
superesse, 167–68, 167n.97
super-man, 89, 89n.28

Tardieu, Michel, 109
Taub, Emmanuel, 59n.47
Taubes, Jacob
apocalyptic legend, 152n.59
on Buber's political theology, 247n.20
on God's enmity toward Jews, 125, 125n.110
on Jesus, 279n.90
Jewish apocalyptic politic thought, 249–50n.29, 271, 271n.80
on messianism, 39n.15, 125n.110, 152, 152n.60, 174–75
on messianism, Scholem's, 139n.21, 140n.24
on messianism, Zionism and, 140, 140n.24
on negative political theology, Rosenzweig's, 101–2
on nihilism, 139n.18
on *novum* and *beginning,* 273n.85
on Sabbatianism, 178
on Saint Paul and the Messiah, 39, 39n.15
on Scholem, critique of, 152, 152n.60
on Scholem, cult of personality, 133n.1
Taylor, Charles, 223
theocracy, 27–28
anarchic soul, 1, 1n.1

biblical, 81
constitutional, 81n.4, 81–82
Jewish, 28, 29–30
Josephus on, 140–42
natural right, 31n.39
pagan political philosophy and, antinomy, 137–47
Philo on, 31–32
political *vs.* religious meaning, 139–41, 139n.21
republicanism and, 81–82 (*see also* Rosenzweig, Franz, religious constitutionalism and)
theological enmity, 82, 84, 93–94, 119, 124n.106, 124–25, 126–27
theologico-political problem, 191, 192–93, 195–97, 197n.24. *See also* Strauss, Leo
theopolitics, Buber's, 245–46, 247–48, 250, 251, 253
throne
empty (*see* empty throne)
political theology of, nationalism and, 150–60
to on, 14–15
Torah. *See also* Scholem, Gershom, mystical foundations of authority
as Aristotelian political science, 205–18
as constitution, 81 (*see also* Rosenzweig, Franz, religious constitutionalism and)
God descended into, 185, 185n.130
as law, crisis, 146–47
Moses, 20, 31–32
nihilistic, 181n.123
Oral, 2n.7, 171, 173–74, 185n.130, 187–88n.131, 206n.46
oral, in state of exception, religious anarchism and, 181–90
as political philosophy, 40–41
as positive law, 133–34
Rabbinical approach, 133–34
study, 40–41, 40n.19
Ur-Torah, 185–86, 187, 188–89
Written, 133–34, 159–60, 173–74, 174n.106, 183–89
Written, *aleph,* 183–84, 184n.128, 185–86, 188, 203–4, 222–23, 293–94
tradition
crisis of, 133–35, 133n.4, 134n.7
crisis of the crisis of, 175–81
Treitschke, Heinrich, 59–60
Trinitarianism, Christan, 18, 36, 36nn.4–5, 56–57, 287–88, 290–91
true religion, 36, 40–41, 44–45, 52–53, 53n.35, 54, 76, 85
T'shuvah (teshuva)
Buber on, 244–45n.12
Cohen on, 75
Luria on, 175–76
Philo on, 28–29
Rosenzweig on, 85–86, 97
Scholem on, 183, 185–86
turning towards. See *T'shuvah (teshuva)*
Twelfth Imam, Sh'ia, 129n.116
tyranny, 18–20, 19n.21, 94, 94nn.38–39

Ur-Torah, 185–86, 187, 188–89
utopian messianism, 144n.40, 151–52, 170–71, 173–74, 175–76, 177–78, 179–80, 183–84

violence, divine
land appropriation, 252, 252n.35
state of exception, 218–28
Virgil
catachresis, 269, 269n.75
civil religion and natality, 264–77
Fourth Eclogue, 265–67, 270–75, 273n.84, 276–77
Voegelin, Eric, 25–26, 26n.33, 42n.23, 42–43, 56–57
von Rad, Gerhard, 120

walten, 94–95, 173–74, 174n.106, 248–49, 248n.23, 250, 252, 260
Walzer, Michael, 40–41, 83–84, 83n.11, 245
on *hesed,* 260, 260n.56
on holy war, 118–22, 118nn.95–96, 120n.101
non-Jewish empires, 106n.67
political freedom and exodus, 251–52
on promised land, 250–51
Weber, Max, 5–6, 196–97, 248–49, 260n.55
Ancient Judaism, 119–20
Weidner, Daniel, 133n.3, 140–41n.26

Weil, Simone, 1–2, 2n.6, 91n.31, 189n.134, 290–91, 291n.13
anarchism, religious, 2n.6, 290–91
"Descent of God," 290–91, 291n.13
divine omnipotence, Pythagorean solution, 290–94
on purpose, 293–94, 293n.15
Weimar Germany, spiritual situation of Jews, 143–44, 143nn.37–38
Wellhausen, Julius, 140–41n.26
Wiedebach, Hartwig, 70–72, 71n.74, 78, 78n.85
Whittaker, Hèlene, 272–73n.84
Wolfe, Judith, 254–55n.41
Wolfson, Elliot, 146n.45, 166n.94
Wolfson, Harry, 12–13, 12n.5, 138n.16, 161–62, 222
Written Torah, 133–34, 159–60, 173–74, 174n.106, 183–89
aleph, 183–84, 184n.128, 185–86, 188, 203–4, 222–23, 293–94

Xenophon, 193n.10, 207n.49, 219, 234
Cyropaedia, 25, 27
Hiero, 14n.10, 18–19

Yaffe, Martin, 211n.69
YHWH
Bickerman on, 156
Buber on, 1, 248, 252–53, 260–61
Goldberg on, 137–38
Heidegger on, 256
leadership, 249
Midrashic, 153–54
Philo on, 3
Scholem on, 156–57, 172–73
Shema and, 156n.79
von Rad on, 120, 120n.100
Walzer on, 118–19
Yom Kippur, 127n.114
Young Hegelians, 82, 86–87n.20

Zadoff, Noam, 178n.112, 179n.117, 181n.124, 182n.125
Zank, Michael, 205n.42
zimzum, 169–71
Zionism, 2, 144n.39
Arendt on, 240–44, 244–45n.12
Buber on, 244–45n.12, 246, 247n.18
Butler on, 239n.5
Cohen on, 58–59, 60–62, 180–81
Fackenheim on Cohen and, 145n.44
federalism and, 240–44
Heidegger on, 256
Hess on, 82, 87–88, 87n.23
Jewish messianism and, 145n.44
vs. messianism, 140n.24
messianism and, Benjamin on, 139–40, 140n.24
Nietzcheanism 198, 198n.27
political, 58–59, 60, 61–62, 139–40, 198–99
Rosenzweig on, 83, 83n.9, 101n.54, 112–13
Scholem on, 143–44, 144n.39, 175, 178n.113, 178–81, 180nn.119–120
Strauss on, 96n.43, 138, 143–44, 144n.39, 191, 198–99, 198n.27, 198n.30, 201–3, 205, 205n.42
Žižek, Slavoj, 39, 113, 125
Zvi, Sabbatai, 135, 174–75. *See also* Sabbatianism